The Education
of Young Donald
T R I L O G Y

DONALD HORNE (1921–2005) was an Australian writer. He worked in journalism, starting as a reporter for *The Daily Telegraph* and going on to edit the intellectual periodical *The Observer* and *The Bulletin*. He was an academic in the school of political science at the UNSW from 1973–86. He chaired public bodies, served as a university chancellor and held a number of other public positions. He wrote more than two dozen books including *The Lucky Country*, *Money Made Us*, *Death of the Lucky Country*, *The Great Museum* and *10 Steps to a More Tolerant Australia*. He also wrote two memoirs: *Into the Open* which covers the period 1958 to 1999; and *Dying: A Memoir*, a portrait of the period before and after his death, co-written with Myfanwy Horne and published posthumously.

'Donald Horne looks down on Australia from the loftiest heights in the pantheon. He's up there with Patrick White as our most savage literary lion. *The Education of Young Donald Trilogy* is a masterpiece and should replace the Gideon Bible in motel drawers.'
Phillip Adams

'... a superb book.'
Peter Coleman, *The Australian*

'I commend it to you quite fiercely.'
Max Harris, *The Australian*

'... an exhilarating inquiry into the sources and quality of the facts and ideas that made him ...'
H.G. Kippax, *Sydney Morning Herald*

'... a master of the autobiography-as-an-art form'
Denis O'Brien, *The Australian*

'In some ways, his personality embodied the Australia into which he was born in 1921: hard edged, wry-humoured, industrious and pragmatic. In a country with a deeply ingrained anti-intellectual tradition ... Horne was a feisty advocate for the virtues of intellectual life.'
Mark McKenna, *The Australian*

'Australia had made him and he was concerned to remake Australia ... it was his country and as such it had no right to be boring or provincial or mediocre.'
Owen Harries, Speech at Horne Memorial

'Like Henry Lawson and Patrick White, his work will live on as a faithful record of our time.'
Manning Clark

'Donald Horne is Australia's special gift to the world ...'
Kenneth Hudson, *Art Monthly*

'His three-volume autobiography is one of the major literary achievements of twentieth century Australia ...'
Meaghan Morris, *Gleebooks Gleaner*

The Education
of Young Donald
T R I L O G Y

DONALD HORNE

NEWSOUTH

A NewSouth book

Published by
NewSouth Publishing
University of New South Wales Press Ltd
University of New South Wales
Sydney NSW 2052
AUSTRALIA
newsouthpublishing.com

© Donald Horne 1998
Foreword © Tracy Sorensen 2021
Introduction © Julia Horne and Nick Horne 2021
First edition published by HarperCollins Australia in 1998
This edition published 2021

10 9 8 7 6 5 4 3 2 1

ISBN: 9781742237299 (paperback)
          9781742245331 (ebook)
          9781742249902 (ePDF)

A catalogue record for this book is available from the National Library of Australia

Design Josephine Pajor-Markus
Cover design Luke Causby, Blue Cork
Cover images (*top right*) Donald Horne as a young man, c.1948–54.
    (*bottom left*) Donald Horne as a boy, 1935. Courtesy Horne family

UNSW Press Literary Fund wishes to acknowledge the generous support of its donors.

Contents

BOOK THREE
PORTRAIT OF AN OPTIMIST

Foreword

Tracy Sorensen

I'm here writing this foreword because some years ago I wrote a book in which a pink and grey galah tears the pages of Donald Horne's *The Lucky Country* with claw and beak. The bits of text float from perch to floor. There is Donald's famous image of the man in the open-necked shirt, solemnly licking his ice cream. Here is the practical man resisting radiations of bombast. Scraps of the famous text litter the floor, spattered with bird shit.

Once *The Lucky Galah* was published, I wondered whether any surviving Hornes might read it, and if they did, what they might think. Yes, it's rude to tear the book to pieces but – I'd argue – I'm doing it in the spirit of Donald Horne.

What is this spirit, exactly? I think it is to do with play. There is always a playful quality in Horne, a glint in the eye that takes the edge off certainty. Ideas must be taken seriously, their contest must be fought with vigour, but it must always be possible to swing around in the opposite direction occasionally, just for the hell of it, like a galah on a wire.

But there was silence coming from the direction of the remaining Hornes. I knew they were there because I'd Googled them, but they were not biting. I reminded myself that Australian writers have been playing around with *The Lucky Country* for more than fifty years and they were probably not in any rush to taste the latest offering.

Then I got an email from Nick Horne: 'As the son of the author of *The Lucky Country*, I can say that there are a few who have tried to tear that book to shreds, but none who have done it so sympathetically.' I sat for a long time in a soft pink glow. In the absence of Donald Horne himself, this was the next best thing.

FROM AN EARLY AGE I WAS RIGHT THERE IN THE HEART OF THE conundrum that runs through both *The Education of Young Donald Trilogy* and, to some extent, *The Lucky Country*: How do you have a Life of the Mind in a Nation Without A Mind?

I am the daughter of a truck driver and a dressmaker (my parents did other things, but I'm simplifying for effect). I grew up in a remote, red-dust Australian town and went to the local schools. As a teenager, I had a weekend job at the local takeaway shop, filling buckets of chips with my silver tongs and pulling out packs of Winfields from the bottom of the wall-mounted feeder, saying, 'That the lot?' In my breaks I read books, sometimes standing next to the wet mop at the back door. I was cultivating a Life of the Mind but if I wanted to fit in, I had better keep it to myself.

Horne's account of his life before *The Lucky Country*, with its exhilarating forays into Australian intellectual and public life in the 1930s, '40s and '50s, returns often to this theme. In talking to other boys at school, he can do an excellent job in conversation with the sports boy and an excellent job talking to the swot, but when both boys are present at the same time, he falls silent. Horne is unable to find a unified self that might make sense in this situation.

The solution is to switch back and forth, to inhabit a series of plausible selves fit for a variety of social situations. There is Young Donald (optimistic, eager to learn) and D. R. Horne (angry shouter). Who is *he*, really? We human beings might like to find a singular essence, something sound and true, but we're more Walt Whitman: containing multitudes. In discussing the problem of his own need to 'appear to be some particular, recognisable and predictable kind of man' Horne notes how 'bits of me would keep on running from behind the mask, as if I were a troupe of tumblers'.

It will always elude us, but we can't help continuing the search for an identity, personal or national, that might help us make sense of it all. The image of Australia may be the man in the open-necked shirt, solemnly eating his ice cream – but an image has no flesh. The man is an idea, an ideal, a trope or a goal. Today, non-Indigenous Australians know that our innocent happiness was carved out of the suffering of others.

Still, innocently or not, Australians continue to live in a nation more fortunate than most. The beach, the ice cream, the long holidays for those in jobs, the universal health care, the four-wheel drive vehicles probing ever further into the bush to 'get away from it all' – these remain, despite bushfire and pandemic, for now. While the carefree word *luck* could be replaced by the more critical *privilege*, the word luck will do. What will we do with the dumb luck that has been heaped upon us? Will we demand that our innocence and ignorance be pandered to indefinitely (electric cars will *steal our weekends*, refugees will *steal our jobs*)? Will progressives let go of their pampered purity long enough to see what's driving their outer suburban and country cousins?

How might we talk to the sports guy and the swot at the same time, as if they were in the same room?

Part of the answer, I think, is in understanding that the Nation Without A Mind is another image without any flesh. It is as much of a trope as the man in the open-necked shirt. The anti-intellectual mask behind which dangerous ideas hide must be lifted away. Horne was making a critique of ideology, not of his fellow human beings. He was not merely describing the dominant culture, but making an urgent case for changing it.

In *The Education of Young Donald Trilogy* we can see how a bookish boy, passionate about culture and ideas, grew into the man who would write the book that lingers in Australian culture: understood, misunderstood, played with, torn to shreds, returned to again, read afresh.

For me, reading this autobiography has been like having a one-on-one conversation with a beloved teacher, over a cup of tea. There is a personal openness that never feels like over-sharing; and there is a teeming mind that is happy to both 'philosophise' and give names, dates and telling details. More than once, he mentions the honeypot that looked like a beehive on his Nanna's table. Why? Just because it was there, and Horne, alongside his ability to generate hot air, is always in love with what is actually there. I thoroughly enjoyed reading this book, and I hope you do, too.

Introduction

Julia Horne and Nick Horne

On the centenary of the birth of our father, Donald Horne (1921–2005), we are delighted to see the re-publication of his autobiography. We hope the book also brings delight to new readers and to those re-visiting this Australian classic.

Donald's autobiography is a trilogy, published as *An Interrupted Life* in 1998. This new edition, *The Education of Young Donald Trilogy* takes its name from the first book, published in 1967. The second, *Confessions of a New Boy*, appeared in 1985 and the third, *Portrait of an Optimist*, in 1988. In bringing together the three books into a single volume, Donald gave the following insight in his introduction:

> ... it gives an idea of what a whole range of things were like back then in the 1930s, '40s and '50s. For that reason, for a while I thought I would call it a sociography – thereby making it clear that I didn't consider that I personally was worth a trilogy, but that there was a trilogy in an account of the times. Later I realised that this word was nonsense: it didn't allow for the fact that this is also a story of individual experience with surprises and oddities beyond stereotypes. Autobiography 'shows life in action,' said Antonio Gramsci, 'not just as written laws or dominant moral principles say it should be'.

In explaining his stylistic approach, Donald went on to say:

> In a sense, fiction is one of the themes of this trilogy – amongst many other things, it's a story about how novels can be used in trying to make sense of existence, whether in reading other people's novels

or in writing novels of one's own. And what I have written has the techniques of fiction. It is a story. But it is fiction within limits. I didn't invent any 'facts' to get myself out of narrative problems. I didn't want anything in it to be false. I didn't invent direct speech conversations to make it seem more real. If I described things, it was, so far as I could manage it, how they seemed to me at the time. I didn't want to use that kind of heightened literary sensibility that can be specious in any kind of writing. What I was looking for was what, for me, is the best autobiographical style (unless you are St Augustine, addressing God) – an unobtrusive style with a sense of detachment that provides a kind of declaration of honesty.

An unobtrusive style seemed essential to a sense of detachment – in which the self of the central character is a different person from the older self now telling the story. And this in turn meant presenting things as they seemed at the time, in all their false starts, and never appearing to have the slightest idea about what would happen next. It also meant no self-pity, no self-justification, certainly no settling of old scores. (Isn't it the first duty of an autobiographer who is concerned with folly to concentrate on follies of his own?) It also meant that presenting transgressions should be enough – one doesn't have to write editorials about what is happening. And if there are contradictions, presenting them should be enough: juxtaposition is the best signpost. It also meant not laying on the emotion too thickly.

He approached the task of writing this 'fiction within limits' with the pragmatic rigour of a modern historian. To strive for historical accuracy, he cast the net wide, talking with family members, reading personal papers, newspapers and visiting all the places he was to write about. He described his investigative methods in *Into the Open: Memoirs 1958–1999*, published in 2000:

As well as sinking back into my own memories, my mother's, my grandmother's, I looked at every piece of paper I had kept from primary school onwards – diaries, school essays, letters, old books, photo albums; to check the status details of a country town such as attendance at annual balls I looked over several years' issues of *The Muswellbrook Chronicle* and then read a year's issues of the *Daily Telegraph* to get down its view of the world in 1936; I revisited all the relevant sites, including railway journeys, that had survived from my boyhood, youth and student days.

Almost ten years after publication of the first autobiographical volume, the State Library of New South Wales sought to acquire his personal papers as part of the Mitchell Library's manuscript collection. The library collected the first forty-seven boxes of papers in 1978 with seventy more to follow during his lifetime and a further 110 after his death. The Mitchell Library soon became not only the permanent home for these papers, but also a temporary place of studious reflection for Donald to read this extensive collection and prepare his next two autobiographical books.

In the 1990s, while in the process of recasting these three books into the trilogy, he once again sat at the elegant, polished wooden work tables of the Mitchell Library, an archival box or two to his right, carefully working through the contents, occasionally rising to stretch his legs, return one box and collect another. When lunchtime approached, he often wandered down to the library's restaurant, sometimes for a quick bite by himself, at other times to meet old friends and reflect on shared memories.

We were, of course, too young to remember visiting the 'relevant sites' for the first autobiographical book. But later, we did accompany Donald and our mother Myfanwy on some of these excursions. During a family holiday to Adelaide and the Northern Territory in the 1970s, Donald revisited sites that helped him reconstruct scenes for some of the wartime parts of the second book. We travelled by train across the same country between Port Augusta and Alice Springs as he did in 1943 while on his way to the then battle zone of Darwin. On our train trip Donald took notes of the passing scenery using his customary black Pentel pen to jot down brief observations in a small cardboard-bound notebook. Now and then he sought Myfanwy's assistance to determine the best way to describe this most unusual landscape of native grasses, sand dunes, dry riverbeds and desert gums:

> flat seas of dry grass ... bare, stony ground with sparse clumps of derelict scrub ... red sand plains with solemn, green shrubs ... dunes rising from plains rippling with pebbles ... desert gums guarding dried watercourses

... corrugated ridges of sand held together by tufts of cane grass ... whole plains of rusted red stones.

On a family holiday to Europe in the late 1970s, we visited the small village of Bow Brickhill in Buckinghamshire where he lived in the 1950s. Trailing behind on a short walk in the surrounding English woods as he gathered his thoughts, wet leaves underfoot, we shivered in the winter cold.

And on a rainy Saturday in the 1990s, our parents organised a Saturday excursion to 'Denbigh' in Arthur Street Kogarah in Sydney's south where Donald was born. We soon discovered the early twentieth century bungalow of his youth had undergone a classic Australian suburban Mediterranean renovation with nothing left to remind him of his grandparents' house. He spoke to the owners to explain his interest, a sociable chat, and then, a little despondent, we headed off to a delicious Chinese lunch at a restaurant on the Princes Highway (chosen by Myfanwy after a favourable review in the *Sydney Morning Herald*) to soothe inevitable feelings of disappointment.

In *Into the Open*, Donald acknowledged Myfanwy as a crucial part of his prolific career as a writer. Donald attributed her emotional and intellectual support to his becoming a writer of books, along with her significant technical support as a trained journalist, including revisions, suggestions, second opinions, proofs. She is not a character in this book but very much part of its production.

The events in the trilogy conclude in 1958, just before Donald and Myfanwy met. Donald was thirty-six and had become editor of an intellectual periodical, *The Observer*, publicly setting him on a collision course with some of the prevailing ideas about the direction of Australia – a course that most famously manifested itself in his 1964 book, *The Lucky Country*. For that reason the trilogy is the autobiography of a 'nobody' who would become a 'somebody' only after the book finishes. It is an honestly presented tale of character development, with positive and negative twists, against a background of changing social milieux where the fate of the central character is always in the balance. Was Donald Horne destined to become a successful writer with a useful working life? The answer to that question is not clear cut, but one can say that the character, views and faiths of his productive subsequent life were shaped by his earliest years and tested by the later education and experiences described in this book. Donald felt that those later experiences were something of an interruption between his optimistic upbringing and the rational optimism of his life as a writer.

Donald started work on the first volume of his trilogy after finishing *The Lucky Country* as a way of testing out some of that earlier book's generalisations against the example of his own life. He had sociographical motives but writing about yourself inevitably involves some self-appraisal. He'd grown up as a happy boy but had become, in his own words, an 'entirely objectionable university student' where D.R. Horne, angry shouter (one part of his make-up) overpowered young Donald, soft-spoken mumbler of witticisms (another part of his make-up). *The Education of Young Donald* is more a description of the early years of an Australian intellectual coming to terms with his environment than an analysis of personal growth, but he felt that writing the book allowed him to control the D.R. Horne part of himself a bit better. Manning Clark said it well in a perceptive review: 'He, who managed somehow to survive possession by that evil spirit, must now get back to the roots of his life which, one suspects, he rediscovered while writing this deeply moving account of his early days.'

The titles for each book of the trilogy borrow from Henry Adams, Jean-Jacques Rousseau, James Joyce and others and reveal Donald's debt to the international literary canon. Donald became famous for advocating an independent Australia but he was never parochial – he believed Australians could achieve their potential with one eye on what makes us distinctive, and the other on what links us to the human condition more generally and he was an enthusiastic reader of what the world's best writers had to offer. The autobiography, with its descriptions of life across many aspects of Australian society, is a fundamentally Australian work, but his concept of what it means to be Australian always saw Australia as part of the whole show.

Donald is usually described as the author of *The Lucky Country*, or perhaps as the creator of the famous phrase, 'Australia is a lucky country, run mainly by second-rate people who share its luck', but the description doesn't really do him justice. It doesn't do him justice not only because he wrote other good books and penned other pithy phrases but also because *The Lucky Country* isn't so much an examination of the role luck has played in Australian life, as an impassioned call for us to be a country where intelligence and imagination are prized as much as the other good qualities that have helped make the place what it is. *The Education of Young Donald Trilogy* is a tale of the formative years of an Australian writer as he comes to terms with his own strengths and weaknesses while growing up in a country that periodically needs to do the same.

Above all, *The Education of Young Donald Trilogy* is a good read. The first book is seen by some as the best thing he wrote, while the second and third books, written a couple of decades later, show a writer at the height of his powers. Intelligent, engaging, nimble-witted and funny. If you're not chuckling at regular intervals you're missing out.

The 1998 edition was dedicated to his mother and we'd like to enthusiastically acknowledge that.

BOOK ONE

THE EDUCATION OF
YOUNG DONALD

PROLOGUE

Making our own fun

In the summer at Muswellbrook, as in other country towns, it was considered not only cooler but healthier and more manly for boys to 'sleep out'. Since my bed was on a verandah beside the room where my parents played cards, this meant that, although I have more conventional memories of sounds that drifted into sleep – of the church clock striking the hours and the quarters, or of the rushing of water in the weir – my immediate and prevailing memory is of dutifully thinking the Lord's Prayer and then losing consciousness to the sounds of the card game of bridge. For Thine is the Kingdom. The Power and the Glory. Forever and Ever. Amen. One No Trump. Two Diamonds. Two Hearts. Your lead, partner.

Our house was one of the centres of Muswellbrook's amusement and triviality. It was said of my mother that 'Mrs Horne entertains as much as a doctor's wife' and while my father took some of his pleasures more seriously my mother's delight in the diversions of the late 1920s and early 1930s had no limits – bridge, mah-jongg, singsongs, surprise parties, mini-golf, tennis, grand balls, car drives, the talkies, golf tournaments, picnics, afternoon teas and late suppers were all there to be enjoyed as she waited for the next new 'craze' to catch up the people we knew in Muswellbrook.

When I came home from school, walking across the big paddock where the horses were kept, I was likely to see the white dresses of my mother and some of her friends as they enjoyed their afternoon tea beside the tennis court. I would take a cup of tea and a slice of sponge cake coated in crushed fruit and whipped cream and walk across the smaller paddock where we ran the cow, then into the backyard and up past the fruit trees to the kitchen, where I would eat the cake and give the plate to the dog to lick. My mother arranged at least three of these tennis parties during the week, mostly for her women friends, although my father usually came home early enough to change into cream trousers and white silk shirt and play a set, and at the weekends there were sometimes all-day tennis parties when a couple of dozen people would gather on one of the verandahs for lunch and we would run a sweepstake on the results. The kind of tennis played at our house created some scandal in Muswellbrook. The puritans who saw tennis as a matter of competitions and tournaments dismissed ours as 'chatty tennis'; too much fun, not enough nation-building.

Although my mother liked her bridge as chatty as her tennis, my father gave a puritan sense of seriousness to bridge, analysing mistakes in play even if they won a game. He was not a good player, but he had learned some precepts from a book called *Teaching Iris to Play Bridge*, and since he expected life to yield its rewards only to those who followed the rules, justice demanded that the player who most closely followed the precepts in this book should win. I had learned to play bridge at the age of six or seven, and during the weekends we would often play the three-handed game, or, if a bridge player dropped in for an hour or two, I would make a fourth. In these family games my father would run us through some of his simple bridge player's beliefs: *Through strength into weakness* or *Lead the third highest of your longest and strongest*. At moments of great exasperation (perhaps when he had gone down after being doubled) he would remind us that *The game in bridge is to score below the line*. My father's simple rules from *Teaching Iris to Play Bridge* provided some of the most memorable precepts of my childhood.

At the gala bridge parties the spirit of chattiness prevailed. For these great occasions, bridge tables and chairs were brought in from all over town and there were great doings in the kitchen as my mother prepared cheese straws, sandwiches, savoury eggs, asparagus rolls, lamingtons and sponge cakes and then boiled water and coffee essence in our biggest saucepan, ready for reheating. (Coffee was coming in as a craze.) On the big night there was so much eating and laughing that only the most puritan players worried about their bridge. In our evening family games other than bridge we paid no tribute to conscience. Mah-jongg, for example, which was 'all the rage' before bridge, could be played without moral concepts. The hospital matron's daughter had taught me mah-jongg at the age of five when I was in hospital with congestion of the lungs, and I preferred it to ludo or snakes and ladders, although in our house it was easy enough to get up a game of either.

My mother had issued an invitation to her friends to 'drop in' at night when they felt like it. (Scarcely anyone had a telephone: we had abandoned ours when my father had to economise after his salary was cut as a sacrifice to the Depression.) After dinner there might be knocks on the front door. *Now who would that be? Merv or Rita? Bill? Irene?* If only one or two dropped in they would just chat, or play bridge. If more dropped in, they might have a singsong. On more formal nights there were solo performances by those who 'had voices' and 'had brought their music'. My father was one of those who 'had a voice' – my earliest memory of song was of him lying in bed, bouncing me up and down on his bent knees as he sang hit numbers from musical comedies. (Later his songs became melancholy, perhaps reflecting the beginnings of what later became a catastrophic shift in how he saw things.) But the music I most enjoyed were the singsongs, if I was able to be the one pedalling away at the pianola, pressing the pp or ff buttons when the instructions on the roll told me to, surrounded by all these singing grown-ups. When 'Mick', my Sydney cousin and greatest friend, stayed with us she and I would sometimes play 'Tiptoe Through the Tulips' or 'Painting the Clouds with Sunshine' after breakfast, before we settled down to a game of poker.

When there were Sydney relatives staying with us – my grandparents or uncles and aunts – there was always a lot of shouting and laughter over dinner. Sydney people were like that: they shouted at dinner. I became a shouter early. I remember once, when I was aged eight or nine, running off to the lavatory, which was 'down the back' at the bottom of the backyard, and sitting there unyieldingly while my grandfather stood outside and tried to persuade me to come back and apologise to my grandmother for shouting at her over dinner. It must have been a matter of some moment; usually I avoided 'going down the back' at night because of the spiders, and peed under the quince tree instead.

On the nights when my parents were not entertaining they might go out to night tennis (with the hard-shelled flying beetles bashing against the arc lights) or to mini-golf while it was the rage, or to the 'picture show', which was built after the talkies had come to stay. Occasionally we would go to the lending library of 5,000 books at the School of Arts, where my mother would get a 'good book', a Warwick Deeping novel, or something like that, while I would borrow a *National Geographic Magazine* or a *Pearsons* or a *Strand* magazine. (The names of the dozen or so books that were added to the library each month were printed as front-page news in the *Muswellbrook Chronicle*.) If we visited other people I always took a book in case I got bored. On Friday nights, when the shops were open until nine o'clock, we would sometimes walk up and down the main street, lit up with its electric lights, with much of the rest of the town, to look at ourselves. On the hottest summer nights we might go to the swimming baths (which had just been opened). My parents enjoyed themselves down at the deep end; I was left at the shallow end, until I taught myself to swim.

The most formal ways of having a good time were the most traditional – the Anglican Ball, the Masonic Ball and the Golf Ball. For these a band was brought up by train from Sydney, 180 miles away, arriving half an hour before a ball started and leaving on the 3.30 a.m. train, half an hour after the ball was over. When there was a ball I waited around until my mother had pinned a corsage on her long evening gown and my father had adjusted his white tie and put on his tailcoat, then I went off for the night to our neighbours, the Jeeveses. While Gwen and Gordon Jeeves and I were playing bobs (the 'poor man's billiards'), a couple of dozen of my parents' 'crowd' would assemble at our house and have a drink – which they called a 'spot' – and a singsong. Then they would sort themselves into cars and drive off to the ball, some of them still singing. The next morning I would wake up in a bedroom in the Jeeveses' house, watched over (as one might expect in a Catholic household) by prints of the Sacred Heart and the Pope. When I got back home my parents would still be in bed, sleeping it off, their finery scattered around them. On the washstand, for me, in a paper napkin, there would be a piece of cake with silver cachous on its white icing, and I would eat it as my second breakfast. In the next issue of the *Muswellbrook Chronicle* we would read descriptions of all the dresses women wore at the ball.

My father's most serious diversions were golf and shooting. His interest in golf overwhelmed even our interest in bridge, mah-jongg, mini-golf, tennis and ludo. Golf was more than mere pleasure, and a great deal of our conversation was necessarily concerned with it. Between hands of mah-jongg, for example. Sometimes we would start the day with me sending golf balls back to my father as he practised putting into a glass tumbler on the verandah. He even had a few small clubs made for me, and from the age of six I spent many tedious hours going round the course with him, or with my mother, who was a 'chatty' golfer. When he won a cup, his one trophy in seven years of golfing, it was put in the place of honour on top of the pianola, replacing a cut-glass vase. I looked at it every night when I was practising my piano scales. The inscription said: MUSWELLBROOK GOLF CLUB. D. HORNE. 'B' GRADE CHAMPION, 1931.

The Muswellbrook golf links was a 'sporting' course, with eight creek crossings during a full game. For me, crossing the creek provided the main relief in the tedium, along with watching the crows that circled restlessly above the club house as if they were waiting to pick it clean; sometimes one of them would swoop on a ball lying in the brittle yellow grass of the fairway and carry it off to a nest in a gum tree. A few cows grazed on the course; occasionally a ball would land in a fresh cow pat.

Although most of them took their actual golfing seriously, the four dozen men and two dozen women who made up the Muswellbrook Golf Club allowed some social gaiety, when the golfing itself was over. When my father went off on a golfing expedition to one of the other country towns he would come back very jovial, with a pound of chocolate gingers or a jar of stuffed olives, or a pewter pot souvenired from a hotel. (For years I drank my milk out of a pewter pot on which was inscribed the name of a Singleton hotel.) I was taken on several of these expeditions. Once I sat on someone's knee in a car on the night ride back from Denman; for a while they sang songs or told jokes about the aviatrix Amy Johnson and the Prince of Wales; then one of them suggested a game of ring-a-ring o' roses. Beside the road, men in plus-fours and women in sensible shoes pranced round in a circle in the moonlight. I was told to stay in the car.

After golfing in his plus-fours on Saturdays, my father usually got into his grey flannels on Sundays and we went for a picnic, with rabbit shooting before and after lunch. There was the same dry grass as on the golf course, the same cow pats, the same crows with desolate cries, the same dazzling skies, but on shooting picnics the carcasses of dead cattle were to be found, or their bleached bones, whereas on the golf course someone carted the cows away if they died. On the way home the man who acted as our host would ask me to recite poetry. As we drove along in the dark on this Australian country road I would recite from the works of the nineteenth-century English romantics, perhaps six or seven poems. My favourites were 'I wandered lonely as a cloud', 'Roll on, thou deep and dark blue ocean', 'I come from haunts of coot and fern' and 'Oh, to be in England, now that April's there'.

We spent about a fifth of the year in Sydney, holidaying there on each of the school vacations. My mother's first city sport was hunting down new things to buy in the shops. Apart from foodstuffs and small household requirements, she bought nothing in Muswellbrook, saving the pleasures of purchase for concentrated indulgence in Sydney. (I did not realise the risks she ran in this diversion until one night back in Muswellbrook I sat on the verandah and listened to my parents argue about my mother's having run up such a big bill at David Jones department store that they had cut off her credit and she had to open an account at Hordern Bros, a store down the scale from David Jones.) To me, the particular delight of the city was to enjoy the latest city crazes – pure orange juice served from green and orange coloured kiosks shaped in the form of huge oranges; then milkshakes, in milk bars of black and white tiles, with a lot of glass and chromium plate (chromium was the latest thing); then, not long before we left Muswellbrook, the hamburger sandwich, the new American delicacy.

What Sydney really meant to us was enjoyment of the natural and the primitive. The demanding bustle of pleasure that occupied my parents in their country town was replaced in the metropolis by the simplicities to be enjoyed in the bushland on the outskirts of Sydney and on Sydney beaches. It was in Sydney that we beheld the delights of nature; in the country (so brown and bare that it seemed unnatural) we enjoyed the pleasures of society. There was a reserve of bush less than a mile's walk from my grandparents' house, which was much more pleasant than anything available at Muswellbrook (where the trees were stripped away so that animals could eat dry grass and make money to reduce their owners' overdrafts). Sometimes my father and I would walk there to eat our sandwiches, drink our thermos tea, sail my model boat and chat about topics such as the Roman conquest of Britain; but the real bushland extension of my grandparents' house was Yowie Bay, an inlet of Port Hacking, then almost deserted, though now a suburb of Sydney, where my grandfather had his 'weekender'. To get to the weekender, we would walk along a sandy bush track (keeping an eye out for snakes) and then climb down the steep stone steps my grandfather had built to the little house that jutted into the bay on stone stilts. We would put the stores in the cupboard and get into the dinghy and row out and fish; or scramble over the boulders picking oysters; or dig around in the mud looking for worms for bait; or, if it was high tide, jump off the verandah into the water. There was a lot of shouting over lunch; in the afternoon we might sit on the verandah and look across the quiet bay and talk until afternoon tea. I would then go to sleep to the light of an oil lamp and to the sound of the water lapping around the house; I might listen for a while as my grandfather discussed getting up before dawn to catch the tide. At Yowie we were simple-hearted fisherfolk, taking our milk condensed in cans like true primitives, and ignoring golf handicaps and bridge scores and the other demands of the high-pressure living that was already considered to be one of the great problems of the age.

The motor car, the most fundamental of all new crazes, also aided our communion with the natural. Two or three carloads, with everybody's children and dogs, would occasionally go for a bush picnic, the men in their cream trousers and blazers and ties and motoring caps, the women in tailored 'suits'. We would go to the National Park, a large bushland reserve south of Port Hacking, or down the Bulli Pass (where somebody's radiator usually boiled over on the steep climb back), or up to the Blue Mountains or the Kurrajong Mountains. At any turn in the road, if a particularly beautiful view revealed itself, we might park for a while and admire it. For lunch we would build a fire of dry leaves, twigs and small dry branches, and grill lamb chops over it on a wire frame until they were black outside, the blacker the better: while we ate the burnt chops, holding them in our hands, a billy of tea simmered on the fire. We were true Australians. If we heard a kookaburra laugh during a picnic we felt even more Australian.

The climax of the year's pleasure was the most traditional. For a week before Christmas Eve my mother would go into the city every day to do her Christmas shopping, while my grandmother prepared for the feasts of the Christmas–New Year festival. She would ice two Christmas cakes, bake dozens of fruit-mince pies, boil three Christmas puddings in the laundry copper, bake two hams, and get ready the dozen or so chickens she had fattened for Christmas: after chopping off their heads, she would pluck their feathers in the garden, draw their entrails in the kitchen, truss them, stuff them with sage and onion, then roast them in the oven, two at a time. On Christmas Eve these delicacies would be packed into boxes and we would go off to the house we had rented that year at Cronulla, then a beach resort isolated from the suburbs by bush, but now, like Yowie, part of them. About ten of us would stay in the house; others would drop in for the day during the four weeks we stayed there. We would decorate the house with balloons and paper streamers, then I would put out an empty pillowcase at the end of the bed, with a note to Father Christmas (I did not believe in him, but kept up the pretence for my mother's sake). When I awoke at dawn the pillowcase would be crammed with purchases from the department stores. Instead of the usual mid-morning tea and scones in the kitchen we would all enjoy a glass (in my case, a sip) of port and a slice of fruit cake in the garden before we went down to the beach, sunned ourselves and had our first surf for the season. Boasting of our appetites, we would come back to find that the day's extra guests had arrived, and when we were seated around the tables, we would cram in all we could of our feast, washing it down with beer. When the last nut was cracked and the remains of the last dried fig extricated from the last set of artificial teeth we would rest for a while, then go for another stroll down to the beach, and another surf. In the evening, after eating exactly the same meal, we would take down some of the balloons and form sides across the table to play balloon handball. On Boxing Day and until the day after New Year's Day we would go on eating Christmas dinner, supplementing it with fish netted near the beach and sold alive. Then it was all gone, and the bones of the exhausted hams were used to make stock for a delicious split-pea soup, which also lasted for several meals.

For the whole four weeks, unless there was something wrong with the weather, we would go the beach morning and afternoon. On the beach there was always the feeling of being part of a friendly encampment; people would drift off into the surf and, when they came back and dried themselves, describe what had happened to them; then they would sunbake for a while and again drift off to the surf. We would discuss the kind of surf it was that day, what the seaweed, bluebottle or sunburn problems were, how the weather looked. Some days 'Mick' and I spent the whole time either on the water's edge, building sandcastles and then tunnelling water into them so that they fell down, or jumping round in the surf. There were other days when it was the sun more than the surf that attracted us, and we could enjoy more sun. We would lie on the beach, our backs turned up, our cheeks pressed down into the sand, to achieve the mahogany stain that marked the true White Australian. We would go crimson quickly, then so quickly brown that the scorched skin came off in long white strips. We would peel it from each other with delight, enjoying the gentle tickle and congratulating ourselves on getting out of last year's skin.

It was at Cronulla every summer that we bore witness to a truth that was self-evident to us every day of the year: that the most important part of human destiny was to have a good time.

PART 1

OUR PART OF THE VALLEY

1927–34

ONE

In the manner of country towns

My grandparents and some of my uncles and aunts would stand outside the carriage window talking to us as we waited for the express to leave. The train would take about three-quarters of an hour before we got beyond the suburbs of Sydney, first passing the slums of little terrace houses whose backyards, with their rusted iron sheds and dunnies, butted against the railway track; then the more 'suburban' brick houses, with their vestigial verandahs and red tile roofs. At the outskirts of Sydney an extra engine would be hooked on to carry us up into the forest ranges that led to the Hawkesbury River. In the summer the hills might be smothered in the dirty yellow smoke of bushfires, with charred trees glowing beside the railway track. After crossing the Hawkesbury (looking down on the large yellow jellyfish floating midstream) we would pick up speed, running for miles beside the mangroves and the pale blue water, in a long farewell to the delights of the coast. At Gosford we would buy bottles of oysters. For the rest of the hundred-mile trip up the coast we would see little but trees – some of them citrus orchards, most of them just dreary scrub.

As we approached Newcastle, the steel-making city at the mouth of the Hunter, there were settlements of fibro and weatherboard houses. Then as we skirted Newcastle, passing the stockyards and the coal trucks, we were back in the Hunter Valley. For the remaining eighty miles to Muswellbrook, apart from the two main towns of Maitland and Singleton, it was mostly brown grass paddocks fenced in with roughly dressed timber, rolling off to bluish hills. Sheep scampered away from the train as it clattered past, or rested in the distance, near a waterhole or in the shade of a tree. Sometimes we would stop beside a stock train: filthy with their own dung, the sheep would look at us through the bars of their trucks and bleat. In the drought years patches of clay-coloured earth, bare of grass, added the colouring of fever and the grass itself was drab with death. It would be dark when we arrived at Muswellbrook. The house would still smell of the naphthalene we had spread over the carpets before we went on holidays. We would light the gas lamp in the kitchen and sit down to our supper of oysters and bread and butter. Holidays were over.

The mouth of the Hunter (first named the 'Coal River') was found by the whites in 1797 by a party that had rowed up the coast from Sydney in a whaleboat looking for escaped convicts. Several years later someone remembered this 'discovery' when 300 Irish convicts, armed with rifles, pikes and cutlasses, rose in revolt near Sydney. The leaders of the revolt were hanged, but it was considered necessary to set up a penal settlement of 'secondary punishment', to punish the others and to act as a general reminder. To this purpose, a small and horrible settlement was established at the Coal River. By the time we were living in the Hunter Valley the coal-pit villages had long since coalesced around it to become Newcastle, Australia's Pittsburgh, centre of heavy industry, producing some of the cheapest iron and steel in the world, and up the valley there were fifty to sixty pits where the miners were establishing one idea for what it might mean to be a worker in Australia.

Because in the upper reaches of the valley sheep and cattle grazing seemed to be the most honourable forms of endeavour available to humankind, to us at Muswellbrook, Newcastle appeared a mean, grim half-city and the pit towns an insubstantial encrustation. Our part of the valley had been 'opened up' in the 1820s by settlers, some of whom were such gentlemen that they stayed in Sydney while assigned convicts did their back-breaking for them, while most of the others were direct from England or Scotland, unstained by colonial birth (which usually meant a convict mother) or colonial ways.

Imagine Muswellbrook first as scrub, brush, forest and a river with its tributary creeks, the land of the Aborigines. Then the whites walk into this 'wilderness' and begin to clear it for their huge sheep and cattle runs. After ten years someone hammers in a few pegs along the valley and on the side of some hills and lays out a few streets. By 1840 there are forty-one houses and 215 people. There are only two edifices that affirm a connection with a wider civilisation – a post office and a barracks for the mounted police. Then, like cardboard cutouts placed together one by one, affirmations of civilisation appear. An Anglican church goes up, then a Presbyterian church. A courthouse is built. Despite opposition from the gentry, the Wesleyans put up a chapel. Something even more challenging happens: the Irish build a Catholic church. By 1862 an eight-roomed private house is taken over and formed into a school for twenty-five pupils. Someone starts a newspaper in the back room of a shop; it doesn't last. A few years later the railway reaches Muswellbrook, running right through the centre of the town. By now there are eleven hotels and three wine shops. In 1871 a School of Arts goes up, with a library of 150 books, readings, eisteddfods and debates. Two comfortable inns are built, one for commercial travellers and one for the gentry. In the 1880s the Catholics open a convent school and the Masons build their temple. By now there are several 'fine residences' and the green trees that were planted earlier are flourishing in the wide streets. Muswellbrook had become a town. In 1900 they laid down a primitive golf-course; they built the first bunkers in 1926 and replaced the sand greens with grass in 1927, the year we arrived at Muswellbrook. If you looked at Muswellbrook from a distance, sprawling along steep hills, with leafy trees, church spires and green thickets on the banks of the creek that wound through it, it looked like something alien that had been set among the bare, brown paddocks.

The typical Muswellbrook house was a four-roomed weatherboard cottage painted battleship grey, with wide verandahs and a reddish-brown corrugated-iron roof, but here and there was a more ambitious old house, with a traditional formal garden and a gravel drive; there were other old houses, made of little bricks, with steeply pitched slate roofs, and a few two-storeyed stone houses with cast iron railings on their balconies. On the fringes of paddocks, or at the back of other people's gardens, there was an occasional shack, the paint blistered off its woodwork, and even some of the boards falling off, flapping down on one nail, with poultry scratching the dirt round it; and there were beginning to appear houses in the Sydney suburban manner, usually in fibro, with a few feet of verandah tacked in front of the main bedroom.

If you walked to the top of our hill you found the doctors' houses, then you rushed down the other side of the hill to the cemetery. There was an even steeper fall in another part of town – I once tumbled down it, head over heels – from a stately home down to the gasworks. In the river flats, between the creek and the railway track, there was a sleepy part – old houses with nothing behind them but paddocks of maize, separated by empty roads wide enough to take six lanes of traffic, shimmering with heat and in summer drumming with insect noises. The blacksmith (who was also the undertaker and for a while the mayor) had his shed alongside the Catholic church; the railway shunting yards were just across the creek from the golf links; when you walked down the main street past Eaton's Hotel and turned the corner you found yourself right out of town, back in the country.

Some of the town's shops were isolated failures, with holes in their flyproof doors and the colour faded out of the flyblown window displays. Across the railway line, in the new part of town, there was a cluster of brick shops which looked as up-to-date as one of the minor shop agglomerations built ten years before in a remote part of a Sydney suburb. At one end of town, near the river, there were some confident shops of old colonial style, wide-verandahed and leisurely, cleanly kept and freshly painted. At the other end of town, near the railway station, there were a dozen or so down-at-heel wooden shops with stilted wooden verandahs, the paint peeling off them, looking like a set from a Western movie. (It did not occur to me that Australian country towns had begun their histories looking like sets from Western movies.) However, it was to the main part of the town that we gave our respect. Here there was a department store, which we spoke of as an 'octopus' as, taking over some of the smaller stores, it spread slowly down its side of the street; there were small shops that sometimes broke into the brief bad temper of price-cutting wars, bringing prices down a penny at a time throughout the day, proclaiming each change with a freshly scribbled placard; the Greek's café was here, with its marble soda fountain, marble-topped tables, home-made chocolates and steak and eggs; it was also here that the banks had their buildings and the doctors, lawyers, stock and station agents and so forth had their offices; and here one could respect the plain stone of the courthouse, the late-colonial floridity of the post office, the barracks style of the Strand picture show and the indescribable style of the School of Arts.

IT WAS OUTSIDE THE GREEK'S CAFÉ THAT I REMEMBER SEEING THE daughter of one of Muswellbrook's landed families sitting back in the seat of her father's car in Muswellbrook's main street waiting for a café waitress to bring her out an ice-cream. One of my eight-year-old friends started to give cheek; then he stopped in mid-sentence and ran off. She had not even heard him, but it was against his very nature to give cheek to a member of an old family. This was one of the few occasions when I saw a bearer of one of our famous names. Like my mother, they did their important shopping in Sydney, and if they wanted people from the town they sent for them.

It is hard to convey the sense of special consideration with which an Australian living in a country town could then regard the large landholder whose property was developed before the town itself began to form. Muswellbrook was particularly concerned with its old families, because we saw it as 'landlocked'. The large pastoral estates on which the old families lived their remote and unimaginable lives ran right up to the town, cramming it in, and engulfing it with a feeling of mysterious presence.

The special consideration we gave them was different from the city attitudes toward wealth: it was partly a recognition of priority (they got there first) and of the sheer importance and bigness of their holdings. There was something of the Norman about them: in the original land seizures from 'the natives', and in the massive indifference of some of them to the townspeople: even in the self confident territorial identification, as when one gentleman named his son 'Hunter' after the river and its valley, as if claiming for his family a title that covered an area as wide as the English North Country.

Even those members of old families who played some part in the town's affairs (perhaps a round of golf, a church attendance or some charity work) still confounded us because we knew they could enjoy luxuries and indulge in eccentricities. Trips to Europe, for example. Or even trips to Tasmania. They belonged to the social life of Sydney, where they stayed at the Australia Hotel or their clubs, and sometimes raced horses at the Easter and Spring meetings. In Muswellbrook Eaton's Hotel was reserved for their purposes. When Ruth White, the daughter of one of the old families engaged in social work in the town her coolness and self-assurance made our mothers feel self-conscious and inadequate.

To cut the old families down to size we invented stories about how they got there. Even though most of these families were established in the early 'gentry' period of land settlement, we would decide that one family was founded by a tramp who walked into the district carrying his swag, or that the founder of another family won his estate at cards. We tried to destroy their aristocratic look (one gave his son the Christian name of 'Squire'); we tried to imagine that these grand seigneurs were immediately descended from Texan horse thieves.

IN ITS TURN, MUSWELLBROOK, IN THE MANNER OF COUNTRY towns, had produced from its 4,000 people its own internal structure of social differences, perhaps not significant to the old families, who scarcely observed the anthill, but with plenty of meaning to those who lived inside it. Since enjoying leisure was so important, it was access to the sources of pleasure in Muswellbrook that became one of the significant ways in which those of its citizens who were eating well were able to distinguish between themselves. Anyone could play tennis, cricket or football who was good enough for the district competitions, but there were some forms of enjoyment that were not available except as privileges or affirmations of where you stood in the world. From this point of view the most serious events of the year were the two-day Picnic Race Meeting and the Picnic Races Ball because almost all of Muswellbrook was excluded from them. It was an invitation to the Picnic Races Ball that settled who was on top. Most of those who went to the ball were the local landholders and their friends from Sydney and from other country districts. To these were added the members of the merchant family that controlled the department store, who gave the town's social structure a peculiar shape; and by right, or by grace, or by power of overdraft, there also came the town's professional men and those, such as the bank managers and the stock and station agents, who most closely served the interests of the landholders. There were distinctions within lesser gentry: for instance, the leading stock and station agent (who wore an eyeglass) outranked even the doctors. Whatever most touched the landholders was most esteemed. Since my father was only a teacher at the government school my parents were not invited to the Picnic Races Ball. 'In the West' my mother would say, as if to suggest that the human race was not altogether without hope, 'the schoolies are invited to the Picnic Races'.

Schoolteachers had to content themselves with membership of the golf club, where they might join the townspeople who were invited to the Picnic Races Ball, along with other claimants to position such as the bank clerks, the mine manager's daughter, a well-to-do grocer, the managers of the two main hotels, the daughter of a wealthy butcher, the oil company 'reps', and the wife of the assistant stationmaster. The bridge players were much the same 'crowd' as the golf players, along with those who could have joined the golf club if they had wanted to play golf. Bridge playing was itself a mark of status, superior to euchre and five hundred. (My mother described euchre as 'a very funny little game'.) There were also implications of where one stood in the world among the lesser balls, notably that the Golf Club Ball was more 'exclusive' than the Masonic and Anglican balls, although the Anglican Ball was 'exclusive' enough to exclude the rector's wife, who was considered a 'bluestocking' and 'a bit of a red flagger'.

Beneath the golf club set another line was drawn, again with overlapping. (My parents lapped both above and below it.) My mother wasn't invited to some of the golfing houses, and most of the people who came to her tennis parties and afternoon teas did not belong to the golf club. Her tennis parties were a kind of cooperative in which her tennis 'crowd' put in 1/6d a week each to buy tennis balls and pay for the marking of our court and brought their individual contributions to afternoon tea. The people she entertained at home at afternoon teas were schoolteachers, schoolteachers' wives, the wives of some of the salaried railway officers, the postmaster's wife, wives of oil company reps, a hairdresser, a piano teacher, and other odds and ends. The way my mother explained this was that 'the moving population kept together', that those who were stationed in the town for only a limited time preferred to make their own fun among themselves. Finally she resigned from the golf club because she considered some of the other women members had insulted her. It had something to do with a committee meeting of the women 'associates' when she and the wife of an oil company rep were left to put away the chairs and clear the ashtrays, as if they were housemaids. My mother decided that the golf crowd were cheap snobs who did not recognise that schoolteachers' wives were as good as the wives of pharmacists.

OUR HOUSE WAS ON A HILL AND FROM ONE SIDE OF IT YOU COULD see, in the river flats, the steeple of St Alban's Church of England; from the front, on the side of a hill, you could see the steeple of St John's Presbyterian church; from the back on the side of another hill, you could see the steeple of St James' Catholic church; and if you looked down into the town's main street you could see the tin roof of the Methodist chapel. A quick walk round our verandahs provided a reminder of the religious history of England, Scotland, Ireland and Wales. Just glancing at these four churches one might think that the religious tolerance that had evaded the old world was at last flowering in Muswellbrook. In fact the town's tone was set by the Anglicans, with some help from the Presbyterians, and its affairs were very largely in the hands of the Masons. It was church adherence that lay behind some of our most significant social divisions, even if most of those who took pride in their Anglicanism might attend church only on Anzac Day, the national day. To be Anglican was not necessarily to go to St Alban's. It was to see oneself among the ascendancy.

The Presbyterians were accepted as collaborators but it was hard for Anglicans like us to understand why Presbyterians didn't just change churches: there didn't seem much point in remaining a Presbyterian. (My father, born a Presbyterian, had been converted to Anglicanism by marriage.) The Methodists were unimportant – not quite as unimportant as the Salvation Army (which mustered a small following among the miners) – but unimportant. Their notorious Bible-banging and wowseristic opposition to card playing, dancing and enjoying oneself represented an underground threat to those who found part of the meaning of life in having a good time. But it was by our difference from the Catholics (who made up about a fifth of the town) that we members of the ascendancy most clearly distinguished ourselves. In the Masonic families it is doubtful if we considered 'the Micks' to be fully human. My schoolfriends and I believed that the 250-or-so boys and girls who went to the convent were different physically from us; their faces were coarser than ours – more like apes. I can still see my childhood image of a Catholic boy: flat-nosed, freckled, scowling, barefooted, tough and as white-skinned as a grub (a white skin was an evil in a sun-worshipping society); he is about to throw a stone. That the Catholic church occupied the most commanding of the Muswellbrook hills was seen by the Masonic families to be evidence of the Catholics' 'pull'. *Trust them to get the best positions in town*, our parents would say. *There's no doubt about Catholics they stick together.* This belief was held despite the fact that there was only one Catholic family of any significant wealth or position in the whole district. I believed that Catholics had some special words of their own. Through the paling fence that separated our house I heard Mr Jeeves cursing his lawnmower. I misunderstood 'bastard' – a word I had not heard before – for 'custard' and deduced that for Catholics 'custard' was a swear word.

Our intolerance had no necessary relation to special cases. One of the priests visited us on some charity work, and we were inclined to consider him a fine, sincere man. When I was sitting in the sun at home recovering from bronchitis (with brown paper soaked in camphorated oil sewn to my singlet to make me better) some nuns called, and these black figures of superstition spoke quite pleasantly. Much more important: Miss Irene Morley, my teacher for four years at school, was a Catholic, yet, after my parents and grandparents, I considered her the most admirable person living. And Gordon and Gwen Jeeves next door were great friends, even if they went to bed in a room decorated with pictures of the Sacred Heart and the Pope; and even though, for a while, Gordon dressed in red and lace robes at his church and gabbled words I did not understand, reciting his altar boy's Latin as we played in the cowshed. And Mr Jeeves, who was a railway fireman, seemed splendid when I thought of him striding the plates and shovelling coal into the furnace as the train rumbled across the valley through the night, up through the hills and out into the world that lay to the north.

For that matter, our Anglicanism also lacked application in special cases. The rector was not an Anglican at all, really. You would often see him sitting on the floorboards of the verandah of an old wooden house in the main street chatting to the workless men who sat there most of the day; or you might see him leaning against one of the verandah posts of a shop talking to men who didn't play golf or bridge or get invited to the Anglican Ball. In his T-model Ford he visited some of the cockies who lived in shanties squeezed between the big estates, but he was not invited to the houses of the old families. And because of her reputation as a radical and an intellectual – she wrote letters to the *Muswellbrook Chronicle* about the town's unemployed – the rector's wife was not invited to play any part in the church's social affairs. The respectability of Anglicanism was maintained despite this democracy in the rectory.

OUR CLASS ROLE AS ANGLICANS AND GOLF AND BRIDGE PLAYERS had its hazards. As I was getting onto the merry-go-round at the Muswellbrook Show it was hard to believe that I had in fact heard a woman say: 'There's that stuck-up, fish-faced Mrs Horne.' Stuck-up! This was my mother, not one of the cheap snobs who married pharmacists or doctors. In the manner of a young child I said nothing about this: but I continued to turn it over in my mind for several years. As a family we remained ignorant of the lives of the shop assistants, railway workers (apart from 'salaried railway officers'), miners, and the other people who made up most of the town. Mr Jeeves was the exception. He lived next door and he was a friend. He was a good tennis player, and he sometimes had a family game with us, when the tennis 'crowd' were not around.

Although the two small coal-pits at Muswellbrook were closed for most of our stay there, and although most of our stay coincided with the Depression, I did not know much about what was happening to the unemployed in Muswellbrook. The heads of about a hundred households, something like one in ten, were out of work. Some drifted into the half world of odd jobs – a bit of work on one of the estates, some rabbit shooting and the like; a few obtained government sponsored 'relief work'; most simply filled in the day as best they could and drew food relief from the police station. It was not until 1933, and then largely on the initiative of the rector's wife, that any attempt at community relief was made. There were appeals for old blankets and old boots, and the Boy Scouts ran a drive for old clothes. A concert for relief funds brought £20, and an empty shop was taken over for regular sales of goods; enough money was raised to open a lunchtime soup kitchen and to give milk to the children of the unemployed. As a family, we did not seem to take much of this into our comprehension. My father had taken a twenty per cent cut in salary. That was our contribution to the Depression.

Despite its two mines and the railway workers, Muswellbrook was presented as a pastoral market town, and the unemployed didn't exist as a group. It was different on the big mine fields farther down the Hunter Valley, nearer the coast. It was here that for years most of the men in whole townships were out of work – in one town, Greta, ninety-five per cent of the men were workless – and where, in the Rothbury disturbances of 1929, a miner had been shot dead. Altogether in Australia at the depths of the

Depression, nearly a third of the work force was unemployed. I have one memory of a number of men marching down Muswellbrook's main street behind a red flag, but I think they may have been the railway men going to their annual picnic. Plenty of swaggies who had hit the track passed through town, sleeping under the bridge or in the pig pens at the showground, where they had a galvanised-iron roof over their heads and a concrete floor under their backs. If they knocked at our tradesmen's door asking for food, since vitamins had become a craze, my mother would give them oranges. When my grandfather was staying with us on one occasion he walked into the hall to find that a swaggie had come through the front door and was walking towards him. My grandfather shouted: 'Go to buggery!' The swaggie ran out of the house, and possibly out of town.

More within our comprehension than the unemployed were the drifters and scroungers, then a normal feature of country towns and an essential part of some Australian short stories and some movies, in which they were represented as the people who alone saw the falsity of the gentility that surrounded them. One of my best girlfriends at school, one of the smartest kids in the class, had a father who was one of the town's most notorious scroungers, and a notable chook thief. The family lived in a rickety shack with hardly any furniture; when the head of the household got drunk he would sometimes beat his wife and kids, until the boys got big enough to hit him back.

IN 1931 A PHOTOGRAPH WAS TAKEN OF THE FOURTH CLASS OF Muswellbrook District Rural School. There we all were – forty of us – posed in front of the pepper tree, the two smallest boys sitting cross-legged on the ground, and to the right of us a German heavy machine-gun, shipped from some battlefield in France to be set up as a trophy of war beside the school tennis court. The photograph showed how the clothes our parents put us into could seem to divide us – but it was not a real division. About half the boys did not wear shoes, but being barefoot, if a distinction, was a distinction of worthiness. Barefooted boys were tough; you didn't look down on them. None of the others present in the photograph was the child of a golf player. In fact, the only time I remember playing with the child of a golf player at Muswellbrook was at a golf function. He was the son of a bank manager. He became so objectionable that one of the other golfers gave me a penny to punch him on the nose.

Usually we would walk home from school down the main street chattering about the town with the high scepticism of children and sometimes giving cheek to the shopkeepers (until one of them, the manager of a Cash 'n' Carry store, told on me to my father, who gave me a belting). But sometimes we would sneak home from school along the railway line, preferring the grass and the weeds of its ditch to the tar pavements of the main street, and discuss a favourite plan of ours, that one weekend we would run away to Denman. Even when I got out of the railway ditch I could avoid the town, by scrambling along an old drain that ran under its main street and into the paddock, behind our tennis court, where the horses were kept.

As the town's community of children we had a public life, in which the grown-ups could see what we were doing. But there was also a private town we had of our own. Some of it consisted of hiding places: there were river banks in which we could lie in the grass and gossip; old sheds and stables where we could pass on secrets and look at each other. Some of us had made cubby houses. Even climbing a tree and gossiping was to create part of the children's private world. Around our house there were several old sheds and a number of trees available for various negotiations but the two special places were a large clump of cannas into which one could creep with a friend and remain altogether hidden – and the children's realm of 'under the house', an extensive cavern, since the back of the house was propped up on piers on the side of a hill, and provided a whole range of the pleasures of privacy. But we carried around with us our private world even when they could see us. One could stand for hours in the water at the shallow end of the swimming pool with a girl and they didn't know what we were talking about. At children's parties we could giggle and whisper behind our hands. And in the school playground there could be a private web of subversion as enormous as that of a prison yard. If nothing else was available, there were always private looks, secret signs, riddles, double meanings.

It was with the more intelligent of the girls that I could do the most pleasant talking (in our class none of the boys matched, in wits, the brightest of the girls) – in the classroom, in the playground (until we reached the age of segregation), at children's parties, at the movies, sometimes in the backyard, and best of all, when we were organising an act for a classroom play. But except for the girls in our street (who became honorary boys) it was with boys that I was supposed to spend most of my time out of school, except at children's parties. As boys we could swing on the weeping willows on the banks of Muscle Creek, making Tarzan cries, or compete in throwing stones so that they skimmed along the water; or scoop up frog spawn in a bottle and take it home to watch it grow into tadpoles; or lie on the sand and watch the dragonflies; or sit under an old tree and have a yarn, chewing dried stalks of grass. If we were in a paddock we could kick dried cow turds at each other or chuck stones, or we might try to put burrs in each other's hair or push each other into clumps of nettles; then we could run around like mad and practise flying tackles, or see who could pee highest against the fence, or catch a grasshopper, hold it in his fist and let it fly into someone's face when he wasn't looking, or pull its legs off and watch it wriggle. When one of the town's bitches was on heat several dozen of the several hundred dogs (there were more dogs than Methodists) sometimes formed into a pack and followed her; a pack of boys might follow them, roaming all over town, yelping with the dogs, until they got bored and ran over to the Common to try their hands as bullfighters with the cows.

When we were old enough to be segregated into boys' and girls' playgrounds, in the boys' playground, by sheer force, toughness was the strongest code, not only as a test of adventurousness (climbing to the top of the tree) or of bravery (fighting on although your nose was bleeding), but as an assertion of contempt for all other standards. A 'real boy' was a bully: he went barefooted; he had warts on his knuckles and scabs on his knees; he defied classroom instruction and carried a lump of resin in his pocket to rub on his hands before a caning; he asserted his toughness with his whole body, lurching and pushing, scorning even to speak, except to mangle the language in a jargon of his own. In this sense I was not a real boy: I wore shoes, I didn't have warts, I welcomed classroom instruction, and I chattered all day, priding myself on my command of language and collecting new words with more enthusiasm than I collected stamps and, on the whole, unlike a 'real boy', I preferred conversation with some of the girls. Fortunately there were only two real boys in the class and the rest of us tried to keep clear of them, not only because we didn't want to have to explain to our mothers why we had come home with a thick ear, but also because their surliness and taciturnity prevented them from even entering into our games. The rest of us could not parallel their standards of masculinity, and usually we left them to fight it out with each other to see which of them was the most male.

What sometimes made me feel ill at ease as a young male was an occasional physical timidity: I could pull the wings off grasshoppers with the best of them, and I enjoyed pushing boys into nettles or being pushed into them myself, but when it came to bullfighting in the Common I was a bit frightened of the cows, and when it came to climbing a difficult tree I tried not to go first, preferring to leave some other boy to grapple with the perils at the top. I tried to conceal this hesitance about risking my neck, partly by adopting the vocabulary of toughness and partly by forcing myself to perform deeds of derring-do if there was no way out, but I wished that it were not so. To be a real boy one had to conceal part of oneself and pretend to be something one was not. I was terrified that I might lose my nerve if in the next war I had to go over the top at the front into the murderous crossfire of the enemy's machine guns, although I consoled myself that if I could get into the cavalry like my father and fight in the desert against the Turk rather than in France against the Hun, war would seem less frightening because I would be riding a horse. Yet I had not yet learned how to ride a horse.

IN THE FASHION OF THE TIME, I HATED THOSE PARTS OF Muswellbrook that were old. The verandah posts on the shops, the cast-iron balconies, the stone courthouse, the gravel drives, the old houses, the marble soda fountain at the Greek's – I would have liked to have seen all these pulled down. I had the Sydney suburban belief that this should all be replaced with the modern. It would then be substantiated and real. We had no sense of Muswellbrook's past: no one told us anything about the history of the Hunter Valley. Apart from some false legends about the landed families we knew nothing about how or why or when Muswellbrook had been founded and how it had grown to be what it was. I knew more about the Roman settlement of Britain than about the settlement of Muswellbrook.

But I respected the Hunter River. I had a sense of its little streams rising in the bush-covered hills and growing into rivers that freshened thousands of square miles of grazing country, and of how the Hunter ceased to be ours once it left Maitland, where it had to strain itself through mosquito-infested mangrove country to reach the wide, shallow, sandy outlet where the filth of Newcastle was cast into it before it reached the Pacific. Part of the significance of this river in our imagination was that it was the Hunter that made us a 'flood town'. In fact Muswellbrook township was hardly ever inundated by the Hunter – this was more often the lot of Maitland, where, swollen by the waters from its main tributary, the Hunter from time to time broke its banks and burst down the streets and into the shops and houses and out across miles of the surrounding country, occasions so remarkable that postcards were made out of them. But at flood time the Hunter – otherwise a pleasant river, rippling with sunshine as it flowed past the weeping willows – would turn brown and swell to the top of its banks as it rushed past Muswellbrook, sweeping debris along in a roar and bursting out into the river flats beyond the town. When the Hunter was in flood, instead of drifting off to sleep to the sound of bidding at bridge, I would listen to the roar of the river. The caprices of the Hunter added to the sense of impermanence that came from the long periods of drought, and from the bushfires that swept through the scrub on the coast. There were times when washaways of the railway track and the roads cut us off, for a few days, from the rest of the world.

Sometimes, although I loved Muswellbrook, I saw it as only an insubstantial staging camp between somewhere and Sydney. You could sense its insubstantiality in the very town noises. Along with the insects, and the town's roosters, and the church clock, you could hear the clatter of trains in the shunting yard, the sighing of steam engines, the rattling of goods trains and stock trains, the roar of expresses. The highway ran through the town, and you could hear the lorries rattle down it. Even the Hunter was leaving us and flowing down to the sea.

To begin with, at Muswellbrook, we had lodged in a boarding house, with our furniture in storage, and then in an apartment in an old two-storey stone building with some kind of a history behind it (that we knew nothing about); then my parents rented the flimsy weatherboard bungalow where we were to live for six years – a wooden, tin-roofed box of two bedrooms and two living rooms, with unlined wooden walls and ceilings, illuminated brilliantly at night by gaslight, and given a sense of space by the verandahs that surrounded it, by the large kitchen at one end, and by the suites of furniture and the names we gave the rooms. The front living room, which we called the 'drawing room', was too small for our expansive Sydney 'lounge suite', so one of the chairs was placed in front of the fireplace, thereby putting the room out of action for winter nights: however the fireplace in the 'dining room' was free, so in the winter one end of it became the 'drawing room'. And since we had all of our family meals in the kitchen, the 'dining room' itself became the place to eat only when we had guests, and brought into play the 'dining room suite' of oak table and sideboard. In my parents' bedroom there was a brass bedstead and a 'bedroom suite' of oak wardrobe, dressing table and marble-topped washstand (not used except as the place where they kept their chamber pot). However in the room where I slept in the winter (lit by a naked gas jet and with the floor covered by linoleum), there was nothing beyond a curtained cupboard and – what mattered most – the bookcase containing the books bought each Christmas with my moneybox savings. The bathroom (an enclosure at one end of the widest verandah) was tyrannised by a 'chip heater' which, when it was alight, pulsated like a ship's engine, with intimations of explosion. However I had only one bath a week, on Sundays. Usually I sat on a mat on the bare bathroom floor in front of a large pudding basin full of hot water and washed myself, part by part, in a predetermined order. The packing case in the bathroom, used as a cupboard for my toys, would come in handy when we moved from Muswellbrook (we would say); on another verandah there was the packing case in which our pianola came to Muswellbrook: that would also come in handy when we moved.

The kitchen, a large room with a small store room off it, had a disused fireplace at one end where we kept our home-made ginger beer, and, at the other end, an ice chest. (The Jeeveses could not afford an ice chest; they had a hessian chest Mr Jeeves had made, with water dripping over it.) Above the ice chest, on a hanging bookshelf, my mother kept her sixteen books. We drew our cooking and drinking water from a tank fed from the guttering on the roof; a little tap projected from it through the wall into the kitchen, about two feet up from the floor. There was no sink. Washing-up was done in a tin bowl, and when it was finished we threw the dirty water down the tradesmen's steps off the kitchen verandah. As well as eating we did much of our daytime living in the kitchen. If friends dropped in during the morning they would sit on the hard wooden chairs as my mother baked cakes for the afternoon and then served them tea and hot scones. On Mondays the washhouse – a lean-to at the back of the house, where there was a fuel copper – billowed with steam, and later in the day the clothes that had been washed were pressed in the kitchen with a flat-iron that was heated over the flame of the gas cooker.

We congratulated ourselves that we were not house-proud, and we told scornful stories of women who became slaves to the upkeep of their homes. We would joke about the shabby condition the house was in – the loose ceiling boards that rattled, the flaking paint. Apart from a bookcase we did not buy anything for the house in the six years we lived in it. Although a couple of hundred households in Muswellbrook already had wireless sets, we did not buy a wireless. At our house we knew how to make our own fun.

On one side of the house were the remains of an orchard. Hardly any of the trees still bore fruit, although one year a barren tree strangely produced one perfect peach and another year another barren tree unexpectedly bore a pomegranate, thereby solving the problem of what kind of tree it was. The trees were mainly for climbing, but as we got older my friends and I preferred a bigger tree alongside the pepper tree on the other side of the house. There was an old swing near this tree, but it needed mending and no one had mended it, and a stretch of dirt that was very good for marbles and 'flips' (a game played with the tops of boxes of wax matches). Since I was bad at marbles, it was a house rule that we didn't play for keeps at the Hornes.

The main part of the backyard was used for playing with my dog, Zac, who was a cross between a cattle dog and a kelpie, and very excitable, or, as we put it, 'highly strung'. One of my happiest memories of the backyard is of just running around with Zac while he barked and I laughed. There was not much knowledge of dog training at our house, so I trained Zac myself; he was not very obedient (except for obeying the order 'Sit', which he would do even in the middle of the most exciting game), but he liked me, and he was obsessed with the idea of running after tennis balls.

Our paddock, which surrounded two sides of the house and garden, offered the advantages of paddocks – grasshoppers, burrs, dried cow turds, stones, nettles, and so forth – and at the bottom end, near the tennis court, there were an old stable, an old cowshed, and another old shed, all of which gave us the chance to swing from the rafters, to lock each other in or out, or to shut the doors and have private talks, or open our flies and look at each other. On one of the side verandahs I would sometimes play with my Meccano set or the clockwork trains that were handed down to me by two cousins of my mother's, but I did not become a very advanced student of Meccano and the only really enjoyable game we had with the trains was when we pulled one of the engines to pieces.

Sometimes there were afternoons of ennui, when I would sit silently in the plum tree unable to imagine that anything was worth doing, or idly sift my collections of cigarette cards without seeing them. I might go into the bathroom and take my toys out of the packing-case, and then put them back again. Then I would play a game of patience or read a book. Since books came only at Christmas, I re-read and re-read my books; I saved my children's comics (*Film Fun*, and then Billy Bunter) and re-read those, too.

My love for my parents was ideal. The three of us seemed undivided, except when my father beat me, which he would do in a formal ceremony in which he placed me over his knee and slapped my buttocks with the sole of one of his leather slippers. These occasions left me with no sense of crime or punishment – although with some sense of the capriciousness of being caught out – but it did leave me with a terror of loneliness and betrayal. The same fear would come when my father lost his temper with my mother, when I would sit on the verandah and listen, as if to one of the thunderstorms that sometimes struck across the valley. My earliest memories of my parents – pre-Muswellbrook memories – are solely of my father. I can remember how, as a very young child, I sat on the bed and leant forward to touch his cheek and his black hair, and to look at his brown eyes: he then sang a song for me. I adored talking to him, or listening, watching his tobacco smoke spiral and turn blue in a shaft of sunlight, or pottering around with him in the garden, probably getting in his way. I loved his carnations so loyally that I pulled 'Mick's' hair when she plucked a bloom off one of them. As I got older what I enjoyed most was holding conversations with him that seemed more serious than conversations I held with anyone else. I also greatly admired him in company when he made people laugh or sang a song; there were other times – when people were talking about their motor-cars or their businesses – when he seemed inadequate, but when talk switched to the Great War, which it often did, he more than stood his ground. I respected his importance at the Muswellbrook school, where he was second in charge, and when he blew his whistle in the playground we would all stand still; and as a sportsman, although this was more remote and sometimes dull. He called me 'Donald'. My mother called me 'Don'. Although there was sometimes a certain sudden reserve in my father's manner, a thud of silence as if he were suddenly contemplating something within himself, my mother's personality invariably flowed out amongst all of us. I have not one early memory of her, but as a growing schoolboy I admired and associated myself with her appetite for hospitality and her incessant desire to do something. When my mother talked we would all shout inconsequentially, hopping from one subject to the next as if we were playing hunt-the-slipper in a game in which we were never to find the slipper. However, it was not all that often that the three of us were able to enjoy our own company together. Some of my most contented times were at the evening meal when the three of us would sit in the kitchen with no one else there, the tennis party behind us, the bridge party still to come.

The planting of memories

My mother's father (whom I called Pa) was baptised Edward Horatio Carpenter. For Pa the main meaning of life lay in the plain, blunt style. If there seemed any humbug around, Pa would sniff at it, to give it warning; if the sniff did not work, Pa might issue some concise reprimand; if it seemed a hopeless case of humbug, he would simply retreat into his gaunt face, looking very Norman with his white moustache and hooked nose, indicating that he had chosen to have nothing further to do with the matter. He might even walk out of the room. It was as if there were some situations so inflexibly dishonourable that the best a man could do was to remove himself from them. Pa had practised this style from an early age; in 1872, at the age of eight, he had quarrelled with his father because he was living with his mistress in a house on his vineyard estate at Camden, out of Sydney. When, from the dignity of his eight years, Pa spoke up for his mother, he was horse-whipped. He ran away to live with his grandmother. A few years later he went off into the outback, droving, 'to get his colonial experience'.

Pa was remote enough to be my principal hero. His sense of honour in upbraiding his father, the injustices he had borne with a sniff, his laconic outspokenness and unpredictable pride had a quality of excitement lacking in my father's innocent honesty. Speaking one's mind and pursuing one's convictions seemed an attractive style. When, a few years later, I became spectacularly rebellious, I decided that – although the issues were different – I was a true grandson of Ned Carpenter.

Pa seemed to have learned early how to keep his own company and his own counsel. He would usually spend the day by himself in his workshop, or in attending to his garden. At night he would read a library book, using an eyeshade. Some of his most affectionate recollections were about horses rather than people. He had sold the only car he owned shortly after he bought it because he did not choose to accommodate himself to a mechanical contraption which, when you tugged on its steering wheel, did not respond to the pull of the bit. When the annual show was on at Muswellbrook he would come up and stay with us, spending every day watching the horse events.

Despite the aloofness in which he could wrap himself, Pa would sometimes sit down on the back verandah or in the breakfast room with me and tell stories of his youth, when he looked for adventure and knowledge in the bush, a lad of fifteen, riding along the outback stock routes with the drovers. He would tell me the things a man could do with a stockwhip, imitate dozens of bird calls, roll off Aboriginal words, describe the creeks and rivers he had crossed and the stars he had slept under, and make me write down long lists of names of Australian trees and wildflowers. His enthusiasm for Australia was for Australia as a place; he was more selective in his enthusiasm for those who lived there. Australians like us were all right, if we were proud of our descent and our continent. Among us true Australians, outspoken and with no humbug about us, there was a real democracy. Then there were the riff-raff, whether millionaires or paupers, who connived and twisted. They weren't 'straight', so they could all go to buggery. ('Go to buggery' was our favourite swear phrase.) And there were the English, the 'Poms'. Pa loathed 'Poms'. They could not even pronounce Aboriginal place names like Goondiwindi or Booligal and they did not know the difference between a thin-leafed stringy bark and a forest red gum. He was particularly contemptuous of governors-general and governors and their ladies, and told stories about some of them as if they were old personal enemies.

It was significant that Pa's father, who was a great scoundrel, was a gentleman. There it was on someone's birth certificate (we often took out old documents such as birth certificates and paid our respects to them): under the heading of 'Rank or Profession' Pa's father had simply written 'Gentleman'. *Some gentleman!* we would say, as we retold the injustices done by him, repeating our sagas like any other clan. Sent out to Australia from Gloucestershire in 1861 at the age of thirty-three on a remittance to marry a distant cousin. Flouted her by living with his mistress in a house on top of the vineyard's wine cellar. Then deserted her to live with his mistress in Sydney.

Mortgaged the property without telling anyone, and the property saved from foreclosure only by his wife's wealthy sister. *Some gentleman!* And yet when I took out from the box of family records a portrait of him as a young man and looked at the long curling hair, the casual crossing of the legs, the way he lay back in his chair as if he owned it, his air of jaunty self-indulgence, even the big, confident ring on his finger, he seemed a memorable villain. In contrast, his wife, 'Granny Carpenter', Pa's mother, the only family saint, seemed unreal enough for me to keep on forgetting who she was.

We saw Pa's family – the Carpenters – as 'hard': unsentimental, haughty people who with proud sniffs took pleasure in stalking out of rooms, situations and lives. They were not 'hard' in the sense that they calculated where their self-interest lay (quite the opposite) but in the sense that they were above all concerned with the honour and pride of 'face'. The 'hardest' of all the Carpenters was considered to be Lila, Pa's eldest sister, and the ogre of my mother's girlhood, a spinster aunt who became more and more indifferent to human frailty as she grew older, a splendid rider of horses, able to swear like a trooper, and the tyrant of St Mark's Church, a little wooden chapel that had been built right next to her house, allegedly because she had quarrelled with the Rector of Camden and wanted to have a church she could keep her eye on. She walked out of the lives of Pa and his family because she and Pa quarrelled over who should possess their great-grandfather's sword. Lila took the sword with her, saying (in these words) that she would never darken her brother's door again.

Also 'hard' – with the haughtiness of the rich – was Pa's aunt, known as 'Aunt Lloyd', the *grande dame* of our saga, widow of C.M. Lloyd, a grazier, with a property in the Riverina and a mansion in Toorak, so grand that she lived as much in London as in Australia, altogether making eight trips to London. When my Uncle Loy (who was named after her, although we abbreviated the Lloyd to 'Loy') visited her in London during the Great War he found himself, although a private, hobnobbing with bishops and generals. Having no children of her own, Aunt Lloyd had promised Pa she would remember him in her will, but as she lay dying in London in 1926 she had made a codicil, leaving her whole fortune, apart from a few legacies worth about £10,000, to the widow of her husband's nephew, who had been a bishop. It was said to be the opinion of Pa's family solicitors that the will was 'most iniquitous'. 'A most iniquitous will', we would repeat, some of us stumbling over the word, as we retold this part of the saga. And then: 'you know, Dad, you should have fought the case.' 'Yes, Pa, you should have fought the case.' A sniff from Pa. While we recalled the Riverina property, the Toorak mansion and all those deed boxes with 'C.M. Lloyd Estate' written on them, Pa would get on with reading his book. As a Carpenter he knew it was no good whingeing.

To Pa's wife – Laura May Carpenter, known to me as 'Nanna' – life had also been 'hard'; Nanna's father and her uncles and her father's father and her father's uncles, the Sellars, had all been builders, some successes, some failures, but in one of the great depressions of her girlhood they had all been temporarily ruined. For a while Nanna helped her mother make up posies of flowers to be sold in the street. Nanna's father, Frederick Sellar, drank too much. When Nanna married Pa he was drunk for a week. Nanna could remember her Great Grandfather Sellar, an old man who lived a street away from her when she was a girl, who would give her a shilling if she visited him, show her the cat-o'-nine-tails he kept on the wall as a memory of his days as an official at the convict settlement at Norfolk Island, and tell her how salt used to be rubbed into the convicts' wounds after a flogging.

For my mother the symbol of ideal happiness in her family's past was Fernside, the house Pa had left at the age of eight after being whipped. My mother and her family spoke of Fernside as if it were a person, although they did not all see it as the same person. Pa's stories were of its cruel days. Nanna spoke of it with kindness: she would recall how, when she and Pa were married in 1892, they drove in a pony and trap from Sydney to Fernside to spend their honeymoon and how they walked into a drawing room heavy with orange blossom while Lila played a wedding march on the organ. But to my mother and her sister it seemed a reassurance of memory, and they would talk of morning prayers, of the wistaria and banksia roses in the garden, of how Billie the horse would put his head through the drawing-room window, and of how they enjoyed trips into Camden in a fourwheeler. For me Fernside was three or four sepia photographs. I had not seen it. After it was sold we scorned to go anywhere near it; the proud Carpenters weren't going to be caught looking at their family house now that it belonged to someone else. The photographs showed what looked like a large English farmhouse before which tight waisted young ladies of great beauty poured tea for gentlemen in grey hats seated on hard chairs.

In recalling the pride as well as the 'hardness' of the past Pa told stories of Camden, the old settlement out of Sydney, where the eighteenth century lasted longest in Australia, and where he was born in 1864. They were stories of a static society, pre-ordained, and of Pa's pride that he had been born in it, at Macquarie Grove, his grandmother's house at Cobbitty, near Camden, built on a 400-acre property her father-in-law had received as a land grant from Governor Macquarie in 1812. Several times we went to Cobbitty for a picnic and walk in the graveyard to look for collapsed family tombs bearing names famous in our sagas. Having been partly brought up by his grandmother, Grannie Howell, who was born in 1800, when the European population of Australia was less than 6,000, most of them convicts, Pa also had a few of her stories to retell, of a colony with a population no more than that of a large town, and most of them convicts or ex-convicts. There were stories of convict floggings, of 'the blacks' planning massacres, and of bushrangers. A gang of bushrangers once demanded food from Pa's grandmother and played cribbage while they waited for it. They left their crib board behind them when they left, and there it was now in Nanna's sideboard for all to see. My cousin and I learned how to play cribbage on it. Pa taught us.

Among the birth certificates, copies of wills, newspaper clippings and old portraits in our box of family relics there was a miniature of Grannie Howell, stern, proud, 'hard', in the family fashion. She looked like an aged queen who had just ordered her rebel sons to be executed. She was the woman ancestor to whom we paid the greatest and most particular respect. If we were reciting extracts from our genealogical table someone might ask: 'What relation was Grannie Howell to Don? How many "greats" was she?' I could count on my fingers: Pa, father of Mum ... *Grandfather*. Granny Carpenter, mother of Pa, father of Mum ... *Great-Grandmother*, Granny Howell, mother of Granny Carpenter, mother of Pa, father of Mum ... *Great-Great-Grandmother*. Two Greats. There were a lot of people who didn't have as many Greats as that. Her special significance to me was her connection with the land: she represented the natural state of things, that we should be landowners; she belonged to that golden age before the profligacy of Pa's father had brought about our dispossession. I knew nothing about her. She died in 1882 when even Pa was only eighteen. As often as not we spoke of her not as Grannie Howell but by her maiden name, Lucy Mileham, or even as 'Old Lucy', giving her an identity of her own and stripping her of her husbands so that we could get nearer to her. She had married twice, first to Samuel Otoo Hassall, then to John Howell, described on somebody's birth certificate as 'grazier'. Neither of these husbands seemed to matter to us. They took their turn in giving her children (nine altogether), then they died. They had done all that was required of them. John Howell was dead by 1841, when she still had half her life to live. We knew nothing of him, although he was our own progenitor. Gone without a trace. And all that was left to us of Samuel Otoo Hassall, her first husband, was a newspaper clipping describing his wedding to Lucy Mileham, in 1819, and another clipping describing how he got his middle name of Otoo, in honour of a Tahitian chieftain – his father, Rowland Hassall, having been a member of a Congregationalist mission sent to Tahiti in 1796.

The Hassalls were footnote material in Australian history, and we laid some kind of claim to them. 'We're some sort of relation to the Hassalls,' we would say, although we were not. Our requisition of the Hassalls was reflected in the name of my grandparents' house, Denbigh, originally the name of the 1,000-acre estate Thomas Hassall bought at Cobbitty. In corrupt versions of the saga among younger generations the name of Pa's house was taken to commemorate a large estate our own family had owned at Camden; in extremely corrupt versions it was taken to be the name of an estate that 'some sort of relations of ours' had owned in Britain. Although Pa's Denbigh was a suburban house in a suburban street, I gave it the emotional values of an ancestral hall set in its own park.

It is customary for seafaring immigrant peoples in the South Pacific to trace their descent through named generations to great heroes, the famous founders of their families, the first people of their race to set foot on some new island. We were no exception. Our sagas began with James Mileham, our founder, father of 'Old Lucy'; he arrived in the colony as a surgeon in 1797. It was his honour we preserved when we walked out of situations or told people to go to buggery. It was over the housing of his sword that Pa and Great-Aunt Lila had their irrevocable quarrel. Mileham was not even thought of in terms of the number of 'greats' that divided him from me. His significance was that he was a measure of generations of my Australianness. 'How many generations

Australian are you, Don?' Don ... *one*. Mum ... *two*. Pa ... *three*. Granny
Carpenter ... *four*. Old Lucy ... *five*. James Mileham ... *six*. James Mileham was
the reason why we were so very Australian.

We imagined him as we chose. In my imagination I put him into breeches
and a wig, but most of the family put him into respectable twentieth-century
dress: since he was one of the early surgeons of the colony they spoke of him as
'Dr Mileham' and thought of him as one might think of a wealthy and famous
twentieth-century medical specialist. In Sydney society such a person was near
the top of the tree. It would have been better if he had owned a large estate.
But to be a doctor was very good. In his human form he was sometimes spoken
of rather cosily – 'Old Dr Mileham', as if he were that dear old retired doctor
who lived down the road.

When I was somewhat older I came across references to him in some
Australian historical records. He was a Frenchman, and left France at the time
of the revolution. He was posted to various stations in the colony, including
Norfolk Island, where the convicts unsuccessfully planned a rebellion in
which they hoped to kill him and the other officials. His was the third of
the 100 signatures demanding the arrest of Governor Bligh. When he was
passed over as Chief Surgeon of the colony he began writing most miserable
complaints of his position: the agents in London who had been appointed
to receive his pay had defaulted and his bills had been dishonoured; he had
bought a horse for £120 and the horse had died; 'I am *ruined* !!! ... I can only
deplore my misfortune and look forward to the Grave as my Refuge.' When
Mileham died in 1825 Governor Brisbane reported of him that:

> ... his latter years were pinched by penury; his declining health was
> alleviated by no comforts; and he terminated his mortal career after a
> lingering and distressing illness ... Devoted incessantly to the duties of his
> appointment, he saw his companions hourly improving their opportunities
> of enriching themselves which he allowed to pass by unheeded himself;
> and he remained a solitary instance of one who had continuously resided
> in this Colony nearly thirty years, and yet was in want.

So I was descended from the 'solitary instance' of an official of the colony who
had not made his fortune out of it.

Nanna also had a feeling that she had come from a 'family', or, rather, two families – the family of the house-building Sellars, and her mother's family, the Blackmores, who had been coach-builders in Jamaica and spoke of an Indian princess among their ancestors. (I learned later that 'Indian princess' could be a euphemism for a descendant of one of the black slaves – somewhere amongst the mysteries of the past of the Blackmores was there 'a touch of the tar brush'?) But what mattered most was being Early Australian and the best Nanna could contribute to that distinction was Great Grandmother Sellar's cat-o'-nine-tails. My father didn't claim anything for the Horne family: they were not remarkably Australian, since his father and mother were immigrants from Scotland. In any case, my mother had ruled the Hornes out of the picture: after my father's mother and father died, she quarrelled with his sister and, except for my father's eldest brother, we saw nothing of them, so, just as, from being a Presbyterian, my father had married into the Church of England, so, from being a Horne, he had become a kind of honorary Carpenter. His zeal as a convert to Carpenterism was so great that he moved our genealogical tables from oral to written culture by preparing a family tree so that I could know exactly where I stood in relation to Aunt Lloyd, Old Lucy and Dr Mileham, and he would sometimes examine me about it.

There seemed a simple innocence about my father's childhood that contrasted with the land grants, officers' swords, remittances, cat-o'-nine-tails and Indian princesses of Pa and Nanna; he had to walk three miles to and from school each day on a bush track from the pit village in the Hunter where they lived; he became a pupil teacher, that is to say he taught at school while he was still being educated, and then came to Sydney to study at the Teachers' Training College. He lived with his brother Bob in Sydney. Uncle Bob had 'done better' than any of his brothers, and my father was able to 'do better' too. When it came to the Great War, however, all the younger Horne boys did well – so well that, of the five of them, one was killed, one went mad and my father's life was blunted. His father had come to Australia in one of the gold rushes, and when he left the diggings he worked at a coalmine, being number two or number three in a small pit in the bush out of Newcastle. Despite his humble eminence at the pit he associated himself locally with the union movement and with local cooperative societies, building societies and the other kind of forces that so quickly suburbanised Australia. In this sense this old man with the white beard, living as a small boss in a pit village, may have been the most distinctively Australian of them all. But it was in the patrilineal-matrilineal-matrilineal–patrilineal line of descent of my mother that we proclaimed our Australianness, and we saw its living exemplification in Pa.

Pa had been a sleeping-car conductor on the railways. His brothers had been educated into professions by Aunt Lloyd, but there had not been much education for Pa. When he came back from his droving days he joined the railways. He was in his retirement as I remember him, but for most of his married life he had gone off to work in his conductor's uniform and stayed away for his spell of duty, usually working up to the state border at Wallangarra. When he came back from duty he would throw on to the kitchen table the small bag in which he kept his tips. 'Here you are,' he would say. 'Now you can count it.' It was from his tips as a sleeping-car attendant that he bought the land at Yowie Bay and built his weekender. This proud man would clean his passengers' boots and bring them a cup of tea in the morning. Then they would give him a tip.

FOR FIFTY OR SIXTY YEARS AFTER THE FIRST SETTLEMENT AT SYDNEY the land around Botany Bay, only five miles away, was still given over to forests of ironbark, swamp mahogany, turpentine, blackwood and gum, except when the charcoal burners cut down trees to keep Sydney warm. Its mangrove flats and sand dunes were used only by the limeburners who burnt shells to give Sydney lime, although occasional shooting parties might go there for wild fowl or kangaroo. Then, by the middle of the century, when Sydney's population was 54,000, clearings began to appear in the forest, quickly joining together to form a collection of market gardens and dairy farms. Private tollroads were put through, to connect the bush tracks from the farms, and a village of sorts was established at Cooks River. No sooner was all this done than in 1884, when Sydney's population was 270,000, the railway went through and a dozen suburbs began to sprout. At first hundreds, then thousands of families living in the rented terraces that crammed the hills and flats of Sydney took a free trip to the auction sales of the new subdivisions, put down ten per cent on their allotments, and satisfied their aspiration to own a four-room cottage and garden of their own. Near the railway stations a street of shops would assemble along one side of the line. A butcher. A draper. A blacksmith. A hairdresser. An Italian greengrocer. A coachbuilder. A newsagent and stationer. A produce merchant. A confectioner. A haberdasher. A milliner. A chemist. Then some more ambitious tradesmen would establish an emporium. A doctor or two would set up a surgery; banks would put out branches; a post office would be built. Underground, the gas mains were dug in, and then the water mains. Where the new houses had coagulated most densely a few streets and footpaths were paved and telephone lines were strung out on poles. Police lock-ups were built. The hand litters of the volunteer ambulance and the horse-drawn engines of the volunteer fire brigades were housed. Small schools were built, and a few years later much larger schools. Old wooden churches were replaced with edifices in Victorian Gothic. As some sense of identity developed from the settlements of cottages, new and smaller municipalities were founded. Forms of sociability were being established – a few hotels and billiard saloons, a racecourse, a bowling club, sports ovals and public tennis courts hired by the hour. At the end of the century (when Sydney's population was 480,000) there were several Schools of Arts, with lending libraries, lectures, meetings and dance halls. In 1908 there was established a branch of the Boy Scouts.

It was two years after this event, in 1910 (when Sydney's population was 615,000), that Pa and Nanna paid £60 for two blocks of land at Kogarah (Aboriginal: 'place of the bulrushes') and raised another £300 to build a weatherboard house, naming it Denbigh. Kogarah itself (which was about nine miles from the city) had begun to form in the 1880s and the 1890s, but Arthur Street was part of a new subdivision on its fringes, still out in the farmland. An estate had only recently been subdivided and only six houses had been built in Arthur Street when Pa and Nanna moved there; it took about ten years for the street to fill up. There were two dairies and two Chinese market gardens nearby. No shops. A horse bus provided a service to the shops at Kogarah station. When the house was built Pa put down a lawn of buffalo grass and alongside the paling fences planted Cootamundra wattle, jacaranda, silver wattle, poinsettia and frangipani. He put in an olive tree, a mulberry tree, a guava tree, a fig tree, two lemon trees, two mandarin trees, a peach tree and an apple tree. He planted wild olive from Fernside along the front fence and set up a flagstaff in the front garden. Lattices were built to separate front from back. Beside the side verandahs he set up a fernery of staghorns, maiden hair and palms. Along and over the path in the back garden he built a rustic arch, with a grapevine running over it and shrubs and ferns alongside it. In one corner of the back garden he built a chook run, in another corner a run for his pony. He built a workshop, a shed and a stable, and took a cutting from the Fernside wistaria and planted it alongside them. He was planting his memories around him.

Nanna and her children built up memories into the house itself, so that it became a kind of spirit house where the past was stored and, when required, summoned to give some meaning and shape to present action. Denbigh began to be seasoned in this way by its first death. A big room had been added at Aunt Lloyd's expense so that Granny Carpenter could spend her dotage in it. She was not long dying, but for a while this unfortunate old lady, her memory mainly gone and her senses awry, shared a house with young people to whom a year seemed a long time. My mother and her sister were now 'flappers' and they added gayer memories to the house. In their ankle-length black skirts and white blouses, with black bows at their collars and black bows in their long hair, they had a few years' devotion to enjoyment, working as typists and acquiring some of the ways of the city. They turned their parents' new house into an instrument of hospitable frivolity. When Granny Carpenter died, what had been her death chamber was turned into a drawing room, and here the 'flappers' and their friends would roll up its carpets and dance the foxtrot, the waltz, the barn dance and the lancers. They had 'musical evenings' when people brought their favourite music scores and took turns at playing the piano or singing, and 'surprise parties' when their friends would invade Denbigh for impromptu parties. And they had 'send-offs' for the boys who were sailing to the Middle East or France, to the war, parties of twenty or thirty young people, each of 'the girls' bringing her contribution to the supper. When their brother Loy had his sendoff in 1915 he left behind him a studio portrait of himself in private's uniform; they framed it and gave it a place of special honour in the dining room by adorning it with flags and his battalion colours of chocolate and green and putting it on a lace cloth on a small table of its own. They saved his letters and postcards from France and the telegram that told them he had been wounded. When the war was over, and in 1919 Loy returned to Sydney, they planned the biggest of their 'Welcome Homes'. They strung a big sign, 'Welcome Home to an Old Digger', in chocolate and green satin, across the front gate and pinned big 'Welcome Home' signs to the curtains inside. The house was saturated in red, white and blue paper decorations, and from the flagstaff in the front garden they flew the flags of all the allies. About fifty people were at Denbigh to welcome Uncle Loy; Nanna had spent days in the kitchen preparing the chickens and plum puddings. Loy confessed later that when he walked into the house, straight from his troopship, he felt like a stranger among all these people and wanted to walk out again. Now he was not only the eldest son; he was also a 'returned man' who could talk about the Hun and the trenches in short sentences, wryly, between draws at his pipe. He knew something his father didn't know.

After the send-offs and the welcome-homes the big room that had been built for Granny Carpenter to die in was clearly established as the family's meeting place or hall of ceremony. Its most traditional use became that of formal banqueting chamber. After the furniture had been piled into a bedroom, trestle tables, which were hired from the School of Arts (along with the china and cutlery), were arranged in a big 'U' to seat thirty or forty people who would tuck into cold chicken and ham salads, trifle and cake, served with beer or sherry. Not long after Uncle Loy was welcomed home and they had been to all the Peace Balls, it was here that my aunt and then my mother and then Uncle Loy had their wedding breakfasts. (There were eighty guests at my mother's wedding, and they ate in two sittings.) After the bride and groom had changed their clothes, the guests danced around them, holding hands, singing 'Auld Lang Syne' before the married pair went off on their honeymoon to the Blue Mountains.

TO ME, THE VERY WORD 'DENBIGH' SUMMED UP MY WHOLE SENSE of family – not only uncles, aunts, Pa, Nanna, second-cousins-once-removed, but the dead as well. It was the family temple – the whole meaning we gave ourselves as a family. Denbigh lasted more than fifty years before it was sold to a builder so that he could pull it down and build two brick bungalows on its land but I remember it best when it had entered its third decade, in the early 1930s (when the population of Sydney was rising to one and a quarter million). That was the time when we would stay there on school holidays from Muswellbrook. With three bedrooms, drawing room, dining room and breakfast room it seemed a bigger and more important house than those I knew in Muswellbrook, and with Sydney refinements, such as the fact that the walls of its rooms were plastered (although not its ceilings) and that, since electricity had come to Kogarah in 1923, there was electric light. It was at Denbigh that I first saw electric appliances in use: Nanna had an electric hot-water jug and a wireless and, later, an electric iron and an electric toaster. There was an old hand-winding gramophone ('Turkish Patrol', 'Hallelujah, I'm a Bum!' and the 'Dead March in Saul' were my favourite records), but singsongs were mainly provided in the form of broadcasts of the community singing sessions that were held every day in the city during the Depression so that people could cheer themselves up by gathering in a hall and singing some old songs. Sometimes 'Mick' and I would have our own singsong in the morning, by adding our voices to the community singing as it came over the wireless. One of Denbigh's splendours was that it was sewered, while at Muswellbrook we still had dunny men. (The Denbigh lavatory was set in the middle of the garden, at the end of the red-painted concrete path that ran under the rustic archway; it was still 'down the back' but there was a twist in the path and a hedge walled the lavatory in so that only its roof could be seen from the back verandah. Nanna would cover the walls with pages she had cut from the coloured supplements of the Sunday papers, changing them from time to time.) In the bathroom there was another city refinement: Denbigh had replaced its chip heater with a gas heater for bath water. Like our bathroom at Muswellbrook the bathroom was a walled-in part of the back verandah. There was a tiny cold-water basin in one corner, barely large enough for a pair of hands, and a white marble-topped table, where there was a shaving mirror, with a chair in front of it so that the men could sit down while shaving. Here Pa's 'cut throat' blades were laid out, with his strop, and alongside them was the more modest box covered in black cloth where my father kept his safety razor. (I would look at them, and touch them and think about becoming a man.) The drawing room at Denbigh was much bigger than our Muswellbrook drawing room, and it was not so overcrowded that its furniture covered the fireplace. Its dining room also seemed superior to ours, for whereas we used our dining room for almost everything except playing the pianola or playing bridge, the Denbigh dining room was so dignified that it was not used at all; eating was done in the breakfast room or the kitchen.

The nature of Denbigh as ancestral hall was accentuated by the fact that Nanna had hung about 250 framed photographs on its walls – of her family, Pa's family, and the family they had themselves created, along with photographs of friends and family animals. In the sitting room and her bedroom the walls were thick with photographs. Whenever 'Mick' and I decided to inspect her collection it might take us an afternoon to do justice to it, without even opening the photograph albums and the wooden boxes.

The garden at Denbigh was much more varied and better kept than our Muswellbrook garden and more of the trees bore fruit. It was in this garden that 'Mick' and I spent a lot of our time. As we played in the garden we would hear the familiar sounds of street trade: the slow clop of the milkman's horse and the rattle of his cart and the clink of the can as he poured our afternoon milk into the billy that hung on the lattice; the rattle of the greengrocer's lorry drawing up outside the house so that Nanna could stand in the street and choose her fruit and vegetables; the rattle of the baker's horse and cart ('How many today, Mrs Carpenter?'); the iceman's footsteps as he hurried round the side and into the kitchen, holding the big block of ice on his shoulder in a hessian bag; sometimes the cry of the clothes props man ('Clo-props! Clo-props!') or the Bottle-oh (calling, 'Bottles! Bottles!' with a glottal stop instead of a double 't'). When the Bottle-oh arrived we would run into the street and yell at him to come in. Empty bottles were stored under a hedge near the garbage tins, and the money for them was a perquisite of ours. We would watch him count out the pennies; then we would go down to the ham and beef shop round the corner in Prince's Highway where they sold lollies.

We always had our morning tea in the kitchen, often quietly, between the morning's tasks, sometimes dramatically, because the kitchen was a place for family news announcements. On Sunday mornings tea in the kitchen made a quiet sociable beginning to a day of sometimes demanding sociability. Since four of Nanna's children and her sister lived within a few minutes' walk of Denbigh, at least one person always seemed to drop in for a cup of tea on Sunday morning: sometimes a whole family might arrive to have a chat while the scones and cakes were being made and the roast meat and the apple pie were cooking in the oven. We would make our Sunday morning cup of tea last as long as we could; we had some of our biggest laughs over Sunday morning cups of tea, crammed together, sitting or standing around the kitchen table (our cups placed between pudding bowls and apple peelings, the thick dobs of butter melting into our hot scones), looking into each other's faces, trying to maintain our intimate conviviality as long as we could before habit demanded that the visitors should go home and Pa and Dad would retire to the back verandah to read the Sunday papers while Nanna and Mum finished the cooking. Our hot midday dinner was served in the breakfast room. We did not do much talking as we ate our way through the roast meat, the baked potato, baked carrot, baked sweet potato, boiled peas and boiled beans, and the apple pie and whipped cream. After the washing-up was done it was Nanna's and Mum's turn to read the Sunday papers before we all went off to our bedrooms to change into better clothes to be ready to receive those who had been invited to afternoon tea or who would just drop in on the off-chance. There was always some excitement when we heard the click of the front gate on a Sunday afternoon: who would this be? Sometimes there might be a dozen or more for afternoon tea, including people who came from the other side of Sydney. We would eat our tomato sandwiches, buttered scones and sponge cake in the garden, sitting in our good clothes in a big circle of deckchairs, wooden garden seats and cane chairs brought from the house, or in another big circle in the drawing room; then people would split up into smaller groups – two or three women might retire to a bedroom to discuss someone's illness, some of the men might wander around looking at the garden. Afternoon tea seemed to fade away rather than end. There was all the noise, and then there would be a quiet time when the only people who remained were those who had accepted our invitation to stay for the evening meal. (Everyone who dropped in for afternoon tea was invited to stay for the evening meal.) They became individuals for a while, some of them looking over the Sunday papers in case there was something they had missed before they again formed themselves into a group – this time in the breakfast room, to eat 'Tea'. Tea was always a party. Soup first. Then a lot of passing of undressed shredded lettuce leaves, sliced tomato, sliced gherkins, pickled onions and chutney, to be eaten with the cold meats. Then fruit salad and cream. Then cakes, with our cups of tea. It was at the cake-and-tea stage that conversation expanded; we might linger over it until there was a click as the front gate shut, another click as the lattice gate shut, and footsteps were heard coming down the side path, indicating that the first of the night's visitors had arrived. The women would retire to the kitchen to wash up and gossip, and the men would group themselves in the drawing room for men's talk. When the women rejoined the men and perhaps some more visitors arrived we would cram ourselves into one big circle and get on with the conversation – shouting and laughing – until supper-time. More tomato sandwiches. More sponge cake. More cups of tea. When they had all gone home (although visitors arrived by the back door, they always left by the front door), Mum and Nanna would have a quiet talk for a while about what they had learned during the day, while Dad washed his false teeth in the bathroom and went down the back and Pa put out the cats and hung the billy can on the front fence for the morning's milk. We would see each other again when we had our early morning cup of tea, before breakfast.

In our great mêlées of conversation you had to be quick off the mark and you might have to shout to get attention, although once you had the floor everyone would hear you out. There were conventions of what should be said where and when. The kitchen, preferably in the morning, was reserved for intimate or red-hot news, worthy of special release, and for most family arguments. Afternoon tea was the time for a simple exchange of information, disconnected statements about what everyone had been doing lately, not usually anything very important. Around the table at the evening meal we were likely to philosophise, although philosophising might break out at other times of the day, particularly in the drawing room, if anyone felt like it. There were social trends to talk about: how the talkies were killing the live theatre, the length of dresses, the agonies of the Depression, women smoking in public, and the like. Was money all that mattered? was an issue over which debate could go on for hours. (Most of us felt that money did not matter all that much, but money had its supporters among us.) Where did real human happiness lie? Could this ideal style ever be achieved? Who was best – a kind or a clever man? What was the real nature of human wisdom? Which was best – to get on in the world or stick with one's friends? There were no conclusions. Over the cakes and cups of tea we simply affirmed our values and confirmed our suspicions of those who did not hold them.

In the drawing room, people often put on a turn, mainly in retelling famous anecdotes. Someone would say: 'Come on, Unk, tell us about the time ... ' and we would all settle back to enjoy a well-told and well-remembered yarn. At some stage of the evening I might be put up to give a comic recitation. On these evenings we were a tribe amusing itself by retelling famous stories: no new material was required, unless someone was good at impromptu wisecracks. (Of the group, for a while, my father was best at this.) On evenings when we seemed to be short of good raconteurs someone might fill in by describing the plot of a good picture she had seen or of a good book he had read lately. There were other evenings when it was understood beforehand that one or two famous storytellers would be doing most of the talking. When a great-uncle and great-aunt and their two sons came back from their annual trout-fishing holiday, they were expected to come round and tell us all about it. There would be a full house that night. Every Christmas they went camping with two other families, and we would listen to them all evening. Uncle Loy went camping every Christmas at Shellharbour, and when they came back he and Auntie Jan would also report on their holiday, although with more restraint and to a smaller audience. The best of all at this particular kind of storytelling was Aunty Con – a cousin of Nanna's – who for twenty years spent every Christmas at the same boarding house at Katoomba in the Blue Mountains; Aunty Con could fill in the whole evening performance to a packed drawing room on the subject of her experiences at Katoomba that year.

Specialist topics – clothes and diseases for women, sport and motor-cars for the men – were discussed within the sexes only if the general discussion broke down and smaller groups formed within the circle, or when the women were in the kitchen doing the washing-up or in the bedroom trying on hats. But there was not usually any break-down of general conversation as between men and women: some of our best performers were women. We treated women as human beings more readily than they did in some of the more polite suburbs where, I learned a few years later, you were supposed to stand up as women went in and out of rooms and hand them things, hold things for them, give them chairs – as if there was something wrong with them. In general we managed with a minimum of etiquette. You didn't eat peas off your knife or speak with your mouth full, but to be natural was what mattered. You had to be yourself.

Sometimes there were dead days at Denbigh, and there seemed to be more of them as I got older. There were days when things were so quiet that you could hear the sitting room clock tick from the back verandah. Mum and Nanna would be in town shopping, Dad would be playing golf, Pa would be working in the garden. Pa and I would talk to each other in the kitchen, for morning tea and lunch, and then we would go our own ways. I would wander around the house by myself, touching things or looking at them. I would take out all the decorative buttons that Nanna had cut off old dresses and put into a drawer in a front bedroom and forgotten. Then I would take out some of the pieces of string that were kept in a calico bag that hung from a nail in the laundry, lay them out on the lino, and look at them. I would take out the flour bin and look inside it, feeling the flour with my hands, and examine the contents of the pantry shelf by shelf, reaching over to the back of each shelf before passing to the next, and climbing up to the top shelf to get a good look at the discarded kitchen equipment there; then open the doors and lift up the hotplate of the disused fuel stove; or peer into the fireplace of the fuel copper in the laundry. I would hide myself in the fernery and rub the green palm leaves between my fingers, or sit on the back verandah and look at the shell of a dead tortoise that was nailed above the doorway. When the others came home Dad would tell me about his golf and Mum about her shopping. We would sit around the fire in the sitting room after dinner. Pa would put on his eyeshade and read his library book; the others would listen to the wireless. I would sit on a hassock and look at the china door handles, the coloured glass of the hall door, the ornaments on the mantelshelf, the dog sleeping beside the hearth, the cats sleeping in the easy chairs. I would listen to the clock tick. I would put the poker between the pieces of coke in the fire, wait till it reddened, then take it out and watch the red turn to black.

'MICK' WAS THE FAVOURED COMPANION OF MY CHILDHOOD. (She was called 'Mick' as a family name: for the rest of the world she had a name like other girls.) 'Mick' was about my age, about the same height and colouring and the person beyond all others with whom I could feel my 'self'.

My earliest memories of 'Mick' went back to our first explorations of the world and of each other as we came out of babyhood, but after Dad and Mum and I migrated to Muswellbrook, although she would visit us there, the main scenes of our friendship were at Denbigh and in whatever beach house we rented each year at Cronulla. Whenever we came down to Sydney, three or four times a year, 'Mick' would usually be at Denbigh as one of the welcome party. We would run down the back garden, and, beside the fowlyard, exchange whatever new information we had received about the world. Then we would sit on the verandah and make out a long list of the games we would play for that holiday season. Some were conventional ('hidings' or 'chasings' or French cricket), or playing Nanna's gramophone records, or poker, or joining in the community singing on the wireless. But a number were dressing-up games, based mainly on re-enactments of what we had read in books or seen at the movies. We had pirate games, Red Indian games based on Joan Crawford movies (which 'Mick' liked and I didn't). Some of them were satirical imitations – we particularly liked satirising Shirley Temple. Some were private enough to bear code names. Unless there was a special occasion, each day we met we would go through the list again (sometimes arguing over it, or adding to it) and decide which game would be played that day. Some of our dressing up games were merely knockabout. Others could be character studies with plots complex enough to pass from one day to the next until we tired of them. As we grew older we would usually devise a concert built around a dramatisation of popular songs – 'Shuffle off to Buffalo', 'The Man on the Flying Trapeze' etc., to be practised as a game and then put on for the grown-ups.

The two favourite places to stage our dressing-up or satirical imitation games were the back verandah and the main part of the back lawn, where the clothes props held up the clothes line. But 'exploring Denbigh' could itself be one of the games – checking the photographs on the walls, going through the postcard albums, hiding in the fernery, climbing the fig tree, counting the hens. Sometimes we might play in Pa's workshop, warm with the smell of the pollard that was mixed with scraps from the kitchen and fed to the chooks. We might take out and admire the tools that Pa kept in a chest on which were pasted drawings cut out of Cole's Funny Picture Book. Or we would look for new props for our games (sometimes finding new props would suggest new games) among the discarded things stored in the old stable. Next to the stable there was now a garage that had been built to house an uncle's T-model Ford. Sometimes we would play the game of 'Old Denbigh', made out of memories of snapshots and family sagas re-enacting the life of the historical Denbigh of ten or twenty years before. The greatest of the Denbigh games came when there was no one else in the house: there it all was, a background to our pleasure. We could even explore the secrets of Nanna's and Pa's bedroom.

We would go to the movies, and the regular outings – the zoo, the museums, a day's visit to Manly, 'a lunch in town'. We would sit together with as much honour as the others at all the great family meals and other family gettings-together, sometimes silent or giggling if a great tale was being told, sometimes brought into the conversation or even asked to put on a turn. We would go 'for a spin' in family cars and be photographed at family picnics. At Cronulla we abandoned dressing-up games and played mainly the part of swimmers, surfers, sunbathers, ice-cream eaters, ginger-beer drinkers and makers of sandcastles, but since the others were also having a holiday we could persuade them to join us in French cricket or even 'chasings'. What mattered most was our companionship. It was not imaginable that we could have secrets from each other.

In December 1932, after Mum and Dad and I had again arrived at Denbigh from Muswellbrook and had our cups of tea in the kitchen with the welcome party, I went with 'Mick' out into the garden and stood beside the wire netting of the fowlyard. We each had a secret. It was the same secret. We had learned how babies were made. Knowledge of this fell like a shadow between us. At first only a light shadow, but something that grew, until we knew that things between us would (as they said in the Joan Crawford movies) never be the same again.

THREE

Country, King, God

In the bottom right-hand drawer of his side of the dressing-table Dad kept the symbols of his most important beliefs. When there was no one in the house I sometimes took them out and wondered at them. There were his Masonic apron, his Bible, his war medals, a Bedouin's knife he had brought back from the Palestine campaign, an army revolver, his spurs. One day I put on the Masonic apron and the medals. Holding the revolver in my hand, with the Bedouin's knife at my waist and the spurs on my feet, I looked at myself in the mirror and saw an Australian.

In the photographs he kept in this drawer columns of horses marched along the desert; Dad, in his hat with the emu plumes, rode down a desert wadi; a desert plain was studded with Australian bivouacs; in Cairo there were men in sun helmets and Sam Brownes or fezes and galabeahs; there was a background of mosques, minarets and British lions; in Sydney the troopship was leaving for Suez, its paper streamers billowing up in the air. There was also a newspaper clipping of pictures of Dad and four of his brothers in their uniforms – a private, a sapper, a trooper, a lance corporal, a sergeant – and a photograph of the grave of one of them.

The Great War and the ethos of the Australian soldier cast a bright light over our house. We lived not only with clear memories of the past war but with thoughts of the wars to come. It was assumed that when my turn came I would also play my part. One night, when we came home from a pacifist movie, as we had our cup of tea in the kitchen Dad was silent. Then he looked at me anxiously and said: 'You'd fight if you had to, wouldn't you?' Often there were rumours of war in the Sunday papers and, home from a day's rabbit shooting, we might discuss the prospects of war before I went to bed.

The only day of ceremony in our year was Anzac Day, the day we commemorated the Australian landing at Gallipoli in 1915, seen as the occasion when Australia 'came of age'. On Anzac Day Dad would put on his three medals and join the other 'returned men' who were forming up in the main street behind the Muswellbrook brass band, the Boy Scouts and the Junior Red Cross. They would march up and down the street to the music of wartime marching tunes, then bifurcate – the Catholics to St James' Church, where the priest would remind his congregation that life was eternal and that they should pray for the souls of the dead soldiers; the Protestants to St Alban's Church, where, as the rector processed, with the gold cross held before him, and the choir sang 'Onward Christian Soldiers', we knew that soldiers like Dad and his brothers, by volunteering to sail across the Indian Ocean to fight the Turk, had given the word 'Australia' meaning. The rector would remind us that Australia was young in the company of nations but that its nationhood had been earned in the glorious epic of Anzac bravery. 'The history of Australia begins with a blank space on the map and ends with the record of a new name on the map, that of Anzac.' While we sang 'Fight the good fight with all thy might' the returned men would move in procession to the Soldiers' Chapel, where in front of the flame of remembrance the roll of the Muswellbrook dead would be called. The Last Post would sound, then the Protestant returned men would march to the war memorial, where the mayor would preside over another ceremony and we would sing 'O God, our help in ages past, our hope in years to come'. One of the Protestant clergymen would then remind us that Anzac Day was a solemn sacrament of mateship, commemorating our heroes as a band of brothers who for the first time in history had shown a final understanding of the essential humanness of mankind. However impatient they were of saluting and ceremonial, they could rise to the occasion, do the right thing and never let down a mate. We would observe two minutes' silence in honour of the men who had escaped calculation and ambition by dying blameless and young, in the simple act of men following their destiny. The Last Post would be sounded; wreaths would be laid; we would sing Kipling's 'Recessional'; then the bugler would blow Reveille and the ceremonies would be over until the reunion dinner at night, when the rector would again remind his audience that Anzac Day was the birthday of our nation, commemorating forever the nobility of men who took something on and saw it through without whingeing; other speakers would remind themselves that Australian soldiers were uniquely independent-minded and adventurous, uniquely able to display initiative, uniquely healthy in body and bold in spirit, uniquely *men*. Australian soldiers were the greatest men in the world.

Dad had fought in the desert with the Australian Light Horse. It was not on the Western Front and with the infantry, but only in the desert and with the cavalry, that war seemed fully to assume the heroic meaning we gave it, that things renewed themselves when young men went off to risk death. Dad had not reached Gallipoli; he had got sick on the island of Lemnos and by the time he was better the Gallipoli campaign was over. When he campaigned in Palestine he was so reduced by the sicknesses of the desert that at the end of the war it was noted on his discharge certificate that his physical condition was one of 'general debility'.

Much of the Australian history we learned at school, particularly the record of exploration, seemed to concern itself with virtues similar to those of the Anzac spirit – endurance, commitment, the expression of will. (The school syllabus spoke of liberating the child's life force.) As men struggled across deserts of stone or sandy wastes Australia seemed the dead frontier, the land of the dogged gesture. Even the Gallipoli expedition, the savage act of national self-recognition, had failed.

We were living through a run-down time. I was seven when prices fell in Wall Street. The worst the Depression did to our own family was that Uncle Loy, who had been an agent for Borsalino hats and a few other Italian lines, was put out of business by high tariffs and for a while worked as a floorwalker at a city department store, another Carpenter forced to eat his pride. But the Depression seemed to drain the whole country of its spirit, and for some years most of what I was likely to hear was pessimistic. There was an occasional glint of sardonic wit: merely to say 'Prosperity is just around the corner' could set a roomful of people laughing. But despite the happiness with which I was immediately surrounded, there was nothing invigorating to hear about Australia. Australians may have been the best people in the world, but the best, apparently, was no longer very good. The Depression had a sense of inevitable calamity about it, like floods farther down the valley, or bushfires on the coast.

The main contemporary enthusiasms lay in admiration for our sportsmen and aviators, particularly the cricketer Don Bradman and the aviator Kingsford

Smith. Even here it was their will that was most admired. Bradman was the boy from the bush who had battled his way to the top; he was a calculating, implacable batsman; a granite idol. Kingsford Smith showed more dash. As he and other Australian aviators crossed continents and oceans in their improvised aeroplanes we marked their positions on maps and pasted their pictures in scrapbooks. This was 'exploring' – very Australian. When some of them died, lost with their planes, no one knew where. This also seemed very Australian. They were great men, capable of iron-willed Australian failures.

Perhaps the most human thing we felt at school for our newly established nation was an admiration of our plants and animals. We were proud of kangaroos and platypuses and koala bears, gum trees and flannel flowers. These were ours. The waratah seemed a proud symbol; we celebrated spring by festooning the classrooms with wattle; at Christmas we decorated the table with Christmas bells and put a sprig of Australian Christmas bush on the plum pudding instead of holly. Along with the English nature verse we also learned poems that boasted that our Australian seasons and countryside were different from those of England. The Anzac spirit had its place in the school syllabus, but it did not carry conviction at school; you needed a father at home with a secret drawer to do that. And it did not finally carry conviction anywhere. It was just a belief. We believed in the Anzac spirit. But we didn't believe it existed. Not any longer. The Anzac spirit was a failure, too. On the evening of each Anzac Day Ruth White subsidised the attendance at the reunion dinner of any 'old diggers' down on their luck who were passing through town. After their free dinner they could go back to sleep under the bridge or in the pig pens.

AS WELL AS BEING AUSTRALIANS WE WERE ALSO BRITISH, FIRST-class citizens of the Empire, and at school this was what we were most taught to admire. One of the themes of the history curriculum was 'The growth of an empire based on liberty'. In this growth the campaigns of Clive and Wolfe, the Indian Mutiny and the Boer War led up to the climax of the Great War, in which the imperial dominions joined the mother country in fighting for freedom. A large part of the geography curriculum was given over to the theme of 'Australia and the Empire'. Jute in India, huskies in Canada, geysers in New

Zealand, springboks in South Africa, rickshaws in Singapore. We learned the names of the British naval stations, the principal sea routes that linked them, the names of the great imperial cities, and we learned nothing about the rest of the world. That came later – in the newspapers, when, nation by nation, year by year, the rest of the world demanded that we pay attention to it.

On Empire Day we would assemble in the school playground, clattering the tin mugs we were taking to the picnic. Arranged in classes, we would stand easy while some of the children gave Empire Day speeches. We stood to attention while Dad conducted us in singing patriotic airs, and then we would march to the Strand picture show, where we were joined by the boys and girls of the convent. Here we would sing 'Land of Hope and Glory', 'Rule Britannia', 'Three Cheers for the Red, White and Blue' and 'Advance Australia Fair', a song between each speech. When the three Protestant clergymen and the headmaster spoke to us they would suggest that the empire held together only because of some particular moral virtue. To the Presbyterian minister it was truthfulness; to the Methodist minister, the belief that if a thing was worth doing it was worth doing well; to the headmaster, love and good feeling; to the rector, unswerving loyalty and devotion in our sacred duties to King, God and Country. The rector would also tell us the story of the Indian prince who poured his tea into a saucer and blew on it when he visited Queen Victoria at Windsor and how, to put him at his ease, the Queen then poured her tea into a saucer and blew on it too, thus showing that the empire was a commonwealth of peoples. We sang 'God Save the King', then the convent children marched off to their picnic and we marched off to ours – sandwiches, jellies and lemonade provided by the Parents' and Citizens' Association. If we had been able to eat a meal when we got home and had tried pouring tea into our saucers we would probably have got a clip over the ear.

On Empire Day, 1933, I was one of the schoolchildren who gave a speech in the playground. This was the speech: 'When we speak of the British Empire what do we mean? We mean all those countries that are ruled over by our King, George V. They are scattered all over the world. There are tiny islands like pinpoints on the map, and great stretches of land, such as India, South Africa, Canada and Australia. It is a mighty Empire. All the people who live in our Empire are not white; yellow people, black people, red people and brown people own King George as their King. They do not all speak English as we do; but there is room in the Empire for men of all colours and creeds. Now, think of the heart of this mighty Empire! It is away to the north in a little country called Great Britain. There lives our King, and from there come the men who have made our Empire what it is. They were brave, those men who left Great Britain to come across the seas. Some carried the flag of Britain to places always hot under a burning sun; some went to lands held fast by the frost and snow of the icy north. In lonely stretches of desert country, in great forests, amid the hum and buzz of great cities, they raised the flag of Britain, and thousands have died to keep it flying there. Why were they ready to die for it? What does the Union Jack stand for? First of all, it tells us that we are free. No one is allowed to keep slaves under the British flag. It was not always so. Less than a hundred years ago, all slaves in the British Empire were set free, and, one by one, most of the other nations have done as Britain did. That was a great achievement for our Empire to lead the way in doing the right thing by making all her peoples free. Our flag, too, stands for right. Of course we all make mistakes, and our country has made mistakes: but we do our best to be honest and fair in all we say and do, and to help the weak against the strong. In a few years we will be men and women, and we will have to keep up the fame of our Empire. Upon us rests the task of keeping the flag flying high. How can we do this? We must lead a good and noble life; we must be honest and fair; we must do what is right; we must do unto others as we would like them to do unto us; we must work while we work and play while we play. These are some of the things that will help.' I was very proud of this speech, particularly the phrase 'the hum and buzz of great cities', which I had taken from an essay about city life I had written at school. I rehearsed myself for days before delivering it, sometimes to my parents, sometimes to the dog.

In Muswellbrook, out there in the brown grass of the Hunter Valley, we had never seen a ceremonial parade, or even a uniform, except the khaki of the 16th Australian Light Horse, the Hunter Valley militia regiment. In every classroom, however, there was a world map, with much of it covered in red. We lived in an empire on which the sun never set. That seemed a good kind of empire to belong to – the biggest. We always stood up for King George V when his image appeared on the screen at the beginning of the programme at 'the pictures' and we often saw this remote and taciturn monarch, to whom we owed our loyalty, in the newsreels, dressed as an admiral or a field-marshal or in morning dress. King George did not laugh in public or display a 'personality'. This more modern requirement of royal persons was met by the Prince of Wales, who came through as someone who knew how to make his own fun, just as we did in Muswellbrook. One could not imagine sitting down to mah-jongg with King George V or joining Queen Mary in a singsong around the pianola. But Mum spoke of 'Teddy' as if he were someone who might drop in for a spot before they all went off to the Masonic Ball. Perhaps our most demonstrably 'British' period was when Noel Coward's *Cavalcade* came to Muswellbrook. It ran for a special season, and many of the shops in the main street carried Union Jacks in their windows. The father of a girl friend at school considered the talkies immoral; but when *Cavalcade* came to town her whole family went to see it, dressed as for church.

AS WELL AS BEING AUSTRALIANS AND BRITISH WE WERE ALSO Christians, but the formal practice of Christianity ran a bad second to Anzac stoicism. Apart from on Anzac Day the church seemed to be in the grip of elderly women. On the rare attendances we made there I could not make head nor tail of the form of service, being unable to follow the intricacies of the prayer book. Before we took up shooting on Sundays I went to Sunday school, but it seemed to be just a place you went to: there were songs to sing, there was money to collect, there were words to say, and then they handed out coloured pictures of Christian saints which I would throw away as I walked home to afternoon tea. I could not understand why I was supposed to be there. There was nothing to learn, no exams, no esteem for being clever: the kind of children who were esteemed at Sunday school seemed to be those who at school were remarkable neither for physical dexterity nor for cleverness. There was about all this some mystery I could not comprehend. I made my protest by joining the delinquent set: before the bell rang we would gather at the back of the church hall, where nobody could see us, and throw stones at it, as if it were a martyr. At home Dad sometimes suggested that I should read the Bible, but the print was too small, the pages were too thin, and the archaic language repelled me. The most meaningful religious instruction I received was from a textbook on the main anecdotes from the Bible read to us at school in 'scripture lessons' – by our Catholic teacher.

From my earliest memories I had recited the Children's Prayer to Dad or Mum every night. *Gentle Jesus, Meek and Mild, Look upon a little child, Pity my simplicity, Suffer me to come to thee. Amen.* To this was later added the Lord's Prayer and the Creed. As I got older I was allowed to recite these to myself silently. ('Have you said your prayers, Don?' 'Yes, Mum.') After a certain age I dropped the Children's Prayer in these silent recitations, as being beneath my years. There was one brief stage in my boyhood – somewhere around the age of eight – when I practised a great deal of private prayer. *Please God, don't make it rain today. Please God, don't let the teacher find out. Please God, forgive me for that lie. Please God, don't make this cup of tea too hot.* This period passed, although I went on reciting the Lord's Prayer and the Creed to myself until I went to high school.

Such personal addresses as I made to the divinity were to God the Father, never to God the Son. There seemed no point in praying to the simple man called Jesus to stop the teacher from finding out; his weakness and goodness made him seen an unlikely recipient for pleas for action. When he felt inclined to discuss religious matters with me it was the man Jesus that Dad always spoke about. Perhaps this gentle Jesus reflected Dad's own simplicity, put aside so that he could become an Australian and suffer in the war. When he spoke of the meekness of Jesus he spoke of a man who had failed, a simple, good man whom everybody had set upon. For a while we would contemplate our compassion, then retreat into the banality that was such a treasured part of our lives. The creed of this meek, gentle Jesus, Dad would say, was that you should do unto others as you would have them do unto you – or, as Mum would sometimes translate it, you should show more consideration for other people, Don.

When, in fantasy, instead of imagining that I was the unknown elder son of King George V or the true descendant of Bonnie Prince Charlie, I would decide that I was Jesus Christ returned to the world, this time determined to win, it was as the throne-sitting Christ the King rather than Jesus the Man. But we Protestants knew little of the triumphant Christ at Muswellbrook; it was not only Dad who saw Jesus as the unfortunate sensitive man who failed: this was the prevailing concept. While we might pray to God to break a drought it was Jesus' name that was invoked if we were asked to spare a thought for the unemployed. He wasn't supposed to *do* anything about them, except to join us in sparing them a thought. God, the father of this decent-minded son, was unimaginable. Dad deprecated the idea that God was an angry, bearded old man dressed in a long, white sheet. So if I addressed him or tried to imagine him, all I saw was a big glow. However, I maintained a belief in the anger of this unpredictable and powerful God of Destiny, Lord of his own far-flung battle line. The Bible anecdotes, and for that matter the prayers for rain, suggested an arbitrary God, laying about him right and left. This was a puzzle I did not often take up, except in an occasional spasm of fear. But the general rules, as revealed to Dad and passed on to me, fitted most civilly into the context of our life in Muswellbrook. If I showed consideration for other people, and was obedient, truthful, diligent at my lessons and neat in my personal habits (taking my castor oil every Friday night), I would probably pass muster with God. Dad was punctilious in his own neatness. Perhaps more than anything else it was his sense of tidiness that was affronted when he gave me my biggest belting – for writing 'shit' in indelible pencil beneath the red roses on a white box of chocolates. I was aged eight and I did not know what the word meant.

BOTH OUR AUSTRALIANNESS AND OUR CHRISTIANITY INVOLVED us in some doctrinal affirmation of human 'brotherhood' although this was not necessarily a matter for our daily lives and it existed in contradiction with other things we believed or were supposed to believe. Brotherhood was, of course, a matter for men and it reached its most ambitious moments on Anzac Day, when we attempted a formal synthesis of Australianness and Christianity, but the image of the Rev. Mr J. Christ, the sincere clergyman who served as a chaplain in the Australian Light Horse, was not convincing. The meekness of the man Jesus made him un-Australian: he was obviously not tough enough for the Light Horse, and toughness was one of the most important parts of brotherhood. God was the essential deity for Anzac Day: he would always see to it that we won. Our attempt to mix brotherhood with Britishness on Empire Day also failed: we did not really see ourselves as the mates of all these foreigners in the empire, least of all of the English, who were notorious as stuck-up snobs: opposition to people who asserted their superiority over us was also one of the most important parts of brotherhood.

At Muswellbrook, where invitations to the Picnic Races Ball made it clear that bank managers had something that schoolteachers couldn't get, and membership of the golf club showed that schoolteachers could enjoy something that shop assistants couldn't, the sense of social position as something that divided our parents was nevertheless an oddity that had nothing to do with children, and even among their parents it was something that one was supposed not to talk about or to display in personal relations. Although recognition of social difference was almost universal, and when it was asserted it might be with considerable crudity, there was a bad conscience about it. Open affirmation was rare. When pharmacists' wives openly showed their contempt for schoolteachers' wives at the golf club by expecting them to clear up the ashtrays it was breaking the rules. At Denbigh over Sunday tea we would often laugh at the snobberies of Muswellbrook and wonder that people could divide themselves in this ridiculous way. There was Pa, who was both a member of an old family and a retired sleeping-car conductor. There was Nanna's brother, Uncle Alf, dentist, mayor, and once almost selected by his party to stand for election as a senator, who sometimes dropped in on us and displayed the wit of the big world, amusing us with anecdotes of power in Manly. And there was Nanna's Uncle Tom, so poor that he lived in a one-room shack in a paddock on the outskirts of Sydney which we called 'Uncle Tom's Cabin'. Life was just a gamble. Australianness was what mattered at Denbigh, and we reserved our snobbery for mocking people who claimed to be better than us: governors-general, for example.

I do not remember being sustained by any of the explicitly stated beliefs of Australian 'mateship', or even hearing the word regularly used outside Anzac Day. Mateship had meaning for me only as a greatly admired relationship existing between Australian soldiers when they went off to war. When I became a soldier and went to war I would find out about mateship. From the Australian short stories we read at school we realised vaguely that mateship was also something practised in the old pioneering days in the bush, but we were not specifically taught anything about it at school: as a term used in civilian life 'mate' was simply a slang word and if you used it you would lose marks in an English composition. According to the official syllabus the virtues that were to be inculcated into us were not mateship but courage, prudence, perseverance, self-control, self-respect, cleanliness, orderliness, obedience, kindness, gentleness, fairmindedness and truthfulness. One of the ways in which this purpose was to be achieved was through instructing us during history lessons in the fables of 'noble persons', such as Leonidas, Cincinnatus, Haroun al-Raschid, Richard the Lionheart, St Francis, Joan of Arc, Sir Thomas More, Sir Philip Sidney, Captain John Smith and Helen Keller. We learned about such people and passed examinations in their nobility, but they were all toffs and the only one of them who cared about his mates was that proto-Anzac, the wounded Sir Philip Sidney, who gave his drinking water to another wounded soldier and died.

At Denbigh we believed that one should not talk about politics or religion, and so far as religion was concerned, since we were all agreed the Catholics were up to no good and the wowsers were a menace and we should all be kind to each other, there didn't seem to be much to say. But we sometimes talked politics – several times with a bitterness that proved temporarily disastrous to our amity and when we did there was a division between those of us who held the worldview that 'the workers' were the salt of the earth and those who considered that money was what mattered. Most of us temporised, but when the extremes were stated brutally most of us supported the workers. The two greatest extremes of our view of the struggle between Capital and Labour were represented in my Uncle Ted (for Labour) and (for Capital) 'Mick's' mother, Aunty Lil, and her husband, Uncle 'Candy' (an abbreviation of his proper name, 'Alcanda', an odd name we wondered about). In the early days of the Depression Aunty Lil and Uncle Candy had travelled New South Wales in a car, with their dog sitting on the running board, and, strapped to the luggage rack at the back, and on the roof, the trunks containing the women's dresses that they sold in country towns. When they decided to make their own dresses in Sydney and send travellers out to sell them they rented rooms in a city building and installed machinery and work-girls in it, and thus became capitalists. My Uncle Ted, in contrast, was an electrical fitter at the Chullora railway workshop who saw something splendid in his relationship with his mates; to dramatise his contempt for money grubbers he kept the few shillings of his savings tied in the corner of a handkerchief so that if people started talking about money he could bring out his handkerchief and show us his entire capital, demonstrating that he was a worker. There was a shouting match one night when Uncle Candy talked about the mugs who rode to work on their bicycles while he rode by in his car. The rest of us were scandalised: we knew that Ted rode to the railway workshops on a bicycle. On another night the capital-versus-labour controversy was expressed in such cutting and directly personal terms (one of our richer relatives shrieking defence of labour) that Pa told everyone to go to buggery.

A form of division on which we were nearly all agreed was that Australians were better than foreigners. Not that we knew much about foreigners. Only 140 of the Muswellbrook people were born overseas, and of these 130 were British, and at Denbigh we knew no foreigners apart from Uncle Loy's wife, Aunty 'Jan' (short for Jeanette). Aunty Jan, Noumean–French as we were Australian–British, and perhaps married by Uncle Loy because on the Western Front he had picked up a taste for things French, with her uncertain temperament, sometimes generous, sometimes grumpy and always smelling of very strong scent, was all we could handle in the way of foreigners. Like the English, we saw ourselves as superior to 'continentals'. The Germans were the traditional enemies of Australians, and our fathers and the many war stories in the boys' comic books told us that the Hun made a tough enemy and it took us to beat them. As proof of this, there was the captured German machine-gun beside the school tennis court and the many German field guns in the parks of Sydney. We knew that in beating the Hun (which we might have to do again) there was not much help to be expected from our allies. The Belgians were all right as a gallant little ally, but the French (whom our fathers called 'the Frogs') were too excitable and the Mediterranean peoples (whom we all called the 'dagoes') were only good for running cafés or fruit and vegetable shops. The Yanks were all right in their own way, almost as good as Australians perhaps, but too boastful and upstart; the Yanks still had a lot to learn from us.

Insofar as we thought about it, our principal concern was to distinguish ourselves from other white peoples. We did not take Asians or Africans into any kind of account, or discuss them in any way, except when my father, in the course of an anecdote about the war, might refer to the 'Gyppos', whom we saw as rascally street beggars, or the nomadic Bedouin, for whom we had a certain respect. I do not remember being told that there was a White Australia policy. It simply seemed part of the natural order of events that we should be 'white'. My feelings towards 'Asiatics' were drawn mainly from books. Some 'Asiatics' were important people – maharajahs, mandarins, sultans and Hurree Jamset Ram Singh, the Indian boy at Greyfriars in the Billy Bunter stories – but they seemed more like English toffs than

Australians, stuck-up snobs who treated their own people badly. Apart from these few toffs, all the inhabitants of Asia were called 'coolies', a class of person for whom I felt vaguely sorry. Both the Chinese and the Indians seemed very old-fashioned peoples, colourful, picturesque, living in the past: they had had their day. The Japanese were a different matter: their warships had visited Sydney Harbour; their manufactured goods were on sale in the shops; and we read in the papers about what they were doing in some distant place called Manchuria. Apart from sultans or ships' crews, the peoples of South-east Asia were almost unimaginable, and I was only vaguely aware of New Guinea and other Melanesian islands around us; these were inhabited by 'kanakas' who, as a result of our British love of liberty, were no longer exploited by blackbirding expeditions. Central Africa was all jungle and its native residents, the niggers, were happy savages, harmless to anyone except themselves, not as exploited and unfortunate as coolies, but even more remote from Muswellbrook. I did not see any Australian Aborigines, or give them any thought. At the front of our school atlas there was a map of Australia showing it as all black before the British arrived (meaning that it was 'undiscovered') and then a series of maps showing the spread of civilisation as a golden advance, ending with a map of Australia in which all the black had turned to gold. I was taught at school that since we were all brothers the Empire was a giant cooperative run by the fortunate for the benefit of the unfortunate. Sometimes, as in the Indian Mutiny or the Boer War, disloyalty had to be put down, but most of the maharajas, mandarins, sultans, coolies and niggers were loyal, and some day, in some way, they would move into equal partnership with us. Meanwhile we bought their jute and the English rode in their rickshaws.

Our intolerance was directed in effect almost exclusively towards the English, the 'Poms'. We looked down on Poms almost as much as we looked down on Catholics. At our house, where how men shaped up to the tests of battle was what counted, the Poms were considered too deferential to their officers and lacking in initiative, physically puny compared with Australians, and inadequate in personal hygiene. Their officers, of course, were effeminate, incompetent and dictatorial. The Poms did not make such good soldiers as Johnny Turk. Of all the peoples of the world living outside Australia, those we held in the highest regard in our house were the Turks.

FOUR

'Be yourself, Don'

I had no doubt that acquiring knowledge was one of the most admirable of human activities and that the institution in which I acquired much of my knowledge, the Muswellbrook District Rural School, provided that service efficiently. One of my favoured rooms – equal to the rooms of our house at Muswellbrook and even the sacred rooms of Denbigh – was the school classroom where, all around us, were reminders of knowledge, order and the virtues of improvement: the main dates in British history, maps of Australia and of the world, lists of principal exports, botanical specimens. On the wall alongside the 'model block' where the cleverest girls and boys sat (more girls than boys) were printed in black ink on white cardboard the names of those who came first, second and third in each subject in the written 'tests' set each month throughout primary school. What divided us in this room was not our sex or the social standing of our parents, but cleverness – which seemed to me the only fair division among human beings. The daughter of the chook thief was one of my closest competitors in the monthly tests.

The Muswellbrook District Rural School consisted of a brick main building and half a dozen prefabricated wooden classrooms, called 'portables', that were placed around the playground, three of them along a bank of the creek. Here the inculcators of knowledge were the primary-school teachers, the second or third generation of the bearers of compulsory education, briefly trained in teachers' colleges and controlled by a Department of Public Instruction that moved them arbitrarily from one town to another, perhaps hundreds of miles apart; they were people on the move, living in boarding houses when they were single and rented houses when they were married, their furniture being carted all over the state; they were controlled remotely but in detail from Sydney, tyrannised by annual visits from inspectors; in whatever town they settled they were never part of the permanent scene. In old photographs, posing under the trees in a school playground, their very clothes seem to say: here we are, upholding standards. Whether I would have liked them so much if I had met them only at school I do not know, but as it happened some of them were in and out of our house much of the time and I saw them not only as purveyors of facts and upholders of standards, but as part of my mother's 'crowd', delighting in bridge, mah-jongg, golf, or singsongs around the pianola.

It was they who taught us (or failed to teach us) how to write cursive at a slope of seventy five degrees to the line, how to divide 1.08 by 12, or 22 by 5½, how to multiply 4½ by 24 or to express ten per cent of three acres in chains, or work out what was left when 2s. in the £ was taken off 7s. 6d., or what the simple interest on £1 was for a month at five per cent per annum. We were instructed in the person, number, gender and case of nouns and pronouns, in the tense and voice of verbs, in the use of the past participle, how to identify a principal clause or a relative clause or an adverbial phrase. We were given poems to learn and 'compositions' to write. Our teachers campaigned against usages such as *ain't, brung, drownded, drawed, would of, uster, says I*; they distinguished between *may* and *can, don't* and *doesn't, lie* and *lay, rise* and *raise, teach* and *learn, shall* and *will*; they fought against what they considered inelegant uses of *start* and *got*, and tried to dissuade us from redundant pronouns and misplaced modifiers. It was on these questions of speech that we began to divide among ourselves: there were the boys who went on using *ain't* and the other forbidden words and usages defiantly and with ideological fervour (they were proclaiming their independence not only of grammar and arithmetic but from Leonidas and Joan of Arc); and there were those of us who said *aren't* instead of *ain't*.

Whatever I lacked in loyalty to sporting teams was compensated for by loyalty to the Muswellbrook school. The school returned my loyalty. Each month, from third class to sixth, I came top of the 'test' in every subject, except for the month when I went down in arithmetic. Any information that anyone cared to present was taken in with pleasure. I was several times called into a senior class and asked to read something or answer some problem on the blackboard, not realising that this was to show up the slowness of my seniors, and I was encouraged by my parents and my teacher and all the Carpenters at Denbigh to cultivate my cleverness. To be myself was to be clever. As other boys delighted in being good at running I delighted in being quick-witted. Without feeling either vain or guilty, I enjoyed exercising a talent. We learned at school that life was mostly froth and bubble, two things stood like stone, kindness in another's trouble, courage in your own, and that one should be good, sweet maid, and let who would be clever, do noble things, not dream them all day long – but we also knew that it was prudent to have a good head on your shoulders. I had a good head on my shoulders. When he heard of this clever boy at the public school the principal of the town's merchant family took the trouble to urge my father to make sure I had a good education and even hinted that he would give him the money to see me through.

In the dining room, as well as the sideboard and the traymobile there was a bookcase with a frosted and lead-lighted front, where we kept the mah-jongg set and all the pianola rolls, and also three sets of books – the four-volume *History of the British Nation*, the eight-volume *Cassell's Book of Knowledge* and the two-volume *Dr Vertue's Household Physician*. This meant that my devotion to learning wasn't confined to school. I could read and re-read *Cassell's Book of Knowledge* with their more than 2,000 articles and 10,000 photographs and drawings. Sometimes I would supplement Cassell's with Arthur Mee's *Children's Encyclopaedia*, borrowed from the school library. I kept on returning to favourite bits and reading them again, passing from 'Caesar, the Man who Crossed the Rubicon' to 'Strange Hats of Many Lands' to 'Brave and Thrifty Belgium' to 'Kinematograph, the Wonders of Moving Picture Land' to 'Marx, the Originator of the Modern International Socialist Movement' to 'Mighty Russia's Rise and Fall'. There did not seem much more to learn.

The world as it presented itself in *Cassell's Book of Knowledge* was more diverse than the simple ideas we used at home or at Denbigh or on Anzac Day or Empire Day or the more complicated but still highly patterned ideas introduced to us at school. I passed from the language of one world to the other without thinking about it. I did not speak to anyone else about the world of Cassell's. It was my own. It was a matter of private knowledge, personal to me, that 'Strange Empires had Flourished When the World was Young' or that 'The Protoplasm was the Beginning of the Wonderful Story of Evolution'. It was only I who admired pictures of 'The Basilica of St Anthony at Padua' or of 'The Curious Striped Bacilli Which are the Cause of Dreaded Tuberculosis'. I thus began a habit that was to remain with me: that some of the things in which I was most interested were matters that I could discuss only with myself. I did not then consider that I was any better for this kind of special knowledge nor even different. It was simply a secret delight that could not be practised publicly without embarrassment. While Mum and Dad and their friends talked about their golf scores, who was to know or care that, as I sat there with them, my nose in a book, I might be reading that 'if we could discover a means of making atoms break up at a fast rate we should discover the key to unlock enormous stores of energy'?

The principal pattern of events we learned at school was one of inevitable and desirable change. Year by year we learned the history of change. Month by month we sat for examinations in it. (When did Hargreaves invent the spinning jenny? When did Vasco da Gama sail to India?) Our teachers taught us change out of a book, from a syllabus of instruction that – if some of its principles had been expressed in the British Isles earlier in our history – might have led to transportation in chains to New South Wales. We were offered a view of life based on an optimistic belief in inevitable improvement, an improvement that would proceed of necessity, without our doing anything in particular about it. It was the officially expressed belief of the New South Wales Department of Public Instruction that there was a natural 'sense of growth and development' in human affairs, and that 'the human race ... was developing towards better and happier conditions of life'. This meant that one of our schoolroom views of mankind was optimistic, progressive and radical. We were on the side of revolution, exploration and innovation. We were for the barons against King John; for Wat Tyler against Richard II; for Sir Thomas More against Henry VIII, and for Henry VIII against the Pope; for Cromwell against King Charles; we supported the Bill of Rights, the Declaration of Independence, the Declaration of the Rights of Man, the Toleration Act, the Catholic Emancipation Act, the Factory Acts, the Reform Acts of 1832, 1867 and 1884. (Many of the dates that we had to learn by heart commemorated the passing of famous Acts of Parliament.) Some of the greatest people in our pantheon were explorers, inventors and reformers: Prince Henry the Navigator, Columbus, Magellan, Hudson, Cook, Livingstone, Scott; Galileo, Copernicus, da Vinci, Caxton, Newton, Watt; Lincoln, Plimsoll, Howard,

Nightingale, Damien, Wilberforce. Human history was a story of discovery and reform; innovation served the welfare of the ordinary people in a sure evolution from serfdom to having a good time playing tennis at Muswellbrook.

The sense of inevitable improvement taught at school was tempered by the many hours I spent at home studying the four volumes of *The History of the British Nation*, a work that offset the sense of reason in *Cassell's Book of Knowledge*. This work had come to us first in weekly instalments from the newsagent. Then it was bound into four volumes, each of 600 pages. Its special appeal was that it had 3,000 illustrations – the whole range of paintings of English history along with hundreds of illustrations 'specially painted for this work'. Its text told the history of progress, but I did not read much of the text; I read the lines beneath the 3,000 pictures, and these told a story of inhumanity, treachery, stupidity and meaninglessness. I was as familiar with most of these 3,000 pictures as if they were cigarette cards, so that, along with the optimism of school history, I taught myself another view of life: of disconnected, discordant, irrational and unpredictable events, and the possibility of failure, from lines such as:

> Edward II, one of the most incompetent of English kings, aroused
> the opposition of the barons by entrusting the government to foreign
> favourites, such as Piers Gaveston, who passed their time in pleasures
> and frivolity. Gaveston was so hated for his insolent behaviour that he
> was murdered in 1312. Edward continued to govern by favourites and
> reduced the realm to such disorder that in 1327 he was deposed, and
> shortly afterwards was murdered at the instigation of his wife Isabella.

Or:

> Like most forms of trial by ordeal, the judgment of the nine
> ploughshares was treated as a religious rite and took place in a church.
> The exact method is disputed, but the most reliable accounts suggest that
> the ploughshares, having been made red hot, were laid on the ground.
> The accused had to walk upon each in turn, and if after three days the
> blisters were healed he was considered innocent. A judicious gift to the
> priest would probably have been the most effective solution.

Sometimes, while Mum was chatting with her friends over afternoon tea, I might fill in my time reading *The History of the British Nation*, my imagination excited by the procrastinations, incompetence, favouritism, murders, depositions, superstitions and dishonesties that had gone into its making.

The view of the world I obtained from the pictures in *The History of the British Nation* was confirmed in some of the discussions on politics I heard at Denbigh. We liked to tell stories demonstrating the venality or the stupidity of Australian politicians. In fact, we delighted in any stories of misbehaviour, often swapping yarns about the high jinks of Kingsford Smith, or the girlfriends of the Prince of Wales. Nanna gave historical depth with tales of Sir Henry Parkes ('Oh, he was a real old devil!'). This cynicism combined with our despair at the calamity of the Depression to lead us to the view that, so far as politicians were concerned, none of the buggers was any good.

I remember reading newspapers, but it was from a weekly news magazine called the *Sydney Mail* that I seemed to get the most coherent impressions of what was supposed to be happening in the world outside Australia. At first the main use of the *Mail* was to provide pictures of great events, to be cut out and pasted in a scrapbook – Kingsford Smith flying somewhere, Don Bradman scoring a century, Uncle Alf as Mayor of Manly greeting a visiting duke at a surf carnival. But the *Mail* also ran regular commentaries on foreign affairs that gave more connected and interpretative accounts than appeared in the newspapers. Some of this was what any student of *The History of the British Nation* might expect: assassinations in Eastern Europe, for instance or the Japanese invasion of Manchuria. But what seemed improbable was Adolf Hitler. A piece I read on Hitler when I was aged eleven seemed meaningless: it explained the *Führerprinzip*. How could that be true? How could people deliberately believe in one man absolutely, and surrender all their liberties to him? Accidents could happen so that people lost their liberties. But to develop a principle of surrendering one's liberties voluntarily seemed very unlikely as late in history as 1933.

The sense of accident and of the indifference of events to human values that I learned from *The History of the British Nation* were strengthened by reading Dickens. Apart from a children's version of *The Christmas Carol* I first came across Dickens at the age of ten in an extract from *Oliver Twist* in the school magazine. I turned the extract into a play, adding it to the repertory I had written for classroom performance. That Christmas I came across the full text, in a shelf of cast-out books in Nanna's laundry. (This assortment of volumes, which consisted mainly of books picked up by Pa from sleeping-cars when he was a conductor, was my grandparents' library.) I was so fascinated that I read it through twice, and daydreamed about its characters for days. I wondered whether to risk asking for it, or whether I should simply steal it. Thereafter my moneybox savings were invested heavily in Dickens, who more than took his place among the *Chums Annuals*, pirate novels and Billy Bunter stories. This was a *History of the British Nation* view of life: things were unpredictable, catastrophe was always imminent and the existence of evil and horror was a matter of course. I had to summon Australian manliness to withhold my boyish tears whenever I re-read the description of Oliver's farewell to Dick. I asked Dad to buy me a notebook and I began writing a novel about a little barefooted boy who ran away from Muswellbrook by hiding in a freight train. After some pages were done I read what I had written to Mum and Dad. Mum did not think the subject was very nice. I was scolded for writing about a boy whose parents couldn't afford shoes. It was wrong to draw attention to boys who were worse off than I was. I brooded about this misunderstanding and lost confidence.

What seemed to me most 'lifelike' about Dickens was his sense of grotesquerie. The people in his books were as grotesque as the people in *The History of the British Nation* or the people I knew in Muswellbrook and Sydney. I had a child's sensitivity to the self-caricature and repetitiveness of most external human behaviour. Most of the people I knew seemed static representations of a few simple and predictable 'characters'. Human society consisted of people whose 'characters' were unchangeable and obvious. They would go on being the same: the interest was in the wonder of the display of what they were, and of their relations with each other. It was like a game of cards. This feeling for character was most intense when we were staying in Sydney: there were the people who visited Denbigh to stimulate it then. I would sometimes sit in the sun on the front steps of Denbigh and make out lists of 'characters' – Dickens people combined with Denbigh and Muswellbrook people – and then imagine stories in which they were all shuffled together.

The melodrama of Dickens and *The History of the British Nation* left me at times with the fear that I might end up in the workhouse or on the executioner's block in the Tower of London, but it was Dickens's sense of the comic that most affected me: in what usually seemed the certainty of my own life, to make a joke of things was what seemed of supreme importance. To talk about the things one respected most it was sometimes necessary to make fun of them. Thus if I wanted Mum to take some interest in *The History of the British Nation*, I made a joke of it. We giggled at these peculiar people in their old-fashioned clothes making this ridiculous fuss – beheading people, burning them and the like – all over nothing. If you could make a joke of things everything seemed more comfortable. At school I preferred the boys and girls who liked to have fun; at home I liked to do imitations of people to amuse Dad and Mum; and at Denbigh I was so surrounded by jocularity that an important way of distinguishing between one person and another was to categorise their senses of humour. Most of the Carpenters were laconic in their humour: Uncle Loy, for instance, was a master of the wry humour of the trenches, front-line wit, clipped like his moustache and cropped as close as his hair: but the people they married and our other relations practised other types of humour – chyacking and leg-pulling, sardonic anecdotes, jolliness and exuberance, wise-cracking, cheerful vulgarity, ruminative humour, crazy inconsequence, and gentle observations of absurdity. We abhorred whingers who could not laugh at their misfortunes. I detested all serious people, seeing them as straitlaced sobersides who had nothing to say.

Except when I feared the workhouse I had as strong a sense of my past and my future as anyone could have in even the most static society. I saw 'Mick' and me as being happily just two of the smaller people stitched into a huge tapestry behind me, where the tapestry stretched back beyond sight, apart from the distant flash of a Viking battle-axe, the first people I could see were Great-Great-Great-Grandfather Mileham with his sword and Great-Great-Great-Grandfather Sellar with his cat-o'-nine-tails, except that now and again, once a year perhaps, I might notice a distant Blackmore marrying his Indian princess. With a face of granite, Great-Great-Grandmother Howell was sitting at the head of a table; Great-Grandfather Carpenter was leaning back in his chair with an insolent smile; Great-Grandmother Carpenter was on her knees in prayer; Great-Great-Aunt Lloyd was discussing the western front with generals and bishops in London; Great-Aunt Lila was galloping her horse across the paddock; a host of Sellars were on their building sites, constructing bits of Sydney; Grandfather John Horne was founding a cooperative society; my unknown Uncles Horne were in their new uniforms, off to the war; and closer to me all my Denbigh relations and Muswellbrook friends were laughing at my jokes.

MY LIFE WAS TO BE A MATTER OF MOVING FROM CLASSROOM TO classroom. I had moved from first class in the main school building to second, third, fourth and fifth classes in the 'portables' that surrounded the playground. At the age of eleven I was now back in the main building, in sixth class, preparing for the Primary Final examination. To go to high school I would leave all my friends behind me (they would leave school at fourteen) and accept a new continuity in which for five years I would again move predictably from classroom to classroom. Then I would go to Sydney University, take an Arts degree, spend a year training at the Teachers' College, and become a teacher like my father, although, being a high-school teacher, of a higher grade. There was nothing unpredictable about this, since there was no doubt that I would pass the necessary examinations.

However, this sense of progress was to be disturbed. Dad tried to conceal his sensitivity by irony and wit, but somewhere in the process of pulling himself up into the world he had come to express belief in truth and in knowledge for its own sake. He was not learned and he had little natural curiosity of his own. But his life would have lost some of its meaning if he had not believed that he was encouraging curiosity in me and encouraging me to speak 'the truth as I saw it'. He had chanced to read an article on modern education in the *Cassell's Book of Knowledge*, and when he began to think of writing the thesis that might gain him promotion he copied it into an exercise book. He did not write his thesis, but in his handling of me he had decided that what they said in the Cassell's encyclopedia was true: education was growth. None of us knew what this meant, but the practical effect of this belief was that while I was still expected from various quarters to pay respect to God and the King by obeying orders, dressing neatly, writing neatly, talking neatly, thinking neatly, and emptying my bowels daily after breakfast, and to pay respect to Jesus by showing some consideration for other people's feelings, and to pay respect to the Anzac heroes by not whingeing and by always doing the right thing, along with this I was also expected to *be myself* ('You have to be *yourself*, Don,' my mother would say), read, ask questions, tell the truth, and always say what I thought. But if I wrote 'shit' on a chocolate box I got a belting.

Dad's admonitions to me to express myself meant that I was encouraged not only to enjoy exercising my wits by regurgitating on demand what I had learned: I was also encouraged in my eagerness to invent things of my own. Like my mother, I could bounce around, impatient to find out what I might do next. I liked to air my views in school lecturettes, at Sunday teas at Denbigh and the like. Then there came a new opportunity: with my teacher's cooperation I was able to run a drama club, with its headquarters at our house and its principal performing space at school.

Several years earlier, before my piano lessons had begun, I had taken a year's elocution lessons from Miss Alma Doepell, who, with a name like that of a character in a novel, and a supply of exotic shawls and fans and an assured and professionally modulated voice, seemed the most 'cultivated' person I knew. I would visit Miss Doepell once a week in her 'studio' (a large room at the top of one of Muswellbrook's oldest stone houses, which she also used as a living apartment) and there I would be trained in posture, gesture and how to speak with expression; I would recite the special exercises she gave me (full of tongue twisters) and when she thought I was ready for it, she began giving me a new 'piece' every week, which I was to learn and then recite to her the next week, with the appropriate gestures and expressions. After a year it was considered that elocution lessons had nothing new to teach me and I was put on to piano lessons. But now I had a whole repertoire. 'Don's recitations' became one of the regular turns at Denbigh, when at one of the large gatherings I would be asked to stand up and 'recite something'; 'Mick' and I put them into concerts; they were used at children's parties at Muswellbrook; and once a year, at the annual concert of Miss Doepell's students (piano, violin, elocution), as well as doing a very uncertain turn at the piano I would put on an assured performance as Muswellbrook's best schoolboy reciter, enjoying the uncertain delights of applause.

This assurance made me feel the star of the few plays we put on at school (seen in the syllabus as an encouragement of 'self-expression') and gave me the idea that I would produce a show of my own. I decided to turn Charles Lamb's *A Dissertation on Roast Pig* into a play. My friend Rosemary Hart would be my collaborator and we would rehearse in the large space under the house. Our mothers made our costumes and we made the scenery at home, lugging it in several journeys through the streets of Muswellbrook to the schoolroom for an after-school dress rehearsal before the great day of the first performance. The show was so successful that we put it on for other classes – with such praise that the girls who were my two main competitors in 'the tests' joined us in forming a drama club to produce other shows. Later, even a couple of boys joined in, although usually, since we had too few boys, girls had to play some of the male parts. Our plays became part of the school's routine. When we put on a special performance for the annual visit of the school inspector our teacher's obvious talent for cultivating 'self-expression' helped gain her promotion.

As entrepreneur, author, producer and chief character actor of our group I could see a clear road ahead for my own 'self-expression'. It was not about my cleverness but about our drama club that I was vain. I was bossy with the members of it, a show-off who wanted to get things right so that the audience would applaud, but wondering whether they meant it. But sometimes I could feel afraid that as an only child I might be 'spoiled'. When I looked around me it could sometimes seem necessary to ask if showing-off was what God, King, Jesus and the Anzacs expected of me.

The audience reaction about which I became most vain, however, occurred when one of the teachers, as punishment for my making fun of the way he said 'Left, right, left, right' in the playground, told me to stay in after school for three consecutive afternoons. I was to write on the first afternoon a page composition beginning with the word 'left' and ending with the word 'right', on the second afternoon another composition which began with 'right' and ended with 'left' and on the third afternoon a third composition that began with 'left, right' and ended with 'right, left'. I wrote all of them in the one afternoon and he was so pleased with them that he took them home and kept them. This was really holding an audience.

To Dad the world of action, with its necessary calculations and assessments of the use of fraud, was a mystery. We would often compare him favourably with Uncle Candy as our materially most successful relative who had made a whole philosophy based on being sharp-witted. The result was that from an early age I was to regard business, politics, success and the whole conduct of affairs as the discreditable side of human activity. There were the ordinary decent people, making their own fun; and – with an occasional exception like Cincinnatus or Haroun al-Raschid – there were the rogues and survivors, the expediency men, the con-men, the cheats. Disinterest was what mattered – doing things as a service for others or for their own sake, with no reward. Although Dad believed that the men who had volunteered to fight the Hun or the Turk were the only real men in Australia, he also despised ex-soldiers who tried to cash in on their war service. Volunteering to fight was simply doing the right thing: it was not done in any sense of reward. The simple innocence of his theory of outspokenness, independence and utter honesty appealed to me so much that by the time I had reached adolescence in Sydney I argued with him most of the time, saying what I thought. Finally it was almost impossible for us to have any conversation about anything.

FIVE

Extracts from the diary of ...

DONALD RICHMOND HORNE,
HILL STREET,
MUSWELLBROOK,
THE HUNTER VALLEY
NEW SOUTH WALES,
AUSTRALIA,
THE BRITISH EMPIRE,
THE WORLD,
THE SOLAR SYSTEM,
THE UNIVERSE.

19TH OCTOBER 1933

This morning I made the usual full stop mistake. Miss Morley remarked 'I hope you lose ten marks for that.' (I wonder if she did.) Here's some blind justice. I helped Mabel Tucker with a mistake (permissible) and Miss Morley commanded me to stop talking. I tried to tell her why I did it but she told me I was the worst talker in the class.

20TH OCTOBER 1933

Some trouble at the court today. I expect there will be some kind of row tomorrow. Dashed if I know what. I told mum, as soon as she started tournaments there would be trouble. Some people don't like to be beaten. What a jealous world! I was going to ride on the merry-go-round, but we changed the library book and my magazine instead. Went to sleep 11.30.

24TH OCTOBER 1933

Tuesday scripture. I asked Mr Campbell where animals go when they die. He replied that they went to heaven, as animals. I wonder what our cow, dog and canary will be like.

26TH OCTOBER 1933

I was pretending to throw some ink at Peggy's book when some ink did come off. She told Miss Morley, and before I had time to explain, I was bundled out of the 'Model Block'. It is called a 'model' block, but there isn't much 'model' about it. It includes the girl who came last in the class.

27TH OCTOBER 1933

I had a restless sleep last night and this morning. It must have been from all the worry of not being amongst the 'Models' (?) Rosemary and I are practicing in full force for the concert. Went to Trevannes tonight and received some ginger-ale and cigarrete cards. Mum also changed the library books, and I, my magazines.

31ST OCTOBER 1933

The sketch was a huge success. Miss Morley was presented with the flowers also. After the presentation we sang 'For She is a Jolly Good Fellow'. Then she suggested we sing 'For We are Jolly Good Fellows'. Carried unanimously.

15TH DECEMBER 1933

Back to the diary again. On the way to Sydney for holidays. The only occupants of this carriage are the Hornes and Rita and Tipp, two of the women teachers. The good-byes are just finished. Some of the boys were here to see the girls off. Rita and Tipp are going mad at present. Dad is rolling a cigarette preparatory to reading the papers. They've placed some box-like arrangement across the seats and will be playing bridge after a while.

I haven't written anything in the diary for more than a month. I will mention several of the things that happened at school.

1st November. Examination Day. I woke at 7.30. The sharpening of pencils had taken place the night before. I told mum I half wished I had a mascot. She then told me there was one on the dressing table. I hopped out of bed and found it. The 1st time I read through the English Paper I thought it was dashed hard. The second time I did it appeared easier.

3rd November. We had the picnic today. It was good. I brought 2 bottles of ginger beer, a cake, two oranges, 6d. lollies, packet chips and sandwiches. There were 8 in my party. In the afternoon, just after dinner, I farewelled Audrey and Hilda Bailey who are leaving Muswellbrook.

There was some trouble with Peggy but it was all cleared up before the holidays. She called me a 'dirty pig' and a 'filthy scoundrel' & such nice names so I retaliated by calling her a 'common liar'. Her mother sent a note to Miss Morley & she investigated. When she found out the true circs. she pardoned me.

We have had several children's tennis tourneys. I presented the trophies.

We received the examination results. The class went mad. Only 5 failed.

We had our 'Farewell to the Primary' concert last Monday. My parts of the concert were a recitation and two sketches. I presented Miss Morley with the present and Judith pres. her with the flowers.

Tuesday. We had our party today. I brought my share. My word, the kids gorged.

Wednesday. Speech Day. I came first in our room and received a book, *The School Jonah* as prize. I also made a speech. Before I made the speech I was sitting up on a chair with my legs crossed like Mr Campbell & the rest of the old pots.

Thursday. My Last Day in Muswellbrook District Rural School. Oh dear! I have enjoyed myself immensely in all those past School-Days & I said 'Good-bye' to Miss Morley with a lump in my throat. I recited to the class and while I was doing it my eyes roamed round my classmates who had been my friends for 61/2 years. I walked up the paddock coming home from Muswellbrook school for the last time in the afternoon. As I walked up I thought of all the things I had enjoyed at that school. I hate leaving the Primary School of Muswellbrook. Therefore I say LONG LIVE MUSWELLBROOK DISTRICT RURAL SCHOOL.

I am still writing in the carriage. Dad and Rita are asleep. Tipp is looking at me and mum is looking out the window.

21ST DECEMBER [DENBIGH]
I've been into town Monday, Tuesday & Wed.

1ST JANUARY 1934 [BONDI BEACH]
It's an awful day and the surf is rotten. Mum and I went to the Museum this afternoon. The various things, mummies & so-forth there are all very interesting. This is the 3rd time I've been. Mum had a pain in the neck – she called it 'tired feet'. She didn't seem to understand the mummies and half-believed they were 'fakes'. I didn't see the New Year in – that's a lot of 'bunkum'. My smile hasn't been in the *Sun* newspaper 'smile' contest yet. Dad went to the cricket match. He wanted me to go, but I wanted to go to the Museum. Bradman made 122 runs not out. The three of us went to the pictures in the night. 'Moonlight and Pretzels' was on. Mum and myself liked it but I don't think Dad did. I've read 4 of my books and will begin 'Coral Island' tomorrow. I finished 'The Talisman' today.

2ND JANUARY 1934
The surf is still bad as ever. Bradman scored a double century. The Queenslanders will be licked (I think & – HOPE). We played cards tonight. Dad won 3 times out of three. Mum came second every time. And son came LAST EVERY TIME.

3RD JANUARY 1934
We went down the street tonight. 'Mick' & I went on the 'Scoota Boats'. 'Mick' went on the 'Chairoplanes' and the two of us went on the 'aeroplane'. Those dashed things are a waste of money.

4TH JANUARY 1934
I had a row with Dad tonight. I made a mistake in cards and he lost his temper. He started to roar so I went outside to cool off for a while. Not much else happened except that episode. I went into the surf. We are going to go on the Harbour Trip some time during the holidays. As well as that we will be going for a day at Taronga Park to see the Zoological Gardens. 'The Solitaire Man' will be one of the pictures we will see tomorrow night. I've begun reading 'The Last Days of Pompeii'.

7TH JANUARY 1934

The surf was very rough, VERY rough. We played Five Hundred and Bridge in the night.

8TH JANUARY 1934

Mum has taken a loan of 3s 2d from me. I think I will charge 8d interest. I went into the surf both morning and afternoon. I had a bath at dinner-time after my surf and felt nice and glowy. 'Mick' is hungry at present. I want to go for a walk with Dad. Dad is lying on the bottom part of the bed scratching his head and reading Poppie. 'Mick' is lying across the top part of the bed reading 'Ben Hur'. Mum is gawking out of the window. I want to go for a dashed long walk but nobody seems inclined. I must have a 'Hamburger Sandwich'. I am more than halfway through 'The Old Curiosity Shop'.

9TH JANUARY 1934

We went to the amusements tonight. I haven't got a 'Hamburger Sandwich' yet. 'Mick' & I went on the 'Scoota Boats'. And what do you think?!! We were shoved in with someone else! I am not dashed well going to go in with anybody any more. I also had a go on the darts.

10TH JANUARY 1934

I've read 8 of my books.

11TH JANUARY 1934

Dulc., Unc. & Nanna arrived today. Letter from Miss Morley. She has been moved to Tempe. Well, Good-bye, Miss Morley, you've been a very good teacher to me. I have spent a very many of the happiest days of my life under you as a teacher. Sometimes I have not liked you as well as I should but most of the time I have liked you with all my heart. Therefore – Good-bye. Good-bye, schoolroom. I can see in my mind's eye Miss Morley's desk, her charts, everything! I can now see Miss Morley as we 1st met face to face as pupil and teacher. Ah! I can see everything as if it were but yesterday. Good-bye, Judith and Dione! I've always been your friendly rival in position in class. Thank you for your help and cooperation in the Dramatic Club. Good-bye Peggy! Good-bye Ken! Good-bye Jacko! Good-bye Rosemary! Goodbye Alwyn & Clive,

Maud & Elsie, Margaret and Audrey, Mabel. Good-bye to all of you! God bless you!

12TH JANUARY 1934

We went into town today. While there I bought 2 new books 'The Escape of Monte Cristo' and 'The New Boy at Greyfriars'. As well as other shopping Mum paid 2s off my copy of Shakespeare valued at 21s. We enjoyed lunch at David Jones restaurant. I had chicken in Jelly and Salad, peaches & cream, roll & butter, coffee & orange drink. We went to the pictures tonight. 'My Lips Betray' was light, snappy and impossible.

13TH JANUARY 1934

It is the afternoon. We went into the surf about 1½ hours ago. Quite suddenly the rain began to pour. Everybody ran into the shelters like frightened rabbits. The announcer was yelling out 'Hullo! Hullo! Esplanade Cabaret speaking' with nobody listening.

16TH JANUARY 1934

We heard the strident clang of the shark bell. Dulce & I, on seeing other people rushing down to the beach decided that we, ourselves, would follow their example. Forthwith, without further delay we rushed as quickly as possible down to one of the cement Piers. Both of us had slippers & Dulce had a torn frock to match the effect. We saw the shadow of the fish in the water. It was rumoured that it was a blue-nosed shark 14 ft long. The surfboat, with a harpoon & two other smaller boats were out. When the boat came near the fish it rowed ashore again. We read in tonight's paper how Bondi was tricked by a school of FISH, GARFISH OR MULLET!

17TH JANUARY 1934

Mum and I went in the surf both morning and afternoon. I read in today's *Herald* that the fish in yesterday's episode was a shark. There was a row tonight. They intended going to the concert. I told mum I was tired of wearing my long cream trousers and voted a change. She started to lose her wool and call me a lot of names and naturally I didn't keep my mouth closed. I said I wouldn't go to the concert if she went down there to sit on the grass. So I stayed home and read in bed. I am going to put the light off.

20th January 1934

Back at Denbigh today. I wouldn't mind this house and its grounds, 3 bedrooms, a lounge room, dining & breakfast rooms, Hall, kitchen, bathroom & laundry, a back, side & front verandah, a garage, two large tool sheds, & a carpenter's room, not to mention paths, lawns, gates, fowl yard, fruit trees & a lavorary as well as other things. Nanna has 6 tables, not counting small ones. I can always remember this place since I was a very small child. Everywhere I look brings back a flood of memories. I left a bottle of ink in Uncle Arthur's car. I received sixteen books for Christmas presents on the 25th 1933.

21st January 1934

The big crowd were here again. Aunty Jeanne was as bad tempered as ever.

23rd January 1934

We went into town today. Mum paid the rest of the money to be paid on my Shakespeare. When we were lunching at David Jones we met two people who came from Melbourne. Amongst other things they told us that the little girl had a party with over a hundred guests. They were accompanied by a nurse. Their governess was at Melbourne. Ho hum!

27th January 1934

Mrs Schofield was here today. She gave me a shilling & promised me a pound if I go to the University.

29th January 1934

Back to Muswellbrook. I spent a good part of the morning tidying up the room. I have already packed my port ready for my week at Maitland High School. Mum will have to pay my railway fare down and I will receive a free ticket. Mum has given me some pocket money.

SIX

En avant

If she wanted to make it clear to me that I was being a nuisance Mum sometimes said: 'If you're not a better boy, Don, I'll send you off to boarding school.' Since Dad did not have enough money to send me to an expensive private school (the only proper boarding school) it was understood that this was simply a way of reminding me that affection could be withdrawn, that what a mother gave, a mother could take away. Because to get a secondary education I had to board at Maitland Boys' High School, a different line was now adopted. As she now had paid off, at two shillings a time, the collection of Shakespeare's plays she had put on the 'lay-by' for me, she now presented as a privilege what had previously been a threat: boarding at Maitland was something that most of the Muswellbrook boys were not lucky enough to enjoy.

Maitland High School was a government school at which attendance was free, but it was sixty miles from Muswellbrook, so I was to board during the week (with Dad paying seventeen shillings a week to the government for my board, and the government paying my train fares) and come home to Muswellbrook on Friday nights, thereby avoiding 120 miles of train travel every day. Only three boys from Muswellbrook, brothers from the same family, went by train daily to Maitland High. They did their written homework on Maitland railway station and read textbooks on the train. They travelled 600 miles a week, 24,000 miles a year, 120,000 miles for a five-year secondary education.

The 'port' that I packed on the eve of my departure to Maitland High School contained a number of new purchases: a soap holder, new sheets and towels (on which Dad had printed D.R. HORNE in black ink), thick exercise books with hard covers, a geometry set and a new foot rule. My first fountain pen was in the jacket of my new suit. To proclaim high-schooldom I had been measured for a navy blue knickerbocker suit with breeches that fastened with buttons below the knee and tucked into long socks. Knickerbockers, known among boys as 'poop catchers' or 'shit catchers', were a proclamation of higher education and good taste. To further emphasise my high-schooldom, for use at home I had two pairs of long trousers – one cream, the other dark grey.

We woke up before dawn at Muswellbrook on 30 January 1934 and as I got into my new knickerbocker suit and while Mum and I made the train trip to Maitland, with the suitcase on the luggage rack above us containing my new towels and sheets, my new exercise books, and my new geometry set, I wondered what it would be like to be someone who was familiar with algebra, whatever that might be, or could read Latin. What was the texture of chemistry? How would geometry or French feel once they were inside my head? I was sure that I was about to become a new person, knowing not only new things but new kinds of things which I could not yet imagine as being part of my own experience. As it turned out, after Mum handed me over to Maitland High School, I was not to learn anything that week except that I was alone in a new world and I must quickly find some consolation in it.

The place where I was to board was first built as a private residence, but it was now a government-owned hostel, called 'Hinder House', being named after Maitland High's most famous headmaster. The master-in-charge lived in the front portion, which still looked like a house; the back part had been rebuilt and added to, providing on the first floor three dormitories, a bathroom of three showers and some washbasins, and a master's room, and on the ground floor a big dining-hall and kitchens. It was shabby and bare, slippery with dark linoleum and drably painted, but when I looked around I tried to turn it into the Greyfriars of my Billy Bunter books. I unpacked the contents of my suitcase into the drawer I was allotted in a chest which I shared with two other boys, put my pyjamas under the pillow of the bed, which was at the end of the dormitory, overlooking the asphalt playground, and then went downstairs and wandered round the school. Bells would ring, but they did not seem to be ringing for me. Someone told me to go and see the headmaster. Someone else said the headmaster did not want to be bothered by new boys. I was told to go and get a free rail ticket. I joined a queue formed for this purpose, then when I had got my ticket I sat down on the side steps of Hinder House with a second-year boy who told me his nick-name was 'Sparrow'.

'Sparrow' explained that one of the first things I would have to be fixed up with was a nickname, that surnames of the younger boys were used only by masters, or by other boys only in disapproval, and that Christian names were not used by anybody. The nicknames of some of the other boys were 'Gandhi', 'Mutton', 'Weed', 'Aggie', 'Peastruck', 'Magsman', 'Sheila', 'Goofy', 'Scram' and 'Fungus'. For a while we tried to think of a nick-name for me. All the best nicknames seemed already to have been chosen. 'Sparrow' then told me that as a second-year boy he should not be talking to me in this friendly way, that at Hinder House everybody was expected to ostracise first-year boys apart from whatever human contact was needed to bully them and order them about. Term did not begin officially until the next day, however, so it would probably be all right to be friendly to me for a day, then I would have to wait until I had served my first year before he could be friendly to me again. He explained that during the week my manliness would be tested in an initiation ceremony and that by this means I would be introduced to the 'head-test', which consisted of bringing the knuckles of a clenched fist down sharply on another boy's skull. The head-test came in three main forms: as an open game, in which two or more boys tried to hit each other over the head; as a bullying device, in which a boy was held down while another boy hit him; or, in its most insidious form, as an unexpected attack from the rear. 'You've got to have eyes in the back of your head at Maitland High', said Sparrow. When some of his old friends of the year before arrived, Sparrow left me on the step. A gong sounded. I sat down to the worst meal of my twelve years.

When we were allowed to leave the table I went up to my dormitory (which I was already calling 'our dorm') and made a meal from the cake and biscuits Mum had baked for me at Denbigh. Another boy was in the dormitory, a boy from Scone, the next main town up the line from Muswellbrook; he was also a golf-playing schoolteacher's son. In an afternoon we became such friends that by the end of the week I already had my nickname. Since his surname was Whiting it was obvious that his nick-name was to be 'Fish', and since I was obviously to remain his inseparable companion it was equally obvious that my nick-name should be 'Chips'. I congratulated myself on drawing something better than 'Weed' or 'Aggie'.

The next day the deputy headmaster (whose nick-name, I was told, was 'Schnozzle') lined up all the new boys according to our place in the 1933 Primary Final examination, and then walked down the line, numbered us off, and cut us up into classes. I was surprised to find that, by examination, I had proved to be only the third most clever twelve-year-old boy in the Hunter Valley. 'I hope I can bring that up a little higher', I wrote in my diary. Having been apportioned into classes, we were marched off to what were to be our classrooms for the year. Although there were only about 450 boys at Maitland High (with twenty-three teachers) the old school, a simple brick building, had proved too small. There were 'portables' in the playground, and the first- and most of the second-year boys were marched off down the hill to Cumberland Hall, a mansion built by Alexander Brown, one of the Hunter Valley's coal barons, and bought by the Education Department two years before. There were no other 1As in New South Wales, I reflected, who were housed in a coal baron's best bedroom with the marble fireplace and bell-pull still intact (although with inkspots all round them) and out of the windows a splendid view of the valley.

At Cumberland Hall things were so higgledy-piggledy for the first week that no one taught us anything. We met the teachers who were to instruct us, most of them wearing dustcoats to save their suits from the chalk, and each of them exhorted us to be enthusiastic about being at high school. We analysed the characters of each of them and learned their nick-names. At Hinder House things were higgledy piggledy, too. Nick-names were handed out, but the initiation ceremony proved to be nothing more than each of us being stripped, insulted, hit on the head, and flicked over the naked body with knotted wet towels. When I got home to Muswellbrook on the Friday night I spent an hour or so in the kitchen amusing Mum and Dad so successfully by being funny about the bad food and doing satirical imitations of the teachers that the next day Mum wrote to Nanna that I had settled in nicely at Maitland High and that I 'had them in fits' in the kitchen when I told them all about it. Mum had got me a *National Geographic Magazine* with a good article about trapdoor spiders in it: I read it on Saturday morning, and on Saturday afternoon I played tennis; on Sunday I wrote a 'composition' for the English master and read the Sunday papers.

We would wake up at four thirty on a Monday morning, and after getting dressed and eating breakfast in the kitchen Dad and I would walk down to the railway station in time for me to catch the North West Mail at five thirty. Each day at Hinder House we were woken at seven o'clock. We breakfasted in the dining-hall, walked down the hill to Cumberland Hall for lessons at nine o'clock, up the hill to Hinder House for lunch, down the hill for lessons at Cumberland Hall until three thirty, up the hill to Hinder House, where we had free time until the gong sounded for our evening meal. After the tables were cleared we got out our books and bottles of red ink and settled down in the dining-hall to do our prep under the supervision of the assistant housemaster. On Wednesday afternoons we played sport. On Friday afternoons we caught the Brisbane Mail and I got back to Muswellbrook at eight fifteen. Over supper I would describe the funny things that had happened at school that week, and perhaps do some new imitations.

In the train we were put in 'dog boxes', self-contained twelve-seater compartments that had no communication with each other, each with its own lavatory. We small boys would all try to get together into one compartment without any of the bigger boys, so that we could play noughts and crosses in peace, but if bigger boys travelled with us we were likely to be bullied much of the way to Maitland. Sometimes our hats were filled with water and the water then thrown over us, on the assumption that we would dry out before Maitland; or we might be held down and pinched or slapped; or our trousers might be taken off so that our genitals could be mocked and our bottoms smeared with boot polish. Sometimes two or three of us might lock ourselves into the lavatory for safety and stay there all the way to Maitland. On one heroic occasion we had an isolated big boy with us: we swarmed over him and got some of our own back, first planning our assault in whispers in the lavatory, then coming at him in force. Playground bullying was a minor matter. Hinder House boys stuck together in the playground and this made us collectively unbullyable. At Hinder House the bullying usually meant being head-tested, with some amount of ceremony, perhaps being called into the smallest dormitory, where the big boys slept, and being put to the test to liven up a dull day. One big boy took a dislike to the way I pronounced 'r' with a 'w' sound. I was called into the little dormitory. 'Say rubber, Horne.' 'Wubber.' Clonk went his fist on my head. 'Say rubber, Horne.' 'Wubber.' Clonk. And so on. By the end of the year I had learned to pronounce the 'r' sound. At Hinder

House first-year boys were supposed to submit to these indignities without struggle or protest, with the solace that there was only a year of it and then they would be initiates who could help put next year's batch to the test. When I hit one of the big boys who was head-testing me, this was considered an act of cowardice. Most of the time we were not bullied, apart from being pushed over or flicked with a towel; but we were always on the lookout, waiting for the real bullying. We led an uncertain and peripheral life, formally despised and unwanted by every boy who was not in first year. It was the proper thing to cut us out of conversations, or crush us with a word, or send us out for a meaningless run round the playground as a punishment for our existence. Even the food expressed its indifference.

It was not within our range of comprehension that any first-year boy would complain so when after a few weeks I gave up pretending I was having fun and asked Mum and Dad if I could leave Hinder House I did not give them the real reason: I made up a reason and complained about the food. Mum said she would try to get me into one of the small private boarding houses, run by widows, where some boys stayed, only four or five of them to one house, sleeping two or three to a room. There was no bullying in these places; in fact, we Hinder House boys despised the boys who stayed in them as softies. During the week in which Mum made her inquiries, whenever I was bullied I would think of how quiet and friendly it would be when I retreated to a boarding house. At other times I miserably contemplated how I was not living up to the standards of the Billy Bunter stories or acting like the son of a trooper in the Australian Light Horse, and how I would lose the companionship that, along with the bullying, I was also beginning to find at Hinder House. I was ashamed that I was not proving myself a real Hinder House boy through thick and thin, taking the rough with the smooth. On the last day of what had proved to be my unhappiest week, the assistant housemaster came up to me and said coldly: 'I hear you don't like us, Horne. They tell me you're going to a boarding-house.' 'No, sir, that's not true', I said. 'I like it here at Hinder House.' When I got home that night I told Mum I would stay where I was, angry with her because she had agreed to let me do what I wanted to do.

AFTER THIS STRUGGLE WITH MY CONSCIENCE I DEVELOPED A GREAT pride in my membership of Hinder House and Maitland High School. Most of the bigger boys were getting bored with hitting us; for our part, we began to learn how to keep out of the way of the indefatigable bullies, and, if we found ourselves with them, to proceed with a crafty reticence. I was incompetent at this and showed such a talent for provoking one of them that he continued to hit me for the rest of the year. Now it was just being hit, however, and this was not so bad as feeling lonely. 'Fish' and I kept each other company, and divisions were appearing in our environment that provided solace. The principal of these was that the fifteen of us who went home for the weekends were all in the one dormitory, separated from the thirteen boys who stayed at Hinder House over the weekends, and, irrespective of whether we were only first years or not, the fifteen of us all became reasonably friendly.

I was ashamed that I went home at the weekends instead of staying at Hinder House, but proud that I stayed at Hinder House instead of living in one of the small private boarding houses, although on Mondays and Fridays when, on the train, we joined the boys who lived in these places, we all combined in despising boys who lived at home during the week. As a Maitland High boy I looked down on all other high-school boys (not that we ever saw any). Having been founded in 1884, our school was the second-oldest government high school in the state, and we knew that it had a famous history (although we did not know what this history was) and that it had many famous old boys (although we did not know who they were). It was clearly the pride of the Hunter Valley, Australia's best valley. The main reasons we were given for loyalty to the school (apart from the most significant of all reasons, that it was the school we belonged to) were provided by the school song: 'Some talk of their high schools and colleges too, from Brisbane right down to Geelong, but the school on the hill is the best of all still. En Avant, Maitland High, En Avant! From town and from country, from minefield and farm, our fellows are mustering strong, and together will pull for their district and school, to which they are proud to belong. On the red fields of Flanders, on Palestine's hills, our motto was carried along, by chaps side by side, who have fought, bled and died, in a glorious fight against wrong.' The refrain to each of these stanzas inspired us onward: 'En Avant! En Avant! En Avant! We'll carry this motto along. With efforts untiring and ever-inspiring, there's room at the top.

En Avant!' Pride in my membership of this school became emblazoned in my dress. At my request Mum knitted me long socks with the school colours. The Maitland High crest was stitched to the breast pocket of my knickerbocker suit, the Maitland High badge was stuck in my lapel, the Maitland High tie was at my throat, and the Maitland High crest reappeared on my hatband.

Although I liked most of the other masters as 'characters' – this one for his meticulousness, this one for his whimsy, this one for his conviviality – my hero was the master in charge of Hinder House, Frederick Alexander Elgar, known to us as 'Zander' or 'Froggy', although I spoke of him respectfully as 'Mr Elgar' when I talked about him back at Muswellbrook. Mr Elgar seemed the kind of person it was most desirable to be. He walked with a deliberative tread, and at moments of concentration he had a habit of lifting up his head and slowly pulling at the loose skin of his neck with thumb and forefinger thus seeming to emphasise that he was giving full consideration to his next action. He dressed carefully, and gave the impression that he had polished up his vowels before speaking. It was particularly impressive that he pronounced 'here' as 'heah'. He spoke dryly, and with emphasis, in a firm voice, but aloofly; his manners were more 'English' than those of the other masters, and he appeared to wear his learning as if it had been there all the time. I saw him alone every Monday evening when I paid him seventeen shillings for that week's board. We would be sent out, one by one, from the dining-hall where we were doing our prep, through the swing door that separated his part of the building from ours, in among the antique furniture. My hero would be at his antique desk. While he wrote out a receipt with his gold-topped fountain pen he might speak a sentence or two as I wondered at the old furniture: the armchairs that were slim, not fat like ours, and did not match each other, the old woods and the oil paintings. It was my introduction to 'good taste'. He spent a long time each afternoon exercising Peter, his Alsatian dog, whom he seemed both to respect and to adore. When Peter made as if to attack a visitor he was locked in his kennel, the vet was called, and Peter was killed by cyanide. The sternness of this event impressed even Mr Elgar's critics.

Bank managers' sons were thick at Hinder House, some of them sent from distant parts of the state because their fathers were old boys of the school. We were golf players' sons to a boy, talking about our fathers' handicaps and comparing impressions of the golf courses of our respective towns, and at Muswellbrook in the weekends I now played mainly with the few Maitland High boys in Muswellbrook: we would go back to calling each other by our Christian names as we made rotten-egg gas together or walked grandly through the town to visit girls.

In our lessons I was learning new languages. Not only French and Latin but the languages of algebra, geometry, chemistry and physics. The 'feel' of this new knowledge was now familiar inside me. In geometry I learned the language of triangles (congruent, acute, right-angled, obtuse, equilateral, isosceles and scalene) and how to think in terms of $\leq$, Δ, $\therefore$, or $\because$. Geometry took on the symmetry of its own surfaces and abstractions, moving smoothly with its peculiar arguments with itself to reach neat verifications of what it said was going to happen. Geometry moved vertically in argument; algebra moved sideways, more opaquely, sorting things out, always in balance, but with different arrangements of the components in the balance, as we contemplated the relations of equality of all these letters of the alphabet, now deprived of their old meaning. In chemistry I learned the language of Na and O_2 and H_2SO_4, and watched the minuet of the elements, cold, orderly and prearranged as, held together in one partnership, they would then break off when the music sounded, shuffle around and then hold together again in new partnerships on the other side of the floor. Physics spoke both the language of intricate measurement, as under instruction we manipulated calipers and screw gauges, spherometers and balances, or measured relative density or specific gravity, and the language of perfect order as we learned by heart Archimedes' Principle, Pascal's Principle or Boyle's Law, learning the language of certainty and underlining it with double rulings of red ink. By 1934 scientific knowledge had gone just about as far as it might be expected to go. There seemed more interacting complexity in French and Latin. In both of them I absorbed batches of new words every week, and as knowledge of their inflexions and their relations with each other grew they developed some life of their own: they could be manipulated infinitely and unpredictably. In French I felt the verb grow inside me, like a second skeleton, as we learned the positive, negative and interrogative of the present, imperfect, past indefinite, future, immediate past and immediate future tenses of the indicative and the imperative of the regular conjugations. I learned to regard Latin as a kind of jigsaw puzzle to be put together ('composition') or pulled apart ('translation') in an ordained order: principal verb, its subject, adjectives matching the subject in number, gender and case, object of transitive verbs or indirect object of intransitive verbs, adverbs and adverbial phrases, then the same thing all over again for the subordinate clauses. We were expected to regard Latin as a discipline that would make us think more clearly, but with French we could have a bit of fun. In the playground, or even at Hinder House, we jokingly threw around words and phrases such as *Qu'est-ce que c'est?*, *Donnez-moi*, *Où est?*, *voilà* and, in particular, *derrière* (a very funny word), and we even learned some French songs. With Latin there was not much fun in *hic, haec, hoc, hunc, hanc, hoc, huius all genders, huic all genders, hoc hac hoc*. I liked all these subjects, along with arithmetic (in which old problems had suddenly become more complicated), geography (in which we forgot about the British Empire and looked up at the sun, moon, stars and down into the earth's crust) and ancient history (in which we drew Osiris in our exercise books in coloured pencil, with the corn sprouting out of his body). In English, at my suggestion, we turned *Kidnapped* into a series of plays, writing a script for some new part of it each week and acting it impromptu. At the examinations I tied with another boy for first place in 1A.

At Hinder House enthusiasm for learning had to be concealed. The general tone was at the best indifferent but more usually hostile towards the idea of becoming educated. Whatever values the master-in-charge held, to the dominant boys education represented false values thrust on us so that we could become bank clerks or something better and then be able to afford to join golf clubs. Among these oracles of Hinder House's general will there was not even all that much enthusiasm for school sport. There was no strong belief in the 'team spirit', or the manly or character-building qualities of sport; head-testing was a better way of encouraging the team spirit and making men out of boys than playing the game; insofar as sport was important it was roughness that gave it appeal. The important things in life were to be tough, to be like each other, and not to talk too much. Swots were despised, but it was understood that they did not really like their education; they were simply working at it. For my part I also despised swots, scorning boys who did well in examinations simply because they worked hard, preferring effortless brilliance. But this very idea of brilliance, even more than swotting, went against how we were supposed to see things in the dormitories of Hinder House, where if we insisted on doing well at lessons it was better to do it because we were stupid but worked hard rather than because we liked lessons and enjoyed exercising our talents.

It was easy enough to conceal an interest in study, less easy to conceal a liking for quick-wittedness, especially when this was combined with the habit of saying what came into your head and trying to make a joke of it. Unlike my Denbigh family, some of the Hinder House boys did not like my sense of humour. I respected the values the masters were supposed to stand for (although it was fun laughing at their eccentricities), and instead of rebelling against them I expressed my effective person-to-person rebelliousness against some of the bigger boys, who, unlike the masters, were allowed to hit me over the head. Other than this, I fell in with our way of life and enjoyed its companionships and conformities.

If we could avoid the bullies, the period between the end of lessons and the evening meal was the time when we could most easily amuse ourselves in our own company. We might sneak down to one of the shops, buy a packet of cheap cigarettes, smoke them in a barn; or get a whole watermelon for sixpence or ninepence, then, after eating it, throw the rinds at each other; or break bounds and wander out among the lucerne farms; or run around on the grass hitting each other, or climb trees. A lot of our conversation was just lung-exercise: a lot of the rest of it ritual leg-pulling or gossip about the masters, playing the clown, adopting the cheery cynical style, a mode we also adopted when we shouted out ribaldries at each other in the dormitory before 'lights out'. Sometimes we would talk more seriously, breaking through our group cynicism, although the more of us there were, the less this was likely to happen. There was one boy, a bigger boy, whom I would help poke fun at when we were in groups, because he was a sissy but with whom I particularly enjoyed talking in private, relaxing in seriousness. If no one else was looking he and I would spend time pleasantly arguing about politics. Even one of the train bullies, another bigger boy, talked seriously with me when we once found ourselves alone in a railway carriage – until I discovered he was trying to make a pass at me. Sometimes there were just two of us in the dormitory together, two twelve-year-old boys sitting on a bed looking out on an empty asphalt playground and talking about what we knew of the world.

From time to time we received an official exhortation from some master or other to be manly – clean-living, with healthy minds in our healthy bodies – but this kind of manliness seemed to us a form of anti-masculinity. We did not want to be manly. We wanted to be men, with dirty minds in our healthy bodies. For the boys of my age our personal apparatus was not yet ready for this purpose, but we would talk about our ambitions, using information we had picked up from older boys (one of whom gave a demonstration lesson), waiting for the moment when our bodies gave the signs that they were ready. Into this atmosphere of innocent intention there broke an example of the extraordinary passions these matters could arouse. During prep one of the boys tossed a note to another boy. The assistant housemaster picked it up and read it. We all looked at him out of the corner of our eyes as he led the two boys away. When he came back he announced that these two boys were to sit alone for the rest of the week and that anyone seen talking to them would be caned. As we went up to our dormitories we heard the swish of the cane. After lights out we discovered what was in the note. One of the boys had written: 'Down in the valley, where nobody knows, someone was lying, without any clothes.' The two boys ate by themselves for the rest of the week and sat silently side by side in the hall in their spare time, an example to us all. On the following Monday we were assembled in the dining-hall, warned that we could be expelled for filthy conduct, and then the father of the author of the note caned his son in front of us.

My own attempts to be like everybody else were inhibited by my ineptitude in team games. In winter I played tennis instead of football, and I felt somewhat guilty about this, although I was delighted to find that even the 'chatty tennis' I had learned at home made me play better than some of the boys. In summer, instead of going swimming, which I would have preferred, I acted like a true son of Hinder House and tried to play cricket, a game I had not learned, although I was a keen follower of Don Bradman and the other Australian cricket heroes. This meant that I established myself as one of Maitland High's worst cricketers. When our team was fielding I was placed in some remote part of the park where the balls were least likely to appear. For a while I would strain every nerve trying to look as if I was interested in what I was doing: it was only when my attentiveness had disappeared and I was chewing grass and watching the ants scurry around that the ball would come bumping towards me, looking as if it were going to hit me. I would run after it, and throw it back feebly while our opponents scored three or four runs. When we were batting we sat under a tree, awaiting our turn: when my turn came it took me only a few minutes to strap on the pads, address a ball or two, then get bowled out. In a summer's cricket I may have hit the ball five or six times. I scored one run. I tried to make amends in athletics by entering almost everything a first-year boy could enter, apart from jumping, which seemed too hard: Mum made me a pair of black running-shorts, with white piping in the school colours, and I trained for some weeks – how to get off the mark quickly, how to hop around in a sack, how to hold in my mouth a spoon with a china egg in it, how to make a last spurt at the tape. I was placed in several heats and to my great delight came second in the 75 yards handicap under thirteen years, the proudest sporting achievement I was to attain in my life, and the last I was to attempt.

I ENDED THE YEAR WITH A DISPLAY OF CONFORMITY THAT MET even the standards of Hinder House. I was being held out of the Hinder House dining-hall by some of the bullies while their friends poured water on me from the first floor – they had pulled a window down over my thighs to hold me in place – but I managed to kick their hands out of the way, release my legs and fall out of the window onto the asphalt pavement. When I got up there seemed to be something wrong with my arm. We tried to reduce the swelling and the pain by holding it under a cold water tap, but it was obvious that this was no use and that I would have to report my arm to Mr Elgar. As I went through the swing doors into his part of the house the bullies' eyes followed me: Would Horne take the blame? Or would he tell the truth? A doctor was called. He said the bone was broken, and Mr Elgar drove me in his Hillman Minx to the hospital. On this car ride I was questioned about what had really happened, and again after I had woken from the anaesthetic to find my arm in plaster of Paris, and again on the next morning when, after sleeping at the hospital, I was taken back to Muswellbrook by Mum. I announced that I had jumped out of the window deliberately to 'show off'. My heart swelled with dishonest pride.

Back in Muswellbrook, I learned that Dad had been transferred to Westmead Junior Technical School, in Sydney, and that I would therefore leave Maitland High and go to Parramatta High School. We would be leaving Muswellbrook for Sydney in three weeks' time: removalists were already giving quotes for the cost of packing and removing our furniture. I insisted on saying good-bye to Maitland High School, going back to Hinder House for a couple of days, where, with my plaster of Paris arm in its calico sling, I received acknowledgment of my integrity in not peaching on my chums or ratting on my mates. I went through the swing doors for the last time to make a sad farewell to Frederick Alexander Elgar, my hero. I was astounded when he told me that he had hoped that if I had stayed at Maitland I would have become captain of Hinder House, and perhaps captain of the school.

As I surveyed my first year at high school I was very pleased. I had been vice-captain of 1A. I had moved from being the third most clever twelve-year-old boy in the Hunter Valley to being one of the two most clever twelve-year-old boys. When my mates broke my arm I had not told on them. I was learning cricket and I had come second in the 75 yards handicap under thirteen years. And here was Mr Elgar telling me that if I had stayed at Maitland I would have become captain of Hinder House.

As they were packing up our furniture and stowing it away, on the morning we left Muswellbrook, I stood on the verandah of the only house I was to think of as a home and sang the Maitland High School song right through several times. *En avant, Maitland High, En Avant!* Maitland High was to be the last institution of my youth to which I would be proud to belong.

PART 2

A BOY IN A STREET

1935–37

SEVEN

Usurpers in the family

On my first day at Parramatta High School I arrived early and, after visiting the main school building to enrol in 2A, I was sent down to one of the 'portables' at the bottom of the school grounds where I sat on a bench under a tree and looked at the stretch of grass (green grass, not brown like Hunter Valley grass) that made up Parramatta Park on the school side of the railway line. Between my legs was an attaché case in which I had stowed my old geometry set, a bottle of red ink, some old exercise books, some sandwiches in a tin, and my two Maitland High school reports. Another boy arrived early, and he took me out into the park to walk beneath a row of trees near the roadway. He said he went there every morning to look at the French letters left on the grass. We counted them, compared the tally with the situation obtaining before the Christmas holidays, then walked back to the precincts of 2A, where, in a desultory kind of way, I met some more of my new classmates, neither they nor I taking much interest in each other. I learned that boys did not head-test each other at Parramatta High, although they lunged with their hands at the flies of each other's trousers to unbutton them, and that although Parramatta was a co-educational high school, the only one in Sydney, the girls had a separate playground and we would see them only in the classroom. What really surprised me was that Parramatta did not bother to have a school song. Lessons were late beginning that day, and when I heard that a master from Maitland – they thought his name was Elgar – had been transferred to the teaching staff of Parramatta I went to look for him, hoping that two exiles from Maitland High School, pride of the Hunter Valley, might share their sorrow at being cast into this nondescript city school. When I found Mr Elgar he told me how lucky I was to be at such a good high school as Parramatta.

For the sake of politeness I agreed with these treacherous remarks, and walked back to 2A feeling even more lonely.

For the next few months I did not make friends with anybody. I talked a lot to the boy who arrived at school early every morning to count the French letters, but he was far too content with his disillusion to be concerned about friendship. He and I would go part of the way home together down the asphalt pavements of the Great Western Highway, and into the asphalt pavements of Marsden Street, where we now lived, kicking stones, pushing each other, swinging at each other with our attaché cases, pulling stalks off privet hedges, lunging at each other's flies, and pouring our scorn on the world. At the age of thirteen there was nothing that did not seem farcical to him, although he was good-humoured about it. It did not worry him that things had turned out so badly: that was all he had ever expected. I invited him home once for a cup of tea, but Mum did not like him. A month or two later he left the school.

The language of city boys seemed different, more like tough talk in American movies. In particular, conversation was made barren with a constant repetition of sceptical 'Oh yeahs?' Like 'OK', 'Oh yeah?' was only just coming in, and boys would spend minutes trying to out scorn each other with its use. 'Oh yeah?' a boy would say, pulling himself up and glaring at his rival as if that was the end of the matter. 'Yeah!' the other boy would reply, equally challenging. 'Oh yeah?' ... 'Yeah!' 'Oh yeah?' ... 'Yeah!' ... and so on, until someone tired of it. There was no bullying and nobody got hurt. But some of these boys talked so bleakly that it seemed to deaden the senses. At first the allusive phrases that made up much of their conversation seemed meaningless, until I learned that these were catch-phrases from their favourite comic radio serials. They sang songs I had never heard of until we got our first wireless and I discovered that these were the song hits of 1935. When we bought the wireless I would listen eagerly to all the serials the other boys talked about (especially the funny ones), thereby establishing some understanding of their minds, soaking myself in the shared revelation until I talked like the other boys. After the hour when I would have started doing prep at Maitland I might still be arguing with Dad that I wanted to listen to yet another serial; when I had hurried through my homework I would be back at the wireless to listen to one more programme before going to bed, drawing my chair close to the wireless in affection, my face almost rubbing against the polished Bakelite of its cabinet.

After a while I used the wireless more moderately. I now saw things as they did at school, but apart from the programmes that became established as my own favourites I could not be bothered putting myself to any more trouble to share their experience. The popular songs, repeated ad nauseam on the wireless and by the boys at school, did not seem as good as such favourites as 'Broadway Melodies of 1932', which we had liked in the old days when we had singsongs around the pianola. The pianola now stood unused except when, for old times' sake, I might play a roll or two when I came home from school.

I despised my new high school, but in a tolerant way. No one seemed proud of it. We were not expected to burden ourselves with any loyalty. At Parramatta we acknowledged that we were the most inferior of the city's dozen or so high schools. We were stuck out on the edge of the city, at the end of the Western Suburbs electric railway line, with only some straggled suburban settlements west of us, some of them only the beginnings of suburbs, and then other settlements that were more country than city. Being both a girls' school and a boys' school seemed to make us neither one thing nor the other. When Mum asked me if I would like to buy a school tie I said no, and affected some dotted silk ties instead. At sport on Wednesday afternoons I now performed badly with bad grace, whereas at Maitland I had performed badly with great enthusiasm. Now and again the headmaster called us together to exhort us to show more school spirit; when he asked us to write suggestions for a school song I wrote the following: 'Some talk of Sydney High School, And some of Fort Street too, And some of Sydney Grammar, And some of Riverview, But of all the schools in New South Wales, If only we would try, There could still be room at the top For Parramatta High.' I wrote IF ONLY WE WOULD TRY in capital letters to make my meaning clear.

Apart from the history master, who seemed to lend some enthusiasm to teaching British history and Australian history, I disliked all of the teachers, this one for being pompous, that one for being stupid, this one for being a bully, that one for being bored with the subject, that one for disliking me. French, in particular, had become an expanse of dreariness: we spent much of our classroom time simply copying into our exercise books what was already in Heath's *Practical French Grammar*, word for word, with double lines of red ink under the major headings and single lines under the minor headings.

Latin had also become a grind, like mathematical tables, something just to be learned. Mathematics and science began to fade into school report stereotypes. English seemed to survive only because of the qualities I myself gave it. In all these lessons there seemed to be remoteness, even indifference. We were expected to recast ourselves as people who could satisfy examiners' demands if we wanted to. Whether or not passing examinations mattered was something we could determine for ourselves, but this was what education was about – if we wanted education.

Uprooted and hastily replanted, I was looking for someone who would show some interest in my desire to find acceptable ways of exercising my talents; but it was the convention of the time that high school teachers should not pay any personal attention to their pupils. They were to move from class to class and offer instruction, and that was all they were expected to do. Examinations were a test of how talent survived this aloofness. Talent had to be trained and toughened. I declared war on two of the teachers, attracting their interest by defying them, and thereby also attracting the interest of classmates who might otherwise not have noticed that this new boy had joined their class. From identifying myself with schoolteachers I now identified myself only with the subject matter of my education, defying the educators in the name of education. When I was sick in bed – I had managed to persuade myself and my mother that I was sick enough to stay away from school for what added up to two weeks in the first half of the year – I would spend hours imagining that I was a teacher giving lessons with the enthusiasm with which I considered they should be given. In my head I would give long lessons to myself, in English grammar and, for a time, in algebra (I had read the preface to our algebra textbook and discovered what algebra was supposed to be about). If my mother was out of the house I would give these model lessons out loud.

The conglomeration of streets of bungalows edging into a large shopping centre that made up the suburb of Parramatta confounded us with its indifference. We did not meet anybody. I was no longer a boy in town. I was a boy in a street, and a street in which I did not know anyone else. There was no method by which we could bring to the attention of Parramatta the news that the fun-making Hornes were now resident and that we would like to make some friends. All we belonged to was this long street in which the main intra-connections were the telegraph poles. Parramatta was supposed to be 'historical', but it seemed nothing more than acres of red roofs merging into the acres of red roofs that belonged to other suburbs. It had no beginning or end. We were not sure whether where we lived in Marsden Street was really Parramatta or the adjoining suburb of Harris Park.

We did not like the street we lived in, with its little houses crammed into their little gardens, nor the house we had rented, a four-roomed weatherboard house, painted cream and green, with a high privet hedge mounting guard over it, keeping watch on us and subduing us with its darkness. It was my job to keep the hedge clipped, and each time I attended to it I tried to bring it down an inch or two, not so low that my father would notice, but with the hope that eventually I would humble it and destroy its dominance over the house. We did not entertain anybody. No tennis. No afternoon teas. No bridge. Nobody 'dropped in'. At night we listened to the wireless and then went to bed. We had stopped having a good time.

PERHAPS IT WAS SUDDENLY BEING THROWN IN ON OUR OWN company in this way, without Muswellbrook to save us from ourselves, that made me begin to see Dad as if he were someone I could not talk to openly any more. At times he was as jovial as ever but there were other times when he could seem a stranger in our house. He would stop listening to Mum and me, or even seeing us, and just look in on himself, sitting among us silently. Then he might wake from this, and lunge out irritably. At other times I would catch him frowning as he looked at me, as if there were some inadequacy in me so great he would not reveal it.

Perhaps there really was something wrong with me that only he could see? But then for the last two or three years there had been a background of conversation about his health: perhaps it was not my fault at all. I had only overheard bits and pieces, as if he had the toothache and would get over it soon. He had begun to go deaf, and there was talk about that, but there was even more talk about a mysterious disease called 'nerves', which I could not find any reference to in our *Household Physician*. Two years before, he had taken six weeks' leave to recover from this mysterious complaint. Perhaps he had not done so.

Now that this strange, worried man was living with us, not sharing his worries, I stopped talking about school to Mum and Dad, and I did not do funny imitations for them any more. In any case I was beginning to feel that I was not fitting properly into my own body. It was growing into somebody else's body. I began to worry if I might not be too skinny. I would examine my thighs in the bath wondering if they were sturdy enough, and I was so concerned with what I feared might be the thinness of my wrists and forearms that I would try to get my arms close to another boy's and, as I talked about something else, silently compare them for width. I wondered what I looked like to other people, and peered at parts of my face from unusual angles in mirrors and worried about what I saw. What did my voice sound like? At times I would try to listen to it, but I couldn't hear it. One day at school I saw one of the boys imitating the way I walked. Did I really walk in such an exaggerated style? It looked like Mr Elgar's walk, not mine. I tried to watch my reflection in shop windows, to find out how I did walk. I read articles in the newspapers about the problems of adolescence, but they did not provide any advice about how to make your body fit you. When Mum and Dad were not looking I read a great deal of our *Household Physician*, absorbing knowledge about my viscera and muscles and bones, and diseases such as gonorrhoea, leprosy and St Vitus Dance. I worried that, for some unknown reason, I might have been infected with syphilis without detecting the primary symptoms, and I would wait with dread for the secondary symptoms to appear.

BECAUSE IT TOOK TWO ELECTRIC TRAINS AND A BUS, UP TO NINETY minutes travelling, to get there, when we went to Denbigh we stayed for a whole weekend. At Denbigh the three of us could forget the new loneliness we were now finding in each other. I would see 'Mick' there, my only Sydney companion. 'Mick' and I fabricated an ambitious series of concerts out of popular songs, staging them in our relations' houses, miming 'Pettin' in the Park' in silhouette behind a sheet, or 'Shuffle off to Buffalo', with a couch signifying a railway sleeping compartment. We always produced 'The Man on the Flying Trapeze' as finale; in my Maitland High running shorts and singlet I would jump around the room and, in climax, over the audience.

'Mick' and I were playing ping-pong one night in the breakfast room at Denbigh when someone spoke to us so severely about the noise we were making that we realised it was true that Pa, who had gone to bed that morning after feeding the hens, was very sick. We went into his bedroom to be nice to him and, in the Carpenter fashion, tell him a joke, but his gaze was so beyond all concern that we came out again without speaking. When he was taken in an ambulance to a private hospital at Kogarah, the house seemed empty, although Denbigh was crowded with relations. It was unlike Pa, so self-sufficient, to be the occasion for so much consideration. In the middle of the night, alone in the dark of his hospital room, suffering his last loneliness, Pa died. His body was brought back to Denbigh and laid out in state, surrounded by flowers from his garden, in the room in which there had been so many weddings, surprise parties, send-offs and welcome-homes. That night my uncles and Dad kept vigil all night, sitting in the drawing room, talking in low voices in front of the fire and drinking cups of tea as if they were at the Front and would soon go over the top. The next morning, before the lid of the coffin was screwed down but after all the wreaths had arrived, we walked in turn to this large room, now perfumed with flowers, to look for the last time on Pa's body. I contemplated in amazement the dead, proud face of this hero, unbelievably put into a polished box and cushioned on lace. Death had added an unexpected delicacy to his skin that contrasted with the aloofness he had kept up when he was alive. The first part of the funeral service was conducted in the drawing room at Denbigh. At the cemetery his sons carried his body to the grave. That night back at Denbigh our shock released itself in laughter. 'Mick' and I were sent down to buy some stuff at the ham and beef shop and over a tea of cold meats we all paid respect to his memory by recalling the happiness of his house. As I was going to bed I heard one of my aunts say: 'Don took it well. He didn't cry.' I had been too startled to cry, but I doodled coffins at school for months afterwards, finally stylising them as boxes, a habit kept for years.

IN MY FIRST HALF-YEARLY EXAMINATIONS AT PARRAMATTA HIGH my school report said '1st – Excellent' against history and '4th – Very Good, class work very good indeed' against English, and that was how I expected things to be. But for the first time in my life there was also the damning faint praise of 'Very Fair' – against science and algebra; 'Could do better than this' was against geometry; and 'Fair – should do better' was against Latin. What astonished me even more was that I had failed in arithmetic ('Disappointing – capable of better work'); and what seemed unbelievable was that I had failed so badly in French (twenty-nine per cent) that the only comment was 'Very Weak'. When I read this report I could not imagine how I could show it to my parents: to be in this new position of a boy who could fail in a subject made me seem as big a usurper in my own family as my father now seemed. It was beyond my understanding why, when I had summoned enough courage to hand over the report to my parents, they made no comment on it.

I began to accommodate myself more to Parramatta High. Acquiring some of the city vocabulary, I found it was easy enough for us to avoid each other by using this cynical, jocular form of noncommunication. I was not such a master of its meaninglessness as some of the boys, one of whom in particular could chatter brilliantly for a long time, in puns, snatches of song and allusive phrases without saying anything, but I found a better audience for satirical imitations than I had found in Hinder House. However, to be able to mock authority was not the true style of Parramatta; the true Parramatta boy did not so much mock authority as amuse himself with its peculiarities: that we considered our masters to be no good, for example, was a matter not for indignation but for jest. What did it matter? The whole school was no good. Parramatta was no good. What was good? I took up such school debating as there was and enjoyed it, although with some disdain for both the other contestants and the audience, as if a great star from the Hunter Valley was now patronising a suburban amateur theatrical company.

I made three particular friends; one was the boy who came top in 2A (the kind of boy I used to be); another was 2A's most talented and amusing exponent of city humour, as good as the wireless; the third was a quieter boy, a good listener who, when he spoke, spoke briefly and dryly. We formed a group in the playground, delighting ourselves with our flippancy as we talked together in the mid-morning break and over our lunchtime sandwiches and piece of fruit. The schoolyard seemed better now that I did not have to wander around looking for somewhere to sit and then make an excuse for joining the group sitting there. However, this was a different friendship from earlier school friendships, more tentative. Did these new friends really like me? Did they see me differently from how they saw each other? I would look for significance in some slight detail, taking this as a sign that they liked me, or as a sign that they were tolerating my company in some kind of hoax which they would talk about between themselves when they retired into that place, wherever it was, where *real* friends met. At Maitland I had still seen people as friends or enemies: now I was becoming uncertain. These doubts and hesitations did not stop me from being talkative, but I was acquiring the habit of conducting two conversations at once – one with my friends and one with myself. For the two and half years I was at Parramatta High I did not invite my schoolfriends to our house. They did not invite me to theirs.

ONE NIGHT IN THE SECOND HALF OF THE YEAR, BEING INCREAS-ingly dissatisfied with our home behind the hedge in Marsden Street, we went to look at a house that was advertised as being to let at Westmead, a small unfinished suburb, more a suburb of Parramatta than of Sydney, Parramatta's west meadow, where Dad was deputy headmaster. We found it hard to believe that the splendours of this house were being offered to us. A double frontage, with lawns, rose gardens and cement paths, a backyard three times as long as those of the surrounding houses, and set in these grounds an edifice in solid liver-coloured brick, with mosaics of red and brown tiles on its brick verandahs, redbrown tiles on its roof, and six white-walled rooms inside, along with a white-tiled kitchen and a white-tiled bathroom and spacious halls. There were leaded panes of diamond-shaped glass in the windows, natural brick surrounds for the fireplace and varnished wooden picture rails running around each room, with a wallpaper dado beneath them and a 'china rail' above them for *objets d'art*. Dad accepted it at once. Too good to miss. A bank inspector owned it, and since he was moving to the country he wanted someone as reliable as a schoolteacher to take it over.

There was new furniture to fill it out – a light oak 'breakfast room suite' replaced our old kitchen table and chairs, and a glass-fronted light oak cabinet replaced our old kitchen dresser; there was a light oak 'lowboy' for my clothes and a light oak desk for me to do my homework on in the spare bedroom, which I now thought of as my study. In the dining room and lounge room Dad stained the floorboards with dark varnish to set off the new carpets, and Mum made new cushions to be placed on top of the newly upholstered 'lounge suite' to show when we weren't sitting on them. We bought a 'standard lamp' to put beside the wireless cabinet and some earthenware vases to place on the china rails. We laughed at the primitive way we had lived at Muswellbrook.

I became as enthusiastic a home-maker as Mum, checking her taste and going on shopping expeditions. In creating our new home we were creating for ourselves in reddish-brown tiles, leaded window panes and wallpaper dadoes an aspiration of what our new life should be. Everything would be all right once this monument was perfected. I had gone to an Electrical and Radio Exhibition at the Sydney Town Hall and my mind was now extended by a realisation of the potentialities of the age. There were not only electric toasters, electric hot water jugs and electric irons to admire – we had those ourselves by now – but one might also aspire, although with little hope of early fulfilment, to electric mixmasters, electric cookers, electric room heaters, and even electric ice chests, called refrigerators. With the reverence of a tourist passing from one chapel to the next in an old cathedral, I passed from one exhibitor's stand to the next, collecting the 'literature' on the exhibits, which I took home and put in a folder as a testament to the progressiveness of our times.

My sense of participation in this home-making gave me some of the feelings of a young husband, starting life all over again. This feeling was to be given extra substance at the end of what was my first – and only – conversation with my parents connected with sex. We were sitting in our breakfast room one morning, surrounded by the light oak of our breakfast suite, and I was eating toast and honey, taking the honey from the crockery honey bowl designed as a beehive I had given Mum for Mother's Day. I had been noticing that her breasts seemed to be getting bigger, so I decided to ask her: 'Are you going to have a baby?' She was. I tried to become Mum's principal adviser in babycraft, reading some of the most progressive booklets, and insisting on modern dietary techniques, such as orange juice. I could not make up my mind about the comparative advantages of breast-feeding and bottle-feeding, but I mounted a long and at times intemperate campaign, in which I met firm and insidious opposition from Nanna, against the use of a dummy. I was very concerned that our baby should be born into the world of the Electrical and Radio Exhibition and enjoy from birth all of a baby's equivalents of the mod cons we were now ourselves enjoying.

EXCEPT THAT THE BABY WAS YET TO COME, EVERYTHING IN OUR palace was now in its place and we wished we had a camera so we could give it a final reality. But our new house did not save us. Dad moved even further from us as he became preoccupied with the claims and appeals he was now making to various tribunals in the Repatriation Department: he was trying to have it established that his deafness – which was becoming worse – should be recognised as being due to war service so that he would qualify for medical treatment and a small pension. The documents thrown up by these negotiations he kept neatly folded in the drawer where he stored his war medals, his Bedouin's knife and his Masonic apron, sometimes bringing them out and turning them over, as if finally to discover their real meaning. Much of the conversation in our house was now concerned with 'Dad's case'. War still cast a light over us, but what concerned us now were questions such as whether the quinine with which the army treated Dad's malaria in 1917 was likely to have made him begin to go deaf in 1932. When he was not discussing his 'case', his most enthusiastic approach to our occasional visitors was to retell anecdotes about the Great War. Several times I cut into the middle of an anecdote and quickly finished it for him.

Mum and Dad did not make any friends in Westmead. Its half formed streets lay around us, but they were inhabited by unknown people. For evening entertainment we again sat silently by the wireless, as we had done at Marsden Street, as if we were inwardly praying for some great revelation. Now and again, entertaining ourselves as visitors in our own home, we played a family game of bridge or mah-jongg. The pianola was still there; its outer woodwork still highly polished; it was to continue to stand in the houses we were to live in until the felt in its insides became so eaten away by moths and its metal so eroded that it was sold as junk. Sometimes we made the long trip to Denbigh. Sometimes Kogarah relations visited us. This was our only company, except for the rare occasions of visits from old friends from Muswellbrook who were now living in Sydney. On these nights, when we talked about old times, we might even take out old snapshots of Muswellbrook and wonder what had happened to the people in them.

Although Dad maintained the grass lawns and rose gardens in the front of the house so that they still looked as good as a small second-rate public park, despite an occasional show of interest he neglected the backyard and a lot of it was still paddock, excellent for my dog, Zac, whom we had brought down with us from Muswellbrook and who was now my main companion. I played with Zac every afternoon after school, and sometimes, in relief from our lonely liver-coloured and reddish-brown splendour, he and I went for long walks along our new street and the paddocks that still surrounded parts of it. Here I made friends with some of the men who lived in the less pretentious fibro and weatherboard houses that made up most of the rest of the long street. I developed a talent for interesting them in what I had been reading in the newspapers. My only other diversion was to walk around Parramatta Park or across the park to Parramatta shopping centre, sometimes simply to drink a chocolate malted in one of the milk bars and to stand around for a while and look at the people. As often as I could I went to the pictures at Parramatta (usually by myself), either to the Roxy, which was done out as the castle of a Spanish grandee, with its own courtyards, fountains and arcades, or to the Astra, recently built in the new, heavily carpeted 'intimate' style, bringing to cinema architecture what we saw as some of the good taste of the high-class suburban home. The age demanded that, as a token of their maleness, boys should keep their hair cut very short, having it clipped back as frequently as they cut down their father's lawns, so that I was able to visit my favourite barber at Parramatta often, delighting in the relief of tobacco smoke and straightforward men's talk as I delighted in the relief of Zac's bark and the smell of his coat.

As often as possible I went to the pictures in the city – again, often, alone – walking across the park to catch the electric train at Parramatta. During the forty-minute train trip I would contemplate the two dismal shades of brown of the carriage or its dirty dull-green seats, or wish that the girl in the far corner would come over and speak to me, or look out of the window as we jolted and rattled past the vast plains of the suburbs, the roofs of the cottages swirling like a red mist, with here and there a solitary green tree or the stone of an older and bigger house and sometimes the bare brown face of a rock outcrop, unconquered. Stretches of wasteland separated the suburbs from the black and grey plain of the industrial area closer to the city where, with many of the factory buildings walled and roofed with corrugated iron, painted black, and so many of the dilapidated terraces or tumbledown bungalows roofed and fenced with corrugated iron, we seemed to be hurrying to the solid delights of the city through an ugly shanty settlement that, given a stiff wind, might blow away. There was a smell of old smoke as we passed the acres of the Eveleigh railway workshops, then a smell of hops from the brewery as we joined the rest of the twenty-two railway tracks which united Central Railway Station with the rest of Australia and then a smell of old air as we rattled into Sydney's short stretch of underground railway.

CITIES HAVE TO DERIVE A SENSE OF IMPORTANCE FROM SOMETHING. Its cinemas gave Sydney much of its significance. The big 'picture shows' were its true cathedrals. There were not only Clark Gable and Jean Harlow and Myrna Loy and William Powell and Jeannette MacDonald to wonder at; in the most ambitious picture shows there were copies in marble of famous statues, copies in oils of famous paintings, copies in glass of famous chandeliers, copies in bronze of famous suits of armour, copies in wood of famous styles of furniture, copies in mock stone of famous orders of architecture. There were hundreds of square yards of thick curtains, hundreds of square yards of thick carpet. There were kaleidoscopic lighting effects; a full orchestra would rise from the pit on hydraulic lifts, dressed in clothes that picked up the theme of the music they were about to play; and on the stage ballets would be performed before the main feature began. Mightiest of all these effects was the Wurlitzer organ, which also rose on a hydraulic lift. Some of its 250 stops played not only the organ but the grand piano, the castanets, the Chinese gong, sleighbells, the xylophone, horse's hooves, the full range of drums, cathedral chimes, the tambourine, train whistles, the thunder sheet and bird whistles. And beside the big city picture shows were some of the city's most splendid milk bars, exciting to jostle in at interval.

Even more significant to the city were the department stores, which we called the 'retail stores'. It has been usual in the history of cities that a sense of importance should come from the great houses of great families. In the 1930s, while country people drew their sense of importance from their landed families, we Sydney people paid respect to our merchant princes. The families in Sydney that seemed important were the families that had established the retail stores: the picture shows may have been the cathedrals but the palaces of Sydney were the retail stores themselves, whether the founding families still owned them or not. Sydney had few significant mass ceremonies – going to the beach in summer, going to football or cricket matches, going to the pictures, going to the races (where the division between the Flat, the Leger, the Paddock and the Members' Stand made an even more significant statement about the social order than the difference, at a cinema, between front stalls, back stalls and dress circle). To spend 'a day in town', shopping, was to take part in one of the significant ceremonies of Sydney.

Each of the retail palaces had its own character. David Jones had been founded by a family of ancient but not remarkable origin who had suddenly become more vigorous than the others, an ascendant family. The David Jones store was not as grand as Farmers, with its Corinthian pilasters, scrolls and pediments, but no one could any longer remember anything about the Farmer family. Anthony Horderns was the oldest and largest of the palaces, but it was now in decline, although we still talked about the Hordern family even if, in English fashion, they had sold out of trade and acquired land. Mark Foys was trickily fashionable but unpredictable; Hordern Bros reliable but dull; Grace Brothers appeared to have over-extended itself; and so forth. Beneath the great palaces the lesser palaces, the big stores that specialised in furniture or men's clothes or whatever, played an honourable part of their own but the smaller retail stores that tended towards cheapness and the chain stores that specialised in it were a threat to established privilege. With the familiarity of a city discussing its patricians, even schoolboys would talk about the retail families. Many of the heads of these families became knights; several of them had patronised the arts; most of them used their money to acquire power in politics; they often travelled overseas, looking for new things to sell. Between them, they seemed the city's main arbiters of taste.

The city was the heart of a fifty-mile stretch of suburbs, with patches of bushland filling them out, but with already a million and a quarter people living in them. What did it mean to us? As well as visits to the palaces of the retail stores and the cathedrals of the picture shows, there were the two annual pilgrimages across the Harbour – a day at Manly and a day at the zoo. There were the acts of witness at the races and at the cricket matches. There were the outings to the Royal Agricultural Show and Anzac Day (along with the suburban festivals of Christmas dinner, Mother's Day, and Cracker Night, when children let off fireworks to celebrate Empire Day). And there was the Australian Museum, where we could imagine we were walking through an encyclopedia as we looked at stuffed birds, Egyptian mummies, New Guinea head-dresses, Australian opals and dinosaurs' bones; or the Museum of Applied Arts and Sciences, which seemed to suggest that technology had long since come to a stop. And there was the Art Gallery, with its revered bush landscapes, and its even more revered collection of such nineteenth-century historical paintings as *The Sons of Clovis, The Three Sisters of Phaeron Weeping over the Tomb of Their Brother* and *The Visit of the Queen of Sheba to King Solomon*. Two of these (*Rorke's Drift* and *Chaucer at the Court of Edward III*) were so celebrated that there were reproductions of them in *The Story of the British Nation*. Sometimes I would go into the city and seek something else: I would walk around the imitation Gothic of the two cathedrals or the imitation Renaissance of the bank palaces, or various varieties of imitation classical, or peer at the statues in the parks. But this didn't seem real. Sydney was women shoppers jamming narrow pavements between nondescript buildings, some of them carrying large suitcases to pack their bargains in, pursuing their day in town.

EIGHT

Clever in a new way

The front of Parramatta High was a dark brick façade overlooking the dark asphalt of the Great Western Highway. At the beginning of the new school year in 1936, by which time I was fourteen, we moved from the 'portable' where we had been 2A and became 3A in a classroom in the main school building, overlooking the highway. As members of Third Year we had a new importance. We were to be subjected to the 'Inter', the Intermediate Certificate examination, a ceremony of initiation for adolescents then conducted annually by the government of New South Wales.

In November third-year pupils in all the secondary schools in the state would sit down for three hours a day for at least seven days and on special foolscap paper issued by the Department of Public Instruction they would write their answers to the printed examination papers prepared by the department's examiners. Their answers would then be sent to the department for marking and, according to what the results were when they were announced in the newspapers in February, friends and relations would congratulate them or commiserate with them, and employers would sort them out so that they knew who to hire. Printed certificates would be issued recording their passes, to be framed by their mothers and hung on the wall. For a year several hundred classrooms of fourteen-year-olds would be injected with the kind of information the examiners required, and they would be taught the way the examiners liked this information to be given back to them. Since we were to devote the year's lessons to nothing but learning how to pass this examination, all our homework now consisted of answering questions similar to those asked in the Inter. The examination papers were always predictable in form and the same kind of questions were asked each year, so we learned the structure of the examination paper by heart. We were not sure what a 'nervous breakdown' was, but we believed that the Inter was such a test of us that some of us might suffer 'nervous breakdowns' in the course of our preparation. We discussed the possibility of concealing cribs in our pocket handkerchiefs or writing mnemonics on our shirtcuffs.

Although I was still inclined towards my new style of rewarding or punishing my teachers by being good or bad at their subjects according to my personal relations with them, I was impressed by the general hysteria of the occasion, and I still had some memories of those days, even if they had ended as long as twelve months before, when I was the boy who came first, but it may have been only a brush with the French teacher that made me *determined* to do well in the Inter. He was the teacher I hated most and for whom I produced the worst results. I got on his nerves so much one afternoon that he called me up to see him at the end of the lesson and cut me down with a few words: *what would my father think of me if I failed in French in the Inter?* I did not tell him that I had been shocked by Dad's lack of comments on my bad marks in French and that I was losing interest in what he thought of me in this or in other connections, but I went home, got out Heath's *Practical French Grammar* and started working hard at French, a habit I kept up during the year. I was delighted that the hated French teacher had shown enough affection for me to give me a good kick.

In elementary science I was happy enough to parrot off the notes I took down on hydrostatics or pneumatics or on oxidation and reduction or determining the equivalent weight of magnesium by igniting, seeing chemistry and physics as mere memory tests, two separate disciplines, unrelated to each other or to the rest of science, whatever that was, or to anything else. My rebellion against arithmetic in 2A had bewildered me, and I was surprised to find that, even now that I was again trying, I still sometimes got wrong answers. Finding it demeaning that what had been the easiest of subjects had become stubbornly and inexplicably elusive, my resentments against arithmetic began to rub off on to algebra and geometry, and I sometimes did not really care if I solved simultaneous equations involving quadratics or consider it really important that if two chords of a circle intersected, either inside or outside the circle, the rectangle contained by the parts of the one would be equal to the rectangle contained by the parts of the other.

In French, as we continued our struggle inside the skeleton of the verb, and as we continued to assemble the innards of syntax in Latin, we did not acquire any facility in reading or understanding these languages. French and Latin were good for us because our textbooks made them hard and tedious: if we simply learned to speak them and read them, how could we sit for examinations in them? In Latin we turned the first book of *De Bello Gallico* inside out, going through it twice in class, sentence by sentence, but something of the book survived because our Latin teacher, although a woman, delighted in manoeuvre and battle and was pleased to go campaigning with Caesar. She was a supporter of Franco, and sometimes she would draw on the blackboard a plan of the latest military dispositions in the Civil War in Spain (as if it were being fought by Julius Caesar) and give us her analysis of the strategic situation, moving troops around in red and blue chalk as if they were already in history.

For the Inter we had to slice up our history and dehydrate it in the form of short memorised notes that could be stored easily in the mind and then, when the Inter came, watered with the required prose style and put together again for the examiner. What were the three most important causes of the Seven Years War? What were the four most important results of the Industrial Revolution? Write a brief note on Pitt, Clive, Burke, Gladstone, Cobden, Parnell, Durham, Lugard. Describe Sturt's expedition into the centre of Australia and draw a neat sketch map to illustrate your account. The history we were taught was still British history, but the wars of the seventeenth and eighteenth centuries, the French Revolution, Napoleon and the causes of the Great War reminded us that there was a world outside Great Britain. We met this world mainly by learning the story of British colonialism as we marched with the British across the world. In the Australian history course we marched with the British across our own continent.

In English lessons the year was a catechism in which we learned how to answer the seven kinds of question that would be found in the English examination paper. We even learned how much time to devote to answering each of these questions so that we would be able to fit them all into the three hours allowed for the paper. Question 1, which invited us to choose from three essay topics on subjects such as 'In a Garden', 'Animal Pets' or 'War in the Air', was a training in the subtlety of deceit: we affected attitudes we did not hold about subjects we were usually not interested in, saving interest, if one was clever at this game, for imitating the literary style of nineteenth-century essayists and journalists. The strong pleasure of spurious enthusiasm and borrowed belief would take me over as I wrote one of these essays, partly aware of the pretence, partly believing in it, but mainly enchanted by the craftsmanship of turning in the job in the manner required. In Question 2 we would have to pick away at a sentence, analysing the kind and relation of its clauses, and parsing underlined words. *Trepidation: Abstract noun, 3rd., sing., neut., obj. gov. by prep. 'with'.* Question 3 would ask us to 'appreciate' 'The Rime of the Ancient Mariner' and to admire the characterisation of Conrad's *Youth* and *Gaspar Ruiz*. To guide us in 'appreciating' Coleridge the teacher drilled us in examples of 'beautiful expression' and 'beautiful thoughts' so that we could memorise them and write them down for the examiner. To help us discuss Conrad's characterisation he dictated notes telling us what everyone looked like, whether they had good or bad characters and whether they were true to life. Question 4 was easy: 20 lines of poetry or prose from memory, with a choice from subjects such as the expression of joy, a race, the sea, patriotism. In Question 5 we were asked to comment on passages from our texts, in terms of their bearing on plot (*What leads to it? What comes from it?*), their bearing on character (*What the character thinks of himself. What others think of him. What he really is.*), the thoughts expressed and the thoughts aroused, the feeling or atmosphere (*Our feelings. The character's feelings. The author's intentions.*) and expression of beauty (*Vivid scenes. Appropriate words. Smoothness and clarity. Rapid movement. Alliteration. Long or short vowels. Consonants. Onomatopoeia. Epithets. Figures of speech*). Our teacher picked out a number of the most likely passages, mainly from *A Midsummer Night's Dream*, and told us what we should say about them. In Question 6 we would have to choose one of several quotations about *A Midsummer Night's Dream*, somewhat harder because less predictable than the other questions, and in Question 7 we would have to give a detailed analysis of four or five passages from the same play telling the examiner which character was speaking, when, where, and under what circumstances, and giving an explanation of difficult words and phrases, classical allusions, grammatical peculiarities and figures of speech, and then paraphrasing each passage in our own words. The effect of this approach to English was that for most of the year I gave up reading books.

THE READING THAT INFLUENCED ME MOST NOW CAME FROM THE newspapers, in particular a new newspaper called the *Daily Telegraph*, which was revamped in March with a publicity campaign saying it had ten editors. I persuaded Dad to spend an extra penny-ha'penny a day by ordering the *Daily Telegraph* as well as the *Sydney Morning Herald*, and I fell in love with it from the first issue. Its contemporaneity made it part of the age that could produce the Electrical and Radio Exhibitions. The more conservative *Herald* now seemed to belong to Nanna's generation. As the *Telegraph* said of itself on its first issue, it was 'thoroughly modern – as modern as television, wireless and airmail'. Its modernity was partly a matter of busy layout, short paragraphs, comic strips, columns, readers' contests, photonews, and the use of serials such as H.G. Wells's *The Shape of Things to Come*, but what warmed my heart was its rebelliousness of spirit. The *Telegraph* was against red tape, addle-pated bungling, muddle-headed blunders, and stodgy bumbledom; it stood instead for acting quickly on vital questions and avoiding delay in reversing unhappy decisions. It had no patience with clumsy camouflage or fatuous hushing-up; it thrashed issues out so that light might be shed in dark places. It opposed all-talk-but-no-policy, bureaucratic timidity, lags in progress, squabbles and anomalies, but it also knew that we should look before we leap, preferring facts to hysteria as we reach towards new milestones in progress.

True to the primary school syllabus belief in 'a natural growth in human affairs', the *Telegraph* supported the League of Nations, peace, the forty-hour week, collective security, organised disarmament, the extension of airmail services, films for schools, progress on factory and farm, modern marketing, the establishment of a symphony orchestra in Sydney, a flourishing Australian film industry, the drinking of Hunter Valley light wines, air defence, the establishment of a national music authority, modern methods for making marriages stay put, modern art, uniform railway gauges throughout the nation, educating parents how to bring up their children, dress reform, slum abolition, a fairer deal for mother and baby, music concerts for children, serving wine with meals in cafés at reasonable hours, traffic safety, art for the people, training unskilled workers and cheaper telephones. It opposed road deaths, book censorship, smash-and-grab tax policies, scandalous overcrowding of mental institutions, restriction on shop trading hours, taking it out on the motorists, prejudices holding back science, TB-infected cows, hanging, homework, city death traps, buying brains on the cheap, delays in starting television, rent racketeering, the race towards war, the scandalous treatment of the Aborigines, traffic jams, high tariffs, the gambling laws, Sydney's apathy to the arts, prudery on the beaches, and scaring away tourists with poor accommodation and bad manners.

The *Telegraph's* rational optimism lightened even the darkest news of the year – the collapse of Ethiopian resistance to the Italians, Hitler's occupation of the Rhineland, the outbreak of the Spanish Civil War, the Japanese seizures in China. Somehow, the *Telegraph* felt, British diplomatic leadership would bring about collective security leading to world peace. I still accepted one of Dad's central assumptions – that there would be another Great War – so I looked for gloomier comment on foreign affairs, brooding over Mussolini's and Franco's successes, and still puzzling over the unbelievable tragedies of Nazi Germany. What delighted me above all in the *Telegraph* was its steady attack on wowsers, old fogies and fuddy duddies in Australia. One got the feeling that an old, stupid lot was running the country but that any week now, as a result of a particularly brilliant editorial in the *Telegraph*, they would crumble and a new lot would take over.

Unable any longer to identify myself completely with my family, or at all with the suburb where I lived, or with the school I went to, or with its teachers or – altogether – with the subjects they taught, and with nobody to talk to after school and my dog not providing all the company I wanted, I became part of the world of the *Daily Telegraph*, taking the side of progress against reaction or, perhaps more exactly, of intelligence against stupidity. One day when I was in the city I even walked into the *Telegraph* building to see what it looked like. I was astonished at the clutches of untidy offices from which the *Telegraph* daily urged on the march of progress, but I was heartened when I shared a lift with some snappy dressers, in blue double-breasted suits, soft-collared white shirts, red ties, brown hats, who briefly amused each other with their cynicism in an adult version of the way we talked at Parramatta High.

There was nobody I could discuss the *Telegraph* with. I knew from its book pages that sooner or later all the Empire would be self-governing, or that Hitler's troubled childhood was the key to his personality. But I did not personally know anyone who cared. When the *Telegraph* ran a long and fierce campaign against a Minister for the Interior for an act of remarkable injustice and stupidity, none of the people I knew had heard of it. I was forced to indulge my indignation privately – as I read the *Telegraph* before breakfast and as I thought about what I had read while I walked by myself to school across Parramatta Park. It seemed that I alone understood that this was part of the struggle for British liberty, which in history lessons was a matter of examination notes but which here in Australia was still a struggle not yet fully won. I consoled myself in my loneliness by glorifying it. I now felt myself to be 'clever' in a new way. Not as an author of plays, maker of speeches and so forth. That was behind me. Certainly not as an examination-sitter. I was now a clever boy who knew things about the world that other people did not know. I no longer 'showed off', looking for applause. With a secret vanity I provided my own applause.

WHILE I CONTINUED TO TALK AS MUCH AS EVER AT SCHOOL, NOW that I had made the disconcerting discovery that some conversations could be uninteresting I would sometimes become silent in adult company, even shy, complaining to myself about these stupid people who didn't know how to talk. I could still sometimes lose myself in Denbigh conversations with the old gusto; at other times, bored with playing a role in conversation that had been so thoroughly rehearsed before, I would say nothing and listen to nothing, carrying on conversation in my own head until my ears rang. I would become stupefied, my head would ache, and I might even retreat to the verandah and read one of the newspapers or books I now carried with me everywhere in case I got bored.

For several years I had been finding part of my interest in Denbigh by enjoying the tensions of its quarrels, not so much the frightening excitement of the rare moments of climax when relations shouted at each other and sometimes even strode out of the house, but the more chronic conditions – the subtle groupings and re-groupings, the subdued personal rivalries, the quiet, persistent searchings for inferred insult, the insidious analyses of character. We lived in one of the principal observation posts of these tensions. Since Mum was a kind of multiple barometer reacting to them, new reports were coming in all the time. Her widespread indicators recorded states of tension all over her family, including some that existed only in her indicators. We would delight in ripping open the behaviour of relations and peering inside for signs of their true attitude to Mum. But now I would criticise even those relations who were her favourites. Criticising not only my extended family but people in general was now becoming my normal style. Even when I liked people, if I spoke about them it would be to criticise them. Their manners. Their pronunciation. Their grammar. Sometimes their 'characters', as if I were discussing an Intermediate English text. (*What Nanna thinks of herself. What others think of Nanna. What Nanna really is.*) I become scathing about bad taste, developing a particular dislike for popular songs and castigating Mum for letting the wireless run like a tap. After one argument Dad called me a prig. I sulked about this; I was wounded by its truth, pleased – as with the French teacher – that he had shown enough interest in me to attack me; and resentful that, having diagnosed the condition, he offered no remedy.

Being on the side of intelligence and against stupidity did not save me from contemplating how boring my life had become. Beneath my progressivist enthusiasms, and the rhetorical pretences of my English and history essays and the self-satisfaction at my cleverness, I was beginning to make some sort of lonely and fumbling search to try to get closer to 'life' and see how it felt. In this search for my own sense of 'reality' I was tempted to find some of it in what I thought of as the 'poorer classes'. There was an old man who lived in our street – as old as Pa had been when he died – with whom I would talk for an hour or two, standing up all the time beside his fence, shifting from one foot to the other while he leant stolidly over the rail, not moving: when I got the chance I would give him my opinions of things – I was stronger on foreign affairs than he was – but more usually I listened to him explain the superiority of the working class over its exploiters and the necessity for considering the wishes of the 'poor and oppressed'. Of my relations I began to prefer my Uncle Ted. Being an electrical fitter at the railway workshops he was undoubtedly a worker, and he talked in a very down-to-earth way. (I now felt guilty about the year's elocution lessons I had taken at Muswellbrook, and I would smile to myself when I recalled how proud I had been of my 'recitations'.) But my greatest affection was now for Nanna, who established herself as the most 'real' person I knew.

I would sometimes go over to Denbigh and spend a weekend with Nanna alone. I still felt for her some of the simple love of a child, although a fourteen-year-old boy who spent so much time reading important newspapers had grown out of the public expression of such sentiments. We would spend a lot of our time together not talking, just being with each other, in a familiar house full of familiar furniture, part of something that did not change. Nanna showed a determined and forthright loyalty to her own origins. When she went into the city on Fridays, as well as going to the department stores she would also slip in a visit to Paddy's Markets, the city markets, where she would wander around among the stalls and pick up bargains, just as she had done at the Newtown markets when she was a girl; sometimes Nanna and I, instead of eating our lunch at a restaurant in a department store, would go to one of a chain of cheap restaurants, wolfing down meat pie and tomato sauce with a bread roll and a cup of tea for a shilling; we might go to a Laurel and Hardy movie – considered vulgar by Mum – and Nanna would stoutly defend Charlie Chaplin from Mum's criticisms of his bad taste; if there was a bad smell Nanna would insist on calling it a 'stink', when the furthest Mum would go in this direction was to call it a 'pong'; and from time to time Nanna, following Ted, proclaimed her loyalty to labour and the working man. Life seemed more real when Nanna and I sat down at the kitchen table for afternoon tea, our cups and scones on the oilcloth, and then went out and fed the chooks.

These were my feelings for Nanna when I was with her. When I was with Mum I shared some of her criticisms of Nanna for being behind the times and for being too outspoken. As well as liking to hear Nanna say 'stink' I disapproved of it. I was becoming coy about the use of blunt words – not in the barber's shop or in the schoolyard, where we would delight in using them – but among the men and women of my parents' acquaintance. Although I sought the 'reality' of roughness and outspokenness, I shrank from it in old family friends or relations: it was an expression of intimacy, and I was now beginning to want to distinguish myself from these older people, to see myself as part of a younger set (the other members of which I had not yet met). There were chance allies to be found for the adult world in the barber's shop or in the old men living down the street, but in their official role as the older generation I was beginning not to want adults to interfere with me by offering friendship. Although it concerned me that Dad did not seem to be the father he used to be, it was also a relief: the idea that we should share interests was so embarrassing that when, very occasionally, he made some attempt to do this I froze off his advances. I was beginning to develop a talent for shutting people out, defending myself from their intimacy. My happiest times with Dad were when we did something together – went to a cricket match or the pictures, worked in the garden or walked around Parramatta Park – but did not talk to each other. I enjoyed his company then.

MUM'S BABY WAS BORN BEFORE BREAKFAST IN A NURSING-HOME at Parramatta. A girl. Dad learned this from the telephone at his school, at Westmead. He walked across the park to my school, took me out of a French lesson, and then we walked into Parramatta. There was a strange moment when he arrived in the classroom. He was flushed and happy, cracking jokes. The French teacher became flushed and happy and also cracked jokes. Here were two men from whom I felt withdrawn now acting as the kind of men I used to be friendly with – a happy father talking to a happy schoolteacher. We laughed a lot on the way to the hospital, wondered at the little baby in its bassinet, and then had a cup of tea together at a milk bar before we went back to our schools. We would call the baby Janet, just as I was called Donald, to show that the Hornes were Scottish.

Having studied Mum's 'literature' on babies (which was like the brochures handed out with the new electric appliances) and even taken notes on it, I had now decided that it was essential that this new human appliance we were about to acquire should be breast-fed rather than bottle-fed. Statistics showed that nine out of ten babies who died in the summer were bottle-fed babies. But, other than this concession to naturalness, it must be left to cry when it cried; it must do everything by the clock – eat, wash, sleep, play; it must not be rocked; it must be toilet-trained very early. If these rules were not carried out the apparatus might be seriously impaired. I was not sure if Mum was intelligent enough to have a baby.

When the baby came home the wonder of her being such a little animal, seeking and sucking, so different from the illustrations in the baby 'literature', made it seem unlikely that she could be turned into a machine. She was to be bottle-fed after all, since Mum's milk had run out: at least it was not summertime and there were no statistics about the death-rate of bottle-fed babies in the winter. The question of her discipline hardly arose: she was a quiet baby, a pleasure to be with, apparently born with an amenable character. The difference of opinion between myself and Nanna as to whether she should be granted a dummy now came to its climax. I put up all my arguments: filthy flies, malformation of the mouth, bad character training. Nanna's arguments were more persuasive: she had borne six children. 'Poor little thing', she said as she gave the baby her first dummy.

FOR A WHILE AFTER THE BABY'S BIRTH WE FORGOT OUR relationships with each other and became absorbed in the baby and in the growth of her body. The growth of my own body disturbed me more and more. Now that it was the body of a young man I tried to stop older people from seeing it. On the rare occasions when I went swimming, if there were grown men in the dressing-shed I would cover as much of myself as I could with a towel, and when I took a bath I would lock the door so that no one could look at me. Although this new body was different from the old one, it now felt as if it belonged to me, but I did not want other people to judge me by it yet. It was all right for me to examine the hairs that were growing on my chest, but they were no business of anyone else. They asserted a manhood I could not yet sustain: I had been cast into a new role, but I had not yet learned the lines; I could not even find the script. Often I lost a sense of my body's existence. By great deviousness I now usually managed to cut school sport, slipping off to the Roxy or the Astra instead, and I even avoided swimming, with the result that I did not often feel my body through its exertions. When I got into bed or got up in the morning I only uncovered parts of my body at a time so that I did not even see it, except when I took a bath. My clothes seemed my real self: this was the way other people saw me, and most of the time this was how I saw myself, but even my clothes were spoilt because my hands and wrists stuck out through the cuffs, and there was the smell of my body in them. When hair grew on my face I shaved it off secretly, borrowing Dad's razor, unwilling to discuss this new assertion of change. Yet I also sought contact with my body, farting loudly, picking my nose, scratching my bottom furiously, as if to remind myself that a body was still there.

My body's most effective means of asserting itself had now sprouted between my legs but this added further agitation. I would sometimes spend part of Saturday afternoon walking around Parramatta Park, trying to breathe its atmosphere of left-over sex so that somehow, by casting myself into this place that at night was an arena for so much sexual encounter, I might solve its mysteries. I now equated the satisfactory release of sexual urges with public parks, my imagination grown irritable from contemplating the discarded French letters in the park and the newspapers, left on the grass from the night before. For a while I would examine the contours of newsprint, pressed into the grass by passion, and then search the walls of the park's lavatories, looking for the answer to an anxiety that now held me tranfixed in horror. Although I had learned the tricks of manipulation at Hinder House and in the Muswellbrook–Maitland train, in advance, ready for the day, I was now suffering from the lack of a simple piece of information. No one had told me that a fluid would accompany the ejaculation of sperm. The time had come to produce sperm, but when the fluid also produced itself I was horrified that I had done myself some unknown and perhaps serious damage. The *Household Physician* had nothing to tell me on this subject, and I was too ashamed of my ignorance to discuss it with friends at school, where we were in the habit of making ourselves look as if we led sophisticated sex lives once we retreated to those mutually unknown places where we lived. It was only by accident, when I was listening to some boy tell a boastful anecdote, that I felt confident my body had not sprung some debilitating leak. But as soon as this particular anxiety was stilled others took its place, and there was no answer to these, either, in Parramatta Park, however hopelessly I walked around it, contemplating my fears, made anxious by both my ignorance and my knowledge.

Although my juvenile sex experience with girls had earned the admiration of other boys when I boasted in our cowshed at Muswellbrook, I did not connect schoolgirls with the kind of sex I was now discovering. There they were in our classroom, girls, but they were only somebody to talk to between lessons. Sex was something practised by unknown women in parks who left the impressions of their bodies on sheets of newspaper, and its proper consummation would not be achieved until I met one of these unknown women and went with her into a park, taking the *Daily Telegraph* with me to lie on. At my age this did not seem likely. When the time came, what kind of woman would this be? Film stars with beautiful faces were the remote ideal of sexuality, but this kind of face was not often to be seen in real life: the faces of most grown women were very ordinary and their conversation was often about their cooking recipes, their dressmaking, or their false teeth; they had babies from time to time, but it was hard to imagine how women who did not look like film stars had aroused sexual desire. Sometimes in the street or on a train one might glimpse a young woman whose face bore some relation to film star beauty: it should be with a face like this that one went into a park. But did women looking so pretty go into parks? Yet how did one fall in love so that one could go to a park, except with a pretty face? But what did a face have to do with sex? I liked some of the faces of some of the girls in 3A, and I chose one, then another, then another like a sultan choosing his partner for the night, as faces to admire. The faces were only remotely attached to the girls themselves. Whatever face I was admiring that week belonged to a girl of pleasant personality. When I replaced it with a new face the personality of the girl with the old face crumpled into the ordinary, unsatisfactory kind of personality that most people offered to the world. That I should meet any of these girls out of school hours was as unlikely as the idea of meeting any of my friends among the boys.

It did not occur to me that I might discuss any of these matters with Dad. As the year progressed the friendly accommodation we had reached at the time of Janet's birth fell apart. He had taken to shouting me down as if I were in a classroom when I tried to debate with him the question of whether the British Empire would survive, so I shifted the subject to the existence of God, a matter I had not questioned since at the age of four. I was sitting with him in a bus going from Kogarah to Denbigh and had suddenly put to him the puzzle: *If God made everything who made God?* He had been so proud of my asking him this that he retold the story for years afterwards as an example of how he had encouraged me to ask questions. At meal after meal I now insisted that we talk about God, meeting all his arguments with arguments of my own, once shocking Mum by announcing that I was an agnostic. I moved beyond questioning to badgering. If the only way I could reach him was by irritating him, then I would irritate him. I used the arguments I knew would annoy him most, goading him with reason. Our great debate on God lasted several weeks, intermittently: if I had gone too far one day I would put the matter aside for a day or, two, then raise it again, quietly and reasonably at first, then with what I considered to be cutting argument. This ended in Dad shouting so loudly that

I thought he was going to hit me. He thumped the table, making the honey pot that looked a beehive rattle in its plate and upsetting the china toast rack that was designed to look like rustic wood. He jumped up from his chair and out of the room. Mum and I finished our breakfast together. She asked me to stop talking about God while we were having breakfast.

NINE

Extracts from the diary
of a high school boy

5TH DECEMBER 1936

At present momentous happenings are occurring. A crisis has been reached over the King and Mrs Simpson. But I read in this morning's *Daily Telegraph* that there is hope of compromise. Quod demonstrabatur. The *Telegraph* has devoted five pages to the matter, the *Herald* four columns. I think this is very silly on the part of the *Herald*. I also think that their editorial is silly. The first test match was begun yesterday. England started off badly. The war in Spain is still being waged and the Government forces are becoming much more tenacious.

The __ __ __ s are coming this afternoon. Whatabore!

Afternoon: They are here. __ __ __ still has that filthy 'dummy'.

Disgustin', I calls it. I have been listening to the second day's play in the test all this afternoon. The Commonwealth Parliament meets on Wednesday to pass the Statute of Westminster. I am just beginning to realise what this means and will mean to the British Commonwealth. Mrs Simpson is rushing across Europe in motor cars and I hope she has an accident.

7TH DECEMBER 1936

I have had rather a boring day. After reading the papers this morning I continued reading a book, which contained memoirs of the war, until the cricket started. I listened to that until the luncheon adjournment. I tuned in after lunch but the cricket was most painful, and extremely slow. More news about the King was broadcast in the afternoon. After this I finished my book.

8TH DECEMBER 1936

An abdication now appears unlikely. This afternoon I went down to the Astra. There were only a couple of dozen people there. We played mah-jongg tonight.

10TH DECEMBER 1936

The Westmead Junior Tech, of which Dad is the deputy headmaster, held their concert last night. The doors were opened at 5 to 8, and the performance was supposed to start at 8. I was in the front row (which, by the way, was about 3 feet from the back row). The room (not hall) was warm, hot and stuffy. The stage was decorated in a most artistic manner. The wings, composed of two moth-eaten flags and a bit of crepe paper were splendid, magnificent. There was a piano stuck over in the far corner and nine flowers and twenty pieces of fish fern decorated the back. Artificial roses were entwined around the 'footlights', and on either side of the stage. On the stage there was a bowl of roses (on a stand) and a chair which came out of the bedroom in our house. The whole was crowned (or shall we say covered, or obscured from view) by a very holy (i.e. full of holes) curtain which had painted upon it a very beautiful scene, reminiscent of a view of Luna Park, with the Bondi sewer as a background, and Venus de Milo, dressed in a Spooner costume sipping tea in the middle of the picture. Il faisait chaud, with a vengeance.

The King's friends think marriage to Mrs Simpson unlikely. The King and his Prime Minister dined and smoked and talked for five hours in fog-bound Fort Belvedere. A decisive battle is expected in Madrid.

11TH DECEMBER 1936

This morning at seven I hopped out of bed into a dressing-gown and then sat beside the wireless, fully expecting to hear something happening. My hopes began to dwindle when an ominous silence came over the air, and with the Prime Minister's first sentence they fled away. King Edward had abdicated and the Duke of York succeeds to the throne.

15TH DECEMBER 1936

The barber still has the same amount of tales and theories to tell. A new one, and a new type, for every customer. One man had both his legs shot off. His right eye has also disappeared. Another, presumably a poultry farmer, says that eggs have a disease. The man minus legs and eye thought Mrs Simpson a 'slut'. This man was rather unusual. His shoulders were very broad, too broad in fact. His one whole eye didn't look much, it was all screwed up, and the eye-socket of his departed eye wasn't pleasant to look at. His legs were cut off above the knees, and there were two pieces of wood, about 9 inches long, with the black paint wearing off them, affixed to all that was left of his legs. He walked on these pieces of wood, with the aid of a stick. When walking, he was about four feet high. The barber said he drives a car.

16TH DECEMBER 1936

I donned my best suit and went to the Town Hall for Speech Day. Waiting outside the foyer were quite a lot from 3A. Power and Gates both had new suits. Most of the teachers had their gowns on, the Beak had his usual moth-eaten one on (this is the same one as he sometimes wears at school). When the proceedings began the mayor (pronounced by the Beak as May-or) and the Beak exchanged cordialities. Then the Beak read out the report, which wasn't as long as usual and, except for the constant reference to the house system and the house shield, was interesting.

At length the prize giving ceremony began ... My turn came at last. 'Donald Horne,' said the Beak. A ripple of faint applause. (They had clapped themselves out i.e. they were tired of clapping) and I got up and crawled (not literally) along the floor. I put my foot on the step and the silly thing slipped (step, not foot). Willy came down, book in hand, and winked. I then walked up the stairs, which seemed to twist everywhere, and so on to the stage. Mrs Gollan was holding a book in her hand. She opened and shut her mouth. I shook hands and grabbed the book. Then I remembered. I smiled (or shall we say I gave a sickly grin) and stumbled down a couple of stairs and then slid and crawled alternately (again not to be taken too literally) back to my seat. All this, as in the best books, took 47 seconds.

18TH DECEMBER 1936

I went down to the Astra yesterday afternoon and saw *It Happened One Rainy Afternoon* and *Amateur Gentlemen*. The Wilsons were here last night, to play bridge.

19TH DECEMBER 1936

I listened to some of the Test yesterday, but after lunch I became sick. I think I was a bit bilious. Mum went into town in the night, and got some more presents.

21ST DECEMBER 1936

We went into town this afternoon (Dad and I, that is). We were going to go to see the Test until we read in the paper that the wicket would be like a glue pot. Instead, we went to the Prince Edward, and saw *The General Died at Dawn*. There are a number of cricket scoreboards, provided by shops, scattered around Sydney. I received a camera, and some apparatus necessary for developing and printing, from Mum and Dad, as a Christmas present.

24TH DECEMBER 1936

(commonly known as Christmas Eve)

I went out to Kogarah yesterday with some Xmas presents and a ham. I had lunch at Nanna's. Mum and I went to the pictures last night. *The ex-Mrs Bradford* was being screened.

25TH DECEMBER 1936

There weren't any carols last night, or this morning. I gave my presents out at breakfast and went down to Dulce's.

26TH DECEMBER 1936

Today is my Birth-day.

There was the usual Christmas dinner yesterday, though there were only four of us. This was different to some of the former dinners, when Pa was alive or when we were at Cronulla. I was very tired after dinner. It must have been the beer. No threepences have yet appeared. Unc and Dulce came to tea, bringing Joan with them. Aunty Lil and Mick stayed. Tea was brighter, but could not stand comparison to former Christmas teas. After tea Aunty Florrie, Uncle Arthur and Roy walked round. Then came Arthur, Joan and the man who is going camping with Arthur, and finally Ted. The weather isn't very nice. I have eaten one box of chocolates and I am now starting on a tin of toffee.

28TH DECEMBER 1936

We are now back at Westmead. Mum, Nanna and I went to the Carlton Picture Show on Saturday night. That place certainly is antique. I went down to Parramatta this afternoon. Zac was very pleased to see us home again. He did his usual 'over-grown pup' act and ran through the house, tearing helter-skelter, ears down, tail up, mats flying, and Zac skidding.

31ST DECEMBER 1936

I went to the Astra on Wednesday, and saw *The Last of the Mohicans*. Last night we developed the snaps and next morning I printed them, with only one mishap.

4TH JANUARY 1937

Nanna and I arrived at Denbigh about 11.20 on New Year's Eve. We decided to wait up, and at 12 we went out on to the verandah, there to see what we saw. And what did we see? The moon, the stars, the houses, the street, and, here it comes, a boy. That is all. What did we hear? Very little. A stone on the roof, a bang and the old Kogarah tram cock-a-doodle-doo. We then went to bed.

On Friday Uncle Candy asked us to go for a ride in the car. The car explored many of the unknown parts of Sydney, to me at least, then to Bondi, where Nanna, in her usual style, remarked upon the sewer. Yesterday we spent at Cronulla. Uncle Candy came round in the car about 9.30. The day was fine, though a little overcast in the morning. Oh, how chilling! I have very rarely been in such cold surf, and my toes were blocks of ice.

5TH JANUARY 1937

I have had pains, somewhere in the region of my appendix, on and off, all day. I went to Parramatta yesterday morning to have a haircut, and again this afternoon with Mum, to get some film. Mum was going down to the clinic. The Third Test seems to be in Australia's grip.

9TH JANUARY 1937

It's raining, or it was last time I looked. I suppose it will be the next time I look. Who cares? I do, but what's it matter? I just peered out the window. It is not raining, but what's the use? There's a perfect mud patch outside ... and a wet dog, smelling like a polar bear, or dead fish, bounding everywhere, muddy, mud, splosh, over goes a plant, two plants, a whole garden, who cares? I haven't done anything. I went to the Astra yesterday. I observed Eddie Cantor in *Kid Millions*. It was very, very patchy. Australia won the Test. Bradman scored over 200, it might have been over 1,000, I don't know. It isn't raining again, yet. Who cares? I don't.

10TH JANUARY 1937
The incredible happened. Janet woke up. This was the second time since she was born, and everybody was utterly dumbfounded.

19TH JANUARY 1937
It has been very humid today and yesterday, but a southerly change sprang up this afternoon, and everyone is happy again. I have been to the pictures about four times, including the St James, where I saw *Libelled Lady*. Yesterday afternoon I went to the Roxy and saw *The Prisoner from Shark Island*. There was quite a crowd there, the two men in front of me taking off their coats. There was a crowd in Parramatta, all hot, and all perspiring. The milk bar was full, the hotels overflowing. I myself drank two 'Chocolate malteds', and then felt a pain.

21ST JANUARY 1937
The weather is still humid, though today is not so bad as Monday, I went to the Astra yesterday, where I saw the Australian film, *The Lying Doctor*. I was sitting next to a howling baby for a while. As usual the milk bars profited from me.

23RD JANUARY 1937
On Thursday afternoon I went down to Parramatta, had my haircut at the usual place, and then caught the train. I arrived at Nanna's and teaed. After tea, I had just settled down in the breakfast room, and had started to read a *Smith's Weekly* that I had bought, when I heard a car stop. The gate opened and shut. Footsteps along the red path.

The wire door, the other door having been fastened back, then opened. Footsteps in the hall. 'Hullo' It was Aunty Florrie and Roy. After Aunty Florrie and Roy had departed, Nanna announced that Aunty Florrie had whispered to her in the bedroom that Arthur is to become engaged to Joan. Of course, there was a terrible lot of talk and chatter. We then *se couchèrent au lit*. I hope that last bit is right – it seems ages since a French lesson.

We woke on the morrow – Nanna at five, myself at 8, the only difference being our method. No one woke Nanna, but she woke me. After breakfast I walked down to get a *Telegraph* and a pound of potatoes. We arrived in town at last. Nanna had a bilious headache. She did a little shopping, and then I went to Swain's, and bought a book I was after. As it was still early we strolled along to David Jones's, where we partook of an exremely cheap lunch (I paid). Since it was still hot, we sat in a couple of chairs near some windows, which overlooked Hyde Park, and felt the gentle fanning of the breezes as we gazed on the green below. Then we saw the _ _ _ s. We talked to them for half an hour until we were bored to distraction with their talk about themselves, their children and their clothes. When we had become thoroughly bored (please excuse this horrible repetition) we walked down to the Embassy, where *Dodsworth* was being screened. When the show was over, we returned to Nanna's, etc. etc.

25TH JANUARY 1937

Apropos Arthur's 'engagement'. On Friday a car was heard stop outside Denbigh and Arthur came in. After saying 'Hullo', I went out on the back verandah, so that Arthur could tell Nanna what he wished to, without any hesitation because of my presence. Of course, I had both ears fully cocked, but I heard very little, just uninteresting scraps here and there.

But after he had gone I heard it all. Arthur came up to tell Nanna not to tell anyone about the important event, because he, Arthur, will not be engaged for a few months yet since he wanted to save for two years before his marriage and an early engagement would be too lengthy. Anyhow, it's no secret. Nanna has told everyone in the whole family.

On Saturday night we went round to see the Awful _ _ _ s (they are unpopular at present). It was as awful as it was funny. And it was as funny as it was boring. And it was boring! Vulgarly speaking, they skited – first one, and then the other, then the first, and then the other, and so on, and on, and on, and on. Oh my! Also, after deep thought, Oh Yeah!

On Sunday, while we were breaking our fast, Ted arrived, fresh from holidays, with a brown face, and browner ankles. After tea, Ted put on parts of his uniform (he is in the militia, anti-aircraft division). He looked very smart in his uniform. Of course, everyone else had to try on parts of it, and we looked like a roomfull of soldiers.

1ST FEBRUARY 1937

I've been down to Parramatta a couple times. On Wednesday night Mum and I caught the 'bus down to the pictures. On Wednesday afternoon, about 6, I went up to the paper shop, on the off chance that the Inter Country results might be in the paper, and that Parramatta might be included in the country. But alas, and alack, and Alaska! There was nothing. Of course I wasn't terribly disappointed.

On Thursday, about one o'clock, Arthur came up, and had lunch with us. He is now engaged to Joan, ring and all. In the afternoon I went down to Parramatta, to get a pound of peas, when I glanced at the paper shop, and there, glaring at me, wet with the paste, was a placard with the words:

METROPOLITAN

INTER

RESULTS

My hand dived to my pocket. No money! The other pocket! No money! The first pocket! Nothing! The second! A handkerchief! The first! The second! Coat pocket! Trouser pocket! Coat ditto! Trouser ditto! Then, wow! It was in that little pocket near my belt. It was a two-shilling piece, and I walked faster than my legs could carry me, burst into the paper shop, and gasped, '*Sun*, please', and made my exit. The paper was very bulky. There seemed to be hundreds of pages. At last I found what I sought. The paper was upside down, at least bits of it were, other bits were torn, and whole pages fluttered helplessly in the breeze. But I was disappointed. There were only a few schools in, they were only up to 'D'. I had a malted milk, bought the pound of peas and walked home.

Next morning I awoke at 7.11 approximately, and, having waited 59 minutes approximately, I strolled down to where the paper had but recently been flung by our paper boy. Everything in me was jumping up and down, but

I just strolled. I picked up the paper, looked at the headline on the front page, or I thought I did, and then skimmed the pages, and I'm blowed if I could find Parramatta.

I lay the paper out on the bed, and then it hit me in the 'igh– Parramatta 'igh. Horne, D.R. 'A' in English. 'A' in History. 'B' in Maths I. 'B' in Maths II. 'A' in Latin. 'A' in French. 'A' in Science. Thank goodness!

Nanna came out on Friday night, and stayed for tea. She congratulated me. A telegram came from Miss Morley which ditto. Mrs Chaplin did ditto. I met Pitt today, and he did ditto. Joan and Arthur came out today and they did ditto. Tomorrow I return à l'école. ('A' in French, you know.)

TEN

Dad

There was a mellowness about being as old as fifteen and moving up into fourth year at school. We had proved to be the best of our harvest and now we were set aside for further maturing, our superiority established because we had passed the Inter and because our parents had enough money to keep us at school for another two years. Our proximity to the Leaving Certificate, for which we would sit at the end of our fifth year, in the last test of our identity, already made us seniors, distinguishing us from the junior school, but we did not yet have to pay the price of this distinction: we could take things easy in fourth year. This was shown even in the size of classes; they were smaller and more intimate, so that one could loll at one's desk and sometimes even interject during a lesson; some of us now gossiped with the more approachable teachers, condescendingly treating them like human beings.

Our previous lack of concern about who won or lost at sport or examinations was now extending to our relations with each other: we were becoming more friendly, more of a group, suppressing our differences, amusing ourselves in our common contentment with our mildly cynical style. This change came suddenly, right at the beginning of the year: it seemed to have something to do with the more flexible method by which we were now arranged in separate classes for each subject, according to our strengths or weaknesses. We were no longer assigned to special desks or even to special rooms. As we were shuffled afresh after each lesson we lost the loyalties, hatreds and boredoms imposed by the set pieces of fixed classrooms: we could display more of ourselves to each other, sorting ourselves out in ways not related merely to the topography of classrooms.

The small group in which I had sheltered myself from the indifference of the schoolyard dissolved. I made new friends and talked to more boys and girls. Although I was in the 'A' class in English, French, Latin, history and chemistry, the fact that I had got 'Bs' instead of 'As' in Mathematics I and II in the Inter meant that I was in the 'B' class for mathematics. Here in particular I made new friends among people I had not known before, finding it easier to get on with the friendly 'B' class girls than those I had known in the 'A' class. Despite this relaxation in manners, there was still no question of seeing any of these new friends out of school. At the same time this new sense of community made it even more difficult to talk to the people one did meet out of school, viz. the older generation. When it came to things that mattered I was becoming stronger in the art of having a conversation with myself.

In schoolwork I had recovered some of my self-regard. I had lost one hated French teacher only to find him replaced by another, whom we called 'Bruiser' and who seemed determined to shout French into our heads, but my 'A' in the Inter had redefined my attitude to French, and we found 'Bruiser' more absurd than fearsome. In mathematics I had lost another enemy – we did not study arithmetic any more, replacing it with trigonometry – and we had gained a new mathematics teacher, who was determined to banter and charm us into an interest in his subject. He was a smart dresser and a snappy talker, and he stimulated my interest in mathematics to the extent that I studied his suits carefully, intending to have my next suit cut in the same style; I imitated his choice in ties and put some of his words into my own vocabulary. We also admired the laconic style of the chemistry teacher, whose wry wit communicated both his boredom with the subject and his amusement at his boredom, and although I had no sense of direction in chemistry I did well at it, continuing the process of learning to be a laboratory assistant in long 'experiment' periods in which we enjoyed gossiping among ourselves and with the teacher. The new Latin teacher dressed and talked in a way unfamiliar to us: he wore hand-knitted socks and in hot weather an unpressed white suit with stove-pipe trousers, his teeth were yellow, and he pronounced 'were' to rhyme with 'where'. He did not look as if he lived in the suburbs and we laughed at his peculiarities. But although he was co-author of a book with a title as unentrancing as *Latin Prose Composition*, he set as one of our texts a miscellany of pieces in Latin – love lyrics from Catullus, witty anger from

Juvenal, brilliant descriptive stuff from Ovid – and used these to lift us up out of Latin as crossword puzzle by turning it, for a few months, into something one could *read*.

Both the English and history teachers had told those of us who had elected to take these subjects at the honours level to treat fourth year as a 'reading year', reading beyond the course, and I began to do this so enthusiastically that the most important part of these two subjects consisted of the books I read at home. We had been told we could borrow free books from the Sydney Municipal Library so I took out tickets in my name and my father's, and I also went to the library of the schoolteachers' union, of which he was a member; this meant that I could borrow a dozen books from one trip into Sydney, more than I could comfortably carry home, two armfuls of oddments taken from whatever most caught my attention as I passed along the shelves. It was like the days when I used to get sixteen books at Christmas, except that it now happened once a fortnight instead of once a year.

There was always a handful of fiction in my armful of books: I was ready to discover 'the modern novel'. According to information available at Parramatta High, this meant reading H.G. Wells, Arnold Bennett and John Galsworthy, so I read a couple of the comic novels of Wells (lightly 'Dickensian'); passed from his shopkeepers to Bennett's (more 'real', giving dignity to drabness); then ascended the social scale to *The Forsyte Saga* – where I took the side of Irene and Fleur against their unsatisfactory men, and, as one who had, in his mind, turned his own ancestors into fiction, I was delighted by the scope of a three generation story. However I felt most sympathy for the opening chapters of Wells's *Experiment in Autobiography* (which wasn't a novel at all, and certainly not 'literature') because it described, in suitably flat prose, how a boy can create a private world – very realistic, I felt (he even used the word 'masturbation', a word I hadn't seen in print before, except in dictionaries and *The Household Physician*).

By then I had moved to *Tess of the D'Urbevilles* and *Jude the Obscure*, which made the other novels seem chatty, like my mother's bridge. Thomas Hardy, it was now clear, was 'literature' (an opinion confirmed by our English teacher when he warned me against Hardy's pessimism). However *The Dynasts* lost me between the Town Hall and Parramatta railway stations. On the way home to Westmead I tried for various entries into George Meredith's *The Egoist*, but couldn't find one; and although I read Virginia Woolf's *Orlando* right through, I might as well have read it backwards. From time to time we received warnings against modern pessimism, cynicism or decadence. The only effect of these warnings was to stimulate me to read on. I was still inclined to the view that things were likely to turn out all right in the long run, but I also felt that there was something unsatisfactory about the way we lived now. This sense of dissatisfaction caught some of my mood of the previous year, but I was now so busy reading about other people's dissatisfactions that I felt somewhat more satisfied with my own. In Literature (as distinguished from modern writing) I had a simple desire: I wanted to read it all. The last armful of books I was to bring back to Westmead included *Don Juan*, *The Faerie Queen* and the plays of Ben Jonson.

DAD AND I NOW HARDLY SPOKE TO EACH OTHER. I WAS BECOMING ashamed of his irritable silences, but I affected to be unconcerned, stamping on my uneasiness. I would get on with my reading while he went for long walks by himself or at the weekends went alone to watch football matches. There seemed to be a violence in his loneliness; he would come back from a walk angrier than when he left the house. On the evening when I brought back *Don Juan*, *The Faerie Queen* and the plays of Ben Jonson I was not surprised when Mum told me that Dad would be staying away from school for a few days because his 'nerves' were bad. He had developed the habit of getting out of bed during the night and walking around the house and then making a cup of tea in the kitchen: I could recognise the sound of his movements or the faint reflection of the kitchen light along the walls of the side hall, so l paid no attention if I heard him; but one night when I woke up there was no sound of movement: Dad was standing quite still as he looked at me from the doorway of my bedroom, and from what I could see of his face he seemed to be looking at me with hatred. Did he want to kill me? I did not move. I half-closed my eyes until he went away.

There was a slight sound of footsteps, then silence. I guessed he was now standing at the other bedroom doorway looking at Mum. The light went on. They talked for a while. Then he walked to the back of the house and Mum followed him. As I went back to sleep I could still hear them talking.

The next morning we did not speak as we ate our breakfast, although several times Dad stopped eating and stared angrily at his clothes and plate. When he went down the back Mum whispered that Dad had been suspended from his school without salary, because one of the schoolgirls had alleged that when he sat down beside her to correct an exercise he had put his hand under her dress. There was to be a departmental inquiry, and if the girl's allegation was accepted Dad would be dismissed. He came back more quickly than we expected – we could see him through the breakfast-room window – and, although we made sure we were talking about something else, when he returned to the breakfast room he at once accused us of discussing him behind his back. He started shouting at us. I could not stay. I was late for school.

For several days we lived with Dad's fears. After I came home from school Mum and I would try to discuss our predicament. We were certain the schoolgirl was mistaken, or a mischief-maker, or unbalanced. His hand might have touched the outside of her dress, or touched her leg, but it would have been by accident and that was all there was to it. (How could one imagine anything else?) The inquiry would just be a formality, but when he was cleared of this improbable charge we would leave Westmead and he would move to another school. Of course there was the possibility that the inquiry might come to the wrong conclusion ... If Dad heard us talking he would come into the room and sit with us, without saying anything in particular, but with a frown of concentration. Mum began to tell me of the anxieties she had felt about him for many years, of the unhappiness he had shown beneath his old surface of good humour, even in the days before he began publicly to suffer from his 'nerves'. The main chance for Mum and me to talk to each other occurred when he went for a walk, which he did regularly, dressing in his school clothes for the purpose, striding along the streets of Westmead with meaningless determination. If he was away for long I would go out to find him, meeting him as if by accident and saying little as I tactfully walked him home. We would try to eat our dinner without provoking his irritation, and after dinner, while I made my homework last until bedtime, he would sit quietly with Mum by the fire, examining his misery. During the night he would get out of bed and move around the house, as meaninglessly as he moved around Westmead during the day, from time to time standing in my doorway and staring at me. Mum might call to him to come back to bed, or she might go out to the back part of the house to speak to him. I would finally lose consciousness, perhaps to the murmur of their conversation. At breakfast we would try to act as if none of this had happened. I would go back to school.

I had seen that he was making notes in a pocket diary and that he kept it in his dressing-table drawer, along with his Repatriation Department documents, his war medals, his Masonic apron and his army revolver. When he went off to Parramatta to see his doctor I went through this diary. The entries in it (some of them in a kind of code) were printed as neatly as anything else he did: their very neatness gave extra emphasis to the craziness of the suspicions he had written down, day by day, as meticulously as if they had been exact observations of the weather.

When he came back from Parramatta he told us the doctor had arranged for him to enter the Repatriation Hospital the next day. He was suffering from a 'nervous breakdown'. The doctor believed it was due to his war experiences, although this matter would have to be determined finally by a tribunal. This was to be his last night with us. I did not do any homework, and after dinner the three of us sat around the fire, in memory of our fifteen years together, and in a silent good-bye. After a while he tried to talk to me, still looking at me with the same anxious anger, but from his conversation it appeared that it was with himself, not me, that he was angry. He said there were many things he should have told me – he began to weep. I would have to look after my mother now – he began beating his head softly against the brick of the fireplace. He became so absorbed in the rhythm of this motion that he seemed to forget me and he said nothing more.

The next morning I stayed away from school to look after Janet while Mum went with him to the hospital. As we were waiting for the car he became angry with the middle button of his jacket because it did not seem to fasten properly. After I helped him fasten it he sat down on a cane chair in the bedroom and until the car arrived he still fidgeted with the button or anxiously tried to pat his jacket into place. When he left the house and walked down the cement path between the rose beds he looked as neat and ordinary as if he was going off to school. 'Good-bye, Dad,' I said, 'Look after yourself.'

He was lying in a bed in a general ward the first time we visited him in hospital, quiet, but remote, staring through the fruit and delicacies we had brought him. The second time we visited him they had moved him to a room of his own because he had disturbed the other patients. He was weeping most of the time we were there, more lost to us than ever, saying nothing that made any sense except that it was a song playing on the wireless – a song he used to sing at Muswellbrook – which had made him weep. We tried to reach him with our bedside jocularity, but we had nothing to offer. After we left, a doctor took Mum into another part of the hospital while I sat outside in the winter sun. Mum learned they were going to send Dad to the Reception House, the institution where people were certified as being insane. After that he would be placed in one of the Repatriation wards in the Callan Park lunatic asylum.

For several days after he was 'certified' we were not allowed to see him. I tried to imagine him in the Reception House, but I could not. Then we took the tram out to Callan Park, known to schoolboys as Sydney's most famous 'looney bin', and we sat in a cold stone room with bars on its windows as if we were paying a social call on a man who was not interested in us. He was anxious that we should meet a fellow patient, whom he described as his 'new friend', and after some discussion this other patient was brought in, dressed in his three-piece suit like Dad. Dad and his new friend talked to each other. We sat on our hard wooden chairs and watched them.

On the morning of my last day at Parramatta High I said goodbye to our house at Westmead while the removalists were stacking away our furniture. I avoided good-byes at school, and when lessons were over I made the long journey to Denbigh, where we were going to live until we knew what was to happen. The removalists had already piled our furniture into the room where the weddings had been held and where Pa's body had been laid out. Alongside the furniture, at one end of this room, were my bed, lowboy and desk. The next morning I woke up early, looking at the shapes of our stacked-up furniture as they defined themselves against the early light, and then went, with indifference, to my new school, Canterbury High. I handed the headmaster a mid-year report on me from Parramatta so that he would know the nature of the consignment and where to place it. I found myself in a Latin class that was translating a text different from the one we had studied at Parramatta. Since I did not have a copy of the text I sat through the lesson wondering what was happening. The texts being studied in English and French were also different, and the chemistry experiments had been done in a different order. I would have to work hard simply catching up.

By now Dad had been moved into one of the Repatriation wards, each of them a separate building, at the end of the grounds of Callan Park. To reach these we would walk through the rest of the hospital, past buildings with barred windows, and past a big stone enclosure, like an animal pit at the zoo, where insane women in blue hospital uniforms were crowded, ignoring each other as they talked to themselves or stared out into nothing. Whenever we walked past I looked at them sideways, ashamed of my curiosity, but unable not to look. Although I knew I was in a madhouse, and although I was afraid of everyone I saw, nevertheless when anyone spoke to me I was always startled to recognise that this person was insane. The grass was trimmed, the paths were freshly swept, there were flowers in the garden beds. If one looked away from the barred windows and the women's stone pit it all seemed as normal as a public park. A well-dressed woman came up. She was carrying a copy of the *Saturday Evening Post* and began to talk in an apparently normal way, in an educated voice. She was writing with a pencil over the cover of the magazine. She was telling me about a conspiracy against her, a conspiracy mounted in words that were not even words, and she was drawing a diagram on the magazine to prove it, sketching it out quickly and methodically. I kept on listening, afraid of her, but politely making conversation. Even when Dad came out of the ward with Mum she would not go away. Yet she looked as if she was dressed for a quiet day's shopping in town. On these journeys to Callan Park I chilled my emotions, trying to notice nothing, but noticing things nevertheless.

Dad and his fellow patients were locked up inside their ward, spending much of the day in an interior courtyard that sounded like the exercise yard of a jail. When he was let out of the ward for our visit the three of us would sit in a summerhouse on a point of land overlooking a disused cement swimming bath in a bay called Iron Cove. On a dull day the water lay across the bay like a sheet of metal while in the summerhouse we would try to talk as if Dad was simply in hospital with a broken leg. There was a strange formality about our meetings, even at times a certain boredom, as if, instead of being a family sitting together in a summerhouse, we were strangers sitting in the compartment of a train on a long journey, waiting to be relieved of each other's company for ever. Although most of the time he was still listless, Dad was now coming out of his state of confusion and on his best days he was tense and anxious, more like he had been at home. Desperately compromising with our concepts of normality, on these days we thought he was more himself again. One day he asked if there was going to be a war, and then looked at me silently, worried. For most of the time we talked Denbigh gossip to him, trying to make him laugh, our universal remedy for all misfortunes: for his part, if he talked, he told us the gossip of his ward. On the day on which he made a joke Mum and I were pleased all the way home to Denbigh: that was the Dad we used to know. At the end of each visit we would say good-bye to him in the summerhouse. Mum would kiss him, I would shake his hand, and then we would watch him as, dressed in his Sunday best, he walked down the path and knocked on the door of his ward so that they could lock him up again.

I was so shocked by this disaster that I was concerned only with keeping Mum company and with concealing the facts of it at my new school. I retreated into a silent and deceitful pride. I did not want anyone to laugh at Dad or pity me. I did not want to be judged – nor did I want Dad to be judged – by what seemed the improbable accident of this sad affair. Although there was a certain self-importance in being at the centre of some sympathy and offers of help, even at Denbigh I preferred to discuss Dad's illness only with Mum, although when she and I talked together about 'Dad's breakdown' we would do so for hours, just as we had tried to make Pa's death real and comprehensible by the solemnity of words. When I was by myself I tried to freeze away any contemplation of it. If I felt a deeply painful shudder of compassion for Dad I would try to think of something else: it was unbearable to imagine him lying in his ward at Callan Park, locked up with lunatics. For several years I had resented his neglect of me; I now understood why he had acted as he did, but that did not stop me resenting it, especially since I had woken in the middle of the night to see him staring at me from the doorway.

Not long after we arrived at Denbigh I was lying in bed trying to read *The Faerie Queen* when I heard Nanna say to my mother: 'Don will have to leave school and get a job.' I went to sleep trying to imagine what it would be like not to sit for the Leaving Certificate. At this time we had no income at all. Then as a result of our representations we received sick pay from the Department of Education: but the Master in Lunacy, of whom Dad was now a ward, had control of this money. It was obvious that if we were lucky enough for the Department of Education to retire Dad on half-pay we would also need a pension from the Repatriation Department. I was sustaining myself by doing what I could for Mum, and this revived intimacy proved useful when she began seeing to it that we got some money. She went from one official to the other of the Master in Lunacy, the Department of Education, the Repatriation Department and Callan Park, and before she went for any of these interviews we would talk it over and I would try to suggest to her what she should say. When she came back she would describe everything, as she used to describe everything in the movies she had seen – the room, the furniture and in great detail, the official of that day's interview. We would talk about how good a kind official was, or how we might somehow change the judgment of a hard-hearted official who was at present set against us. I learned enough about several of these officials to develop them as 'characters' in books.

When our particular cause – that Dad's condition was due to his war service – had to be stated I wrote a long document. Before doing so I questioned Mum for some hours on what she knew of Dad beyond his public personality, going back to the earliest years of their marriage, even before they were married, looking for significant detail that would establish a connection between the 'general debility' written on the discharge certificate the Army gave him in 1919 and the 'nervous breakdown' he had suffered in 1937. Then I wrote a long report, in the literary style I was favouring in English and history essays at the time, with a strong emphasis on adverbs, but with the special consideration of making it highly persuasive. I had decided not to overstate the case. It should appear to speak for itself. I half wondered how many marks it would get.

WITH MUM, AND AT DENBIGH IN GENERAL, I TOOK IT TO BE unmanly to express any emotion other than in laughter, so I made no open expression of my horror. Things rushed in on me so much from one day to the next – a new school to accommodate myself to during the day, conferences with Mum after school, homework at night, longer conferences, and visits to Callan Park at the weekend – that I began to divert myself with more elaborately staged fantasies than I had known before. In the lavatory, or before going to sleep, or when I was alone at Denbigh I would deliberately tell myself a strong story in which I was the master of all situations, usually a great general, a great statesman, or a great man of the people, lost in conquest or success. These fantasies were so deliberate and so vivid that they alarmed me. I decided I might be going mad. When I found myself alone in Denbigh one afternoon and went berserk, running around shouting and throwing cushions, I decided I *was* going mad.

I had taken a liking to the Ben Jonson plays, with their crooks and shysters and their punchy verse but I found it hard to concentrate on *Volpone* as I was reading it in bed one night because I was also listening to Nanna and Mum as they talked beside the fire. Nanna was complaining about what Zac was doing to the Denbigh garden. She said he would have to be killed. I got up early the next morning and went out into the garden to sit down with Zac behind the mandarin tree. I put my arms around him and cried, my first and only tears. Zac licked my face and hands. As I rattled off to school in the electric train with the strangers who were my new schoolfriends I felt deeply ashamed. This event was too like Dickens, whom I now considered an author like Hardy, who sometimes exaggerated the gloomy side of things.

ELEVEN

More serious inside

At first at Canterbury High I seemed to have been seized by a machine as some kind of raw material. At one end there entered boys and at the other end these boys would be ejected, having been processed into Leaving Certificates. The entrance to the machine was the electric train at Kogarah railway station (for the first time in my life I could not walk each day to school). These trains were usually so crowded that we would stand near the doorways, jostling each other and pushed together whenever the train jolted. The principal subject of conversation was masturbation, shouted about in code language so that the other passengers could not share knowledge of this secret amusement. We got out at Sydenham station, sorted ourselves into new groups and boarded another train to Hurlstone Park, where, when we got out, we might again arrange ourselves into new groups for the walk to school. The school building was one big brick barracks, set in grounds of asphalt. We would assemble on the asphalt like a battalion of troops ... Attention! ... Right (or left) Turn! ... One! Two! ... Quick March! ... Left, right! Left, right! Left, right! Left! ... Left! ... Left! ... Left! ... Boys would stamp down corridors. Masters dressed in dustcoats would slam on their desks. The processing would begin. We were exhorted to study hard so that Canterbury would do well in the Leaving Certificate and we could get good jobs when we left it.

Out of this mechanism I began to sort faces, and the types of people who were caught up inside the darkness of the machine. At first there seemed to be an extraordinarily high number of toughs at Canterbury. Since we were seniors, there was no question of being hit, but some of the boys used words and lurches of their bodies so effectively that a flick or two of their lowered eyelids might kill a conversation. One of them lived near Denbigh, and I was sometimes caught with him in the bus that took us to Kogarah station. If I talked to him he just glared until I shut up; or if I went on talking he would cut me short by saying: 'Listen, Horne, *don't try to bullshit me!*' I would go to any lengths, even waiting for another bus, to avoid sitting beside him.

Then it became clear that there were very few bullies, that the more numerous kind of enemy was the sport, the boy who, apart from masturbation, saw nothing in life except his own success in team games. At Canterbury, it now appeared, there was not only the chute that ejected Leaving Certificates; there was another equally important chute that ejected the future stars of grade football, grade tennis and grade cricket, who might become the stars of interstate matches, or even play for Australia in the cricket tests or the Davis Cup. It was simply beyond the comprehension of these boys that anyone should consider that the final reality did not lie in success in games. Between them and someone who did not share their views there was no possibility of communications. I soon discovered, however, that I was not so surrounded by enemies as I thought: among those who appeared to be nothing but toughs or sports some were also cynics, who liked talking so long as it was in the sardonic, chyacking style. I made my first friend among the cynics. Then I discovered that a number of the boys were not toughs or sports at all, not even cynics, but humorists. With this discovery I took up the humorists, with whom I found more possibilities for conversation than at Parramatta.

Things were sharper and more competitive at Canterbury and as well as the boys determined to be successful sportsmen there were the clever boys determined to do well at examinations. Some of them were swots, anxiously obsessed with quietly chewing up information and turning it into high examination marks, but there was also a handful who delighted in their special subjects and unashamedly pursued their interests. I had not met this kind of boy before. I envied particularly the Greek class, only four of them, with what seemed an open friendship with the Greek master. It took me a couple of months to emerge as anything in particular, but when I did it was as one of the clever boys, with a special penchant for being clever without being a swot, rather offhand about the processes of study, but taking a greater zest in cleverness than I had ever attempted at Parramatta. There were regular arrangements for debating and I took part in them, winning a medal: when one of my friends among the humorists began staging a one-act play satirising some of the more improbable masters I happily collaborated. I was cast into the most satirical role, playing it with such venom at the school concert that the headmaster walked onto the stage, stopped the play and closed the concert.

Finding my own life unsatisfactory, I invented a new one. I would drop hints among the Canterbury boys about my success in dating girls. I invented three liaisons, placing them at Parramatta, well beyond the scrutiny of anyone at Canterbury, and proved the truth of what I was saying by carrying around a class photograph taken at Parramatta High. I would sometimes take this out of my pocket and point to the faces of two girls with whom I had enjoyed no greater liaison than conversations in the classroom, and tell anecdotes about them. My story was that I had discarded one of these girls but was now pursuing an active relationship with the second, meeting her in the city over the weekends or even going out to Parramatta. The truth is that over the weekends I was occupied with comforting Mum, with conspiring with her about the pensions we needed to pay our bills, and with visiting Dad at Callan Park, but I would support my story by recounting circumstances – a movie I had seen, a description of Parramatta Park. I had been so impressed by the moodiness and cynicism of what I had read of *Don Juan* in odd snatches during the first two weeks of Dad's collapse that I had bought a tattered secondhand collection of Byron from a city bookshop for sixpence, and I would sometimes privately see myself as a very lively fellow, potentially Byronic. I had also summoned my Australian ancestry, and I was now inclined to adopt the lordly airs of one who was of old family (although not the grandson of a sleeping car conductor). I invented an ambition to become a lawyer, and repeated it often enough to begin to believe it, although I also knew that we did not have enough money for me to satisfy this 'ambition'.

At the very time that I was cultivating a carelessness in outward style I was also feeling more 'serious' inside. Dad's illness seemed a big and important as well as a terrible thing, and I saw it in relation to myself as if it were one of the those dividing lines that historians draw, marking the end of one age and the beginning of another, something like the Renaissance or the Industrial Revolution. I was sure I must now be quite changed, another person, and I spent time thinking about this, although never talking about it: what had happened to Dad seemed a horrible secret I would never tell anyone, although when I was by myself I was often impelled to take it out and look at it.

My concerns about human society were becoming so large that I might even have talked about it, if I had been able to find anyone who would have listened. To the *Daily Telegraph* criticisms of Australia I now added the attitudes to English society of Wells, Galsworthy, Bennett, Hardy and Shaw, not to mention the more general criticisms of the human condition provided by Ben Jonson, Byron or whoever I happened to be reading that week. While I was now impressed by the sense of accident in human affairs I was also concerned that everything in society should be made better at once ... Left Turn! One! Two ... Quick March! ... I developed a very private public-spirited concern with the fate of the world, to the extent that in some of my new-style fantasy-spectaculars I played the role of the courageous reformer, righting wrong and shedding light in dark places, sometimes as the outspoken author (*J'accuse*), sometimes as the great statesman. I saw reforms as mainly a matter of words – of a scathing denunciation of existing evil and a lively expression of sublime aspiration. If the words were good enough, if the right things were said in parliament and in books and newspapers, then reason would prevail. Events proceeded along an unsatisfactory course only when there was ignorance. I managed to say a little of this in some of my English and history essays or in school debates, but the main expression of this new indignation took the form of long editorials I would write in my head often in the bus on the way to Kogarah station after stoking anger by reading that morning's newspaper. I would dictate these editorials to myself as I rattled along in the bus and arrive at the station in such a fury at the need to dispel falsity that it would take me several minutes to remember that I was only a boy on his way to school.

BEFORE THE BOTANY BAY DISTRICT BURST INTO SUBURBS THERE had been an attempt to turn part of its southern shores into a fashionable watering place. English trees were planted beside the beach; swimming baths and boatsheds were built; a hotel went up, and Sans Souci was created. By the 1930s Sans Souci was an ordinary kind of suburb, with the relics of its pretence at fashion now grown decrepit, and alongside it the suburb of Sandringham had formed. When both the Education Department and the Repatriation Department granted us pensions we found a house to rent at Sandringham. It was right beside Botany Bay; beyond the front fence there was some grass, and then the water; we thought it would be relaxing for Dad. There were only four main rooms along with kitchen, bathroom and laundry, so we had to cram six roomfuls of furniture into four: our breakfast-room suite was broken up, some of it going into the kitchen and the table into my bedroom to be used as a desk. There was a front verandah where, in the summer, I would be able to sleep out, as at Muswellbrook, this time going to sleep to the sound of water lapping along the shore. Zac had been spared, but he was now contained in a tiny backyard, where he become fretful and barked for much of the day.

Just as, at the Muswellbrook school, movement around the playground from one 'portable' to the next had heightened the sense of progress, so at Callan Park the six buildings of the Repatriation wards were formed in an order that represented the degree of seriousness of illness. Dad had been placed at first in the 'worst' ward; it did not seem long before he had graduated to the 'best'. The patients in this ward were not locked up, and after a trial they were allowed to go home, at first only for the day, and then for longer periods. Some of them did not get beyond this stage, still falling back on their ward to save them from the world, although making regular expeditions out of it. However, Dad's progress over a few months was so rapid that they declared him sane again, and he was sent home to live with us.

What had happened seemed so improbable and had passed over so relatively quickly that it was fairly easy to resume old habits. Even in his weeks of collapse, when we visited him we had tried to treat him as if nothing had happened, and we continued with this fiction. For years afterwards I was to go on seeing his breakdown as the dividing line that marked my life into two parts, but this particular Dad who was now living with us again was not the same Dad I had seen weeping in his hospital bed. He told jokes and recounted long anecdotes again; he was devoted to Janet; he went swimming and fishing in Botany Bay; he played golf occasionally; we took up bridge and mah-jongg again; although instead of going to school he now filled out much of his day in the basketwork they had taught him as occupational therapy. But it did not take us long to realise that he seemed to have become like one of his own baskets, sturdy enough to look at, but empty inside. He went on much as usual, repeating old habits, but with nothing new happening. It was as if the hospital had handed us back an almost perfect imitation: it fooled us for a while, then we realised it was not the real thing. But it was all that was left, our only souvenir. Whatever else there had been in him was lost in that hospital bed and no one could find it.

He was not to do any more teaching. The tenseness of his anxiety both kept him together and made him snap under even a small strain. I was careful not to argue with him any more, but this seemed to leave us with very little to say. Because I knew what had happened I could no longer resent the fact that I could not open out to him, but neither could I learn to make conversation as if we were strangers passing the time of day. I was evasive, avoiding intimacy. I had the suspicion he was trying to do the same with me. Sometimes when I tried to sneak a look at him I would catch him trying to sneak a look at me. I had relinquished my role as acting titular head of the house, but now, if she was worried about something, Mum was less likely to discuss it with Dad than with me. We treated him with the honour due to a constitutional monarch, but we had to see to it that the business of our house went on without his being concerned about it over much.

Mum and I turned to dieting as a relief for our despair. Food fads were becoming the vogue, and we adopted a diet that was meant to punish our bodies by removing all the wastes and poisons from them: for twenty-four hours we were to eat only apples, then eggs, then go on to a more balanced but still very light diet. We laughed over this together comparing notes on the rumbles of our stomachs. Mum saw the diet through, but I soon dropped out, preferring my body's poisons to purified intestines. Thus partly purged of wastes and poisons, for some weeks we went to spiritualist seances. Although I no longer believed in God, I still had a shapeless hope that, somehow or other, I might nevertheless manage to live for ever: I had read *The Expanding Universe* by James Jeans, and by spelling science with a capital 'S' and considering its mysteries with a capital 'M' I vaguely hoped that the mysteries might include an immortal me. On the night I went to them nothing much happened at the seances – more seemed to happen on the nights Mum went by herself. We were regularly addressed by a Red Indian maiden and an Irish priest who spoke through the medium (a suburban housewife) to such little effect that it seemed a waste of their time to have made the journey. We sang songs and held hands, and at the end of each seance there was a kind of guests' half-hour in which various spirits took over the medium in turn to see if anyone would claim them. We were on the lookout for Pa, and when we were asked to concentrate our thought-waves so that they emanated from our heads I tried to emanate so hard that my eyes dazzled, but this did not seem to produce Pa. Once a week the medium visited our house to treat Mum's neuralgia, which she did partly by massage and partly by emanations.

I ceased to believe in the immortality of the soul on the night we buried Zac. His body was lying stiff and cold in the laundry when I came home one afternoon. He had been killed by a poison bait someone had thrown over the fence, presumably because he had barked so much. I sat on the cement floor of the laundry with his body for most of the time until it got dark, still not believing my dog was dead. Then I helped Dad put the body on a wheelbarrow, the stiff legs sticking over the side from under the hessian, and we buried him in a paddock near our house, Dad shovelling the dirt while I held the lantern. When I went to bed, in the offhand way in which these things are sometimes settled, I decided that since there was no God there was no immortality. For some time I did not give this observation any further consideration.

PEOPLE BEGAN TO 'DROP IN' ON US AT SANDRINGHAM ON SAT-urdays and Sundays; on a good day it became a little like Denbigh in its prime. We were so close to Kogarah that a full range of old friends was at hand, with quick access by car, trolley-bus or pushbike, and Mum was now making her first new friends since Muswellbrook. Some of the drop-ins would have a swim, and the wet towels and swimming things hung out to dry reminded us a little of the old days at Cronulla. We began inviting friends to night-time prawning parties – our only new diversion – in which we would scrape a few feet of net along the bottom of Botany Bay, one of us walking ahead with a hurricane lamp, and then boil the live prawns in the kitchen and settle down, with bread and butter, to a 'good feed'. Dad retained only one friend from Callan Park, a thin, jumpy little man who had suffered shell-shock while serving with the artillery on the Western Front and had never quite recovered. Sometimes he lived with his wife and daughter, sometimes he retreated to Callan Park to regain his poise. I considered his daughter, who was a year older than me, to be so beautiful that I contemplated going to the pictures with her: but whenever we met we seemed to be surrounded by our parents and their anecdotes about the Great War (which now consisted more of stories about pension claims

against the Repatriation Department than fighting the Hun or Johnny Turk)
and nothing came of it; I began to drop hints about her at school.

For the first time since we had moved to Sydney I invited a schoolfriend
home, then repeated this experiment several times. We would have a swim,
sunbake on the front lawn and talk. I seemed to have regained some sense
of possession of my own body. In the winter I had taken to playing non-
grade football at school, not fully aware of the rules but enjoying the running
around, and I went swimming with the school in the summer. Although
swimming-trunks officially were still illegal, they were coming into the shops,
and I intended to buy a pair when my swimming-costume wore out. When I
went on long walks along the shore of the bay I would now sometimes break
into a run, for the pleasure of feeling my muscles ache and my heart pound: for
a while I read the body-building ads, wondering if I could Be Strong, like the
man in the ad. This new sense of feeling that I was myself received sustenance
in the annual examinations, when I did creditably in all subjects and came first
in English and history, scoring an 'Excellent' in each. When school broke up I
went with one of my new friends for a holiday in a farmhouse in the Kurrajong
Mountains, where we rode horses most of the day and met some girls with
whom, when we got back to Sydney, we went to the pictures. Absorbed in the
feel of leather and horse, and the quietness and sweet air of the hills, I felt so
happy that I decided I was now on the other side of the dividing line. Things
would be better now.

TWELVE

Extract from the diary

Friday 7th January 1938

Time has passed since last I took up pen to this book – much of it has been unhappy time – time without hope some of it – and I look to the future with hope in my heart that this year, at least I shall be spared misery. To relate my personal experiences through the year would be tiring and difficult and unnecessary. Therefore I shall busy myself with the present. This year I sit for the Leaving Certificate and I see a year overcrowded with work ahead of me, too much work. It is my aim to get an 'A' pass in Latin, French, Chemistry, Maths I & II and First Class Honours in English and History. Whether I shall accomplish this the future alone can tell. And then after this, my last year at school, what? It is my desire to do great things, but I have not yet decided what great things. At present I tell people my ambition is the law – but hardly anyone is enthusiastic. My ambition is not the law, it is to use the law as a stepping-stone to Parliament. I regard lawyers as useless things for what good is ever done for civilisation in a lawcourt? But then I have other positions in mind. If I knew I could write well, I should write. But I am afraid that, if I wrote, the stuff I should write might not bring me much in the way of money – on the other hand it might. If I write I want to write literature. I want to write for Australian Literature too. But by that, I do not mean copy Henry Lawson or this piffle-monger Thwaites or such people as Idriess (he has never written Literature). And then I may become a University lecturer or a journalist. And so the list goes on.

PART 3
YOUNG DONALD
1938–40

THIRTEEN

Two days

In the winter of 1938 I got into the habit of arriving late at school, having discovered it was more pleasant to lie in bed and let reality take over from fancy with a warm, private gentleness than to be punctual for what was usually a boring lesson. On the morning of 26 July 1938, however, I got up at seven o'clock, half an hour earlier than usual because my watch was fast. In the bathroom I rubbed some water over my eyes and cheeks, rinsed my hands and then tended my hair by rubbing lotion into it, parting it meticulously with a comb and then brushing it back. At school, like cats sheening their fur, even the most slovenly boys were careful to keep their hair neat and glossy. It was a cold day so I could wear my old suit, hidden under an overcoat. I put on the silk shirt that was patched at one elbow (nobody would see that, hidden under two wrappers of clothes) and the new floral tie I had bought out of my pocket money. The tie would make me look new. I had my breakfast in the kitchen, listening to the wireless, and then caught the early bus.

I went to the top deck of the bus and on the way to Kogarah station read in the *Daily Telegraph* that Australia had won the fourth cricket Test against England, that Hitler would adopt a more peaceful foreign policy because he knew Germany was not yet a first-class fighting power, and that the cost of living had gone up in nine months by eight-and-sixpence a week. Sitting in front of me was Freddie, another boy from Canterbury, with his girl. They always rode in the bus together, and in the afternoon Freddie's girl waited at Kogarah so that they could ride back together. After they left school they intended to save enough money to pay a deposit on a house: then they would get married. One afternoon Freddie had lectured me on the importance of superannuation. At school one hardly noticed Freddie, but in the bus he secured attention just by sitting there, pleasantly sure of himself, day after day, with his girl. While I sat behind Freddie, reading that 20,000 Chinese had been massacred by the Japanese in Nanking, I wished that I 'had a girl'. While I was reading the comic strips (Brick Bradford had entered the Fortress of Fear) I reminded myself that the girls I dropped hints about at school did not exist.

At Kogarah station I stood with a sport and a swot. I might have been able to talk to either of them separately, but I could not talk to them together because I would have to speak in two languages, revealing a double disloyalty. The three of us stood there saying nothing and when the train arrived we walked to different carriage doors. At Sydenham station, as soon as I saw Aub, my latest friend, I walked over to him, thinking how much more important Aub looked than any of the other boys, with his brown pork-pie hat on the back of his head and his camel-hair overcoat unbuttoned to show a new grey suit. Aub's parents 'had money'. As Aub and I talked in the train on our way to Hurlstone Park I wished that my parents 'had money' so that I could dress like Aub. When Aub told me he was going ice-skating that night I wished I could go ice-skating.

At school the boys seemed to be drooping on the grey asphalt. The group I joined were comparing masturbation scores, boasting either of indulgence or, if they were training for sport, of abstinence. The bell rang. In the Latin class we translated some of a Cicero oration, concerned with the argument that a consolation of life and a prompting to action was that one might build a monument to oneself for posterity. In the maths class the teacher took us a little further into what I thought of as 'the wretched binomial theorem'. Despising the binomial theorem as not worthy of concentration, I talked in an undertone. But how on earth was I going to get an 'A' in Maths II if I talked to one of the boys throughout a lesson on the binomial theorem? Then playtime. After I bought two mince pies and a fruit tart at the tuckshop, set in the cement and raw brick of the school basement, Aub and I paraded around the asphalt, important Fifth Year boys. Aub had taken off his overcoat, but mine was kept buttoned, to hide the shame of an old suit. Then 'eternal and infernal French'. I had not done my prose. As the teacher (whom we called 'Basher') wrote the answer up on the blackboard in an elegant handwriting that came oddly from his big hands, I pretended to be correcting a prose I had not done. Usually

I 'played the ass' in French lessons, but today I worried about what might happen. French 'had me wet'. There were thirty-six mistakes in the last prose I had done. At this rate I wouldn't get even a 'B' in the Leaving. Then English. Very boring. The English swot gave the lecturette that day. This swot came second to me in the English examinations, but only because he was a swot. He wasn't really clever. I considered that his lecturette was crushing a light and airy little essay with pedantry. After the English lesson I stood in the corridor and discussed T.S. Eliot with the English teacher. I had been reading Eliot over the weekend – I had found a copy of *The Waste Land* and some other poems in the school library – and I now affected to despise them because of their pessimism, although I congratulated myself on knowing they existed. The English teacher accused me of escapism. I told him he was too cynical. A meat pie and an apple pie for lunch, eaten as we again walked around the asphalt of the schoolyard, most of us still in our overcoats. One of the boys produced a filthy postcard, the first I had seen. I pretended to glance at it as if I knew all about that kind of thing, but as it passed from hand to hand I kept glancing, and after lunch I thought about it during the chemistry lesson, as we prepared a decinormal solution of sodium carbonate from pure sodium bicarbonate.

Going home was like running a film in reverse. Walk to Hurlstone Park station. Train to Sydenham. Train to Kogarah. Bus to Sandringham. Freddie and his girl. Kitchen. Afternoon tea. Bedroom, where I sat down to what used to be the breakfast-room table and felt both pleased and uncomfortable. I was trying to reconstruct myself from what was left of my past in a box – photographs, a clipping of the *Muswellbrook Chronicle* report of my school Empire Day speech, letters, school reports, examination papers, scrapbooks, school magazines, Pa's pipe. I turned these over, looking for the meaning in them as if they were the possessions of someone who had just died. For a while I flipped through the piles of the *Sydney Mail* I had kept, moving them from bedroom to bedroom as we moved from house to house, then I took out my diaries and re-read parts of them. Feeling different from the person who had written the diaries, I even despised the 'myself' of only six months before, writing 'Pedantry!' against a pretentious syntactical construction and 'Sordid money grubber!' against a statement of ambition. Alongside a description of a happy day spent swimming with a friend that summer I wrote: 'The record of what seemed an eventful day in an uneventful life! (Not that my present life is any different.)' Then against the praise I had written down six months before I wrote: 'The big kid! I can't stand him now. Very tiring! God save us! Those childish ways! Personally I feel quite out of touch!' I wanted to remove this discarded friend and the myself of six months ago from my existence.

What existence? After dinner Mum and I did the washing-up and then I sat by the fire and decided to start writing my diary again so that I could honestly describe what I was, good and bad. (The only good marks I gave myself were for honesty.) I began by writing down that day's happenings and thoughts. When I had finished, Mum told me to fetch some more wood for the fire. I got the wood, then went to my bedroom, finished translating the *Aeneid*, Book VI, did some algebra exercises, decided not to do a French prose and started reading Carlyle's *History of the French Revolution*. At ten o'clock I listened to my favourite radio news reviewer, on 2GB, give the opinion that optimistic forecasts of an early settlement of the Czechoslovakia issue had now lost some of their strength. The Czech–German gulf was far from bridged. I went to sleep thinking of the filthy postcard.

The next morning I got up late and missed the bus. Late bus to Kogarah station. Late train to Sydenham. Late train to Hurlstone Park. Walk to school. A quarter of an hour late for French. 'Basher' just kept writing the translation of last night's prose on the blackboard, and again I pretended to be correcting a prose I had not done. How! Oh how! I asked myself, shall I pass in French? In English the teacher tried to interest us in Conrad's *The Shadow Line*, but the suggestion that one got wiser as one got older seemed so improbable that I recited poetry in an undertone – continuous poetry, non-stop, until the boy whose copy of *The Shadow Line* I was sharing moved to another desk. I thought this was amusing. At playtime, a mince pie and a lemon cheese tart, and a talk with Aub, who was tired after his ice-skating. As I sat on the seat with Aub, I decided that I was bored, and I remained self-consciously bored during the maths lesson. While we were being told how to express sin C + sin D as products, to help me in my boredom I solved the *Daily Telegraph* crossword puzzle, ignored an old friend, and talked to a new one. In Latin we reached the end of the *Aeneid*. I became sufficiently unbored to make a small speech to myself, deciding that at last – in a very modest way – I was beginning to understand why *Aeneid VI* was the noblest book of one of our greatest epics. Having congratulated myself that I was the only person in the class to have made this discovery I jotted down some notes on the main failures of modern education.

At lunchtime Aub and I went to the school library for a meeting of the magazine committee. When the previous year's magazine had come out eight months late, on the day after its issue we had spent more than an hour sitting on Sydenham station deciding what should be done about the magazine. We had appointed ourselves to the magazine committee and now were going to tell them what to do, but at the meeting in the library while we seemed to please the master in charge, the other boys were not interested in what we had to say. When the meeting was over Aub and I went to an empty classroom to decide whether we might withdraw from the committee; obviously it was totally unfitted to its responsibilities.

From the window of this classroom I saw three boys in the schoolyard miming some of the more exaggerated gestures of oratory – sweeping movements of the arms, decisive thrusts of hands into pockets, contemplative holding of jacket lapels, pointings of forefingers. Obviously, they were mimicking the theatricalities of my debating style, so I acted out an expression of mounting disgust and then slammed the window down, as if in anger. They all laughed. That was good. I had got a laugh. Also good: more evidence that I was making a hit in the debating club. As if I needed it. Boys were now asking me if I was debating before they decided to go to one of the club's sessions! Perhaps I might drop into next week's debate and liven it up. There were plenty of laughs in the subject: 'The modern Miss makes the best Mrs'. On the other hand – if I continued to be interested in it – I might be too busy with the magazine.

Aub and I went to a sports reserve where the school played some of its tennis and non-grade football. We sat on a stone and talked solemnly about the writing of books, and the characters of our classmates. I decided Aub was advanced beyond his years. One of the masters blew a whistle. All the other boys lined up. We talked on. The whistle blew again. We sat on, pretending to be so busy talking that we had not heard the whistle. After a few more whistles we looked up and smiled. Aub walked down to the tennis courts, I moved to the non-grade football group with what I took to be insolent slowness, making it clear I was not the kind of person who jumped just because some fool of a master blew his whistle. At the last moment I put on an exaggerated spurt, as if just realising what had happened. When he shouted at me, I decided I couldn't help laughing at this stupid man. Then he shouted something that seemed unbelievable to an admirer of Virgil, reader of T.S. Eliot and celebrated debater: he told me to stand outside the headmaster's office until three-twenty and report to him the next morning. I gave what I took to be an insolent grin and walked with an affected slowness back to the school. When his back was turned I made the gesture with my thumb that meant 'Up your bum!' The boys laughed. I had got another laugh.

How would I save the headmaster from embarrassment? I decided to play the puzzled innocent. My only line was: 'I was sent up to stand outside your door for grinning.' The headmaster was tolerant, but he told me to stand outside the door nonetheless. I satisfied my dignity by sitting outside the door, and by taking out the *Daily Telegraph*. I learned that Australia needed a stronger batting side for the next cricket test, that Hitler was planning a German Commonwealth of Nations similar to the British Empire, and that the loyalists had checked the rebels in Spain. Whenever a master walked by I made wisecracks to assure him that I realised that masters were not as silly as the one who had treated me like this. Then I read in a feature article that there was a 'suburban neurosis' in which lonely women developed functional disorders because their sympathetic nervous systems went astray.

At Sydenham station that afternoon Aub and I decided we were too bored for good conversation. We talked on for fifty minutes nonetheless. At Kogarah I drank a chocolate malted and bought the latest *Sydney Mail*. In the bus, sitting behind Freddie and his girl, I read that the Maginot Line made France's frontier impregnable; it was just as much a defence-work of the British Empire as was the British fleet. At home I wrote down the day's events in my diary, in the hope that I might improve myself by chronicling my follies honestly. As part of my homework I wrote an essay on the subject *What is Literature?*, concluding:

> My own view is based on what I personally have found in literature ...
> When wearied with my fellows I have sought in books an escape from
> life and a relief from thinking. I have made excursions into lands more
> ideal than my own ... with Yeats in his nine bean rows, or with Endymion
> in his search for Ideal Beauty, or with Shelley in his impassioned appeals

to the elements. But at other times I have felt embittered with the world and contemptuous of mankind. It is then that I travel with the cynical Childe Harold, seeing with him the littleness of man in the greatness of nature. It is then that I read Galsworthy, emphasising the disintegration of modern society, or Shaw, satirically mocking it with a devil-like playfulness. But most of the time life seems a great battle worth fighting. It is then that I deepen my understanding of life by reading Shakespeare, with his great number of living characters, or Lamb, with his whimsical comments on life, or Burns, with his democracy, or Walton, with his cheery good fellowship, or Browning, with his intense optimism, or Hardy with his equally intense pessimism.

I went to sleep thinking about the filthy postcard.

FOURTEEN

A rapid growth of
true understanding

Just as my new body had grown up inside my old one, at first painfully and grotesquely, and then bursting out with such finality that I wanted to decorate it with floral ties and new suits and sun it in swimming-trunks, I now had a sense of a new 'self' that was swelling and spreading, sometimes making me do things that startled me, at other times stopping me from doing anything. I still saw my dividing line, my secret and decisive sorrow. But what was on this side of the line?

Usually I was pleased with what I thought I looked like, although if I had a pimple I would feel conscious of it. I would examine photographs and see myself as intelligent, remote, thoughtful, 'interesting'. I was Canterbury's cleverest boy in English and history, and received 'Very Goods' or 'Goods' in most of the other subjects, but what delighted me was that I did less work than many of the others. I congratulated myself that I was interested in reading for its own sake, and I was enthralled by cheers at the debating club, laughter at wisecracks, praise for English and history essays, but even more by getting someone interested in what I was saying. On walks along Botany Bay I would talk with old men of forty or fifty, leaning across their fences to try to interest them in my views on Hitler, or the premier of New South Wales.

Figures of rebellion appealed, if they made enough fuss about it. Even in fantasies of failure, in which I died a glorious death, it was with a happy boast on my lips. In recompense for the times when I was just another Canterbury boy with a pimple I would dream about myself as a centre of things.

It was self-satisfying to consider that, with exceptions such as the *Daily*

Telegraph and the 2GB news reviewer, I lived in a world full of idiots. I hated the premier of New South Wales, the prime minister of Australia and, above all, the prime minister of Great Britain. The Munich settlement in September was a personal insult. I became so angry that I wrote denunciatory 'essays' on Neville Chamberlain, treating him as if he were George III or some other famous blunderer in history. I thought I had come out of the Munich crisis so well that I wrote in my diary: 'During the Munich crisis, after three hours homework, at ten o'clock I would switch on the wireless and for fifteen minutes as I listened to the 2GB news reviewer I would tear my soul with sorrow and hatred. With tears in my eyes, I would helplessly hear him tell of the Czechs' betrayal. In these moments at least I rose above myself and became noble, even if I was far away, on the shores of Botany Bay, with the sound of its waves dashing in my ears.'

Great revelations of stupidity came to me daily from print and over the air. I saw myself as someone who would in due course make his name in the world and right wrongs, serving the people, but although I expected great things, I had no particular plans. There was nothing within reach worth having, except to go to the university. When I made speeches or wrote books, or whatever else it was I was going to make a career out of, some transformation scene would have occurred: I would then be able to serve the people.

But from what I could see of myself, I was not up to specifications for this task. I did not always speak the truth, and this frightened me. And although I was pleased that I was a show-off, I was also ashamed. Even worse – I felt lonely among some of the very 'people' I wanted to serve. When I thought of 'serving the people' I criticised myself for concerning myself at all – as I sometimes did – about what I would do for a living; at the same time I worried that I had only the vaguest interest in this, compared with the kind of boys at school who were already thinking of their second mortgages. While I congratulated myself on not working hard I also worried that I might not do as well as I should in the Leaving Certificate. I was pleased with getting up late and arriving late at school, but this added to the worry that I might not be prepared to make the sacrifices necessary if one was to serve the people; especially since there was the possibility that I might go mad through self-abuse. When I thought of myself as a great writer I wondered – apart from the showing-off in school essays – if I had anything to say. I could delight in being lighthearted, but I regretted that often I was still lonely and not lighthearted at all: or, alternatively, that I was too frivolous and no good would come of me. I would express in my diary contempt for my own secret rottenness. Against acts I had recorded because I felt I should be honest about them I would later write comments such as 'Hopelessly self-conceited prig!' or 'Why did such a miserable worm as I was ever live?' The only good mark I gave myself was: 'His only virtue is his stifling honesty.' I recognised that this self-honesty was also inhibiting.

In my diary I wrote: 'If I am with the wrong people I now feel a lot more comfortable than of former times, albeit still a little out of things. But by not saying much I now get on all right. Generally I feel best in a crowd. I hate to be alone with most people, unless they are practically strangers – and so know nothing about me – or people I have known for some time.' I was obsessed with my inability to make conversation with 'wrong people', that is to say, people to whom I could not say what I was thinking. On the other hand, as soon as I got to know people, and did speak to them freely, I became critical of them, as I became critical of whatever I learned of myself from day to day; and when I did talk or act, I might burst out with something I did not mean, or say something I meant, but with more anger or jocularity than was appropriate. The conversations that indicated what I really thought were those carried on in my own head. I would go for long walks determined to think a thought, so that I might begin to know what 'life' was 'like'.

Sometimes the most 'natural' seemed the most real. Sitting in the sunlight on the kitchen steps, eating with my fingers a blackfish Dad had caught only an hour before and Mum had just fried in butter, or watching the light of the hurricane lamp bring a gleam into the dark water as we pulled the prawn net along the bay – these seemed real. In English exercises I was still gushing about nature, as if reality were to be discovered only in European vegetation and bird life: there was not even the cement of the kitchen steps in this type of 'naturalness', or the kerosene in the hurricane lamp, yet in my own life, as distinguished from the literary enthusiasms of the schoolroom, what we meant by the 'natural' was unpretentiousness, often the assertion of those out-of-date man-made things that now seemed symbols of human sincerity and brotherhood: the simple oilcloth of the kitchen table at Denbigh was 'natural' in the days when we used to sit around it and lick the butter that had melted on the hot scones; so were the cans of condensed milk we had used in the weekender at Yowie Bay. Nanna was natural when she went to Paddy's Markets instead of one of the department stores. Dad was natural when he rolled his own cigarettes instead of buying 'tailor-mades'. This feeling for the natural was a desire to maintain some of the apparently more simple and real Australia of the time before there were Electrical and Radio Exhibitions.

Yet when I took up regular smoking on the bus on the way home from school I did not roll my own; I smoked 'tailor-mades'. I preferred tablecloths in the dining room to oilcloth in the kitchen. If virtue was to be found in old things it was because of their literary associations, and very few of my literary associations were with Australia. Part of the charm of the hurricane lantern was that it reminded me of a line from 'The Burial of Sir John Moore at Corunna'. How people dressed, the kinds of houses they lived in, their furniture – I believed both that these were mere artificialities and that they were an essential part of what people were. I still delighted, with my mother, in making catty comments on clothes, property and manners. I was ashamed of my old suit – and also ashamed of my shame, because I now yearned more strongly than ever to 'be myself'. Yet when I was myself people didn't like it. It still seemed that what mainly mattered was to say what I thought. But what did I think?

'REALITY' WAS TO BE FOUND MOST SATISFACTORILY IN BOOKS and in talk about them. This was the way to know what you were supposed to say and do. But a problem with the books that made up 'literature' was the hollowness of what had to be written about them in school exercises and examinations. I entered into this dishonesty with great enthusiasm. In English, we were expected to be more bogus than ever. The Leaving Certificate honours paper was a test of the effrontery with which a student could suggest an acquaintance with all English literature, as if it were something picked up in spare time reading. Some of this merely involved swotting things up: *Define and give examples of pathos, euphemism, allegory, farce. What are the idyll and ode? Discuss the essential qualities of each.* But most of it provided opportunities for writing what at Canterbury High we called 'magnificent bullshit' *1. Who is the greatest English lyrist? 2. Milton is unique. Discuss. 3.*

Romantic poetry is always the poetry of youth. Discuss. We were taught the tricks of answering such questions. Study a textbook history of English literature so that you could drop names; study a textbook of literary criticism so that you could drop opinions; scatter with 'quotes' from poems; throughout the year practise putting these three elements together in typical examination answers.

I had been well trained in pretending to knowledge I did not have and quickly constructing a pattern out of it and gumming it together with expressions of enthusiasm or distaste for works I had not read. In one of the essays written as part of our training for passing the Leaving Certificate English honours examination I gave my view in one paragraph on the dramatic works of Scott, Wordsworth, Coleridge, Byron, Shelley, Coleridge, Shakespeare, Arnold, Lamb, Byron, Swift, Dickens, Burns, Pope, Tennyson, Browning, Yeats, Galsworthy and Shaw. What I wrote about the books I *had* read – all those armfuls of library books – was not usually my own reaction. This was too unlike what was supposed to be said, and too hard to think up in the time it took to answer an examination question. I had read most of the plays in the volume of Shakespeare my mother had bought for me on the lay-by five years before, and of them I preferred *Henry IV* (because it made England 'come to life'), but I could not imagine writing this freak judgment into an English essay.

Writing English essays to order gave me an opportunity to defend most vehemently those attitudes I was about to reject. The use of nature by romantic poets played a big part in our literature course and I angrily defended 'Nature' because this was now part of the 'magnificent bullshit' of English that, in a sense, I most doubted. It was a 'belief' that impelled me only when I wrote an English essay. In one of these essays I wrote:

> The pleasures of company and good fellowship may be great but rare is
> the man who never tires of his fellows. How pleasant it is for a weary
> man to bathe his body in the sea or hide somewhere in some deep, dark
> forest. What matter if the sea tosses in a wild storm, or if the branches of
> the forest rudely sting his face as he pushes on? Is he not man enough to
> stand up and exult in the name of the glory around him?

Against this paragraph the English teacher had written: 'Very good writing'. Yet what I 'meant' was something like this: 'When I get bored with being at home with Mum and Dad – and this happens often – I can get some relaxation by having a swim by myself in Botany Bay or by going for a walk among the spindly trees of the Dolls Point park. Sometimes I feel angry and the water seems flat; sometimes I even hate the way the paint had blistered off the bandstand in the park. But what does it matter? This is the life I lead. I'd better make the most of it.'

In my subterranean reading of 'modern' work I was looking for images that seemed to have something to do with the life around me, but what I found were mainly images of despair. In the 'appreciations' we had to write on great works of literature the kind of words I used about nineteenth-century works were *deep, intense, heroic, gorgeous, glorious, surging, lofty, beautiful, majestic, longing* or *simple, carefree, peace, rest, happiness, freedom*. To describe the few twentieth-century works we studied I used words such as *bleak, miserable, frost-bitten, fierce, uncompromising, hated, grim, grey, misty, stark, tragic, poor, hard, clear, deadly, flat, spiritless*.

This search for some kind of a sense of *now* made me continue to read 'free verse' after I had 'discovered' Eliot: 'Free verse' was one of those newfangled things, like women smoking or modern pessimism, that were not publicly practised in Australia and there was no reference to it in our syllabus, but I now affected to see it as such a natural part of my life that I took up the usage *vers libre*. Yet as I read furtively in this latest example of modernism I was startled by a problem: if poetry did not need regular rhyme and rhythm where would we all end?

The particular form of Eliot's apocalyptic vision astonished me. I did not dislike unhappy endings. Wells and Huxley had suggested to me that things might get startlingly worse – and there was Hitler in the newspapers. What seemed incomprehensible was Eliot's flatness. When I read 'The Hollow Men', in the *Oxford Book of Modern Verse*, I could not believe it meant what it said. It was easy enough to imagine the world might end but, if so, it would be with a bang. We would all be very angry, and until the very last moment there would be daily editorials in the *Telegraph* and nightly denunciations by the 2GB reviewer. As, after seeing the filthy postcard, my imagination kept returning to it, so, with Eliot, I kept on returning to this peculiar flatness, wondering at it, and in my English essays I denounced Eliot (thereby also indicating that, alone in the class, I had read him). But the more angry I became, the more I began in some way to accept his verse as an expression of the low-key quality I detested in my own life. At the end of the year, as I was reading over my English essays, I wrote in the margin against one of the denunciations of Eliot: 'I think that, after all, Eliot may be poetry.'

By then I had received another shock in my reading but this time something for which I was ready. It was my own style – when I wasn't writing English essays or editorialising in some other way – to recall events either with a wry flatness or with a heightened but simplified consciousness, a caricature. Either way, a good story was one that brought out some absurdity. Life was full of them. Being taken out of the 'model' block by Miss Morley at Muswellbrook, having a nincompoop like Neville Chamberlain as prime minister, being stood outside the headmaster's office at Canterbury, having one's father go to a mental hospital – at times life seemed a string of ludicrous anecdotes. I had enjoyed reading Ben Jonson and the comic Byron of *Don Juan*, but it was when I read Evelyn Waugh's *Vile Bodies* and *Decline and Fall* in a Penguin edition that I felt I had found someone who saw things as I saw them. Unlike Eliot, Waugh laughed instead of whingeing, thereby meeting one of the few of my surviving childhood standards.

However, my most significant discovery was history, seen in its widest scope in the seventy-one little chapters in H.G. Wells's *A Short History of the World* (which I read in a Penguin reprint), beginning with 'The World in the Universe' and taking in revelations such as 'The First Americans', 'The Life of Gautama Buddha', 'King Asoka', 'The Dynasties of Sui and Chang in China' and 'European Aggression in Asia and the Rise of Japan' – and there was, in John Gunther's bestseller, *Inside Europe* (which I bought for myself as a Christmas present), an encyclopedic reminder that history was still being 'made'. At school, history became an immense multi-generational European story stretching from the Renaissance to the Leaving Certificate examination. My personal discovery of the Renaissance came in Walter Pater's essays, borrowed from the Municipal Library and opened on the train home: as we rattled through the suburbs I began contemplating beauty, art, life ... images, sensations, perfect form ... the possibility of an existence of constant and eager observation ... and of burning always, with a hard, gemlike flame. (Wonderful words to put into an English essay!) Our key textbook was *History of Modern Europe*, written by Stephen H. Roberts, the history professor at Sydney University and it was Roberts who introduced us to some of the celebrities Pater wrote about. Three paragraphs on Leonardo ('universal genius'), two on Michelangelo ('awe-inspiring rather than beautiful'), one on Raphael ('harmonious, restful') – not to mention Dante, Petrarch, Erasmus, Bacon, Copernicus, Galileo, Rabelais, Shakespeare, Cervantes. 'Thus', said Roberts, 'the New Learning triumphed over the Old.' And amid the details of the wars, triumphs and defeats of the European kingdoms Roberts then showed us the way to four other great signposts: *The Reformation* (Luther, 'brave and outspoken'; Calvin, 'too extreme'); *The Enlightenment* (Montesquieu, 'shrewd'; Rousseau, 'a serious thinker'; Voltaire, 'animated only by destruction' – given this distinction, I chose Voltaire); *The Industrial Revolution* (capitalists, factory hands, the class struggle); *The French Revolution* (Robespierre, 'coldly inhuman'; Danton, 'impulsively audacious'; Marat, 'dreadfully bitter'). The French Revolution also led to an armful of books from the Municipal Library.

Then, in fifth year at Canterbury, in the history teacher, I found a teacher I could respect. In history lessons he simply told us how he saw things, leaving us some cyclostyled notes of all we needed to know to pass the examination, if that was what we wanted to do, but I would forget myself entirely as he talked about the accidents of history and offered to us, without urging them on us, some of the patterns historians had tried to impose on events. He was not only *Cassell's Book of Knowledge*; he was also *The History of the British Nation*.

Of the patterns of history he gave us, the Marxist seemed the neatest. It seemed to fit in with the Darwinism I had been defending against my father for several years, both in its sense of struggle and its sense of progress, but I merely contemplated the neatness of the diagram. I did not accept it or reject it, but I learned off the notes he gave us on Marxism and read a couple of banned books he lent me, their titles concealed in brown paper covers. What I came more or less to believe, as my history teacher did, was that the absurdities of history – which amused him and angered me – might later be dissolved by world revolution. There was nothing new to me in the idea of revolution: that things could be improved by revolution was one of the accepted ideas of my education. Since my childhood at Muswellbrook, history lessons had been filled with useful revolutions. The concept of world revolution was, however, new. It was a very shadowy idea – it did not even have anything in particular to do with Stalin's Russia, which seemed something of a backwater, or even with communism, but with some general, vague liberation of the working class. But despite its shadowiness – or because of it – this idea of world revolution allowed me to combine my cynicism towards the past and my optimism towards the future. Everything had been stupid. In the future it might become intelligent. By the end of the year I considered I had been blessed with true wisdom.

When I wrote in my diary a description of my last day at school it was only to the history teacher that I paid tribute:

> After it was all over we walked around for a while, very important-
> like and at last went home, having a last look into the old 5A room
> on parting – scene of my intellectual awakening owing to the wide
> scholastic resources and tremendous breadth of knowledge of the full
> flood of history of my history teacher. He foretells eventual world
> upheaval – perhaps he is right – for, as he says, the working classes have
> now been educated to a sufficient level as to begin to try to understand
> present conditions. After that I have forgotten what he was saying so I'll
> have to turn back – hence a prophecy of future upheaval – not in his
> lifetime but in mine – and he is a very widely read man. On the other
> hand such prophecies have been continually made through the ages.
> The thought of some self-satisfied government shining benignly in its
> own stagnation is highly amusing, still more amusing is the comparison
> of its self-complacency and its belief in its inevitability with its future
> (sure) downfall. As Tennyson says: *The old order changeth yielding
> place to new, lest one good custom should corrupt the world.* I'd like to see
> Lyons, Stevens, Chamberlain all toppled over. There is a bitter attack
> on Britain being waged in Germany and more talk of the firming of the
> Rome–Berlin–Tokyo pact into a veritable Triple Alliance against Britain.
> Mussolini, however, hesitates. The Spanish War, no doubt, is still in
> progress. They don't say if the Chinese are succeeding in their attempt to
> recapture Canton. Today, as I said before, school was officially finished.

First rural delight at Muswellbrook – why I even directed plays! Then
Maitland and Hinder House with its discipline! Then Parramatta with
its laxity! Then Canterbury and a rapid growth of a true understanding!

A few days later I was working in a city bookshop as part of the extra staff
employed for the Christmas rush, and here I was to fall over some more 'true
understanding'. My first job was in the basement, unpacking imported books,
cutting the overseas prices off the jackets and writing the Australian prices
into them. Things seemed sexy down there in the basement, down to earth,
fundamental, true. Another boy, also a temporary hand, talked a great deal
about girls. He had no more experience than I had, but he would recite his
fantasies – which were as vague as mine – as we prised open wooden cases
of books and slapped the books down on the steel tables. The kind of mating
episodes we imagined were those in which the two partners simply leapt at
each other. I fell in love with the girl cashier's lipstick and breasts – bright red
lipstick and breasts which, I was able to inform my new friend, gave promise
of pneumatic bliss. Most of our conversation about the girl was in more direct
terms: as we wrote prices in books we would look at her and tell each other
our thoughts. (In these fantasies we fell short of actual coition. One had to
be practical about it.) What puzzled me most was how one could ask a girl
like this to come to the pictures when one was too shy even to speak to her.
To take her out would make demands on social accomplishment and it was
beyond my imagination how I could ever master them. This girl came from the
North Shore, where there were supposed to be many 'beautiful homes', and I
had never been inside a 'beautiful home'. When I was promoted to salesman
and went upstairs into the shop's juvenile section, selling Biggles books and
Billy Bunter books, snapping string and tucking brown paper, I would still
sometimes go down to the basement at lunchtime to read one of the books.
One day my new friend told me he had found a very sexy book, written by
someone called Havelock Ellis. We hid it, and read it in snatches. I had not
known such a book could be written. It not only stilled some of my anxieties;
it also suggested a whole approach to life I did not know existed. But it left me
wondering how to ask this girl to come to the pictures.

AFTER CHRISTMAS MUM AND DAD RENTED A COTTAGE IN THE Blue Mountains, and while we waited for the Leaving Certificate results we tried to cast ourselves back into the roles we had played five years before when we had last had a holiday together. It was in the Blue Mountains that I was finally able to think a thought. Dad and I set off on a day's walking expedition – down a mountain track into the valley and then up another mountain track. For lunch we stopped in a small cave near the end of the downward track. We did not have much to say to each other, so the conditions were good for thought-thinking. When we finished our lunch with a bunch of grapes this reminded me of the grapes Mum and I brought Dad when we first visited him in the mental hospital eighteen months before. He had not even noticed them. I then remembered eating grapes with him when I was four, before we went to Muswellbrook. For some reason I had been left at the Kogarah school with him, and I sat in a class of big boys and listened to Dad tell them about Julius Caesar's invasion of Britain. Then we sat in the empty classroom while he shared his sandwiches and grapes and told me some more about Julius Caesar. Now what was left of him was sitting on this bush track, saying nothing and looking along the valley. Since the grapes also reminded me of John Keats, when I looked at the valley I wondered how Keats would have described it. Australia was an inadequate country, not written about in good literature. As we tidied up and continued our walk I felt bored with Keats and bored with the walk. I thought about hospitals and death. I had not thought much about death. I feared hospitals and pain, not death – the terrifying sharp smells of a hospital, the blood and the muck running down its drains. When I had broken my arm at Maitland and they put me in hospital I had seen, as I was leaving the hospital the next morning, a woman being wheeled away from the operating theatre, her face white and her mouth open, a patient etherised upon a table. I remembered Pa's face, dead, in its box. I looked at my hands. How could these hands ever rot away into the earth? I tried to imagine dying. 'We just die like dogs,' Uncle Candy had said, and I believed him. But I couldn't imagine it. Yet I would die and that would be the end of me. Then I thought my thought.

If I didn't believe in God and I didn't believe in life after death why was I always worrying about everything? What did it matter what I was? If there was no good and no bad why didn't I just be bad if I wanted to? I could be as selfish as I liked, plan everything just to please myself, be unscrupulous, just take what I wanted. What was the point of believing in anything? Everything is meaningless. Why should I act according to beliefs if I didn't believe in them and they got in my way? Beliefs were a lot of bullshit. There was no reason whatsoever why I should act one way or the other. What did *should* mean? Nothing. I was going to die. There was no God to punish me. Nothing meant anything. I could do what I liked. But I would have to be careful. Other people expected you to have beliefs. You should act as if you had them. That would be smart. You could act as if you believed in honesty and so forth, and all the time you were lying. I considered these thoughts so important that I kept on repeating them for the rest of the walk, so that I would remember them. Now I felt optimistic about the future.

FIFTEEN

An answer to everything

In my first fortnight at Sydney University I knew I was now a man. Like a piece of rubbish found unexpectedly in a pocket, youth was an embarrassment to be discarded quickly and furtively. Nothing in it seemed precious. Its only distinctions were those of which I was ashamed. Before Christmas we were boys and girls. In March, by beginning our first term at university, we became men and women.

To me it was even more important than the instant acquisition of maturity that the whole body of knowledge was represented within the imitation architecture of the buildings scattered around 130 acres just beyond the central part of the city (which we now called 'downtown'). 'University' was one of those words like 'life' or 'revolution' that I could feel inside my head as a special sensation, and when I enrolled in Arts I, along with 160 other Arts 'freshers', I knew that, at the age of seventeen, close as I had come to true understanding at Canterbury High School, I was now to walk the corridors and backrooms of wisdom and I would come away from them changed for ever.

This sense of importance was strengthened by the fact that there were only six universities in Australia, one in each state, so, in New South Wales, if you said 'the university' you meant the University of Sydney. I spoke of 'the University' with a capital 'U' and with a slight emphasis on the definite article. Most of the university's 3500 students were there because their parents had enough money to buy them careers as doctors, lawyers, dentists or engineers. At its top the university's governing body was largely controlled by judges and doctors from downtown. Some of the professors were members of Sydney 'society'. Orthodoxy was prized: university men and women were expected to

keep their feet on the firm base provided by the unchallengeable wisdoms of
Sydney in 1939. Most student activities seemed dominated by conventional
men and women from the private schools and 'good suburbs'; some of the men
even dressed alike – in tweed jackets dyed in the colour known as 'ox-blood',
white shirts with woollen ties, grey flannel trousers, and wide-brimmed brown
felt hats with narrow crowns. To me these 'sports clothes' came to be such a
symbol of status that I regarded all casual dress as a form of pretension.

My first class honours in English and History in the Leaving Certificate
had given me one of the 200 free places at the university, but no money went
with it for living expenses, so I had also taken a Teachers' College Scholarship
of £40 a year. This involved baring my chest to an Education Department
doctor's stethoscope, baring my crutch to his hands, and pissing in a test-tube
behind his door; it also involved signing a document binding me to teach in
government schools for five years after I graduated, so that, along with four
years spent doing an honours course in Arts and another year taking a Diploma
of Education, I was now handed over to the Department of Education for the
next ten years. When I found out that they wanted me to do physical training
once a week down at the Teachers' College (which was in the university
grounds) the idea of touching my toes in singlet and shorts while I was looked
over by some lout in his ox-blood tweed jacket was so repugnant that except
when they complained about my neglect of them, I acted as if the Teachers'
College did not exist.

Having already learned how to forget that my father had been in a
mental hospital, I now found it easy enough also to forget that he had been
a government schoolteacher, or that I had been to a government school, or
that I did not live in a 'good suburb'. I simply acted as if all this were not so,
not telling lies, but not speaking the whole truth either, as when I would say
of my father simply that he was 'retired'. In the Medical School there was a
plaque of Dr Mileham, founder-hero of Pa's family, commemorating him as
one of Australia's first doctors: I saw myself as a member of a family that was
in Australia before the families of these upstart medical students had been
heard of.

Although my native woodnotes had already been somewhat changed
by elocution lessons, I still spoke with a more 'Australian' accent than some
of the men and almost all the women from the 'good suburbs'. I decided to

change this – partly to put myself at ease, perhaps even more because it seemed a negation of education to speak 'like an Australian'. One of our textbooks was in phonetics – pure analysis, but I used it to train myself quickly into some new diphthongal sounds. I would practise one diphthong for several days until I mastered it, making the sounds over and over again – in my head when I was with other people, and out loud when I was by myself: *ei, ei, ei, ei, ei, ei,* I would say to myself, *ei, as in 'may'*. I did not go too far. I did not want to over-anglicise. After several weeks I had mastered my new diphthongs. Not long after I had changed my accent in this way I nevertheless began to defend the view that there was nothing wrong with the Australian accent; it was just that some of us did not happen to use it.

The wisdoms of western civilisation were to be communicated to us primarily through lectures, with the lecturers speaking slowly and carefully – or even at dictation speed – so that we could get it all down, learn it off, and pass it back to them at the examinations. The first notes I took were on what my lectures would be about. Latin was to be some Livy, some Virgil, some lessons in prose composition, with the only novelty a course in Roman architecture and social customs. In history we were to gallop from the Age of Palaeolithic Man to the Fall of Constantinople in ninety one-hour lectures. In English we were to learn some Anglo-Saxon, some phonetics, something about the history of the English language, study some Chaucer and some Shakespeare, and two portmanteau courses, one on English narrative verse and one on a few modern – but not 'experimental' – novels.

At lectures in all three subjects I got into the habit of sitting with Bill Pritchett, who was to be the first friend I made at the university. Pritchett came from one of the private schools, and, having been brought up by English parents, had an accent fruitier than almost anybody's. But his private-schooldom did not seem to matter. In fact, when we first met he thought I came from a private school, although one despised as being bad at sport and producing softies. Pritchett was more heavily built than I was, with a full, robust face, a sharp nose and old-fashioned spectacles – his face was a mixture of beefiness and intelligence – and when he laughed his cheeks reddened and his glasses flashed. We were both great laughers, roaring with laughter at our cutting remarks, Pritchett sometimes laughing in the middle of a sentence, or breaking off for an interrogatory 'Ha?' Even when we were sitting in the cafeteria in the men's Union, making a meal of meat pie and mashed potato (fourpence) and coffee (twopence), Pritchett would approach his meat pie with an enthusiasm it did not deserve. At times he would break off to sing 'Boom-da-boom. Boom-da-da.' Or to whistle something from Bach. The music of poetry entranced him, and he might recite some of the border ballads we were studying in our course in English narrative verse, or a passage from *Paradise Lost*. Sometimes he would quiz me. 'Ha? Yes. Donald? Ha?' If he quizzed me for too long I would answer him in my debating voice, now enhanced by its new diphthongs.

We shot off our received ideas at each other, delighted by the companionship of talk. We might carry on this way all day, sitting through a lecture on early civilisation in the Indus Valley or on the great vowel shift in English, but otherwise talking most of the time, satisfied with our brilliance. If it were a long argument I might try to bombard Pritchett with my intelligence, trying to win every point, but it was with Pritchett that I began to forget myself, seizing outwards. It was only on those days when he went to the office of *Honi Soit*, the student newspaper, where he was a sub-editor, that our worlds divided. Several times I walked with him as far as the door and saw the long table, with the editor at one end and men and women from good suburbs sitting along its sides. The gothic of the oldest university buildings, built eighty-seven years before, formed a particularly large quadrangle, grassed over, big and simple, walled in by quiet brown stone. In the cloisters there was brown stone to feel, leaded glass window panes, carved cedar and the long sweep of grass in the quadrangle. Just as our university was 'the University' the main quadrangle was 'the Quad'. I quickly became a 'Quad lounger' and it was here, rather than in the lecture theatres, that I was to be prompted to most of my university education.

MY FIRST ENCOUNTER IN THE QUAD HAD BEEN WITH ANOTHER man who had just come up to the university. After we talked for a while about what a lot of bullshit our school lessons in English had been he told me of a wonderfully dirty book called *Ulysses* he had stolen from a public library. Although I skipped some of it, *Ulysses* startled me as much as Eliot's verse, but by now I was eager for shocks, and *Ulysses* seemed the world's greatest novel, making me doubt the value of everything else. Its texture evoked the very sensations of existence, and the confusions through which its characters stumbled illuminated my own confusions; it seemed the most 'real' book I had read, demolishing the barriers between reading and experience.

I soon became ashamed of these unprompted reactions. When I began to read what other people had to say about *Ulysses* I discovered there might be a great deal more to it than I had innocently believed. It was by this means that I began to acquire the first of the new habits that were to seize me in the next few months: the habit of assuming that no literary work was ever what it seemed, that literary works had to be ransacked to find out what their themes *really* were, a matter about which there were infinite possibilities of dispute.

I came across my first explanations of what *Ulysses* was supposed to be really about in some back copies of *Hermes*, the university literary magazine, in an article by John Anderson, the Professor of Philosophy. I was informed that Joyce's main concern was with exile, the hell of mental dissociation, something grave and constant in human suffering, the nightmare of history from which one could wake by *affirmation*. The form that affirmation took was to present things in themselves, and this, the aesthetic object, was to be pursued for its own sake. That the aesthetic object was to present things in themselves and that this object should be pursued *for its own sake* seemed the most important thing I had ever read. This was to be a year in which almost everything I read was to have this characteristic in its turn.

The university carillon had been built as a memorial to graduates who had died in the Great War, and when there was a carillon recital three of the university's most conservative professors usually made a point of standing in the middle of the Quad, as much to safeguard the sanctity of the dead as to listen to the music. They were on the lookout for students who did not stand up for 'God Save the King'; however, it was notorious that they were also watching for the same Professor John Anderson whose articles in *Hermes* had informed me that the aesthetic object was to be pursued *for its own sake*. Anderson would sometimes walk through the Quad when 'God save the King' was being played and defy the three professors, who had become three of his many enemies. On the day I first arrived at the university I saw Anderson walking along the cloisters in the Quad: someone pointed him out as the Scottish radical who was the university's main rebel, a renowned atheist, not long ago a communist, censured in the New South Wales Parliament and by the university Senate. Anderson seemed the most important person at the university. When he walked by, my skin might stiffen and my hair prickle at the roots. He was in his forties, very tall, stooped, gangling, striding loosely past in a brown suit and a green hat with an upturned brim, usually sombre, with his pipe jutting out from between his teeth. He seemed an embodiment of what was grave and constant in human suffering, but sometimes he would wave an arm at a student, loosely, as if it were a puppet's, and smile, strong teeth bursting out beneath his full black moustache. His huge, sad brown eyes seemed to sag right into his face, pulling the cheeks down with them, lost in wisdom. Sometimes he seemed very tired, both tough and fragile, bearing a great load, but still walking briskly. Then he would laugh, or wave his arm. I was gripped by the need to know him.

Light came into the philosophy lecture theatre, where the Literary Society held its meetings, through leaded glass windows, and on either side of the blackboard there were murals, one of classical and one of modern philosophers. There was the sense of an inner temple about this room when early in term Pritchett and I sat in it to hear Anderson give his annual address to the Literary Society, of which he was president. When he began speaking in an urgent Glaswegian singsong the room seemed stilled by significance. Most of the time he spoke strongly, but occasionally his voice hovered and fluttered while he stuttered for words, by this hesitation building up a pressure that then burst through into a confident and sustained high note. The style of his address was intensely serious, but lightened now and again with a wisecrack, or with sarcasm. Most of the small audience took notes of what he said, and in the discussion that followed some of them stood up and elaborated parts of what they had just heard, holding their notes in front of them without referring to them, in the manner of someone at church who sings from memory, but with the hymn book open at the right page. Anderson sat silent, hunched over the rostrum as he wrote on a piece of paper, looking up from time to time, deep-eyed and intent. Then, when the discussion was over, he made a triumphant ending, flowing strongly again, correcting errors and confusions and bestowing agreement like a final blessing. It took only an hour, but we felt we had just witnessed an important new contribution to the theory of aesthetics.

The subject had been 'Literature and life', but the obvious importance of the occasion had so confounded me that I was not clear what it had been about. After reading Joyce and then Anderson on Joyce in *Hermes* I returned to a report of Anderson's address, and then read other articles he had written, and articles by his followers. What I learned now became the most important thing I had read yet. I discovered the entire romantic movement in literature was rubbish because romanticism was illusion, whereas the true role of literature was to expose human illusions. 'There are two kinds of poetry', one of Anderson's followers had written in *Hermes*. 'The true and the false.' The judgments of romantic critics were arbitrary and unscientific whereas in a 'realistic aesthetic' one was scientific in judging works as good or bad according to their structure. By these tests a good literary work was one that *developed a real theme*. According to Anderson's 'realist aesthetic', *beauty in literature lay in the development of a real theme*. That beauty in literature lay in the development of a real theme was to remain with me as a belief for years.

The realist aesthetic was more a weapon of attack than a method of appraisal – apart from Joyce, not many writers had as yet been established as passing its tests – and I developed an assassin's vocabulary in literary criticism, using as bludgeons distinctions between 'reality' and 'illusion', 'true' and 'false', 'scientific' and 'arbitrary', even imitating some of Anderson's fierceness, as when he dismissed Dickens as 'poor stuff' or all Wordsworth as 'drivel'. By now we were in second term and there seemed so many important things to discuss in the Quad that I began to drop lectures in English since they were unscientific and arbitrary.

IN THE FIRST TERM AT ABOUT THE TIME I BEFRIENDED PRITCHETT I had also made a friend of a man who had already been at the university for a couple of years and was studying psychology. He was small, thin and spidery, with brown eyes in a thin, brown face, the skin tight across the skull bones, and with a thin, tight smile. He spoke very dryly and meticulously of 'extroversion', 'introversion', 'exhibitionist', 'inhibited', 'superiority complex', 'inferiority complex' and so forth – words that seemed to extrude human life neatly and then shape it into measurable and observable patterns of opposites. This prompted me to read a textbook in psychology – enough material for a three-year university course, read over one weekend. I decided that I was both extroverted and introverted. I had an inferiority complex and a superiority complex. I was an exhibitionist and I was inhibited. Having acquired some of my friend's vocabulary I joined a group of his associates in examining our own and other people's behaviour in psychological terms. As with books, so with people. Nothing was what it seemed.

I fell in love with one of the psychology students, the daughter of parents who were refugees from some earlier European error and now a woman with light-brown hair to which the sunlight in the Quad seemed to give a brilliant sparkle. Whenever she was with a group in the Quad I would join it, staying on as long as she did, to talk about inkblot tests or extroversion instead of going to a lecture on Hammurabi's code or the Egyptian Middle Kingdom. My imagination was drenched with her brown hair, the rich, sticky red of her lipstick, her deep sexy voice and her air of amused reserve, as if she were a possessor of secret wisdoms. I would even dream about her. One day I followed her in a tram, imagining some great adventure. A private conversation about books perhaps, leading to the climax of a 'date' (an event I knew all about from the movies, but could not connect with my own life). And then, perhaps – a kiss? When she got out at the Municipal Library I followed her distantly and discovered her, as by surprise, among the bookstacks. 'Hullo, are *you* here?' she said, speaking with the voice of one who knew something of the ironies of the Old World. I had intended to ask her to have a cup of coffee – perhaps that was how the negotiations for a 'date' began – but I just passed the time of day and chose some book at random. I continued to crave for her from the safety of the group in the Quad, where sometimes we would talk about sex and virgins (although we were all virgins, we discussed virginity in the third person) until the sun began to set and we went home to our mothers and fathers.

My non-relation with her reached its climax when I boldly invited her to come with me to a university dinner (three-and-sixpence each for four courses). I went home early on the afternoon of the dinner (tram–train–bus) to have a bath and change into the dinner suit my father used to wear on Masonic Lodge nights at Muswellbrook, then back to the university (bus–train–tram), uncomfortable in the stiff-fronted shirt with its stiff stand-up collar, but excited by the prospects of the night. As if I smoked nothing else, I bought a packet of imported Turkish cigarettes (which cost me several pence more than my usual brand) and marched confidently towards 'my woman'. When I escorted her to the dinner she hardly spoke until she managed to whisper to me that I should have told her I was going to wear a dinner suit: in relation to me she was underdressed. The triviality of this complaint puzzled me slightly, but I was so delighted by a story in the afternoon newspapers – one of my favourite enemies, the premier of New South Wales, had been dislodged from office by his own party – that I tried to rush her into a conversation about this unexpected event. She said it didn't make the slightest difference to her who governed New South Wales. When I offered her one of my imported cigarettes she said they were too strong. I began to talk to my other neighbour and she to hers.

I had never eaten a four-course meal before – the idea of a small entree helping served between soup and joint was new to me – and I had not tasted table wines, previously knowing only beer, or fortified wines at Christmas. Through reading novels I was mistily aware that more than one kind of wine could be served during a meal, but I had not realised that the wines might be of different colours, nor had I known that pudding could be eaten with a fork, held in the right hand, without a spoon. At the end of the meal, 'my woman' chatted with her own group and I with some people I had not met before, one of whom offered me a cigar and then invited me to have some coffee with them 'downtown'. I was indifferent when 'my woman' went off with her friends, and I went off in a tram to a downtown coffee shop where we sat until closing time, in our black ties and stiff shirts, drinking more coffee than I had ever drunk before. I was sure it would keep me awake, but there was so much to think about. Several days later I fell in love with a different woman.

By the time of this dinner I considered myself well on the way to becoming a Freudian. Freud was not a normal part of intellectual discourse in Australia, but John Anderson and his followers had taken him up and there was a lot of talk about psychoanalysis in the Quad, which seemed to provide an opportunity to be bitchy while also being scientific. Once again, people were not what they seemed: look hard enough at them and you would find they would give their real selves away by some word or action, thereby revealing that they really possessed the anal character or showed signs of substitute oral eroticism. Our prime hunt was for signs of latent homosexuality. After someone read that green was a homosexual's colour, when we saw anyone in the Quad wearing even the slightest touch of green we would smile knowingly. I was afraid that, by some accident of dress or gesture or slip of the tongue, I might be accidentally mistaken for a latent homosexual.

This gossipy side of Freudianism extended to literature. Literary works were examined as if they were reports of dreams in a psychoanalyst's notebook. *Kubla Khan* was obviously an intrauterine phantasy, *Hamlet* a phantasy of the Oedipal situation (we always spelt 'fantasy' with a 'ph'). Again, nothing was what it seemed. In this shadow play of opposites we Freudians alone could see through the screen with our analytic vision to what went on inside. Freudianism was part of the technique of the 'realist aesthetic': to find out what a literary work was really about you had to give it a kind of preliminary clinical examination. If it was found contaminated by phantasy it was not worthy of any further examination.

I read *The Psychopathology of Everyday Life* and *The Interpretation of Dreams* in Penguin, skipped through the Modern Library Giant selection of Freud as if it were a novel, and then decided to make a complete, careful reading in the long vacation. I was reading so many books (none of them now in my university courses) that I would just skim through some of them, using quick wits to connect this and that together into a general idea, as if for a school English essay, and then promise myself to study them more fully in the long vacation. With some books or articles the first tentative general idea I put together was all I was ever to know, a simple remembered diagram. Even if I read more thoroughly, marking passages, underlining words, taking notes, memorising structure, puzzling out difficulties, the hastily patterned impression of a rapid first reading might still cast such a dominating shadow that I might as well not have read on. By the end of the year most of these new patterns of belief had been cast into me in iron.

AS WELL AS FREUDIANISM, A FEW OF US IN THE QUAD, WOMEN AND men, also talked some of the language of sexual freedom. This had nothing to do with love, of which we were inclined to be scornful because, like everything else, love wasn't what it seemed. Nor did it have anything to do with our actual behaviour – with each other, or with anyone else. Occasionally, women and men together, we might discuss 'seduction'. 'Seduction' was seen as a male making a female drunk without getting drunk himself (otherwise we wouldn't be able to 'do it') and without getting a 'knockback'. But none of us had even been into a hotel. Our very language was usually indirect. When discussing a matter of such intellectual importance as sexual freedom we usually spoke formally of 'copulation'. *They went into the park and copulated*, we might say, as if two railway carriages had been hooked together.

A lot of our concern with sexual freedom was with perversion, a cause we disinterestedly took up in the general interest of freedom. We were determined that perversion should be quite uninhibited. People should be allowed to do whatever they like with themselves or each other. Homosexuality. Lesbianism. Incest. Sado-masochism. Voyeurism. Exhibitionism. Pornography. If it didn't do anybody else any harm, perverts should be allowed to practise perversion. One afternoon we discussed the question of public masturbation. Why shouldn't people practise what they liked in public? We were not ourselves, of course, homosexual, incestuous, sado-masochistic, voyeuristic, exhibitionistic, or pornographic or public masturbators. We were heterosexuals, and our concern was with free love, a matter not only of freedom in fornication, but of freedom in practices and positions. Some of us acquired some abstract knowledge of heterosexual practices and positions, but only in terms of principle. We talked about repression as if it had nothing to do with our own situation and about sexual experiment as if it did.

In the Quad the most learned rhetoricians of free love (although not its practitioners) were the freethinkers, members of the Freethought Society, which John Anderson had formed eight years before when he was a communist and which he had transformed in his Trotskyist period and which had now been switching around into something else, since he had finally broken with the Trotskyists two years before. As with the rest of the university, in 1939 the Freethought Society had passed its best days. But although its greatest glories were behind it, echoes of past explosions still gave it significance and it still had as its president the greatest living philosopher, for as well as being freethinkers, members of the Freethought Society were 'Andersonians'. To be an Andersonian was as self-sustaining as being a Marxist or a Freudian: it provided an answer to everything.

The first freethinkers I met in the Quad were mere outriders of Andersonianism, but they were such zealots that after I had spent my first afternoon with them I felt skinned. For weeks afterwards I nevertheless subjected myself to their logic and bullying. It was as if the Quad had been turned into the playground at Maitland High and I was being head-tested all over again. I was learning new reflexes and manoeuvres in conversation, new ways to duck and jab, which I would then practise on others. 'Ah!' I was learning to say in the Andersonian fashion, 'but what do you mean by that?' Pouncing on a careless phrase and tearing at it for meaning – 'relative terms' were particularly good for this purpose – could jolt almost any conversation to a stop. If definitions were offered it was easy to shoot them down from the hip. Or one could detect a 'confusion' in an opponent's argument, as if pointing to contradictions settled the matter, or restate the argument as a 'position' in terms that made it simple to get rid of. I hoped to become a laconic analyst, clarifying discussion, sorting out confusions, clearheaded, cold-hearted, objective … scientific. But I also enjoyed attack, and the Andersonian weapons seemed irresistibly strong.

I had been a believer in Darwinism ever since I had read in *Cassell's Book of Knowledge* that 'The protoplasm was the beginning of the wonderful story of evolution', and when Pritchett and I stayed back at the university one night to attend a symposium on evolution at which Anderson would be speaking I expected that, since a Catholic priest was to be one of the other speakers, Anderson would launch all his fury against the ignorance and superstition of this clerical bigot. The large lecture theatre was brimming with people, and Anderson sat intent, silent and sad-eyed, while the priest jumped on the theory of evolution and a scientist picked it up. Anderson sprang into the ring and floored the priest with a couple of blows. I was astounded when, after an obeisance towards Darwin because, like Freud, he had rejected the dualism of man and nature, he then pummelled evolutionary ethical theory, on and on, blow after blow, because it was full of progressivist illusions. Things might not get better. They might get worse. With Anderson one did not know where one was. It was the same with the Quad freethinkers. We could exult in our atheism, scorn the 'slave's morality' of the Student Christian Movement or the black, implacable puritanism of the Evangelical Union, and attack the sinister, fanatical conspiracies of the Catholics, then I would say something wrong and find that the freethinkers were bashing me again. Didn't I realise I had adopted a mere 'humanist position'? Didn't

I realise it was as much an illusion to see things as man-centred as God-centred? Didn't I realise *there was no centre to things*? I might then find that I was accused of slipping into 'progressivism'. Didn't I understand that the pessimism of religion was an antidote to mere sentimental optimism? With the freethinkers I was learning not only the language of rebellion but also how to rebel against other rebels, still using the language of rebellion.

Freethinkers attacked both right and left. On the right they attacked sexual taboos, obscurantism, superstition, repression, patriotic belief, absolutism, capitalism. Simultaneously, on the left they laughed at the very idea of progress that had been fundamental in my education at school. To suggest that one might plan for social amelioration was mere 'voluntarism'; it was *movements within the structure of society* that determined events, untouched by human wishes. Humans were mere vehicles of social forces. It was ridiculous – even worse, it was 'atomist', 'individualist' – to think that there was anything we could do about whatever displeased us in society. Things *had to take their course*. To try to make things better was a sickly product of Christian moralism and rationalist humanitarianism: one must account for things, not try to change them. To plan for the future was sheer phantasy. It was a particular and necessary delight for freethinkers constantly to expose the confusions and illusions of liberalism. As with dogmatic communists, the particular enemies of freethinkers were those with whom they had most enemies in common.

Thus while mysticism was an enemy, so was 'materialism' – because there was not a single entity, 'matter'. In the same way relativism in ethics would make freethinkers run both right and left simultaneously. Right – to attack such terms as 'ought', 'duty', 'right', because these were mere expressions of moralism, *relative terms* that were simply part of social codes. Then left – in defence of the use of the term 'good', which was not a relative term, but a *quality of mental activities*. Ethics was a *science*. Just as there was a realist aesthetic there was a realist ethic.

The ideas put together three months before when I went with my father for a walk along a bush track in the Blue Mountains that I would die, that it didn't matter what I did, I might as well have a good time – had been joined by a sceptical suspicion that there could be doubt in everything, that the very perceptions of the senses were no final authority, and that, in the irony of belief, in any general position there was bound to be error. But it seemed to be such attitudes as these that most irritated freethinkers. They made short work of demolishing my flimsy arguments for hedonism – apparently my position was compounded of *logical confusions*; and, so far as my scepticism was concerned, one freethinker (Elwyn Lynn, already in third year) tried to bully it out of me. He walked me round and round the Quad for a whole afternoon while he tried to still my doubt that seeing a book on a table necessarily meant it was there. 'You simply *take it to be the case*,' he told me over and over again. 'To assert is to *take something to be the case*. If you say you see the book on the table you suggest that what you perceive has characteristics of its own. You simply *take it to be the case*.' I did not understand what this was supposed to mean. But I began to act as if I no longer had any doubts. I attacked scepticism as well as hedonism, and when in difficulties I began to say: 'You simply take it to be the case.' In the name of disbelief I was losing my belief in disbelief.

Nevertheless I became a critic of the Freethought Society. My platform was that it had fallen on bad days; it was not active enough; its discussions were sterile; it was living in the past. I was tired of people suggesting that things in 1939 could not be as interesting as they used to be. Here was I in 1939, and I wanted things to be interesting again. I volunteered to give an address on 'What's wrong with the Freethought Society?' They accepted. Signs went up in the Quad: FREETHOUGHT SOCIETY. DISCUSSION MEETING, 'WHAT'S WRONG WITH THE FREETHOUGHT SOCIETY?' SPEAKER: D.R. HORNE. The night before the meeting I tried to plan my speech. I couldn't think of anything much to say. I didn't know enough about the Freethought Society, and I became terrified that the little I wanted to say would be exposed as rationalism, humanism, progressivism, relativism, materialism, hedonism and scepticism; that my position would prove to be made up of illusions and confusions. The next morning I stayed home. At lunchtime a few people came to the meeting, stayed for a while and went away. I arrived after the meeting time was over 'I'm sorry,' I said. 'I forgot it. It must have been a Freudian slip.'

AS SOMEONE WHO HAD LEFT HIGH SCHOOL BELIEVING IN THE probability of world revolution I had been delighted when, in first term, I met Oliver Somerville. Somerville looked as if he had just come from serving on the barricades. During even the most dreary conversations in the Quad his dark eyes flashed as he made the generous gestures of a street orator and he wore the clothes of an Irish rebel – no tie, collarless shirt fastened at the neck with a stud and covered with a white scarf tucked into an overcoat. On some days he wore white sandshoes. At the slightest opportunity he would sweep off his hat (which had several holes in it) with such theatrical gallantry that he might also sweep away some of the bystanders. Somerville, too, was a freethinker, but his very theatricality distinguished him from the tight-lipped fundamentalism of some of the others. He was more likely to recite passages from English or French *fin de siècle* poets than to set up an inquisition on the true and false in literature. He was an old freethinker from the great days of several years before, already graduated, and now a freethinker martyr who had served Anderson so well that he was still resolutely detached from the guiles of the commercialist society around him. In fact, in Anderson's cause, he had suffered a nervous breakdown. Beyond a little private coaching of secondary-school pupils Somerville did not earn a penny. Usually he lived with his parents. Sometimes he took a room in a slum. His immense integrity in rejecting society so wholeheartedly made me feel guiltily frivolous. To show my earnestness, I had a three-course meal for ninepence with him one night in a slum café, but I marvelled at the fortitude of a man who could eat in such surroundings when I knew he came from a 'good home' in a 'good suburb'. There were times in the Quad when I feared he had decided I was unredeemably bourgeois. He would become abstracted and stare at me silently, or stare at the stone floor of the cloister and silently shake his head. He might even walk away without a word. My fraudulence was discovered! I was lost to the revolution! But the next time we met he would again bombard me with high laughter and baroque compliments. Even Anderson would chat to Somerville in the Quad. Somerville even called Anderson 'John'. He even criticised Anderson's position. 'It is said of a certain university professor that he is getting more liberal every day,' he once said knowingly at a Freethought Society discussion group on Trotskyism, conducted in the University Park. There was only one possible unsoundness in Somerville. Although he was already in his early twenties he was rumoured still to be a virgin.

The Quad freethinkers were in disarray in their attitudes to the revolution. This particular generation of them had been at school at the beginning of the 1930s when Anderson had retreated from Moscow, but his final rejection of

Trotskyism was still in some of their memories. None of them seemed more confused than Somerville, but it was more through his imagination than anyone else's that I tried to cling to the consolation that there was assuredly still to come a great turning of everything upside-down which would destroy the bad, cleanse the good and rid us of the injustices and absurdities of human existence. In his Trotskyist moods Somerville seemed to believe in world revolution in the Marxist sense, although this event was still unimaginably in the future. In his anarchist moods he seemed to regard the revolution as an aspiration of excellence that was too good for humankind to accomplish, although the idea of it might illumine our lives and give meaning to our actions. One thing stood clear: in Russia the revolution had been destroyed.

THE FRENCH REVOLUTION, THE COMMUNE, THE RUSSIAN Revolution – all destroyed.

For those who were still possessed by revolutionary impulses the purest revolutionary act was to abominate Stalin the betrayer, assassin not only of the revolution but of the revolutionaries, the unintellectual cynic who did not know what the revolution was supposed to be about. Some of the Quad freethinkers carried in their briefcases part of the literature of anti-Stalinism, and when they gave me a book or an article to read, they seemed to expect me to read it on the spot as if the scales would drop at once from my eyes on to the brown stone of the cloisters. After going to the Freethought Society discussion groups on the purges, the Moscow trials, the frauds of the 1936 constitution, the deceit in Spain, and the vilification of Trotsky, I quickly learned how to replace the world 'Communist' with 'Stalinist', a member of the Stalin gang, an impostor. Since it was social forces, not people, which moved events in their mysterious way, freethinkers were supposed to deny the individual a role in history, but in the case of Stalin some of them placed on him an entire personal responsibility for all the disasters and hoaxes of the Russian reaction, although others speculated historically as to whether it was always thus with revolutions that they should fail. And although in the case of Hitler it was agreed that Nazi doctrine did not matter, that one must merely examine the social forces moving through German society, in the case of Stalin there was a perpetual, detailed nagging at Stalinist propaganda and at the un-Marxism of the Stalinist switches in the party line between adventurism and dogmatism. Whether or not we were still Marxists was a matter for conjecture, but it was one of our criticisms of Stalin that he had ceased to be a Marxist. Somerville was inclined to attack the whole idea that the revolution could have started in Russia. According to the recipes laid down by Marx and the younger Lenin, Russia was fit only for a bourgeois revolution. The Bolsheviks should have left Russia to Kerensky.

The freethinkers' indignation with Stalin was magnified when they confronted the dupes of Stalinism. Sydney and Beatrice Webb were the main clowns in this morality play and the Dean of Canterbury the principal villain. We laughed at the Webbs and hated the Dean, who was a Christian as well as a fellow-traveller, and so doubly damned. In confronting the innocence of the fellow-travellers there was an angry despair that people simply could not understand *what was the case* in Russia. It was like arguing with people who believed the earth was flat.

Although their books could be discussed at Freethought Society meetings, it was not possible to arraign Beatrice Webb and the Dean of Canterbury personally in the Quad. For this purpose the freethinkers had to be satisfied with members of the university Labour Club which had been re-established by the Stalinist cell at the university early in the year. Freethinkers argued only with fellow-travellers or innocents from the Labour Club, not with Stalinists directly. Between Somerville and the few student Stalinists there was a strange courtesy: neither side took the other to be a serious person, so that it was possible to banter allusively without any attempt at conversion, cracking Marxist jokes, like emigres who meet in a strange country and for a while enjoy the cordiality of vilifying each other in their own language.

Images of Trotsky and Lenin haunted the freethinkers in the Quad. Trotsky – brilliant, courageous, passionate, the Trotsky who wrote himself up in exile rather than the earlier Trotsky of action. Lenin – intellectual, precise, puritan, somehow more of a sound, tough-minded Sydney pragmatist than Trotsky. There was no bullshit about Lenin. When Somerville talked about Trotsky, and the Trotskyist Party in Sydney, I felt myself a Trotskyist – Somerville's Trotsky wanted to make my revolution. When Elwyn Lynn talked Leninism I felt excluded – he and his Lenin wanted to make a revolution *against* me.

The Russian Revolution still caught the imagination, especially after I read *Ten Days That Shook the World*. Except for the Smolny Institute, which was bright with lights and hummed all night like a gigantic hive, the two colours of the Revolution were grey and black. Skies were grey and windless, with a few hesitant snowflakes; nights were black, cold, nervous, with people hurrying along the streets of Petrograd, or clustered briefly beneath a flickering streetlight. Black was also the colour of the masses – black rivers of men surging forward, silent but for the shuffle of feet. Their leaders were unshaven and filthy after three nights' sleepless work, eyes burning in their harassed anxious faces while the samovars stood cold and foul blue clouds of cigarette smoke hung in the thick air. The sounds of the revolution were distant – the sharp crack of rifles, scattered bursts of firing, the rattle of a *yunker* battery along the streets, the rumble of a big armoured car flying a red flag, the dull thud of guns. Only the words of the revolution were immediate – the long speeches from the tribune of the Petrograd Soviet, the telephone calls and telegrams, the proclamations and bulletins. SOLDIERS! WORKERS! CITIZENS!

I bought a secondhand book on anarcho-syndicalism and glanced over it. The guerrilla warfare of sabotage and the ultimate revelation of the general strike stirred me. For want of something better to say, I began to call myself an anarcho-syndicalist: we would do away with the State altogether, we anarcho-syndicalists. Property was theft and the State was a predator and a parasite. Producers' groups should themselves organise production. Among the freethinkers, however, there was now some doubt as to whether the workers were not already so corrupted by their concern for nice homes, baby clinics and old-age pensions that they were no longer worthy of the ideals of anarcho-syndicalism, and there was even some doubt as to whether producers' groups *could* organise production. But I decided to believe that the workers were like warriors and artists, that they were heroes in their dispossession, showing initiative, disinterest and a craftsman's exactitude. There was a literary flavour about this belief, a force of words that pushed me beyond my liking for and my understanding of my Uncle Ted, who pedalled his bicycle to the railway workshops every day, and beyond the other workers I knew, to the idea of workers as an abstract. At the same time, and in contradiction, I maintained a sentimental desire to do good for the people, to help the people, by attending to their security and welfare, in particular by demolishing the slums and setting the people up in suburban homes of their own, but this aspiration was difficult to express to either freethinkers or Stalinists, both of whom seemed to be contemptuous of those who urged such considerations as being mere *humanitarians* and *meliorists*, suffering *illusions* because of their *confused social theory*. Was I expressing no more than suburban bourgeois prejudice?

After I read some of the back literature of the Freethought Society I took up a hero's code in which the heroes were the producers – the scientists, artists and workers. Since I saw myself as moved both by the spirit of inquiry and the love of beauty, I was both scientist and artist. It was because we hero producers followed our pursuits for their own sake that we could distinguish ourselves from those who merely held to a consumer ethic, and were concerned with getting things. All we producers wanted was to engage in our productive activities, and we didn't give a damn whether anyone else wanted what we produced (if we produced anything). It was most important to this sense of heroism that we should not be concerned with meeting 'the demands of society', and we had to maintain eternal vigilance against those who tried to take us over, in the name of practicality, and pervert our ways of life by trying to manage us. As producers we did not need managers. We could manage ourselves. We knew we might fail; the barbarisms of the age might destroy us – but like warriors we should be brave in the face of the enemy. Not only did Anderson walk across the Quad when 'God Save the King' played: he had also been known to jump on to the station platform from an electric train while it was still moving. We were isolated and few. It was possible that workers had deserted us, corrupted by their trivial concern for their own security and welfare. It was likely that many of the scientists did not understand us, befouled as they were by commercialism, practicalism and rationalism. It was true that many of the artists were lost in mysticism and romanticism. But those of us who had been taken up by the spirit of inquiry or the love of beauty would still follow our ways of life for their own sake, and, as Pa would have said, everybody else could go to buggery.

EARLY IN THE FIRST TERM I HAD MET JOAN FRASER IN THE QUAD. 'Fraser' – it was progressive to call women by their surnames – dressed modestly, in the intellectual fashion, and even put on her lipstick modestly, but this modesty in embellishment seemed to bring out the whiteness of her skin and the warmth of her eyes. I was put at ease by her maturity – she was already graduated in Arts and was now taking a Diploma of Education – and, since I had never been taught to treat women with any special respect, as if there were something wrong with them, the affirmations of feminine equality – rolling her own cigarettes, or paying for her own cup of coffee – instead of disturbing me, settled one of my anxieties about women; that they might cost money. I did not imagine I had to have a 'date' with Fraser. She talked softly, in a monotone, using not pitch but a certain kind of word stress to create emphasis, but she talked very amusingly and wryly, introducing me to the throwaway style of soft, confident underemphasis. There were times when it could seem that I had been there forever with Fraser, this older woman of twenty two, so kind to a seventeen-year-old – sitting in one of the sandstone cloisters of the Quad, looking out at the lawns rather than at each other, chatting softly, with Fraser showing me how to speak wittily and throw lines away, so that one had to listen to the words themselves. I read some *New Yorker* profiles, James Thurber, Lytton Strachey. One of my new key words was 'amusing'.

When it was clear that I was lucky enough for Fraser to have taken me up, our companionship moved beyond the Quad to the Union refectory, where for fourpence you could be waited on and served at a separate table. I now learned how to spend a couple of hours happily lounging over a pot of coffee, the cigarette butts filling up the ashtray, while Fraser was amusing – reciting Dorothy Parker or A.E. Housman, or telling pointed anecdotes or jokes, or making wisecracks. I tried to develop a laconic style, talking softly out of one side of my mouth, and saying nothing at all unless I had a witticism to offer, and then mumbling it so that if they wanted to hear it people would have to lean forward. This seemed to come off. I seemed to be amusing Joan Fraser! I wanted to say whatever came into my head, but in Sydney one had to look to one's defences. To appear to take nothing very seriously was one way of evading sceptical cross-examination, or, as I put it to Fraser, to speak softly and carry a big wit.

It was after Fraser took me up that I began to get another sense of the importance of the university: that as well as housing the greatest modern philosopher it was also the scene of what might prove to be one of the world's significant literary traditions, a tradition that had begun with Chris Brennan, a bohemian professor and symbolist poet who had been dismissed by the university in the 1920s. That Brennan began writing symbolist verse under direct influence from Paris and that he had been victimised by the authorities were both relevant to this tradition: it showed that, like Anderson, Sydney poets could be in the van of world movements, and that, like Anderson, they were totally without recognition.

This Sydney University literary tradition was now embodied in *Hermes*, and as I read and re-read back copies of *Hermes* I assured myself that, as one of its editors had said, *Hermes* was the best magazine of its kind in the English-speaking world. I had never seen an intellectual magazine. I knew that Steele and Addison's *Spectator* was 'literature' because we had read about it at school as part of the 'Age of Pope' and I had known about the *Edinburgh Review* because Byron satirised it in a poem. But here was a magazine printed in Sydney, that would publish articles with beginnings such as:

'In these days of unabashed commercialism with utility treated as the touchstone of all worth ...'

or   'Sociology, like all sciences ...

or   'At the end of Plato's *Symposium*, it is recorded that Aristodemus ...

or   'Now that T.S. Eliot's *The Waste Land* has receded into the background ...

or   'The existence of a gulf dividing economic theory from economic fact is happily no longer disputed ...

And ran on its back cover an ad for Toohey's oatmeal stout illustrated by a drawing of Socrates. In format, it was the most handsome looking journal I had seen – not even a title on its cover, simply a moderne stylisation of what I learned later was a famous sixteenth century bronze statue. Appropriately, it was hated by many of the students. There had been demonstrations against it when a more than usually rebellious editor had brought out one issue entirely in verse, and the first big student meeting I attended was one at which *Hermes* survived only by the chairman's casting vote. Fraser was indifferent to *Hermes* now. The great days were gone. It no longer seemed to matter much what happened to *Hermes*. The main criticism at the protest meeting was of a satire that had appeared on the Catholic Mass (done in a style that was also a satire of *Finnegan's Wake*), with the blessing *in nemine pompous et Filthi et Spurious* and many other blasphemous (and cryptic) jokes. This had been done by one James McAuley, already my hero among the *Hermes* poets as 'J.Mc'. I read his verse so often that, without meaning to, I soon had some of it by heart. 'J.Mc' seemed to convey the sad emptiness of metropolitan youth, lost between beliefs. *A howling desolation feeds that pride at whose dead centre sits a child that weeps, lost and disconsolate, and never sleeps.* In 'J.Mc's' verse the late sky cleared and wet pavements shone with hard blue light; the night was fearful and empty; dawn burnt low and pale upon its wick. *Morning for both of us would shine like insult in the eyes.* Walls crumbled, faces blurred as one passed to the black abyss, contemplating, with fearful eyes and a scarred and weary heart, dusty passion and dissolution. Lips were cold and shadowed, smiling with a sad, slow smile, or in an agony of contemplation. *The fizzy drink that love provides changes quickly and goes flat, so quickly, sour and flat.* Close to mad lust was death, sunken skin, wrinkled breasts. *Oh! thou dead come not in dreams, your cold mouth to my mouth.* I most admired a sequence called 'Aspects of the Moon':

I

SELENE ON LATMOS
Late through the suburbs wandered the blonde moon
With disenchanted gaze, a little wild,
And lonely gentlemen most courteously
Saluted her. She only shook her head.
'Ah, not this evening, my dear', and smiled.
But at the silent house she paused and cast
Her brilliant nubile glance within. In vain.
The unsleeping figure turned towards the wall
And did not hear the whisper through its pain.

II

HECATE

Now from the crossroads of the heart
Softly the dead arise.
Who then is she that from above
Looks down and lifts their eyes?
Ah, Lady Hecate! Must you steal
Another's form for show?
Those eyes, those lips were never yours:
I kissed them long ago.

III

HONEY MOON

His Majesty the Golden Moidore
Conducts his court with cheerful grace
Nor is his dignity impaired
By twigs that scratch the royal face.
His sovereign sway illumines all
When Mrs with her man conjoins,
Defies connubial attitudes
And summons vigour to the loins.

At the end of first term I squeezed into a spare seat in a small balcony up near
the film projector to watch McAuley in his role of pianist in the orchestra
at the student revue. The tobacco smoke was as thick as at a meeting of the
Petrograd Soviet, and beery shouts drowned much of the dialogue (in which
the principal laugh lines were to shout 'bugger' or 'bastard'), but I kept him
in the corner of my eye for most of the revue. He was placed below the stage,
in a dinner jacket, playing the piano, undulating up and down on his seat
with the rhythm, his fair hair caught by the stage lighting. I had gone to the
revue mainly to see McAuley, and I left with the same urge I had felt towards
Anderson: *I must know this man.*

McAuley was known to Fraser as Jimmy, and he was the central figure in
her reconstruction to me of the university's golden days gone these two years.
Jimmy was now twenty-two and although memories of him were still lustrous

enough to light up Fraser's sadder moods as we spoke softly over the coffee cups, the bright gilt of Jimmy's youth had now faded. Nevertheless Fraser rebuilt for me the romance of Jimmy the jazz pianist – at bottle parties, playing 'St James Infirmary', cigarette in mouth, hair falling over his forehead, glass of neat gin on top of the piano, perhaps playing blues and jazz for hours, but stopping before dawn to sit and smoke beside the grey window and talk softly. After a party he had once gone on to the university and played 'Rhapsody in Blue' on the carillon. Jarring bells clashed sardonically while surburban people woke up to eat their breakfast cereals. He was happy, and sad, and sardonic – and also a great charmer, and enlivener. Fraser still talked of what had been his greatest university love affair, its heyday, its fall, little incidents still remembered, as of the dead. There was Jimmy for whom parties went on too long, and there was 'J.Mc', a genius whose brilliance shone like the sun.

Jimmy was now away on a country property, tutor to the son of some landed gentleman, an inadequate ending. Fraser spoke about the lonely rooms he had lived in, how he sometimes spent the hours before dawn at the cafeteria on Central Railway Station waiting for the first train. He had written a piece of 'prose' in *Hermes* in which the railway cafeteria was the setting for a meaningless re-encounter with a past love, so I stayed up all one night to see what things were like at the railway cafeteria. After going to the pictures I got there at midnight and waited till dawn, filling in the time by drinking sludgy coffee, smoking cigarettes, sometimes walking around the big, cold empty station at which we once used to arrive with great excitement from Muswellbrook eager for good times in Sydney. I imagined that I was Jimmy McAuley, for whom parties went on too long. I took notes – on the prostitutes eating fish and chips, on the sailors who boasted about beating up a homosexual who had accosted them in the lavatory, on the ordinary people who sat in front of their empty cups and saucers, waiting for a train. On the back of my notes I wrote a poem which began *The suddenness of seeing this before: that melancholy ever walks without its breeches, stark against the dawn, that doubt proceeds from tray to tray and out the door* and ended *The matchstick down the urinal is tossed, for roses grey from dung, the story said.*

When I was with Fraser I had no doubt of my inadequacies compared with the giants of the past, and of the greatness of former times compared with the meaninglessness of the present. One had to get on with one's life as best one could, however, and I became determined at least to learn how to drink. In alcohol I might find both the secret of good times and the romance of disillusion. The great drinking place of the past – a song had been written to it – was the Park View Hotel in Myrtle Street (in legend this pub was simply called Myrtle Street), so that when I got one of the £1 notes from my Teachers' College scholarship I decided to spend some of it getting drunk in Myrtle Street. With an equally innocent companion I found Myrtle Street in a slum down from the university, several streets away from a view of the park. We went into the parlour, a small room with a leather horsehair sofa, an aspidistra on a wooden stand and a few hard wooden chairs, and then began to order. Some people boast of the instant success of their first sexual act. I can only boast of the instant success of my first act of drunkenness. Like a child at a party, I was going to have one of everything. We started with a sherry. Then a whisky and water. Then a beer. Then a gin squash and soda. Then a port. Then a rum and milk. We looked over the bottles on the bar, and then went on to try whatever other drinks we had heard of. We laughed and even sang a little. The background blurred, but I saw my companion's nose as I had never seen a nose before, and the horsehair sofa. When we went staggering back to the university, delighted by our wise conversation, I felt I had seen a street for the first time. 'I have seen such a vision of the street as the street hardly understands,' I shouted to Fraser when we found her back in the Quad.

We went on talking and laughing. Catching an unexpected echo, even Fraser took on some of our gaiety. Perhaps it again seemed 1937 and not a dull year like 1939. And then, as if by getting drunk we had performed the ritual that would cause the godhead to manifest itself, Jimmy McAuley, back from the country, came walking down the Quad, walking up to us, joining Fraser, meeting me, and shaking my hand. I was too talkative and my vision was too selective to register much more than a pair of very steady eyes, but when I arrived at the university the next morning Fraser told me that I had made an impression on McAuley and that, if he seemed sad, it was only because my happiness reminded him of his lost youth. I was so pleased with myself that I got a party together – one of the women freethinkers, a Stalinist, Oliver Somerville, a couple of others – and we all went off to the little parlour at Myrtle Street again. Before lunch I was again drunk.

Walls rushed by and the floor sagged. Talk was just clatter, along with the rumble of blood rushing through my head like an underground train. In the lavatory when I vomited I spattered my clothes. Pretending nothing had happened. I tried to drink again, then again hurried off to the lavatory. Fraser, who found me in the street, walked me round and round the block to sober me up. As the houses hurried past I made her a speech about how the slums must be ripped down and replaced by 'decent homes'. When she returned me to the parlour she said: 'Donald wants to start a slum clearance programme.' The Stalinist seemed as amused as the others. I was ashamed of my error. I had forgotten that slum clearance was mere social amelioration. I had revealed myself as a repressed humanitarian.

Like someone at a party who without apology leaves the group he has been talking with and hurries across the room to join the more interesting guests who have just arrived, in the next few weeks I spent little time with Pritchett and other old friends in the Quad, delighting instead in being taken up by the new friends Fraser had introduced me to – but I was afraid they might drop me as quickly as they had taken me up. When McAuley or one of the others appeared at the far end of the Quad, walking towards the cloister, it was as if the lattice gate had clicked at Denbigh after tea on a Sunday night, or there had been a knock on the front door at Muswellbrook; with a visitor everything was about to come to life. My new patrons called me 'Young Donald' and I re-enacted young promise surrounded by its elders. I spoke softly, even more out of the side of my mouth, and I tried to confine myself to witticisms. If I amused them they might let me stay.

Just as once I had developed a simple, caricature sense of the 'characters' of my relations, I now developed a simple, caricature sense of the 'characters' of the new friends Fraser had introduced me to. McAuley had some of the mannerisms of a hypnotist – a careful but slight gesture, sometimes nothing more than a significant stiffening of his long pianist's fingers, would emphasise a point, or he would lower his eyelids, then suddenly raise them, confronting me from beneath blond eyelashes with a piercing stare, his face muscles well controlled to register significant emotion. There were times when his whole body would seem to stiffen and expand, erectile, as if to strike. Like Fraser, but even more pointedly, when he spoke the words would bunch up, quick and monotonous, then there would be the briefest of pauses before the key words struck out, slowly stressed. This was 'J.Mc', who wrote verse. Jimmy the jazz pianist was golden haired, laughing, sometimes frenzied, but behind even the frenzy there was a resilient toughness, a kind of rhythmic control. Metre seemed to be built into his body. Harold Stewart, seemingly second-most significant poet, who had been at Fort Street High School with McAuley, was short and almost without mannerism. With black oiled hair parted in the middle above a cheery reliable face and dressed conventionally, he looked like an honest man of the suburbs come to make some repair to the house, yet his attitude to verse was more purely aesthetic than anyone else's. Stewart lived very sparely and was concerned with little except writing verse or reading verse or looking at art books. To save money on books he sometimes took his typewriter to the public library and made copies of poetry he admired. He was friendly – he seemed to enjoy telling me what to read next as we moved from Ezra Pound to Hart Crane to e.e. cummings – but he could also slash out in conversation, although still smiling. I had no doubt of Stewart's genius, but of A.D. Hope, who was known in this group as 'James', one was less sure, mainly because he went so far back in time – he had graduated in the dark ages of the late 1920s – that he might now be 'burned out'. It was assumed that he was frustrated in his lecturing job in the Teachers' College, but he gave no sign of it. In one of those secretions of external 'character' that protect the young from what may seem quite trivial dangers but thenceforth determine who they 'are', Hope had thrown up around himself ramparts of imperturbable anonymity. He talked softly, with deliberation, but as if he were thinking of something else, faintly smiling as if at some memory, his eyes searching the distance and wisps of hair pointing in other possible directions. Hope had gone on to Oxford from Sydney University, and to me he seemed the finest flowering of European civilisation in Australia, not least because he would talk to me directly and listen to what I had to say, so that I would sometimes talk for a long time, angry that it was all coming out in such a jumble but happy that James seemed to be making something of it. That James was married, had a child, and lived in a house but had not yet 'settled down', gave some hope that one could get older and not lose intellectual integrity. Usually the suburbs seemed quickly to claim back their own.

Ronald Dunlop, another friend of McAuley's, was a case in point. Dunlop seemed undoubtedly a talented minor poet, his verse seemingly as slim and dry as his wit, but although he was still writing he also played golf, almost unimaginable in a poet, and Somerville in particular watched Dunlop like a crow, waiting to swoop onto signs of respectability. Somerville himself had been redefined in my new context – from a revolutionary to a very minor poet – and since an afternoon when he and I had got drunk and I had saved him from a policeman and then taken him back to his parents' house moaning all over me, he seemed a very minor poet who could not hold his liquor. There was another act of redefinition. Although Fraser was writing a novel and there seemed no doubt it would prove very amusing, she did not write verse, and it was only writing verse that mattered. Even Fraser now seemed only a minor figure – little more than a novelist.

SIXTEEN

Do it all at once

On the Sunday afternoon of 3 September it was obvious that another Great War was about to begin. It was still night in England, but when the English had woken up and eaten their breakfasts Neville Chamberlain would tell them they were at war with Germany. When I went to the Domain, Sydney's open-air orators' forum, the Trotskyist speakers were sure that capitalist reaction in Australia was about to strike them down. 'I'm going to hide in the mountains,' one of them said as he took down his revolutionary banners and stacked them into a cardboard box. The Domain was nearly deserted. I went home in an electric train that was almost empty, past the factory where years before someone had daubed up the big slogan

$$\text{NOT} \begin{cases} \text{A MAN} \\ \text{A SHIP} \\ \text{A GUN} \end{cases} \text{FOR BOSSES WAR}$$

and when I got home and had tea I settled down with Mum and Dad to a game of bridge. We kept the wireless on and we stopped playing when Chamberlain came on the air and told us we were at war. 'Ah well, it had to come', Dad said, and he shuffled the spare pack while Mum dealt a new hand.

Like the generals, we on the liberty front had prepared ourselves to fight the previous war, and in the Quad our immediate concern was for the preservation of our liberties against outbreaks of jingoism, war hysteria, white feathers and false atrocity stories. When a German member of the teaching staff, alleged to be a Nazi, was interned, John Anderson immediately called a protest meeting of the Freethought Society, and among the desks in the philosophy lecture theatre we waited with courage for the first onslaughts on academic freedom. Democracy, which in the 1930s seemed to have only a chance of survival, might now be destroyed, not by the Nazis, but by the forces of reaction in Australia who would use the war as an excuse. Would Anderson still be able to walk across the Quad when the carillon played 'God Save the King'?

Poland had been seized so quickly that it was almost as if it had not happened. And now nothing was happening. Hitler could not fight a long war, we believed, because he did not have the gold reserves, and the German generals were not behind him. The Allies had called his bluff. In protest against a 'National Register', in which all males of eighteen and over were to register with the government and which was clearly the thin edge of absolutism, I tried to burn a National Register card in the Quad, but its thick cardboard would only smoulder. One of the main interests in this non-war was to attack the university Stalinists for the switch in the party line: according to the Stalinists and the fellow-travellers Russia had struck an enormous blow for freedom by saving the White Russians and Ukrainians from Polish oppression, and it was obvious that the war was nothing but a clash between rival imperialisms, of no interest to the working class. Some of the freethinkers were as suspicious of the war as the Stalinists because they knew all governments were predatory. One of them detected an immense Stalinist–British connivance in which Winston Churchill, although only First Lord of the Admiralty, was the main manipulator, dealing secretly with Stalin, provoking Hitler into war.

I had put the *Daily Telegraph* war map on the wall of my bedroom to follow the progress of the fighting, but with nothing happening on the Western Front, and with the Eastern Front turned into two huge and tragic prisons, there was nothing further to look at on the map and nothing more to think about the war. The Siegfried Line and the Maginot Line were clearly marked, so I would know where they were in case I needed them. What now mattered was that there were problems of conscience to solve in my attitudes to verse. I liked Eliot's early verse, but the freethinkers attacked it as mere poetical journalism, meretricious rhetoric. They maintained that, even in expressing the incoherent, one still had to be coherent, that one should distinguish between the *real presentation of distortion and the distorted presentation of reality*. This incantation was to go on rattling in my head for years afterwards, but McAuley found a way out from the particular back alley of Eliot's early verse, telling me that it was true that the scenes in it dissolved into each other disconnectedly, as in a surrealist movie, but there was an underlying connection – a connection of emotional continuity. It was as if I had found an escape clause in a difficult piece of legislation.

I skimmed several of the 'metaphysical poets' who, after being packed away for a couple of centuries as far-fetched, were now to the modern taste (although not yet in Australian high schools) – Donne, sometimes, astonishingly direct (I quoted 'For Godsake hold your tongue and let me love', in and out, for a season) and some Marvell (very 'fresh' writing); and then, picking up a clue from somewhere, a few 'minor Elizabethan dramatists', Marlowe mainly (very 'readable'), on whose death in a tavern I wrote a poem. Then I settled down to Baudelaire, who in the Philosophy Room had been declared a realist. Given this dispensation, I was able to enjoy images of Baudelaire's romanticism – the fragrance of sultry breasts on warm, autumn evenings, the stink of filthy clothes, the cold teeth of a woman's chopped-off head, flies buzzing in the rotting belly of a hanged man. *Oh, Satan, take pity, on my long misery*! Convinced that only putrefaction of the soul could ennoble it, I wrote a long poem in my Baudelairean period to ... *a vicious Negress, bare, except for clumps of stinking rusty hair*. I began to invent fictitious sadness, claiming the sorrows of Charles Baudelaire or Jimmy McAuley rather than my own. Thus I would write *She yields him the earth, the monotone of growth, but yet the torture etched upon his brain equivocates the warm of summer rain and tempers any spring to winter's sloth*, but I knew that as yet no 'She' had yielded me anything.

It also seemed important that Baudelaire regarded virtue and beauty as matters that had to be contrived with the concern for minute detail of a dandy attending to his dress in front of a mirror. The idea of contrivance and artificiality appealed, as it did while I was reading Oscar Wilde. I needed, in Ezra Pound's word, a persona, a mask, a 'character': I must appear to be some particular, recognisable and predictable kind of man who always did the same kind of things. I did not know what the mess of motives was that pushed me around, but I knew that I must hide it behind some kind of front, so that whatever I did would seem to be something I meant to do. I wanted to be like James Hope, apparently as impassive as an effigy carried in a street procession, undisturbed by the jolting from below and the comments of the passers by. And yet bits of me would keep on running from behind the mask, as if I were a troupe of tumblers. Even 'naturalness' was contrived: it lay in reciting border ballads in a misty voice or singing nineteenth-century English music-hall numbers or 1920s American Syndicalist songs. Above all, being 'natural' consisted of singing blues. I discovered the blues one afternoon when we sat in Fraser's mother's house while Jimmy played 'St Louis Blues', 'St James Infirmary' and some other blues numbers on the gramophone. I stared ahead, my line of vision adjusted a few inches above the gramophone on the floor, but keeping my eye on McAuley's foot so that my foot would keep time with his. The toes of my right foot pressed my right shoe up and down, a fraction of a beat behind McAuley's.

When I first looked through Laforgue's verse I had to seek help to supplement the inadequacies of Leaving Certificate French, but I was entranced by this poetry of metropolitanism, allusive and ironic, restless, 'modern'. The habit of inserting literary quotations into school essays now extended to coffee table conversation, so that when I picked up from Eliot a line like *Que la vie est quotidienne* I used it as a kind of special punctuation point, thinking of life in the suburbs of Sydney. I stopped reading Eliot when it occurred to me that in some of his earlier pieces he had simply stolen Laforgue's imagination, his rhythms, some of his phrases, representing them more heavily and sadly, without Laforgue's lightness. Eliot seemed a hoax poet, a counterfeiter, going beyond 'influence' to theft.

I heard talk of Rilke, Novalis, Verlaine, Rimbaud, de Nerval, but I had read only a few snatches of them, although for a season I took every opportunity of reminding my listeners that de Nerval was once found outside the Palais Royal leading a lobster on a blue ribbon, because, he said, it knew the secrets of the sea and did not bark. It was from Mallarmé, the very fountainhead of disconnectedness, (borrowed from the Municipal Library, with French on one side and an English translation opposite) that I tried to work out something that would allow me to like what I liked while staying faithful to the realist aesthetic. As a secret vice, I was privately attracted by the idea of the *frisson*, the shock of an image, or of a violent juxtaposition of images, and I yearned simply to shock irrelevantly, to shock for shock's sake. But this would be mere rhetoric. I decided that *frissons* were all right if they shocked attention towards a real theme, and I seized on the idea of 'objective correlations', concrete images that symbolised subjective emotional states, thus talking myself into believing that the 'real theme' of a poem could run silently beneath its surface with the lucidity of an algebraic equation, but it had to be puzzled out, like symptoms in a neurosis, by examining the broken surface for indications of what was going on underneath. Again, nothing was what it seemed. For a while I wrote verse according to this theory. I considered I had solved the problem of my approach to verse when I wrote the following:

The chantry emptied, all its bells now ring
Their loud hosannas to a new born king.
The penitent who shades his cheeks with grey,
Can look with terror on the coming day.

The promise of the apple, brought to fruit,
Has now reduced to slavery the Mute
Who in his temple once could shake a sword
Where now he dumbly serves an upstart Lord.

The cloth is disarrayed, and spilt the wine.
The crumbled loaf is cast upon the floor
That lustful youth, commensurate with law,
May bounce upon a bed to mock his crime.

While through the streets there walks a steadfast bride,
Her vision lost ... discomforted her smile ...
The strangeness of her beauty floats awhile
Until before a door she stills her pride.

Who would know what that meant?

Perhaps I was sufficiently aware of the triteness of what I had to say to prefer to hide it. I felt anxious because at the age of seventeen no new and original awareness of the human condition had yet come to me. I had the feeling I must pretend to something rather than be nothing. Later I might know how I was going to see things. The greatest anxiety lay in the idea of a 'real theme'. If I had a real theme worth stating, why not state it in logical form rather than obscure it in verse? Some of the freethinkers saw verse as an inferior form of literature. What if they were correct? There were times when it was tempting to consider that perhaps what I had heard of Novalis was true, that poetry might exist altogether without intellectual meaning, that it was a 'reasoned derangement of the senses'. I was not courageous enough to discuss this heretical view with anyone except Harold Stewart, who – to my surprise – regarded it with equanimity. As in a kind of Black Mass I secretly wrote two sonnets that were deliberately meaningless, one of them expressed in colours (*The yellowed masses and the darkened brown now shade into the twinkling greens which splay the steadfast silver. Red can then stream down to speed the inertness of black and grey*), the other in geometrical forms (*The broken lines have rolled into their sphere; the nervous tangents, falling ever past, are strengthening into spirals in the rear ...*), but I was not bold enough to show them even to Stewart. When Stewart instructed me in surrealism I secretly entered a surrealist period and wrote a long poem with the refrain *And Romeo to Juliet will spill it on a serviette*. Since I had written something that was a distortion of reality I was afraid I might be caught out, as I was when I had written 'shit' on a chocolate box. Stewart was my guide to the experimentalism of the immediate past – dadaism, gagaism, art exhibitions in lavatories. But to be concerned with deliberately shocking and provoking seemed *vieux jeu* (although one might shock by accident). It was amusing enough in its old-fashioned attempt to make it new, but by 1939 nothing seemed so obsolete as novelty.

Among McAuley and his friends there was a contempt for anything that was now happening. There was a particular distaste for the shoddiness of practically everything at that time being written in England: Eliot, Pound and Joyce had declined; contemporary American literature was a clamour of affected primitivists; England had been seized by literary smarties, some of them Stalinists; and Australia, of course, was a literary dungheap in which a few featherless cocks crowed with literary nationalism or puffed themselves up with the second-rate. The times were so bad that one did not bother to talk about them.

WITH THE FREETHINKERS THERE WAS THE SAME DISDAIN EXT-
ended to McAuley, whose verse they attacked behind his back. As a member
of the Freethought Society and of the Literary Society I was now sometimes
talked to by Anderson in the Quad. He had a habit of laughing nervously
while still talking, and he adopted this style when he held up the latest *Hermes*
between thumb and forefinger, the pages flapping. 'What's McAuley trying
to say?' he asked us. 'He seems to be sad about something. But what does it
mean?' I said nothing. I had been moved by McAuley's prose piece in *Hermes*
about how he went home, but could not talk to his parents. 'Terrible stuff ...
terrible', said one of the freethinkers. I said nothing.

In being a freethinker I now shared with a small group of people the
exclusive revelation of a 'thoroughly worked out philosophical position' which
cast the only true light on all fields of inquiry. Ideally its truths were passed on
in lectures, from the voice at the rostrum into pen and paper, then by being
learned off at home they passed into the body for ever, but since I was not yet
enrolled in the philosophy courses I had to content myself with conversation
in the Quad and reading some of the fragments of Anderson's 'position' that he
had written into articles. I was thrilled by his implacable lack of compromise
and the way he argued stubbornly and passionately against almost everything
said by anyone apart from the freethinkers at Sydney University. From our
oral culture in the Quad I had now made my own sketch of what, apart from
the realist aesthetic and the heroism of the producer ethic, most interested
me in Anderson's 'position'. I understood vaguely that as a philosopher it was
important to him that 'there are only facts, that is occurrences in space and
time' (although I had no idea what this meant), but what seemed of more
importance was his belief in 'pluralism' extending into his theories of what
constituted human minds and human societies.

I now believed that the mind was a battleground of passions, of complex
impulses striving to relieve their tension, warring with each other and with
the objects of their striving. The 'self' was the ground fought over, nothing
more. In any other sense there was no 'self'. What we 'were' at any particular
time was simply a progress report on what passions were occupying the
commanding heights at the latest stage of the long battle. And just as there
was struggle within the mind, there was struggle between the mind and what
went on outside it. To 'know' something was not to mirror it in the mind

but to strive with *complex occurrences in space and time*. This view of the mind as a vast complication of passions, struggling for supremacy with each other and with the objects of their striving, was repeated in a view of society as an arena of tension and struggle between *social forces*. The approach to any particular society was to ask 'Of what *conflicts* is it the scene?' as, in passing the Colosseum, a Roman might have asked, 'What's on today?' Both in the mind and in society life was a matter of unceasing *conflict*, in which all that seemed certain was uncertainty. Had not Heraclitus, Anderson's favorite pre-Socratic philosopher, said that one should expect the unexpected? To expect immunity from risk, to demand safety, was simply to engage in phantasy. Worse, such demands threatened the very existence of a high culture, which was generated from incessant struggle. When society became secure liberty and culture declined. If there were no evils in society life might not be worth living.

For both Anderson and McAuley, to be a certain kind of recognisable person in external behaviour – to maintain a certain purity of style – mattered more than any other particular achievement. Nothing could be sacrificed to their pride in remaining 'themselves'. McAuley was saved from destruction by his brilliance and, when that imperilled him, he was saved because other people looked after him, conniving and arranging on his behalf. Anderson had all he wanted, a professor's freehold with the chance to build up his 'school' of philosophy, so he could delight in his almost unparalleled record of defeat in everything else. He was a no-man, to whom to be political was to engage in *phantasy*. Events were determined by their history. There was nothing to be done about them. No point in trying to influence them. Social forces *just had to fight it out*. What mattered was talking about things rather than getting something out of them or trying to change them. Anderson did not want to reform anything. He wanted to oppose everything. To him democracy was opposition. Beyond a few chosen fields, he despised anybody who did anything. What mattered was to sustain the style of an Andersonian, as to Pa it had mattered that he should sustain the style of a Carpenter.

IN THE WORLD OUTSIDE IT WAS AN AGE OF SIMPLE JOURNALISTIC alternatives – communism or fascism? Catholic or communist? evolutionary socialism or revolutionary socialism? – and one of the more gentle alternatives was Barbara Wootten's *Plan or No Plan?* The word 'planning' was already obtaining a small vogue among a few university-trained people. There had been an article in *Hermes* suggesting that the government should recruit university graduates as officials (to Anderson this represented a threat to academic freedom), and now there was talk about planning for the war. To freethinkers any kind of planning was 'social engineering' and therefore voluntarist and based on invalid argument by analogy, but I began to meet those who thought otherwise. One of these was Alan G. Crawford, another poet, whose time at the university stretched back almost as long as James Hope's but who, even when he had set up as a solicitor downtown, still acted in the background of student politics, among other things playing the role of poet's politician to ensure that *Hermes* survived the indifference or hatred of most of the students. As with Hope, the fact that Crawford's age had not thrown him back into the suburbs gave promise for the future. Fraser introduced him as a poet's politician, and, just as Crawford had taken up Jimmy McAuley in his first year in Arts in 1935, I was now beginning to hope that he would take up Young Donald in 1939. I would listen to him for hours, as he told the behind-scenes history of *Hermes* speaking softly and quickly, with the same use of stress as Fraser and McAuley, but adding 'you see' for extra emphasis, and knocking off ash with his forefinger as if he were striking a sharp note on the piano, his moustache moving sideways with his mouth, his glasses glinting, and his left hand thrust confidently into his trouser pocket, folding part of his jacket back under it, in one of the classic poses of oratory. Crawford stood for intelligence against stupidity, but the cause of intelligence was not to be carried forward in a reckless crusade but as a matter of infinitely careful contrivance. *Pas trop de zèle.* He had spent years in student politics trying to manipulate things so that somewhere intelligence would survive. He was a master of committee manoeuvre – when to move the previous business, when to get consideration of the matter adjourned, how to pass a note significantly across the table, when to impress by remaining silent, how to give an opponent enough rope to hang himself. He would also entrance with anecdotes of lobbying – when to flatter, when to tell a white lie, when to point to the possibly disastrous consequences of a certain kind of action, or alternatively to the limitless possibilities that might open out, when to lobby someone else to lobby someone to lobby someone else – wheels within wheels. He delighted in the idea of backroom influence, exhorting me to stay out of the limelight and carry out my policies through others: his special delight was that a loose network of persons, privately helping each other, had continued to exert their intelligence, keeping a bright light shining in the darkness of Sydney University. To this cause he had entirely devoted his enormous political skills, but now there was a chance that, through 'planning', intelligence might begin to shine into the black recesses of government.

Perhaps one of its vehicles might prove to be Alf Conlon, a friend of Crawford's, and of much the same age, graduated in Arts some years before, but now back at the university as a medical student. The generous curves of Conlon's face, his slow, thoughtful speech, the bluntness of his style and his mannerisms with his pipe – sucking it between words, pointing it at someone he was talking to, rubbing the back of his neck with it – hypnotised with their straightforwardness, softened by a surprising mildness and good humour. He seemed the ordinary man, yet when he talked he could conjure up great visions, as if the smoke from his pipe was being shaped into mirages of wisdom. In his speech he had a trick of Laforgue's – unexpected juxtapositions of slang and technical terms. 'I've got a feeling in my water ... young Donald ... that what this country really needs is a good sociology.' He would linger over 'sociology', with a long stress on each syllable, chew on his pipe for a while, then point it. 'And it's people like you who will provide it.' I had scarcely heard the word 'sociology', but I would wave my glass of beer in general agreement and wait silently to see what Alf wanted me to do. He spent an hour or so at a party outlining the theory of functional disorders – something I had once read about in the *Daily Telegraph* but could not properly understand – explaining everything slowly and carefully, brushing aside interruptions as if we were conspiring over some great deal. Conlon was the students' representative on the university senate and he was meeting there people who knew people who ran things in Australia. He was talking some of the language of planning, using words like 'scientific manpower control' that did not seem to have meaning – enlivening the imagination with the romance of manipulation and the language of change, peering into the future of the war for exciting possibilities. New ideas were coming. New things would happen. And we would be in among them. Perhaps it was true that this was only voluntarism, that it was social forces that moved men, not men who moved social forces, but, speaking some of the language of scholarship, Conlon eyed events speculatively and in a way that promised fun.

I was drinking coffee in a city coffee shop as I looked over UNI EXAM RESULTS in an afternoon newspaper: I had come only tenth in English Honours and History Honours. Ah well, I hadn't done much work ... There was more than that to think about. In particular: How could I be all things? How could I think everything and do everything, first this, then that? How could I exercise myself in contradictions? In the Philosophy Room, Anderson was right. In the Quad, McAuley was right. In the pub, Conlon was right. I would pass from group to group and take on some of its colour, seeing the attractions of one side, then feeling what it was like to be this kind of person, and then betraying him to the next. Always what *moved*, what *rebelled* was best, but there were so many rebellions within these rebellions. I could not put them together and so achieve an enormous subtlety: instead I could only blurt out simplicities, only part of what I saw, and then – somewhere else, in some other company – some other part of what I saw, some contradictory simplicity that made me a traitor to my earlier self. If, as I went off home in a train, all these complexities could push together in my head so that I could feel their opposition, why could I not put them together in conversation and speak in the kind of depth I felt in my mind? But then who could I speak them to? I could no longer think thoughts of my own, as I had done at school. In my head now there was nothing but the impressions of other people's opinions.

STEWART HAD LENT ME A BOOK OF WORLD-FAMOUS PAINTINGS AND I had wandered through them as through a gallery, staring at the chiaroscuro of *Giorgione's Concert Champêtre* for longer than if I had been looking at it in the Louvre or examining the precise fantasy of Bosch's *The Temptation of St Anthony* more carefully than if I were inspecting it in the Prado. As my guide Stewart would point to the serenity of the breast in Fouquet's *Madonna and Child* or the sense of movement of Rembrandt's *Polish Rider*. But now we had something that went beyond books – an admirably complex exhibition of more than 200 French and British post-impressionist and late-impressionist paintings. It seemed to be all modernity in one go, an amazing show put together by the *Melbourne Herald*, on the instructions of Sir Keith Murdoch, and brought to Sydney, as one would expect from our only progressive newspaper, by the *Daily Telegraph*. I went to it on some spare afternoons during the week, but it was on our Saturday visits (every Saturday) with Stewart as guide, that it most 'came to life'. In theory, we specialised in four isms – cubism, surrealism, pointillism and, of course, impressionism itself, even if that term seemed too wide – and, in just looking at paintings, we specialised in Picasso, Braque, Matisse, Léger, Modigliani, Cézanne, Van Gogh, Bonnard, Dali, Chagall, Toulouse-Lautrec, Derain, Chiroco, Dufy, Roualt. In one visit Stewart spent much of the time simply on the nine Picassos. I also liked the pieces by Vlaminck, Marquet, Utrillo and Sickert, but since Stewart had nothing to say about them, I had to look at them by myself during the week. In the hours I spent in this exhibition I seemed to pick up interests and perspectives equal to those I had gained in the year's reading.

Much of our talking about cubism or pointillism, along with French symbolist poems or Trotskyism or other enthusiasms of the year, took place at Sherry's, a nondescript café where we happened to go after our first visit to the exhibition; it was run by a couple of refugees but they did it in a way that made it seem, in appearance, as Australian as possible. I began to look forward to Saturday afternoons at Sherry's as I used to look forward to Sunday afternoons at Denbigh. Somerville later wrote some couplets about it ('Within a café where they sit, baking by halves the pie of wit' ... 'Occasionally they make a pun, merely to show it is not done', etc) but they were about a later, more dispirited period; in the summer of 1939–40 it became for me a symbol of predictability, like memories of Pa casting his line into the water at Yowie Bay, or Dad rolling a cigarette. I am sitting at a table at Sherry's: McAuley's fingers tighten with emphasis; Somerville mimes sorrow, bending over his coffee cup; Hope looks across the room and smiles and sips his China tea; Stewart tells a feline joke; Fraser frowns slightly before softly reciting several lines from a poem; one of the woman freethinkers rolls a cigarette; Crawford leans forward and points a finger. Norma Abernethy, McAuley's 'girlfriend' smiles as beatifically as a madonna in one of Stewart's art books.

It was from Sherry's that I went, with McAuley, to my first allnight party. Among the bottles and glasses and people I staggered from group to group, forgetting to mumble, confident in every wild thing I said. I vomited over the lavatory floor, bringing up the pineapple I had eaten at supper, the first time

I had eaten pineapple as a salad vegetable; but I would not go home or stop drinking. The woman I had taken to the party went home with someone else. As dawn approached almost everyone had gone and the drink had run out, but by mixing together the leftovers in the people's glasses we kept on making it a party. McAuley was at the window, talking intently; I could not hear what he was saying. Now it was dawn and I could go ... I awoke several hours later and clattered home through the sultry haze of the suburbs in one of the almost empty electric trains of Christmas Day. It had been my job to put out the decorations, but Mum had done it. Dad had set up Janet's Christmas tree. The next day I would be eighteen. It had been a long year.

SEVENTEEN

Extract from a student's notebook

Summer, 1939–40

It took a long time to free myself from Oliver Somerville. We had been drinking sauternes at a sly groggery until the girls drifted off disconnectedly. Somerville, in sandshoes and without socks (a gesture to a world that would otherwise have failed to see him), led me around the city, cursing his empty pockets in high-pitched, cultured tones while I pointed out to him the droll workings of his neurotic mind. Somerville began moaning a dirty song. He collapsed on the steps of the General Post Office as we watched a drunken businessman (who looked like a Roman Senator) twist in and out of its colonnade. Somerville began to tear off his sandshoes. This was too much. Somerville was a fool. It was time to play another part. 'Oh for Christ's sake!' I said. 'Bugger off. Go home!' Somerville looked up. 'Lost all initiative,' he wailed. I smiled. 'I'll be your initiative, Oliver.' I walked him down to Wynyard station, put him on a tram and waved him good-bye.

Pleased at having pushed the wreck of the rocks, as I walked up the ramp I wondered what I would do next. I wanted to see the sun rise across the Harbour, but it was not midnight yet. I looked in a bookstall but there was nothing worth reading. It was raining slightly when I caught a tram. Why did I have to be lonely? Not one person in a million would force himself into these hours of boredom. I got out and sat in a tramshed. A drunk was talking to me. A man's best friend is his mother, he told me. I agreed with him energetically and shut off my mind. Yes. Yes. Now repeat the last thing he said. Give him a cigarette. Still talking about mothers. He never married. He has a mother fixation. Probably thinks I am listening. Probably likes me. He went to the last war. Love your mother and go to the war. No don't go to the war, he tells me. Too young. Don't go to the war unless you get a commission. 'Well, good-bye, old man.' Amusing hypocrisy. He's just an animal. I stretched my body and walked along to another tramshed.

I hoped I didn't sit next to a syphilitic. An old abo was playing a gumleaf mouth organ. Told me his leg was gone. When your leg's gone yer no good. The blackfellers used to own the place. Dinkum Aussies. How about a drink of metho, Sandy? Sandy was too drunk to reply. I walked off. A drunk was trying to seduce a woman into a taxi. No, she was going by tram. She stroked her gloves for reassurance. She was too busy for men. She pulled her gloves tighter. Further on was a drunken harlot, crying and cursing and smoking. Sandy's cobber was with her, speaking Great War French. I went up to the railway cafeteria. I was hungry.

Sodden food. Sleeping drunks. Too much coffee. Loud talking workmen. Women smiling at me when their soldier 'friends' weren't looking. I began to tremble as I walked around outside. I was tired of the whole thing but it was too late to go home now. The stupid attendant on the fruit stall kept nervously rearranging his fruit. Lorries were unloading. I went back to the cafeteria.

There were a number of us at the table now. The sailor was buying more pots of coffee. The police had taken away a man. 'You can't look sideways at this time of the morning,' said one of the coves sitting at our table. 'I'd better do me shirt up,' said his cobber. I had never expected to sit with such people, but, now that I was, the only worry was what to say. I pushed out my bottom lip significantly. The woman – the sailor's pick-up – was singing softly. She was eyeing me with a mixture of amusement, curiosity and hatred. It must be of some significance that she had put my hand between her thighs and held it here. I felt my lips moving. I told some dirty jokes and everyone laughed. Perhaps she would take me into the park? But she might have syphilis! Then the sailor and his pick-up got up. She patted my cheeks and pulled my nose. 'Good-bye, little weasel-face.'

As I walked down to the Harbour the city seemed beautiful. Even its nineteenth-century statues and imitation skyscrapers and milk carts. There was a breeze coming in from the Harbour. This was what I wanted. Peaceful solitude. There was a ferry waiting at the wharf in the half daylight. Some of its lights were still on. I gave one of my last threepences to the attendant. I smoked fretfully, leaning on the rail of the top deck. I was back in the world now and I had to strive to be happy or poetic or something equally foolish. I went into the cabin and sat looking at the few men and women, already dressed for work. I sneered at them but I wished that I had the money for breakfast ...

TO DREAM A DREAM AND THEN, STIMULATED BY THE DREAMING hours and neglecting the waking hours, to work all one's life for its execution. It is not a matter of success or failure, or profit or loss, it is the joy of execution, the knowledge that one is living the only life one will have with all the speed and tempo of modern music and all the colour of a modern painting.

WHEN I ARRIVED AT SHERRY'S ONLY DUNLOP WAS THERE. WE talked for a while and then Ron went off to play golf. I wonder if he will go on writing verse. I hated being by myself at the table so I rushed outside – without even a rationalisation for doing so. Big storm in my head. It was better on the pavement, with all the people walking by. When Stewart and the others turned up, we went back in. That dreadful ejaculation _ _ _ came in. We tried not to talk to him but we finished the afternoon by going to Adam's Marble Bar, where he shouted us some drinks. Then we got rid of him. We had hamburgers and eggs for tea. Then we went back to Sherry's to talk for a while, then caught a tram to Norma Abernethy's. (Her parents are away.) Arrived too early. It was a good party. Everyone there. Except for some awful bastard who broke up what was left of the party by throwing bottles over the fence.

I was going to spend the night at McAuley's parents' house. A long walk to Stanmore station with McAuley and Stewart. Norma's dog followed us until we chased it away. It seemed strange walking down suburban streets with them. A train journey and another long but fascinating walk. We ate some watermelon at McAuley's, discussing Joyce and Yeats, and so to McAuley's bed and he to a bed on the verandah. Awoke at 7.30 and read some of the Laforgue he had on his dressing-table. Very simple room. Clean. Neat. I absorbed its atmosphere. Found McAuley's mother in the kitchen. While he was still asleep she talked about him. She calls him 'Jim', which makes him sound like some other person. Like my mother calling me 'Don'. She thinks that 'Jim' is even better than he thinks he is himself. And so he is. As a very young boy she used to read him *Tiger Tim*. One day she was too busy. Said McAuley in a rage: 'You wait! I'll read it when I go to school!' He learned to read in two months. By the time he was seven his father was exhibiting him – Jim reading leaders from the *Sydney Morning Herald*. N.B. Mothers and fathers ...

Why do I sometimes still give a horrid sneer?

THE SIX OF US WALKED DOWN THE STREET TOGETHER. I STAYED outside the coffee shop for a moment or two to read the headlines on a news stand. When I walked in Dorothy was pushing the spare chair away.

She didn't want me to sit there. Peter had pushed her hand away. While she was busy demolishing her repulsive air of hard-boiled sophistication to assume a more kittenish air I sat down on the disputed seat. She was wearing that stupid, pretentious hat. I tipped it down over her eyes. I would have liked to smash her in the teeth.

I had a hell of a headache. Perhaps they were all going to turn on me. The struggle between Dorothy and me for a place in this group was becoming too obvious and ugly to last much longer.

When the orders for afternoon tea were taken I ordered nothing, not having more than the fare home. I couldn't borrow money this afternoon. It would put me at a disadvantage. I didn't talk much. I'd sooner have had a sleep or a bath than shift around in this uncomfortable chair smoking too much and occasionally trying to say something. But I must last out and settle the matter. I swung back in the chair and played with somebody else's coffee spoon, clumsy, nervous and worn out. Now and again I mumbled unintelligibly. There were long silences in the conversation. Then too many words. I hated Dorothy. My mind was barely functioning, but I made some near-insulting remarks to her. More from habit than anything else. She defended herself. I surprised her by agreeing. Of course. Of course. She had got the point. I could make things pleasant now. Nobody else had noticed. The others were talking to each other, obscurely, making secret references to some mysterious subject. They were trying to push Dorothy out of the conversation! She was the one they didn't want!

She liked triumph. She had thought she was going to defeat me. Now *she* was being defeated. She sat it out for a while, trying to direct all this spite against someone else. She was grimacing and taking it all with a vulgar, clownish assumption of good-humoured mystification. Using some of her pet phrases like 'What a lovely thought!' But she couldn't get way with it. She was the bad smell of the party. Not, as she had hoped, me.

The conversation blundered on. When she got up she said she thought she'd have to go. Two of us said good-bye to her. I smiled at her. The other two ignored her. I'm sure that as she walked away she congratulated herself on the clever way she had got out of it. Ostracism is a fearful thing. Some overcome it with some wretched pomposity or other. Most don't understand, of course, or are too stupid to have the experience. A sense of injustice always surrounds it. You can get used to it. It's the first moments that hurt the worst. When you realise they don't want you ...

ALAN CRAWFORD HAS THE ABILITY TO WALK INTO A ROOM AS IF HE were descending a magnificent sweep of stairs. I wish I could walk into a room like Crawford.

He can add drama to stirring a cup of coffee, or silence a conversation by pursing his lips and making a slight sucking noise. People wait to know what he is going to say ...

When I got home I found that everyone was out. I dreaded being by myself at home. I sat down and turned on the wireless. Someone was talking about God (pronounced 'Gard'): '... and it's only in moments of complete quiet and solitude that you find Gard.' Next station. Something about our brave boys. Next station. Swing music. Next station. Mozart. Next station. Off the air. I left the wireless tuned into the station that was off the air and went into the bathroom to look at my face. Hated it. Smash it to pieces, tear it up. Pour flames over it. Make it look *older* ...

EDITH AND SOMERVILLE AND I WENT INTO THE SARGENT'S CAFÉ, famous for its meat pies. Somerville, with his hands in his pockets, his shoulders laughing at the world, his hat well down in the approved proletarian manner, stalked in with an evil air. My fair hair was falling down on my forehead at the correct poetic angle and my necktie was appropriately loosened. I was dreaming of nothing in particular except the engrossing problem of looking like myself. Edith, her face brown except for her red splashed lips, walked in smoking behind us. We sat down and ordered three famous meat pies.

'There is, of course', I said, 'a distinction between the person who eats famous meat pies because he likes them and doesn't know the difference and the person who eats them because he thinks them amusing.' I wasn't sure whether I had said that as well as I should have. 'Don't be ridiculous, Donald,' said Somerville. 'That's a snobbish attitude.' I thought of how Somerville had told me that he sometimes dreamed of himself as an Irish gentleman and of how he would sometimes say of someone that he should be horsewhipped. Somerville was telling Edith that she was beautiful. She laughed at him. He told her she was an ignorant bitch. 'The force of that phrase is almost lost now, Oliver,' she said. 'Yes ... yes ... yes ...' Somerville was silent for some time. Then he began coughing so violently that he made his nose bleed. He pointed out to us what a disgusting sight he was. I watched the blood. 'Stop watching me in that morbid manner, Donald.' 'Middle distance, middle distance,' I murmured back, pleased with the answer. Edith asked Somerville if he had any dreams lately. 'Yes, I dreamed I was walking down a long, dark tunnel with you, Edith, and halfway down you pushed me out and told me to go back and sell suitcases where I belong. I always said you were a bastard.' 'You always dream the most obvious dreams, Oliver.' 'Ah, Edith, you are always in my dreams.' 'But I'm sure I'm only a symbol.' 'Ah, too true!'

I changed the subject. 'Did you hear some thunder this morning, Oliver?' 'Yes indeed. Blow winds and crack your cheeks rage blow you cataracts and hurricanes spout till you have drench'd our steeples, drown'd our cocks.' I laughed. 'You utter bastard, Donald.' I had asked this question of him before: 'What do you think of *Lear*, Oliver?' 'I try not to; slovenly pieces of dramatic workmanship to be found and the rest not much better.' 'Yes, I think so too,' said Edith. I had forgotten the point I was going to make. I felt tired. 'Give me a cigarette, Edith.' 'Oh, Donald, you're a bastard. I'm sick of being the gentleman. Why don't you buy a packet yourself?' I smiled and took the cigarette and lit my own and Edith's and blew smoke over Somerville. 'Do you know anything about the physical characteristics of homos?' I asked him. 'No,

Donald. The three homos I have met had entirely different characteristics.' 'Do you know anything about lesbians?' Edith asked. '*The lesbian shall find a man, the fornicator turn woman-hater.*' 'Oh shut up, Oliver. We've been hearing that all day.' 'Every woman should hear it three times a day with meals.'

We got up, Edith and Somerville putting their chairs back under the table while I left mine sprawling. As we went through the park I tried to walk like McAuley. Edith was humming a tune. Somerville was carrying on an obscure monologue, occasionally broken by fits of coughing or cries of 'Christ! Oh Christ! Oh Christ!' I began to think how beautiful Edith was. All I said was, 'I want a gin squash.' Was I just becoming a habit with these people? A nuisance? I didn't say much, except when I was drunk. Why did they let me stay with them? Nothing was said when Edith said she was going. I watched her walk away, gently poised. 'I wonder ...' said Somerville, shaking his head. 'Wonder what?' 'Ah, Donald ... you'll find out some day.' Somerville went off, too. I stayed by myself, smiling at nothing ...

FILLED IN A NUMBER OF NATIONAL REGISTER CARDS IN SPURIOUS names. A spanner in the bureaucratic machinery. Read Thucydides until tea. A quarrel with my father, whom I answered back in a bullying way. Curse me! Read several pieces by Catullus after tea ...

THE WORLD IS MINE AND I MIGHT TURN MY ATTENTION TO ANY part of it. But my gaze is still turned inward, too numbed by the sudden loss of the tawdry rubbish that it still treasures. I walk through a grand emptiness for many hours like a clumsy clockwork doll, mouthing what the clockwork makes me say. Both friends and enemies scorn me. I can do nothing except represent the merest scraps thrown away by others.

Where you think the actuality of yourself lies, there lies nothing. When you look for yourself both hunter and hunted disappear. No man can know himself but he sometimes has a feeling of recollection of undergone experience. But this is no more himself than anybody else. He knows what he remembers but he cannot know what it is that remembers. Within memory there is true and false. The struggle goes on. Why should the true win? ...

WOKE UP WITH A SWOLLEN EYELID. THE HOPE OF SEEING LILY MADE me go into town nevertheless. Bought an eyeshade at Kogarah Station and being an exhibitionist enjoyed the pipe–eyeshade combination. Into the city where I handed in four library books. In Repin's coffee shop met Nield and Pritchett. Remember discussing Byron, Shelley and Keats. Nield likes Byron, thinks Shelley is a 'bastard'. Pritchett likes all three. The glorious Lily joins. She makes some comment on my eyeshade. Then she doesn't look at me. They discuss a psychological question. Then, looking at her all the time, I discuss the war. Some others join us and we have lunch. Talk about Freud and Trotskyism. I had a Russian salad. Price, a shilling. Talk for a couple of hours after lunch, mainly anecdotes. Fraser joins us and the conversation burns even brighter. Then Lily went. Won't see her until Monday. Fraser recites Housman. Then home. God! Will I ever do any work! ...

EIGHTEEN

Lessons from life

I had framed and put on my desk a flattering picture of myself taken in a street in Sydney, an eighteen-year-old striding along in new light grey double-breasted suit, cigarette in mouth, a glint of sun in hair, eyes set straight and firm, mouth ready. I would often look at this picture, seeing myself as the hero impelled forward from something forgotten towards something unknown, alert to the strange beauties and unimaginable threats of his mysterious journey. Experience! Once I had penetrated its secrets, I would really have 'something to say'.

In the meantime there was a move to reform the student revue. I had heard a great deal about this, and wanted to be part of it. In the running of the revue, intelligence must now take over from stupidity. Instead of a series of disconnected and independently arranged acts, there must be a script, thoroughly planned, with a theme and an integrated cast, and instead of indulging in undergraduate horseplay the revue must satirise the follies of our times – wartime censorship, military stupidity, Neville Chamberlain, air raid precautions, secret diplomacy – all the absurdities of the phoney war. So many curtains had gone down between me and an audience since I had produced plays at Muswellbrook District Rural School that the idea of writing sketches did not occur to me. I did not now want to amuse audiences but to mystify them or insult them. It was the glamour of the revue that pulled me towards it – the stage lights, the music, the make-up, the drinking – and the necessity to associate myself with the idea that it was time totally fitted people took the revue over. I unofficially attached myself to a committee and sat in the office of the Students' Representative Council, at the centre of things, agreeing that there must be a script and a plan and a theme and an integrated cast, that the revue must be placed on a proper footing. Out of these meetings only scraps of the script emerged and there was no proper footing, but the talk went on about how a revue should be produced. One by one the wardrobe manager, the house manager, the musical director and so forth were appointed and such script as existed was retyped – it was the first time lighting directions and musical cues had been put down on paper – but when the casting meeting was held hardly anyone turned up. We held further meetings about how things should be put on a proper footing.

A few days before the dress rehearsals were due, when it looked as if the planning of the revue had been so thorough that the show would not go on, Alan Crawford, receiving reports in his solicitor's office downtown, picked up his phone and in a few hours bundled it all together. Flicking his pencil as he flicked his cigarette, Crawford made lists and then hurried me into the lift and along the street, dropping into some of his favourite downtown pubs and casting the revue from among the friends he happened to meet in one bar or the other, ending his efforts over dinner by scribbling out a new verse to a revue song he had written called 'There'll Always Be a Menzies'. In the meantime the planning of the revue continued independently of what was happening. The script was not fully typed until the revue had been on for two nights, but an important objective had been achieved: for the first time in the history of the revue there was a fully typed script. That as a result of one afternoon's rush we had a revue told me an instructive story.

THAT WAS THE WAY TO DO THINGS. DON'T LET THE PLAN BECOME a cause in itself. Improvise – hustle everyone along. *On s'engage et puis on voit.* Get going and see what happens. With this incident I began the habit of framing episodes of my life into moral anecdotes that had taught me something. Throw myself into something, enjoy it, then perhaps later think about what it 'meant', arrange it into an anecdote. Then there was the excitement of what the next empty frame might contain. As soon as I thought of doing a thing I had to rush towards it. A single coherent pattern would flash in my brain, linking memories and freezing into something new, thereby making sense of immediate decision. After I had read Osbert Sitwell's *Triple Fugue* and made some notes, one thought led to another and I had to call a meeting of the Literary Society to give a paper explaining what had happened in the development of the English novel since Samuel Richardson. A month later (as the new secretary of the Literary Society I had decided to give one paper a month myself, to set an example) having read a freethinker's article on the essentially unsatisfactory and second-rate nature of poetry, I saw how the structure of his argument could be turned upside-down and used to support a quite different view – of poetry as the barbaric initiator of other writing – so I had to call another meeting of the Literary Society to launch D.R. Horne's theory of 'The Heroic and Barbaric Role of Poetry'. I would be overwhelmed by some push to action, washed off on the wave, tumbled to the beach, and then rush back into the water to see which wave would hit me next.

When it was all over there was some exemplary anecdote.

FIRST, I MUST EXECUTE AN ACT OF FEARFUL REVENGE AGAINST the Arts Society, which was in the power of men and women from good suburbs, because its literary magazine, *Arna*, had rejected some verse by Jimmy McAuley. For the sake of his honour I was determined to start a blood feud: I spent several days drafting and redrafting a letter to *Honi Soit* to make sure that, in the name of the producer ethic, all error would be scarified and the truth would be held up for all to worship. Insulting and infuriating, I must now make events tremble at the shake of a pen, stinging with angry phrases and refreshing with rage. It was essential that the letter must be written in bad taste. Prevailing social norms were part of the enemy: I must break through the comfortable conventions of life in the Arts Society and destroy them.

How would I sign it? Who was I going to be: It was an age of initials – T.S. Eliot, V.I. Lenin, e.e. cummings, J.P. McAuley. I would be 'D.R. Horne'. To his friends – 'Young Donald', soft-spoken mumbler of witticisms; to his enemies – implacable 'D.R. Horne', angry shouter.

ARNA – PLEIADE OR CABAL?

Sir, The most lamentable activity of the Arts Cabal is its control of *Arna*. University pretensions to culture reached their cesspit depths in the latest issue of this journal. For a Faculty which provides a more liberal education than any other, it is amazing that nothing better could be produced than this footling effort, comparable in its literary and scientific values to a school magazine or the *Sydney Morning Herald* literary pages. On glancing through its pages one finds that most of the poetry was written by Mr Muir Holburn, poems which in common with the rest of Mr Holburn's published work are Poems of No importance. Mr Holburn is the most unintellectual poet for many years, and the gap has not been filled by 'intuition'. Mr Holburn's schoolboy themes are left undeveloped, and as a stylist his ugliness is deplorable (much more so than that of any of the University's 'modern poets' against whom our contemporary Philistines never fail to raise the sword and the spear – would that I could give the carcase of the host of the Philistines this day unto the birds of the air!) ... *Arna* should be in the hands of people who have a genuine interest in culture. The Editor, the Business Manager and the Sub-Editor should all be practising literary artists or scientists and the committee should be quite free of the Arts Cabal itself. If its own cultural activity is removed from the non-cultural way of life of most members of the Cabal and the producers of literary and scientific work are allowed to control themselves *Arna* may be restored to a position of some cultural importance.

I am, etc.
D.R. HORNE, Arts II

It was my first letter to a newspaper! I admired the look of it, and continued to glance at it, as if it were a first child.

Several days after it had been published, when I saw McAuley in a downtown pub I stood silent, waiting for somebody to say something, but the group continued its conversation until, half an hour later, McAuley turned to me in an aside, eyelids lowered, mouth taut, and brushed me off with the words: 'I believe you are now writing for the public prints.' He went back to the general conversation, ignoring me for the rest of the afternoon. My disappointment was comforted when I read the attempts at replies to my letter. When one of them suggested that I was a 'dogmatic, conceited know-all full of puff and bombast' Young Donald called a meeting of the Literary Society and put up notices advertising that D.R. Horne would be opening another attack on *Arna*, to lambast the poltroonery of his critics.

The crowd in the Greek lecture theatre, where the Book Club held its meetings, was spilling out into the corridor. I could see James Hope beyond the doorway, looking as if he were not there. Stewart and Pritchett and others had arrived and were sitting in the front row. I winked at them. I was their boy. I was glad that Hope had come, but it increased my excitement and anxiety about how I would perform. In a green suit, green shirt, green tie, Muir Holburn was at the other end of the lecture dais. He would speak first in this lunchtime dialogue arranged by the Book Club after my feud against Holburn's verse and against *Arna*. Like the debating club at Canterbury High, the crowded lecture theatre reminded me of an engraving of one of those famous halls in the French Revolution in which the citizens bunched together to decide what they would do next. As he began his address, with his talk about orchestrated rhythm, Holburn seemed to be playing into my hands. I made some notes on what he was saying: *Unintellectual ... Themes of no importance ... He subordinates sense to rhythm ...* I had him there! HOLBURN HAS LOST ALL FEELING FOR LANGUAGE IN HIS SEARCH FOR RHYTHM. Essential weakness! I've got him! *H. doesn't understand should be definite striving for exact word express exact meaning.* I underlined more key words. Holburn had not mentioned me: probably thought it would be bad taste to turn it into a debate. Well, I'd give them some bad taste. I'd attack him from the start. What was he doing now? He was dancing! To explain his theory of orchestrated verse Holburn was dancing! I could make fun of that. I could begin by saying I wasn't going to give a physical demonstration of my verse. Pleased with this unfair play, I spent the opening part of my address attacking Holburn, then elaborated my 'central position' from my notes. Artistic and intellectual approaches. ARTISTIC: *My debt to Mallarmé. Sustain feeling and atmosphere poem. Sounds and symbols must be appropriate to sense and fit whole tone of poem. Not just shock, cf. Eliot, Auden.* INTELLECTUAL: *My debt to John Anderson. Explain 'real theme'. Like logical form or rhetoric.* ROLE OF ARTIST: *Find out what living is like and try to interpret poetically. Putrefaction of soul may be necessary.* NO OBSCURITY: *What matter if have to read poem 25 times to extract meaning?* I concluded by reading some of my most obscure verse, explaining that I was going to recite it through clenched teeth to make it even more difficult.

This attack on Holburn had launched me as a Quadrangle celebrity –

and it brought another instructive anecdote: there had been no plan to attack him – it was just last-minute debater's ad-libbing occasioned by his dancing and his talk about orchestrated verse – but now people were suggesting I had done it deliberately to get publicity. How tiresomely stupid! I was *naturally* provocative! Excited by all this, I picked up gossip about myself and enjoyed exposing its absurdities. I may not have chased publicity, but I enjoyed it now that I had got it. And to criticisms, as a freethinker, I had an answer for everything. Thus when the official report of the Book Club meeting broke with the tradition of such reports to include a reprimand to me for displaying an intolerance unfortunate in a university, I warily replied that 'to hold to any position was to be intolerant of any other position'.

Such attacks strengthened a sense of anti-audience, the pleasure in saying things people would not understand, of perversely withholding satisfaction, or alternatively of speaking insults with such clarity that relationship was achieved through anger. The more I was attacked, the more self-satisfied I became. Here was another moral anecdote: If you want people to stick to their opinions attack them! As with other precepts, to acknowledge the truth of such a matter was all that was required. My precepts were not for acting on; they were not to have anything to do with behaviour. They were not useful, but true. I would go on attacking people's opinions, indifferent to the results. As I had written in a school essay, life is a great battle worth fighting.

WHEN I WAS MADE SUB-EDITOR OF *HERMES*, WITH DUNLOP AS editor, it seemed that *Hermes* should be hustled together as peremptorily as Crawford had hustled together a cast for the revue. No one volunteered anything usable, so it was filled with the work of our friends. We did not have enough friends. To fill the gaps, at the last moment I wrote four articles, signing them 'D.H.', 'Donald Horne', 'D.R. Horne' and 'Aristaeus' – I had already used 'D.R.H.' for my three poems. Because Dunlop had signed his verse 'D.' and Hope had signed his 'H.' their work was credited to me as well as my own and it soon became one of the jokes of the university that I had written almost all of *Hermes* myself. I denied this to individuals – just another foul attack – but I began to enjoy it as the rumour expanded so quickly that within a year's time it was already a legend that D.R. Horne had filled a whole issue of *Hermes* with nothing but his own verse. For several years after I left the university this was to remain one of the central legends of what had by then become, in retrospect, a golden age.

From this anecdote, giggling about its cynicism, I would lecture my friends that, whatever the truth, people would simply go on believing what they wanted to believe. If they didn't understand you, you might as well pretend you were what they thought you were, because this was the only way they would ever see you. However, when a letter in *Honi Soit* from a woman student made a disguised attack on me as an effete show-off, a poseur languishing in the Quad, considering lectures above him, adopting a pure accent, affecting to 'taste life', but completely above everything that excited the appetites, interested in life only in an abstract form, I could not altogether comfort myself with my own cynicism. What if what they said was *true*?

WHEN A HISTORY LECTURER AND A GROUP OF STUDENTS FORMED an 'Anglo-Saxon Society', to preserve in the university, as their contribution to the war effort, an understanding of British traditions, we freethinkers got together with the Labour Clubbites and the Stalinists, determined to wreck this new organisation. We sat in the audience firing off shots at the slightest movement among the Anglo-Saxon enemy, and after a couple of meetings we had seized their position, giving papers ourselves and taking over most of the discussions. When my turn came to give a paper on 'The Freedom of the Press' I sarcastically instanced censorship as a fine old Anglo-Saxon tradition. I saw myself as the sharp-shooter of our gang. The speaker would give his paper; I might make a note on some of its greatest weaknesses, and then I would sit silent while the rest of the gang moved in to attack and played both Stalinist and freethinker patball with the few Anglo-Saxons who still came to the meetings.

FREETHINKER: Can't you understand that there is no such thing as 'the good community'? There is no such thing as the 'community'! There are simply conflicting social forces that have to fight it out.
ANGLO-SAXON: We must all sink our differences in the common cause.
FREETHINKER: There is no such thing as the common cause.

ANGLO-SAXON: That means we should all be cutting each other's throats.

STALINIST: That's what the revolution's about.

ANGLO-SAXON: Why can't there be concessions on both sides? Why do you have to advocate a revolution?

STALINIST: I am not advocating a revolution. Can't you understand I am simply saying a revolution is historically inevitable whether you or I like it or not?

EVOLUTIONARY SOCIALIST: The governing class doesn't legislate for society as a whole but in its own interests. The question is simply one of evolution or revolution.

PSEUDO-TROTSKYIST: The capitalist class will not voluntarily surrender the means of production. The means of production must be seized from the capitalist class.

TIME FOR ME TO INTERVENE. I HAVE BEEN SITTING THERE SO enraged that I have not followed all the details of the discussion, hot with hatred for this stupid thing that was said half an hour ago. I burst into the middle of someone else's speech, throwing words 'inadequate' ... 'obscurantist' ... 'ignored the real issues'. This interruption makes everyone talk at once. My rage over, I try to make some sense of myself by interrupting again to give everyone a lecture. 'Politics,' I explain, speaking at dictation speed, 'is the struggle to maintain or create rights. It is when the rights of one section of society come into conflict with the interests of a stronger section that suppression is instituted.' That should fix it.

The moral of the anecdote of the Anglo-Saxon Society seemed to be that the result of the formation of an anti-radical body was that, by bringing Stalinists and freethinkers together, it had become the most effective platform for the expression of radicalism.

I HAD NOW DEVELOPED A BLOOD FEUD WITH THE HISTORY lecturer, partly because he was the most prominent Anglo-Saxon, partly because he had started calling a roll. Because we were simply covering the same ground as we did for the Leaving Certificate (although not as well) I preferred to spend history lectures in the refectory, over a cup of coffee, talking about the history lecturer, but now my liberties had been infringed and I had to attend his lectures or I would be expelled from history. I walked into the lecture theatre with an insolent stare and sat in the front row, both arms spread out along the desk behind me, so that everyone could see I was not taking any notes. At a university dance that night I spent much of my time attacking this outbreak of 'authoritarianism' and as soon as I woke up in the morning I started talking about it again, having spent the night on the floor of a friend's room in a slum boarding-house. I got back into Dad's dinner suit and stiff shirt, borrowed for the dance, and put an overcoat over them, and a scarf around my neck to hide them, now and again during the day surprising people by flashing my overcoat open. I borrowed a mortar board and gown, and, when the afternoon's history lecture began, walked into it in black tie, stiff shirt and dinner suit, gown and mortar board. Buffeted by tiredness and excitement, I sat through the lectures wondering how it would all end, occasionally interjecting to keep my spirits up. At the end of the lecture I stood up and cross-examined the history lecturer. Was he aware I was the only correctly dressed person in the class? Was he further aware that not to be correctly dressed was not in accordance with Anglo-Saxon tradition? Etcetera. Etcetera. Last question: Was he aware that I was now resigning from History II? And so, abandoning the Renaissance, the Reformation, the Enlightenment and the French Revolution, I walked out of my favourite subject.

At home my mother complained that I had stayed out yet another night without warning, how worried they were about me. Etcetera. Etcetera. Nag. Nag. Nag. I slammed the door as I went into my bedroom, changed out of the dinner suit, and began to read *The Revolt of the Angels*.

It was as if the great days when things happened were with us again. This episode caused another flurry of gossip at the university which was also to harden into legend, and this time I found it easy enough to play the role the legend demanded, magnifying my actions into being the character people now recognised as D.R. Horne. I added this episode to my moral anecdotes in a way I had not expected. The only conclusion I could draw from it was that a gesture of freedom could limit freedom. I liked history and I had wanted to continue studying it.

AS I ADDED TO MY PRECEPTS, THINKING OF THEM AS 'LESSONS FROM life', I saw myself as someone who could both act and think, both experiment and experimenter. Young Donald would go off on some fresh expedition, and when it was over D.R. Horne would be its historian. Collected like butterflies on a chart, the precepts themselves were simply a hobby; they were not part of me, neither a guide to behaviour nor worth including in my writing. They were fit only for amusing conversation. For this reason my conversation was a great deal better than my writing, but James Hope was almost alone among my older friends in paying attention to Young Donald's paradoxes: now I usually put up D.R. Horne to talk to the others.

What seemed much more important than conversational paradoxes were lectures in formal logic (I had now enrolled in Philosophy I. How otherwise could I gain true wisdom?). Why the traditional formal logic we were learning was 'a description of the general structure of facts themselves' was a matter we would discuss in Philosophy II; in the meantime I simply learned it all off, in good faith, with great pleasure, chopping down my opponents' arguments with logic as with a magic sword. There was a physical satisfaction, like carpentry, something one could do with one's hands, in putting statements together into logical form or thinking up the contradictory of a proposition's contrapositive. I did not this year despise the subject matter of the English literature course – late seventeenth- and eighteenth-century literature, Shakespeare's histories and, for the honours course, six nineteenth-century writers – and even did some reading in it, although, of course, skipping the lectures, but I was neglecting the language course on the assumption that Beowulf and Middle English wouldn't take long to pick up when I turned my mind to them. Over the weekends or on vacation I would often lie in my bed all morning, smoking and reading, then after lunch lie on top of it still reading until I got back into bed at night to do some more reading. This reading went beyond concerns with 'literature' to a tasting of *styles* – perspectives on existence, ways of looking at things ... Put together newspaper headlines, hit songs, unrelated scenes, *Ulysses*-like interior monologues, bung in a lot of characters from all over the place, who are united only by their indifference to each other and their materialism, and you have Dos Passos's *USA*. (One way to write a novel.) ... Move into a provincial French town, take up a silly bourgeois love *affaire*, meticulously close in on the drabness and follies of bourgeois life, but do it with 'detachment' and you have Flaubert's *Madame Bovary*. (One way to write a novel.) ... Go out and get 'the facts', then, by an enormous imaginative effort transform your notes into a tale of working class struggle and you have Zola's *Germinal*. (One way to write a novel.) ... With a calculated clarity and coolness, and a comic style, look into the sense of status and of 'reality' professed by the American upper class and you have Thorstein Veblen's *The Theory of the Leisure Class*. (One way to write a social critique.) ... It was wonderful to arrive at the university on a Monday morning and for Pritchett and me to talk for a couple of hours in the Quad about what we had been reading over the weekend.

What interested me most in reading was to find some of the texture of experience, not in the sense of 'naturalism', nor of Anderson's 'realist aesthetic', but in some sense that was more difficult to talk about and that I therefore did not talk about, since among the people I could discuss it with, a halting and necessarily confused statement about anything was loudly laughed at and fell to pieces. This did not stop me from reading what I wanted to, but it meant that I talked only about those books that lent themselves to no-nonsense exposition. Mostly. I fell into reading as a relief from the rigours of the realist aesthetic, going through some of Proust in this way, for example, without thinking about aesthetics, simply experiencing what I was reading as an example of how existence might seem to be. Bits of books became lodged in me as much as the incidents out of which I made moral anecdotes, becoming absorbed as part of my view of things.

I could not always find in myself some of the texture I was seeking in books but I recognised it when I was stupefied with boredom, as once I had sat dispiritedly in the plum tree at Muswellbrook unable to think what to do next; or when I had a hangover, examining myself and regretting what I found; or when partly literary melancholy seized me so strongly that I was given to horror, romanticising suicide. But now that I had become a freethinker, with an answer for everything, I could become angry when I was in the company of those few students I knew who could see no point in living. Whereas I had been stripped of my old beliefs and clothed in new ones, they had been left naked and unsupported, seeing no point in doing one thing rather than another. I had to agree with them that, in theory, there was no meaning in life. Slumped around the coffee cups, we could empty ourselves into silence, but I would not allow myself to do so thereby cutting myself away from the kind of experience that might have enabled me to fill my greatest ambition: to think a thought.

As people talked more about me there was secreting, like a crustacean's shell, a hardness of behaviour that stiffened action. I was becoming a 'character', with 'traits', like someone in an Intermediate Certificate exam paper. When I still attempted to contemplate myself it was only when I felt out of joint. In these moods I still saw myself as not put together properly, so that I could be shocked when people seemed to assume that I was self-contained, hard-hearted and beyond insult – although as soon as this was suggested, I would pretend that it was so.

JUST AS, IN THEIR HAPPIER, MUSWELLBROOK, DAYS, MY PARENTS HAD found an important part of the meaning of life in making their own fun, to me it was equally important that I should have a good time, and I threw myself into it with equal thoroughness, although in different forms. I had launched myself into the serious goodtime business during the revue, when I had hired a bedroom, at a hotel near the university, to which students would drift up from the bar every afternoon, bringing drink with them, so that I did not have to buy any. The room would soon be packed with a babble of men and women, many of whom I did not know. I congratulated myself that I felt like a character in an Evelyn Waugh novel when, on the afternoon of my biggest party, one unknown 'guest' tried to throw me out as a gate-crasher. At the revue each night I would sit in the band with McAuley, turning the pages of music for him at his nod until it was time for the act I was in, when, as the make-up was put on, I would gulp neat rum from a bottle and then stumble through my lines and back to the band, the music bouncing through my brain as McAuley undulated to its beat, and grotesquely painted faces dazzled and blurred and feet thumped near my head. At the end of each night we would sing dirty songs around a beer keg until it ran dry. When I woke up in the morning some students would be asleep on the floor of my hotel room, and after breakfast we would go into the bar to talk about what a good time we had had the night before, trying to remember what had happened.

It was only on the Saturday morning after the revue, when I went home and read the newspapers, that I realised that the talk I had heard at the revue – about blitzkrieg, panzers, stukas and the invasion of France – meant that Europe was falling to pieces and that the Nazis were marching over the rubbish. In the manner of my revolutionary heroes, they were pushing and thrusting and toppling things over, but this was the Nazis – who would shoot me! I wrote a poem about how I died in the war.

Much of our drinking was in bars, and these were for men only, with the extra crudity that since all hotel drinking after six o'clock was illegal we had to cram down as much alcohol as we could before the bar was cleared. We practised this form of a good time in the bars in slum hotels around the university, where students and labourers jostled together and men fought on the pavements outside, or in businessmen's bars down town, among men in hats and waistcoats, straight from their offices. The favourite of these was the long bar at Ushers Hotel, a posh bar where lawyers and doctors drank as well as businessmen, although we sometimes preferred to its cream tiles the old brown wood of the Brooklyn, a Victorian pub down near the Quay, where the barmaid made sure that the sailors did not mix us up in their sudden brawls. On Friday afternoons the whole male cast sometimes assembled at Ushers, and I would lose myself among familiar faces in the fuzz and hubbub of late afternoon drinking, jostled and pushed, trying to keep a place beside the bar, near our favourite barmaid, hardly hearing what was being said or knowing what I was saying, determined to soak myself in as much beer as I could get my hands on before the bell rang at six, staggering out to the lavatory where the word TOILET on the door seemed to flash into TSELIOT, pissing into a urinal stamped FOWLER WARE, then staggering back to find my place lost and my companion talking to someone else, then pushing into some other conversation, talking endlessly, or thinking nothing while someone else talked endlessly. We floated gently in a trough between brown waves of beer, men together, sucking in comradeship with each new glass, lost in repetitive motion.

Drinking with women (mainly older, and freethinker, women) would take place in the 'parlour' of a slum hotel, or in the 'lounge' of a fashionable city hotel, where after-hours drinking was safe because the police were not likely to raid them. A few times we went to one of the tough speakeasies, where there were prostitutes and, allegedly, the bosses of razor gangs. We would sing and shout, aware of our risks. Sometimes at night if we were with freethinker women, we went illegally to a favourite wine shop, entering the owner's house from a back lane on the slope of a hill, and then going down several flights of stairs to the shop, at the other side of the house down on the main street level, where we would sit with the wineshop keeper and drink in his hock and his wisdom. Or, if it were all men, when we ended our bar drinking we might go to a back alley in a slum, to a sly-grog shop, and buy quarts of beer in brown paper parcels, and then burst in on some women we knew who had a flat, or on the wife of a friend, our arms clutching the bottles, and announce that we were going to have a party, quickly grouping round the piano. When the party was over we might go to sleep in chairs or on the floor.

I was making dozens of new friends, not remembering the names of some of them until weeks after I had met them, and I was now saying what I liked to anyone I drank with, bold enough to try to talk them into believing it. I would run out of money, but all my new friends were older than I was and did not mind seeing to it that Young Donald got a drink (although honour now seemed to demand that I should always carry my own cigarettes). Money was not something to which one gave any thought. If there was some of it around it didn't matter whose it was. The fact that rapid bar-drinking almost invariably gave me the hiccoughs was, however, a matter of desperate concern until I learned how to hold my breath long enough to get to a lavatory cubicle, where I would poke my fingers down my throat and quickly vomit the hiccoughs away as nonchalantly as if I were merely blowing my nose, then walk back pretending that nothing had happened.

For some of those I was now drinking with, delight in the recklessness of drunkenness had become the main affirmation of pride. Our heroes were those who preferred to assert their purity and incorruptibility in drunkenness as a way of rising from the illusions of the ordinary world into the heightened consciousness of companionship. It was in drink that one became oneself.

Around us was the hostile city, surrounded by the hungry wastes of the suburbs where we might yet be lost forever and where, it seemed, empty little people displayed their emptiness proudly, bundles of trained reflexes. Even those parts of the city that served our purposes seemed dowdy and second-rate. The overcrowded bars with their lavatory tiles, the tawdry women's lounges, the hamburger joints, the nervous furnishings of the coffee shops – and around them were the meaningless buildings, neither new nor old, nothing buildings where suburbanites earned their livings for no good reason, all set among the sudden suspicions and angers of these surly Sydney people, constantly seeking offence, suspecting that whatever you said was an attack on them, waiting, like bandits, to cut you down. In its heroic style, our drinking was glorified into an act of contempt for all suburban ambition, indeed for all ambition: there was no greater hero than someone whose talents had been destroyed by drink. We saw ourselves as alienated from all Australia, a rubbish tip of European culture where all that was native was the suffocating dust of a third rate nationalism. We were even alienated from the twentieth century, a junkyard of hastily repainted nineteenth-century ideas and tinpot novelty items that fell apart in your hands. 'Look at us,' someone boasted one night. 'There isn't a twentieth-century face among us.'

ALAN CRAWFORD HAD INTRODUCED ME TO *JURGEN* AS A BOOK THAT displayed the charms of 'walking quietly down pleasant ways' calculating how to take one's amusements where one found them. For a season, I quoted from it a great deal and idealised such personal cynicism as I found in myself and my friends into Young Donald's romantic view of the hero as a charming utter bastard. But D.R. Horne detested charm as a type of untruthfulness and dishonour, and instead of walking quietly down pleasant ways he was prompted by pride to rush along public thoroughfares shouting out abuse. D.R. Horne nevertheless did what he could with Young Donald's latest enthusiasm by adopting a new style of verse. Driven out of the excesses of his obscure period by the publication of *Hermes*, in which almost everything he wrote, under various names, was equally unintelligible, he entered his songs for the charming utter bastards period with a poem that began:

> Girls and ladies, come and play,
> Desecrate your holiday.
> You have money. I am bold.
> Come on in! The water's cold.

But D.R. Horne prevailed over Young Donald. The idea that utter bastards had to be charming was soon discarded. An essential part of being an utter bastard became refusing to engage in what my mother called 'showing consideration for other people', in particular to avoid small talk and refuse to be polite to those whose conversation seemed boring or stupid. There were enough boring and stupid people around for them to be able to bore each other without requiring any assistance. At other times I gloried in the idea of pretending to like people, to talk to them in their own terms and then to laugh at them later. I saw myself anchored to my friends, loyal to them, part of them. Everyone else in the world was open game.

When people boasted of the details of the private manipulative ways in which they had done things I found this both abhorrent to my ideals and highly attractive to my intelligence, so that, while continuing to attack manipulation in enemies and outsiders, and while still advocating full discussion of everything, as if life were a huge Petrograd Soviet and the only good way to conduct practical affairs was by newspaper editorials, I also, with great amusement, began to practise deceits and to applaud them in my friends. As if I were under the influence of a drug that magnified sensation, even the slightest trick or white lie of commonsense became a gigantic fraud, so that the only way to conduct affairs seemed to be by deceit and hypocrisy. This seemed a clever and exciting way to arrange everything – do it by cheating. Not only was the hero brave; he was shrewd and resourceful, and when it came to fighting he enjoyed fighting, like Hercules, without scruple. What else was fighting? So I was both an onrusher, heroic and careless of risk, shouter of slogans, reckless of consequence – and a private plotter. The plot I told many times as an anecdote was concerned with getting rid of an unwanted sub-editor of *Hermes*. He had been appointed along with Dunlop and me, and it seemed ridiculous to lump us with this stranger who did not share our 'position'; so, to get rid of him, I decided to exclude him from all the planning of *Hermes*, puzzle him by ignoring him, and then, when the galley proofs were ready, ring him up and tell him to collect them that afternoon, correct them, paste them up in the dummy, and be quick smart about it. He would resign, and that would be the end of him. When I boasted of this manoeuvre to my advisers they acknowledged it as something they would have been proud to claim themselves.

But even plotting must be reckless. Cheating was fun, and could be pursued for its own sake but after a victory, one must risk destroying what had been achieved – by rushing at it all over again publicly, thus enjoying the thrill of public debate as well as the pleasure of private manoeuvre. Even if I simply fluked something I would then act as if I had carefully and unscrupulously planned this success. Of course two matters were above deceit – namely, art and science. With art and science, it was essential to remain implacably uncompromising, an Andersonian, not a sceptic.

Yet favourite daydreams remained those of the defeated hero, the intelligent, courageous, idealistic but sometimes cunning revolutionary who achieved great success and then grew tired of the subterfuges necessary to success. He would then startle everyone by returning to a pure statement of his ideals, denounce all subterfuge, and be immediately hacked down by his followers. In bed, before going to sleep, I made dozens of elaborate plots, some of which might go on for weeks, all following the same form: the early struggle, the success, the disdainful sacrifice. I cast my hero in the Egyptian Middle Kingdom, in democratic Athens, in Imperial Rome. He was the leader of a peasant revolt in the Middle Ages, a Renaissance prince, an American rebel. But the scenes to which he most often returned were the French Revolution or the Russian Revolution, although, to provide variety, these two revolutions were sometimes shifted to other countries. He met his downfall by being burned alive, strangled, beheaded; he was hurled from rocks, he walked the plank, he was shot in the back of the neck. He always made a final speech, denouncing error, upholding the truth, and telling everyone to go to buggery.

WOMEN, ESPECIALLY FREETHINKER WOMEN, OR WOMEN ON THE fringes of free thought, continued to be significant conversation companions, but they were for talking with or, sometimes, drinking with. One did not 'do anything else' with them. 'Doing something' with a woman was one of the many secrets of 'the date' and I had not yet acquired any of the arts of 'making a date'. At a party while everyone else was singing 'Frankie and Johnnie', I had declared my passion to the woman I then loved, getting down on my knees beside her chair so that she could hear my whispers, but she only laughed and explained to me that these things were not done in this way. Shortly afterwards at a university dance, done up in my father's stiff shirt and dinner jacket, like a knight in black and white armour, I became more direct when I persuaded another woman to climb through an open window into the dark, empty *Honi Soit* office. Once we had got in I told her in a bored, matter-of-fact way that if she lowered my trousers I would copulate with her. She laughed and explained to me that these things were not done in this way. There seemed to be some subtlety in relationship with women I could not yet understand.

I now had my eye on a woman who, though I did not love her, might settle the question. She did not look like a film star, and she wanted conversation to be about emotional relations between people, a subject that bored me as meaningless and non-discussable and she was scarcely aware of any of the secrets of free thought. But there she was. In the afterglow of the revue we kept on having parties at her flat, and she and I had got into the habit of engaging in long kisses and caresses, even if I lost her to someone else later in the evening. When the party ended early one night, apart from a drunk who was asleep in a chair, his face and glasses scrawled with lipstick, we were alone.

She was a long time in the bathroom while I lay naked in her bed, looking at the shabby carpet and the cheap furniture with as much glee as if I were lying in the bedroom of a duchess. When she came to bed my delight was reached with a puzzling suddenness, but I was immediately proud that I had now fulfilled one of the technical requirements of adulthood, performing an act that many in Arts II had not yet achieved. Since there seemed to be nothing more to do in bed I got up and, sitting on the end of the bed and using her fountain pen, corrected a poem I had been writing and then we had a talk. The next morning, after we had woken up the sleeping drunk and sent him off to work, I gathered all the empty quart beer bottles into a suitcase so that I could take them up to a hotel and get the refund on them and buy breakfast. It was a cold day and it had been raining. Walking up the street, I looked at all the young people I passed and wondered if they had yet been 'in bed' with a person of the opposite sex. Then I began to compose another poem in my head, getting as far as *The march of life had come to this and you ended it with a kiss, that all the faces in the street might seem a crop of rotting wheat.* As I stood in the delicatessen, buying coffee and eggs with the money I had got for the empties, I wondered what I would rhyme with *You and I were bred from slime*, and as I walked back to the flat I thought of the couplet *The cooling star, the sodden weed, inherent in our misspent seed.* There was a man in her sitting room, another guest of the night before, returned to talk about the party. While we were talking I noticed the headline on the front page of the *Daily Telegraph* he was carrying: It said: PARIS FALLS.

This anecdote of life imitating art was not one I could tell my friends, since I could not confess to the novelty of my situation.

PART 4
I HAD TO BE MYSELF
1940–41

NINETEEN

Summer of an anarchist

Having noted (almost with indifference) before Christmas that I had dropped from tenth place to twentieth in the exams, in the summer of 1940–41 I took a vacation job as 'tutor' to a mentally deficient youth, aged sixteen to my nineteen, living in the house of his wealthy family in their good suburb. I sufficiently respected their bluntness and diffidence to trouble to be polite to them, and even cooperated with them in keeping the conversation going in a lordly and remote manner about the little nothings of their household. We saw each other only at meal times when, following family convention, we were expected to report on what we had done since the last meal – pruned the roses, gone for a walk and so forth – and make the latest predictions about the weather. Despite myself, I fell into the rhythm of this progress from one meal to the next. I respected the structure of their boredom and their disdain for enthusiasm.

Every afternoon the youth and I went for a long walk, and I began to admire my health and brownness, sucking in fresh air and delighting in the hotness of my body, imagining the shower I would have when I got back, and the clean shirt I would put on for dinner so that we could talk about what we had done since lunch. Having enjoyed the pleasures of drinking, I was now enjoying the pleasures of not drinking. On most nights, and on some of my days off, I did not go out. I would go, instead, to my room and 'do some work' – none of it connected with my university course.

One part of this 'work' was to gain instruction from my experiences with the mentally deficient youth (whom I spoke of to my friends as 'The Idiot'). When I described these incidents – the remoteness of my situation, the strange house with its minuet of meal times and its rose gardens, the Idiot and our mysterious clash of wills – I did so amusingly, because this had become the only way I could talk, but in fact they became for me images of horror, which I memorised, making them part of me. If I was to 'know life' I must ingrain into myself its sadnesses. When he trembled towards me, playing with words like a baby with blocks, building by accident, offering his anxiety, seeking comprehension, I would speak slowly, reaching out to seize what he was trying to say, hoping to find our common humanity. But it was all emptiness. From such episodes I would make general assumptions about the human predicament, writing them in my notebook, as I used to write down the results of chemistry experiments. *Shades of people form in our minds*, but we cannot touch them. There was a little bit of imperfect something in him, a hopeless demi-awareness that twisted and strove to ensure his misery: when he was most relaxed he would rake around in his mind and talk about garbage and excrement. Reflecting that all that had lodged in his consciousness were a few scraps of the refuse of human culture, I would write down: *It is our necessary condition that we must be isolated and unloved; 'Love' is merely one more cloak for our self-interest*. At his seven-year-old's lessons he sometimes broke his pencil in frustration, with a sixteen-year-old's hands. When I stood in the bathroom, instructed to see to it that he did not masturbate, I would look at his long body, longer than mine, and the genitals that would never touch another person floating on the soapy water. I would write down: *It is undignified to complain about our loneliness: we must happily accept its consequences*. At lunch, when we were talking about the garden we heard a scream from the corridor. Someone had provoked him into a tantrum. He was thrown to the floor and we all threw ourselves on top of him. He bit his mother's leg savagely. I wrote down: *Only neurotics crave affection*.

There was one scene that froze into me and that I talked about again and again so that it seemed the most significant *tableau vivant* of the summer vacation. The Idiot is jolting forward, aiming the gardening-fork at me like a bayonet. Young Donald wants to run away, but D.R. Horne stands firm, stares at him coldly and shouts with the firm voice of command. 'Paul! Put that down!' Full of fury, he hesitates and the gleaming prongs of the fork fall away hurling up and then curving down on to the rubbish heap, while he lopes into the house and Young Donald hurries after him, to coax him from his implacable and unstatable miseries.

In this new mood of both vigour and detachment I began to shuffle around the dozens of poems D.R. Horne had written in the last eighteen months, examining them for meaning as if they were fortune teller's cards. They were retitled, pruned, rewritten, typed out, given a good wash and hung up to dry. There they were. So what were they? They read as if they were written by somebody else. The question turned over and over: What were these poems like? Someone should give them marks like a school English essay – so much out of ten – and write down comments: 'Shows decided promise' or 'Disappointing – should try harder'. It was boring re-reading them. A bulldog clip was snapped on them and they were put away. Now there was a new style to try out, knowledgeably bored:

> With lunchtime gone, the dull perspiring haze
> of long suburban afternoons was tricked
> upon a street of houses, newly bricked,
> whose windows firmly winked with dirty gaze
>
> upon an early guest, whose tepid grin
> could counterpoint the wisdom of the stars
> or gain him drinks from gents in cosy bars
> as, haste upon her breath, she let him in
>
> that on a bed beneath the sejant blinds
> the flesh might voyage along a charted path
> until, replete, it yawned and took a bath
> to wander back among the Neon Signs.

There was also the question of my anarchism, to be contemplated, in my new, reflective mood, after dinner. Overall, it was simple enough: society should consist of loosely cooperating producers' groups, impelled by various forms of the spirit of creativity, with their own forms of organisation emerging from their own discussions. But how this, the only ideal human society, was to be achieved was mainly a matter of imagination. I could look out at the rose garden of this rich family and see the predatory State blown away by the dynamite of revolutionary destruction 'terrible, complete, universal, ruthless'.

There had been, for a while, several decades before, a syndicalist movement in Australia in which dynamite could be seen as a metaphor of human liberation, but in the Australia of the summer of 1940–41 this was merely something in books and, even in books, mainly repressed. No reason, however, for not berating all prevailing forms of political error. One of the tasks I decided to set myself when I retired to my room after dinner was to write an anarchist manifesto. I even sketched out some parts of it. The right was easily eliminated in a few phrases: 'stupid reaction' … 'incipient fascism' … 'rogues' … 'creatures of monopoly' … 'predators' …, and the Labor Party, in the grip of Catholics and brewers, was merely 'one of the state departments of capitalism'. With the right disposed of, praise came for Marx, Bakunin and John Anderson, even if they were pointing in different directions. Otherwise, on the 'false left' it was essential to reveal the despicable illusions of evolutionary socialists who, in 1940, seemed the main enemy:

> It is ridiculous to say that to change the social order by revolution is to throw out the good with the evil. Meaningless words! The overthrowing of bad social forces does not necessarily entail the overthrow of the good, and as every revolutionary knows, the destruction of capitalism does not mean the stifling of enterprise but the unleashing of it. 'The scientist,' says Lenin, 'works much better under Socialism.' Society should be organised from the essential basis on which it works, that is production, not from the ignorant Christian ethics of consumption. When you get a government which clears away slums for a while and gives free milk to one generation of children you do not get socialism: you get much the same benevolent despotism as you get under capitalism, or you get a benevolent fascism. And talk of 'education' is no way out. When the same class controls the press as controls the jails, *who will educate the educators?* Ask an anarcho-syndicalist! A couple of tons of dynamite distributed under appropriate desks throughout the world would achieve more in two hours than 2000 years of evolutionary socialism. The workers must look after their own interests. No one else will do it for them. The way to socialism is not to be found in parliamentary lobbies or the aisles of Christian Socialist clergymen or in the jails of Stalinist counter-revolutionaries. It is to be found only among the men who work

in the factories and in the fields. That is why we probably won't get it in our life time.

But what of the Stalinists? D.R. Horne had no doubts. He knew they were counter-revolutionaries, alternating between the errors of adventurism and opportunism, in Russia assassins of the revolution and in Australia purveyors of the consumer ethic. Young Donald knew all of that, too, but he was personally friendly with a few Stalinists. And the banning of the Communist Party because it opposed the war had given it a certain romantic seriousness. When the party press was published illegally it seemed so much more attractive that I had begun to read it, although, of course, disapproving of its theoretical unsoundness. It was amusing to sit with respectable people who did not know seditious literature was stuffed into your hip pocket, buttoned down so that the police could not see it. The Stalinists had become principal speakers-up for freedom, opposing the dictatorial system of censorship, suppression of the labour movement, and menaces to civil liberties, and the Stalinist-led miners' unions had called a long strike to prevent fascism from succeeding in Australia. I was still anxious to gallop forward in the Freethought Society against prevailing illusions with the battle cry OBSCENITY! BLASPHEMY! SEDITION!, but Anderson was so quiet – there were rumours he was working out a new political 'position' and didn't want to be disturbed – that the Freethought Society was regularly concerned with little more than psychoanalysis, on which we had an evening study group. We weren't even sure where Anderson stood on the war. We knew he opposed all restrictions on liberty, but even here he was ambiguous – he desisted from attacking restrictions on Stalinist liberty. We exchanged rumours about police raids on bookshops and private libraries, and Alf Conlon sent his extensive collection of 'working-class literature' to a library in case his house was raided. I went around carrying copies of Trotsky's *The Proletarian Revolution* and Lenin's *State and Revolution* for all to see, as an act of defiance of the absolutism that was just around the corner.

I got my copies of party literature from my main Stalinist friend, an Arts student who was older than the rest of us and, before he came to the university, a worker; even, for a while, in the Depression, a swaggie. He seemed more real than we did, like someone from a Steinbeck novel. That he had been roughing it out in the world also made him much wiser than we were on a number of practical matters, and we valued him as a shrewd-head. Although as a Stalinist he was of course deluded about the Soviet Union, it was nevertheless his integrity that I now respected, rather than Somerville's. Somerville now seemed a childish figure from the past, and I had discarded him. I was also avoiding Fraser; I discovered, when I read parts of her novel without her knowing about it, that she had included in it a silly young man who seemed to bear some remote caricature resemblance to me. Obviously Fraser did not understand me!

EVERY SEAT IS SOLD. SOME OF THE AUDIENCE ARE STANDING AT THE back. We look around. Some of Sydney's most famous Stalinists are pointed out. The audience is mainly Stalinists and fellow travellers. Their talk dies down as the band begins playing. McAuley is at the piano, his body moving to the beat. His hair shines yellow as the curtains draw. The talking stops completely. Father Christmas is on stage. Father Christmas sings (slow and stately):

> Oh, I come from freezing Lapland
> To Sydney where it's hot.
> The retail trade employs me
> So I must be on the spot.
> I urge my reindeer onward
>
> And ride
>   right
>   down
>   the
>   map
>
> (slowly) With a bagful of English and Birmingham toys
> (quickly and loudly) MANUFACTURED BY THE JAP!

(Father Christmas skips round the stage, now frenzied, singing on, concluding):

Oh, the rich man gets a Buick And gives it to his wife
The poor man gets a lemon And he can suck it all his life
No kiddin!
He can suck it all his life!

LOUD AND PROLONGED APPLAUSE.

The New Theatre League Revue, *I'd Rather Be Left*, has begun. Father Christmas is wanted for National Service and skips through act after act as the Intelligence Man chases him. (*The Intelligence Man that's who I be, the girls they all done fall for me.*) Journalists cynically fabricate the news. (*Writers of the Daily Pulp, we write the stuff that makes 'em gulp.*) War profiteers rejoice. (*And at this time when we are all rejoicing, rejoice with those who profit from cement. In war they make the pillbox and the shelter, in peace the tombstone and the monument.*) Elderly dowagers boast. (*Every morning we give thanks that our husbands are directors of the very biggest banks.*) Popular culture is praised. (*There is pie in the sky, and in God we trust that Shirley Temple soon will develop her bust.*) The GNATS (the Girls Night Attack Training Squadron) are raided by General Copperbottom (*We're the GNATS, we're on parade, our sleeves are lined with golden braid, and every private is first grade while we're playing soldiers.*) Climax: General Copperbottom sings 'Doing' the Reactionary':

It's blacker than the blackbottom / It rumbles more than the rhumba /
If you think the two-step's got 'em / Just take a look at this number /
It's got that certain swing / That makes you want to sing.

HAND HELD HIGH
ABOVE YOUR HEAD!
YOU'LL SOON SEE RED!
DOIN' THE REACTIONARY!
DOIN'
    THE
       RE
         ACT
           ION
             A
               RY!

Hair over forehead, hand extended, dictator-strutting General Copperbottom accepts his encore. The applause continues. Father Christmas is arraigned. (*Every tooth in his head gleaming with Moscow gold.*) Finale (Stalinist propaganda): *Keep on going left, don't meander to the right tho' things look black, don't turn your back, the workers' might is right.* Last song, last laugh:

> Oh, the workers' flag is deepest Red ... /
> (The rest of this we'll leave unsaid.)

WE HAD KNOWN SOMETHING ABOUT THIS REVUE. MCAULEY HAD sung us some of the songs he and his friends had written for it, and those that had been taken from the International Ladies' Garment Workers' Union show, *Buttons and Bows*, in New York. But we did not expect it to be as good as this. This was a theme revue, properly planned. I went to it on a number of Sunday nights, never tiring, laughing again at every joke, clapping every song, remaining silent only when obviously Stalinist propaganda intruded. We talked even John Anderson into going to see it. The New Theatre League was a Stalinist front, but they seemed to be friendly Stalinists. After the show we would go to Stalinist parties, still reciting whole lines of the dialogue, or singing the songs all over again of a wartime conspiracy of racketeering retailers, corrupt journalists, war profiteers, stupid society women, reactionary politicians and buffooning generals. There seemed no doubt that the running of the war was in the totally wrong hands of men who had not read Tom Wintringham and Liddell Hart. In the war, as everywhere, stupidity was in command and all that intelligence could do was to write books about it. We talked over and over again about the fall of France, seeing in it all the rottenness of a stupid society. At one Stalinist party we talked about it for so long that I stayed there the night, sharing a couch with a Stalinist woman, feeling against me the softness and warmth of her long, slim Stalinist body.

THINKING ANARCHISM BUT LYING DOWN WITH STALINISTS, IN a fuzzy kind of way I also found myself in a third contradiction: I could also sometimes speak some of the rhetoric of the new reformism. Menzies, the prime minister (whom we saw, of course, as a fascist) had almost been defeated in the elections; his own party was attacking him and the *Daily Telegraph* was thundering at him every day from its front page. For a while the Stalinists had seized the NSW Labor Party; when they were expelled they formed a front party with a reformist language of its own. To me all politicians were Tweedledums and Tweedledees playing deadly games with each other in the mad-house of the predatory State, but there was the thrill of the chase. My old enemies the premier of New South Wales and the British prime minister had been toppled ... now for the prime minister of Australia!

From under the surface we saw things darkly and mysteriously through the imagination of Alf Conlon, now University Manpower Officer with filing cabinets, staff and a suite of rooms of his own in the university administration block, up there under its pseudo-Gothic roof doing God knows what, but respected by Pritchett and me even when we merely looked up at the leaded windows and thought of all this busyness of Alf's humming benignly in its hive. Conlon seemed to be seeping into the precincts of power with an historical inevitability – his use of the names of men in power had become as much one of his mannerisms as his play with his pipe – and now he was said to be advising the Minister of the Army on matters too secret to discuss and also, we feared, too mysterious for us to understand. When a plane crash had killed three cabinet ministers whose names I hardly knew, Alf had stood with his noggin of beer in the pub and astounded us with his personal knowledge of them. Now Conlon, apparently inventor of the concept of 'manpower', was using a new phrase – 'army education'. It might be necessary for intellectual integrity to put on a uniform, he explained, and hide oneself in the army for the duration of the coming barbarisms, against which Alf could be seen as a main bulwark. 'Have you ever thought ...' he pulled his ear thoughtfully as he spoke to us in the pub. 'Have you ever thought of ... chaos? That's a word we should get used to, boys. Chaos ...' I tried to explain that hardly a day went by without my thinking of chaos, but the conversation changed. In these rumblings of power, stratagem and purpose only so much was revealed, then no more. 'There's toys abroad ...' Conlon would chuckle as he quoted from *King John*. 'Anon I'll tell thee more.'

We saw less of him now, but at a party in his flat held just before my summer job there was Alf, reassuredly the same despite his power, leaning back in a chair by the keg, shirt off, stripped to his singlet, pipe alight, noggin in hand, softly talking sociology. 'I love him, I love him,' some drunk said to me. My one anxiety was that Anderson may have quarrelled with Alf, who had once been an Andersonian but was now clearly a voluntarist, but this anxiety was stilled when Pritchett and I, drinking in one of the slum pubs near the university, had opened a door off one of the bars to see what was behind it and found a tiny parlour big enough for only two or three people. Sitting in this back room of a back room, beers in front of them, talking so intently they did not notice us as we quickly but reverently closed the door, were Alf Conlon and John Anderson.

IT WAS A TRADITION IN THE FREETHOUGHT SOCIETY THAT student politics was one of the many refuges of scoundrels, but my own reputation with the freethinkers was by now of such unreliability that it was no surprise to them when I tried to take up this triviality of trivialities.

I still understood that planning to make things better was mere 'voluntarism' and that one must try to account for things, not change them, but this didn't stop me from responding to the call to reform outdated anomalies that had come to me from the *Daily Telegraph* when I was at Parramatta High. There were a few anomalies at Sydney University that needed changing. First, no more segregation of the sexes between the men's Union and the women's Union. The refectory in the men's Union (which charged twopence extra for a cup of coffee) was the only eating place where men and women could eat or drink together and, for that matter, the only place where they could sit down on chairs together. But I saw the Union as a haven of fuddy-duddiness and reaction and the separation of the two unions as a childish survival of Victorianism. Egged on to it by Alan Crawford, as one of the prophets of a 'mixed Union', I had got together a number of influential signatures to a petition for a referendum. Combining with another Union-hater, who guaranteed a big bloc of votes from the medical faculty, I had spent several days daubing invitations to VOTE YES on dozens of pieces of cardboard, and on the day before the referendum the two of us, now cracking jokes about ourselves, suddenly taking it only half seriously, had hurried around the university, putting up the notices. On polling day we had toured the polling places to encourage the gangs of supporters who were supposed to bully a YES vote out of their friends but many of whom seemed to have disappeared. When the counting finished that night, everyone was satisfied: 909 had voted YES, 795 NO. The forces of progress had outnumbered the forces of reaction, so that pleased us. However, the YES vote had not got the required two-thirds majority, so that pleased the forces of reaction. Things were on the move. We could strike again.

Next I stood for the position of representative on the Students' Council of the men of the Faculty of Arts (nominated by Pritchett and another friend). I had seen myself as someone who knew everything there was to know about the Students' Council (because Alan Crawford had told me all about it). My simple message to the electors was 'Remember this – things have been done at this university in the past, and, given support, they can be done again.' In the interests of office I was prepared to defy the freethinkers, so I proclaimed in my policy statement that all we had to do was see what was best to do – and then do it. I had previously been somewhat ashamed of my leadership of the Arts debating team in the Inter-Faculty debates; I now pointed to it as proof of my ability as a representative, hastening to assure the electors, however, that I would resign if I felt myself out of touch with their opinion. In giving my *cursus honorum* I suppressed my connection with the Freethought Society. Now that, although still secretly an anarchist, I wanted to play the role of a responsible reformer to see what it was like, I anxiously hoped that everyone would forget my rebellious past. There was a different D.R. Horne now.

It was a preferential poll, and the first candidate to be eliminated was the one who had promised the abolition of hidebound conservatism in student administration and the substitution for it of a policy that was flexible to the needs of the hour. The second to be eliminated, an Anglo-Saxon, offered a policy of increased military training for students. The third to be eliminated was D.R. Horne. The fourth to be eliminated had proclaimed that his policy would be the policy of his electors. The winner was our friend, Gordon Jockel, who had cried for new blood, for the ruthless elimination of back-slapping politicians and of petty office-holders who were paralysed with the inertia of bureaucracy and a slavish adherence to the powers that be. 'Progress', Jockel had said, 'is my platform.'

Progress had been my platform too, but while I had policies (mostly borrowed) for pulling to bits and reconstructing everything from the National Union of Australian University Students to the layout of the revue

programme, Gordon Jockel had excited the imagination by projecting the
very aspirations and style of progress. He was an idea. His election to the
Students' Council meant defeat for the good schools and the old order – his
supporters had manipulated most of the Teachers' College vote on his behalf
– and in itself his election made it obvious that things were about to become
more democratic, more pointed, more relevant to the times. Did he not wear
a polo-necked sweater in the Quad?

Pritchett and I had already respected Jockel as one of the earnest thinkers
of Arts II, and I both respected and was disconcerted by his gift of silence. Taller
than I was, older-looking, with a moustache and a long face to my round face,
stern when he wanted to be, he could fall into a thoughtful silence, brown eyes
staring ahead, which would make me feel juvenile and frivolous, and I would
try to bait him. He would neatly puzzle out his problems by writing long notes
in the margins of books on politics and history, and he was so concerned with
being methodical that when he decided it was time to have a girlfriend he
began making out lists of prospects, gradually whittling the list down as if he
were voting for his 'woman' under the preferential system (but, we suspected,
finally choosing the woman he had decided to choose anyway). He was
suspicious of my literary interests. 'Take that stuff away,' he had said, as if I
were offering him poisoned meat when I tried to interest him in the complete
body of my poetical works – and he disapproved of my spendthrift ways and
drinking. At lunch one day he refused to lend me sixpence to buy a slice of
beefsteak pie and a cup of coffee, lecturing me instead on my improvidence.
When he started on the two slices of pie he had taken for himself I diverted his
attention, grabbed one slice and started to eat it. He was gently amused. It was
the kind of thing he expected from me, part of the very basis of our friendship.

AN EVEN GREATER DEVELOPMENT: PRITCHETT IS MADE EDITOR
of *Honi Soit* and I am to be at his right hand. We celebrate his victory by
drinking hock and soda (I had recently read about this as a favourite drink of
Byron's) and playing Debussy while we make out our lists of staff. My body
shivers with excitement as I daydream of how *Honi Soit* will look like the
Daily Telegraph and sound like my conversation ... First, we appoint Jockel as
news editor: he will send out reporters on assignments (just like the movies)

instead of waiting for copy to come in ... New typefaces must be chosen and the whole layout changed ... Shorter paragraphs ... More serious (but more controversial) 'feature articles' ... A really planned newspaper. Pritchett and I sometimes meet at night and plan for the day when we will march into the *Honi Soit* office and take it over.

In the meantime, another change. Since I had been tossed the editorship of the *Students' Handbook*, a guide to student activities, I go ahead with revolutionising that (not answerable to anyone) – how surprised everyone will be when they see what I have done with the *Students' Handbook* – and (another change) Pritchett and I are planning a coup in the Literary Society which will make me president instead of John Anderson, so that we can really get the Literary Society marching again. We have many other plans afoot for 1941, and when we discuss them with Jockel he becomes more gentle, as if he is carefully nursing a baby to estimate its weight. When we talk some of the connivance of student politics – voting lists, estimates of who has the numbers, calculating and scheming – we all laugh anxiously, both excited and trying to conceal our excitement, or make a joke of it, as if we are all three going off together for the first time to a brothel. (Not that any of us had been to a brothel.)

THE SUMMER THAT BEGAN WITH MY PLANNING AN ANARCHIST'S manifesto now ends with me working every night in my bedroom in my employer's house bullying the 1941 *Students' Handbook* into its new and only possible form, giving it an intensity of interest it does not seem likely to get again. A pattern had formed ... click-click ... its shape is quite clear now ... now I must rush towards it ... there are no other possibilities ... D.R. Horne is *right*: what the *Handbook* needs is a *philosophy of relevance*. I will alter it more than anyone has ever imagined possible, but – clever! – it is going to cost less than it ever cost before. Cut thirty pages of rubbish out of it ... slash-slash-slash-slash ... that will save enough money to reset the headings in the right type, give it a proper layout, improve it with blocks, panels, sub-heads, rewrite the main articles as they should be written, write new articles that nobody had thought of but that are clearly essential; polish it and polish it until it gleams.

TWENTY

All in, the whippy's taken!

Dressed in undergraduate gowns with the badges and facings of the Students' Council on them, Pritchett and I were talking in the university administration block, important senior students carrying out my next project, the Freshers' Information Bureau, something the university had not seen before. When this was over I would plan an information service about the university for the schools. I was intoxicated with the pleasure of thinking of new things and improvising immediate fulfilment, developing a momentum, do this, do that.

Life seemed simple and lively now that I had come into my own: I could think of some new thing on the tram on the way to the university and, minutes later, I could hurry to the *Honi Soit* office and start doing it. There was little possibility that it would be wrong, and if there were some obstruction it was good exercise to jump over it boldly. Had I not stared down an Idiot? Or, for that matter, replaced John Anderson as president of the Literary Society? There had been a hitch in this coup. At the last moment Elwyn Lynn, an Old Guard freethinker, had nominated Anderson, and although Anderson had agreed to stand down for me on the unanimous recommendation of the committee, he hesitated, looked round the room – and accepted nomination. It was embarrassing that we had to put it to the vote: we knew we had the numbers. It was D.R. Horne, of course, who nominated Anderson as vice-president. Now we were pushing ahead in the Literary Society – arranging for all my friends to give papers (McAuley, Stewart, Hope, Jockel), getting things going again after the years of neglect. In his presidential address on Oscar Wilde as critic, D.R. Horne spoke up for poetry against the freethinkers' distrust of it: 'poetry is essentially barbaric ... the poet is a discoverer with all the imperfections and virtues of discovery ... even jaded poets who merely elaborate tradition make certain symbolic and linguistic discoveries almost despite themselves ... true poetry feels towards things imperfectly perhaps, but for the first time ...' This showed the freethinkers that poetry did not always have to develop a real theme to have a place in intellectual life. Anderson seemed older now – and, in conversation, surprisingly awkward and shy. There was his public implacability, the feeling that he was in the command post, planning endless rolling barrages – More guns! More ammunition! – determined that all illusions must be destroyed, but in person he hesitated, cracked lame jokes, laughed nervously, fiddled, fell silent. From their huge pouches his wide brown eyes seemed almost gentle and anxious. Perhaps his best days were over.

On *Honi Soit* the excitements of our revolution push on. Paragraphs are lopped. Black indented pars spring up. The heading types turn crisply into sans serif in the *Daily Telegraph* way. Pages are enlivened with new blocks. In the composing room Young Donald lightly touches the shiny metal of the new blocks with his fingers as if they were a woman's skin, dreaming over them. Reporting breathes with the new atmospheric style. McAuley and Stewart write controversial articles, and every day Jockel sits ruminating over his news editor's diary. Ridiculous letters attack the new *Honi Soit*, but we see to it that our friends write letters of praise. It seems longer than a summer vacation since D.R. Horne was not welcome in the *Honi Soit* office. He now acts as if he had been born in its ante-room and has now come into his part of the inheritance.

It is our rhetoric that billows out at student meetings and settles down as a sediment of print in *Honi Soit*. The new order at the university begins to bloom. It is mainly words that come into flower – 'the University must link with the progressive forces in society' ... 'we must consider our studies in their social context' – but even if we don't think about them the words are our words. That the right kind of words should be used is more important than that anything new should actually happen. We are different from all those grey generations of students who have trudged on before us and left behind them only a litter of old words. We seize on improvements at the Men's Union as external proof of the novelty of things. The Arts Faculty Society (for years moribund in the control of people from the best schools) awakes from its long slumbers and runs a weekend summer school on intellectual themes at one of the northern beaches. The president of the Union is now Jim Plimsoll, an economist with the Bank of New South Wales, who has spent years as an evening student (taking two degrees), but has also become a connection of Alf Conlon's and he seems to be getting things going. He orders reproductions of modern paintings for the walls of the Union and starts a series of lunch-hour music recitals in the Union Hall with McAuley in charge. The student societies go musical: the Literary Society puts on jazz, the Labour Club Soviet and Aboriginal music, the Book Club sings madrigals. It is a new world when, after a lunch-hour recital of Handel in the Union Hall, we can stroll past the new reproductions of Matisse in the Union ante-room and then sit in the refectory and order, as a first course, that novelty of novelties, chilled soup. An art exhibition is arranged in the Union by Ian Hogbin, an anthropology lecturer ('sophisticated' in striped suits, and a noted reader of Jane Austen novels): it is the work of William Dobell, a painter who has come back to Australia after a spell of some years in London and has been seen by Stewart, and therefore most of the rest of us, as one of the signs of the end of nationalism in Australian painting. (Stewart finds other signs for us in the Contemporary Art Society exhibition of 1940, and in Sydney painters like Desiderius Orban, Sali Herman, Wolf Cardamatis, Rah Gizelle, James Gleeson and Donald Friend.) 'There's a warmth of human values in Dobell,' says Stewart '... very Daumier': for us the exhibition is dominated by *The Red Lady*, a harridan–grotesque who would never have been allowed to pass through the doors of Sydney University Union.

In this new world there are new friends, and new feelings of importance. I drop into the rooms of lecturers such as Hogbin, and talk; a woman student I know who is having an *affaire* with a lecturer introduces me to him and we gossip. We have afternoon tea with the vice-chancellor and I have lunch with the chancellor's wife, Lady Halse Rogers, after Hogbin and I take her around the Dobell exhibition: over the chilled soup she says that when she was a child she was given a paint set and she could have done better than this. 'You must have been a very talented child,' says Ian Hogbin. (An anecdote.)

One of my friends now is Bruce Miller, a tall, thin, economics student wearing very thick glasses of a kind that seem appropriate to evening students, but with a resonant but mellifluously seductive voice that rises above the shouting in crowded pubs. He is an oddity amongst our acquaintance: like other evening students he is working – as a cadet radio announcer on the ABC.

But that doesn't stop him being into it all with us (at times) – the Student's Council, *Honi Soit*, drinking sessions, arguing, talking about ourselves – and with him I have become a regular at the Union Night debates, on Wednesdays, debating academic freedom, war aims, strikes, the barrenness of Australian cultural life. I seem to have caught Plimsoll's eye. He tries to run me as secretary of the debates committee but a fellow economist runs a ticket for Miller, the more conventional candidate, and wins. How Miller and I laugh about this in the pub! As a result of Plimsoll's reforms, from being an opponent of the Union I become one of its propagandists. Plimsoll sometimes seems to crane up even higher than he is when he peers down thoughtfully and remotely to speak softly to me, his pleasantness covering all that tough plotting and planning he must be going on with up there in the Union boardroom, talking all those Union fuddy-duddies into Handel recitals, Matisse reproductions and chilled soup. His air of thoughtful interest in my future breaks through my pride, and I listen to his advice, reflecting how quiet and pleasant it is to be standing here with someone who is not simply trying to buffet me. I get the same feeling with Les Philpott, secretary of the Students' Council, enjoying his light, ruminative humour, which touches on human oddity more with a tickle than a sting, and sometimes I stand in his office for an hour or more, gossiping enjoyably, as if we were leaning over a backyard fence talking about our neighbours. His shrewd gentleness also dissolves my pride and, not conscious of any anxious self-definition, I speak to him as a descendant of the happiest of my former 'selves'. At times I feel somewhat ashamed of my friendship with Philpott. My friends patronise him as a middlebrow.

For some time, when I think about it, I have been troubled because talking seems to come more easily with people for whom I have no intellectual regard than it does with my friends, whom I respect so deeply that I must constantly honour them with outspokenness, while they ensnare me with an amused distrust that makes me thresh about, trying to kick free of their suspicions. With these other people, not bothering to be my 'self', I recapture some of the neglected joys of relaxed companionship, talking for talking's sake, sometimes, it occurs to me, idly philosophising about mankind in what is little more than an educated version of our Sunday tea discussions at Denbigh, hopping from this topic to that. None of us worries about who is the cleverest. We know that, in certain things, I am.

It irritates me, in particular, that some of my old friends and the Stalinists and the freethinkers should see me as calculatingly *ambitious* when I see myself as deliberately contemptuous of my future. Is not Plimsoll already advising me not to neglect my courses completely, not to push at things so often, or to insult people so regularly? ('Yes ... Yes ... Yes ...' I say.) This kind of talk deprives me of my shape; but it is only when it comes from Plimsoll that I even listen. I live merely for the day when I can persuade Pritchett to use a seventy-two-point heading in *Honi Soit*. I have forgotten by now that I am supposed to become a schoolteacher. When I begin writing, everything will fall into my hands. Alternatively – I shall die in the war. (Pritchett and I go to see Conlon one day, saying we would like to enlist, but he assures us that such an impulse is an attack on government manpower policy. It is our job to fight on the academic front, not to take the easy way out.) The belief in my ambition is strengthened as a result of the anecdote of Brian Penton ...

This begins when Pritchett writes an editorial saying that the universities are 'not exempted from the dirty work of war because they are full of nice lads who can drive cars fast'. When, in a 'quotes of the week' column, the *Telegraph* cuts the 'not' out of this sentence we all prepare ourselves for the ignorant and malicious town as it marches up Parramatta Road to destroy us. Since I am now the university's resident *enfant terrible*, the embattled Students' Council appoints me as its spokesman, to argue the point with Brian Penton, the editor of the *Telegraph*, a man of fierce reputation, said to be both sharp and rough in argument.

Penton is what I had hoped for. His hair and eyebrows stick up and out as if electrified, and a terrible impatience seems to seize his body and his face. While I am lodging my protest he breaks off to speak on the phone ... something goes wrong ... he buzzes his secretary ... she doesn't come ... he bangs on the wall. Now he is comradely and jocular, talking to me quickly and warmly. Surely I must understand that it was a mistake, that the *Telegraph* wouldn't be crazy enough to do this deliberately. This has not occurred to me. I go on arguing, but with less conviction. Penton asks what I expect him to do about it, for Christ's sake. Stop the attack, I say. 'For Christ's sake. What attack? There's no attack. If you don't want that kind of publicity you shouldn't write that kind of editorial!' I can see this now, and I feel like some crank who has walked in off the street to waste the editor's time. I go on arguing, but with a faint smile as if to suggest: 'You're a man of the world; you understand my position.' Penton switches the conversation around. What do I think of this? Of that? We go for a quick gallop over rough ground as he tries me out. 'I know what', he says, 'We'll make you the *Telegraph*'s university correspondent.' Phone. Buzzer. I am appointed university correspondent on £3 a week! I feel like Napoleon contemplating the riches of Europe.

To me the moral of the anecdote of Brian Penton is that life is full of ridiculous accidents and paradoxes – and that it is natural enough that able men will recognise my talents. In the meantime, to test them, I must constantly throw these talents away, to show there is plenty more where they came from. When the new revue comes up I lose myself again in the movement of bodies, the hypnotic repetitions of song, the absorption in exaggerated personality and sharpened gossip, the improvisations, crises and self-congratulations. Again there are parties every night, rolling from one place to the next, and I go to sleep wherever the party falls to rest. Waking up late one morning in a flat shared by two women unknown to me, I hurry off to a champagne tasting at a vineyard and become quickly drunk on an empty stomach, reeling out of the cellars to sit in the sun. As we break speed limits driving back to town we put the hood down and I stand up, alternately giving Nazi and Stalinist salutes, and shrieking insults at suburbanites coming home from work. When the revue is finished that night, my mother, who has come to watch it with a friend, stays behind in the empty hall. It is extraordinary to see her here at the university. She praises the revue and then asks me to come home. Dad is worried about me. After a while I simply stand and say nothing, waiting for her to go away.

I take even greater comfort in the anecdote of the Union bust. Sometimes, if no one is looking, as we pass the Union's most valuable and revered work of art – a bronze bust of a professor whom we particularly hate as an arch-reactionary, jingoist, obscurantist persecutor of John Anderson – we stab a cigarette butt into its vacant eyes, as a gesture of progressiveness; or if one of us is strong enough he might try, unsuccessfully, to rock it loose. This bust was bolted on to its supporting column and the whole thing anchored to the floor after some students hid it in a Union lavatory and pulled the chain on it several years before. There it now stands, embedded into the Union. One night, drunk and wild after a party, I take a running jump at it, as a symbol of reaction. There is a loud crack, the marble-faced supporting column is sprawling and splintering, crashing down, breaking all over the floor, and the bronze head, like an assassinated king's, spins across the floor and bounces down the steps. We all run – some this way some that – and the next morning, over a hangover and coffee, Young Donald sits around, waiting to be denounced and then expelled, and trying at the same time to write a poem in his own honour (*His monuments all sway, and sprawling – foolish crash ... some thing something ...*). He is trying to suggest that chance acts can be frozen, like a snapshot, into arbitrary but inordinate poses. After all, he didn't mean to break the bloody thing. Earlier D.R. Horne had stood in the crowd around the shattered column, pulling a long face, his new prominence leading him to be addressed by an old Union director, a lifelong friend of the decapitated professor, who assures him that this is a deliberate crime, planned by criminals with a tow-rope and a car. Someone tells me that detectives are looking for me in the *Honi Soit* office. I hand over the subversive literature in my back pocket to a friend, and like a patriot marching towards Madame Guillotine I walk through the crowds standing around the *Honi Soit* office. They part before me. The detectives want to summons me for being caught in an after-hours police raid at Ushers Hotel. I see Alf Conlon, throned like a bishop behind his desk in his pseudo-Gothic chamber, sacred among his files and served by his staff. Chuckling and reassuring, he plans smokescreens to conceal my crime. He'll get onto it at once ... light a fire here and there ... (he points with his pipe as if it were a fire-stick) ... he'll create diversions ... he'll see to it. When Plimsoll talks to me again, pleasant and direct, I reflect on how clever I am not to let him know what I have done. But when Young Donald gets drunk his rough play still goes on. He tries to strip a tree in the Quad, branch by branch ... he stamps through gardens and pulls out shrubs, throwing them at friends ... chucks glasses into fireplaces, or even at people ... pushes and shoves ... pisses on things he doesn't like ... and, when D.R. Horne takes over, he shouts everyone down.

Sometimes I agreed with Baudelaire that virtue must be learned, like fashion, and contrived, like a dandy's toilette, but most of the things I might have taught myself were those that once came 'naturally', particularly open-heartedness, and that my education had now destroyed. I would secretly yearn, in particular, to be absolutely honest – but such disasters accompanied my honesty that I began to see it as an anti-social vice. Honesty was attractive because it was a crime. I wanted to be remote from things, uninterested in gossip (my chatter sometimes terrified me: it would blow us all up); contemptuous of gain. A person apart was a virtuous person. My love of James Hope's imperturbability increased: here was a man who had made himself into something that was good: his actions carried out his findings on life. Compared with him, I felt a clown. Gabble, gabble, gabble. Sometimes, remotely, I wished to be kind, but kindness was something for which there seemed no intellectual justification. It was a suburban virtue. It was intellectually much easier to defend hardness. Everything had to be fought out. It did not occur to me that fighting it out could simply mean an endless repetition of the same old battle cries and rallying calls so that finally one heard nothing in the din. Nor did it occur to me that sympathy with other people was a way of understanding them and might provide something about which one could write. Loyalty to friends still mattered, the rest of the world could be cheated.

Even loyalty to friends was challenged by my belief that true virtue lay only in the acceptance of anarchy, which was an essential characteristic of existence. It was only convention that prevented us from knowing our minds and our societies were in chaos. To be an anarchist was to see this chaos and to welcome it, finding freedom in the anarchy of one's own soul. The soul must be brought into life by being pushed to unexpected extremes. Sometimes drunkenness or degradation or rage or dishonesty might strike off some of its fetters, but freedom was best achieved by the fiction of decision. Since it was only phantasy to imagine that one could predict the results of one's actions, decisions were best made on the spot, without thought, although it was essential that if one were turned into something new by accident one should add some apparent choice to it. It was by methods such as these that I could discover, in what would be my brief life, some of the things it might mean to be my 'self'.

ALTHOUGH PRITCHETT AND JOCKEL AND I WERE DELIGHTED WITH our new *Honi Soit*, we were on edge because of the vacuities with which the Students' Council was now opening old wounds with resolutions of dissent from the chairman's ruling and motions that the question be now put, collapsing into the ash can of university history because it could not either make itself relevant to the new order our rhetoric had invented for it or be satisfied with its old role. In the middle of this meaninglessness, when I sat behind Pritchett at council meetings, I would start at the slightest movement that might suggest interference with *Honi Soit*. The night came. The attack began. *Honi Soit* was ordered – ordered! – to give more publicity to the Students' Festival. Interference had begun! With editorial freedom challenged, Pritchett came back with a scathing editorial, 'The Council in Possession'. They interfered again, bold enough even to criticise a Pritchett editorial, then followed it up with attacks on the increased costs of *Honi Soit*, made inevitable by our new policies, and with more complaints about lack of cooperation. After a row at one council meeting someone said: 'If Mr Pritchett is not satisfied, it should be possible to replace him.' Pritchett manoeuvred by promising an interim report.

As if this were not enough, I had begun quarrelling with Pritchett privately. Surrounded by the reminders of our revolution of the last two months – the long varnished table covered with copypaper, paste pots, scissors; the galley proofs hanging from bulldog clips on the cream-painted wooden wall; the blue-bound volumes of previous *Honi Soit*s stacked in the glass-fronted bookcase – we held long debates about the future of our revolution. In this two-man Petrograd Soviet I played Bolshevik to his Menshevik. The revolution must continue. There must be constant change. Since such a dispute about general style and approach demanded some concrete issue over which I could squabble, our debates became concerned in particular with the question whether we should have a six-column headline each week. I was determined we should; Pritchett was determined we should not. He would say that we should have streamer headlines only when the lead story demanded it, to which, exasperated with such a lack of zeal, I would shout back: 'Then we must simply see to it that we have a lead story each week that is worth a six-column streamer headline!' 'That's easier said than done,' replied the power-corrupted Menshevik Pritchett. 'We must commit ourselves to it', I would say, 'then we will have to do it.' Pritchett would then infuriate me by quoting from *The Shadow Line*, suggesting I was not yet mature. 'Maturity!' That was the end of all decision! The issue became further and fatally refined one afternoon when, against the heading STOUT GIVES A.R.P. PLANS, I wrote the type directions '60pt Gill Sans caps, 6 cols', making it a streamer heading. Pritchett reduced the size of the heading. The *Honi Soit* office itself was empty, so that we could shout at each other without worrying about staff morale, but I walked over to shut the door. I did not want them to hear us from the next room. My whole body craved a sixty-point streamer heading in *Honi Soit*. I could feel the excitement of sixty-point Gill Sans in my bones. For several hours I darted and encircled Pritchett with all the tricks of debating and Philosophy I. He surrendered, but next week he shrank the main heading down to three columns and it whispered in a mere twenty-four point. The *Honi Soit* revolution had been betrayed.

When I put in an ultimatum – greater status and responsibilities, or I resign – Pritchett promised an interim report. Although we were jostling each other in this way, we still roared with laughter at each other's wisecracks and for most of the time forgot our dispute, but I was affecting to discover a contemptuous edge to his witticisms, believing he was translating what I said into the salesmanship of a bullshit artist. One evening in a pub I threw a beer at him, and its glass too, cutting his face. No one seemed to take my side and I began privately to play a role I had forgotten – of the man from a government school, son of a pensioner, his talents suppressed by privilege, expected to make himself useful as an obedient understrapper to this gentleman from a good suburb. So far as *Honi Soit* was concerned, all my friends were mere Mensheviks – telling me that I must stay with Pritchett, consolidate our gains and so forth – but to me this seemed contemptible opportunism. If we did not press on, what did it matter if I went or stayed? Besides, there was the excitement of decision: by resigning I would know what it was like not to be on *Honi Soit*. Alan Crawford talked to me about Pritchett on and off for two hours at a university dance, drawing on all the weaponry of his persuasion. We faced each other, standing up, each with a foot on a chair, looking into each other's face while he assured me that the practice of power could be best indulged from behind the curtain. I should manipulate Pritchett, become his *éminence grise*. The suggestion horrified me. Power? I had no interest in power! I simply wanted a permanent revolution, with streamer headlines. I said nothing more. When Pritchett announced that he would not increase my status and responsibilities on *Honi Soit*, I drifted around for another day or two while we had our last arguments, picking up at the last moment some new principles to ennoble our sad quarrel. Thus stuffed with principles, I resigned. I would finish that week's work, or next week's too, if he hadn't replaced me by then (replaced *me*! Ha! Ha!), and then I would go.

TO UNDERSTAND WHAT IT WAS LIKE TO HAVE RESIGNED I NOW had to enact the emotions of resignation over and over again, melancholic with loss – by one decision losing many others. Either by their silence or directly, my friends suggested I had let Pritchett down. To this I must be indifferent – if that was what they thought, then let them think it! Their opinions were no longer significant. Who would I be now? Who would I even talk to? I strolled slowly through the future wreckage of *Honi Soit* and contemplated it mournfully. Where would our new order be? What did it matter? I would give up drinking, enjoy for a while the reflections in the mirror of my own company, then make new friends, to whom I would talk at length and quietly, real friends with whom I could sort out the muddles in my head. They would listen to me and I would listen to them. Since I would no longer know or care what was happening at the university, I would have lost my £3 a week as the *Telegraph*'s university correspondent, but this would help teach me to be more provident and to live more sensibly. And, since I had done no work in my courses, I would write the essays that were already late, then settle down to do some reading, perhaps even go to a few lectures.

I spent more time at home. On Sunday, walking along our part of the shores of Botany Bay, I found a band playing in the park, near the little creek. On the farther bank of the creek a young man, who looked like a woodcut of a village youth in a volume of Wordsworth, was half lying on a nondescript girl, his trousers pulled up to his knees. Ah! I thought, the stallion age. He will then be married, with wet nappies hanging on the line six months after the wedding reception. There were children and ill-dressed virgins sitting around the band and ugly old men and women tapping their feet out of time. The conductor of the band moved his baton and moved it up and down sideways, backwards, forwards. Very Freudian. I would write a satire in which the hero died, to find himself in this Freudian park: it would turn out to be heaven. My busyness of the last few months had begun to show me how things went in the world. I would now reflect on my experiences and write about them. I wrote five pages of my satire.

I was quickly parched by lack of talk. I must go on talking.

Because, earlier in the year, I had got into the habit of talking to people whose conversation I did not respect, I talked again to them. By this accident I found myself in the middle of an anti-Pritchett faction. Now I learned what it was that had caused these surface movements of opposition against Pritchett on the council. What people resented in private about Pritchett was something different from what they said about him in public. And while it was one of the beliefs that bound my friends together that it was I who was uniquely inept in dealing with people, it appeared that in the anti-Pritchett faction, it was I who had become the candidate of good fellowship. Even at the printer's they preferred Young Donald, mumbler of witticisms. (D.R. Horne, with his bullying ways, had not been allowed into the printer's.) In the interest of cosy chattiness I was now offered the editorship. Another decision! Now I could know what it was like to be editor!

When disputes as to the method of Pritchett's execution began, I strongly opposed dismissal. Pritchett must be allowed to die by his own hand. I told him of these manoeuvres, deprecating them, and he agreed to resign. At the supper break of the meeting in which he had just resigned 'because of pressure of academic work', he leaned back against the wall, winded, put his feet out and kept saying, 'Well, Donald ... Well, Donald ...' Across the room Jockel's brown eyes looked back at me reflectively: the man who had stolen the beefsteak pie had now stolen the editorship. After supper, when I was made editor, I surprised the council by lecturing them on the necessity for my utter independence. They must not think I was their grateful servant. I would never forgive them for what they had done to Pritchett.

To me, talent, efficiency and intelligence were now rewarded. Pritchett had been done for anyway. Now only my editorship would save *Honi Soit*. By accident, the times had brought to the helm the tough-minded government-school man. But another of my decisions was now to make everything that had happened look like total ambition, coolly planned. There was a block of Pritchett's face in front of me on the composing room stone, and a blank space in his last issue of *Honi Soit*, where the editorial would have been. Pritchett's eyes looked up at me from the block, as quizzically as they had looked at me in the Quad when we had first discussed *Ulysses*. I would praise my friend's memory in the blank space of his unwritten editorial. I remembered how, in games of hide-and-seek in the Denbigh garden, 'Mick' and I would hide while someone stood at the 'whippy' and counted slowly up to twenty and then went out to look for us, and how the game was to try to sneak back to the whippy, seize it and cry triumphantly: 'All in, the whippy's taken.' I told the printer to put Pritchett's face in the blank space, put some heavy rules around it, set above it the heading GOODBYE! OH, GOODBYE! and beneath it the caption 'All in the whippy's taken!' This self-irony mystified the people who did not know what the word 'whippy' meant and, since I had forgotten to put in the comma, to others there seemed to be some special meaning: Horne had gone back to symbolism. To my friends it confirmed their suspicions that I had resigned cunningly and deliberately as the first careful move in what was already a fully planned conspiracy to replace Pritchett. I did everything I could to confirm these suspicions, thus making my acts seem more clever than they were, more intentional and planned, more intelligent.

TWENTY ONE

Every dog has his day

Now, to find out about power! This would be my education! First lesson: the greatest pleasure it gave was that I could make my own fun, playing with ideas and typefaces as my parents had played with golf balls and bridge cards, trying a new layout or a new literary style as they would have tried a new brassie or a new bidding system. With this new freedom to play, the making of decisions seemed enormously expanded: by saying what I pleased I could find out what it was like to say it. In my first editorial I warned the university I was going to offend it, then told my friends I was going to offend them, too. ('Take comfort, boys, it's all in the search for truth.') As one month's pandemonium passed into another I published anti-Christian articles, anarchist editorials and attacks on the Catholics and the Stalinists. Now I could really feel as if I were my 'self'. If I wanted to try a seventy-two-point streamer headline, all I had to do was to order it from the printer. I could both defend the Labour Club from its critics and attack its attacks on its critics. New features started, written by me, and folded when I got tired of them. It was fun to model the layout and typography of an article on the format of a series that Brian Penton was now writing for the *Daily Telegraph* – because that was the thing I would like to try out that week. When a magazine called *Angry Penguins* came in from Adelaide it was fun to clear columns of space for the biggest review *Honi Soit* had ever seen: 'Courageous little publication ... much that is pretentious, wordy and meaningless ... vague kind of surrealism ... grappling with great problems that don't exist ... their copulation with reality has not taken place ... their façade is all compensatory anxiety and obsessions ... they should study Symbolism and Psycho-Analysis.' It was equally fun when, momentarily bored with Gill Sans and Cooper Black, for amusement I produced *Honi Soit* in the types and layouts of ten years before, to see what they looked like.

The composing room was my ideal world, where I could be by myself, away from the university, and through the medium of the comps and their metal be concerned with the rhythm of layout and the metaphor of type. The printers allowed me more flexible procedures than they had allowed Pritchett, and I could do much of my work along with them rather than in the *Honi Soit* office. Sometimes I spent two days at the printers, not bothering about the university, playing around so happily that they joined in my game. At lunchtime I would eat with them and, deviously, sprinkle my conversation with light traces of syndicalism, without the dynamite. Like editors, printers were producers.

Writing editorials was a special delight, and I found they could be written best in the composing room, where I could stand up and use a corner of the printer's stone as a desk, writing the next par while the first was clicking on the linotype machine, keeping a word count so that there was no overset. When I scrubbed up as editor I washed my verbal obscurity away: I quickly learned how to cut up a subject neatly and sew it together again in a few pars. Apocalyptic warnings of catastrophe were in vogue – one of the Australian best-sellers of the time being Brian Penton's *Think Or Be Damned* – and I learned the trick of the final admonitory warning, sounded off at the end of an editorial like an anti-benediction. 'Go on growing like unhealthy little mushrooms in your cosy tunnel,' I told the students at the end of one editorial. 'Don't mind the world as it flows past the university on Parramatta Road, or the slums that fester around us ... Stay safe in your little tunnel, my mushrooms – and then you'll be ripe for the picking!' The neatly abusive clarity of my new style reached its finest form when I told the students that they owed their existence to the fact that I enjoyed bringing out *Honi Soit*:

> *Honi Soit* has to rely on you for its copy. So we exaggerate your propensities; we play you up as much as we can. We put you in 7pt, 8pt, 10pt, 12pt type, and we give you 282 headings in anything from 14pt to 72pt type. We put you in capitals or lower case. We use the best of our imagination to arrange you so that you make a good page. We illustrate you with photographic blocks, and give you sub-heads. If we possibly

can, we inflate your importance by putting some of your remarks in black type. But the main reason why we go to such pains is that we like the look of a page that has balance, that is done out in typefaces big and little, bold and light, and broken up with sub-heads and blocks. If it were not for certain typographical traditions you would probably cease to exist as a student body.

Another of the benefits of office was that it brought me more feeling for the texture of power in the university. As I had once learned about the human body by opening the overlapping diagrams of muscles, organs and bones in our *Household Physician*, I could now see into ante-rooms of power in the university. My stock of moral anecdotes increased. On the one hand, for the sake of the jocular, I developed a greater cynicism towards the conduct of affairs, so that I would tell more funny stories; on the other hand, for the sake of anger, I became more indignant, so that I would write more angry editorials. Young Donald confirmed the view of the blocklines to the pictures in *The History of the British Nation* and accepted muddle, stupidity and deceit as amusing and necessary characteristics of the conduct of affairs; but D.R. Horne, faithful to the style, if not the beliefs, of Leonidas, Cincinnatus, the Muswellbrook Anzac Day ceremony and *Cassell's Book of Knowledge*, remained morally outraged and still dreamed, vehemently, that all this evil might be blown up.

Declaring loyalty to Pritchett, Jockel had at once resigned from *Honi Soit* (and there were rumours a few weeks later that he was now saying I was a 'political charlatan'); several others deserted with him. The women stayed, so did the sporting editor and others who had their own sections of the paper, and Bruce Miller was still around to tell me where I was going wrong. To fill the gaps, I searched for new blood (viz students a year or two younger than me); and made one of them news editor – Douglas McCallum, a remarkably handsome Arts II student. (Nobody else in our group – if we *were* a group – seemed handsome.) Like Bruce Miller, he was also working at the ABC, as a cadet reporter, but on the night shift, so that he could drink in the daytime (although he read his way through the weekend at the Public Library, to keep up). When he had astounded Pritchett and me earlier in the year by writing a letter to *Honi Soit* agreeing with everything we had done, we at once sought him out, as an obvious leader of a younger generation that could take up our task when we had gone, but he was already moving almost up with us: as editor of *Arna*, the Arts Faculty magazine, he produced an issue that was forty per cent verse – McAuley, Stewart, Hope, Dunlop, Crawford, (even me); *everyone*. He was pleasant to have around, and he had read a lot of books (although he began to wonder whether he was a Stalinist). I saw myself as a true leader, by my enthusiasm attracting true people. There might not be many of them, but their zeal would increase their individual worth. I doubt whether I could have worked with anyone of such zeal, but the question did not arise. I preferred to do most of the work myself, otherwise I would lose most of the fun, and I enjoyed feeling deserted and demonstrating my own self-reliance; at the same time it was fun planning what the shape and functions of a perfect staff would be. Sure that I would be reappointed editor in 1942, I would sometimes write down the duties of the new staff I would then recruit; in the meantime so much was happening that it was exciting to jump from one improvisation to the next.

It was a hierarchic time and, sitting at the head of the table, editors were supposed to throw their weight around; I had the memory of my interview with Brian Penton to reinforce my belief in this role and the tableau of D.R. Horne staring down an idiot; John Anderson led the Freethought Society with the distant assuredness of a prophet on a faraway mountain; Jimmy McAuley would exact respect, like a praying mantis, by one fierce gesture, held immobile. I would play the role of leader, remote at the head of the table, irritated by stupidity, trying to blow it up to clear the trail. Then I would wish for the democratic methods of discussion, calling for opinions, getting angry again if the wrong things were said. I preferred young people from Arts I on my staff, perhaps as an Arts II man, McCallum was too old. I could teach them the secrets of such things as when to use a black indented par, but they were expected to have minds of their own. If they wanted to become 'followers', I didn't want them.

Outside *Honi Soit* I enjoyed easier, because predefined, relations with people. That my accepted role included unpredictability merely increased my immediate unconcern with what other people expected me to be. Whereas two years before at the Arts dinner I had wondered at a four-course meal with red and white wines and had been puzzled that my partner was offended because I had worn Dad's dinner suit, now my friends and I arrived already drunk at the Arts dinner and disturbed its decorum by throwing bread rolls, juggling with bottles and making mock speeches. Jockel, who was standing for re-election the next day, tried to quieten us, but McAuley took over the piano and played 'The Ballad of Joking Jesus', and when some people walked out in protest another of us rose to make the point that a more academic form of protest would have been to make a pro-God speech in reply. It seemed related to how I saw myself at this dinner that when we went to the railway cafeteria after it was over we read in the midnight edition of the *Telegraph* that *Ulysses* had been banned.

My sense of role expanded further when, with Bruce Miller, I was part of the Sydney team at the inter-university debates in Canberra. (We arrived at Canberra on a freezing late afternoon, drunk on rum, having come from Goulburn on a freight train, but sobered up when we were assembled with the teams from Brisbane and Melbourne and shared out among spare bedrooms in some of the most significant households in the Canberra bureaucracy.) The chairman of our first debate was someone called Sir Robert Garran, whom I had never heard of until Miller told me he was one of the founding fathers of the Constitution – which seemed to me a small reason for having to spend a polite hour or so with Miller while he arranged to visit Garran at home and ask him boring questions about the Constitution (*the Constitution!*) over a cup of tea. The chairman of our last debate was someone called Whitlam, a solicitor-general apparently (whatever that was). In the debates I worked hard to contrive tough fortifications of dramatically oversimplified argument from which I could hustle out as soon as an opponent revealed his weaknesses, seize him and shake him to death. When I was praised as 'brilliantly destructive, analysing, with an acidity that aroused the enthusiasm of everyone present' and even as 'Sydney's wild young savage' this seemed to expand self-acceptance into a new degree of magnitude. When, with a concentration on attack in every speech, we bit our way into the finals, and then went down by a few points to the charm and good humour of the Melbourne team, who did not bother about our analysis but appealed to emotion and, when they referred to our attacks, did so in gentle fun, the teams from the other universities told us that we had the 'Sydney style'. I had not heard this expression but if this was the 'Sydney style' it meant that I should be the pride of my city and that my enemies should go and live in Melbourne. It was in this unexpected role as a 'Sydney man', unexpected because I still despised Sydney as a nothing city, that I began to write to Max Harris, the editor of *Angry Penguins*, whose verse I patronised as 'most encouraging', and to student editors in other states, seeing a confraternity of editors in which I was now the 'Sydney man'.

Whenever I risked my power, the danger of losing it added excitement and increased pleasure. The prospect of risk confirmed the rightness of a decision. When I won my bets, which I continued to do, only increasing the stake could maintain the same level of pleasure. I attacked so strongly that there were threats of libel. When I was locked in a room in a university building by 'Jock' Marshall, that year's editor of *Hermes* who, in the course of his threats, took out a revolver and spun its chamber at me, this was sufficiently interesting to attract Alf Conlon from his momentous preoccupations. He puffed his pipe with the calmness of a highly placed courtier who did not wish to disturb me with the thought that he was keeping the prime minister waiting, but would be obliged if I would get on with it. (He then disappeared, floating up on the clouds of stratagem, high above my vision.) When the Students' Council seemed to be falling to pieces, with old friendships broken and new ambitions manoeuvring, I kicked the pieces, at first tentatively, and then, when I was praised by some of the councillors for kicking them, in my most wild young savage of Sydney style, further revenging the downfall of Pritchett (although also joking about the bad old Pritchett days with some of the councillors), I insulted the new council even before it held its first meeting, warning them in *Honi Soit* that:

> some of the new Councillors will sit at meetings in dumb and bovine simplicity, scarcely heeding what is going on; others will wax garrulous and fiercely gabble about subjects at whose existence they never guessed before they saw them listed on the agenda paper – and, worst of all, they will make petty, minor, ignorant complaints about the activities of those who do the work, and quickly sow the seeds of personal bitterness.

That would call their bluff.

I had discovered one of the familiar ironies of power: that one can take over the very policies on which one's predecessor has been defeated. Although

I had been made editor of *Honi Soit* because Pritchett had attacked the council and run up costs, I could attack the council with ten times his force and run up extra costs and nobody complained. But what seemed the most important lesson was that, if I were bold enough, there was nothing I could not now do. However much I insulted the students, they still queued at midday for *Honi Soit*, and sometimes within half an hour it was cleaned out. We increased the print order.

IN PROTEST AGAINST THE *ULYSSES* BANNING I WROTE AN EDITORIAL, 'Sex isn't it dreadful?' in which, for the first time in the history of *Honi Soit*, the word 'masturbate' was used. Chronicling the sexual growth of university students, I wrote:

> Youth begins to masturbate. Some (grim thought!) never stop. Others effect a clumsy congress, are forced into marriage and lead a wretched life. Some remain virtuous, marry frigid maidens and live without sex altogether. Others are devilishly promiscuous and dash from dissatisfaction to dissatisfaction. Some can obtain satisfaction only from their own sex. Others, as a result of a sudden gust of lust, are thrown into gaol ... You can get much more filth in an hour's stroll around public lavatories than you will ever get from reading the whole of *Ulysses*.

I concluded by recommending lectures at the university on how better to enjoy the sexual act.

Although I was entranced by the uproar, protests and demands for my dismissal, coming from outside as well as inside the university, the sheer weight of noise was beyond my expectation, and I wondered if the university administration would discipline me. So many letters came in that I devoted a large part of the next two issues to them, thereby solving for two weeks the increasing problem of producing *Honi Soit* with a reduced staff. 'Morbid and unsavoury ramblings of a sex pervert of the lowest type' ... 'Puerile mind, now silted up to the nth degree with sewer-like filth' ... 'Mental masturbations' ... 'An indication of the limits to which uncontrolled writing can go' ... 'The exhibitionism of an ill-educated youth' ... 'Give up the editorship for which you are unfitted' ... 'Startlingly dirty' ... 'Pitiful sophisticated challenge to chastity' ... 'The biography of a pervert' ... The protests carried me into a new intensity of excitement, and I ran two editorials on the same subject in the one issue, one on the front page and one inside, so that no one would miss what I had to say in reply: 'False and harmful superstitions' ... 'bigotry and ignorance' ... 'weaknesses of our existing society' ... 'arrant cowardice' ... 'small, contemptible minds'. The vice-chancellor again called me in for afternoon tea, this time to tell me how successfully he had resisted demands from outside religious and women's groups that I should be expelled. With audacity, one could achieve anything.

I did not usually see *Honi Soit* as a way of influencing anybody to do anything. It was simply a means of saying what I thought. In my D.R. Horne editorial style, as part of the general D.R. Horne public address system, I preferred to be implacable, idealistically unconcerned with reactions to what I was saying, having in any case been taught that one could never accurately estimate the results of any action. In my Young Donald conversational style I might sometimes be more conciliatory, bilingual like a politician, disclaiming the excesses of public style in the interests of private conversation. At first feeling guilty at this betrayal, I then drew from it a conclusion which I wrote down and would produce time and again in conversation as my discovery of the year: politicians can be both sincere and crooks. However, there could be no tampering with the principles of *Honi Soit* for matters of mere expediency, unless it was in my own interests, as it was when the new *Hermes* came out and I seized on 'Jock' Marshall's statement that 'It is the best issue that has appeared for many years – but it is still bad' and turned it into the heading 'My *Hermes* is Bad – Says Its Editor' (it was after this that he took out his revolver); or as it was when I did not publish among the many letters of attack on my sex editorial the one that suggested that I myself had a bit more yet to learn about sex. I felt self-justified about the *Hermes* heading – it was just part of a battle against evil – but I could not forgive myself for suppressing the sex letter.

Just as I had decided that the 'themes' of poems, when put down in a sentence or two, sometimes sounded less interesting than quotes from a desk calendar, and that there must be something more to poetry than this, I was now also wondering whether the morals I was drawing from my anecdotes might not also be discovered in Stevenson's *Book of Quotations*. Perhaps all it meant to learn from experience was that I could verify that some old saw was true and understand the texture of its wisdom. In this mood I would reflect that the desk-calendar motto for my successful editorship of *Honi Soit* might simply be: 'Every dog has its day.' At every banquet the ghost of Pritchett was still present. There were times when I had premonitions that, having deposed a rightful king, I might fall victim to the very disorder I had called to my cause. As I waited for something to wash this blood off my hands I also waited for new conspiracies to form. None did. I could not test my hypothesis that the starer-down of an idiot could stare any conspiracy out of countenance.

AN ANECDOTE BEGAN WHEN, HAVING HELPED CREATE THE rhetoric for the university's new order, I was nominated as one of the Students' Council's representatives at a 'Youth Parliament' in which delegations from various youth groups were to follow parliamentary forms in debating four 'Bills'. I accepted the nomination but issued a statement making fun of the 'Parliament': 'While I think that the amateur theatrical atmosphere involved in using parliamentary forms is pointless and may seriously hamper investigation of the problems to be discussed, it should at least show up some of the absurdities of parliamentary procedure.' Although I knew that the Stalinists were behind this affair, after the first morning of the 'Parliament' I was drafting amendments, making speeches, whispering tactics and, at lunch, scribbling on paper napkins. In the afternoon a Stalinist praised me for seconding an amendment to the Education Bill, and by the end of the first day I *belonged* to the Youth Parliament – because a small commando of Catholics had begun obstructing its business, making it impossible to debate our bills in an orderly way, setting traps all over the place, and smearing the Youth Parliament as a Front. In the evening I drank beer with some of the Stalinists, infuriated by the unscrupulous red-herring tactics of the clerical fascists, who were not concerned with the constructive work of the Youth Parliament but with disrupting it by obscurantist Gestapo methods that were destroying its parliamentary forms.

There were cheers and counter-cheers, boos and counter-boos throughout the last day of the Youth Parliament as the Catholics charged again and again in their final assaults on the Post-war Reconstruction

Bill. Their dead amendments littered the field, shot down by our steady fire. Although, to maintain unity and to show how reasonable they were, the Stalinists themselves had helped defeat an amendment that collective farms should be introduced into Australia after the war, the bill had been attacked by the Catholics as 'communistic'. I had scarcely read the bill, simply glancing over it, but I was seized by rage and fear that these shouting and tedious fanatics might win. I became so excited that their very faces seemed old and ugly. Their last shock wave came in the form of a cunning amendment that affirmed 'unswerving loyalty to Australia and the Empire, complete adherence to the principles of democracy, and repudiation of all totalitarian ideologies, whether Nazi, Fascist or Communist' and pledging 'to help the Australian war effort in every possible way'. They were jumping at our throats – this amendment would take away the whole democratic right of criticism. The oldest Stalinist present rose and pointed out that freedom of speech was one of the most important British traditions. 'When the King takes his Coronation Oath,' he said, speaking slowly and quietly, his pipe held lightly in his fist as further evidence of his sincerity, 'his first pledge is to safeguard the historic and traditional rights of the British people. Whoever abrogates these historic rights is guilty of treason to His Majesty the King.' As delighted by its duplicity as by its effectiveness, we cheered this speech again and again. Wise older Stalinist to use the Catholics' own deceitful tactics against them! When the amendment was defeated we cheered for a couple of minutes. That night we went off to the Trades Hall – it was astounding to be alone with so many Stalinists and Labour Clubbites – and in its shabbiness and ranting I again dreamed for a while of the Petrograd Soviet and its failure.

Just as it was only the attacks of the Catholics on the Youth Parliament that made me believe in it, it was only their attacks on the Labour Club that made me defend it, although even Catholic attacks could not make me believe in the Labour Club's meliorism. Whenever the name 'Catholic Action' was mentioned I would fall quiet with hate. We didn't know much about it, but there were rumours of hysterical meetings and secret plottings in some kind of conspiratorial anti-communist campaign that was going on in Sydney. Any student who wore a Holy Name badge seemed a servant of a black and unscrupulous clerical reaction which, under the subterfuge of anti-communism, represented an ambition of Francoism in Australia – the kind of thing that, along with the Stalinists, had caused the fall of France. This was given extra credibility by the way one of the two most notorious 'Catholic Action' priests dined in front of us, with no shame, at the Florentino, a basement Italian restaurant that, serving a set menu of minestrone, spaghetti bolognese, veal cutlet and salad for 2/6 (zabaglione, 6d extra) – my introduction to a 'continental cuisine' (supplemented when, during our friendship, Pritchett would shout me lunch at the Latin Café after he had received a monthly allowance from his father). There we would be, several tables of us; and at the other end of the room, with his half bottle of red wine, the priest, openly conspiring against us.

When some university Catholics attacked 'subversive influences' not only in the Youth Parliament and the Labour Club but even in the Students' Council and *Honi Soit*, I saw myself as part of a small garrison of freedom beleaguered by fanatical superstition, and when they attacked me as a secret communist I used Stalinist tricks in reply, covering up what I knew with a debator's *reductio ad absurdum* ('Do they think the president of the Students' Council is a communist?') and by irrelevant counterattacks ('The Church backed Franco'). It seemed a matter of honour to engage in these deceits – to protect the Stalinists from the Catholics while still seeing them as betrayers of the Revolution – and I entered a double world in which publicly I was attacked by the Catholics as a communist and privately I was distrusted by the Stalinists as an anti-communist. The attacks of both enemies entranced me. Never explain. Let them think what they like.

The pleasures of this private disdain were such that after I wrote my real beliefs down on a piece of paper I showed it to no one. 'The Labour Club', I wrote, 'is a hotch-potch of Stalinists, Christian Socialists, Social Democrats and Muddled Well-Wishing Fools. It is necessary for both its supporters and its opponents that it should seem more important than it is, thus feeding the vain and foolish conceit of both. As its support grows, the number of its enemies grows. Both sides feed on each other, lost in enthusiasm and hostility.'

When there was talk of banning the Labour Club and demonstrating students wrecked one of its meetings by booing continuously, I shouted my way into their attention, challenging them as louts and hooligans and then, in an editorial headed 'Fascisti At Bay', unloaded my abuse in print: '... discontented scum of the university ... Stormtrooper movement ... absurd suggestions that the Labour Club is communist-controlled ... if the demonstrators' loyalty is as great as they say, they can go and enlist and rid a peaceloving and democratic community of their presence.'

'We want Horne! We want Horne!' The feet of the demonstrators pound the floor as they chant. Although I am still walking to the lecture hall where the Labour Club is supposed to be holding its latest meeting, already I can hear the rumble of this war dance. Jostling a way through them as they stamp, some of them swaying their bodies to the rhythm, I climb onto the platform and yell: 'Here I am. What do you want?' The booing begins, a prolonged, ecstatic sexual moan, rising and falling. They have seized the meeting, appointing their own chairman, and as the booing drifts away several dozen of them jump to their feet to denounce my editorial, drowning each other out until only the loudest stays afloat. I am still on the platform, abusing them when I can get a word in and quote Voltaire, as they shout themselves into a purpose: they are going to grab me and carry me off to the university lake in procession and throw me into it.

There is an embarrassing quietness when this is decided. Here they are, crowded in the hall; here am I, on the platform. Which of them will be the first to grab? While they glower and the sunlight comes through the windows, I give someone my watch because it is not waterproof, congratulate myself that I am wearing my new underpants, and reflect that I can write an exclusive story for the *Daily Telegraph*. There is a kind of softening in the crowd ... it dissolves into a normal meeting ... the vice-chancellor has come in through the back door. He assures them that this is the last meeting they will break up. One more sign of hooliganism and he will expel the lot of them. He repeats this several times and walks out. I get my watch back and put it on again. I decide that, by bringing things to a crisis, my editorial had brought this affair to a successful issue. Never compromise! Be extreme! Now the Labour Club has the right to go on making a fool of itself with its compromises and reformism.

And then, when the Nazis invaded Russia, the Stalinists seized on what was now 'our alliance' to urge the banning of anti-Soviet statements as criminal slanders on a great wartime ally, and the new Party fronts that were springing up were preaching mere social democracy. Instead of demonstrating for freedom against wartime restrictions on liberty, after changing its leadership in a quiet purge the Labour Club began a campaign for more deep air-raid shelters – a meliorist programme if ever there was one! Crawford and others were now drinking downtown with Stalinist trade-union officials, whom they began presenting as the kind of men who would soon be running Australia, not revolutionaries at all, but keen-witted and intelligent exponents of efficiency. New men for the new order. 'This is the choice', one of these friends said to me, rigid with confidence: 'The Communists or the Catholics. There is no other.'

Like clowns who could not learn a new joke, the Catholics went on attacking me as a secret Stalinist even after I dropped reports of Labour Club meetings from *Honi Soit*, and even after I opposed the Students' Council's sending delegates to a congress of the Aid Russia Society. When the council sent delegates to the congress I put a satirical caption over a picture taken at it, but apparently the Catholics couldn't read: they saw only the picture, and they attacked me for giving the congress publicity as part of my secret communism. Repelled by the complete switch in the Party line, and deafened by what I considered the ignorant clamour of most political dispute, and disheartened that there was no one with whom I could any longer discuss politics honestly, I began to keep a kind of private diary of political belief, recording my principles in all their contradictions between dreams of a syndicalist society and an anarchist individualism.

Part of my difficulty in talking to anyone about politics came from another irony of power: the rhetoric of a new order that I had helped create in *Honi Soit* earlier in the year was now beginning to be taken more seriously, and, now that it was happening, I didn't like what was going on. There was now actually a 'Left' in the Students' Council: Jockel (with his Labour Club connections) had become a deputy president, there were new alignments, breakings of old friendships, private talks to which I was not privy, new schemes, a puzzling sense of practicality ... And above these rose the star of 'Jo' Collings, grandson of a Labor senator, a medical student with restless, enthusiastic eyes and a quick way of talking that suggested he was really going to get things moving. He had connections with Conlon, Crawford, and plans for operating out there in the world. It all seemed part of a bigger something: now that the Labor Party had taken over government, the rhetoric of the left had a statist ring. Worst of all, like any other rhetoric, it was being given practical meaning in the only possible form – as part of the avenue of personal ambition. Bruce Miller was strong on the details of all the new jobs that were going around. My dreams of a stateless society formed of generous-hearted brotherhoods of producers' groups freed of their chains by dynamite and then exploring the potential of the human soul when they were not fighting it out were now affronted more by the left than by the right; for the right, apart from the minority of clerical fascists, seemed suddenly to have disappeared. Perhaps it had gone to the war. I began to speak against the absurdities of the left; if the left were moving into power, they were the people to attack. That's where the risks would be. I joined forces with the centre to try to defeat a manoeuvre of ambition that was using exclusively the rhetoric of our new order; the D.R. Horne–Centre Alliance was defeated, and as a result of this reckless act, which I had known would fail, my reputation for being ambitious increased. As a last blow, the new false left seemed to have become more prudish; it was wearing its face longer. It did not do any serious drinking. Seen by these new puritans as frivolous in my personal habits as well as a nuisance in my beliefs, I found myself drifting from the left into the centre in one most significant way: the centre were becoming people I drank with. When, for the purpose of drinking conversation, I restated my anarchism in the form that all politicians were rogues and that all their policies were a lot of fraudulent bullshit, the drinkers of the centre were happy to agree. My conscience was satisfied: I had not sacrificed my beliefs. I dreamed of Alcibiades, betraying one side, then another, then another, learning more about life by all this changing of sides.

AS I WENT BY BUS WITH MUM TO THE HOSPITAL WHERE MY UNCLE Ted was suffering from appendicitis, I got more and more cranky about the chequerboard of privet hedges and four-room bungalows, despising the boredom of this land of dull dreams ... Nanna and some uncles and aunts were around Ted's bed. Because Ted's appendicitis had been at first mistaken for a simple stomach ache and he had been put on to castor oil, his inflamed appendix had burst and his body was now decaying with peritonitis. His face was a dark grey, and his head lay listlessly on his pillow, but his eyes were bright and he told me he had been reading something about me in the *Daily Telegraph*. We talked about this for a while. Ted, usually sharp and shrewd, now lying so languid, finally fell silent, his eyes sad and averted. Mum called me outside: Ted was dying; I must get some more of the relations so that they could say good-bye. I went in again. Ted was still lying back on his pillow, his eyes skewed sideways, but he had just smiled a little, making a joke with Nanna. His hand brushed mine. 'You're doing well, Don,' he said. 'Good on you!' This came slowly, his gaze remote and his face taut. When I returned to the hospital with one of my uncles everyone was on the verandah, looking through the window at Ted's face. There was an oxygen tube strapped to his nose, and a nurse was wiping away black ooze coming from his mouth. His eyes were open, but distantly. We stood quite silent, we didn't know for how long. Ted's head was lying on his pillow, completely still. We were inside again. Nanna pulled off the oxygen tube saying, 'Let him die in peace.' The nurse made some sign. We said the Lord's Prayer.

At Ted's four-room bungalow with its privet hedge, the bike on which he used to ride to the railway workshops leaning against the wall, the undertaker demanded down-payment before starting the funeral, and male mourners pulled pound notes out of their pockets and wallets.

PLIMSOLL WALKED ME ROUND AND ROUND ONE OF THE SPORTS ovals, springy-footed, gravely inclining his head like a semaphore as he signalled that if I merely followed every enthusiasm some triviality might carry me off, senselessly destroying everything. Balls! I must throw myself into this, then that, then that. At some drunken dinner Hope gave me his most remote smile as he told me that if I did no work at all I would fail in the examinations. Bullshit! And this from Hope! I would again work hard in the last three weeks and bluff it out. McAuley transfixed me with a bitter-melancholy stare: If I challenged everyone about everything they would all hack at my shins and bring me down. Cock! I could stare anyone out of countenance. I collected opinions about myself. *What did you think I looked like when you first saw me? What are people saying about me this week?* When I heard criticisms I pounced on them, usually reacting to them from a different part of me from whatever it was that caused the action that had been criticised. Good! Everyone misunderstood me! Bugger them!

WITH THE ANECDOTE OF THE STALINIST I RECEIVED THE FIRST item in the reckoning of my decisions. Appropriately, it was to be a reckoning of accidents ...

When I see him having afternoon tea in the refectory with this and then that student politician a drunken memory comes back. I was sitting down; he was standing up, telling me about the position in a student organisation that had privately been offered to him. It was a complete secret ... not a word! I thought no more about what seemed an unlikely story. But now these manoeuvres at afternoon tea in the refectory fall into pattern. The pieces are being moved into position in a rallying of support. This calls for Horne's counter-gambit – boldly knock out a key piece and thus, with an unexpected move, win another game. I take my key piece, a female member of the left-of-centre, to afternoon tea in the refectory. At the next table the Stalinist is being introduced to yet another potential supporter. A nod in his direction. *Are they lobbying you to support him for this position?* Yes. Next and last question: *Did you know he is a communist?* The indignation I have aroused in the key piece is so immediate that I can walk away and leave the rest of the manoeuvre in her hands. At the next committee meeting one of the Stalinist's supporters, purely by the way, like someone idly calling for a new pack of cards, suggests the position be left open until a following meeting. There is difficulty in finding a candidate. Young Donald has won! And his hand remains hidden!

But D.R. Horne's body sweats and itches. Young Donald has won by deceit. D.R. Horne must now dash out and shout battle cries in front of the enemy, so that everyone will know where he stands and those who are good and true-hearted can rally round him. If he is defeated he will go down where everyone can see him, honourably. In this second role I begin obscurely '... certain mysterious circumstances surrounding this appointment ... suggestion of underhand methods ... highly undesirable ... full discussion ...' Someone has tossed me a note. I open it as I am speaking and read: 'SHUT YOUR MOUTH.' The words drum like a battle march, and I speak directly: 'This man is a Stalinist ... the fact was concealed ... people should know who they are voting for ... if you want to vote for Stalinists, go ahead ... but you should know who you are voting for.' There is an outburst of discussion, someone shouts, then it is all hustled away. Another note is tossed over to me: 'THAT IS THE

FOULEST PERSONAL ATTACK EVER MADE IN THIS UNIVERSITY.' Despite the absurdity of this exaggeration, it occurs to me that I may prove to have been defeated after all, but privately in the future, not where everyone can see me and not necessarily honourably. Young Donald reflects that if D.R. Horne had remained content with deceit, this would not have happened.

It is a few nights later. After a university dinner we have gone on to the *Honi Soit* office, where there is a keg of beer. Although it is already nearly midnight, the Stalinist surprisingly appears and, even more surprisingly, is welcomed by my friends as if they had expected him. While they crowd around, laughing and talking, he and I look at each other, at first sideways, then defiantly. At my end of the office there are only four or five people, and as I talk I have the anxiety of an actor who is sure he is about to forget his lines or that he is reciting dialogue from a wrong play. I ask a stranger to stay with me, but he makes an excuse. I ask him again, but he goes off, and now there are only two of us. A space separates us from the others, who are now singing leftist songs with the Stalinist.

When the party is over I let them go out first, but in the lane outside the Stalinist is waiting for me. Everyone else has gone, except Les Philpott, who is locking up, and my friends, who are arranged in a curve across the lane, watching. Moving round and round and insulting me, flicking out his fist but not hitting me, the Stalinist challenges me to a fight. Young Donald wants to run away, but D.R. Horne stands with his back to the wall, perplexed by one thing: although he can kick, slap, shove and tussle, no one has taught him how to box, and now, at one o'clock in the morning, in this dark lane, here is someone dancing around, challenging him to a boxing match. Feeling like a gentleman who scorns to fight a duel, I get out of this by folding my arms and telling the Stalinist to hit me if he wants to, but I am not going to protect myself. I must stand quite still ... I feel a smack over the face ... he hits me by accident ... I must not move ... someone pushes me, and he again hits me accidentally ... I double over, the wind knocked out of me, holding my chest ... other shapes move in the lane ... improbably, McAuley is waving his fists at him ... now Philpott is there ... my other friends stay where they are ... Saying that I am not worth fighting, the Stalinist joins my friends as they wheel off down the lane, off to the railway cafeteria. Philpott takes me to his house to sleep for the night. My face is beginning to ache, and my body is sore. I clean myself up, and over a glass of beer D.R. Horne rants like a character in minor Elizabethan drama; then, to his shame, Young Donald begins to cry, mourning lost friendship.

The next day I chatter about this incident all day ... it is all over the university ... I am privately assured that majority opinion in the Labour Club is against terrorist tactics ... I refuse the personal bodyguard offered by a Catholic Action supporter ... Jockel (who was not at the party) stands in the Quad, a serious-faced Weimar man fearing violence in the streets. As I chatter I seem to hear my mother talking out of my own mouth. Chatter. Chatter. I am back on the verandah at Muswellbrook; I am my mother, darting here, dashing there, lost in activity. Chatter. Chatter. I am gossiping about myself as my mother used to gossip about the latest talkie. Now I am my father, suddenly uncertain, fallen silent, staring, not understood. Now I am the ideal father of my childhood, joking. I am making wisecracks about myself as my father used to joke about his golf score. What else am I? Kegs instead of pianolas ... *Honi Soit* instead of school plays ... Hobbes says we go on making the same motions like dead engines ... my friends instead of the Denbigh crowd ... what friends? ... I am Pa, stalking out of rooms ... the hero of Hinder House, set upon. But I talk too much, just like my mother.

USUALLY AT THE END OF THE YEAR *HONI SOIT* PETERED OUT INTO small issues. (Douglas McCallum disappeared early, to prepare for the exams, so I let him know he was sacked by taking his name out of the staff panel.) What was left of my staff began to drift off to study for the exams, but I kept up the size of the *Honi Soit*; for my last issue I intended to produce the biggest issue yet, partly for the fun of it, partly because now that I lived in hostile territory I must produce such superb final issues that, on the only grounds that mattered, those of efficiency, my reappointment as editor could not be contested. To consolidate my position I telegraphed the student editors at other universities to send me their comments on *Honi Soit*, confident they would say it was better than their own papers. I intended to print their replies in my last issue, and as they came in I read them with pleasure, like an actor bowing to good reviews. 'Most vigorous of the university publications' ... 'easily the best' ... 'mastery of type amounts pretty well to a fine art'. I read over and over again the congratulations from the editor of the Adelaide student paper:

> Not only does the whole get-up make it a pleasure to look at, but the matter is well-balanced and varied, the articles the correct length, and the right emphasis put on the right places. Instead of the signs of strain and frayed nerves discernible in our paper the appearance of *Honi Soit* suggests a willing cooperation and harmonious staff relations.

Although I was by myself in the *Honi Soit* office when I read this I laughed out aloud. When one of the few remaining members of the staff came in, he laughed too. He was Peter Gibbons, whom I saw as my only protégé now, an Arts I man, brilliantly quick to learn and pleasantly mixing obsequiousness with an ironic send-up of his own obsequiousness, so that he was not really a 'follower' but an independent-minded man. After I had served my second year as editor in 1942 I would see to it that Peter was made editor in 1943. I felt that by the exercise of my will and my keen wits I would survive my present predicament. Although my enemies had humiliated me it was useful that they had once been my friends. I knew their ways. I must be everywhere, staring people out of countenance so that I would not lose the support of my new allies, the centre.

And now I must quickly prepare for the examinations. I would start doing this as soon as I had finished reading my present volume of Dostoevsky. I had begun reading Dostoevsky a few weeks before, more startled by his novels than by anything I had read for a couple of years ... something new to learn again, when it did not seem possible. I paid no attention to his 'themes', absorbing myself into the feel of the secret, obsessive drives that push people into catastrophic actions, the storms of conversation, words jumping out of the brain from strange impulses. This seemed so like the real texture of living that, like an addict granting himself one more day of his drug, I put off work from one night to the next to read some more Dostoevsky.

I slept badly, trying to read myself to sleep, then discovering that it was already three o'clock and I was still wide awake, my head tingling with excitement. My dreams were of threats. Gangsters stand around my bed and one of them undoes his cuff-links, rolls back his sleeves, flexes his fingers and, while the others hold down my arms and legs, he starts breaking my neck, like a hen's. I scream and kick ... the screams sound far off ... the electric light is on ... there are books scattered all over the room. Dad and Mum and even Janet are telling me it is only a dream. I have been fighting the bookcase. After they go and I have picked up my books, I lie awake in the dark.

At the beginning of the study vacation I have to get out an emergency issue of *Honi Soit*. The reactionaries on the senate are opposing the appointment of two professors to the Law School – there is talk of anti-Semitism; we must push the senate out of the way, publishing this *Honi Soit* at once – to show our strength and unity, sending it to members of parliament, prominent people, influencing opinion. The streamer headline jumps up to ninety-six point in a condensed type I have been longing to use.

On the day it goes to press my arms move like lead; I eat nothing, but I am not hungry, standing in the composing room all day, subbing copy on the stone, sometimes forgetting what I am doing, flushed with some mysterious heat, eaten by fatigue, words jangling in my head, skin tingling into pimples. I wait until I can OK the page proofs and give them exclusively to the *Telegraph*. Like some rubbish on the tide, I drift home and then lie in bed and contemplate what is obviously to be my 'nervous breakdown'. I have cracked up. It runs in the family.

The next morning it is clear that I have chickenpox. It is a virulent attack, and I remain feverish and peevish, unable to study. There is no chance I can pass my exams. I wonder how I ever thought I could. Conniving with the doctor, we work it so that he will not let me sit for the exams. This way I will save face and avoid failing. Daubed with calamine lotion, itchy, unable to shave, I lie in bed, sweating, smoking cigarettes, reading Dostoevsky novels and sleeping. Sometimes I improvise plans for next year. When I repeat Arts III, I shall have my money from the *Telegraph*, and that will see me through. The *Telegraph* have been ringing me for several days, at a house down the lane, on our nearest friendly telephone, and now I walk up in my pyjamas and dressing-gown to take one of their calls. Where have I been? ... *The Senate bust-up was the biggest university story for years and they were scooped by the* Herald *on the special issue of* Honi Soit *when their own correspondent was editor of it*. I try to explain that, with chickenpox sprouting at every pore, I had taken the proofs of the special issue to the *Telegraph* office, but the telephone disconcerts me; I have not used telephones much, and I get so excited by its unfamiliarity that I cannot hear what this other voice is saying. My mother had rung them up to say that I had chickenpox, but perhaps she got excited, too. I cannot speak too loudly because I am in someone else's house. He's saying something ... I've been sacked ... OK.

Forgetting the question of what is going to happen to me next year, I lie in bed writing my report as editor of *Honi Soit*, twenty single-spaced foolscap pages of it with forty-three recommendations – the best report, I am sure, ever written by an editor of *Honi Soit*. When I am reappointed editor, with a new staff and with Peter Gibbons by my side, we shall see to it that I do less of the donkey work myself. Lost in dreams of efficiency, I plan new schedules, new ways of keeping the news editor's diary, new procedures in proof correction.

At other times I am terrified. Now that I am away from the university, not exercising my will and my wits, not staring people out of countenance, what is to stop them from getting together and putting someone up against me? I torture myself with the shadows of the conspiracies I imagine to be forming ... and then with the fear that perhaps I am going mad. Is this persecution mania? I indulge in hideous fantasies, making up details of how I would go about such a conspiracy if I were conspiring against myself, of how the left and the centre could join in casting me out, stripped and cold.

To take my mind from these fears, I try to write some verse, but it seems impossible: I have no talent for it. When I gave all my poems to McAuley he kept them for days, then handed them back to me, making a long point about a false rhyme. This seemed to be leading to some more general remarks, but the conversation changed, someone else arrived, and he went off, leaving the poems with me without another word. And all James Hope has said is that I seem to lose interest in poems as I write them, leaving the ends flapping in the wind a bit. Since this is what their ends are meant to do, I am again puzzled and disheartened. Dreaming of complete defeat, I write doggerel songs of farewell and then start assembling phrases for something I have entitled 'Last Poem': *No more to thunder with that old desire ... storm-hungry night ... grown tired with panic, wandering far from home ... When all his world retreats in light of day, no man recalls the moon when it was gay.* There is another telephone call for me. I go up the lane in my pyjamas and dressing-gown again. It is Les Philpott. They have nominated Peter Gibbons against me as editor.

WHILE THE STUDENTS' COUNCIL IS DEBATING WHETHER D.R. Horne should remain editor of *Honi Soit* Young Donald cannot find anywhere to sit comfortably. To his relief, the Union closes. It has been lonely sitting in a leather chair in the empty common-room, and he walks around in the dark, across the Quad and around it several times, up and down roads, walking quickly, as if hurrying somewhere, sometimes looking up at the night sky. He decides to go to the meeting chamber and sit on the step of its ante-room. Some of the voices sound loud. He goes over to the wooden wall and puts his ear to it. One of the councillors (Jockel's girlfriend) is complaining about keg parties in the *Honi Soit* office ... 'There was a terrible smell of beer in the morning and the office was wrecked.' ... 'Did this happen often?' ... 'It happened often enough. Mr Horne always liked a party.' ... They all laugh. Someone else takes up the attack, and Young Donald reflects that some of the councillors were with him at these parties ... He stumbles against a chair, making a noise ... Jo Collings comes out. In the most unexpectedly melodramatic manner, at which Young Donald smiles despite his horror, Collings says: 'What are you doing here? Get out!' D.R. Horne joins the argument, and they jostle each other. When Collings pushes D.R. Horne, D.R. Horne stumbles into the doorway, loses balance and falls down the steps. Collings tries to shut the door, but D.R. Horne catches his hand in it, only distantly aware of the pain, and pushes, body against body, bursting across the ante-room into the meeting chamber. He strides to one end of the table, puts his hands on his hips, and as a kind of D.R. Horne squared he starts shouting a speech: '... thrown out of this office like a criminal ... personal attacks to which I have no right of reply ...' For a while D.R. Horne is so angry his words jar his own eardrums. Then he quietens down: 'Why don't you consider my editor's report? ... forty-three recommendations ... you haven't even looked at it ... efficiency or personal spite?' Another shudder of anger makes him shout again: 'I'm not going to let you talk about me behind my back. I've got a right to attend this meeting and I'm going to sit here and listen to what you all have to say.' He pulls a spare chair towards him and sits down, for the first time seeing faces round a table, and not swirling shocks of anger. Some of his old friends are in the audience, now disturbed and whispering. Alan Crawford is there, obviously on the other side. Jockel looks at him appraisingly, as if to say: 'You've managed to do it again!' Bruce Miller is at his most statesmanlike (and perhaps still sympathetic?). Points of order are raised ... Crawford has whispered some advice to Jockel ... someone is making a speech ... 'Might I through you, Mr Chairman, suggest that perhaps the best course might be ...' So D.R. Horne has surprised them all again. He argues back. They don't know what to do now. They didn't expect this! This daring action will save the editorship! D.R. Horne has the initiative now!

Young Donald's hand hurts and his muscles ache. His shoes are too tight. His skin feels clogged with grime. His bum is itchy and his shirt is wet under the armpits. He gets up. They can do what they like, Young Donald tells them. He's going home to have a bath. It is surprising for Young Donald to find, when he wakes up in the morning, that he has slept soundly all night and he is now enjoying his breakfast.

The phone call with Les Philpott tells me nothing I had not already imagined. I have been defeated for the editorship. The right voted solidly for me, but after I had burst into the meeting and insulted them some of the centre shifted to the left. If I had stayed away from the meeting I would probably have won. The moral of this anecdote seems to be that I talk too much.

I GO INTO THE CITY TO SEE BOB HOPE IN *CAUGHT IN THE DRAFT*. I have chosen this movie because I have been called up and tomorrow I will be in the army for a summer camp. I buy *The Enormous Room*, and when I get home I begin to read it, but then something distracts me, some unsettled business buzzes in my head, something I should do. There were a couple of pieces of doggerel I had written while I had chickenpox. Farewell poems, written because I felt in a farewell mood. I must look at them again, perhaps put them together into one piece. It is as if I must leave something behind me, here in this bedroom, with the desk that used to be our breakfast-room table before Dad had his breakdown, and the bed from which I used to listen to the water running in the Muswellbrook weir or the sounds of my parents bidding at bridge. I dedicate my farewell song to the Students' Council, and sign it 'D.R. Horne, December 3, 1941', and decide that, unlike most of the other things I have written, this is based on experience:

You made what you liked of me, boys,
But you didn't make me your friend
For I lived in a world full of toys
And discontent, played without end.

My style was to reach for the moon
In a poem or two full of death,
Or talk for an afternoon
Until I ran out of breath,

To make my friends by the dozen
And talk to them late in the night,
To eat all the food in their pantries
And never turn out the light.

My life was a half-tone screen,
Dotted and broken at heart.
People could make nothing of it,
It wasn't significant art.

Make who you like of me, boys,
Make what you can of me, do.
You'll get no reward for your trouble.
My father's not in Who's Who.

I made my friends by the dozen
And talked to them late in the night
And all they got for their kindness
Was a bill for electric light.

For I sold my soul to the devil
In a temper, some time ago,
For a pot of pride and a mirror
And I knew I'd have to go.

I put on a show for you, boys,
That cannot be put on again
For now they've packed up the toys
That I used, in default, for a brain.

SOMETHING ELSE DISTRACTS ME ... SOME MEMORY OF SOME OTHER farewell. I look up the diary of the child who grins confidently at me in photographs of myself at the age of eleven, and I read his description of his farewell to Muswellbrook District Rural School, ending, 'Goodbye to all of you! God bless you!' I finish *The Enormous Room* before going to sleep, and report to the army at the required time the following morning, carrying the sandwiches Mum has cut for me in case I get hungry on the train. Everyone's there ... Pritchett ... Jockel ... Philpott ... Miller ... McCallum ... even Crawford ... Stalinists ... Catholics ...

Squad! ... Atten-SHUN! ... Right turn ... Quick MARCH! ... Left, right, left, right, left ... left, right, left, right, left ...

BOOK TWO

CONFESSIONS OF
A NEW BOY

PART 1

THE MAKING OF GUNNER HORNE

1942–44

Scenes from the life of
an occasional malingerer

1

The training depot at Ingleburn was a desolate city of wooden cabins and dusty parade grounds, with so many army units drilling in such a confusion of stamping and shouting that we didn't seem to belong to anything, and when we were not on parade we were exposed to the demanding emptiness of life in long, bleak 'huts' in which I felt we were providing a parody of the theatricality of character and the individual loneliness of e.e. cummings's *The Enormous Room*. (It had been a good idea reading it just before I was called up.) We learned to live in the pandemonium of 'our hut', a monkey house tyrannised by short-tempered extroverts whose bullying and rantings decided who the rest of us were to be. After lights-out, one of them, when he began masturbating, would call out his sexual fantasies as if telling the rest of us exactly what to do. We washed together under groups of showers and sat in rows in the lavatory, where there were no cubicles, smelling each other and hearing each other's farts. The drill and the marching so stupefied me that at times I could not eat. I could not speak. I could not sleep. And to exhaustion were added the trials of neatness: the polishing of boots and scrubbing of webbing, the fear that a speck of dust might be found in a rifle barrel, the rolling up, in the prescribed manner, of palliasse and blankets and the meticulous arranging of all other possessions so they became a 'kit', ready for inspection.

As one out of eight pairs of boots in the centre file of Fourteen Platoon, 'C' Company, Sydney University Regiment, I was learning that what was required of me was to know that when the whistle blew this was where I would fall in, and that when the Platoon Sergeant said 'Quick March!' it was in this file that I would march. I must keep in line, keep in step and, when ordered, slope arms, right wheel, number off or about turn; this was the beginning of becoming a soldier. If I walked even a yard from my given place I would be breaking ranks; if I persisted they would lock me up. Based on the experience of the solid squares of the redcoats, this was the essential wisdom of training: to fall in when told and march in the correct file. The function of the 'instruction' we received was not to teach us how to strip a Bren gun or what to do if the enemy used mustard gas – as university students, if we had been given a drill booklet it would have taken us only a few afternoons to learn all of that. Our instruction was carried on in such discomfort and presented with such rigidity that its main function was to turn us into people who were being so obedient that they couldn't understand what they were being taught.

In retaliation, five of us found we had become the intelligentsia of Section Five, Fourteen Platoon: Gus, with the *savoir faire* of one who was already twenty-two; Lou, a Stalinist and wise-cracker and, on route marches, a talented clown; Jock, a musician, who brought out such feelings of protectiveness that we felt he should be saved from the worst of the army; and Dave, a schoolteacher with a friendly face of rural wisdom that had little to do with his nervous disposition.

Walking along the road back from the pub we five would devote ourselves to complex, subtle mimicry of our training and those who gave it to us, shouting out absurd orders, singing satirical songs. We knew how to make fools of the army, even if we still had to get up in the morning and go on admin parade. After some discussion, the members of the Section Five intelligentsia were now agreed that the sort of drilling we were given was an example of the military dry rot that had led to the fall of France, and a majority felt that what would be needed in Australia was guerilla warfare from a 'people's army'.

But if there were a guerilla movement it would probably be conducted by hard-riding, straight-shooting typical Aussies who hadn't read a book. How could they be guerillas? The only revolutionary talk I had heard from soldiers was from some privates from one of the other units sharing the training depot with us. They were 'sick of being buggered about'. The whole country was 'up to shit'. It was time 'the fucking soldiers told all these bludging war fucking profiteers where to bloody well get off'. We needed 'a fucking good clean-up of all these bastards' who were rooting the whole fucking show – and we could start with 'the fucking refugees and the fucking Jews'.

2

It was six weeks later. The 'Japs' had attacked Pearl Harbor, a naval base none of us had heard of, and we had been trucked down to a 'front line' to the south of the heavy industry centre of Port Kembla. Now, as the dawn came up behind the black shapes of 'C' Company's field kitchens, where Jock and I were setting the fires, it brought, fresh as dew, the pleasure of being different from the others as they still slept in their tents. Whistles blew and feet stamped, but instead of going on PT parade, Jock and I loafed around backstage, unshaven, drinking tea, talking to the cook. We were in the know – the only ones who had seen what was on for breakfast. While the rest of 'C' Company was on admin parade we ate by ourselves and then washed our mess gear without having to queue for the tap; we could shave and clean our boots as if our faces, even our feet, belonged to us. This was official malingering. But, after 'mess parade' I 'fell in' with the rest of Fourteen Platoon and we marched in a 'wiring party', wearing 'tin hats' as if we were about to 'face the Hun'; we were to work on a double-apron of barbed wire alongside a tank trap that stretched between the hills and Mullet Creek. (Mullet Creek! We were descending to farce!) The tank trap undulated across the dried, yellow grass of innocent Australian paddocks: it was as if someone had cut a photograph of a tank trap from a foreign magazine and pasted it onto an 1890s Australian impressionist landscape. This tank trap, with its double-apron of barbed wire, was part of the defence of Port Kembla from 'the Jap'. *The defence of Port Kembla!* If it weren't for the awkward rhythm, the words would have sounded like a line from a satirical song in a Sydney University revue.

Now there was a chance for some unofficial malingering when we found there weren't enough sledgehammers and pliers. Using army issue words, we said: 'Just like the fucking army'. Then, acting out a predictable comedy, Jock and Gus and I hid behind some trees and decided to 'make ourselves scarce', do some 'spinebashing' and 'have a yarn'; when Lou and Dave joined us we talked of deserting, for half an hour, to a nearby general store to drink ginger beer and ice-cream.

Lying on their backs behind the lantana, hidden from the working party, the intelligentsia of Section Five now said what they thought about the Platoon Sergeant, the Japanese infiltration tactics in Malaya and the decline of the West. I began a lecturette on how the Australian army had not learned the lessons of the Spanish Civil War ... Then we heard the sounds of the enemy coming up the other side of the hill. For the next half hour, in 'evasion tactics', we worked our way behind and between lantana bushes and across several rusted barbed wire fences. Scratched by lantana and gashed by barbed wire, we congratulated ourselves on our initiative. For the first time we had 'engaged in realistic training'.

THE WIRING PARTY HAD AN EARLY KNOCK-OFF – 'C' COMPANY WAS to march out in full battle order and, with bayonets fixed, spend the night at combat stations. Section Five's combat station proved to be two short, shallow trenches alongside the railway line, arranged in a 'V', looking over a cornfield with some small hills beyond. They were placed, we told each other, in a way that meant the rest of the company would 'shoot right up our arses'. The trenches had room for only half the section: during our hours of 'stand to' the rest would have to squat in the dirt of a crawl trench. According to instructions, our 'V' was the southernmost outpost in the defence system of the Newcastle–Sydney–Port Kembla industrial area: all ground south of Section Five was to be yielded, 'in the first instance', to the enemy. It was our task to 'check the advance of the Jap' and 'test his strength'. When, from orderly room gossip, we had heard that the OC, a Great War man, had dictated a long memorandum explaining that our regiment was so thinly spread that when the Jap attacked we would all be killed, I had put the details in a notebook, along with a sketch map of 'C' Company's battle positions, lettered with words from a Great War novel ... 'Barbed wire', 'Farm house', 'HQ'. Among the intelligentsia of Section Five there was talk of a 'Maginot Line mentality': were the concepts of manoeuvrability and of defence-in-depth understood, let alone the possibility of a genuine people's resistance?

We discovered that the large tree above our two small trenches was a resting place for hundreds of flying foxes. As we stood-to they flapped above us like large leaves and, making literal an army-issue metaphor, 'shat upon us from a great height'.

ALTHOUGH THE RED ARMY WAS FIGHTING A WINTER OFFENSIVE and the Japanese were cycling through Malaya, on the New South Wales coast one night in the trenches was enough battle duty. After breakfast we were given the morning off, and in the afternoon there was a swimming parade in Mullet Creek. At night, we were granted leave to go to Wollongong, the shopping centre of this coastal strip of coalmines, steelworks, surfing beaches and holiday places. Gus, as one would expect from someone with his sophistication, told our group that the 'only' restaurant in town was the dining room of the Illawarra Hotel, the eating place of the local gentry (such as they were), so we booked a table there before walking down the main street, where Lou, as one would expect from his talent for clowning, mimicked how the OC should call 'C' Company together and announce that, 'after inspection', it had been decided Wollongong wasn't worth defending and the company would retreat 'in orderly fashion' to the bars of Sydney. At the Illawarra, we arranged ourselves as a group for the first time around a table with a cloth on it. Jock, as one would expect from someone with his sense of sympathy, read us a letter from his mother describing fears in Sydney of an immediate 'Jap' invasion and Dave, as one would expect from a man with a wry view of the world, further analysed the character of the Company Sergeant-Major, a schoolteacher with a face of iron.

Here in the hotel dining room, sitting around our table as if we really were ourselves, we re-enacted the reassurances of a family Sunday dinner. We ate asparagus soup, lamb cutlets, roast beef and Yorkshire pudding, apple pie, then jelly and cream. With the coffee we ordered brandy and cigars and then, in the hotel's drawing room, stretched back in easy chairs, put our legs out, and again turned ourselves into critical observers. After sipping beer for a couple of hours, we turned back to being soldiers, went to a hamburger bar and ordered two hamburgers each, with two eggs and two rashers of bacon. Filled with all this food and drink, we dozed in an unlit bus as it took us back to our camp at the Kembla Grange racecourse, where we slept, the aroma of cheap cigars in our hair, on our sacks of straw. In this warm circle of intimacy we seemed to have been friends forever.

This was the only outing we shared.

WHEN I HAD RELUCTANTLY ACCEPTED MY CALL-UP, THERE HAD been a brief medical examination and at the end of it the doctor had asked if there was anything wrong with me on that day. I told him my antrums were stuffy, so he wrote down in his report: 'Says he has antrum trouble'. When I got my paybook I found a clerk had copied this onto the front page – N275356, Pte Horne, D.R. (*Says he has antrum trouble*) – as if, when I was killed in action, this was what I most wanted people to remember me by. When on the morning after our night at Wollongong, the whistles blew at 06.00 hours, my breathing was heavy, my voice slightly hoarse and there was a mild ache in the front of my face. I decided it was antrum trouble, put my head under the blanket and, after the others had gone off to PT parade, went back to sleep. Their voices came through hazily when they returned – I could hear Lou's wisecracks – but when they left for admin parade I heard the Platoon Sergeant's voice. 'Where's Horne?' 'He's sick.' 'Why didn't he report to me?' Silence – then (softly): 'But he's sick.' Another voice, the Company Sergeant-Major's: 'Fourteen Plat-*oon?*' Platoon Sergeant: 'Twenty-three men on parade, sir. One man sick.' They were coming into the tent – Platoon Sergeant's voice, Section Corporal's voice, Company Sergeant-Major's voice. 'Hey, Horne! Hey, Horne! You sick?' When I accepted the commitment, the Regimental Aid Post Sergeant – noted in our gossip for his private aloofness and his public bellowing – clumsily but softly tried to play the leader comforting one of his wounded men.

An ambulance came for me at 10.00 hours and it seemed obvious that symbols of tragedy were to continue to be turned into farce. As part of the complex of battle stations along the coast, an Advance Dressing Station had been set up at a school in Wollongong. Instead of bloodied bandages there were ink-stained papers and instead of the groans of the wounded there was the quiet gossip of a few soldiers sitting in a queue on a wooden form. The MO examined me, wrote down a classification, handed it to an orderly, and told me I was to go off in another ambulance – it would be leaving at 12.30 hours – to the Main Dressing Station, in the hills. It took us an hour to get there, with another half hour on a windy verandah before an MO appeared. Of my four fellow disabled, one had a crushed foot, one had gastritis, one had gashed his scrotum on a barbed wire fence and one, with a sore ear, had been told authoritatively that his army days would soon be over. The MO ordered the bandages on the crushed foot and the gashed scrotum to be changed, sent the man with gastritis to the lavatory, ordered the man with the sore ear to go back to his battle station, looked down my throat, and ordered the four of us who remained to get back into the ambulance and go on to the Casualty Clearing Station at Ingleburn, where we waited for another half hour on a verandah. I spent two minutes with an MO. He said I had a cold, wrote me an order for some cough mixture and told me to go back to camp at Port Kembla.

This 'shitted me off' completely: I had 'spent the whole fucking day being fucked about by experts'; I had been 'properly buggered up'; so far as I was concerned 'they could all go and get well and truly stuffed'. I had read *The Good Soldier Schweik*: I knew what to do. I went to the Regimental Sergeant-Major, showed him, as evidence, the doctor's order for cough mixture and said I had been sent back from the coast to Ingleburn for medical reasons; the Regimental Sergeant-Major attached me to 'B' Company for rations and discipline until 'C' Company came back from the coast.

For the next two days, when my only task was to malinger at morning sick parade, I was able to loaf around, go to the lavatory when no one else was there, shower and shave in the shower block when it was empty, sprawl in a cane chair in the recreation hut reading a volume of verse and magazines from the year before last. I felt that the incident of the ambulance had turned into such an exemplary tale that I could go home now. I had nothing more to learn about the army.

3

Where six weeks ago there had been blisters on my hands and feet there were now the beginnings of callouses. My body was brown. The uniform seemed part of me. I could survive a route march. I knew how to strip a Bren gun. Had I become more of a soldier than I had expected? Not, of course, like my father or my uncles; they had been real soldiers and finally there was nothing real about any experience of mine, since experience, for me, was merely part of the study of comparative literature. But had I gone too far in compromising with the army?

In his latest letter Max Harris had written from Adelaide that he had enjoyed in my last note its 'volatile common sense', 'the quick appraisal of experience and ability to evaluate a situation with a sure touch'. Then he added something that was about more than mere common sense: he said there was evidence in my letter-writing of a 'strain of neurasthenia' and a 'sense of the theatrical'. *A strain of neurasthenia!* – that seemed to suggest that I had not overcompromised!

But was I merely pretending to neurasthenia? Was the impression I had given of neurasthenia nothing more than the skill of a letter writer? There seemed no saving trace of neurasthenia in my becoming an obedient pair of boots in the middle rank of Fourteen Platoon, in admiring the callouses on my hands and feet and the brown bloom of my skin, and in trying for competence, insofar as army instruction would allow it. There seemed 'common sense', or at least an outraged rationality, in being rebellious about saluting, disdainful about all the eager stamping and shouting, and contemptuous of 'crawlers' who wanted to get their 'stripes' or their 'pips'. But was this scepticism merely personal accommodation within what had proved to be, to my surprise, my general conformity? In any case this might merely be the conformity of the Australian soldier as larrikin. However unexpectedly, perhaps I was just another stereotype of the Australian as bronzed Anzac. Self-criticism could go no further.

THESE REVERIES WERE OF A KIND (PRIVATE HORNE, D.R., TOLD himself) that Balzac might have put into the mind of Lucien Chardon in *Lost Illusions*. (Private Horne had not read the novel, but he had read an article about it.) He was sitting in a 'B' Company hut, playing the role of malingerer. He got up and went to the ration store where several of his friends had found a 'soft cop'. Instead of the coffee shops and hotel bars of the city and the university pubs, the quadrangle and the Student's Council offices, the ration store was now the meeting place for what was left of his friends.

In the ration store we could speak without envy of how satisfactory it was that Jimmy McAuley and Harold Stewart hadn't been caught in the draft. We could imagine Stewart peeling potatoes as he thought about the *haiku* but how could one imagine McAuley standing to attention in Section 5? In fact we had heard he had been posted to a front of his own, to teach English in a high school at Newcastle. In the ration store we also talked about those who had already been discharged. Alan Crawford had been in camp for a few weeks, presenting himself, by the way he wore a forage cap and by the arrogant tilt of his cigarette, as a Republican Spanish Civil War General; now he had 'got out' (did Alf Conlon do it?) to engage in work in the Department of War Organisation of Industry so confidential that he seemed to have disappeared. Bruce Miller, all gawky knees and knobbly elbows in army uniform, had been given special training in how to co-ordinate arm and leg movements when marching (which hadn't worked), but now he was out, back at the Australian Broadcasting Commission, reading the national news from Canberra as part of a government initiative to improve morale. Douglas McCallum had played the soldier perfectly – tall, browned, handsome, a veritable 'digger'; but now he had gone off to the Malaya Broadcasting Corporation in Singapore in a way that seemed so sad that I had sat in the recreation hut trying to write him a farewell poem on YMCA writing paper.

In the ration store we spoke of those who had got commissions through family 'pull', of corporals who had crawled their way up to sergeant, and of idiots who had been promoted to lance corporal. Then we took up our oldest ration store theme: perhaps, despite the Japs, at least some of us would be sent back to the university? Civilised values had to be maintained. Otherwise, why would the war be worth fighting?

I visited the sergeants' mess where Bill Pritchett had been sent because of his eyesight; he had become barman and was strutting around as if he had three stripes of his own, while in the background one of the Labour Club Stalinists sulkily lit fires, and another friend, a minor poet and wit, dabbed at the floor with a mop. As we ate stolen bananas, he and I argued whether it really was possible to formulate a theory of aesthetics, then vilified a storeman who had boasted of how, in distributing stores, he favoured the officers' mess. He seemed a character from the fall of France.

When I went out among the men, in the Machine Gun Company I

found Gordon Jockel sitting beside a hut cleaning a Vickers heavy machine gun and looking like someone in a creased and faded photograph from my father's Great War album. Then, in his company's cookhouse, Alf Conlon's brother Arthur was peeling potatoes as if born to do so. As mess orderlies clattered pans Arthur said there were rumours that Alf was making plans for a resistance movement against the Japs, with a scorched earth programme and a dividing-up of Australia into localised zones of control, each with its own underground HQ. We might see a great national revival. As Arthur moved to slicing pumpkin, I reported gossip that Alf would use his pull with the army brass and go into the army himself, and other gossip that he now had the ear of the prime minister, who had some big task for him. With each rumour of a new Conlon scheme, as the mess orderlies sloshed their mops around, we reflected that Alf might yet save the best and brightest from the meanness of the army.

4

The day after the rest of 'C' Company came back from the coast in trucks we were given our first overnight leave. Seven weeks before, when I had left home with my packet of sandwiches, I had been a pale-faced son whose university career had moved into fiasco. Now fiasco was normality but my face was browner than it had been for years, so, when I arrived home, the first thing that had to be done was for Mum and Dad to admire how brown I was. Looking healthy was my contribution to the war effort. Mum piled up unfinished sentences with great spirit to show her pleasure; Dad put on an expression of joviality that was basically tired and unsure. While he was out of the house Mum and I discussed his 'condition': No change. Appetite good. Obediently doing his basket work. Regular habits. Reading newspapers. Listening to the wireless. On Saturdays, playing bowls. His schoolteacher's retirement pension was safe, but Mum said there was word that his war disability pension would soon be up for review.

While Mum cooked the dinner I walked alongside Botany Bay so that Janet could show the barbed wire put up to hold back the Japs; with the nimbleness of a five-year-old, she scuttled through the wire and onto the beach, then showed me a place where I could get through. We danced on the sand and sang the satirical leftwing songs I had taught her, then went back to the house and sat around the oak table in the dining room to eat a celebratory dinner of roast chicken and apple pie. It was followed by tea and iced cup cakes in the sitting room as we listened to the wireless, where Bruce Miller was reading the national news. (The Japs had bombed Rabaul – Rabaul! for Christ's sake! They were almost here!) Mum served chocolate gingers with our game of three-handed bridge; then, when the game was over, she brought in a supper of tomato sandwiches and grilled cheese on toast, her last love-offering for the night. I lay in a bed for the first time for seven weeks and fell asleep over some difficult passages from Mallarmé, chosen because they were remote from army camps, without being mere entertainment. In the morning my voice sounded hoarse enough for me to get from our doctor a certificate for three days' sick leave. If the Japs were bombing Rabaul I might as well have a good time.

But who will I have a good time *with*? What is there to do? Go to a movie. Buy some books. I can find no one at Sherry's or our other coffee shops, nor in any of our hotel bars: even at Ushers the only person I know is the barmaid. As Mum would have said of a tennis club, 'the old crowd has broken up'.

The next two days are spent at home, sluggishly, mostly in bed, sleeping, nursing headaches, reading, writing, crumpling up paper. When a second visit to the doctor obtains more sick leave, I go into the city and take a tram out to the university, where in the main quadrangle I find nothing but green lawn and brown stone, but in the Students' Council office, there he is, Jo Collings, now master of all. 'How well you look,' he says, as if to say that if I had looked as brown and normal as this last year, well things might have been different. I decide I must dissimulate. Well, that's all water under the bridge, I pretend to think. (The bastard!) When we go to the union to have a coffee he talks about national student politics, the confidential work he is doing for the government, the room the university has given him, the secretary, the typewriter, the latest about Alf Conlon. I tell him the ambulance anecdote and other stories, with imitations, with such enthusiasm that I look up Ian Hogbin, the anthropology lecturer, and tell the anecdote to him so successfully that we go down town and have a few beers at the long bar of the Australia Hotel. Sergeant I-forget-his-name from the regiment is in the bar. (How did *he* get in?)

There is a woman I know who lives right in the city, in a terrace house down near the Quay. Perhaps she's at home? I tell the ambulance anecdote to her, and her mother, and the three of us chat about the shape of things to come for a couple of hours. The mother leaves. I attempt what I think of as a 'half-hearted seduction' and as second-best she takes me to a coffee shop and buys us supper. She was in love with me once, for a few days, she says.

The doctor again extends my sick leave. Apart from a lonely trip into town in which I take myself to dinner and then to a movie (where two 'homos' – one military, one civilian – are having a cuddle), I stay in bed, making notes on Freud on humour, Kant on the comic, Aristotle on the ludicrous and Max Eastman on the Sunday funnies.

5

I returned from leave with such an extended contempt for 'C' Company's lack of understanding of the principles of modern warfare that when a sergeant went along the huts shouting for volunteers to join the regiment's battery of museum guns from the Great War, I paraded and, having listened to him tell of the opportunities for greater expertise offered by the artillery, volunteered and spent my last night in the infantry, expecting that, as a gunner, I would again be using my intelligence. But when we reported to the battery and they entered us in their books, we found it was not our intelligence they wanted. The battery was going on a 'shoot' and they needed us in the kitchens to work as 'slushies'. After the guns clattered off each morning, we slushies stayed to clean the huts, peel potatoes, wash dishes, scour pots, and slice food. Our encounter with the guns was at lunchtime when we rode out to them on the cookhouse trucks. When the gunners came back after the shoot, ready for their showers, we were at it again, peeling potatoes.

On the last day, they let the slushies stay at the gun position to listen to the final cannonade. This proved also to be a salute to the end of the university regiment. It was announced that the regiment would now be disbanded: 'reserved' students would be returned to the university, most of the rest would train for anti-aircraft work (after which, it was hoped, they would become officers or NCOs), but battery slushies and a few others would reinforce 'chocko' artillery regiments in the Newcastle Defence Area. The university regiment was itself a 'chocko' unit: as a militia unit of conscripted 'chocolate soldiers', our shoulder patches were not rimmed by the grey border denoting a volunteer for overseas service with the expeditionary Australian Imperial Force; our hatbands were of a drab khaki cloth, while the AIF had stylish linen pugarees; our gaiters were cloth, theirs were of webbing; and unlike members of the AIF we were not permitted to wear a shoulder badge saying AUSTRALIA. But we had not felt like a chocko unit; for better or for worse, we had felt like a university regiment. Now I had become a 'chocko'.

Ambition again arose. The field artillery regiment we had been posted to was in the Hunter Valley, and I now became a Hunter Valley boy again, who knew what needed to be known about the town near our new regiment's base camp. The day after we arrived I wrote to Mum saying how much better organised this new unit was. I praised the view over the green pastures, the companionship of tents compared with the loneliness of crowded huts, and spoke of prospects of promotion and of joining the 'battery staff', the people who made the calculations that kept the guns raised at the correct angle and pointing in the right direction. Mum wrote back that she was pleased I had taken a step up from infantry to artillery.

This was the kind of son Mum, and even more, Dad, would like to read about – someone concerned with getting on in the world. Perhaps I even meant it: 'battery staff' work didn't involve strutting, bellowing, crawling or bullying; it was simply a matter of expertise. I could use my intelligence after all. The day after we arrived a 'school' began: we took notes on how to set up an artillery board; how to compile a target record form; how to assemble and use a director; what the duties were of the observation post officer's assistant, the command post officer's assistant; what was meant by 'angle of sight'; how to work a 'position correction table'. The methods of instruction stupefied me. Before I consented to learn how to complete a target record form I wanted to put my hand on a gun, walk around it and find out what it looked like and how it worked; but all the guns were out on the coast at battle stations, defending Newcastle. There weren't even any battery staff instruments to look at: we wrote notes about how to set these instruments up, without seeing them. We were to learn all our notes on trust, before they had meaning. I retreated from ambition. Faced with such a vacuum of imagination, when we sat for the exam, I came last.

6

For a few more days after this fiasco we still talked together, ate together and, when we had night leave in town, drank together as if we were not soldiers but students in uniform. Waiting for us was this new regiment, into which we would be absorbed as soon as we were told what it was they wanted to do with us. For the moment we knew scarcely anything of 'the regiment'. All three batteries were at their 'battle stations' out on the coast: what was left at the camp were the members of its headquarters, whose main offices reminded me of the club house of a country golf club, and whose principal officers seemed somewhat like 'older members' in a Punch joke. But I kept a belief in the regiment's efficiency. On the night of our transfer, although we had not arrived there until well after midnight, they had been waiting up with something hot to eat; palliasses were filled with straw and laid out with blankets and groundsheets in our two tents; hurricane lamps were alight. I could not imagine the university regiment achieving such efficiency, and when we woke up in the morning for mess parade I had my first good breakfast in the army.

Although the regiment had been one of the first field artillery regiments to go to the Great War, its fighting history, whatever it was, had been inherited by its brother unit, a field regiment in the second AIF that bore the same number as our regiment, but with the word 'second' in front of it, to indicate, like the grey shoulder patch or the puggaree, that it was a real military unit, not a chocko outfit. There was a later part of the regiment's history we also knew nothing about – its between-the-wars period as a militia unit, with a drill hall, annual camps and regimental balls. Its present history had begun only in December, when there had been a call-up to meet the Japs in Newcastle, and in the surrounding coalfields, market towns and small farms. What this now meant was that when we were posted to our battle stations, I would be among 'the workers'. When I learned that, because of my failure in the battery staff exam I was to be posted to the gun, I knew that among these conscripts from the steel mills and coalfields I would be among at least some reminders of a great conflict between the classes.

TWO

A series of vaudeville acts

1

It was on a Sunday morning that I was posted to the artillery troop where I was to be part of the six-man crew of a 25-pounder field gun. We arrived by truck at a cleared patch in the scrub which, apart from the 25-pounders in their pits, looked like a devastated picnic area: men, lying around in tents or half-built shanties surrounded by their own rubbish, were sleeping off their hangovers, talking sex or food, or simply staring at the earth. Some were wearing civilian clothes mixed up with army issue; what they had of uniforms was so holed and tattered that they looked like refugees in a newsreel. A gunner called 'Snow' took charge of me. Before showing me the tent where I was to sleep he stood in front of a board in the improvised mess hut and derisively pointed to the Battery Routine Orders for that morning:

09.00–10.00 Gun maintenance
10.00–11.00 Gun drill
11.00–12.00 Laying practice
12.00–12.30 Rifle drill
10 minute spell every hour.

Then he pointed to the men sitting around talking, playing cards or sleeping. All the 'trumps' (the officers) were away, and so was the troop sergeant-major (a real 'mug lair', a 'smart bastard', but Snow 'knew enough to fix him'). The other NCOs weren't game to give any orders: they were 'too shit-scared of the men', so the men had taken the morning off; fancy expecting you to work on a

Sunday morning, anyway. Snow said no one knew much about 25-pounders: the guns had just arrived and although some of the trumps had done schools in gun mechanism they hadn't told the men about them yet; the troop hadn't had any real training, and it hadn't been on a manoeuvre. No one was to touch the guns. Then Snow let off about the trumps: all bastards. They'd go off to Newcastle in their smart uniforms, but the sheilas knew they were just bullshitting. They weren't real officers. They were just chocko officers. After finishing with the officers, Snow got on to the NCOs: none of the buggers could be trusted; they could be great ones with the boys, but they'd all put you in as soon as look at you. As we were walking to the lean-to where the crew of Number One gun lived, we found a bombardier asleep. Snow explained he was called 'Donkey' because he had a big penis, then shook him awake so he could undo his fly and show it.

It was half-past ten and 'Skeeter', a skinny grasshopper of a man with a rasping voice, had just woken up. Snow explained that Skeeter had got stuck into the steam (cheap wine) last night and come home reeling, rotten drunk. They tried to put him to bed, but he fought them. He slept for a while, woke up, vomited, staggered off to the fringe of the gun position area, passed out beside a bush, slept there for the rest of the night, and moved to a gunpit for more sleep while the others had breakfast. Now Skeeter staggered into the centre of the gun area with the confidence of an old Shakespearian actor playing a comic. (I was making comparisons with the recruiting scenes in Shakespeare's *Henry IV*.) With a sense of theatre, he paused until everyone was looking, then, in a thin screech, gave the call for a two-up game: 'We want a spinner! We want a spinner!' Others joined the mime, making motions of tossing coins into the air and watching them fall. The chants went on: 'A bob in the guts to see him go.' 'A zac or any part of a zac to see him go.' 'A brown he heads them.' Then: 'Set on the side?' ... 'Fair go spinner.' Skeeter again pretended to toss coins in the air. They all mimed attention, looking up, looking down, miming gains and losses.

The play acting went on for a while, then disintegrated. Some went off to sleep, some talked. Skeeter still held a small audience, who moved into a kind of corroboree. Now and again there was a ritualised question and response: 'You see that tree?' 'Yes!' (in chorus) 'Then belt it up yer!' The troop relaxed in its own way until someone noticed it was lunchtime and the men lined up along the road rattling their mess gear, making a sound like prisoners rattling bars; most hadn't received army issue mess kit (or perhaps they had thrown it away) so they carried ordinary tin plates, as if waiting for grilled chops at a bush picnic. 'How would you like a nice big juicy steak?' Skeeter shrieked. '*Yes!*' 'With oyster sauce?' '*Yes!*' 'Well you won't get it!'

A young lieutenant arrived on a motor bike. At once Donkey shouted to Skeeter: 'Stop that talking, gunner!' The men accepted this attempt at command with good-humoured contempt. After lunch, in a working party ordered by the lieutenant to clean up the gun position area, I discovered that, while in a university regiment working party I had been one of those who could seem busy while doing nothing, on this working party I was one of the few who did any work at all.

WITH THE DIM LIGHTS OF ITS BROWNOUT, THE SIGHING AND rattling of its shunting trains, its slatternly waterfront bars, the mournful siren-cries of the dark ships in its harbour, and the presence of the iron and steel mills and the coal loaders, Newcastle at night had become, in my imagination, a dirty, provincial town from a French novel. Now, more than before, the fall of France seemed a pointer to our condition. It was while we were at the battery staff school at the base camp that Singapore fell; four days later the Japanese bombed Darwin; now they had occupied Australian territory in New Guinea.

On leave in Sydney I found Douglas McCallum, who had been evacuated in a Dutch cattle boat from Singapore to Batavia just before Singapore's surrender and then, just before Batavia's surrender, evacuated from Batavia to Perth in a small coastal ferry. What he had to say in *Honi Soit* about the British defeat seemed worth reading again and again, because someone I knew had written it. Such phrases! 'The European contempt of orientals' ... 'British ostrichism and wishful thinking' ... 'blockheaded refusals to revise strategy' ... 'the antiquated Victorian imperialist outlook of the hollow men of the colonial administration' ... 'the apathy of the exploited native population and the ultimate defeatism of the high command'. The 'real fifth column' were the British themselves, 'those in the administration who insisted *ad nauseam* upon the servile status of the Malay, those myopic fools who failed to appreciate the hostility brought by their alien rule because of its injustices and invidious system of privileges, its only justification faith in the celestial mission and the destiny of the chosen British few'.

There was consolation in these moral tales of how the fall of Singapore was so well deserved. And here at Newcastle, one of the coal ports of the industrial revolution, where the Japs could destroy most of Australia's heavy industry in a spare afternoon, there seemed images of folly greater than any in the fall of France. Even in France there hadn't been an artillery troop where the gunners weren't allowed to touch their guns. The regiment reflected the long-ritualised rejoicing in social difference in this part of the Hunter Valley. The officers – insurance clerks, bank clerks, schoolteachers – had gone to high school, played golf and bridge and knew who they were. 'The men' despised the officers as 'no-hopers' and the NCOs who served them as 'crawlers'. This resolute contempt was expressed in an insolent slovenliness made easier by the fact that the men were only half-equipped – some had no rifles; none had the full issue of webbing – and they were scarcely one-tenth trained. It was left to the farm boys to do the digging and cleaning, which they did in a good-natured way, despite ridicule, because it was the natural thing to do. But there were no heroic images of class struggle. There were no real 'owners'. Nor were there any real 'workers'. The men from the industrial areas and the coalfields were unskilled labourers. Skeeter's job in civilian life was to sweep floors. The heroic had turned into a series of vaudeville acts. No one spoke of 'the workers'; the talk was about the pubs of Newcastle and the 'chromos' (easy lays) who went to them. Getting boozed on beer or steamed up on plonk was what kept life going.

I wrote to friends that I was lost among 'an effete elite of golf-playing petit bourgeoisie,' a 'boozing lumpen proletariat' and 'dimwitted bucolics'; but 'lost' was too positive a term. Apart from a few chatterboxes like Snow, who would talk at anyone, the others would say nothing at all to, or even at, me. Skeeter was, of course, too grand an actor to be able in the ordinary sense to converse with anyone – as a tribal incantator he could speak only in public audience – and this was apparently the source of his power: he set up another world, of derision, which denied the existence of the regiment. The others, when they weren't performing a corroboree with Skeeter, did talk among themselves but, based on a private language of shared, and exclusive, Newcastle experience, their conversation was so allusive there was no part in

it for people from Sydney. The three of us who had come from the university
regiment learned to speak our own allusive language, now based on a common
sentiment of contempt for the regiment.

2

Oliver Somerville, now even more out of tune with the times, stirred
sufficiently from his anarchist's despair at my backslidings to send me, from
Sydney, a *ballade* and a *rondeau*, which seemed to catch a mood. The *rondeau*,
called *Fall of the House of Ushers*, celebrated the future fate, when the Japanese
bombers came, of our part of the bar at Ushers Hotel and its barmaid, Nell:

> Say, Nelly, shall the explosive bomb
> shatter the drinker's full aplomb?
> and loungers on the brassoed rail
> consume a Molotov cocktail?
> The debauchees of gin and lime,
> committing an unheard of crime,
> forsake their drinks before it's time,
> enchanted by the siren's wail?
> Ah, Nelly, say!

The *ballade*, *The Ballade of Lost Phrases*, a more ambitious affair
commemorating the decline and fall of the Left into mere social patriotism,
used the refrain 'Where are the phrases of yesteryear?' and carried as its *envoi*
the quatrain:

> Comrades, we argued, fought and swore;
> We might as well have stuck to beer.
> The Japanese are in Johore:
> Where are the phrases of yesteryear?

As soon as I could I showed both *ballade* and *rondeau* to Jimmy McAuley.
When I had a half-day leave in Newcastle I would go first to the house where
McAuley was living, three floors up with a view of the steelworks across the

bay, in a rented room that would have suited Somerville's mood of intellectual proletarianism; usually McAuley wasn't in, but on the day I brought him the poems Somerville had sent me, he was there, marking essays from an Intermediate Certificate class. In the pub, as he read the verses, it was as if we were back in Sydney and a poem had been handed to him for judgment. The lowering of the eyelids showed concentration; the slow, controlled widening of the lips pleasure ... a quick, high laugh ... it was all right! McAuley liked them. More than that: he told me it was he who had written the *ballade*. With our Smith's Potato Chips, we chewed over the symbols of betrayal by the Left and the rottenness of the Right. We bought more beers as McAuley contemplated the disasters of the age, both the corruptions of the Stalinists and the corruptions of the Labor reformists. And then, in retreat, like shy lovers unable to say what they meant but equally unable to stop talking, we would use, in a manner both comforting and irritating (because what, after all, were we talking about?) the words of what we saw as 'philosophical anarchism'. As more beers went down the hatch there was comfort that we still had a critique with which to distinguish ourselves from the present and, however cloudily, to imagine a better society, even if it was one that was not going to happen.

On the bus journey back to our battle station I slowly moved out of the sense of enchantment that came from being with McAuley and again became Gunner Horne, turned from butterfly to grub, but also D.R. Horne, tremulously his own critic. This time had I really talked too much? Had my worthlessness been finally revealed? I could become frightened by the excesses of conversation – its hen-like pecking, its squawking and clucking and crowing: when it came to wisecracks and set-piece exemplary anecdotes, I knew I had good timing, but everything else was too spontaneous. I would be so overwhelmed by the love and playfulness and generosity of talking that I could shout out sentences from the sheer embarrassment of silence, jump meaninglessly from this to that, and yet at times not speak about what I knew most, as if something known by me was not worth knowing. Faced with complexity, I would either speak softly and without meaning, or get so angry that I would shout out something that was clear and, later, be ashamed of its clarity. But McAuley controlled all conversations by our knowledge that if we offended him, he would no longer receive us. This time (I would wonder this each time I saw him) had I offended him with some fatal revelation of my own naïveté?

In the gun position, from which we were expected to defend Newcastle with guns we were not allowed to touch, conversation was still dominated so impenetrably by the anecdotes and jargon of lumpen Newcastle that sometimes my skull would ache. Then need to talk began to find one outlet – in gossip about the officers and NCOs. Not with Skeeter and his most devoted cult associates. They seemed scarcely aware that there were officers and NCOs; but with most of the other gunners I could now join in the ever-continuing conversation, obsessive and venomous, about the follies of the whole outfit, from lance bombardiers to generals, and in particular about the follies of all those in our own regiment who had stripes on their sleeves or stars or crowns on their shoulders. This conversation roared on, permanently and predictably.

Occasionally those of us from the disbanded university regiment would spend a night's leave together in Newcastle, engaging in pleasures of the mouth: we would eat at the Great Northern Hotel, whose dining room was a gentry eating place; we would drink a few beers, moderately; then we would talk immoderately about the follies of our troop. At our dinners it could again seem – as it had at the Hotel Illawarra, if with different people – that I was with those who would remain companions forever. Some of the most companionable nights, rich in vicarious conversation, were spent at the pictures. The stars and styles of Hollywood had followed us to Newcastle: Robert Taylor was there in *Billy the Kid*, Alice Faye in *That Night in Rio*, Betty Grable in *Down Argentine Way*, Bing Crosby in *Birth of the Blues*. There were the reassuring names of the Royal, the Civic, the Strand and the Victoria and there were half a dozen other picture shows in the suburbs. It was a time of 'aviation movies' – *Dive Bomber* ('Filling the sky with glory'), *Bombay Clipper* ('A fortune in jewels and a plane packed with drama and thrills'), *I Wanted Wings* ('Four hot pilots and the blonde bombshell, Veronica Lake'), *Flying Blind* ('The most thrilling aviation story of all time') – and, as ever, of musicals. For weeks after we saw the musical *Lady Be Good* our gun position echoed with the words:

Oh, sweet and lovely
Lady be good,

Oh, lady be good
To me.

But we preferred movies that were meant to be funny. Claudette Colbert in light comedy, the Marx Brothers in heavy farce. Famous comedians were now being called up: the latest Laurel and Hardy at Newcastle was *Great Guns*, the latest Abbott and Costello, *In the Navy* and the latest Hal Roach, *Tanks a Million*.

In Sydney, where I spent two days' leave once a month, there were chances for 'sensible' conversations with Mum and Dad, uncles and aunts – expository discussions on the state of the world, like wireless talks – and now that there were again people in the bars and coffee shops (even if they were mainly the wrong people) there was the opportunity for correcting error. In the interests of cool reason and clear vision, I could, once a month, carry out my public duty of cutting out the bullshit, chopping arguments with logic and shouting down irrelevance.

Then, through Douglas McCallum, there came the chance to do my public duty in its most satisfying form. I was asked to write for *Honi Soit*. McCallum was no longer a protégé; in fact he could now seem a leading figure, someone succeeding where I had failed. He was still on salary from the Malaya Broadcasting Corporation and was using it to lead an enviable life in an apartment in an old mansion at a smart address in Potts Point, with a sunken bath in it, like a set from a Cecil B. de Mille movie. He had money to spend on records and books; he was building up an acquaintance with writers and painters; and he was going to use some of his leisure in helping keep *Honi Soit* radical in the way I had made it. I wrote for *Honi Soit* a denunciation of the award of the university's Henry Lawson Prize for Poetry to some doggerel on 'freedom' written by someone I saw as a reactionary Catholic. It was like the old days of several months before. Disguising himself as 'D.R.H.', D.R. Horne was again in his angry mood: 'As worthless and unimportant a bit of writing as has ever been awarded a prize, these verses typify the neurosis of the male and female schoolgirls who stalk abroad in our educational institutions as Florence Nightingales to bourgeois culture. As a thesis on Freedom it might well have been subsidised by the Police Department. Once again the university has come out on the side of falsehood, of inferiority and safety, rather than of truth, initiative and enterprise ...' etc.

Back at the gun position, I could follow with joy each week the letters in *Honi Soit* set off by my attack. But I was also now enjoying the best of all conversations – 'conversation' with nineteenth-century novels that I felt were telling me some of the things I really wanted to know. On my previous leave in Sydney I had gone to the Roycroft bookshop and stooped down to the bottom shelves where there was a cache of Everyman's Library and Modern Library novels and books from the World Classics series. I held various volumes in my hands, turned over the pages, then bought *The Charterhouse of Parma* and *The Red and the Black*. I scarcely knew Stendhal's name. However, when I began reading *The Charterhouse of Parma* on the train journey back to Newcastle, sitting beside a soldier who for a long time played with himself under his greatcoat, I found that this novelist was talking to me directly with a personal understanding I had not found in any other novel. I was reading it in the gunpit when I fully understood how much I had enjoyed the section on the battle of Waterloo; I was so gratified by its understanding of lack of consequence that I read this section again that night in the tent, by the light of the hurricane lamp, while the others played euchre: Stendhal, I was sure, would have understood the significance I had given to my ambulance anecdote.

Later, sitting in the gunpit, or in the tent, or, several times, in the back of a truck as part of a working party, I read of the court of Parma, delighted to find in Stendhal's cynicism about liberals and about ambition the lessons I had learned from my year on *Honi Soit* and the Students' Council. Because of his talkativeness, the character of Fabrice held my attention to the point of terror. Count Mosca might say to him, as Alan Crawford might have said to me, 'If a brilliant argument occurs to you, remain silent', or he might remind him that 'it is such dull brutes who are going to decide my fate and yours', but, like me, Fabrice spoke his heart to people who didn't understand him and in the middle of his own words he could throw himself away, as if words could be the most deadly of all actions.

By the time I finished *The Charterhouse of Parma* there was an end to the pretence that we were at battle stations. Regimental Headquarters stopped us playing with field guns we couldn't work and sent us back to a training camp to learn how to use them. After a day's training I would read *The Red and the Black* squatting cross-legged on my palliasse. It was another novel that seemed to be speaking to me more deeply than I had known novels could do, so that I now used Julien Sorel, as well as Fabrice, to think about myself. Obviously, both Julien Sorel and Young Donald had been objects of ill will among the mediocre. We both needed as patrons self-assured, clever people like the Marquis de la Mole or Alan G. Crawford because they were not envious of our talents. And we were both, at heart, so generous that even when we took up some of the deceits of a hypocritical world we would do it with spirits so high that people would see what we were up to, and our deceits would fail. We were both of humble origin – Julien a carpenter's son, and I, although a schoolteacher's son, the grandson of a coal miner and a sleeping car conductor, and in any case from a government school, with a government school accent, in a university dominated by people from private schools. With enough Crawfords or de la Moles, we were bound to make our way in the world; and then, with great honour, we were bound to be defeated. For us, defeat was a way in which we could show our disdain. But what would my form of defeat be? I went back to *The Charterhouse of Parma*. I was proud of how over the last two years I had thrown myself away to profuse enthusiasms; now, in this novel about the impulsive commitments and obsessions of Italian aristocrats there were enactments of how, by an offhand commitment to something one knew nothing about, one might rashly waste a whole life. That seemed to me the kind of thing I might do. How would I throw myself away, for the sake of making conversation?

3

Just as after the Battle of Waterloo Fabrice could ask 'Have I really taken part in a battle?', for us it was only a matter of inference that we were part of a 'regiment'. There was a joke that the commanding officer had visited our regiment's battle stations and a gunner had asked him who he was, but in fact there was no evidence that the CO had visited any of the battle stations – he was said to be busy with the paperwork at headquarters.

Yet while this imagined entity, 'the regiment', remained an amorphous generality, week by week our gun position life was less dominated by Skeeter's nihilist performances and it was taking on more of the outward forms of a military unit.

Our first entry into these mysteries came when we were issued with a gun drill book and then taught gun drill. 'Number One' would order the other five in a crew to line up at the rear of the gun and we would 'number off', calling out the numbers from two to six. On the next order, 'Take post!' we would run to set positions – then we would enact laying, loading and firing the gun; then we would run back to where we had started, re-shuffle ourselves, call out our new numbers, and at the order 'Take post!' kneel in new positions. A sense of professionalism increased when reinforcements arrived from an AIF training depot. There were enough of them, along with those of us from the university regiment, to set up an opposition party with its own rituals of conversation: we broke Skeeter's hegemony.

As rapidly and restlessly as ghosts, we began to move from battle stations to training camps to bivouacs. At one bivouac all four of our troop's guns and their crews were lined up, side by side, and, in turn, each of us was tested as a gunlayer. I came top in both speed and accuracy: at a troop parade it was announced that along with three others I had now become a permanent 'Number Three', a gunlayer, a 'Group Three Specialist', at an extra shilling a day, whose job it was to set the gun's instruments and then turn wheels to move the barrel up and down and from side to side; then slap my right buttock, call out 'Ready!' and hold a clenched fist above the gun's trigger, bringing it down with a thump on the order 'Fire!' We would then hear a small click. We had not yet used live ammunition.

In camp our gun was wrapped in a canvas cover and lined up with other 25-pounders in what the drill book called an 'artillery park' and for a day or two we might not see it; but at one of the battle stations or on bivouac, we would sleep beside the gun as if it were one of us, and on 'manoeuvres' we would attach it to its ammunition trailer, attach the trailer to our truck, and, wherever we went, the gun would follow us around. At times we would manhandle it with dragropes, or our hands; on bivouacs or at battle stations we would cover it with camouflage nets, to keep it from the eyes of the enemy. But the gun's most important function was its demand for constant maintenance – we were always testing its tyres or washing its wheels, its shield, its carriage and mobile platform, the outside of its barrel, and then rubbing them over with kerosene; the delicate insides of the barrel and the breech mechanism would be oiled like a baby, hidden sections were stripped and put together again; and with a grease gun we would lubricate the 'nipples' of its most private parts.

The innards of the gun were unfolded before me in final detail at a Gun Mechanism School, for which I was sent to Sydney Showground for a week. I learned how to strip all the sections we were allowed to handle and was even shown what went on inside its forbidden parts, and I learned in correct order the words that officially described the sections of the gun and their functions. Thus, if asked why the top of the breech block was curved, I would stand to attention and instead of saying simply that this allowed the shell to be put in, I would reply politely, 'The function of the curve at the top of the breech block is to facilitate loading.' I came top of the school. A gunner who was much better than I could ever be at looking after a gun lost points because, parroting the required answer, he pointed to the curve in the breech block and said it was the 'persiliate loading'. This shaped into the first part of my exemplary anecdote from the Gun Mechanism School. It reached its punchline when I returned to our regiment. Our Number Two – a farm boy who had grown up with machinery rather than words – was the gun's mechanic as well as its loader. There was to be no practical use for my training: when I got back to our troop I was congratulated on my success, but he was the one who went on looking after the gun. It was my job to come top of the school; his job to 'maintenance' the gun. However, I was now qualified to tell him, in the official words, what he was doing.

Comprehension that I belonged to a 'regiment' had moved out from knowing something about our own gun, to an awareness of the other three guns and then, more widely, to the idea that we belonged to a 'troop'. At battle stations there didn't seem any meaning to the word 'troop' – we could see ourselves only as separate gun crews – but, just as I had learned the parts and functions of a 25-pounder gun, we were also learning the parts and functions of an artillery 'troop'. On an exercise I could not only feel that I was part of a 'gun position' of four guns and know the various kinds of drill that this could mean; if more tenuously, I now also had some understanding that signal wires and wireless connected us with an 'observation post' (although I didn't know what that would look like), and that somewhere behind us were 'transport lines'. In camp, the 'troop' unfolded on parade, arrayed in our hierarchy – the troop commander, his officers and the sergeant major, then the sergeants, bombardiers, lance bombardiers and gunners. We would fall in, click our heels, perform our ceremonies, shout out our reports, then receive our orders for the day. The veneer of professionalism would fade, however, when our troop commander attempted, either by entreaty or by harangue, to persuade us to become better soldiers. He so carried with him the air of a plump, boozy old *habitué* of the clubhouse bar that although he was in uniform his khaki trousers could seem plus-fours, his swagger stick a Number Two Iron, and his rhetoric that of 'the nineteenth hole'.

On a more complex level of existence, we also belonged to a 'battery': another troop joining with ours through a shared hierarchy of battery commander, battery captain, battery officers, battery sergeant major, quartermaster sergeant, and other specialists, but the 'battery' existed as yet only in our largest form of ceremony, the 'battery parade'. I could now imagine what a 'troop' might do in action but, outside its ceremonial function, we had had no experience of ourselves as part of a 'battery'. Then at one of the training camps there was talk for some days of a 'battery manoeuvre'. In the mess hut there were hurried lectures for officers and NCOs on 'the deployment of a field battery', and on the day of the manoeuvre, which was appropriately rainy, evoking ideas for me of Flanders, we drove out of camp in correct groupings just like the diagrams in different colours of chalk we had seen on a blackboard in the mess hut, and different sections of the battery moved away from us along different roads just like the arrows on the blackboard. With the other gun crews from our troop we then sat in our trucks, parked in a farm paddock for most of the morning, doing nothing. It began to rain harder. When the order came to move, one of our trucks bogged down, as in a real war: after we had manhandled it out of the mud, we drove on for half a mile or so, then stopped in another paddock, where we sat in our trucks, again doing nothing. Several hours passed. No lunch. Heavier rain. We were ordered back to camp. Pure Stendhal.

The next week the troop commander disappeared. It was rumoured that he had been posted to one of the coastal garrisons where old soldiers were pledged to a last ditch stand against the enemy. The new troop commander adopted a laconic style in which a cool stare was more important than words. There were more orders of the day, but no harangues. We seemed to have taken another step towards becoming normal. Shortly after, we began holding regular battery parades and when we again attempted a 'manoeuvre', we seemed to work together, more or less, as a battery. As the last act of the 'manoeuvre' we were to imagine enemy tanks attacking us; according to the referees, we destroyed five of the enemy's tanks before we were destroyed ourselves. We had not yet fired any live ammunition.

A hidden hand was plucking away the Falstaffs, Bardolphs and Pistols among our officers and occasionally there would be a redrafting to a labour battalion of the Mouldys, Shadows, Warts, Feebles and other Shakespearian clowns among 'the men'. I could no longer use *Henry IV* as a way of describing the regiment. A few university and AIF men were sent to officers' schools and came back with their 'pips'; others were given 'stripes'. We were moving from the bizarre to the merely second-rate. There was still a division between the old Newcastle crowd and the new university and AIF men, but some of the Hunter Valley boys had joined us. Skeeter was now well in the minority party. Later, he was drafted to a unit in New Guinea.

In the three months I had been with the regiment we had still not been on a 'shoot'. While a battery parade and even a battery manoeuvre now had meanings, these meanings were related to various types of drill, and to our relations with each other (itself a kind of drill), not to digging gunpits, or getting tractors out of the mud, or choosing gun positions, and certainly not to firing guns. What we were learning was how to 'be in camp'.

This reached a climax when we moved to a large training depot at Greta. With its parade grounds and suburbs of long wooden huts, it was as large a complex as Ingleburn; our whole regiment was there, fitting into one 'suburb', and even though we had no regimental parades, as we lined up outside our huts in various smaller formations, there could be the feeling that in all this strictly ordered muddle we perhaps belonged to something more rational than what we could see with our own eyes.

'Off duty', I belonged to the enormous room of 'our hut', from which the main relief was to mope with boredom among the cane chairs and old magazines of the YMCA. Sometimes four of us might sit on the floor of the hut and play auction bridge. Often I would sit alone, cross-legged on my palliasse, reading. There was always the excitement of gossip about the troop or, more remotely, the battery, or even more remotely, some idiot from regimental headquarters; and there was the reassuring sameness of dirty stories. If we had night leave we could go off by bus to Maitland or Cessnock and play our own mild version of the brutal soldiery. If we went to Maitland it was to 'have a feed and get pissed' – on one drunken night when the only alcohol we could buy was schnapps I came back to camp so drunk that I went to sleep under the hut because, I said, I preferred the company of spiders. If we went to Cessnock it was 'to look for a pickup', a process made difficult for me by the embarrassments of the inextricable banality of conversation with these female strangers. There was a special sense of the military spirit when some of us were posted as guards at the camp's jail. Here at the brutal heart of the military we sat in the guard room chatting to the prisoners behind their steel bars; we gave them cigarettes and they lent us the handwritten pornography with which they amused themselves.

WHEN WE LEFT GRETA TO RETURN TO A 'BATTLE STATION', I FELT I was back home. It was at 'Mosquito Valley', a name we gave to a stretch of flat, dry land at the edge of a limitless swamp, said to be used as an air force bombing target, where at night we burned cow dung to keep away the mosquitoes. Once a week we went on leave to Newcastle to get drunk, on the way home singing again and again our song of discontent:

> So, good-bye General Sturdee,
> And General Blamey, too.
> Since we have joined the army
> We've been fucked about by you,
> The AIF is up to shit,
> The militia is a farce,
> And as for this fucking regiment –
> You can shove it up your arse!

At night in Mosquito Valley we would lie in the tent and, by gossip, share our knowledge of the world, surrounded and protected by the homely smoke from the small fires of burning cow dung.

THREE

The accident anecdote

1

Early in May a truckload of us were singing 'Balls to Mr Winckelstein' on our way from Mosquito Valley to the mobile bath unit. Another truck approached; it was only a narrow bush track – our truck swung to the right.

I was on the right-hand side of the truck and when we swung over, at about forty miles an hour, my head hit the branch of a tree. The tree slashed a cheek, ripped an eyelid, cracked an eye socket and threw me to the floor of the truck, where the back of my skull hit a pick. The gunners told me later that blood splashed them as I thrashed around 'like a headless chook' and then, 'screaming like mad', tried to throw myself over the side of the truck.

First memory: I am floating through dark air, held up by gunners' voices. Someone says we are at a medical post on an airstrip. Next memory: I am lying, sightless, on a stretcher, vomiting, my skull aching and my body shivering. From somewhere there is a voice. I tell the voice I have 'shock'. I have read about it in a book.

Next memory: through the bandage over my eyes I feel a strong light. Some people discuss the signing of a form. I try to say I will sign the form. They put a pen into my hand, hold it – and there's my signature. Before I pass out again there is a rustle of anxiety amongst all this aching: there is something I mustn't forget. It is lost, in emptiness ... then there is a prickle of memory. What I mustn't forget is that this is an anecdote.

Last memory: I wake up in private darkness in the ambulance. Blood is clotting my nostrils and wetting my lips. I am going to die. As I lay in 'B' Ward in the casualty clearing station at Greta, I reconstructed these scenes as if I were painting them as panels in a tryptych of the kind Stewart had shown me in art books. Gasping for air, aching, dribbling, drugged, I would use the moments when I 'came to' to rehearse details so that I would have something to remember. When someone held a looking glass up to my face and I could see that the right eye had sunk into purple and yellow pulp, the nose had spread into the torn flesh of the cheek and the lips had burst into a pink mess, I memorised the colours and added these to my rehearsals. An orderly showed me my blood-stained tunic: it seemed as real as any object in a war museum. This was the awesome presence of the *authentic*. Part of the story I was telling myself was that when I had first been made to understand that I was in a hospital ward I had thought, 'At least they can't say this is psychosomatic.' This could be the punchline of the anecdote. Several days later, a question from myself as audience: what would I say if some friend commented that it might have been a death wish? In a moment of later clarity I decided I should make this comment myself. It would provide a turn-of-the knife *dénouement*.

MUM AND DAD STOOD BESIDE THE BED, DAD WITH HIS ANXIETIES, Mum with a bottle of oysters. On Mother's Day, a few days before, they had received a telegram signed by the Minister for the Army pronouncing that I was on the 'Seriously Ill' list (On a casualty list! More evidence of authenticity!) and now they were lodging at a hotel in Greta. Dad found it too much for his nerves to see me so injured and went back to Sydney, but Mum stayed for a week, arriving daily with chicken and fruit, gossip and praise, cigarettes, the *Sydney Morning Herald* and the *Daily Telegraph* to read to me – and information, gained from the staff, about what was likely to happen to my head. There had been an operation on my eye on the night I arrived, she said (this was not one of my memories), and 'the sight had been saved'; I would be able to breathe through my nose when the swelling went down and they made adjustments inside my nostrils; they didn't think my face would be badly scarred; my teeth were only chipped; the paralysis that made me dribble would probably go; as soon as I could be moved they would send me in an ambulance to the x-ray unit at Maitland to search for cracks in my skull. Apart from sleep, I was now conscious all the time, and aware of my new way of living. 'B' Ward was a Seriously Ill and Dangerously Ill ('SI & DI') ward: it was filled with men with broken bones – some of them (concussion cases) unconscious, or mad. Each morning I would wake up with fear: where was I? On the most fearful morning I knew I was a Bolshevik, hiding in an empty railway station ... outside, the White Guards were waiting ... I screamed. A nurse told me it was time to get washed.

The wet warmth of sponging was one of the pleasurable things they did to me, along with the healing sting of eyedrops, the prick of injections, the smart of wound dressings, the tickle of nostril probings, the moistening of dried lips and the clearing away of dead skin, but my desire to get a good mark in the calm authority of the doctors' rounds made one of the two pivots of the day: the other was the daily visit from Mum, with new talk about 'how marvellous everybody is being', from the doctors to the driver of an armoured personnel carrier who gave her a lift from the hotel. As she sat there beside the bed there was the hope that, again, we were mother and son. At night, in the dark, there were the screams from concussion cases gone mad and the long attempts, by keeping my mouth shut, to try to force a trickle of air through a nostril, and an accompanying panic that I would suffocate – and, when I fell asleep, nightmares that I was being hit over the face. After I had gone by ambulance to Maitland for my skull to be x-rayed, my doctor discovered it was not my skull that had been x-rayed but my right collarbone. This was added to the anecdote, as an afterthought to follow the *dénouement*.

Life became normal. Nightmares and dawn fears stayed but now I joined in such sociability as there was among our broken bones; we called out jokes across the bodies of the unconscious and, by this, imagined we were something called 'Ward B'. Ritual sociability softened into intimacy when I talked with the soldier in the next bed – a concussion case, like me. On and off, between sleeps and shouts, we chatted most of the day, friends for life.

A sense of the authentic remained, except for one suspicion: when Mum wrote that my name had not yet been printed in the newspapers' casualty lists this was to her as if the Leaving Certificate results had come out and my name had not been among them, but to me it brought back general fears about my own fraudulence. If it wasn't in print, was I really 'Seriously Ill'?

The problem of authenticity became a crisis when I was loaded into an ambulance, taken to Greta railway station, and then off-loaded into a bunk in an ambulance train that would take us to the 103rd Army General Hospital in

Tamworth. As I dozed through the journey, with a stiff face, halted breathing and a headache, this could seem the necessary reality for which so many Anzac Days, Great War movies and returned soldiers' anecdotes had prepared me: we were wounded soldiers lying in our bandages in an ambulance train; as we sped through a deceptively peaceful countryside Red Cross aides offered cigarettes and sweets; at the railway stations where we stopped in unexplained delays the civilians were uncertain whether to smile encouragement through the darkened windows or turn their backs to avoid embarrassment. But when I was more properly awake, this daydream was replaced by the reality that the stations we were passing through bore names I had grown up with – Singleton, Scone, Aberdeen, Murrurundi, Werris Creek, even Muswellbrook. I wasn't a wounded soldier. I was merely someone who had been hit over the head.

AFTER A FEW DAYS IN THE ARMY HUT THAT HAD BEEN CONVERTED into a hospital ward of the 103rd AGH, a letter from Mum gave some reassurance: 'You will be pleased to know your name was in the casualty lists in Monday night's *Sun* and Tuesday's *Herald* and *Telegraph*. I have kept the clippings.'

In this new ward I seemed to be back in another version of the monkey-cage life of the army hut at Ingleburn. Since we were in bed there was no physical bullying, and no kits to lay out uniformly, although there were daily inspections for neatness during which, on the order 'Attention!', we were expected to *lie* at attention; but most of the soldiers were well enough for shouted conversations to become rituals, in which by tough talk they remained strangers. As at Ingleburn, there were those who, when playing with themselves, shouted out their sexual fantasies, forcing them on the rest of us; this process of uniformity was helped by the circulation of a set of dirty postcards.

As in the casualty clearing station, in the bed next to me there was a soldier with whom I could talk with such intimacy that, after a week or so, we felt like individual persons with our own histories. And, daily, there was a small, dapper doctor to talk with, once for almost five minutes, about new surgical techniques, new drugs, the state of the world, as if we were equals standing at the bar in Ushers Hotel. We reached such an appearance of reciprocity that, when he left the ward, jokes were shouted out about crawling to officers: it was part of the wisdom of the ward that doctors, since they were officers, were all shits. My particular *confidante* was the day sister-in-charge, a tall, thin young woman in glasses, who read books. One afternoon we talked for almost a quarter of an hour in a way I had talked to no one else in the army. When she left, there would be shouts from the ward about how we were meeting at night and secretly fucking or, alternatively, that when she pretended to be talking to me she was unobtrusively pulling me off.

She had just finished reading *War and Peace*, and some of our conversation was about that – or hers was: I hadn't read it. She lent it to me, in the Modern Library edition, weighty for an invalid's hands, and again I had the impression that a novel was giving me a prism with which to simplify existence. What I now imagined I was simplifying was the idea of leadership, that the leader must accept it as inevitable that there would be absurdity and bungling and mean, ambitious pushings and shovings, but must also understand something of how absurd he himself was as a creature of events. On the eve of a battle, as Kutuzov knew, a good night's rest was more important than planning, because in the muddle of battle the leader must be fresh enough to react to events and in any case the battle was likely to be won by 'the side that has firmly resolved to win'. I had accepted Napoleon's *d'abord on s'engage et puis on voit*, but now I had to set against it Kutuzov's *dans doute, mon cher, abstiens-toi*. I decided they were the same thing. The question was not whether one acted, or refrained from acting. With either commitment the wise leader recognised that events were stronger and more important than reason or his own will. The one task was to preside over events with dignity, as if he knew what was happening, and give them meaning. I wrote off to tell my friends that it was not only in war that leaders must learn to preside over events as if they knew what they were doing, but in politics more generally. The greatest political talent could be to give meaning to confusion: in this, politicians were artists. Even the 'influence' of artists and other intellectuals – to my mind, the greatest of all reality-creators – was a matter for humility: they would be 'influential' only if what they had crystallised was already in people's minds, waiting to be expressed. Failing this, people would seize on their works and give them meanings the artists had not intended.

I NOW BREATHED NORMALLY. THE PARALYSIS TURNED INTO A tickle, then went. They began letting me up for a while each day, but I had headaches; my temperature went up; I was put back to bed; there was talk of an infection. They gave me a new drug, 'M&B'. When I complained of the food, and didn't eat, the dapper little doctor put me on a 'light diet'. I still didn't eat, but the headaches went and my temperature came down. When it was over, the doctor admitted he didn't know what had been wrong with me. But he had presided over my recovery with a competent grace and that was enough.

2

Letters came from friends, bearing rumours that I had been near death and that half my face was permanently paralysed. To cheer me up, Hope and Somerville sent me a parody of *Finnegan's Wake* (it was as if Joyce himself had sent me a get-well note). But my main concern was to learn how many of my friends seemed to be proceeding with the careers the Japanese war had brought them. Alf Conlon had enticed his friend the adjutant general to set up an 'Adjutant-General's Research Department' and Alf was now its director; other friends were with him, in uniform, bearing various ranks. One of them, Jim Plimsoll, gave news in his letters of friends who were controlling this, or rationing that, or had gone into the army as officers and were educating it, or providing it with 'amenities'. Plimsoll himself was doing research into why people went absent without leave, and asked my opinion on this. Bruce Miller wrote of his busy life in Canberra with the Australian Broadcasting Commission – reading news bulletins, reporting, sub-editing and gathering political gossip. He described how he had written an article, unsigned, for *Honi Soit* praising the government. This was part of some highly civilised ploy of Jo Collings' to placate the politicians and save the universities. Collings himself was now conducting an inquiry into the manpower position.

Friends were not only selling out to careers: they were getting married. That Alan Crawford had got married was seen by Miller as 'a definite end of an era'. The impression of an end to an era increased when Jimmy McAuley sent me a letter: he was also getting married, to Norma Abernethy. He tried a stilted jocularity: 'On! On! Past things have done for me! It is with this thought that we say: Farewell! to sunny Bachelordom. (Fade out on a scene of two clean-limbed Australians facing the future with a smile.) I am unable to be amusing on such a solemn theme. Only the music of Mozart does justice to my emotions. I am deep in the study of Tennyson and Coventry Patmore!' Enclosed in the letter was a copy of the latest poem he had written, 'Landscape of Lust'. At least Harold Stewart wasn't getting married, or following a career: he was completing his *Phoenix* series.

Once I became a walking patient I was able to do what might have provided a basis for research work for Plimsoll: I began going AWL. When I had first arrived an orderly had hidden my field service uniform (now cleaned of blood) behind the lining of the hut, explaining that when I was able to get up I could sneak into Tamworth for a few hours of beers, girls and steak-and-eggs. Although the girls proved merely a rumour there was reality in being able to stand up in the bar of a pub and order a beer or sit down to a feed at the Greek's. When I was transferred to a nearby convalescent depot more of my 'self' returned, in particular in finding ingenious methods for avoiding the diversions the army offered as ways of spending a convalescence.

I had been in hospitals for almost three months – Mum was writing letters complaining that she had made my bed weeks ago in the hope that I would 'blow in' (as if I were a student again, refusing to come home). Now the army sent me on a six-hundred-mile train journey to Albury, to a re-training centre made up of rows of tents, haunted by transients waiting for repostings and set out in a valley so damp that by the time I got the eight days' leave due to me I had caught a cold. After this turned into a mild bronchitis on the night train journey to Sydney, I spent most of my leave in bed. As recompense I got a two-day extension from my doctor, then wangled another two days by lying to a Transport Officer. After that, I simply took another three days off, so that when I got back to the dismal, haunted camp at Albury I was paraded on an AWL charge. The officer accused me of deserting in the face of the enemy and wrote his decision in red ink in my pay book. It seemed as improbable as when, in my second year at high school, I had failed in French. I did not report the episode to Plimsoll.

MY FACE HAD TAKEN ON A NEW NORMALITY. THERE WAS A SLIGHT scar and twisting of the skin on the right cheek and, from the stitchings to the torn eyelid, a slant to the right eye. With the left eye, I was level-eyed and equable. With the right eye, I was crooked and angry. When I was shaving I would look at myself, inspecting one side, and then the other – two people: that seemed correct.

How had being hit on the head changed me? What had I now become? Surely, after all that, I must have become something? In bed when I was home with bronchitis I was sweating and thick-chested enough to feel 'Dostoevskyan'. I decided to re-read some Dostoevsky. I turned over again the questions I had asked myself in 1938 when I had gone for a hike with Dad in the Blue Mountains, before the School Leaving Certificate results had come out: *If there was no good and no bad, what mattered?*

But now I had lost this youthful idealism. Cynicism had seemed easy to a high school boy, but after three years at university I had more beliefs than ever. When my fever went I became Stendhalian: I decided that, like Julien, I could speak idealistically the language of cynical ambition, but, like Fabrice, I could throw myself away on generous impulses, so that in what I saw as my most noble, or most crazily unpremeditated actions, my friends looked for self-interest.

When I was up again and able to go into the city and move among relics of the old life (although I now wanted to distinguish myself from 'the old life') in bars and coffee shops, I would point to the difference between my right eye and my left eye and ask questions: Did they think I had changed in personality? Did I seem more worldly? More *what* then? No one cared to say much. I was pleased when Peter Gibbons volunteered that I now appeared less of a wit, more of (in what he said was 'the good sense') a humourist. So that was it: I was more humorous. I decided to change the subject: one difference I would like in myself was that I should become more patient, both in talking and in writing. I wanted to be the 'detached observer' with 'a cool eye for detail'. I wanted to talk and write without the kind of irritation that merely broke up conversations and froze me so hard that I couldn't write. Perhaps it was not so much that I wanted to be a better person, but that I wanted to be a better writer and conversationalist.

FOUR

Gunner Horne finishes his training

1

I would brood over the anarchist writings I had copied into my notebooks. It seemed obvious, as Bakunin had said, that 'there cannot be a good, just and moral State; only a weak State could be a virtuous State': but could I really believe that the state could be overthrown by a social upheaval of the working class and that this would produce a more loosely organised society, arranged from below upwards by way of free association? Probably not. But in one part of me the answer became for a while, entrancingly: 'Well, why not?' I was prompted into a public declaration of this by one of the results of Douglas McCallum's attempts to make *Honi Soit* controversial. He had startled a student whom we saw as a Catholic Actionist into attacking the University Labour Club as 'a public nuisance which had in it the seeds of anarchy and bloodshed and fervid misunderstanding between man and man'.

'What a little shit!' I spent hours, with cheerful anger, drafting an attack on his misuse of the word 'anarchist' as a description of the Labour Club. It was as good as the old days. Dismiss the author as 'an ignorant little muezzin' who didn't know the difference between anarchism and communism, even though Bakunin had made the distinction quite clear at the second Geneva Congress. As to 'bloodshed': if he opposed bloodshed, why didn't he oppose war? Having fired that off I then released a barrage of anarchist writings on violence. 'The brigand is that true and only revolutionary – the irreconcilable, unwearying, untameable revolutionary in deed', and so forth, for three paragraphs. For several weeks afterwards *Honi Soit* groaned with angry replies and counterattacks.

When I got back to my own unit, now bivouacked in a pleasant, lightly wooded area not far from Newcastle, I received letters telling me that south of Newcastle, at Marks Point, was an anarchist poet, Harry Hooton. An anarchist poet! McCallum described how he and Oliver Somerville had gone up to Newcastle to spend the weekend with Hooton. They had been delayed for four hours in the Cricketers' Arms Hotel, where they got drunk with McAuley, leading him back to Norma laughing, singing, dancing, gesticulating; then they spent an hour and a half on their pilgrimage journey by bus to Marks Point, where they stayed up until the early hours talking anarchism with Hooton, strongly playing Chris Brennan as the great Australian poet against Hooton's Henry Lawson, a dispute renewed the next day when McAuley and Norma arrived. There was a theory in Sydney that McAuley was founder of our anarchist revival, McCallum said, but in the Cricketers' Arms booze-up McAuley had produced bitter jibes against him and Oliver for their anarchism.

As soon as I had a day's local leave, I took the bus to Newcastle, and another bus to Marks Point, to see Hooton in his little weatherboard cottage. Black-haired, with a part down the middle of his hair like Stewart, he seemed to belong more to the ordinary world than the rest of us; in manner he was good-humoured and courteous. We talked for hours, disagreeing on his admiration for Whitman and Nietzsche, agreeing on the wonders of Oscar Wilde's *The Soul of Man under Socialism*, and on the importance of poets. The poet, we agreed, feels towards things for the first time. Art is the future. Then we disagreed: I found Hooton's verse too uncontrolled, I said, too many words doing the work of one. Use a dozen words instead of one, said Hooton. Just choose the word you like. The aspects of a work of art are infinite. There are no rules for art. No rules for poetry. No rules for the future. All authority is base.

A week later I received an essay by Hooton on *The Soul of Man under Socialism* and a warning from McCallum about my pronouncements on 'propaganda by the deed'. He warned me against 'atrocitarianism': the true way was not violence, but non-violent non-cooperation. What mattered was the attitude, not what we hoped to get: the essence of permanent militancy was not achieving humanitarian ideals but struggle for the very sake of struggle – what mattered was the being, not the becoming.

IN THE 'REAL WORLD', WHAT I WAS BECOMING WAS NOT AN anarchist, but a more orthodox soldier. I was no longer a 'chocko'. I had joined the AIF. When I had been at Albury they had announced to us daily that the embargo had been lifted on 'chockos' volunteering for overseas service. I had decided to volunteer. I had felt punily naked in a uniform unhonoured by shoulder badges saying AUSTRALIA, and with shoulder flashes not backed by the AIF's rim of grey. I could feel like a thief in the night when I saw the AIF men in their slouch hats with the panache of light-brown puggarees and thought of my own furtive hatband of mere felt; and there was something approaching a sense of genital inadequacy when I saw their smart webbing gaiters and compared them with my own floppy gaiters of woollen cloth. At Albury, even though I had deserted in the face of the enemy, they had hinted that they might be able to fix me up with a special training school if I volunteered, and then I could be posted to a proper AIF unit, rather than go back to the shabby outfit to which I belonged. But I was shamed by a sudden sense of loyalty to this regiment I had despised. I would go back to it, in all its grubbiness. And then I would volunteer.

I volunteered the day after I returned to the regiment, but before I could display the insignia that confirmed my conversion into a true soldier I had to wait for my new army number to 'come through'. As a member of the militia I had been an 'N' number. As a member of the AIF I would become an 'NX' number. It was weeks before the new number arrived: just as Mum had worried when my name was slow in appearing in the casualty lists, she now wrote to me noting that I had not yet got my new number. The day it came, when I changed from being N275176, Gnr Horne, D.R. (AMF) to NX121576, Gnr Horne D.R. (AIF), was the day before I was to see Harry Hooton. I already had the shoulder badges, the shoulder flashes and the puggaree: now I clipped the badges to my uniform, sewed on the shoulder patches, exchanged sloppy hatband for smart puggaree and went on my anarchist's pilgrimage feeling more like an Australian soldier.

2

A HALF-DAY IN THE LIFE OF A GUNNER.

I polish my boots, lay out my kit, then clean my rifle barrel with a pull-through, rub its outside with an oily rag and brush dust out of its trigger mechanism; I clip on my webbing, put on my hat, take up my rifle and, on the whistle, fall in. On parade!

'I'm tired of telling you blokes if you can't come on parade on time we'll just have to get you out here earlier. Why don't you wake up to yourselves?'

Mutterings: 'Christ, it's on!'

'Now, we'll just have to try it again! You've been in the army long enough to do better than that! Come on!'

Officer watches. Descends.

'Troop! ... Your parade, sir!' 'Thank you, Sergeant-Major. I'll inspect.'

Finds dirty rifle.

'Put that man on Defaulters!'

'What are you grinning about? It's not a laughing matter, gunner! Defaulters' Parade for a week!'

'I notice that some of you men have buttons missing. You'll have to sew them on by the next parade. These little things increase a man's self-respect. And you'll have to get the dints out of your hats. I don't know how many times I have to tell you this. We must have uniformity. The sigs, drivers and limber gunners will get on with maintenance. The rest of you will work on the "Q" store. Break the men up, Sergeant Major.'

The officer ascends, and goes back to his tent. The men are dismissed and assembled near the 'Q' Store, waiting for George, the lieutenant in charge of the working party.

'Bloody George! Shit!'

'I don't know ... he's not a bad bastard.'

'The bastard's mad. He works too hard.'

'Well, you'll never kill yourself working, you old shit!'

'I'll tell you what's wrong with George. He needs a good hard fuck.'

'Jesus, he's a bloody kid. These fucking officers give me the shits.'

'But George is bloody thirty.'

'Well, you wouldn't bloody think it.'

'Here he comes. Christ, he's a bloody fool. Look at him carrying that lump of wood.'

'He gives me the shits.'

George gives orders: 'Come on, you fellows. We've got to get this done. You may as well get stuck into it. I'll be back soon. Don't malinger while I'm away.'

Everybody malingers.

George (returning): 'Come on! Break it up! Break it up!'

George distributes jobs, leaving most of the party with nothing much to do. He climbs on the roof and begins hammering the iron.

'Don't stand around doing nothing, gunner! Get on to digging that drain!'

'But, sir, there are eight men on it already and there are only enough tools for four.'

'Don't answer me back, gunner! Do what you're told!'

'I can't dig the fucking drain with my fucking hands, sir!'

'I don't know about that, gunner, but if you don't do what you're fucking told, you'll be under fucking arrest.'

Murmurs of encouragement: 'Good on you, mate!', etc.

Grumbles of discontent: 'Bloody waste of money our being here at all', etc.

'Fuck the bastards!'

One by one, four gunners move behind the trees and, under cover, go back to their tents. They stretch out and, for a while, sleep.

First gunner, awakening: 'I've got a fat.'

'Give us a feel.'

Hands fumble the bulge: 'I've got a fat, too.'

Second gunner, trouserless, struts around the tent.

'Jesus, that's a beauty.'

The gunner takes a hurricane lamp and places it over the base of the erection. He again struts around.

'How would you like to see this on a dark night.'

The whistles blow for lunch. The naked gunner gives a last strut and puts his trousers back on.

3

By rituals we affirmed that one day was no more important than the next: at our bivouac we practised the same drills; on our manoeuvres we went through the same movements; on our working parties we malingered in the same ways; on our route marches we sang the same dirty songs; in the mess hut we told the same jokes; when we got drunk we had the same arguments; in our tents we teased each other by rote. Yet although it would soon be twelve months since I had joined the army, I still had in my mind images of myself as a student.

In Newcastle I visited the McAuleys in their flat with its mattress on the floor and its bookshelves of butter boxes, where, while I tried to show them my new wisdoms, they would give me lunch as if I were a passing waif. In Sydney, when I visited the bars and coffee shops, I found people who had to introduce themselves to me. In letters it was possible to pretend that it was still yesteryear, but in reply would come news of people's careers in cushy jobs or their humble desolation in isolated army units in tropical Australia. Only Douglas McCallum seemed to live life as it should be lived, with controversies in *Honi Soit*, a love affair, friendships with artists, shelves where he could put new books, a sunken bath, and, occasionally, a party spectacularly rich in anecdotes. In particular, there was his penetration of the fringes of the worlds of painting and theatre, from which I knew only Bill Dobell (now drafted as foreman of *camofleurs*).

One night when I was on leave earlier in the year, Stewart and I had visited Dobell in his flat at Kings Cross. For a while we had hidden on the balcony when an art-fancying heiress brought a high ranking officer to see if he wanted to buy any of Dobell's paintings; then we sat on the floor and drank wine. With some giggling and a lot of cajoling, Stewart prompted Dobell to show us some photographs he had concealed in a cigarette tin hidden under the bed. They were photographs he had taken, in colour (a fact that was particularly impressive, since colour was so expensive), of naked young men showing off their erect penises. I thought no more of it – the caprice of a genius artist. When we found we had missed our last trains there was more giggling from Stewart: he suggested we toss a penny to see who would sleep on the floor and who would sleep in the double bed with Dobell. I won the toss, stripped myself down to my underclothes, got into bed, and slept soundly until breakfast. It was only later, when I thought about the innuendoes that had passed, that it occurred to me that 'sleep with' may have been intended as a euphemism. I recalled the night when we were drinking wine in a Sydney park and Stewart reminisced with delight about the mechanical details of schoolboy masturbation; then there was his friendship with a handsome lad whom one of our women friends claimed to have seduced and so rescued from a 'homo'. Was Stewart a 'homo'? Was Dobell a 'homo'? When Dobell said he would like to paint my portrait because I have beautiful shoulders, was that an advance?

WHEN WE WENT TO THE PICTURES THERE CAME ONTO THE newsreels images of Australian actions against the Japanese on 'the Kokoda Trail' in the mountains just to the north of Port Moresby, now the main Australian base to have survived in New Guinea. We knew the forms of trench and desert warfare, but no one had imagined an un-Australian 'jungle warfare' in which the majority on each side were laid low by malaria and dysentery and in which 'the front' was a long, thin track of sloping mud. We saw spurts of death from machine guns ... soldiers up to their waists in rainforest muck ... single files of pathetic relics of ambushes, lamed, blinded. We would be there soon. There were rumours that artillery was useless in these mountains of dense rainforest, so we would be disbanded and sent off, piecemeal, as reinforcements to various infantry battalions, as they needed us. There was a week in which rumours were as thick as flies: movement orders of some kind were coming up. We were to pack and be ready to go. The exact news came at evening mess, brought by the battery sergeant major. He had been born and bred in the Hunter Valley – it was a good enough world for him, and now he was being thrown out of it. 'You gunners will have to toughen yourselves up now!' he shouted. 'You'll have to get off your arses! The movement orders have come.' We waited for it ... 'The whole regiment has been posted to Sydney!'

OUR REGIMENT WAS STATIONED FOR EIGHT MONTHS IN ONE OF the most fashionable suburbs of Sydney, on a golf course, where each battery was concealed among its own fringe of trees. Between them lay the forbidden fairways, cutting communication; the symbol of our unity was the club house set up, as regimental headquarters and officers' mess, as if it were a French chateau in the Great War.

There was a brownout, ships had been torpedoed off the coast, Sydney Harbour had been penetrated by midget submarines and there were American servicemen all over town, but the strength of our belief that the Japanese had immediate plans for capturing Sydney was now sinking. For the first time in my life, I had no sense of progress. There were no exams to pass, no advancement from one academic year to the next, no poems or articles to write, no loves to declare, no projects. Not even anything more to learn as a gunner. I had even forsaken my belief that if I read enough translations of Russian and French nineteenth-century novels I would finally decide what life was like. I still visited bookshops and bought books, but I didn't always read them. The best there was to look forward to was a party, where drinking might produce some unpredicted excitement. There weren't many parties. There were always bars: my main diversion was to get drunk in a bar and, in the process of continuing revision, argue over old causes. Anarchism was fading. There wasn't anything new to talk about. Although the heroes and heroines of my student life were gone, one of them would, now and again, reappear and I was remembering the names of the surrogate people who had emerged as stand-ins. My conversational style had become anecdotal when it was not argumentative. Bruce Miller wrote to me that when I told stories people could be impressed by my 'charm of manner'. Perhaps this was what I had learned from being hit over the head.

If I drank with the gunners it was likely to be in the heroic style, a test of endurance, with prospects of adventure. When a group of us had a leave day in Jervis Bay – we were down on the south coast on a manoeuvre – I challenged another gunner, a student, to a drinking duel. We stood in the bar of Foley's Hotel and drank whisky as if firing bullets at each other, glass by glass, each glass counted by the gunners, until my opponent went off to the lavatory and passed out in a cubicle, lying in his own vomit. After sleeping in the sun, I showed off by going back to the bar and drinking beers; by vomiting, I was able to survive this ordeal and even eat some hamburgers, although I could not keep them down. In the truck on the way back to the guns one of the gunners composed a song. We yelled it out, over and over:

We went to Jervis for our holiday,
Holiday, holiday, holiday.
We went to Jervis for our holiday.

We went down to Foley's
And drank all his beer,
Drank his gin and whisky,
And it filled us with cheer.

The older I get
I will never forget
That day we spent at Jervis Bay-ay.

Compared with boredom, drinking (which gave one many things to do with one's mouth and hands) was so irresistible that when I had a night leave, although I would feel I should go home to spend a few hours with Mum and Dad and Janet, I would be likely to go instead to a bar, or a sly grog place, and cling to whatever company I could find in a shabby city taken over by strangers. Although home was only two suburban train rides away, on one occasion I had been so long gone that Mum wrote me a letter. A week later she wrote another: Why hadn't they seen me? 'Every night we keep hoping you will blow in.'

I elected to take a one-day leave on Boxing Day rather than Christmas Day because it was my twenty-first birthday and Mum had planned a family dinner – not the grand kind of occasion she would once have expected for a 'twenty-first', but a few of the relations I had been most intimate with as a child were to be there; the dining room would be decorated and the lace tablecloth put out; chickens roasted; drink ordered; it would be a reminder of former happiness. But on the way home I dropped into Ushers bar and found a friend I hadn't seen for thirteen months. We at once re-fought the great student issues of the year before, in particular the takeover of *Honi Soit* by Bill Pritchett and me and then, in circumstances people still argued about, my replacement of him as editor. The friend had a new theory to explain these events. After each new drink I would decide that this would be the last – the underground railway station was just across the road and home was only twenty minutes away – but with each new drink I also felt that I could again feel for Pritchett the friendship which *Honi Soit* had taken from us. I could imagine a reconciliation ... Drink after drink ... There was no phone at home: I rang a neighbour with an excuse. Mum and Dad, Nanna and Janet and the relations ate their celebratory dinner without me.

McAuley had joined Alf Conlon's research section and become a lieutenant; Stewart had become Conlon's Corporal–Librarian; Crawford was said to be deep in trades union liaison work; Collings's mysterious research had now become sufficiently serious for him to be given a room in the vice-chancellor's office and a second secretary; another friend had been made OC Army Education Correspondence courses; another was said to be conducting surveys for Conlon of a kind so secret that even Conlon didn't know about them. Another friend – notable both for being married and for still living in Sydney – was an official in a department that issued permits: American staff officers gave him 'presents' of cases of bourbon, cartons of Camels or Chesterfields; Australian businessmen sent him crates of lobsters, sacks of oysters; when we went to his house for a drinking party it was like Christmas in a pirate's hideout.

I was surrounded by rumours and tokens of success. One of the officers explained to me one day (looking at me over a neatly trimmed black moustache) that my work was good, but there were no prospects for promotion. I said, politely, that I didn't want promotion. 'Gunner Horne', he said, 'You have the brains of a general. But you're too cynical!' This became an anecdote, illustrating his ignorance of the brains of generals.

A sense of futility eventually became great enough for me to try to pull some strings and get out of this unit. A friend arranged an interview with one of the higher-ups in Army Education, a major who, if he took a liking to me, might arrange my transfer. In the half hour or so I spent with the major in his office in another of the fringe military camps of Sydney I tried to show off, but he seemed more concerned with impressing me and after the interview I didn't know 'how I had gone', although I had been able to give him a splendid list of referees. Then I began to hope I had done badly in the interview. Perhaps I didn't want to leave the regiment. And I didn't want strings pulled. I would sooner come out of the war with what I saw as a kind of Hemingway sense of moral cleanness surrounded by so many unworthy ambitions. How could I leave my comrades of tent and gun – my 'mates'? At the same time there was the suspicion that behind the scenes no one was really pulling any strings for me at all. Perhaps someone was cutting them, or tying them in knots. In letters, I wrote in code of my suspicions: another appointment with the major was made. By this time guilt at the prospect of leaving the regiment and despair that I would never leave it were equally matched. On the day I was to see the major I went instead on a drinking binge, broke the appointment, and sent no apology.

Training was mainly training in accepting tedium, but not on the day when, after more than a year and several weeks after the Germans surrendered at Stalingrad, we were at last to fire live ammunition on an artillery range on the other side of Sydney. The banging of the guns, the smoke, the smell of cordite and the heat of the ejected cartridge cases gave some sense of reality, but firing on an artillery range proved to be so contrived, with all the gun positions chosen in advance and with a number of unwarlike safety prohibitions, that it did not seem as real as fireworks night, where there was more opportunity for initiative and danger. A sharper sense of reality came when, on the way back to camp, we were ordered to pass through the city in convoy, because it would be good training to learn how to 'manoeuvre in city conditions'. The convoy disintegrated among the slums on the southern fringe of the city: our troop lost the rest of the battery; then, gun crew by gun crew, we lost each other. That seemed the only warlike thing to have happened to us that day. Surreal authenticity reached one of its climaxes in the unexplained assignment of a detachment of us to a mountain wilderness where four Great War 18-pounders, of time-honoured obsolescence, were lined up in a bush clearing. We spent several days firing them, shooting off hundreds of rounds of ammunition each day at unseen targets, for reasons that were never disclosed.

This was followed by a period of toughening-up, back in camp, with increasingly large amounts of PT ending in a three-day route march, with full packs, in bush north of Sydney. The climax was reached in a long, stone gorge, when we marched the full length along one side and then came back along the other, singing dirty songs all the way. When new training drills came out to teach us how to dismantle our 25-pounder guns, carry the pieces, then assemble them again, we knew we were soon for New Guinea, but still as artillery: in the mountains of rainforest and mud this was the way the artillery moved its guns.

Then an infantry officer who had served in New Guinea trained us for a week in the new jungle drills for the infantry. So the regiment was to be broken up and we would be turned into infantry reinforcements after all! For once, we accepted the right of an officer to bellow at us. He had 'been there'. We learned from him how to carry out jungle patrols in the light scrub fringing a fashionable Sydney golf course.

On one exercise he ordered me to climb a tree and stay there, with a rifle loaded with blanks: if a patrol passed a certain mark on the track without seeing me I was to fire off my blanks. I stayed there for two hours, loyal to my post, even in my imagination: I imagined Japs coming down the trail ... I would fire on them ... They would scatter ... Perhaps one of them might fall before they 'got me' ... Then I would drop dead, like someone in a newsreel, out of the tree.

My legs were aching so painfully I doubted whether I could use them to climb down, let alone drop dead. I tried to move a leg, gently, but there was a rustle of leaves loud enough to reveal my presence to the enemy. I called out, softly, several times, asking if the game was over: could I come down now? I waited for another half hour. It was dark, and time for evening mess. Guiltily, and in pain, I climbed down the tree and, as one deserting his post, stole back to my tent. I was careful to take cover among the trees. As instructed, I kept off the fairways. Gunner Horne had finished his training.

FIVE

Combat zone

1

Our twelve-day journey to the Northern Territory began on a dark night in a lonely railway siding in a suburb on the edge of Sydney. We were loaded into a troop train so surreptitiously, to conceal our movements from the enemy, that the only light was an occasional flash from an electric torch, and in the dark carriages taking us 300 miles to the Victorian border the only lights were from striking matches and glowing cigarettes. But Albury station, where we changed from a standard gauge New South Wales train to a broad gauge Victorian train, was lit as brightly as Newcastle used to be when we stopped for a pie and a cup of tea on school holiday train journeys to Sydney from Muswellbrook. As we queued in the Albury station refreshment rooms for hot drinks and sandwiches, now that I was saddled with full marching order, battle helmet fastened in the approved position to my pack, I felt again, as I did on the morning I was on fire-making duty on Kembla Grange racecourse, that it was the Great War, and we were our fathers, drinking mugs of steaming tea before our journey to the Front. That the top end of the Northern Territory was designated a 'combat zone', and the Japanese bombing was rumoured to have destroyed Darwin, provided the first indications that my army service might seem real, even if it were not the newsreel reality of New Guinea.

I was having my first experience of foreignness. Victorian railway carriages seemed unnaturally wide, and after dawn I stared at alien Victorian landscapes, seeking difference. They looked very much like our own New South Wales landscapes, even if the railway stations were strangely designed and the newspaper billboards had peculiar names. All day, four of us, sons of bank clerks and schoolteachers, played auction bridge around a makeshift table, a blanket placed over some of our stacked kits; meanwhile the train took us across Victoria and into South Australia and a darkness from which we emerged at dawn in the approaches to Adelaide. Here, 550 miles after Albury, we 'dismounted' and were driven to the showground for showers and breakfast. When we 'remounted' it was into a train with carriages of South Australian design, even more outlandish than Victorian carriages. As we went north along the 200 miles to Quorn, the landscapes also appeared curious – at first, flat and thin and faded, with clumps of trees only where there was a small township, or some old, grey stockyards or a wheat silo, then red sand and sombre shrubs that sadly ornamented the scene as if planted in a gentlemen's park. At Quorn we marched in style along a wide road to a hall where we sat at long trestle tables and women served corned beef, salad and lamingtons. Someone made a speech wishing us luck in the Darwin 'battle zone'; then we were reloaded into a narrow gauge train with thin, mean carriages in which the only seats were hard benches, facing each other, and running the whole length of the kind of carriage sometimes seen in cowboy movies. We lived in this train for four days, passing through claypan desert, stony desert, sand desert and mountain desert, stopping for mess, which we ate beside the train, and stopping sometimes beside an artesian bore, so that we could wash; at night we slept on top of the piled-up kit over which, for most of each day, our group played bridge. It was a 'foreign' landscape now: flat seas of dry grass ... bare, stony ground with sparse clumps of derelict scrub ... red sand plains with solemn, green shrubs ... dunes rising from plains rippling with pebbles ... desert gums guarding dried watercourses ... corrugated ridges of sand held together by tufts of cane grass ... whole plains of rusted red stones. Sometimes, on the horizon, came perversely shaped ridges, like paper cutouts, and, for one stretch, there was nothing but desolate hollows and hills of meaningless dirt. On the fourth day, the MacDonnell Ranges came up, across a plain of golden spinifex and sombre trees: the train slowed its pace to pass through two red cliffs, where the khaki sand of a broad, dry river bed swept away, leading us to Alice Springs.

We were unloaded, and put into tents in a dusty camp on a small hill looking over a plain of stiff, sunny spinifex and dark trees spread out to old, rusted-red ridges. Alice Springs itself was a scattering of galvanised iron roofs among the trees. An officer paraded us and read out the penalties for giving drink to the blacks and for attempting to have sex with a 'lubra', but when we walked into the little township, with its low buildings with long, sloping roofs coming down over wide, fly-screened verandahs, its water troughs and hitching posts, all we were looking for was a pub. At night when we sat in deck chairs at an open-air cinema this seemed yet another example of Alice Springs' outlandishness but, of the many oddities, the one we joked about most was an army invention, the 'pissaphones', funnels a yard wide fixed into pipes dug into the ground, placed here and there in the staging camp for use as urinals. We had now joined a civilisation of which a distinctive artifact was the 'pissaphone'. The next day we were loaded into army trucks, to travel in convoy along the thousand miles of the North–South Road, built from Darwin to Alice Springs in a crash operation after the bombing of Darwin, but not yet paved. Around us the mulga, small, sombre-coloured but confidently upward-thrusting bushes, spread like dark clouds, but we were passing through our own storm of red dust, set off each time the convoy started, thickening the air, blocking noses, smarting eyes and reddening us, from battle helmets to boots, so that each night, when we 'dismounted' at a tented staging camp, we stood under the showers in our clothes, washing them before we washed our bodies. At Larrimah, reached after four days, the railhead of the line from Darwin, we were loaded into a train of cattle trucks, drawn by a comical engine with a funnel like a pissaphone. We rattled through the night, past the black shapes of spindly trees, to Adelaide River, where tents and huts and boots stamping in the dust signified a military base, and two officers walking side by side carrying briefcases suggested a certain remoteness from battle. We heard rumours of a Jap air raid that morning further up the line and of four chaplains being killed by crocodiles while swimming in a waterhole. Between Adelaide River and Darwin, as well as dispersed airstrips for bombers and fighters, there was an army division deployed in camps among the skinny trees, ready if the Japs attacked on land. In our new regimental area, the three batteries were as well spaced out as they had been on the Sydney golf course. After twelve days and nearly 3,000 miles we now saw ourselves as a new people, who had shared new sorts of experiences; an account I wrote of our journey was pinned up to the battery notice board so that the gunners could feel they had all gone through the same thing.

WE SLEPT IN TENTS UNDER TREES, THE CAMOUFLAGED 25-POUND-
ers parked among the pissaphones. The guns had been packed in grease and
sent by ship to Darwin, but for a picturesque week, instead of our own guns,
we had the guns of the regiment before us: obsolete 18-pounder field guns
and 4.5 howitzers from the Great War. When our own guns arrived we parked
these exotic specimens together, at one side of the camp, as if we had set up a
zoo. The sight of them could make us feel members of a thoroughly modern,
well-trained, well-equipped unit compared with the chockos who had been
there before us, with their outdated equipment.

As concern about air raids and crocodiles vaporised into clouds of rumour
we learned that our true enemy was the climate. The open air showers area
was not just where we washed; it had become a place for practising 'tropical
hygiene'. After a shower we sprinkled talcum powder under our armpits, in
our crutches and between our toes; the first signs of skin eruption were to
be reported to the Regimental Aid Post. We were to boil our clothes daily;
all waste was to be burned and buried, to discourage flies; we were taught
preventive measures against termites and ants; chin straps were not to be
worn because they could cause facial rashes; we were to wear long trousers and
shirts with the sleeves rolled down, to prevent sunburn and protect us against
mosquitoes. Above all we must remain active and hopeful – otherwise we
would 'go troppo' (a mental disease of unlimited proportions). 'The tropics'
were a persistent enemy.

Meals in the mess could be a *mélange* of stew, cabbage, black tea, slushies'
sweat, and bread and jam, but the significant meals were morning and afternoon
tea and supper, when we would make our own tea or coffee or cocoa and eat
tinned fruit bought from the canteen, or fruit cake sent by our mothers or wives.
Our bodies quickly became brown. (Whenever we could get away with it we
wore shorts and took off our shirts. As often as they could, some of the gunners
went around naked.) We adopted laconic manners, using our bodies to lounge
around in – even jumping into a truck was to be done nonchalantly, with a
hand rest and a light hurdling movement. We left shirt buttons negligently
undone, so that our chests could assert there was more to us than clothes. To
emphasise action we would pull up our shorts a little, tighten our belts, pull our
hats down over our foreheads. To emphasise relaxation, we would slacken our
belts, stretch out our legs, idly pluck at hairs on our arms.

Constantly, we handled our genitals through the khaki drill of shorts or trousers, either to hitch them, or simply make sure they were still there. They would swing between the legs of those who played deck tennis, naked outside their tents, before they took their showers at night; we would soap them under the shower and rub them dry; aim our penises at pissaphones; display the bulges that signified erections, or perhaps unbutton our trousers (if asked) so that others could have a look. The size of these dangling objects could be as important as badges of rank in the ways we classified ourselves. By one measure, there were the stripes and crowns and pips that established who gave the orders; by another measure, there were the lengths of our penises. (In a moment of frankness, one of my tent mates told me how he hurried to the showers in the morning while his penis was still extended from its morning erection, so that it looked longer than when it retracted.)

Several of my Sydney friends had asked for details of homosexuality in the army. I had scarcely thought about it. Some of the farm boys paired off and slept together, but we did not even think of speculating about what, if anything, they did with each other; one of the timbercutters had got drunk on looted whisky and jerked himself off in front of anyone who cared to look when we were unloading a ship's cargo in Sydney; there was a sergeant who was obviously in love with one of the drivers – a handsome, pouting youth built like a classical Greek statue who seemed to wander around naked more frequently than most, sometimes standing still, with the hint of a pose – but we didn't know (nor did anyone seem to care) whether there was anything more to it than that. He was the closest we had to the classic, or Renaissance, ideals of male beauty. Once, when I saw him posing naked except for a battle helmet and boots, he reminded me of a reproduction of Donatello's *David* I had seen in one of Stewart's art books. My own view was that if homosexual acts were to be performed with any grace it should be between consenting Greek or Renaissance statues – and amongst all of our bodies – whether of bank clerks, cow hands, tram guards, labourers, tradesmen, schoolteachers, timbercutters – his was the only one which met this specification.

What we held most in common was simply the comradeship of just being there, together; in a few cases there was deep friendship but what united us most was the chatter and laughter and general rubbing together of conversation, and in particular the intricate rituals of gossip about those fools, the officers, whose faults saved us from examining too much the many differences between ourselves. I made notes on the obsessive fantasies of gossip, an addiction that would drive us mad with its tedium, but which we could not get away from. Whenever we were thrown together we could all, with equal depravity, obsessively invoke the most absurd rumours about the officers. Although I took notes on it and could feel detached, I found this kind of gossip as irresistible as the others did. We would exhaust ourselves in our excesses until our brains were numb with boredom.

Manoeuvres seemed more real now that the country seemed foreign. We drove along dusty tracks among reminders that it was 'the dry' – the browned, flattened spear grass was all that remained of the luxuriance of 'the wet', and the wide swamps where the buffalo lived in the wet season had become acres of dried mud; the creeks were down to their sand, the waterholes had dried to dust. As part of a cult of simplicity, I gave up wearing underclothes – if I were boiling my shirt and trousers each night, why should I wear underclothes? Then I stopped wearing socks and washed out my boots each night instead. I tried to learn the names of plants and imagine I was in audience with them, but while I could achieve some intercourse with a parkland of stringy barks because this was the 'nature' I had been brought up to expect, most of this place was just spindly trees that failed to meet the forms of beauty I had learned at school. It was the kind of land that should be *cleared*. I preferred to teach myself about the large and diverse insect and reptile life that surrounded and threatened us, providing many metaphors of the human condition. However, I found I could enter into communion with the quirky individualism of the pandanus palm and wondered if I could build a poem about it. I would stand and look at a lone pandanus, or a thicket of them, and wonder what to say.

The disciplines of the regiment and its society were too complex for the regular pursuit of the simple and the natural – if I stood alone with a pandanus palm for too long the gunners would think I had gone nuts. There was only one whole day when I was able to imagine myself at ease with nature. One of the batteries was having a shoot and I had been deposited on the side of a track to act as sentry. After the truck had gone I built a shelter of tree branches, took off my clothes, and spent the day lying naked under the shelter, fraternising with nature and reading *Anna Karenina*.

2

Plimsoll (now a captain in Conlon's research section) wrote to me that 'many so-called liberals may have to abdicate any claims to leadership after the war simply because they are not showing leadership now.' The army was a good place for me, he said, because serving in the forces was the best contribution intellectuals could make at the moment, and it was an experience that would help me understand human nature and rid myself of intellectual arrogance. I marvelled that Plimsoll seemed to question the need to protect intellectual life from philistine wartime conformities – we had all used the figure of speech that intellectual culture was not like electricity: once you switched it off you couldn't switch it on again. But although the tedium of army life reduced me to headaches and, sometimes, private paroxysms of misery, in occasional moments of optimism I also felt that, as with being hit over the head, experiencing this boring life might change me, somehow, for the better. At least I was pleased that I had not looked for a cushy job. I wrote to my mother that I hoped Alf Conlon was 'impressed' that I had not 'chased' him.

The officer who had told me I had the brains of a general had now become the 'battery captain', second in command of the battery. As a new broom, he wanted to sweep in some of his own team and, as part of his plan, he had me taken off the guns and 'seconded' to the 'Q' store. He said I would be doing only the more interesting work and was to see myself as one of the innovators responsible directly to him; he outlined his reform programme and promised me almost immediate promotion. The work would release me from parades, working parties and 'training', and would leave me more time for reading. It would give me some initiatives. But how could a reader of Tolstoy who disdained the petty go-getting of army careerists accept promotion to bombardier storeman? ('Do you think, sir, that I've now got the brains of a quartermaster-general?') I was 'seconded' to the 'Q' store nevertheless and for a fortnight amused myself as one who had nothing to lose. I didn't shave until after lunch. I greeted the battery captain by raising my hand in the Indian salute and calling out: 'How! Big Chief!' I kept people waiting at the 'Q' store – and solved the problem of what to do about a few howitzer spare parts by throwing them into the scrub on the grounds that if they could not be identified in the handbook they did not exist. After a fortnight the battery captain sent me back to the guns. I had written a mournful letter to Bruce Miller about the threat to promote me to bombardier storeman. It was disagreeable to receive a letter in reply congratulating me on the greater leisure I would now have. Did Miller really understand me?

Stewart wrote from Melbourne that he was living in a neat little bed-sitting room decorated with Japanese silk scrolls only five minutes from Conlon's research section where he ran a filing system, a newspaper cutting service and a small periodical library; he was delighted by the bookshops of Melbourne, by the prints and records he could buy, and the Chinese food. Each night he read in the public library or played records in his room. He asked me to write down the words of the dirty songs the soldiers sang and send them to him for his archives. McAuley wrote of the influence of Stalinists in Melbourne intellectual life and announced that, for him, the 1930s were now over: he felt a certain relief that their spirit had never got as far as his written work, even if it had got in the way of his thinking. But, he warned, after the smart aleck smattering mouths of the thirties we now had the arty-farty forties.

Even I now had a touch of intellectual life. An Army Education Service lieutenant was visiting us regularly and, as with the bookish sister in the Tamworth AGH, I at once saw him as one of us. Because the North–South Road had been built and because the army was successfully growing vegetables in the Northern Territory there had been an outburst of rhetoric about 'the development of the north'. In his first lecture to us, with quotations from history, government white papers and statistics, this lieutenant peeled away all the illusions about 'northern development' with such sceptical wit that I asked sympathetic questions and, when the lecture was over, went up and talked to him. I enjoyed all his later visits. He put me in charge of a library and a discussion group and then wrote saying that as a lieutenant he was entitled to a batman clerk and although he would do his own 'batting' – he would be embarrassed by having a servant – I might become his 'private clerk'. I could give lectures and lead discussion groups and would, he expected, be quickly promoted to sergeant as a lecturer in my own right; he said he would send a formal request to the battery commander asking if he could have me. I began going to sleep each night imagining myself making things clear, bringing up issues, asking questions, encouraging discussion. I planned some of the lectures

I would give. Nothing authoritarian. Questions to be allowed throughout lectures.

He did write to the battery commander and the battery commander 'had me paraded'. For half an hour I stood to attention in front of him and put my case. When I had finished he asked a few questions, but did not contest anything. (Good! He was going to agree to my transfer!) 'Gunner Horne, you have provided very rational and logical arguments ...' (I would bring up issues! Make things clear! Ask for questions!) '... but I'm not going to allow you to make this transfer.'

All that remained was to turn this into an anecdote.

AFTER TWO MONTHS THE REGIMENT TOOK ITS TURN AT 'GARRISON duty' in Darwin itself where an extended brigade group was settled among the wreckage of the early Jap raids. It was like coming into a house where no one had yet cleaned up after the party the night before. Funnels of sunken ships stuck up from the shallow harbour; oil tanks were crumpled like paper; bombed buildings looked no more real than in a newsreel film. Rumours of panic after the Jap raids – looting, desertions, the flight down to Adelaide River – had something of the political retribution of the fall of France, and rumours of the idiocy of military higher-ups recalled the fall of Singapore; but the stories of Darwin's opium dens, its brothels, grog shops and Chinese gambling dens, along with symbols of indulgence – waving palms, soft tropical breezes – added something that in its mood of decadence was closer to a Victorian moralist's story of the fall of the Roman Empire. Our troop was stationed in a small cluster of wide-verandahed houses with sloping roofs set around a beaten earth square, with the guns in pits dug into a cliff that overlooked neglected backwaters of the harbour merging into distant mangrove swamps thick, it was rumoured, with saltwater crocodiles. Gossip told us that this inward-looking little settlement had been part of the Chinese quarter most notorious for gambling dens.

There were rumours that Jap bombers were still carrying out raids – somewhere – but the air raid alerts we received produced nothing more dangerous than bites from mosquitoes in the slit trenches. An air raid alert became an occasion for discipline, with sergeants noting the men to be put on defaulters' parade for not crouching in their slit trenches. Sometimes at dawn we would be ordered to stand-to as if the Japs were about to attack, and a regular part of night guard duty was for a gunner smeared in mosquito repellent to sit in a cane chair and watch for the Verey light that would be the signal to fire 'B' gun, trained on the distant beach where the Japs were most expected to land, and then run to the other guns and fire them as well; the rest of us would then rush to repel the invader by laying down a programmed barrage.

After a night's duty of this kind we would be 'stood down', which meant we could go for a swim, visit the recreation hut (where I would read the American papers *PM* and the *New York Times*), stroll back to the gun position, shower, do our hair (we all used hair pomades of some kind), wash our plates, have lunch, sleep – then be woken by the clatter of cups for afternoon tea. I would read, have evening mess and write letters. On the wall beside my bed (we had real beds – commandeered – and even commandeered chests of drawers) were pin-ups put up by those who had been there before us: I pasted a photograph of John Anderson between Betty Grable's legs. Sometimes we swam naked at a wide beach of clear yellow sand fringed by ferns and palms, but more usually in the saltwater baths, reminiscent of the design of the polar bears' pit at the Sydney zoo, or at a small beach sheltered by steep cliffs where a pontoon was moored offshore. We would swim out and sunbathe on it. The weather was exactly the same every day: generously warm, evenly dry, with a clear, cloudless sky.

I WAS HAPPY TO LIE ON THE PONTOON AND LOOK UP TO THE SKY, but among many of the gunners there was a nervous itch: wanting the weather to show some progress, they were bored by 'the dry' and fretted that 'the wet' hadn't arrived. One afternoon I was lying on my bed with a towel over my face, almost asleep, despondent after a morning of being 'fucked about' on the parade ground: I had dosed myself with aspirin to cure headache, sadness, nausea, weariness. Even the air seemed oppressive. Then on the iron roof there were a few heavy, ponderous sounds ... Huge raindrops! ... followed by a brief deluge in which rain pelted in through holes in the walls and the roof. The gunners yelled with pleasure. Some threw off their clothes and danced in the wet.

It was a false promise. There was no more rain and, in the nervous debilitation that followed, the word 'troppo' was being used so frequently that the battery commander persuaded the garrison commander that a manoeuvre in the scrub was essential to restore morale.

Although I wasn't a sergeant, it had become the practice for me to be put in charge of a gun crew during manoeuvres. On this occasion I was posted as Number One to one of the other guns, and as usual, it was by cooperation rather than discipline that, like Kutuzov at Borodino, I attempted to preside over events: the gun crew knew what it had to do and would do it whether I was there or not. I had been thinking about military leadership, reading from the works of military philosophers – Sun-tzu, the Marechal de Saxe, Frederick the Great, Napoleon, Tom Wintringham, the Duke of Wellington – and, as I went to sleep under the stars while the sentry watched for the Verey light that would tell us the Japs had landed, I saw myself that night as philosopher of an anarchist approach to battle in which we were soldiers who would cooperate through choice. This time we would overcome the mistakes of the anarchists in Catalonia.

It was the gunlayer who shook me awake. It was one a.m. Someone was blowing a whistle. To improve our morale, we were being ordered to 'take post' and pretend to fire the guns. I decided to leave the rest of the crew in their blankets. While the gunlayer sat in his seat, I would shout 'Fire!', open the breech block, slam it shut, and run around as if I were doing the work of four men ... While I was hurrying around pretending to be all four gunners at once, it became clear that the figure standing beside me was the gun position officer. The best I could say to him was that it was all a misunderstanding: I didn't know the whole crew was to be woken up. 'Is that true?' he asked the gunlayer. 'No, sir,' said the gunlayer. I was charged with wilful neglect of duty ... When I was 'paraded' several days later I was found guilty and stripped of my Specialist Grade Three pay as a gunlayer. Immediate objection: 'But, sir, what has gunlayer's pay got to do with behaviour as an acting unpaid Number One?' Objection overruled. Well then, direct action. A friend and I composed a protest song to the tune of 'Twenty-one Today'. For several days friendly gunners stamped around the parade ground from time to time, singing:

Lost his pay today!
Lost his pay today!
They took it away from him.
Just what you'd expect of them.
Poor unfortunate Hornie
Lost his pay today!

I was posted by a sympathetic troop sergeant-major to gun maintenance duty for a week, which meant I could lie in the gunpit and spend the day reading Frederick the Great or the Duke of Wellington.

WHEN IT WAS LEARNED THAT A BATTERY STAFF SCHOOL WAS coming up and it was proving hard to get candidates from our battery, there was scandal among the gunners. Why hadn't they picked the obvious candidate, Horne? Horne had himself 'paraded' before the troop commander. After a delay, he was posted to the school.

The five weeks of this school were to be Gunner Horne's successful period in the army. The high-ceilinged Larrakeyah Barracks with its tall, elegant, shuttered windows was built in the style of colonial military rule; the food was comparatively good; the weather was splendid; there was a daily swim; conversation was intelligent; the instruction was exhaustive (after this, there seemed nothing more to learn about the artillery); and, at the end, I came top. The school was run informally, with practically no 'army bullshit'. Three whistles would tell us it was time to wake up, shower and shave, polish our boots and lay out our kit; another three whistles would tell us to go and eat breakfast; then we would sit on our kits and wait for the three whistles that would announce our only regular daily parade. But at this parade there was a reminder of the reality that lay beyond the intelligence and rationality of the school: day by day, we students were expected, in turn, to take charge of the parade and shout out orders. When my turn came, I would use the same kinds of ingenuity to avoid parade as I had used to avoid roll calls on sports afternoons at high school. It seemed better to be shouted at than to shout.

3

Mum was sending me the *Sydney Morning Herald* and from Bruce Miller I got the *Standard*, the *Tribune*, *Progress* and *Century*, the weekly newspapers of the four main factions in the labour movement. I had voted Labor in the national election (scarcely a gunner confessed to voting any other way), but without belief: Labor politicians, it still seemed to me, were just 'reformists' and 'careerists'. The other side, of course, seemed fascists or madmen. This sense of personal purity extended to the whole age: there was a feeling of foulness about the war itself; some of the rottenness of the 1930s was being burned away, but new forms of corruption were growing. In Australia there was the dirtiness of wartime careerism (I had marked significant passages in Evelyn Waugh's *Put Out More Flags*); even the Stalinists had now moved into good jobs and were excusing censorship and opposing strikes. The enemy were fascists, but so were Stalin and Chiang Kai-shek. In this world in which militarism seemed to have warped almost everything, there was, however, an occasional kindly light. I found some articles by Dwight Macdonald, the editor of *Partisan Review*, a New York magazine we had heard of in the Sydney University Freethought Society because it shared some of our left-wing disillusionment with Stalinism and our enthusiasm for Joyce and Freud: he had set the right mood for me when he wrote that the policies of the United Nations were 'merely opportunistic adaptations to a reactionary status quo' and that the war itself had become 'a vast nightmare from which our hopes and illusions had now leaked away'. I had read James Burnham's *The Managerial Revolution* and taken up with great verve the idea of the enemy as the new technocratic class. And now Macdonald was writing that the bourgeoisie were being expropriated, but not by the workers; the political bureaucracy was the new ruling class. I felt that, in his 'Ballade of New Orders', Oliver Somerville caught the atmosphere of general sellout:

> Good literature's the daily press,
> intelligence is greed for gain,
> and love of truth is greed for cess;
> wash clean in propaganda's rain!
> The plastic artists please Aunt Jane;

the workers work; the wowsers think;
magicians drug the dreaming brain
and put the plug in freedom's sink.

While I was at the Battery Staff School I read Stephen Spender's *Poets and Life*. It was written in what I thought of as 'bubble language', but included the quotation from Yeats about the best lacking all conviction, while the worst were full of passionate intensity. That's me, I thought, as I memorised it. That has caught the spirit of the times.

I read whatever books people sent up to me: classical Chinese philosophy, Swift, Bertrand Russell, Dr Johnson, Villehardouin's chronicle of the fourth crusade, Sacheverell Sitwell, Sainte-Beuve, Graham Greene, Voltaire – and then posted them off to Mum in the tins in which she had sent me cakes, to go on my bookshelves. With each new thing read there might be some old hatred or new enthusiasm: a tough critique of bourgeois freedom brought a tough letter to Bruce Miller ('Freedom is nothing but the *raison d'être* and *sine qua non* of the British financial grandee class'). Miller wrote back, calmly, asking me what I had been reading lately. I wanted to strip myself of old associations but while I could write off to Miller that Oliver Somerville was 'isolated, wild and windy, harsh, crude and degrading' and that Harry Hooton was 'a bag of wind, a crank, just another moraliser' whose verse was 'overdone, undermeant, careless, sensational and unintelligible' and that everything he wrote was 'sticky with mysticism', the furthest I could manage to go in criticising John Anderson was that he was 'no logician – more significant as a kind of critic–historian'.

Novels still provided illuminations so strong they felt like part of my own experience, perhaps the only real part, since my own life only became real when it was confirmed by something I had read in a translation of a French or Russian novel. Now I had found a new form of literary conversation – in one of the few lights still shining in a corrupt world, the English literary magazine *Horizon* whose monthly appearances meant that even in Darwin there was one of us still maintaining cultural values. As its writers talked about the crisis in the theatre or the latest developments in American painting or French and English cultural relations or the future of democratic values, *Horizon* provided me with the highest quality coffee shop conversation, some of it concerned with exactly the same writers I had first heard about in coffee shops ...Mallarmé, de Nerval, Rimbaud.

But now I was playing for an even greater stake: a whole new version of myself, the possibility of which was brought to me by the English quarterly magazine *Scrutiny*. *Horizon* provided, monthly, first-class coffee shop conversation; *Scrutiny* came out quarterly and delivered itself of something more than conversation. Every three months it issued significant and definitive statements. From *Scrutiny* I could get the same excitement I had got from the articles and addresses of John Anderson: here were serious, principled castigations of flabbiness and pretension. Reading them would change me. I had despised the English Department at Sydney University for Andersonian reasons; now, for *Scrutiny* reasons, I could despise English literature departments almost everywhere, because of what I now learned were their 'social snobberies' and their 'bankrupt and decrepit obsession' with the frivolities of a 'scholarship concerned only with editing and annotating texts that were often not worth publishing'. Instead, we readers of *Scrutiny* affirmed the need for 'a life devoted to the humanities'. It was to be a 'vocation', seeking 'mutual enlightenment in literary criticism and sociology' so that 'real standards could be applied to work with real values'.

The belief that 'thinking about political and social matters ought to be done by minds of some real literary education' seemed to give me a chance to construct a new Horne. Here was something that offered tough-mindedness and literary imagination, and also the possibility of action (informed by intellect). I wrote down that 'the vitality of the past could enrich the present' and that 'valuable research was likely to spring only from an attempt to find answers to urgent problems of the present'. But I didn't know what to do with it.

And something else was diverting me. I had discovered an entirely new kind of reading – 'current affairs' – in *The Economist*, my first encounter with 'serious journalism'. With its clear, dry style and neat, sharp argument, and appearance of being in possession of all the world's 'facts', it offered the prospect that I might have an informed opinion on every single thing. I had not imagined such an ambition before. With a mind alight with so many general ideas, I had not thought particular 'problems' required particular knowledge; there were just the general problems that came from being human in an unsatisfactory world, and to discuss these all one needed were a few strong, general theoretical lines. The more general the better, so that they could be applied to almost anything. Now I could sit in a gunpit and have *The Economist* present me with opinion on liberal education in the United States, on the position of foreign companies in Portugal, on prospects for secondary industry in British Guiana, on fascism in Croatia. Not just opinion, but facts, statistics, graphs. From an article on Bulgaria's new government I learned about the Bulgarian labour shortages. To understand the new crisis in Bolivia I had to understand the significance of the new price of tin. Understanding Romania's politics involved statistics on wheat supply.

I was learning familiarity with a world in which the two great measures of human ambition were national income statistics and balance of payments figures. *The Economist* was also casting up for me images of a more rational future for Britain, with a better-planned milk industry, a better-planned machine tool industry, a better-planned housing programme, a better-planned broadcasting service – and, most significant of all, a full employment policy and a national health service. The rest of the world was also being planned – there was intelligent discussion of more rational policies for world shipping, for the British colonies, for world food shortages, for world currency arrangements.

I had also been sent a small book which offered a better-planned South-east Asia – a South-east Asia of politically and economically independent nations with their own arrangements for a balanced internal economy and for collective security. Interesting in itself (we must avoid a Bourbon restoration, of course!) but even more interesting because I had never heard of 'South-east Asia'. It was a new idea that this was a 'region'. Now I could learn off facts on an area about which I had known almost nothing – beginning with names: 'Thailand' instead of 'Siam', 'Malaya' instead of 'Malay States', 'Indo-China' instead of 'French Indo-China', 'Indonesia' instead of 'Dutch East Indies'. The book had been sent to me by Frank Rhodes, a New Zealander who had been a professor of English at Rangoon University and was now in Sydney, an exile on half-pay. I had met him through Miller and now he was writing me firsthand accounts of living in Burma – I had never known anyone who lived in South-east Asia.

In his letters, Rhodes wrote pages about 'Asia'. After the war against Japan, which he saw as conducted by the United States to secure its own commercial hegemony, Western European influence would be eliminated; but then, he said, the millions of Asia would be led by their own charlatans. White Australia was doomed and he would happily swap his lilywhite Australian companions for a society with coloured skins, but with more intelligence, better manners and greater humanity than Australians. In a vision of desired revenge he cursed all the white peoples of the south: 'I shall have to go to China and help the Chinese knock the bottom out of New Zealand and Australia, as they will, no doubt, one day.'

4

After losing my specialist pay I had written Miller a description of 'Arch', the gunlayer who had 'put me in':

> When Arch arrived he had the largest holes in his socks anyone had seen, but the gunners taught him that socks had to be darned, just as they taught him some of the rituals of conversation. He spends a shilling of his pay and hoards the rest. He won't put it in the bank; he keeps it in a fat roll in the left hand pocket of his shirt. He never shares his food parcels unless we tell him to. Arch has an entrancing smile – along with a sniff, it is his main form of communication: once, in a training exercise when we had to swim across a river and we asked him if he could swim, all Arch did was to sniff and give a bit of a giggle; in the water he dogpaddled furiously for five yards, went under and then fought us as we saved him. His face is remarkably noble; his smile is perpetual; his drill movements are perfect. And behind all this there is – nothing. As I had been, he is a Specialist Grade Three: it was only after I lost my pay that I learned from someone from the same town that Arch is the town's most famous no-hoper. He is aged thirty. He has never worked. He used to stay at home, do some cooking for his mother, wash the dishes, grin when spoken to, get five shillings a week pocket money, bank half of it and go to the pictures and buy an ice-cream with the rest. When he came into the army, Arch simply fell into the ranks. I have just read a survey by a United States army captain who says that a mental age of eight is sufficient to complete successfully basic training in the artillery.

Miller asked for more. I wrote another piece:

> I wish people would stop suffering minor attacks of neurosis around me.
> It makes the place dismal and life even more difficult. The latest victim
> is Long Mac, a gunner of great height and little weight, an unhappy
> youth made even more unhappy by his height and by being one of our
> youngest. He is unhappy, unsociable, unoccupied, a ready victim to
> the climate. Wants to go home. Can't. No friends. No interests, except
> Pop, Mom and the pictures. Is no doubt fantasising as hard as he can
> go, building dream walls about himself. Suffered much this morning.
> He was stretched out on his bunk, when up comes something about
> mess orderly duty, rest days and the bill of rights. It would need a long
> Dostoevskyan short story to explain what happened. Everything in the
> army is Dostoevskyan, a point the drill books miss. Long Mac puts up
> an unsuccessful fight, and gives in quickly when authority comes in.
> He spends an unhappy, drooling day being a mess orderly and has now
> retired to his fantasies. I turn in my chair and look at him. Mournful
> Mac lies full length, a long, sad slab. His whole body is turned down
> towards the wall, his arms wrapped around his head, his face pressed into
> the pillow.

In my next letter I wrote about Roy (or 'Woy' as we called him, because he
couldn't pronounce his 'r's):

> Roy's hands are clasped, a slight smile bewitching his stern Red Indian
> face as he watches me write to Miller. 'Silly bastard!' he is probably
> thinking. 'Silly bastard' is one of the expressions the boys have taught
> Roy. When he first came to the unit he had absolutely nothing to say.
> But the boys taught him words. He was in kind hands and he trusted his
> mates. When we faced the river-crossing exercise, he told us he couldn't
> swim, so we told him to float. We told him he would be all right, and
> he floated. He is a good soldier in the sense that he is obedience itself.
> Earlier, with encouragement, he learned the craft of gunlaying. Then he
> joined another gun. No encouragement: his laying went off. If we are
> digging a gunpit or chopping down a tree, Roy is happy if we leave it to

him. His basic creed: The sooner the war is over the better, so that he can marry and settle down ... Drunkenness is unforgivable ... Cowboy movies are best ... Money is meant to be saved ... Everyone should be at parade on time. Above all: Milk must never be watered by the dairyman.

I also wrote about Gunner MacNaughton, whom we called 'Mother MacNaughton' or 'the Mighty Atom':

Although but a lowly gunner, the Mighty Atom, a young man of lower middle-class family, bossy, fussy, scarcely big enough to support his rifle and excused from route marches, got hold of an officer's pistol from the 'Q' store the other day. As he strutted around the camp he put his hand on the pistol and issued orders, as if they were pistol shots, in an upper-class voice of command. The gunners told him to get fucked, to piss off, and so forth, but he would soon be back at it again. After someone took the pistol away, he tried to grow a moustache: it was only a few long hairs, but he would bite at it and pull it as if it were a real moustache. When he was found in his hut reclining naked on his bunk, some passing gunners held him down and rubbed tinned cream, hair oil, boot polish and lemon butter into his genitals; on another occasion gunners shaved off his pubic hairs. They said he played with himself too much and the hairs would drop off anyway. Until the hairs grew again he had showers at night, in the dark. Now he is in the same hut as I am. After lights out we sometimes play the inquisitor with the Mighty Atom. He is a devoted monarchist – not only because 'you have to have respect' but because he believes he has royal blood running in his veins. We baited him about this so doggedly last night that he ran at me with a bayonet. We punched him out of the hut into the rain. When we let him back in again, naked, cold and wet, we cross-examined him on his motives until three a.m.

Miller arranged for me to write up two of these pieces, to be run, at some length, under the heading 'From the Menagerie' in *Arna*, the Arts Faculty literary magazine. What then happened provided the one moment of true hope I was to have in the army: they were praised by everyone I respected. In a review in *Honi Soit*, Hope said: 'These two studies are some of the good writing that has come out of the war.' Rhodes wrote: 'Almost entirely free of theoretical fluff. But your accuracy and sanity of perception bode ill for your future comfort: we live by illusion and you don't appear to have a sufficiency of it.' McAuley wrote: 'Your two fugitive pieces in *Arna* are beyond praise: heart-warming and corrective.' Stewart: 'The simplicity of their malice is superb.' Plimsoll said I should write a book like *The Enormous Room*. 'The novel awaits a new birth. In that resurgence I would like to see you play a part.'

I asked Mum to send me some exercise books: I would write a new poem; or I would write some articles for the army magazine *Salt*; or I would 'get a bit of prose published in one or two of the English journals' – *Horizon*, perhaps, or *Penguin New Writing*; or I would write, when I got out, a novel, in the style of the *Arna* pieces, about army life and I would make some notes for it now. While I was at it, I would also write a documentary observation on Australian life and ways. I would show a new way.

The notebook arrived. I didn't write anything at all. For years afterwards I would sometimes wonder why.

5

By the time the Battery Staff School had ended, the regiment had moved out of Darwin and back down the road to a camp where, before dawn, we would sometimes hear the Australian and American bombers roll out through the dark sky in a long stomach rumble towards the Timor Sea. Our most ambitious collective purpose now was the regimental parade. Held every Monday on a space cleared, in some now abandoned plan, as a strip for Spitfires, these ceremonies took half a day. A borrowed band would welcome each battery as it tramped onto the abandoned space; it might strike up a tune or two when we had assembled, and would then vigorously greet the arrival of the commanding officer. Soft wooing music would be played as he walked past line after line, staring man-to-man into as many of our eyes as he could manage; pert, patriotic airs were played as we marched past him, giving the salute. Then we retreated to the camp we had come from, said what a lot of bullshit that was, and had our lunch.

For the first few weeks after my return from the school, our purpose was to finish constructing our hut. A framework of poles had already gone up, and the earth floor had been cleared and stamped down. We split pandanus logs and nailed them to the poles, making the lower wall, and for the upper wall we plundered the bamboo thickets, hacking a way through to the thin bamboo at the centre, chopping it down, clearing it of prickles, lopping it into lengths, and then, back in camp, splitting it into slats and nailing these to the framework. We also used bamboo slats, laced together with signallers' wire, stretched across poles for our bunks. There was an ovation of thunder, and some rain, on the day we began thatching the roof. For once, I did not revolt with boredom at the thought of working with my hands. Since no one was standing over us, I imagined we were William Morris craftsmen in a commune in which I was skilled in the ancient craft of thatching. In fact our hut was the most incompetently constructed in the battery. After coming top in the battery staff school, I had been given 'specialist' pay again, but this time as a Command Post Assistant; my hutmates were the command post staff. Of the six of us, three were students, two were public service clerks, one was an advertising man, but none was an efficient hutmaker. We gave the advertising man the job of persuading the gunners that our hut wasn't as bad as it looked.

I was back among the sons of golf players. After evening mess, which we sometimes skipped, preferring to eat tinned food bought from the canteen, we had a regular game of bridge. For supper, we would make cocoa on a kerosene heater and share out fruit cake sent from home, or open another tin from the canteen – some asparagus, perhaps, or baked beans. In this hut we were reconstructing, in primitive style, parts of the civilisation in which I had spent my childhood at Muswellbrook, when I would go to sleep hearing the murmured prayers of bridge players … *one no trump, two diamonds, two hearts*. After lights out, we might discuss issues of the day: there was one long debate, running over several weeks, on government control of industry, in which I was able to add to no-bullshit logic-chopping the new habit I had taken from *The Economist* of appealing to 'facts'.

That we had all come from Sydney and had all completed high school provided an aloof sense of shared sophistication which we used to protect pride from the follies and insults of our masters. We became gratified students of absurd statements made by officers or sergeant majors, whether shouted out, or typed up and put on notice boards. There was a special interest in collecting those coming from a battery commander (not our own) notorious for not having even the Intermediate Certificate. Two favourites were announcements on his battery notice board: 'Training will be carried out with enthusiasm', and 'On manoeuvres, troops who wish to masticate will take a shovel'.

ONE OF OUR SET IN THE COMMAND POST HUT WAS SEEN BY THE rest of us as a skite – always talking about the success he would have after the war, how much money he had, the influential people he knew – one of whom, a brigadier, he said had promised him a commission. As he waited for this commission 'to come through', he would talk about it as a way out of all his troubles, like winning the lottery. I now also saw myself as having a ticket in the same lottery. Strings were being pulled ... interviews had been held ... strong recommendations had been made. I wrote to my mother that prospects were good that I would be made a sergeant lecturer in the Army Education Service and transferred to New Guinea. I also had a ticket in a bigger lottery: an advertisement in *Army News* had called for applications for twelve 'diplomatic cadetships'. It was a new idea. Australia was to develop its own diplomatic service which would recruit 'cadets' who would spend two years in a School of Diplomatic Studies before entering the diplomatic service as third secretaries. In the real world I was still bonded to the Education Department to become a high school teacher: in my fantasies I could still see myself sometimes as a successful writer, sometimes, even still, as a failed revolutionary addressing his betrayers from the scaffold (although being even a failed revolutionary now seemed less likely in a technocrats' 'post-war world' in which leftists would become principal supporters of the state). I could not previously have imagined being a diplomat – it would be like becoming a character in *The Economist*. When I applied, I wrote to Miller that I felt like Julien Sorel.

Miller and I had already spent some of our letter-writing contemplating the splendours and miseries of trying to compromise with the world of ambition. For him, ambition was something he could see. He mixed with people who had 'careers'. There was his own career in the ABC; there were the politicians he had daily spoken to when he was in Canberra. He could gossip, as if he knew what he was saying, about what 'the boys in Post War Reconstruction are thinking'. Of the newly arrived 'great men' of our own acquaintance, he could report how they were so concerned with their own affairs that they had little time to spare for those who didn't know how to come in out of the wet; they had gained the confidential manner of men who understood great things. And now Miller had capped all this by getting married. He had bought furniture and rented a house and in its garden he was growing beans, tomatoes, lettuce and rhubarb. As for me, the only ambitions I could see in operation were the desires for stripes or pips, ambitions I saw as so low that they scarcely seemed ambition at all, merely childish perversity. For me, ambition was still a bookish matter.

I still read whatever was sent to me – *The Times Literary Supplement*, Smollett, Byron, Isherwood, Turgenev, Lawrence, *New Statesman* and *Nation*, Ibsen, Mencken, Webster and Ford, Veblen, Namier, books on current affairs, history, biography, Heath's *Practical Italian Grammar*. But for a while I decided to direct my reading so that I could write a manual of conduct in which I would apply to ordinary life the precepts of great generals, since leadership seemed the same whether on the battlefield or the boardroom. (The boardroom came into it because I had read about a book called *Business as a System of Power*.) Sun-tzu's precept that 'all warfare is based on deception' seemed so perfect that I copied out a passage on how to react to the enemy and sent it to Miller:

> When about to attack, seem unable. When active, seem inactive. When near, seem far. When far, make believe you are near. Hold out baits to entice him. Feign disorder and crush him. If he is superior in strength, evade him. If he is of choleric temper, seek to irritate him. Pretend to be weak that he may grow arrogant. If he is taking his ease, give him no rest. If his forces are united, separate them. Attack when he is unprepared. Appear when you are not expected ... To fight and conquer in all your battles is not supreme excellence. Supreme excellence consists in breaking the enemy's resistance without fighting.

In writing my manual of conduct, I decided to draw not only on military and business philosophisers. I had found a copy of *The Woman's Book of Household Wisdom* and took as a significant precept for leadership its injunction: 'It is wiser not to give an order you know will not be obeyed.'

This didactic approach was likely to come through in any letter I wrote to Miller. He was, in 1943, editor of *Honi Soit*, and in the middle of a discourse on the philosophy of a well-balanced page, or the true meaning of the ultra-Bodoni typeface, I might insert some advice suggesting a more universal approach to decision-making, such as 'The aim of editors should be that of gunners – to bring down the necessary fire with sufficient accuracy in the right place at the right time', as if this axiom of Horne were fit to be placed with the axioms of Napoleon, Frederick the Great or Sun-tzu. Similarly, when Miller wrote that although Conlon was now a lieutenant colonel (but still wearing, I was told, a private's greatcoat, an act in the theatre of leadership that suggested he might also be reading some military philosophisers), he had re-contested his seat as student representative on the university Senate. I advised Miller to 'keep in' with Alf's opponent, adding, in my style as political sage, 'To doublecross an opponent, you must first be his friend.'

This didactic worldliness was a way of showing off new public wisdoms. It camouflaged my impulsiveness and dreaminess with clouds of rationality, but I had noticed in my student days that this could give me a reputation for a cool unscrupulousness which, it seemed to me, had nothing to do with the muddle of my own enthusiasms. I was astounded when Miller wrote congratulating me on how I had 'played my cards remarkably well in hanging on to Plimsoll and not whining to Alf Conlon, who retains considerable respect for you'. I had no impression that I had played any cards at all. My own life was so removed from leadership that I was not even prepared to shout out 'Atten-*shun*!' and 'Stand at EASE!' to fellow students at an army school. Apart from being a great writer, or a failed revolutionary, or a Chinese military philosopher of the sixth century BC, I could not imagine a 'career', although I could imagine activity and excitement. I still respected Stephen Daedalus' formula of 'silence, exile and cunning' and wrote to friends that my exile in the army was doing me good, because it was teaching me arts of personal concealment.

Miller invented a career for me. For him, the army was teaching me how to compromise with ordinary things – something, he said, Hope had already learned. As a result of this, I would fit in better after the war. It was like having a job, he suggested, 'in which you have to take orders and sneak and trample on the face of the bloke below you, and so on'. In his next letter Miller rhapsodised on this theme in a way that both astounded and excited me:

There are only two young men among the great Circle of my Friends whom I would nominate as likely to become successes – Sam Cohen and yourself. Conlon might be another, but I don't know sufficient about him to take such a big step as agree with the general estimate of his capabilities. Even in what have been considered your most juvenile, undergraduatish, unfortunate, temperamental and all the other adjectives episodes, you have preserved an attitude of tactics, of strategy, of logical consideration of the possibilities which I cannot but admire.

You could earn big money as a journalist. You have the quality of mercilessness that is so necessary in such a position; your writing is incisive, even brutal, very often; you can examine things critically except in rare cases where you feel inferior to what you are considering, and you set down your observations in the most crystal-clear prose.

And the thing is that you have the business attitude – an eye to the main chance, an appreciation (rather unreliable at the moment, but you really didn't have a fair chance) of the right man to stick to, and a realisation that there is no possibility of improving the world – that is, wasting your time trying to do so.

I felt dirtied by the suggestion that I might engage in something as shady as commercial journalism but in the very same moments imagined the excitement of writing my own *J'accuse* at some time of great scandal. But what else could Miller mean by 'success'? I wrote back that in Australia there were few opportunities for someone like me to be a 'success'. He was remorseless: 'I am keeping your letters. I'm sure you'll want them published when you are a great man in very fact rather than in the minds of your friends.' Later, another surprise: 'Pritchett has decided that the reason why so many others respect you is that you are the only rational person we know – that you do actually shape your actions as rationally as possible, instead of talking about the process as most of us do.'

Rational! This was Miller at his most misunderstanding!

I would write letters of up to twenty pages to Miller, and also to Frank Rhodes, who, as well as sending me *The Economist*, *Horizon*, *New Statesman* and *Nation*, *Scrutiny* and many books, would also write back letters as long as mine, out of peevishness, he said – a peevishness which came from his exile, since there would be no going back to an independent Burma, and no going forward in Australia where all that his Oxford First had brought him was a position as a temporary clerk in the Shipping Section of the Sydney branch of the Commerce Department.

I was flattered to be able to write so intimately to a professor and someone who, at thirty-seven, was two years older than Hope, and delighted to receive in reply reminiscences cosmopolitan enough, I thought, to appear in *Horizon*. Reading sustained outpourings from Rhodes of melancholic memories of Naples in the spring of 1932, or of a tour of castles in Touraine, or his reflections of living in Weimar Germany, was like receiving letters from Marcel Proust. Even the long passages of life in Burma were 'Proustian'. There was one long masterpiece that began, eight years before, among the plum trees and carnations of the pine-clad hills of the southern Shan States and ended, after many delightfully discursive flourishes, in his meeting Collings, then McCallum, then Miller, then Horne. When he sent me a photograph of himself with some lines from Dante written on the back I myself felt like a character in *Remembrance of Things Past*. (Although easily able to imagine myself as 'Stendhalian', 'Tolstoyan' or 'Dostoevskyan', I had previously not seen myself as 'Proustian'; I was grateful, however, that in the letter accompanying the photograph he had translated the lines from Dante so I could know what they meant.) When Rhodes described life in the Shipping Section, he moved from the 'Proustian' to the 'Dostoevskyan' or, perhaps, the 'Kafkaesque'. He saw the eighteen months there as 'the most senseless waste of his life', spent among people 'with rather squalid minds and abysses of ignorance or silliness – petty, vain, improvident and avaricious, drunken, careless, imprudent, dull, warped, fossilised'. When Professor F.W.W. Rhodes, temporary clerk, had lunch with the vice-chancellor of the University of Sydney, he was concerned that the head clerk of the Shipping Section would report him to the higher-ups for taking more than an hour. The head clerk, for whom life took on most meaning at 5.10 p.m. when he would see that no one left the office before the regulation 5.15, was one of the main characters in Rhodes's *Inferno*. The chief character was the Gestetner machine; itself warped and fossilised, it became a source of such complex backbiting that settling disputes surrounding it demanded the intervention, on a journey from Canberra, of the assistant secretary of the Department of Commerce and Agriculture. I wrote to Rhodes asking his permission to put him in a novel; on another occasion I suggested that, after the war, someone might publish our correspondence.

In his letters Rhodes also joined the speculation about who I was and what would happen to me which I encouraged in all my friends – not so much from vanity as from interest in the answers. For him, there was a difference between the Horne he found on paper and the Horne he had met in Sydney. He said I had raised such a rumpus in a restaurant in Elizabeth Bay Road that he had not been brave enough to go there again; at the same time he had enjoyed a noisy anecdotal account of mine, illustrated with actions, giving the history of the university's English Department. He recalled that when Miller had left us in the Elizabeth Bay Road restaurant, I had become quiet, pensive, world-weary: now, in my letters, instead of the abrupt and argumentative Horne he had met in Sydney he found 'a candid, rather fastidious letter-writer, a sensitive and scrupulous individual, peculiarly decent and genuine, serene and good-tempered in attitude and language' (although he corrected occasional mistakes in my spelling and grammar). I would read these phrases over, and wonder about them, and compare them with the opposite kinds of phrases others had used about me. Was I simply inventing, in the strategy of letter-writing, a 'Horne' who might be suitable for Rhodes?

I saw in myself a special problem in which no one else seemed to take any interest: my mind was filled with subtleties and contradictions, but when I argued or wrote I had to hit the nail on the head. Why couldn't I display subtleties and contradictions? I wrote to Miller that I seemed to be moved to talking or writing only out of anger. At other times, despite prickly heat, insect bites and suspicions of inherent fraudulence, I read on serenely, hoping that both my reading and the tediums I found in army life would, like being hit on the head, do me good. I believed that if I could have time to work over what I had read, and what I had experienced, then I would know what existence was like, and what I could believe.

What particularly flattered me in Rhodes's letters were his prophecies (different from Miller's prophecies of 'success') that I might 'fail'. My style, he said, was 'very clear and precise' and my conversation, with its combination of 'laying-about' plus ruthless logic 'was a bit like Johnson and Mencken'. Good! 'It seems to me your mind is desperately analytical and logical: the contests for you between reason and emotion are more vexatious than for most.' Very good! But: 'The sort of knowledge which pleases you and the sort of thing you are likely to write is not likely to please many; it is too intelligent, critical, witty. You are bound to be influential among intelligent people, but opportunities for the free exercise of intelligence become rarer.' *Excellent*!

It was from McAuley that I received a prophecy of coming failure expressed so bitterly that it kept on stinging me for years afterwards. He began linking himself with me (something he had never done before) when he wrote: 'Somehow we never got quite around (you and me) to the more luscious visions for which youth is justly famous.' Then he walked away and left me alone: 'You apparently continue to nurse a sinister longing for something apocalyptic and outrageous in the way of action but your inbred cynicism about "causes" throws you back on yourself; a one-man show. Oh boy, what a show! Even your capitulation to the powers you foresee as something violent, total and lurid. No half measures! But neither side would welcome these fierce gestures which would only discommode their pedestrian junketings through time and space. They hunger for routine, but you like to move in an uproar of your own making, so they'll break your knees to make you hobble to their gait.'

PART 2

A DIPLOMATIC SELF
1944–45

SIX

In transit

1

Water was rushing around us, in pelting rain and swollen watercourses. I was at Adelaide River (where it was rumoured the wet had brought out the crocodiles) to sit for the Diplomatic Cadet examinations. We went to sleep in our tents to the gurgle of the camp's drains and while we sat in a hut for the exams insects screeched outside. For the free-choice essay paper I chose the theme 'Divide and Conquer' in order to display the subtleties of one who had read Sun-tzu. With six questions to be answered in ninety minutes, doing the current affairs paper was like writing for *The Economist*. I declared myself on trade protection, the White Australia policy, relations between the conservative parties in Australia, the future of the British Commonwealth, the significance of the Gipps Mission to India and the meaning of the Moscow Conference. For my five pieces for the general knowledge paper, each of exactly 200 words (no more, no less), I chose the fundamental causes of the Second World War, the likely post-war treatment of Germany, Japan, Italy and Poland, the importance of Britain, the differences between the Soviet and parliamentary systems, and signs of the prophetic in English imaginative writing since 1919. (My choice of Eliot and Auden for the last worried Rhodes, although he admitted that examiners liked novelty.)

Bill Pritchett was also in the Northern Territory, but our first attempt at a meeting had been a fiasco. After a hot, hungry journey of hitched truck rides I had arrived at a railway siding, as improvised and dirty as most places in the Territory, from where, after an hour's wangling, I had been able to get a phone message to Pritchett. I sat and waited on an upturned box, talked to a few loafing soldiers, contemplated patches of spilt and steaming tar, finished off a packet of cigarettes, and got hotter and thirstier, until I was able to bludge a drink from the water bag of a passing truck. When Pritchett arrived on his motor bike, there was not much left of the day. Like strangers, we exchanged a brief, cautious, polite conversation. But now he was at Adelaide River with me, sitting for the Diplomatic Cadet examinations. We were able to wisecrack, sing university revue songs, make allusive conversation and, after each exam paper, talk about how we had 'gone', as if we were back in first year Arts comparing notes on how we had explained the significance of Hammurabi's Code or the great vowel shift.

As in a painting of the Last Judgment, in the examination hut there were only fellow-sinners. Nothing divided officers from the men: the chairs and tables we sat in, the examination questions we were asked, and the paper on which we wrote our answers were all the same; but after each exam was over the officers went off to their mess and we went off to ours. In the exams hut was 'the Brigade Major'. The position held by this beautiful, dark-haired young chap was the most glamorous in the artillery; he was the ideas man and troubleshooter for the field artillery regiments and the tank attack and mobile anti-aircraft units, and his visits to our regiment were like those of a shiny black, exotic bird which had briefly paused in its long flight. In the exam hut in his impeccable uniform he seemed the model of a brilliant officer: but did he know what I knew about the Cripps Mission to Moscow?

While I was at Adelaide River, I saw an Army Education official, a friend, as it happened, of Conlon's: how did things look for my application for transfer to New Guinea? It was a safe bet, he told me. In the bag. As to the Diplomatic Cadets exam, that seemed a long shot. It was rumoured that two thousand had sat, and that of these fifty to a hundred would be chosen for interviews and out of them the final twelve would be chosen. We were spending much of our time in working parties now, sometimes in eight-hour shifts in Darwin, shovelling coal or working on the wharves, sometimes on 'grass fatigues', back at our camp, where we would walk through steaming spear grass up to our shoulders or over our heads, pulling it out by the roots and leaving it in clumps to rot. There were no more weekly parades. The regiment had disintegrated from a 'fighting unit' into a labour detail, working in the wet. There was no news of the Army Education job, nor of the diplomatic cadetship.

Six weeks after I had sat for the exams, while we were shovelling coal in Darwin at night in the rain, wearing only shorts, or altogether naked, a signal came through that I had been chosen for an interview in Adelaide. I was at once ordered back to camp, and told to be ready to move at an hour's notice. I sent off rockets of praise, in letters, and waited. Letters came back. In wishing me luck Rhodes told me how to behave during the interview: I must clean the nicotine stains off my hands but otherwise must 'be myself', except that, when smiling, I must not show my teeth, because they had been chipped when I was hit on the head. The army had told me to pack my kit, but as the days went by and no more news came, my kit became unpacked and I was rostered on to grass fatigues along with the others still in the camp. I had just come back from a grass fatigue when I was told my movement order to Adelaide had been cancelled: something about bad weather restricting aircraft flight. Since the interviewing panel had presumably moved on from Adelaide, I would be put back on to normal duties. The brigade major, however, had gone to Adelaide for his interview. I had myself paraded before the commanding officer. He showed no interest. Distress signals went off to Rhodes and Miller. I was sent back to Darwin, to join a working party lumping crates of beer from a warehouse onto trucks.

Rhodes wrote that he had done what he could with the External Affairs Department. He seemed, in a sense, at ease to find me again reduced to victim. We were back to our normal relationship: he was able to write as if nothing more could be done beyond consoling me with the righteousness of his fury – 'these filthy blows', 'the malice of these impudent military clowns'. I read his letter sitting in a DC-3 pretending calm (it was my first time in an aircraft) as it quivered and pulsated, flying low beneath the rain clouds, over sodden scrub and flooded river flats. The movement order had come while I was lumping crates of beer. I had washed and dressed, and had put my gear together in the back of the truck that took me to the airstrip, where I had been delivered to the DC-3 five minutes before take-off – not, as it turned out, for Adelaide but, I was now discovering, to Katherine, south of Adelaide River, where I spent the night. Next morning I was transferred by plane to Brisbane, and after a night in cattle pens at Brisbane Showground made a two-day train journey to Townsville, during which I read Cecil's *Life of Metternich*. While reading about the shoring-up of the *ancien régime* in the first half of the nineteenth century I would discover that my mind had drifted into fantasies of success and that I had 'read' whole pages without reading anything; I would try to suppress my hopes and compel myself to read those pages again. As an antidote to excitement I forced myself to mark passages and scribble marginal comments. I was not altogether satisfied with Cecil's treatment of Metternich. We passed through subtropical landscapes of a kind I had not seen before, but how could I take an interest in them? When the train stopped at stations other soldiers swarmed around the bar but, like a schoolboy worried the train might leave without him, I would swallow one drink, then hurry back to the carriage and sit there, waiting.

Townsville had been turned into an enormous drafting centre for Australian and United States troops in transit to and from New Guinea. It had become legendary in the stories my friends told of the absurdities of war after Alf Conlon had ordered a survey on the effects on the town of its huge military camps. The survey was reduced to several amusing anecdotes: I was now able to add an anecdote of my own. The Diplomatic Cadets interview was conducted by a tribunal that included Colonel Hodgson, the Gallipoli veteran who was head of the External Affairs Department. During the interview I enjoyed showing off the knowledge of current affairs gleaned from *The Economist* and felt that, somehow, I was coming though as a pretty sincere sort of chap; when asked who my favourite writers were I gave such a long list, with comments on each, that after some minutes I was asked to stop. I was, however, speaking softly – perhaps because it was a manner acquired in my days as Young Donald in dealing with older people, perhaps because in discussing so many interesting questions, I felt, for once, like myself, or perhaps because, as Rhodes had instructed, I was trying to conceal my chipped teeth. Hodgson snapped 'What's wrong with you? What are you mumbling for? Got a gumboil?' I replied, 'Yes sir, I have.'

2

A good anecdote to tell, several days later, in the bars and coffee shops of Sydney, on my month's leave, feeling something of a ghost figure, a spirit-reminder, as McAuley in his time had seemed to me, of a golden undergraduate age of three years before, but feeling also that there was something ghostly about the present, as if it were merely a reflection of the past, or even a shabby imitation, with new people (whose names I would forget as soon as they were introduced) trying to imitate ritualistically but inauthentically what for us had been spontaneous and new. If enough of what my mother would have called 'the old crowd' were around, things might seem the same again. But some of 'the old crowd' were now people with careers, talking about planning community centres for after the war, or how firmly Alf had gained the support of the GOC (there were even rumours of his influence on General Douglas Macarthur), or how efficient the Stalinist union leaders were compared with the old 'Catholic Action' right wingers. As for me, I didn't want to be the same either, but someone made wiser by the tediums of the army, supplemented by a range of reading from Stendhal to Sun-tzu; made more knowledgeable from reading *The Economist* and books about the future of South-east Asia; and made more humorous from being hit on the head.

There were shadows of changes and achievements that seemed omens of my own failure. Verse by Hope, Stewart and McAuley had been published in *Australian Poetry, 1943*: presumably this would be the beginning of world recognition of what we had seen as their genius. When Dobell won the Archibald Portrait Prize I had written to Mum, 'I used to know him: in a few years he will have an international reputation.' Max Harris had got out of the army and *Angry Penguins* was now becoming a large and splendidly produced magazine with international connections. The kinds of people Douglas McCallum had known were being heard of in the world of Sydney painting – from a distance they seemed elegant, amusing, of good taste, and worldly wise. Even jazz, such an obscure cult when McAuley had introduced me to it, was on the climb up: Oliver Somerville's brother was a jazz pianist at the Negro Club in Darlinghurst and he and his friends lived in an eccentric rooming house in the Rocks which had been nick-named 'Buggery Barn' when it was still a hotel.

It was with Miller and Rhodes – because it was to them I had written most frequently and openly and at greatest length – that I now most seemed my new 'self'. This was a 'self' their letters had helped me create. Rhodes told me, however, that I was more constrained in conversation, yet as he and I strode along beaches or on bush walks or up and down the streets of harbour suburbs, I deluged this dapper New Zealander with words. With his solid black moustache and square chin he was not unlike the English comic actor Robertson Hare, and was so anglified that for years, until he came to Sydney, no one except his mother and two aunts had called him by his first name. Unlike Rhodes, Miller was one of us; we now had such strong common experience that he was my only full confidant. In bars, in restaurants, in his parents' sitting room and now in his own house we would talk about ourselves and our ideas and the future. One afternoon, reclining on the grass in the park at Double Bay and looking out to the harbour, we talked the whole afternoon with the full confidence in each other of two young men whose friendship would last as long as their lives.

To my surprise, some of the new generation of students found the new version of myself interesting in itself, not needing to be framed in the faded gilding of the past. Being a soldier, or at least looking like one, could interest some of them: it seemed more real than their own lives. I had a small affair with a woman student of shifting radicalisms. For her, my experience with the gunners had the reality of experience with 'the workers'. When drunk, she would touch my forehead and say 'How wise! How wise!', then touch my skin and say 'How brown!' I was aware of this brownness of my body. When I was showering, I might look down on this brown, healthy and even, perhaps, strong body. I had put away the feeling, grown from the embarrassments of adolescence when my body seemed to sprout as rankly as spear grass, that my body was not my own. This was something I could live in, and wear openly: there was no need to hide it.

It was through Murray Sayle, a lanky youth of immense energy and crushing laconicism who was now editor of *Honi Soit*, that I was meeting this new generation of students. Just as Alan Crawford had tutored me both in wildness and in love for *Honi Soit* and student politics, I felt I should tutor Sayle in drunkenness and in new typefaces, in cutting lectures and in reading books outside his courses. Rebelliousness was the true style for an editor of *Honi Soit*. In return, Sayle treated me with an amused reserve that overcame the gap of four years dividing us.

IT WAS TO MURRAY SAYLE AND THE *HONI SOIT* OFFICE THAT I WENT, ready for revolution in the streets of Sydney, when the government closed down the *Daily Telegraph* and the *Sydney Morning Herald* after the newspapers had broken the censorship laws as a matter of principle. Blank columns had been left in the *Sunday Telegraph* the day before, to indicate that some matter had been censored. Type floating in the white space said:

A FREE PRESS?
THE GREAT AMERICAN DEMOCRAT
THOMAS JEFFERSON SAID: 'WHERE
THE PRESS IS FREE AND EVERY
MAN ABLE TO READ, ALL IS SAFE'.

Sydney, for once, seemed to have entered history. I wrote editorials in my head for a large part of the day. Since indicating that there had been censorship was itself censorable, Commonwealth police officers came to the *Telegraph* building that night, and one of them pulled a gun when a *Telegraph* truck with banned *Telegraph*s in it began to leave. But the *Telegraph* had an old printing press in another part of town where an illegal edition was printed, including a photograph of the policeman with his gun. An illegal edition! An underground press! Sydney had become as real as a foreign country. Parliamentary politics seemed a swindle, with no personal interest for me, but this was the kind of politics I could understand. The books I had read told me what to do next. The people must be roused ... there must be protests in the street. On the tram to the university I imagined manifestoes, posters.

Who was responsible for what happened next was being disputed almost as quickly as it happened, but I had no doubt that it was me. I felt that if I hadn't declaimed in the *Honi Soit* office, no one would have called a student meeting at lunchtime, with a decision to march, in protest, on the town. Later, half a dozen others were to say they had suggested this. There was opposition, of course, from some of the left, to whom the fact that it was a Labor government which had banned the papers excused the banning, or at least complicated things. To me this showed how power had corrupted the left.

When the student meeting began (the meeting itself was illegal), images drifted into a reality that matched the images of political dreams, as fine phrases of freedom taken out of books were given meaning by being shouted through microphones. My own speech was applauded by more people than

I had ever addressed before, then there was a straggling of people into the university avenue – at first not enough, then almost a thousand. Like an illustration in a history book, they went off, marching three abreast. Since I was in uniform, I had not marched with them, but when the gossip came back, I heard that between orations in Martin Place there were chants from some of the crowd of 'We want Horne!' I asked friends what they thought of my actions: Crawford saw it as a newspaper proprietors' stunt; McAuley announced in a letter that his concern in life was the cultivation of a certain sensibility, and it was not served by walkings in the street; Stewart wrote that crowds gave him a headache.

As I sailed north on a troopship, on the way back to Darwin, there was again a re-enactment of what my father had done before, but again without the danger. It was scarcely possible any longer that we might be torpedoed by a Jap submarine, but all the rest could seem real: the two-up schools and crown-and-anchor games, the latrines jutting over the side of the ship where our bums might be sprayed by the sea, the turning of a passenger liner into a container for human cattle. Even at the ship's concert held on deck by the light of moon and stars, the songs and ballads were mainly from the Great War or from the bush. Just before my leave was over, I had learned what had seemed obvious anyway: despite the letters and specially arranged meetings, I was not going to be made a sergeant lecturer in army education and transferred to New Guinea. When at our last meeting Rhodes brushed by accident against the topic of diplomatic cadetships, he apologised for reminding me of my vague hopes. The day before we left, I sent Miller a letter saying, 'I sail for Darwin tomorrow. Fuck it. Fuck it. Fuck it.'

3

To wait our turn for a road convoy to Darwin we had been unloaded from the troopship into one of the transit camps at Townsville. It was like a vast cattle yard with herds of moving men. The public address system thundered music but, like cracks of a stock whip, announcements interrupted the music to order individuals, detachments or whole units to report at the double. In the mornings we were pushed around in fatigues and even squad drill, but after midday mess, the public address announcements seemed to take their siesta, as

if the whole army signals system was digesting lunch; we were told that as no
movement orders had come through for that day we could take evening leave.
We would hurry to a hotel rumoured to have beer and queue at the bar for half
an hour or more waiting for five o'clock when the beer came on. The barmaids
would move down the bar taking orders, but we were allowed only one order
per person for as many glasses of beer as supplies would allow for that day;
then, holding a glass in each hand and keeping an eye on any other glasses we
had (which, in the pushing and shoving, might be snitched by latecomers), we
would gulp them down so we could hurry to a place selling 'steaks' (that is to
say, horse meat).

At one such meal I told an anecdote about the survey of Townsville Alf
Conlon had ordered. Demand had pushed up the price of watermelons so
high that when a surveyor asked a Townsville prostitute how she could justify
her high charges she said, 'Well, look at the price of watermelons.' This set off
a movement in army logic. We were boozed up. We had had our steaks. Now,
said one of the gunners, a bank clerk using army issue language, 'How about a
bit of snatch?' (At last, perhaps, I could seem a real soldier.) Bank clerk, public
service clerk, insurance agent and student, we followed directions to the edge
of town where, set among the paddocks, wooden sheds stood in line, with
soldiers standing outside. When my turn came, I knew I was not going to risk
disease for mere vanity and in any case the conditions were so bleak that I
wouldn't make it. Once I was inside the rough cubicle, with its bed and wash
basin, the young woman in blouse and shorts was so quick unbuttoning my
shorts to give a 'short arm inspection' that I hardly had time to say that I would
pay the fee but all I wanted was to talk for a while, taking long enough to fool
my comrades outside. When I held out the money, she told me to leave, as if
I had proposed a perversion too objectionable for money to buy. I tried to
argue, but she threatened to call the male protector she said was sitting on the
back step. The best I could do as I walked out was to hitch up my waistband
cheerfully. The insurance agent gunner said, 'Jesus, you were quick?' I gave a
wise look, suggesting there was a lot about sex he didn't know.

The next day the public address system interrupted its normal siesta with
the announcement: 'NX 121576, Gunner Horne, D.R. to report to the Camp
Orderly Room. I'll repeat that: NX 121576, Gunner Horne, D.R. to report
to the Camp Orderly Room. At the double, Gunner!' Someone in the army

had found out where I was and now the signal had arrived: I had been chosen as one of twelve diplomatic cadets. I must report to Sydney Showground 'for discharge forthwith'.

On the 1500-mile journey back to Sydney I was suffused with such secret pleasure that I scarcely spoke to my train companions. In Sydney there was a celebration at Ushers bar for those around, but more important was the thanksgiving dinner at home. The meal was merely a Sunday dinner eaten during the week, but as we sat around the oak dining room table at a family meal, eating our roast beef and apple pie we knew I had been born again: once more, I had a 'career'. Only Dad seemed troubled. He said I had been given a second chance but I mustn't throw it away on drink. *Drink!* My mother seemed more sensible. To commemorate my success appropriately, she bought me a leather briefcase.

I was running late for the diplomatic studies course. I had a list of some of the delectable books I wanted to buy – books by Denis Brogan on the American political system and on modern France ... Burke, Hobbes, Locke, Aristotle, Thucydides ... Benham on economics ... Hicks on the social framework ... the Oxford French–English Dictionary ... Rostovtzeff's *Social and Economic History of the Roman Empire* – and I wanted to get to Canberra and read them. But being discharged from the army took longer than being signed up. I would report each day at the Showground, look at lists for my name, be paraded, stand around, and now and again be summoned to perform the next act of divestment of soldierliness; then I would stand around again. It was like being cleaned very slowly – each day less of me felt dirty. Then, at once, all was finished. On this last day, any part of the army processing that was voluntary was abandoned. Intelligence tests? Don't be ridiculous! What *is* intelligence? Cigarette ration? No time to waste filling in forms! Application for a pension for my head and eye injuries? No time for that when I could be reading Thucydides or Brogan!

Sitting in the bus taking me away from the Showground I took off my brown slouch hat whose prototype was a national symbol and looked at it. I recalled the battering I had given it to make it look old, the smartness it had gained when I replaced its felt band with a linen puggaree and the honest sweat I had wiped from the leather band inside. I remembered how at family singsongs my Uncle Loy would stand beside the pianola and sing a song in which an old soldier addresses, with great sentiment, his old army hat (his old 'shako') and recalls the adventures they shared. I threw my old shako out of the bus window.

Instead of waiting for the next day's fast train I would use the travel voucher I had been given to buy a first-class sleeping berth on the night train, a slow one. No time to lose. I had never travelled first class before, nor in a sleeping berth. The only member of our family with any connection with sleeping berths had been Pa, a sleeping car conductor. But there were no sleeping berths. I sat up all night and in Canberra caught a taxi, before dawn, to Beauchamp House where I was to stay.

After five minutes ringing on the night bell a woman still surly with sleep appeared. *Horne? No one by that name.* But there must be. H-o-r-n-e. I'm a diplomatic cadet. *I don't care who you are; there's no one of that name* ... Well, could I sit in the hall with my luggage until the External Affairs Department opens? No. The door was shut and bolted. Across the way, I could see a light. With frost crunching under my shoes, I lumped my luggage over towards the light until, as I got closer, it seemed that the building (perhaps it was some kind of hotel) was in the hands of the police. Closer still, I found that the lowest level of it had been turned into a police station. The sergeant made me a cup of tea. For several hours, until the Department opened, I had the kind of talk with the policemen that I had engaged in thousands of times with the gunners.

The story of these opening hours in the national capital became one of my best Canberra anecdotes.

SEVEN

A political town

1

Beauchamp House, which, in outward appearance, might have been a late-Victorian country house in England, was one of three grandly named hostels in which the twelve diplomatic cadets boarded. A bus ride away across the river valley was Brassey House, whose Corinthian façade looked over a wide sweep of lawn. Across the way from the Corinthian columns of Brassey House was Barton House, whose architects' vision had narrowed to a façade of pragmatic brick. Barton House was a repository mainly for female secretaries and typists from the government departments; Beauchamp House and Brassey House stood larger in the social imagination as places mainly for male officials.

In Brassey House, to which I had been allotted, they had given me a small desk. Its first function: I must write letters of exultation at getting out of the army. 'Your letter was a poem of joy in free verse,' Stewart wrote in reply; but, as if regretting the passing of Gunner Horne, man of sorrows, Rhodes wrote back almost petulantly, 'You seem vulgarly and blatantly happy.' With the letters written, I must now surround this desk with books. In the army I had read books as a secret vice: now I was being paid £275 a year to follow this pleasure. On my second day I went to a small, straight-up-and-down building in the centre of a paddock near Brassey House that was to be one wing of a seven-winged 'National Library', the rest of which, like most of Canberra, had not yet been built and might never be: I came away with an armful of books. On the third day I went to the other side of the valley where there was a former hotel whose lower reaches had been taken over by the police station in which I had sought refuge on my first morning; and whose upper reaches had become the Canberra University College where the twelve of us were to attend our lectures and tutorial classes. I came back from the college library with another armful of books. At the end of the week more books arrived that Rhodes had bought on my behalf in Sydney. Now it was not an army kit I laid out, but books.

All the reflexes of obedience and simulated respect I had learned in the army dropped away as if I had never saluted, reported at the double, or called a fellow creature 'Sir!'. Only once did they return, on my single visit to the External Affairs Department, on the first morning, when I arrived by taxi with my suitcases, wanting to know where I should go next. The head of the department, Colonel Hodgson, walked down the corridor and I felt myself stiffen as if I should spring to attention, but I forced my body back into a slouch. I still took showers rather than baths and my skin was still brown, so that it was only in the morning when I was soaping a brown body under the shower that I could feel like the 'self' I had been in the army.

Most nights were spent in our rooms, two cadets to a room, in our three grandly named hostels sitting at our small desks after dinner, to study. Rhodes had given me a radiator and my mother had given me a spirit stove. After a night spent contemplating the market demand curve or the Battle of Marathon or Hegel's theory of the state I might make some cocoa on the spirit stove and eat some of the cake my mother had sent, although on some nights we would go out into the cold to the room of some of the Barton House cadets, where supper was likely to be more companionable, with a bigger crowd, some of them 'girls'.

My room mate, Bill Morrison, was also Anderson-trained but, in the academic sense, much more formidably than I. As we had our supper he would draw on his profuse resources and cautiously, learnedly and dryly assemble the arguments that seemed most to the point; my counter-manoeuvre was the pre-emptive strike, setting up an argument different from the one he had intended, or a 'simplification' so great it would throw him off balance. When he went to Sydney one weekend I found a letter from his girlfriend, left in a drawer in our shared dressing table. Its advice about how to handle me shocked me so much that I considered writing comments in the margins.

It had taken no time at all for us to accept the label of being diplomatic cadets, but this was not something anyone in Canberra had been before. What was it going to mean? Only one thing united us: we had all spent some time at a university. That was enough. This at once divided us from most of the government officials and, whether we liked it or not, brought us in with the scattering of those 'people with degrees' who now saw themselves as coming to power to modernise Australia. The diplomatic cadet scheme was part of that process. But we didn't feel part of it. When all the others were at their desks modernising Australia we might be sitting outside in the winter sun reading Thucydides.

I took on a Canberra plumage: my favourite clothes became a 'sports jacket' and grey flannel 'slacks'. At Sydney University I had avoided this assertion of conforming casualness because it seemed a declaration of superior social class by the hearties from expensive private schools; I had preferred the urbanity and what I saw as the touch of bohemianism of a light-grey double-breasted suit of the kind McAuley wore. But at Canberra, in the way I now lived, a double breasted suit would have seemed a declaration of hostilities. The best I could do was to affect striped silk shirts with which I would wear white Van Heusen collars. That added urbanity.

Done out in sports jacket and slacks, I felt so comfortably like everyone else that at times my clothes seemed to be giving me an affectionate cuddle. Gordon Jockel, whom I had last seen cleaning his Vickers machine gun at the camp in Ingleburn, had also been chosen as a cadet. In my sports jacket I now felt closer to that overwhelming projection of sincerity Jockel had shown in his own clothes when we were at Sydney University. Perhaps we could be more at ease with each other now. His long face with its sober brown eyes had already seemed 'mature' when he was at Sydney, but he agreed with me that after his time in the army he was even more 'mature', and he granted me a certain 'maturity' too. He still preferred the role of a serious man, and still wrote long disquisitions in the margins of books with the precision of a medieval illuminator, but he would now relax, over a beer or an anecdote, if with the innocence of one who wasn't sure how to do it. He lived at Beauchamp House, away from most of us, on the other side of the river valley, and for a while I tried to move over there to be with him. At first he seemed to agree; then perhaps memories of recklessness disturbed him. Nothing more was said. As well as the long silences into which he would retreat when he was in company, he could still retreat physically, to the other side of the valley.

To me he seemed nevertheless 'one of us' (by which I meant some part
of what I wanted to be), as did Morrison. So did Brian Beddie, another
'Andersonian', who knew as much as Morrison and was as careful in putting
it all together, but who seemed to do it more warmly. He would play with his
forelock and suck his pipe, then out would come a killer argument, hot and
strong, made all the stronger by thunderclaps of laughter. Two other cadets
from Sydney could also appear part of the 'us' I had invented. Brian Hill,
older than the rest, who had two extraordinary attributes – of being already
married and of being able to speak foreign languages – was able to maintain
a good-humoured detachment I envied, as I envied the fastidious sense of
disengagement of John Rowland, who had the extra recommendation of
writing it, subtly, into verse. To these I added David Anderson from Adelaide.
the youngest cadet and the shyest, usually speaking with a wry smile: I didn't
know much about him, but that made him potentially one of the 'us' that
existed, probably, only in my mind.

AS WELL AS LEARNING HOW TO GET ON WITH EACH OTHER, WE
had to learn how to get on with the hostels in which we were living. My hostel,
Brassey House, had turned its back on the road. Its unused front entrance
stared out across an empty paddock. We entered it from its back porch, and
those of us who used the word 'plan' with a slight raising of the eyebrows
liked to joke that Brassey House faced the wrong way through a small error
in planning: it was built back to front. Inside, there were cement floors, dark
corridors, sombre furnishings. A fading aspidistra stood in the main hallway.
In the downstairs lounge the cold leather chairs were used only sporadically;
the chintzy upstairs lounge was cosier, but it was so tyrannised by the oldest
and most tedious residents that scarcely anyone else went there. After dinner
most of the 'older people' dominated Brassey House: the substratum of those
who were young used the ping-pong room as a meeting place. At lunchtime
on Saturday the men took off their ties and wore open-necked shirts to show
that the weekend had begun. Some played sport; most watched the Saturday
afternoon matches; almost all read the sporting sections of the Sunday papers.
On Sundays they cleaned their bicycles.

In Brassey House, the only effective area for sociability was the large dining room. Since all the boarders came back to Brassey House from their offices for lunch, and scarcely anyone went out to dinner, it was our assembly point, three times a day. Here for three-course breakfasts and four-course lunches and dinners, we were being taught what was expected of us in Canberra. Usually a meal would begin by establishing what kind of a 'day' it was. 'It's a nice day, isn't it?' Or: 'My word, it's a windy day today, isn't it?' The oldest official, who served on a standing committee which advised a federal council, liked to discuss sport, a subject on which ordinary citizens might be encouraged to have their opinions – unlike public administration, a boring and technical matter conducted only in office hours. Another, a young graduate working with an advisory panel to one of the more recent boards, was absorbed in statistical analysis. He told me in the ping-pong room that, as a committed socialist, he believed that total planning by a central authority was the only rational and humane way to conduct affairs. He then asked me to keep his socialism to myself. The other young graduate, a research officer in the Post War Reconstruction Department, said that when he was a student he had hung his bedroom with charts illustrating Keynes's *General Theory of Employment, Interest and Money*: if he couldn't sleep he would turn on the lights and examine the charts. He saw Keynesianism and the use of national income statistics as the two main hopes of humankind. This information came from a private conversation, again in the ping-pong room: at Brassey House one did not discuss oneself over a meal. The other person at our table was a woman public servant, who by 'making conversation', controlled us with a cool, amiable skill; she was confident that, if only we had faith, since we were in Canberra we would soon know what everything was about.

In this company I would speak softly, circumspectly and, where necessary, ambiguously, so that I would not seem too outlandish, but after several weeks, at one lunch I spoke like myself. In that morning's *Daily Telegraph* there had been a photograph of Eddie Ward, the Minister for External Territories (whose ear, it was rumoured, Alf Conlon now had) in which he was shown being carried across some water by two New Guineans. Since Ward was a populist of great flair, I made a wisecrack about his being carried on the backs of the people. The woman official turned on me as if I had used the wrong fork (which was also likely) and, bitter-sweet, said, 'You must read the newspapers terribly thoroughly.' She explained that through her work in 'the department' she no longer needed to read newspapers: she knew what was really going on. 'After people have been here for a while they give up newspapers. If you knew Eddie Ward, you'd find that he is a terribly nice chap.' In their own ways the others agreed about how necessary it was not to read newspapers. The Keynesian, however, recognised there must be some provision for the voice of the people; perhaps there would have to be people's consultative committees in the community centres that were to be established after the war? The standing committee official said, 'If the newspaper editors had a go at running the country you'd soon see what a mess we'd be in.'

One of the most satisfying holidays from this existence in which, each day, we had to eat our way through eleven courses of food that, at its best, rose to the indifferent, and with conversation that seemed to become ever more constipated, was to get up late, an indulgence unavailable to people working in 'the departments', miss breakfast, go down to 'the Greek's' for steak-and-eggs and argue venomously about Mr Justice Holme's conception of the role of the Supreme Court or Lenin's theory of imperialism, using insulting language that would have had us expelled from Brassey House, banging fists on the table, shaking the pepper and salt and the Worcestershire sauce. But then at lunch we were back to the tablecloth with yesterday's stains, the table napkins in their identifiable rings, the seven pieces of cutlery laid out in the predictable way, the passing of the same bowl of sugar.

2

Among the congratulatory letters was one from McAuley, with a play on the first name of the external affairs minister who, although universally known as 'Bert' Evatt, was 'Herbert' on his birth certificate, and with several kicks in the tail for me. His letter began:

> Farewell the plumed troop and the big wars ...
> Pride, pomp and circumstance of glorious war!
> So now you are – what? An understrapper to a white washer; knee-high
> to a paper-hanger; a sucker or rootling to that Herb, that Herb of which
> Virgil:

officiunt laetus frugibus HERBAS

But what of that? I am beyond measure rejoiced. What, Donald in frock-coat, sub-assistant-under-secretary to the plenipotentiary to Baluchistan, Peru, or even Cockaigne? And Jockel too? Fine. We shall yet live to see great wonders, old men shall be troubled and the young shall dance like mountain goats.

This seemed McAuley at his best – witty, crammed with learned allusions, brightly hard. It did not occur to me to question that, while to McAuley there was nothing amusing about his taking up a career with Conlon, there was for him everything amusing about my taking up a career in the External Affairs Department. It seemed self-evident that anything McAuley did would be serious and that anything I did would be touched by farce. But some parts of the letter did trouble me, if remotely: after all, I would, some time, be a third secretary. What would that mean? I didn't think about it for long. Two years was too far away. In any case, we were clearly superior to an earlier generation.

As to being knee-high to a paper-hanger, we read about Evatt in the newspapers, but had not seen him, nor did we go to 'the Department'. The possibility of there being an 'Australian foreign policy' was sometimes mentioned in the newspapers. But this was a subject we had not yet reached in our course. For me the nights on which I adjudicated two debates, one in the Air Force officers' mess and one (between two Returned Soldiers teams) at the Canberra Bowling Club, were the most diplomatic episodes of that cold winter.

SOME OF US SOMETIMES 'ENJOYED A SESSION' AT ONE OF THE hotel bars and occasionally had an expensive dinner at the Hotel Canberra (I had a hundred pounds of deferred army pay to get through), after which we might walk back in the dark, across the frosted paddocks, singing, and feeling different from the rest of Canberra. We loathed Canberra, and much of our conversation was about its provincial inferiorities. We saw it physically as a windy waste, and socially as detached in a dream from the rest of Australia:

Hope had written to me that Canberra hovered over the continent like the island of Laputa in Gulliver's third voyage.

Its common social life consisted of three small shopping centres, isolated from each other by paddocks. There was no proper restaurant in Canberra. There were the fixed price meals in the dining rooms of the five hotels, but of these only the Hotel Canberra looked for outside custom. There was one picture show, to which some of the Brassey House people went once a week. There was a regular small town 'hop' at the grandly styled Albert Hall, and an occasional short season of amateur theatricals. With a population not much greater than 10,000, Canberra offered nothing more than the stunted amenities of an Australian suburb or country town.

As a national capital, it offered a temporary parliament house, with two government office blocks on each side of it and, in front of these, lavish gardens with vistas of Versailles proportions; but most of the administration was still carried on in federal government offices in Melbourne and Sydney. On the other side of the wide river flats that divided the town, the Australian War Memorial had been erected so that Australians could believe something about themselves, and an arcaded 'Civic Centre' of two blocks had been built. Separated by paddocks on which sheep sometimes grazed, there was a scattering of garden suburbs; in the mountains large plantations of Californian pine took away some of the Australianness that seemed so inappropriate in a national capital, and there were grandiose plans, expressed in terms of circles and triangles and splendid straight lines, but nothing was likely to happen about these, just as nothing was likely to happen about the plan for flooding the river valley and transforming it, pretentiously, into an artificial lake. After the parliament house had been opened in 1927 it was an obvious wisdom that Canberra was a white elephant. There were flickerings of an attempt at cultural life – hostesses would expect the cadets to go to the play-readings and amateur concerts that were held occasionally – and, overall, among some of those who had come to Canberra since the war began, there was a brooding expectation that, some day, Canberra would 'have' a cultural life; but this did not seem much more likely than its having an artificial lake.

As one of the winter's curiosities, batches of diplomatic cadets were invited to small dinners in small brick houses where we would hear Canberra small talk and be expected to behave as if we were mutually interchangeable. I learned to stand up when others came into the room, to pass things without being asked and to speak quietly. I tried to make conversation with those sitting next to me, raising a subject tentatively to see how it would go and withdrawing it if it went badly. I learned that not everyone liked ironic anecdotes. In all of this there were some of the pleasures of stealth – I could feel that I had stolen so softly into the company of these people that they did not see me – but there were breakouts. Brian Beddie and I stayed on too long at the pub for one dinner so that we missed a bus and arrived late in an unfamiliar garden suburb. We got lost and when we finally reached the house it was from a back lane: we climbed over the back fence and fell into some mud, arriving at the kitchen door, drunken and dirty, yelling and laughing, and then shouted our way through dinner, until we began to feel the silence around us.

Alec Hope had given me introductions to the households of two Canberra scientists. Here there was the same crackle of log fires and the same bristling of hand-woven rugs as in the other houses, but instead of Van Gogh prints there were ironically *risqué* drawings by a Hungarian architect, George Molnar, who had worked in Canberra. One of them showed a thin man, nervously naked, kneeling behind a fat naked woman on all fours who was looking back at him with bovine patience. In his hand he held a book labelled 'Van der Velde', a name I had vaguely heard of, as author of a textbook on sexual positions (which I had also only vaguely heard of). Instead of gossip about 'the departments' there could be amusing conversation about life in general. Both men had diffident manners, one of them withdrawn into some very deep reservations about the worth of existence, the other merely modest because he had spent his life in a field of learning in which he was so specialist that he was unintelligible; but they would have other scientists along who spoke two languages I had never heard, those of radiophysics and nuclear physics, and, besides that, were ready to declare themselves on all the world's problems. Nevertheless, in the drawing room seatings after dinner I would try to sit next to one of two women. One could dominate conversation by the determined gentleness of her wit and the other by outrageous self-assertion, speaking with the frankness of a gunner. Both of these middle-aged women would laugh at the ironic anecdotes I told from my wisdom of twenty-two years, but when one of them asked me, out of the blue, 'What are you like in the hay?', I felt that this was testing the politeness due to middle age.

To the scientists, the fact that Canberra was a political town was what was wrong with it and the politicians were fools who didn't know what they were doing. To those we would meet at the other dinners, the fact that Canberra was a political town was their reason for being there: much of their dinnertime gossip was about the latest delays and compromises in drafting a White Paper on full employment that was seen as one of the world's more worthwhile political and moral activities. At these dinners we were among government advisers who knew some of the ministers, and might be very close to one or two of them: they saw ministers not as 'politicians' but as possible agents of rationality and modernity. But most of the people at Brassey House would never see ministers (who spent most of their time in the state capitals). To them it was 'the departments' that provided the solid matter of their universe and what gave ministers their gravity was that they sat at desks in offices and were connected with serious 'departmental business'. To these people, all public presentations of the ministers, whether in the press or in ordinary conversation, were likely to be ill-informed because they did not capture what really mattered – the conduct of affairs in 'the departments' and the ability of the ministers to sign their names on departmental documents.

I made two visits to parliament and judged politicians on grounds that were mainly aesthetic and intellectual. I found some interest in seeing the ministers sitting together at question time, cartoon characters turned into living caricatures: a few seemed more clever than I had expected; several appeared statesmanlike in repose; most seemed merely grotesque. There was some interest also in seeing the Opposition, some of them cartoon characters I had hated since schooldays – the fallen mighty, using their *ancien régime* voices as if they were still the masters. At my first visit, Curtin, the Prime Minister, made a set speech as part of some theatrical episode I could not understand. As a debater, I felt the speech almost came off: for most of it indignation was projected righteously; but towards the end the elocutionary gestures turned into hollow mime and the action of throwing a pencil on the table seemed a gesture of pique. On my second visit, Menzies, the Opposition leader, also put on a set turn. For reasons I couldn't understand he was praising the soundness of the common people of France: it sounded so like a Menzies imitation that I turned it into one. It was first put on for the 'girls' of Brassey House, but it then became a party piece for many years afterwards.

At least Curtin and Menzies had both put on a 'turn' that could be evaluated. Most of the other performances seemed so poor in oratory and even more in intellectual or practical content and there was so much yelping and barking, simulated anger and genuine sniggering that, to describe this in letters, I used Marx's phrase of 'parliamentary cretinism'. When I went to Sydney for a weekend on the same train as the parliamentarians, they would wait on the platform laughing among themselves, reminding me of the commercial travellers we used to see on the Muswellbrook railway station who next year might change firms and come back to Muswellbrook selling each other's brands. I would feel so lonely in what I saw as a world full of aged go-getters that I would try not to sit near any of them, but one Friday afternoon I found myself in a compartment with some Country Party politicians. I was reading Roberto Michels's *Political Parties*, borrowed from the National Library. While these old men filled in the dreary hours travelling to Sydney with the same ritual inanities as if they had been gunners on a troop train, I took secret pleasure in reading, in their sight but without their knowing it, one of the classic soundings of the shallowness of parliamentary democracy. It was like reading a 'smutty novel' with brown paper over its cover.

EIGHT

Putting myself together

1

Laurie Fitzhardinge, the director of the School of Diplomatic Studies, was a scholar of gentle temperament, for whose eccentricities – his unworldliness in dress and manner, his beard, and above all his unquenchable desire to talk – we developed a protective tolerance: in his lectures 'Fitz' might go on for twice the allotted hour, or even longer, and then follow us out to the bus-stop or the bar, to say some more, with a generous lack of conversational consequence that reminded me of my mother. The eccentricity of Fitzhardinge's interpretation of the subject 'The History and Political Thought of the Western World from the Greeks to the French Revolution' also delighted me: I did four tutorial papers in this subject and worked harder on them than any of the papers in the more 'solid' subjects. We wanted the whole course, with its three strands of history, politics and economics, to be academically sound. There was to be no meretricious 'usefulness' about it.

At first, the academic integrity of the course seemed threatened by one of Fitzhardinge's eccentricities. Although Fitzhardinge was a perfectly sound scholar as a classicist, he was also an Australian historian and one of our subjects was Australian history. In a country where none of the universities offered subjects in the study of Australian history, being concerned with Australia seemed both nationalistic and provincial. Yet when Fitzhardinge, as well as his respectable ramble into some corners of classical and medieval European civilisation, taught us Australian history, I allowed myself to feel at home in this forbidden city, if with some guilt (wasn't I abandoning European cultural tradition for mere provincialism?). In the National Library, after some searching, I found six intelligently written books on Australia.

After courses in statistics and in the assessing of national income, even some of the most obscure sections of *The Economist* now meant something for me and the instruction in statistics was as enjoyable as the logic I had learned at Sydney University; it provided some of the lights of reason and after I bought a book, *The Use and Abuse of Statistics*, I found new rational weapons with which to chop down other people's arguments. And when it came to the lectures on national income statistics, we seemed to reach right into the very brain of the modern state – the place where they stored the figures. Reality seemed to fizzle out, however, in the section of the economics course given over to formal economic analysis. Lecture by lecture we were introduced to new curves – market demand curves, total product curves, total cost curves, supply curves, indifference curves and to new graphs and new abstract concepts. We were being taught a new language, which one had to learn off, accepting its internal coherence without wondering what, if anything, it meant. I tried to do what I was told and master these graphs and concepts so that if in the class I was asked a question I could reply by drawing a graph on the blackboard, but I had the sensation that at times I was reduced to the same stupidity as had come over me when they had tried to teach me battery staff work before I had seen a gun.

Part of the course in 'Political Organisations' was a study of ruins – the French Third Republic, the Weimar Republic, Mussolini's corporate state, the Third Reich, Soviet political institutions; but Brogan's *The American Political System* was as liberating as *The Economist* in the arts of being shrewd and particular. I had never before imagined a whole 'political system' – all these movable bits, overall, coming into some kind of 'together', so that one country's political system could seem recognisably different from another's and, short of catastrophe, keep some of the same shape. More than that: in his description of the White House as a kind of monarch's court, Brogan touched on some of those mysteries of leadership and muddle that had moved me when, in army hospital, I had read *War and Peace*. But as well as *The American Political System*, the book that opened out the possibility of talking about politics both methodically and with imagination, there was another delight, in something I read outside the course (itself a delight). The same James Burnham who had written *The Managerial Revolution* had now come out with *The Machiavellians*, cool and hard-headed in tone, suggesting we could cut out of politics all of its nonsense and, like scientists observing nature, put things down as they are. His targets were, in particular, the illusions of 'representative democracy', and as well as the Roberto Michels whose *Political Parties* I had read on the train as stealthily as if it were a smutty novel, he introduced me to Vilfredo Pareto and Gaetano Mosca, realists both, who assumed that human institutions were necessarily oligarchic and all societies necessarily contained a web of elites. To be practical, you moved on from there. Reading these writers bred a strange ambition: I would sometimes put myself to sleep imagining that I would write books stripping political institutions down to demeaning detail, then describe how they really behaved. In this it seemed an essential pleasure to snatch at new particulars: the role of party bosses in the United States, border customs disputes between New South Wales and Victoria, 1864–77, the failure of Leon Blum – almost anything would do. As soon as you got down to detail, all was demeaning. But I wanted to remain 'literary'. Could one be 'literary' and also write 'political science'?

There was one disappointment: elsewhere in the course, in a subject called 'Introduction to the History of the Political Thought of the Western World', like tourists guided through an art museum, we contemplated, week by week, some Old Masters of political thought. This was one of the parts of the course from which I had most expected enlightenment; it was also the one for which I had spent the most money on books. Through reading political philosophers I hoped to hear the true heartbeats of political discussion. But as we whizzed through the texts – Plato's *Republic* this week, Aristotle's *Politics* next week – it turned out that many of the concepts ('rights', 'sovereignty', 'the general will', etc.) were 'logical confusions' towards which Quadrangle Andersonianism had taught me short, sharp, bitter answers. I didn't have to read the text themselves: I knew what was wrong with them anyway. If anyone mentioned 'rights', all I had to do was chant, 'As John Anderson says, rights are simply *demands that can be made good*' and then glare back convincingly. However I did read the kind of texts that Anderson had probably never heard of: a pamphlet of Gerrard Winstanley's, part of the great political debate under Oliver Cromwell that raised questions that were democratic and radical three centuries ahead of their time, done with simplicity and force; the *Federalist* essays, written in a New York newspaper when the new United States Constitution was being argued about; Pope Leo XIII's *Rerum Novarum*, the Catholic directive on social justice, and of influence, at the time, on the Labor Party in Australia. These were enjoyable, because their theory came incidentally to the great question: *What is to be done?*

Otherwise I was a devotee of the course. As Laurie Fitzhardinge said, it was meant to open a lot of doors, and I began to think that, after all, I really might know everything. I was nevertheless being as diligent as I had been as a new boy at Maitland High School – attending classes, meeting deadlines for essays and tutorial papers, even doing extra reading within the course and when, as I still preferred, I read outside it, the reading was at least parallel. No worries for Dad this time: here I was beginning a career.

WITH SPRING, WE HAD EXCHANGED ANECDOTES ABOUT THE enraged magpies which swooped down from their nests onto cyclists; if it rained we would gather mushrooms and cook them in our rooms. As summer approached we bought season tickets to the swimming baths. To aid him in the diplomatic life that was to come, Jockel took lessons in ballroom dancing, but I would not carry conformity so far. When, one by one, the other cadets bought bicycles and began cycling to the university college, I still went by bus. Bicycles seemed too great a concession to the bourgeois small-mindedness of Canberra.

I began writing sober letters trying to describe the ordinariness of life. In one of them I gave a list of what I did:

Writing essays
Playing ping-pong
Chasing girls
Taking notes
Travelling to Sydney
Talking drivel
Getting drunk
Passing the sugar.

To account for a boozy weekend I made notes on the ordinariness of its context.

> *Wednesday*: Hell of a day. Dry, harsh winds. Woke up late for breakfast. Went to the Greek's for steak and eggs. Missed a bus and waited in the wind for half an hour. Bumped head in bus. Lecture was drivel. *Thursday*: Woke late. To the Greek's for steak and eggs. Read Georges Sorel in the sun. (A myth, says Sorel, can be an inspiring picture of what the world might be like.) To the Hotel Wellington ... tried to talk about Sorel on myth: too much blather. Dinner. Long talk about drought, the Australian land problem, the Chinese land problem, the world land problem. Back in room: read Sorel. *Friday*: Woke in time for breakfast in Brassey House. Read Sorel in the sun. (The myth makers fashion the future, says Sorel.) Missed drivel lecture. Lecture on capital and investment. Lunch. Tutorial on Mazzini and Acton. Lecture on Japan. (Good.) To Hotel Canberra to get full to prepare ourselves for a party in Barton House. More talk about Sorel. (Violence is one extreme of the morality of no-compromise, eg, early Christian martyrs. *Note*: Do we need a morality of violence?) Dinner at Hotel Canberra. Beer, whisky, cherry brandy. Had long talk about life-in-general with Beddie. Double home with him on his bike, precariously and noisily. Quick change. Barton House party. Fun. Good time. *Saturday*: Hangover. Breakfast at the Greek's. Go to Barton House to find out what I did last night. Girls giggle. Return to room. Rest. Feel better after lunch. Go to cricket match. Talk. Afternoon tea. Go to Wellington Hotel. Get drunk. Go to Canberra Hotel. Get drunker. Get nasty. Say fuck this fuck that. Go to Barton House, where there's a dance. Say fuck dancing. Girls say I'm a devil. *Sunday*: Hangover. No Sunday papers. Go to Barton House to find out what I did last night. Afternoon and evening: unsuccessful struggle with economics. Then more Sorel.

2

I was ceasing to think of my parents as 'Mum' and 'Dad', forms of address that seemed leftovers from childhood. By using these words I was rejecting the wider existence given to my mother and father by those who called them

'Dave' and 'Florrie' and the even wider if more superficial meanings of 'Mr Horne' and 'Mrs Horne', or the legal meanings, suitable for official documents and headstones on graves, of 'David Horne' and 'Florence Lila Horne' and that most remote of meanings, seen on envelopes – 'Mrs David Horne'. I had already cleared away the word 'Nanna' from my view of my grandmother: I could see her not as my mother's mother but as a sceptical, earthy woman with whom I could enjoy talking. However, although I no longer thought of her as 'Nanna' I kept on calling her by that name; but I no longer wanted to call my mother 'Mum' or my father 'Dad'. There were no negotiations between us as to some other name. I began speaking to my parents without calling them anything. They had moved in with my grandmother at Denbigh, and as our furniture mingled with my grandmother's, my father seemed to turn into a grandfather. He used the same workshop and sheds that Pa had built, fed the poultry at the same times and looked after the same garden; and to Nanna he was now more than a son-in-law: he was a friend. Calling each other 'Nanna' and 'Dave', sitting over their cups of tea at the kitchen table, a man in his fifties and a woman in her seventies drew on common sympathies that gave him his last (and at this stage perhaps his only) friendship.

When I went to Sydney (for two vacation fortnights and as many weekends as I could manage) I stayed at Denbigh where it seemed that, even though I could speak to my father only in the company of others, and even though I now had no names for my parents, in my relations with them I was becoming more 'mature'. This came partly because in conversation I talked a great deal about affairs of the day. While I recognised that home was no place in which to sound off about the myths of representative democracy or the Marxist theory of the state, during the games of bridge and the late suppers of tea and tomato sandwiches I would attempt cautious popularisations of what was happening in world affairs. In Australian politics I would try to sound as if I were a careful, objective expositor. When, in August, the government lost a referendum calling for more powers for the national government, I gave my parents a state by state account, from an essay I had written, of why the referendum had been lost. We were developing a comfortable family relationship by my acting as if I were a commentator on the wireless.

Like a person who seeks unusual angles in mirrors, hoping for some new idea of what he might look like, I would look for signs such as this that I had become something different and, I hoped, better. When I went into the city, feeling different was helped by the fact that I had new friends or that old friends were rearranged in different proportions. Through Murray Sayle I was meeting students, so that I could gossip with them as if I were nineteen instead of almost twenty-three. Miller, a minor character in the old days, was now my oldest surviving Sydney friend. On one weekend visit I even helped him dig his vegetable garden, an act that without doubt was mature. Rhodes was still new, but already different because I was no longer a lonely gunner waiting for letters and books, and although he sent me copies of *The Economist* and hunted for packets of cigarettes to help me through the 'tobacco famine', most of his long letters were not answered; but I would meet him at times, when I went to Sydney (amusingly, at Proud's Corner, an assignation spot), and we would go to the cinema, then, over dinner, would again try, interrupting each other, to find lost pasts. At Ushers they were mainly imposters ('ghosts, playboys, business men, bludgers in uniform' in Miller's words), turning into ritual our spontaneity of several years before. Alan Crawford would still sometimes appear, but this was a married Crawford, and a Crawford who believed in a government. Plimsoll stopped writing. McCallum was now having his turn in the army. Conlon was not visible. I didn't see Stewart, and was not to see him again. Nor Somerville, who was soon to be killed.

A few old houses had been taken over by groups of intellectuals; one of the Sayle circle lived in a boatshed; in Kings Cross I went to parties in the flats of people whose names I didn't know. Out of our circle – or at least, the circle in which, as 'young Donald' I had once lived on sufferance – a group had formed around Wilfred Cordukes, an affable businessman friend of Crawford, wise to the world. He was an encouraging symbol of how one could live in a suburb but still pursue the life of the intellect and amuse oneself, and it was at one of Wilfred's parties that I saw McAuley again. It was a 'bucks party' of men older than I, all making their way in the world. For most of the night we grouped around the piano and bellowed out songs. McAuley was in a remote, commonsensical mood. He scarcely spoke to me. I hoped for some word from him that I had changed, but all that he said was that, in appearance, I seemed 'more sleek'. This seemed so strange that when I woke up the next morning I looked the word up in a dictionary to see if it had some meaning I did not know. Was this effect produced by my light-grey sports jacket?

The Hopes' house in Manly had become another place where I might go when I was in Sydney. Hope had written only a few letters to me while I was in the army but, compared with McAuley's cold anger, their tone was companionably sympathetic and it seemed another sign of maturity that now I might visit him, not as one in a crowd, but in one of my preferred versions of myself. I sought, several times, to be invited there on a Sunday afternoon before I caught the night train back to Canberra. Usually Hope would be working and I would talk for a while to Penelope, his wife, whose delicate air of detachment entranced me. So that Penelope could get on with her own work, I might then sit on a couch and read to Emily, their five-year-old daughter, or make up a story for her while she remained affectionately quiet. When Hope came in, he would sit at the other end of the room, surrounded by late afternoon sunshine, with his books around him, and the rest of the time would pass as we talked about life as if it were a book, and about books as if they were life; a kind of conversation I usually had only with myself.

AFTER ONE OF THESE AFTERNOONS HOPE WROTE TO ME IN Canberra that I should write a novel. In what had proved to be his last letter to me, Plimsoll, as well as warning that one of the main things a diplomat should know was how to hold his liquor, had also said I should write a book. As it happened, I had now decided what my first novel would be about. It had arisen from an incident with Rhodes. When I had left Sydney, apparently on my way back to Darwin, Rhodes had written me a letter of such admiration that it was like a love letter:

> I found you a great deal more attractive in appearance and with greater skill and *savoir faire* than I had bargained for. Your skin was extremely fresh and clear and gave one a very agreeable impression of health. I have calculated that we met ten times and that altogether I was in your company for 24 hours. Of these I recall in particular three rather happy moments. The first was when you were walking down Cronulla beach. The wind was blowing your hair sideways. Your eyes were bright and sparkling, you were laughing, and your cheeks glowed. The second was when we sat on a stone on our walk in the bush in Kuringai Chase.

It was pleasant, watching the sun on your arms. Then there was the moment you came up to see me with Murray Sayle, so obviously and intensely interested in the paper rumpus, *Honi Soit*, and so forth ... Sometimes I thought of you as a boy, rather young and charming, whom I must help. At other times you appeared a good deal more reverend than myself.

The letter had moved from one army post office to the other and it was not until several weeks after I had been discharged from the army that I read it, and by then I had seen Rhodes several times. Not a word from him of this kind.

I looked over the letters he had written when I was in the army. There was a strange beginning to one of them:

Dear Donald, I'm not drunk, except with ink – but you are a nice chap. I – but no! ... Pay no attention to an old bachelor with his pants down ...

But then in another he said that until he arrived in Sydney he had never been conscious of having known any of 'the homosexual breed', except once, on a P&O boat from Marseilles to Bombay; the anecdote then turned into farce. But what was one to make of this statement, in another letter: 'The idea of tumbling with a woman is horrible – especially with anyone you respected. I dislike being seen unshaven, or in any degree of disorder. If I were married I would insist on separate bedrooms and even separate bathrooms.' But when he said, 'My attitude towards the sexual act is one of intense disgust', perhaps this meant merely that Rhodes was asexual?

These puzzles had no effect on our friendship, which remained cordially conversational. But they did affect my view of the Baron de Charlus in *Remembrance of Things Past*: I woke up one morning and saw M. de Charlus with the face of Professor Frank Rhodes, and therefore of the comical Robertson Hare, so that even the most aristocratic reception scenes in Proust's novel became, for a season, English middle-class farce. Since *Remembrance of Things Past* was a study in deception, I planned a similar novel, set in Sydney. The fantasy that I could write such a novel continued for some weeks: I knew nothing at all about Sydney 'society'. I had never been inside a rich person's house, nor even been invited to a cocktail party. Instead, in two short prose pieces, I went back to writing about army life. Both pieces were accepted by *Arna*. Both were banned by the printer, on the grounds that young girls should be protected from reference to the existence of testicles and masturbation and the use of '– him', '– house', '– off', and 'get –'. The printer said he didn't mind a dirty joke, but this was going too far.

EXPECTATIONS CONTINUED THAT I WOULD SOON BE WRITING a novel. I believed them myself. It was good to be someone of whom people said he would write a novel. But then I was also playing ping-pong, writing history essays, chasing girls, taking notes, travelling to Sydney, talking drivel, getting drunk and passing the sugar. Intending to write a book was almost as regular as these other activities, but even if I could discipline myself to write … what did I want to say? My own experience of existence seemed so tinpot. It could be given meaning by reading other people's books, but was too weak to give meaning to a book of my own. I seemed to be hurrying too much from this to that to understand (or to believe it long enough) that I had the beginnings of a style, and that this style might be what I had to 'say'.

In any case anger was likely to butt into even the most laconically phrased sentence and buckle it up. This was a way of writing that generated itself from apparently inexhaustible reserves of bad temper. It was no trouble to review Max Harris's novel *The Vegetative Eye* in *Honi Soit* and describe it as 'probably one of the worst bits of serious prose ever published', nor to review a poetry magazine in *Honi Soit* under the heading AUSTRALIAN WRITERS SPEAK FROM THE DUNGHILL and send its contributors packing: 'narrow, boasting provincials, an unlovely race of stupid, drum-beating braggarts'. When Harris gave me two pages in *Angry Penguins* I let loose at boasts that Australia was going through a cultural renaissance: 'The watch-our-national-culture-grow attitude is much the same as the soap advertisements, the vitality pills and the toothpaste ads of commercialism', and so forth.

In the 'Notes on Contributors' column in *Angry Penguins* Harris had described me as a 'brilliant literary iconoclast with a legendary student reputation'. Good. Just like the old days. But how long could I go on having a legendary student reputation?

3

Drinking in the Hotel Canberra bar one afternoon, a sense of familiarity came from the soldier's khaki I could see out of the corner of my eye. It was Alf Conlon, pipe in one hand, a 'noggin' of beer (as he would call it) in the other, his generously curved face shining jovially with wisdom. On his shoulders were the insignia of a full colonel, but his uniform was so unimportant a part of him that, after I had talked with him for a few minutes, it dissolved into the more general class of nondescript Conlon clothing. It might have been 1940 again, in the bar at Ushers, with Alf telling me about the need for an Australian sociology rather than, as he was now, the need for an Australian foreign policy. Over dinner there was still the same slow, thoughtful speech diverted now and again by a blunt word, and the same obsession with summoning up great visions that could then be made to seem ordinary because they were presented with such good humour – or perhaps (although this was never stated) because they were no more absurd than anything else. After dinner, in the foyer where small wooden tables were set out with coffee and liqueurs, those movements of his pipe began that, in their tracings in the air, could serve the imagination but that, in their rubbings against his cheek or his neck or his clothes, could be reminders of an earthy common sense. Some of what was said seemed so fanciful, and I was getting so drunk, that for a while I left off listening. Alf went on talking to a journalist who was also at the table, while I talked instead with Alf's offsider, John Kerr, a young barrister I had met once or twice at Ushers; then he had been one of those uninteresting people who were starting a career, but now he was a lieutenant colonel who had been to London with a general. Tall, dark, slim, almost handsome, he bent his head towards me, and made points with his fingers in the air above my wrist, touching it now and again for some particular emphasis. As with Conlon, it was all policy and power he was talking, but without Conlon's sense of absurdity, and also without Conlon's mildness and friendliness. He was speaking to me with great eloquence, but contemptuously, as if he were merely using me for practice.

The journalist was Massey Stanley, one of the greatest heroes in the golden legends of Canberra journalism of several years before, renowned for 'scoops' and the kind of campaigns that had entranced me as a high-school boy when I read in the *Daily Telegraph* of the continuing follies of conservative government, and renowned also for escapades that had become fables. It was with Massey Stanley that I talked after the waiters told us the drink was off and they were closing the foyer; we moved into the billiards room where a tray with two dozen whiskies appeared, obviously ordered by Stanley, although he mimed surprise when it came. I had never before seen such a generous gesture. Two dozen whiskies! Very drunk, Conlon was somewhere in the shadows on the other side of the room with Kerr and a couple of others while, standing beside the tray, Stanley and I, making a mock toast with each fresh glass, drank nearly all of the twenty-four whiskies. Stanley was a man of terse speech with a reputation for straight dealing, and as the drinking went on I was scarcely capable of any speech; so we stood there, almost silent, now and again grunting some sceptical aside about these colonels who were still talking and, in Alf's case, staggering, in the shadows. In doing my own staggering back across the lawns and the open paddocks to Brassey House, I counted out loud to keep awake, but twice lay down on the grass and slept for a while.

When I woke up, just before lunch, on my bed at Brassey House, I was still in my clothes. As I thought about what had happened during the night it seemed even more unreal than the usual drunken anecdote: Kerr and Conlon, despite their talk about power and conniving, seemed, in a way, innocents or, in another way, outlandish adventurers – in either case too ornate to survive in the more ordinary world that would return after the war. They did not talk the language of 'planning', but this would be the language of the post-war world. In Canberra, talk of 'planning' was all around us and, since they were members of the Post-War Reconstruction Department, our economics and politics teachers included some of the most significant theoreticians of planning: the first draft of the White Paper on Full Employment they were preparing was only one of a host of drafts of other papers on 'the post-war'. Although, apart from our tormentor in economic analysis, these individual teachers seemed like other mortals, and although I had never, for that matter, seen the Department of Post-War Reconstruction, nor knew where its offices were in Canberra, I followed up Hope's comparison of Canberra with the hovering island of Laputa by comparing this department with the Grand Academy of Lagado in which there had been solemn pursuit of so many mad schemes. Sometimes it was sufficient to get a laugh by saying slowly, with some eyebrow emphasis,

'I have a plan.' When one friend in the Army Education Service wrote from New Guinea that he had conducted a survey of gramophone records and now knew where every gramophone record was in New Guinea, I turned this into a characteristic anecdote about 'planning'.

The Department of War Organisation of Industry, which Alan Crawford had entered in 1942, had produced what the newspapers and the conservative politicians put forward as the largest crop of follies in wartime planning: at Wilfred Cordukes's 'bucks' party, a jest by McAuley about one of these atrocity stories in this new war of faiths set off a crackle of conversation between him and Crawford that passed before I knew most of what had gone on. At its end, Crawford, still smiling, interjected, 'I wonder how you would behave in a fascist Australia', while McAuley, fiercely serious, was still answering an earlier question from Crawford by saying that he had a business in life, which was the cultivation of a certain sensibility. At his most solemn, he went on, 'I do not judge my activity by reference to the good causes which surround me; I judge the good causes by how they help or hinder my private, selfish and tenacious desires.' That was the end of their friendship.

A certain amount of anti-planning theory had also emerged – I had bought Hayek's *The Road to Serfdom* and marked all the good bits – but for me what most gave momentum to a faith – or rather an anti-faith – that was to impel me for years afterwards was a paper, 'The Servile State', by John Anderson, which had appeared in a philosophy journal the year before. Some of us discussed this as if it were the announcement in *Pravda* of a new party line. In the way in which one sometimes snatches a single image or phrase that one has, as it were, been waiting for, what I most remembered about this article, as if it were its central theme, was the sentence: '... the well intentioned reformer always produces results which he did not anticipate ...' I knew already that things usually go wrong but reading this in the *Australasian Journal of Psychology and Philosophy* and underlining the words and writing a comment in the margin produced a special crystallisation so strong that for many years I did not recognise that, while it is true that any action may bring unexpected results, it is equally true that so might any lack of action.

TO ME, ALL AUSTRALIA SEEMED A DESERT OF REACTION. Businessmen still ruled and now that the conservative parties had disintegrated as a result of what, as a schoolboy reader of the *Daily Telegraph*, I had seen as their imbecilities, the labour movement seemed the main source for reactionary government. As a party dominated by Catholics, the Labor Party was banning books, censoring the press and maintaining sexually repressive legislation, and as a party dominated by unionists it supported the White Australia policy and saw woman's place as in the home; to its left, the Communist Party was Stalinist. And now the 'planners' might produce a new ruling class.

I had been reading Georges Sorel partly because his *Reflections on Violence* was set for a tutorial discussion, but I knew that in 'political philosophy' one needn't read a text to have opinions on it; potted versions in other people's books were enough to get one through a tutorial. I had given Sorel particular attention because, although I had been quoting *Reflections on Violence* for four or five years since Sorel was one of Anderson's favoured writers, I had not previously read it. Now I was taking notes generously: in 'The Servile State' Anderson had used Sorel against the planners. In Sorel's world the good life was that of the 'producers' cooperative, creative, imbued with the spirit of self reliance – but among the 'consumers' the good was not seen as a way of life but as something to be obtained and enjoyed: all that 'consumers' wanted were shoddy things like welfare, prosperity or happiness; the life of mere 'consumers' was based on envy and promulgated by adventurers called 'intellectuals'. The main meaning of Anderson's thunder and lightning was that in the welfare state 'the desire for security and sufficiency is the very mark of the servile mentality'.

This now became a slogan I was ready to use in almost everything I wrote. The review of the poetry magazine included a warning against the repressive tendencies in society; the article in *Angry Penguins* warned that socialism 'from being a wholly libertarian movement had become a wholly authoritarian one'. A tutorial paper on pan-Germanism belaboured Fichte as 'an early welfare planner'; an essay on the revolutions of 1848 assaulted liberals as 'having largely abandoned support for ways of life in favour of meaningless, futile utopias'; notes for a tutorial on Marx castigated Marxists for 'dropping libertarianism, the insistence on social struggle and the assertion and extension of self-organisation'; an essay on economic rationality unmasked the 'sentimental philanthropic polite socialism of today' and warned the worker that 'although he had little free choice in a commercialist society, in a planned economy he would lose such powers of organisation and opposition as he had'. And not only was I ready to carry on the fight for freedom in articles in *Angry Penguins* and in essays, tutorial papers and discussion notes, I was also ready to fight against the servile mentality in the Brassey House dining room over our three large meals a day, and in the bedroom late suppers as well.

PART 3

LIVING WITH A WOMAN

1944–45

NINE

A world of our own

1

At the university I had seen infatuation as something that, like a traveller's luggage, should be openly declared before each new frontier. Each time I had fallen in love I would try to recruit enough courage to make a declaration: sometimes courage failed but if enough boldness were summoned, it would explode so unexpectedly that the frontier was at once closed. There remained intellectual companionship with women, and (what seemed a separate matter) sex with chance partners. With the army, there were no more declarations of love and no intellectual companionship and in the Northern Territory there were no women at all, except in dreams. I would sometimes lie in bed at Brassey House, contemplating failure. At my age! Twenty-two!

Barton House bubbled with 'girls' like a public fountain – for display, not for drinking – but apart from some furtive adventures, mainly fiascos, I began a friendship with a young woman, a professional trainee in one of the departments, which became so intimate that we met in secret, not because we had any sexual relations, but because we didn't. If the others had seen us so much together they might have thought it strange that we were friendly 'without doing something about it'. Sharing a sense of humour, we had become so companionable that it would have been an affront to show how much we enjoyed each other's company.

In Sydney, I met women students through Murray Sayle and one of them, a Stalinist, was so sympathetic that we talked to each other right through a drunken dinner. She was apparently 'well-read'. but knew nothing about painting, so we arranged to go to the Art Gallery together several days later.

When I found two other women students waiting with her I was entranced by the increase in audience and insisted on paying everyone's fares on the tram trip from the university into the city; after showing the paintings to these three 'girls', and giving a lecturette on nineteenth-century art, we went for afternoon tea to a wooden pavilion which had such a nineteenth century look about it that, with three young women grouped around a window, sunshine in their hair, and blue sky and green grass outside, I felt we were picnicking in fields on the outskirts of Paris in a French Impressionist painting. After the 'girls' had left I walked up to Ushers caressed by sensations of young skin, soft smiles and exquisite conversation and, when Hope astounded me by saying that my smile was uncharacteristically seraphic, I extemporised around the phrase *jeunes filles en fleur* and in response he rhapsodised learnedly about the social pleasures of female company. Later I learned that the young Stalinist woman was secretly 'living with' a Stalinist man; she had brought the other two along as chaperones.

We wrote to each other – she wanted me to double my reading to get even more out of the Diplomatic Studies course no matter what I did with it later – and it was through her that I arranged to go to a University Labour Club conference at the beach suburb of Newport at the beginning of the long summer vacation. I decided to go to the conference because I wanted to see her again, but I also wondered what the Labour Club would be like after three years of a Stalinist support of the war effort that had become so cosily Australian that it included a campaign for 'Sheepskins for Russia'.

Since it was Friday afternoon, I began my expedition by drinking at Ushers and then dining at the Florentino; now (was this maturity?) I could afford to order the zabaglione, for which there was an extra charge. However I had still not learned the arts of punctuality: I missed a tram, sat on my suitcase for twenty eight minutes waiting for another tram, then missed a bus connection, with another wait, got out at the wrong bus-stop, spent half an hour searching Newport for the Labour Club conference; and arrived at it, bitterly sober, to be issued with cocoa and an announcement that blankets were ready to be drawn. I found myself in a dormitory where, before lights-out, a discussion was going on about the theory of surplus value. In the booklet issued to us for our singsongs, I began to mark passages like this:

It's going to take everybody to win this war,
The butcher, the baker and the clerk in the store.

and this:

Soviet land, so dear to every tribe,
Peace and progress build their hope on thee.
There's no other land the whole world over
Where man works the earth so proud and free.

The conference, I decided, could be turned into a prose sketch, written laconically, like the pieces I had written about life in the army for *Arna*.

Next day the conference developed a quite different interest when, after fighting a confused campaign through several discussion groups and 'smoke-ohs', I saw at lunchtime a tall blonde woman, somewhat older than most of us, in her late twenties perhaps, whose sunglasses and lipstick brought me across the room to sit near her. When I found she was an amusing conversationalist, speaking some of the language Fraser and I had spoken in the Quad in those April days of 1939, this gave me a chance to shine. The others, even the medical student who had 'brought her' to this conference in which she was so brilliantly out of place, became silent and the three of us stayed on after lunch, missing the first discussion for the afternoon. Now we were being amusing about the conference itself. Since I had already in my mind been turning the conference into a prose sketch, I was ready with my anecdotes.

I learned that she was a poet whose work had already been published in several slim volumes by a small press in Sydney. At the pub later in the afternoon, she told me that when she had finished the book she was working on, she would start writing a novel. Showing that she did not take herself all that seriously, she called it a 'nov-hole'. I said I would soon be starting a nov-hole too. I went to sleep in the dormitory thinking of red lips parting into a quick smile ... The movements of smooth, sun-browned arms and legs ... A quick, accidental, touch from cool fingers ... Blonde hair falling over high cheek bones and then tossed back with a shake of the head. An 'English' voice using smart slang: *He was dumber than dumb ... This comic conference ... I was extremely triste ...* In particular, a repetitive and promiscuous throwing around of the word 'sweetie', scattered all over the conference, but sometimes falling, like a flower, on me.

We were given Sunday morning off, for swimming, and when I saw her settle down with the medical student on some rocks at one end of the swimming pool and then spread around them an assortment of beach towels, dark glasses, bottles of sun lotion, pads of writing paper, books and packets of cigarettes like people who knew where they were going to spend the day, I floated on the water as if I hadn't seen them, then swam over, as if by chance, to where they were, talked to them from the water and then, casually, pulled myself out of the pool and sat down beside them, in a body already again brown from sunbathing at the Canberra swimming pool. And (Oh, my God!) was she looking at it with interest?

At home again, after the conference, I considered it probable that in the smart life in which she lived she didn't go anywhere I was likely to be, and ringing her up and asking her to go out with me was beyond my range of social imagination. Several days later a group of us were singing around the piano of a journalist friend when he mentioned she lived in the next-door flat. I knocked on its door and found her, face washed clean of make-up, and dressed in red cotton pyjamas. After a charade of amusing tipsiness from me, she put on a housecoat and joined us around the piano. Now that she seemed one of us, I asked her to dinner on Boxing Day at the Hopes' house – they had told me I could 'bring someone'. In return, she invited me to a party at her sister's flat on Christmas Eve. At the party there were painters, ballet dancers, writers, actors, journalists (I felt like a character in *Remembrance of Things Past* who had at last gained entrance to a salon). Since the last train had gone, I slept, along with a couple of other late-stayers, on the floor, waking up on a shimmeringly sunny Christmas morning with a bugler playing a Christmas carol on the pavement outside and ahead of me a triumphant train journey through the radiant suburbs back to my family, where Mum would be peeling the vegetables for Christmas dinner.

On Boxing Day I had lunch at home. It was my birthday (*Twenty-three! So little achieved!*) but we had an early lunch because my conference-found friend had suggested an afternoon at Lady Martin's beach. It was unknown to almost everyone in Sydney – nothing more than a strip of sand beside the harbour, barely wide enough for an outstretched body and reached by an obscure lane between houses and flats. The few people there apparently knew each other: I had gained entrance to another Sydney *salon*. By the time we were on our way to dinner, by comic invention we had already created some of the elements of a world of our own, with its own characters and language, and on the taxi ride back to Sydney (with the meter ticking its way into the savings bank account where I kept what was left of my army deferred pay) this private world was extended. It seemed natural that after I had 'come in for a drink' I should stay the night.

2

For the next few weeks, sometimes for days at a time, I was living in an enchanted land in which only we were real and the rest of existence something we had invented for our own amusement. At our small beach, in a world of skin-browning and cooling-off in the green water, in what was now our own private language, we could divert ourselves by making wry comments on the other sunbathers, or I might lie with my eyes closed and think of the long, slim, brown body lying on a beach towel beside me. Sometimes our world moved to the Australia Hotel where, before the war, people from 'the old families' of Muswellbrook would stay during the fashionable horse race meetings; if we were in one mood we would have lunch in the Australia's Wintergarten, thought of as 'the passion pit' since 'the American invasion', and enjoy the public clatter and buzz; in another mood we would say 'Let's get drunk' and go upstairs to the private lounge meant only for people staying at the hotel, unless you knew the waiters – and order round after round of drinks, loudly declaring ourselves on life, and affectionately bringing the waiters into the kinds of conversations they would allow to big spenders who left large tips. In a rare mood we would have dinner in the Australia Hotel's dining room (which I had seen as one of the great centres of powerful people in Sydney). To match its white, starched linen and sterling silver, its glass chandeliers and string quartet, we would speak more quietly. Now and again some society woman or influential man would be indicated to me. If any of the men stopped at our table on the way out to chat to my companion, they were likely to call her 'dear' or 'pet' or 'sweetie', and leave me, standing, unspoken to, but when they had gone we might make fun of them, and give them new names, to put them in their place as part of our private invention. The restaurant at which we ate most often was 'a little place' in a lane in Kings Cross run by some German refugees. It was always full and bustling and at the large, shared tables the side dishes were spread so promiscuously one might find oneself eating someone else's cucumber salad or red cabbage, and the conversation was so densely fused into one loud blur that to speak to each other we would lean forward almost cheek to cheek. New kinds of words floated all around me: *browned off ... oh, pooh to him ... all of a twit ... wouldn't it be beaut, eh? ... I must eat or I shall die .... my hot little hand ... a powerful piece of rich, beautiful prose.* There was this constant chatter of lighthearted self-deprecation, but what were most strange to me were the endearments: *puss ... pusskin ... kitten ... pet ... honey-cake ... honey-child ... angel-cake ... sweetie.* The Americanism of some of them added a touch of international glamour.

The centre of our world was the large, elegant high-ceilinged main room of her flat with a small couch, seating two, in a corner alcove where the casement windows overlooked some large trees. It was here I was nursed when I fell sick with a gum infection (treated by her dentist, a Polish Jewish refugee). I would look through the large window at the green leaves of the exotic European trees and see myself as a young man, dying, but in love, in a romantic European novel. We sat on the couch to eat our meals – sometimes cold stuff from the delicatessen, sometimes home-cooked. We would spend an afternoon sitting side by side on the couch. When she was working on her book she had the couch to herself, with her typewriter on the coffee table and papers all around her and I lay on the day bed and read *Capitalism, Socialism and Democracy* or *The Economics of Imperfect Competition* or one of the other books on politics or economics I had to 'get through' during the vacation.

Coolness and cleanliness seemed essential to her. After a shower she would come out of the bathroom mentally clearer. Doing the washing could seem a spiritual exercise. One night when her book was not going well she scrubbed herself under the shower and then went and scrubbed the kitchen. Housework – which to me had seemed as inevitably timetabled as school lessons, with certain functions always performed on certain days – became a kind of carnival, called on for mental renewal. One night after dinner when she became restless with our talking, she decided to beeswax the parquet floor.

(I had been brought up to see housework as business for women, with only a few heavy jobs such as beating the carpets during spring cleaning as man's work, but I had my share of things to do in the flat and even some responsibilities in shopping for delicacies.)

As well as this enchanted world I had a sense of other achievements: I was beginning to be able to look as if I knew how to order table wines and I could tip taxi drivers and waiters as if there was plenty more where that came from. I had learned the names of a number of mixed drinks and had been taught to serve generous American-size whiskies and to put ice into everything. I was beginning to learn how to get a table if a head waiter said there wasn't one and how to get a taxi driver to do what he had been asked to do. I was teaching myself to type, with two fingers, and how to sit still during a verse play on the wireless. I was learning a little about music (about which I knew nothing apart from a smattering of talk about jazz) and how to use an electric gramophone and call it a 'record player'. The only commercial connection I had imagined with painting was that, like Harold Stewart, I might buy a print of an 'Old Master' or a 'Modern', but hanging on the flat's walls were 'originals' by Sydney painters spoken of by their first names ('Francis', 'Donald', 'Cedric', 'Bernard', 'Wolf').

She taught me how to make coffee which, all my life, had been a symbol of the sophisticated and the exotic. But now I was 'making the coffee'. When I was a boy there had been a 'Ham and Beef Shop' at the end of the street where my grandparents lived and sometimes I would be sent to buy sliced devon sausage or garlic sausage. Now I was introduced to the mysteries of the 'Continental Delicatessen'. I learned what salami was, and leberwurst, how to buy anchovies or olives, smoked eel or dill cucumber. At the greengrocer's I learned about fruits and vegetables I had never heard of – the avocado, the aubergine, the papaya, the globe artichoke. The commandments of enlightened living included rubbing garlic into a wooden salad bowl, grilling steak (having first rubbed it with garlic) so that it stayed red inside and beginning the day by drinking iced tomato juice. I learned how to make French dressing, watched her making mayonnaise, gravely contemplating the oil fall into the beaten egg, drop by drop, as if she were consecrating it, and I saw spaghetti cooked in boiling water rather than heated in a can. I learned the difference between French fried potatoes and German sautéed potatoes and how to make a potato salad. And all of this was supported by cascades of iced orange juice, night and day, freshly squeezed, irrigating our lives, keeping us contemporary-minded and healthy.

I had a new view of myself: at last I was *living with a woman*. And not any woman, but one so glamorous, knowing so much and seeming to know so many people ... painters, actors, designers, the whole Kirsova ballet, poets, even American poets, novelists, editors, film stars, critics, publishers, bookshop owners, all known by their first names. Yet I saw these people only at restaurants or at other people's parties. In my childhood when we had no telephone, one of the great social delights both at my parents' and my grandparents' houses had been to hear the click of the front gate and wonder who was about to 'drop in'. But in this world, scarcely anyone 'dropped in' apart from drunks, one of whom (the sister of a university lecturer) dropped in with a taxi driver, took off her clothes, inserted the stem of a flower between her legs, and while we sat side by side on the couch, danced naked, keeping the flower in position. She said it was a South Seas 'native dance'. Then she put her clothes back on and went off with her taxi driver, whose meter had been ticking over outside.

At times, when I was alone in the flat sitting on the couch looking at the trees I might wonder if she had been 'dropped' by the famous people she knew, because of her *affaire* with someone as young and insignificant as I. But she carried the air of what it might be like to belong to a great world, and I began to imagine what that might be like, too.

I did not take her to see my parents – I could not imagine her at Denbigh listening to my father's stories about the Great War or making a fourth at bridge – and over the period of greatest enchantment I kept away even from my friends. Then we gave parties. ('I don't give food at my parties,' she said. 'People are there to get drunk. If they want to eat, let them eat at home.') Sometimes, if she was talking to one of my friends, I would watch as if I had them in the sights of a gun. She knew nothing about John Anderson, Joyce, Freud or most of the books my friends were likely to talk about, so I was out to protect her intellectual honour with savage, pre-emptive attacks. After one noisy scene in the Florentino when a friend seemed to be mocking her ignorance of Trotsky, I sent him a letter demanding a written apology. I had my own private concern, however, about the nature of her intellect – not her general style and approach to human folly which we shared in the main stream of our conversation – but her lack of bookishness: paintings and gramophone records were one thing, but books were what really mattered. In politics she seemed 'left'. (Had she passed through a Stalinist period?) In one way or the other, everybody was 'left'. But most of them were sloppily so, and so, I was afraid, was she. When I tried to give her what I saw as my tough, laconic views, she listened placidly, without saying much. We were able to laugh together, however, and with real feeling, about economics.

It was with her verse that I was most concerned. I had met McAuley and when I told him whom I was living with he stiffened into one of his most quizzing poses, saying nothing, but looking at me hard, lips in a set smile, head nodding slightly – as if this were the kind of thing he had always expected of me. I began to fear there might be a real fault. Being sloppy in political theory didn't matter much – only a few people in the world, mostly in Sydney or New York, had avoided that: but what if her poetry were not much good?

I had not read any of her verse. The 'slim vols' published by a small press were not visible in the flat and she said she didn't know whether there were any copies left in the shops: it was a very small 'small press' and it had been a very small print run. When she was out one afternoon, with a lover's curiosity I went looking for her verse: in a drawer under the day-bed I found her personal documents (one of which showed her age to be even greater than I thought), a number of manuscripts, and her printed verse. Sitting in the bathroom in case she came home, I quickly read what there was. It was obviously of a school different from McAuley's; I now knew that I was living with a cultural collaborator with both *Angry Penguin* and *New Left* groups, but what most depressed me was that the verse was simply, to my ears, flat. Although I could imagine that if (however improbable this might be) she cooked something I did not like I would be able to praise it politely, even love could not demand that I praise verse of the wrong school and that, in any case, I found flat.

Another enormous room

1

Each time I had gone to the bank after becoming a diplomatic cadet to take out another five pounds of my army deferred pay, I felt like a young man in a Hogarth print on his way to ruin. When there was no money left how would I live on a diplomatic cadet's allowance of five guineas a week, a sixth of which went on tax and of what remained more than half went to Brassey House? With less spending money than I had when I was in the army, I would have to earn extra. That would mean writing. But the one general magazine in Sydney, *The Bulletin*, was lost in bush myths, and it supported White Australia and the British Empire; the afternoon papers were mere gutter press and the other morning newspaper, the *Sydney Morning Herald*, belonged to the world of the old colonial hierarchies of judges, classics professors, bankers and Anglican bishops, so I would have to write for the *Daily Telegraph*.

I had enjoyed the *Telegraph*'s campaigns against conservative governments, and now that Labor was in power, I enjoyed its campaigns against a Labor government, but to some of my friends the *Telegraph* was 'fascist'; in his role as editor, Brian Penton had become that most intriguing of figures, an intelligent rebel said to have sold out. I had had this in mind when, after the student demonstrations against the banning of the Sydney newspapers, I had met Cyril Pearl, editor of the *Sunday Telegraph*, a shining figure from the liberal humanist past, who in 1934 had hired the Melbourne Town Hall for a great debate on censorship. Although he might be editor of the *Sunday Telegraph*, Pearl still seemed one of the most brainy of an enchanted generation of Melbourne progressives and wits, some of whom had come to Sydney to join the new *Daily Telegraph* under an editor, Sid Deamer, whose reputation as liberal, banterer, 'great newspaperman' and quixotic bohemian was so bright that anecdotes about his adventures still shone like stars. They shone all the more brightly because, after several years, he had been fired. When I asked Pearl if Penton had 'sold out' Pearl seemed to grow tired, like a tolerant father who is thinking of a new way of answering an old question; he called Penton 'Brian', as if they were old friends and this surprised me – Pearl and Penton were supposed to be rivals, and in any case the stories of Penton's ruthlessness were so Attila-like that he was always spoken of simply as 'Penton' – and then gave an answer I couldn't follow. At the end of it he suggested I should review books for the *Telegraph*.

Six months later, after I had written a letter reminding Pearl of this, and only a few days before the Labour Club conference, I found myself sitting at his table for lunch, among his entourage, in the solid bourgeois refinement of the dining room of Adam's Hotel, listening to more detailed observations about the claret than I had ever heard anyone make about a bottle of wine.

Then Pearl moved the conversation on to events of the day. He had a controlled style, speaking in short, sardonically arranged paragraphs, sometimes bitterly expressed, but with sad eyes and a loose smile. He seemed to be both worldly-wise, as one might expect of an editor, but also at times world-weary as if he wished that one day it all might end. The others at the table had come along to make up the crowd: what they lacked in sharpness they tried to compensate for by recalling the wisecracks of others. I put forward my anecdotal style. No success. My amusing style. No success. When the meal had ended there seemed to have been no reason for my being there.

As we were walking out of the hotel the fastest talking of Pearl's followers took me into the bar and ordered two beers. He handled the *Telegraph*'s reviews, amongst other things, he said: Cyril had told him I might like to do book reviews. He recited rates of pay and then said that *Daily Telegraph* readers didn't read books: the trick was to forget about book reviewing and look for books from which one might gut a few interesting anecdotes. 'Don't talk to me about book reviews', said this book reviews editor, 'readers don't want book reviews. A book review is just an interesting feature article.'

He said this with a kind of murderer's excitement, speaking quickly and softly as we secretly finalised the details of the assassination; when he took me back to his office we examined review copies of books as if inspecting carcases for a few choice cuts. As well as feature articles disguised as book reviews, the *Telegraph* ran a column which might, in some sense, be described as a book review. It was called 'For Your Dustbin' and each week it rubbished a particular book. Faithful to the critical spirit, I said I would prefer to do a 'For Your Dustbin'.

By the time my review appeared I had begun working as a part-time reporter on the *Daily Telegraph*. My appointment as a reporter had also come from the Cyril Pearl lunch in a process begun when I turned the lunch into an anecdote about a book reviews editor who hated books and told it to a friend of Crawford's, a by-lined *Telegraph* writer who had made his name from a talent for making fools of people by reporting, deadpan, exactly what they had said. Sharp-faced and fast speaking, at 'sessions' at Ushers Hotel he offered an anecdotal world of wits and idiots, in which the proto-wit was Sid Deamer, when he was editor of the *Telegraph*, presented as clever, sardonic and enlightened, and the proto-idiot was Frank Packer (nick-named 'the Young Master'), managing director of the *Telegraph*, presented as a stupid bully.

When I told my anecdote to Crawford's friend he at once turned it, in a way I couldn't understand, into an anecdote of Pearl–Penton rivalry. When I said that if I were expected to turn book reviews into feature articles I might as well write feature articles (my new life of delicatessens and Australia Hotel dinners needed even more money), he said he would get me an interview with Penton.

I found Penton in an office somewhat larger than that in which he had hired me as university correspondent four years before. Then he had seemed like a wild animal in a cage; now he was a wild animal with room to strike. Pearl had been wearily jovial, with a protective reserve, so that he invited friendship but then repelled it: Penton was wearily angry, but beneath the languid surface of his anger there seemed to lie limitless reserves of blazing hatred. When I was announced, he looked up with a quick, unsympathetic glance, then bent his head down over his writing, leaving me to find my way unobserved across the hostile territory of his blue carpet to a seat beside his desk, and then wonder if, instead of sitting so close to him, I should have chosen one of the chairs at the far end of the room. He dipped his pen vehemently into the ink well, scratched at the paper, looked with loathing at what he had written and then, with contempt, crossed it out. I was snatched up into a conversation, the beginning of which I could not understand, but when we took breath and I said I wanted to be a feature writer his face went even angrier and more red: 'Journalism is a profession, Mr Horne! It's a craft! You have to learn it! You've got to serve your apprenticeship! Just because you've got a university degree don't think you can walk in off the street and become a journalist!' There was much more of this – the need for accuracy and precision, the democratic and educational functions of the press, the need for clarity in style – but during a lull in the anger I discovered I was being hired. Penton presented it as a victory: all he would offer was six pounds five shillings a week to do casual reporting three days a week. Take it or leave it. This arrangement would carry on for a couple of months. Then they would (or would not) put me on the staff, on a basis to be determined by actual, hard results. Penton had put me in my place.

I had concealed the fact that I was a diplomatic cadet and that, after a couple of months, I would be back in Canberra. Six pounds five shillings a week! My income had more than doubled! Penton waved me off with a kind of chiding, jovial anger. 'Remember,' he said, 'your Returned Soldier's badge is worth more to you than your university degree!' What an anecdote this would make for my woman friend who was waiting for me in Ushers lounge! Penton punished me – by doubling my income! And then insulted me by saying my Returned Soldier's badge was worth more than my university degree – when I didn't have either a Returned Soldier's badge or a university degree! I would order expensive drinks. I thought we could afford them now.

FOR MY FIRST DAY'S WORK AS A CASUAL REPORTER I WAS TOLD to report at two p.m. when most of the reporters assembled. There was one large reporters' room, with several long, nineteenth-century-looking tables in it, where, I was told, most of the reporters sat, if they could find enough chairs. On two sides of this large room were smarter-looking cubicles, of glass and a fashionably light-coloured wood; the sports department had colonised one set of cubicles and the others were shared by various 'roundsmen'. Along another wall was a row of telephones where, I was told, reporters did most of their telephoning. The fourth side of the room was a wall of glass and light-coloured wood that separated us from the sub-editors' room. Beyond that – a world I could now not enter – was the office of Brian Penton. Beyond that again – although never seen by most of the reporters and unimaginable to me – was the office of Frank Packer.

Like cows waiting to be milked, the reporters stood around as the Chief of Staff called them, one by one, into his cubicle to give them assignments. Murray Sayle was there. His university career had collapsed; he was now trying his luck as a 'casual'. Looking most reporter-like of them all, with his intelligent 1930s face and short-back-and-sides haircut, Harry Hooton was also there. He had been taken up by Penton and also given a chance as a 'casual'. Although I had written of him as a bag of wind and a crank, we now talked to each other amiably: the *Daily Telegraph* reporters' room was no place for the quarrels of poets or anarchists. Sayle codified for me the *Telegraph*'s style: no more than twenty words in an opening 'par'; one sentence per paragraph; always use action verbs and use them in the active voice; concrete, not abstract, nouns; make the clear even more clear; twenty-five sentences was a long 'story'; tell what really mattered in the first three 'pars'. After Sayle ran through all this, there seemed little more to learn about journalism.

When Hooton went to the Chief of Staff for his assignment and came out looking preoccupied, Sayle said they had the chopper out for Harry. By now an hour had gone. All the regular staff reporters had received their assignments and had left the building ('to get pissed,' Sayle said) or were sitting down talking into telephones. Only the 'casuals' – Sayle, myself, and one other – were still waiting. 'They've got the bloody chopper out for me, too,' said the other casual: when he got the call and came out again into the reporters' room he showed Sayle the slip of paper with his assignment on it, a 'follow-up' story on which he had failed the night before. Sayle went in, and came out a few seconds afterwards. He had 'the weather story'. I was called in. 'nothing for you, I'm afraid, Mr Horne,' said the Chief of Staff. 'You can just wait in the reporters' room and see what turns up.' I sat down at one of the long tables. Sayle and the other casual had gone out. Only a few people were left in the office and they were all in cubicles. No one from the regular reporting staff had spoken to me.

WHEN ONE OF THE TWO TELEPHONES ON THE LONG TABLE RANG, I hoped someone else would answer it. In my whole life I had used a telephone only a couple of dozen times and when I did so I found it difficult to understand what was being said. Now I had to answer it. I couldn't follow what it was about, but wrote down a few words: *San Demetrio ... survivor ... F.W. Meeks ... publicity ...* and the name of a hotel. My look of helplessness brought over a reporter, a blonde woman with a deep voice and the classic beauty of an actress in a Pond's face cream magazine ad. She said her name was Rita Dunstan and told me to go to the library and get 'the cuts' on the *San Demetrio*. From the folder of library cuttings I learned the *San Demetrio* was a British oil tanker that had caught fire when bombed by the Germans, but 'miraculously' the crew had put the fire out. What seemed to matter about the *San Demetrio* was that a movie had been made about this incident.

I interviewed F.W. Meeks in his hotel room. Two people from a film company were there, but what they said seemed entirely without interest. Mr Meeks himself wanted to tell me something, but what he was saying was nothing more than I had already read in 'the cuts'. I could see myself going back to the *Telegraph* without a 'story'; I would spend a few more days in the reporters' room, getting nothing. Then they would get the chopper out for me. I asked Mr Meeks if he thought a miracle had saved the *San Demetrio*. 'Yes,' he said, 'it was a miracle.' 'Do you mean that God put the fire out?' I asked, risking everything. (What if he said 'No'? Perhaps he didn't know what 'miracle' meant!) 'Yes, the Lord put the fire out,' he said. (That was concrete!) 'Do you think any human agency could have put it out?' (If he said 'No', I wouldn't need any more questions.) He said 'No', and went back to his own narrative; I kept on taking notes as he spoke and when the two film people said some more I wrote notes on what they had to say, too, but as I went back to the office, with a pocketful of notes and the feeling of exhaustion of one who had escaped a sentence of death, I knew that with the word 'miracle' I had my 'lead'.

It was the time of day when reporters were required to drink in one of the three hotels within a few yards of the *Telegraph*: Sayle took me to a bar lined four deep with shouting men and we shouted at each other, not hearing much, until six o'clock, when all the bars closed. After a quick meal I sat at one of the long tables in the reporters' room, with my notes on one side and on the other side a pile of small slips of 'copy paper' on which to write one sentence to a page. It took me almost an hour to get the first three sentences right. Then, following Sayle's instructions, I had to boil down to a sentence or two the whole story of what had happened to the *San Demetrio*. This would be placed within square brackets. What else? The rest was what Mr Meeks was trying to say himself. None of it seemed to matter, but without it the story would seem too short. I worked over Mr Meek's own narrative again and again, but each time it came out at ten sentences or more. Far too long. As I dropped my story into the wire tray on the sub-editor's desk it seemed absurdly heavy. Fifteen sentences!

There was nothing more to do. I sat talking with Hooton, and watched through the glass screen to see what was happening to my story. One sub-editor took it out of the wire basket, read it, angrily, taking up each page with its short sentence, staring at it, then placing it face down. In front of him was the 'spike' on which rejected copy was pierced through its heart. When he had finished reading, he took up all fifteen slips of paper, squared them off like a pack of cards, put the pin back in, scribbled something on top, and threw my story into the wire basket in front of the Chief Sub-Editor. After that I lost track of it in all the shuffling of paper that went on around the sub-editor's desk, until I recognised that it was my name that was being called out by one of the copy boys. I went into the sub-editors' room and stood beside a sub-editor who was sharpening a pencil with a razor blade. In front of him were the library 'cuts' I had already consulted. The pages of my story were crumpled and scribbled over. He had written his own version in his own hand. He left me waiting while he got exactly the point he wanted on his pencil. Then he said to me: 'Are you a frustrated novelist?' He pointed to my fifteen crumpled sentences. 'You don't have to write a book!' I said something. He pointed to the folder from the library. 'You should always look up the cuts before you do a story.' I didn't answer. 'And you don't say 'Mister' after the first mention. It's not *Telegraph* style. And what about his age? You always give the age!' He pointed to his own neat pile of paper. 'Anyway I've cleaned it up. All we need is his age.' I contemplated ringing up Mr Meeks and asking him his age, but could not bring myself to do it. I went in to the sub-editor and told him Mr Meeks was out. He looked at me with such contempt that I assumed the 'story' would now be 'spiked'.

Later I saw a galley proof of my story, with a single column heading in Metro Bold. Two sentences were almost exactly as I had written them. At eleven the shift ended and I went off in a taxi to the flat as happy as a writer whose first book has just been accepted. Unless something went wrong, the *Telegraph* would be using my first 'story' tomorrow morning! In the morning, I was not sure. Perhaps not having his age would 'kill' the 'story'. I picked up the *Telegraph*, turned over the pages. There it was – in what Sayle had told me was one of the most favoured page positions in the whole of the *Daily Telegraph*.

SAN DEMETRIO SAVED 'BY MIRACLE'

Only a miracle saved the tanker *San Demetrio*, Mr F.W. Meeks, a survivor of the tanker, said last night.

Meeks arrived in Sydney recently. His home is in Peterborough, England.

San Demetrio, a British oil tanker, was set on fire by a German battleship when in convoy in the Atlantic in 1940. After abandoning her, some of the crew returned, put out the fire, and brought her to port.

Meeks said: 'The lord put that fire out on the tanker. No human agency could have put it out.

'The gun crew had not heard the order to abandon ship until the captain strolled across and repeated it.

'We saw the *San Demetrio* the next morning at dawn, but a big sea was running, and we could not reach her,' Meeks added.

'We were picked up from the *Gloucester City*, which also picked up survivors from six other ships on the same voyage.'

The story of the *San Demetrio* was made into a film, which has already been shown in Sydney.

We celebrated with caresses and kisses, cups of Turkish coffee and glasses of freshly squeezed orange juice.

2

Each Tuesday, Wednesday and Thursday, after spending the morning in the flat, with both of us reading or writing and having lunch together (often in a 'continental restaurant'), I would go to the enormous room at the *Daily Telegraph* to earn the money needed to pay my share of the bill at 'continental restaurants'. On these afternoons the mysteries of existence would freeze into a few short, sharp and solid sentences. 'Getting the facts' on the assignments typed on slips of paper produced each afternoon a state of sorrow. To turn a typewritten message into a 'story' meant one or more 'interviews'. Would I again forget to ask the ages of those I 'interviewed'? Or spell their names incorrectly? Or find it hard to understand what they were saying on the telephone?

In the embarrassments of the actual 'interview' I had to place myself against some stranger and pretend it was not I but a 'reporter' engaged in this act of intimacy, with questions that, although they professed interest, lacked it: all that mattered – the hidden climax of an 'interview', sometimes occurring long before the 'interview' ended – was that there should explode in my head some set of words that sounded like a 'story'; even at this moment of realisation I had to go on talking, to conceal that I had got what I wanted, and that this was all I wanted. Sometimes, politely, at the end of the 'interview', I would act as if the interviewee and I had something in common.

In actually writing a 'story', with sub-editors working on the other side of the glass partition a reminder of the indignity that a stranger might rewrite my 'copy', the 'interview' itself drifted off into a dream. Reality was these small slips of paper as, slicing and trimming and whittling, I turned words into a 'story' written in *Daily Telegraph* style. When we talked together, Sayle and I would make jokes about concrete nouns and the active voice, or 'sub down' famous patches of purple prose into fifteen-word sentences, or reduce great events into a twenty-word *Daily Telegraph* 'intro'. In the long lulls that usually came at the end of the evening, we might knock off little skits on *Daily Telegraph* style and show them to each other. As former student editors familiar with typography, we became obsessed by the *Telegraph's* typefaces. 'Don't talk to me in your Pabst Extra Bold voice,' Sayle would say. Or I might say of someone, 'He's the kind of man who thinks in Bodoni Black,' or 'He's a bit Metro Heavy.'

If I was sent to report a public meeting, I would be put in a special place, with other reporters, detached from the audience, and I would ignore everything except whatever would make a *Daily Telegraph* headline. Or the Chief of Staff might simply give me a handout to turn into a few 'pars'. There were several days when all the 'stories' I was given 'fell down' and I would go off to the flat in my taxi fairly sure the *Telegraph* would not bother to keep me as a casual. Worse: the times when a story I had written was not in the paper. As soon as I arrived at the office I would check if the story had 'made the first edition' only to be 'dropped' at the midnight conference when the paper was 're-cast'. Perhaps it had been dropped by Penton himself! (Jeering at it.) If there were nothing in the first edition I would look through galley proofs to see if the story had at least been 'set'. If there was no galley of it the story had been 'spiked'.

The roundsmen in their cubicles spoke only to each other; of the staff reporters in the main room scarcely any spoke to us 'casuals'. We had not 'done cadetships'. We could not even 'do' shorthand. We were blow-ins who would disappear when the real journalists came back from the war. For me, the reporters' room was dominated by a middle-aged man in a dark business suit who sat at his typewriter as if he had invented its keyboard, touch-typing with professional speed and, like a master of his craft, keeping his hat on his head. The women reporters were temporary intruders, also to be got rid of after the war, but when one of them 'went off on a job' she would carry herself with such *savoir faire* that she seemed, without doubt, to be someone who had 'learned her trade'. The women all typed, and took shorthand notes as expertly as a 'newspaperman'.

Rita Dunstan, who had helped me on the first day, regularly spoke to me and, after several weeks, other women might chat during one of the long periods of nothingness. I soon learned which office personalities to laugh at and which anecdotes to tell and found it easy to be amusing with all the women, except the youngest of them who seemed so hard-boiled that she treated my 'humorous' anecdotes as acts of indecent exposure on which she could use her own wit. Sayle thought I was amusing. So did another of the casuals, who made humour out of his own failures. So did Hooton, but after a few weeks Hooton was fired. Even by my last week only two of the male permanent reporters had regularly spoken to me. Neither of them found me amusing.

In the pub, conversations as well as beers had to be finished by six o'clock. Insofar as one could hear anything among all the yelling, and sometimes the brawling and vomiting, I could hear around me parables and litanies of the *Telegraph* – anecdotes of the great campaigns of the *Telegraph* in the golden days of Sid Deamer, before Penton had sold out; heroic tales of the indomitable cynicism of reporters and the sardonic brutalities of managements; the determination that journalism was neither a profession, nor a craft, but a trade; reminders of the fundamental ignorance of the 'readers' whose stupidity we all had to serve, but also respect for their goodness and simplicity; revelations of Penton's betrayals, and praise for his brilliance; gossip about 'heated up' stories, but also pride in being 'objective' and 'getting the facts'. Above all, pride in the *Telegraph*'s short, punchy style, seen as the tightest, best disciplined newspaper style in Australia. The Chief Sub-Editor was in the pub every evening, quick-witted, good-humoured, but back at work after dinner he was prime guardian, hour by hour, of the paper's style: he would talk quickly, joke and drink his beer as if he were just one of us, but I knew that inside his head, there was an unparalleled mastery of the techniques of short pars, Pabst Italic, the active voice, the use of square brackets, concrete nouns, Metro Bold, and all the other marks of tradesmanship that made the *Daily Telegraph* (almost everyone agreed on this) one of the world's best 'subbed' newspapers.

The Chief Sub-Editor was the only 'executive' we saw in the pub and the only one who would have dinner in sight of the staff. Penton, whom I had not seen again after he had hired me, was rumoured to have dinner every night with his mistress at his club. Packer, whom I had not seen at all, would presumably be dining in his mansion at Bellevue Hill, served by his butler like someone in a movie, or again like someone in a movie, this time a 'playboy', he might be dining and dancing at one of the two fashionable night clubs. The Chief of Staff kept himself to himself so much that we didn't know where he ate his dinner, although it was rumoured to be at the Masonic Club.

In his small cubicle, the Chief of Staff sat at his old-fashioned desk inside his large body, like Conlon acting out imperturbability with pipe movements, but also master of the knowing, sideways stare of a shrewd police sergeant: he handed out assignments as if they were summonses. He gave no advice about how to 'get a story' and when, one night, I asked him if he thought I should make my opening par this or that he stared at me, pipe in mouth, without saying anything, as if I had now given him enough evidence for a conviction. Sayle and I suspected he had a guilty secret: he couldn't write in *Daily Telegraph* style. He was an old hand from some earlier era.

But what did it matter? Although at the *Daily Telegraph* they thought I was 'on trial' I knew that this was only a vacation job: the taste of human thinness and meanness which came from the reporters' room was easily washed away by the delights of my love affair. And now I was 'doing some writing'. There had been mornings when I had sat on the couch in the flat and scribbled out fragments of several prose sketches, taken from life, like the pieces in *Arna* – one of them based on the Labour Club conference at which we had met – and now she was going over them with a pencil, cutting the angry parts and smoothing them out. Soon, I might have a style!

There was evidence throughout the *Telegraph* of that serious intent Penton had shown so angrily on the day he hired me to 'serve the public' bits and pieces of solid stuff, but in the mirage of reality that came from creating 'facts' (we pronounced it 'facks') in short, one-sentence paragraphs, nothing very serious came to me. The Chief of Staff confined me to 'food stories' and 'weather stories'. Rumours came from the subs that Penton was asking for more 'bright' stories: there was nothing bright to be found in forecasts of thunderstorms or the movement in pumpkin prices, but sometimes one could coax out enough facts to provide a 'low double' or even a 'page lead', such as: POTATOES, ONIONS PLENTIFUL. Milk Supplies May Increase Later: Meat, Fish Scarce

With the weather stories I would keep in touch with the Weather Bureau and as soon as I learned that something unpleasant had happened I would be on the phone to police stations, looking for facts.

A sense of craftsmanship came with the largest story I was to write during my 'trial': HAILSTONES BREAK WINDOWS, BLOCK TRAFFIC. Crops damaged in cyclonic storm

If the *telegraph* printed a 'story' by me I cut it out and put it into a folder. I was ashamed of doing this. But I was pleased 'they were giving my stories a run'. Into the folder I also put four book reviews, three from the 'For Your Dustbin' column, in its most scathing style, the fourth an exposition to Saturday morning readers of the views of von Mises on the evils of bureaucracy ('Von Mises is that rare person – an Economics professor who does not support government by Economics professors') and it was these reviews that I boasted about when I was having an end-of-vacation lunch with Bruce Miller. Miller was not at his best. He said the 'Dustbin' reviews were too bitter. Too bitter! Instead of praising my reviews he wanted to praise how skilfully I had picked up the tricks of a journalist's trade. Obviously Miller was being corrupted by his marriage and career. As we strode along Pitt Street after lunch, laughing loudly over jokes about my forthcoming diplomatic career, Miller noticed that paint had been used to cover a film star's legs in a poster outside the Lyceum picture theatre. 'There you are,' he said. 'If Penton himself wants "bright" stories, there's a "bright story".' I thought about it. Against doing anything: the embarrassments of asking silly questions; since I was going back to Canberra soon, what did it matter? *A bright story! Penton himself!* After Miller returned to his office I went to the Lyceum and spoke to the commissionaire: yes, that's right, the legs were a bit vulgar. Maria Montez, it was. They had to be covered up. After all, the theatre belonged to the Methodist Church and the picture company only leased it. *How long had he been there?* Twenty years. *Anything like this before?* Never: they had always been very responsible. *Did he think it was right that a young lady's legs should be displayed in public like that?* No, he didn't. I felt like a real reporter.

The Chief of Staff looked at the memo on which I suggested 'there was a story' at the Lyceum, and said nothing. He put it on his desk as if he had impounded it as evidence against me and handed me an assignment slip – the weather story. He said the subs wanted early copy. I rang up the Lyceum authorities anyway, to 'get the facks', and since it seemed to be a day without weather, began trying to turn my notes into a ten-par story in *Daily Telegraph* style, although I didn't know if they wanted it. There were difficulties in telling a 'bright' story in *Telegraph* style: I hadn't even worked out a twenty-word introductory par that was 'bright' as well as 'factual' when the Chief of Staff came back from the late-afternoon conference with the notebook showing that Penton had already made some preliminary commands. *How was the Lyceum story going? The editor was very interested in it. The subs wanted early copy. Fifteen pars!* I would have to go out and get man-in-the street interviews.

FILM STAR'S THIGHS ON POSTER CENSORED

The Lyceum Theatre management has censored the thighs of Maria Montez depicted in an advertisement outside the theatre.

On the management's instructions, a red skirt has been painted over the thighs.

The Lyceum Theatre is leased from the Methodist Church, which watches all films and advertisements displayed there.

The chairman of the trust controlling the Lyceum (the Rev. F.H. Rayward) said last night that Miss Montez's thighs were not acceptable as an advertisement. 'There should be no public display of the thighs like that,' he said. Ron Wills the commissionaire, said yesterday that Miss Montez's thighs were 'a bit vulgar' and had to be covered up.

'I've been here for 20 years and the theatre has always been very responsible,' he said. 'I don't think it's right for a young lady's legs to be displayed in public like that.'

Comments from film goers: A.B. James Crain, RN, 'Good legs spoilt. No one will see the picture now.'

Sig. J. Keenan, US Navy, 'I had to come to Australia to see Maria Montez wearing a skirt.'

Gnr. H.E. Smith, AIF, 'It's just wowserism. The boys like Maria as a pin-up, but they don't paint skirts on her.'

I had four days off and when I came back to the reporters' room for what were to be my last three days as a casual, Rita Dunstan told me that Penton had praised my Maria Montez 'story' at the midnight conference: Why can't we have more stories like that? Here's a man come in from off the street and he teaches us how to write bright stories. There were rumours that Penton would call me in for a talk and put me on special assignments.

I had no interest in this, beyond turning it into an amusing anecdote. In two days time I would tell the Chief of Staff I was leaving. What was more to the point was that I must now leave my love and return to Canberra.

ELEVEN

Perhaps I could become anything

1

It was the beginning of Autumn when I returned to Canberra for my second year in the School of Diplomatic Studies. Because of the many exotic trees in the Canberra avenues (planted to take away some of the shame of being a 'bush capital') it was my first deciduous autumn: yellowing leaves made it the familiar autumn of English nature verse. But symbols of mellowness seen through the flyscreen of a small bedroom in a Canberra boarding house provided no consolation against what now seemed the meanness and bleakness of life away from Sydney. I sat at my desk in Brassey House as if I were pondering demographic trends or the consequences of the Meiji Restoration, but what I was doing, night by night, was writing a long prose poem celebrating the past two months. When her letters came everything seemed as usual. Her book was going well; she was now thinking of writing a new play, about the Black Death. But should it be a 'modern, a but-madly-social piece'? Or should it be 'historical and let the moral point itself'?

We planned that she would come to Canberra for a weekend, but when she came she was staying with two married friends. For most of the time we saw each other only in company, making conversation as if it were the Labour Club conference again, and we had just met, although there was a memorable dinner at which we were classified as a 'pair' in a way I hadn't expected. There were just the four of us, at the 'married couple's' house and here they were, in front of us, staging an argument, at first about the frequency of the husband's farting in bed and then about anything they could think of: I had never known a 'married couple' who argued in front of others. And I had certainly never expected what happened at the end of it: the husband was suggesting we change partners and go to bed, I with his wife, he with my love. I was frozen with uncertainty, but his wife passed it off as a joke. (Another woman approaching her forties!)

I had lost interest in the course. Fitzhardinge had gone to the classics department at Sydney University and with him went much of our intellectual amusement; much of the rest went when the study of politics flattened into a new subject called 'International Relations' with a voguish 'scientific' approach. Attached to it were lectures in international law, taken from a book. Both the new History man and the 'Pacific Studies' man were ready to make careers out of their subjects, thus taking away from the course its earlier delights of spontaneity; we had become part of other people's vocational strategies. In economics we were giving close textual analysis to Keynes's *General Theory*, as if this were the *Talmud* and was all we really need know.

Sometimes I would wonder how on earth I could 'become a diplomat'. What would that mean? What would it be like? But I had already 'become a reporter'. Perhaps I could 'become' anything – thinking about the future when I got there would be soon enough. What pressed on my mind with the fear of a nightmare was a theoretical difficulty: how could I pretend there was a 'national interest' when I knew very well that society was simply an arena of conflicting forces? I could see John Anderson standing up at his rostrum in the Philosophy Room: in his most urgent whine, he was exposing me as a mere 'solidarist' who believed there was a common good. Then I would come back to the loneliness of my present life. I would be taking notes on the economics of international trade or the rise of the Kuomintang and there would come into my mind the glisten of suntan oil on a long body on the white sand, or the bubbles of boiling water breaking through the crust of ground coffee in a saucepan in the kitchen in her flat, or her briefcase, filled with drafts for novels, boxes of pills, outlines for plays, receipts for the rent, poems, lipstick containers. Essays and exercises were not handed in on time: sometimes I would get up so late I would arrive in the middle of a class. Even if I arrived on time I seemed to have entered a conversation begun while I was out of the room.

When I first returned to Canberra, Murray Sayle had sent me a letter, typed on *Daily Telegraph* copy paper, one paragraph to a page:

WELL-KNOWN JOURNALIST LOST
EDITOR CRIES FOR WANDERING BOY

The Chief of Staff of the *Daily Telegraph* last night asked what had happened to Mr Donald Horne.

The Chief of Staff called in Mr Murray Sayle and said: 'Mr Penton wants to know, where is Mr Horne?

'You know, Mr Penton was very sorry to see Mr Horne go,' he added.

'He was a good man. Will you be in touch with him, Mr Sayle?

'We were on the point of giving him a staff appointment when he left.

'Tell him that when he is ready, Consolidated Press wants him to come back.

'Let us know what he says.'

I sent back an ambiguous message through Sayle because I wanted to earn some money by writing an occasional 'For Your Dustbin'. By the May vacation I would sometimes discuss whether I wanted to become a journalist, but mainly as a way of making conversation: why would I want to work in the *Daily Telegraph*'s enormous room worrying that I had forgotten to ask someone how old he was?

The May vacation was far too brilliant a season to waste in thinking about the future. My Sydney friends were throwing parties again; there were parties at her flat; we had met some officers from a British aircraft carrier, HMS *Slinger*, one with literary interests, and this added new faces, new ways of mixing drinks ('pink gins' and 'gin and it') and new forms of gossip. I was re-reading the novels of Evelyn Waugh.

The vacation was over. It was winter. Although I sometimes had to borrow money to buy the railway ticket, I went to Sydney every weekend. Then I made it a three-day weekend, even a four-day weekend. In one week I spent only one day in Canberra between two long weekends. I was not even aware now of the topics of the essays I had not written. The course had got beyond me; it would take a month's study to catch up. I arranged to go back to the *Telegraph* as a casual. On my last day as a Diplomatic Cadet I arrived in Canberra in an overnight train. It was freezing, with a blustering wind. The papers said that John Curtin was dying in the Lodge. I gave 'the Department' my resignation, packed up my things and went back to Sydney on the afternoon train.

2

It was the Manpower Office which had moved me from the army to the External Affairs Department; until Manpower announced its next intention, the *Daily Telegraph* could employ me only as a casual. Since the war was still on, although seemingly near its end, Manpower could even decide to put me back into the army. Now when I went into the reporters' room I felt I was again in a staging camp; what would happen next? They weren't giving me anything very interesting again, mainly, weather and food stories. We were just waiting, the *Telegraph*, Manpower and I.

I WAS NO LONGER SHARING A FLAT WITH SOMEONE WHO WAS writing a book. While I went off three days a week to write about the weather, she went off to write publicity for a radio station. I had loved her too much to pay any attention to her, but now I could sometimes hear what she was saying: at the radio station she was just part of the furniture. Her book was finished, but there was no external sign of success in that – she had been ghosting it for someone else. She had drafted some of her new play, but couldn't summon the belief to type it out. Now she wanted to write a novel, but nothing came onto the page. When I had still been in Canberra she had written to me: 'Puss, I can't write anything and I am not going to write anything any more, I know it. My bones tell me. And there it is. It is too long now since I have not writ a thing you see. It has gone on too long.' I had considered this (insofar as I considered it at all) as merely being amusing, but now it was a theme she came back to. Was her period of success over? 'My prestige is ebbing,' she would say. When she was reading the *ABC Weekly* one day and discovered she was described simply as 'young poet', she told me she used to be described as 'brilliant young Australian poet'.

But there was the company of all our friends to enjoy – eating out, drinks, parties: even Alf Conlon was back in town, and had met her; Rhodes had met her; and I was meeting more of her own friends now. There seemed so much talking to do – and some of it in an exotic language. The officers from the *Slinger* who went to our parties all spoke public school English: I had never been surrounded by Englishmen; it was like being in a foreign language movie. Hope's English began to sound more 'Oxford'; I found myself speaking more quickly. Her English became more 'English'. When they came to parties, bringing bottles of Scotch and Gordon's Gin, they would also bring with them their angular manners, shabby uniforms, rapid speech and secret signs. At dinner in the wardroom of the *Slinger* we would appear surrounded by a sea of foreigners, all speaking English.

At one of these dinners we had been well separated; she had been placed with an Englishman whose public school accent (she and I had decided) was not the real thing. By the end of the meal I was awash with alcohol, eyes out of focus, speech unsteady and, now and again, hiccuping. Where was she? No convincing answer beyond suggestions that she had gone on a tour of the ship. *A tour of the ship!* With whom? The Englishman whose public school accent was not the real thing was also missing. With him? An Englishman who wasn't the real thing? They had been plying me with drinks so that they could go off together. *They were all in this!* Squinting to keep my eyes in focus, shuddering, I invaded the forbidden parts of HMS *Slinger*, looking for her and this English phoney. I looked into officers' cabins, paced around the flight deck, tried to get into the engine rooms. When anyone spoke to me, usually to order me away, I would give a short, grave reply and then square my shoulders and hold my breath, hoping to suppress the next hiccup. Now, fighting rage and tears as well as hiccups and double vision, I ran off the ship, caught a taxi (where I hiccuped with the vigour of someone exercising a long denied fundamental human right), and went back to the flat. Empty. At least not there! Bubbling with self-pity I sat on the couch and in a kind of death rattle, hiccuped and sobbed, the Gordon's Gin pouring out of my eyes and stinging my cheeks. On a wide ledge outside one of the windows there were cactuses in pots. I threw the pots out, one after the other, into the street, waiting to hear each pot crack on the pavement before I threw the next. After this exercise I went to sleep.

By the time she came in I had passed from rage to hangover and sadness – and terror at the thought of destroying all the cactus pots: it was as if I had sacked Rome. I would sooner have gone back to sleep, but now we had to shout at each other, yelling like cats in the night, fighting not only from the positions we had prepared for this incident, but throwing at each other any bit of rubbish that came to mind and by this means bewailing our general condition. It was dawn before we had finished and at last we went to sleep on the couch. At breakfast she squeezed extra orange juice; we tentatively tried our first amusing remarks about Englishmen who weren't the real thing. This would now join our joke repertoire. She went off to write publicity about her radio station; I went off expecting to write about the weather.

WHEN I HAD VISITED THE *DAILY TELEGRAPH* OFFICE DURING THE May vacation I had seen on the wall of the Sub-Editor's room proofs of three frontpage headings with which Brian Penton intended to chronicle the end of the European war. He had them ready, to drop in when the time came. The first was in the *Telegraph*'s largest normal type:

BERLIN SHELLED

The next was of a size never before seen in the *Telegraph*:

ARMISTICE!

The last was in poster size:

PEACE!

The headings had been used and there had been some celebrations in the city at the end of the European war, but in the newsreel theatrettes the films of Belsen and other liberated concentration camps had caught the imagination so sharply that this was to be remembered rather than 'victory'. In any case, to a philosophical anarchist, the symbols of the real 'victory' in the newsreel theatrettes could be images of Stalin triumphantly posing for the cameras.

But now the end of the Japanese war was to get its headline and the whole war was about to finish. A few days before the *Daily Telegraph* had announced on its front page:

WORLD'S GREATEST BOMB ON JAPAN FEARFUL ATOMIC WEAPON

And now, as I walked to the *Telegraph* Office to write the weather story, weary with hangover and fears of lost love, I saw a sign outside a disposal shop:

BIG NOISY RATTLES FOR PEACE CELEBRATION! PRICE 1/- BUY ONE NOW! BE READY!

This could be as good as the Maria Montez legs story! I gave the Chief of Staff a memo; the Pictorial Editor assigned a photographer; at the door of the shop we posed a salesgirl beside the sign, and asked her to twirl two of the gas-warning rattles now being sold as 'surplus'; I interviewed the owner. The next day with picture, there was my story:
RUSH ON GAS RATTLES TO CELEBRATE VICTORY

A couple of days later, when a cable announced that the Japanese would surrender, I and another reporter were sent to Kings Cross to record the actions of 'peace revellers' (mainly roughnecks wanting to do what they would usually be arrested for). We walked the streets noting acts of patriotic vandalism which were to come together under the heading:
BONFIRES LIT AT THE CROSS

He 'phoned the story through', but it was I who drafted the first paragraph while we had a cup of coffee: *Police and firemen were unable to prevent peace revellers in Kings Cross last night from lighting bonfires in the street.*

That was how the war ended.

3

Now that the war was over there seemed no danger that Manpower would put me back into the army, but no form had come through to allow me to take a job. Perhaps in 1946 I would go back to the university? I might finish my Arts degree? Or take a law degree? In the meantime I must get on with my writing. When Bruce Miller had put me into a radio discussion in which we sat beside a microphone and talked about the importance of comic strips in modern society, we had come together so well that we decided to collaborate on a book about Australia. Twelve chapters. Five thousand words in each chapter. Write it in three months.

We began to work out the chapters: Chapter 1: *State and Federal.* Chapter 2: *Economic Planning? – Perhaps!* Chapter 3: *Whitewashed Australia – the meaning of the White Australia Policy.* Chapter 4: *Social Security or Social Oil?* Chapter 5: *Politicians and Culture.* Chapter 6: *Protection – or Not?* Chapter 7: *Government by lawyers?* Chapter 8: *Politics and Wheat.* Chapter 9: *Liberal tendencies in Australia – are there any?* Chapter 10: *Where Does the Money Come From?* Chapter 11: *A Minor Managerial Revolution?* Chapter 12: *The Four Main Political Parties – Labor, Liberal, Country, Communist.*

Miller typed out the headings so skilfully that it really did look like a programme for a book. Over a long lunch we scribbled notes on the list, and added extras. We had forgotten the Press! and there should be a chapter called '*The Myth of the Living Standard*'. And another on education. But that made fifteen chapters and we had agreed on only twelve, all to be done in three months? We decided to write two experimental chapters: I would do the political parties and Miller the 'wheat seats'. Then we would sort out the rest.

In my spare time I sat on the couch in the flat and prepared my attack. After fifteen pages I had explained that the theory of democracy as representative government was a swindle; that Canberra had the mentality of a small frontier settlement; that Australian nationalism was arrogant pep talk; that parliament provided a living exhibition of semi-literates; that the most serious distortion of newspaper reporting of parliament was to make politicians seem better than they were; that John Curtin had not been a great man; that politics was marked by tedium, stupidity and vulgarity; that most politicians were too old;

that too few were university graduates, too few had been abroad, and most showed narrow prejudices against the 'un-Australian'; that many politicians were openly prejudiced against modern trends towards sex equality and saw women as wives and mothers but not as citizens; and not one of them could be described as liberal. They were all book banners and intolerant bourgeois moralists.

Having unloaded my views on politicians in general I turned to the Labor Party: unlike other socialist parties it was not a party with room for intellectuals; its strong trades union prejudices – anticommunism, White Australia, obsession with old age pensions – put off intellectuals, as did the narrow attitudes of the moribund local branches; Labor MPs became divorced from the rest of the labour movement: the party machine was a highly complicated hierarchy organised against the rank-and-file; the parliamentary party was divided and its meetings were a miniature parliament. Then I turned on the conservatives: at least the Labor Party's quarrels were public, unlike those of the conservatives; and at least the Labor politicians showed some responsibility to the party that put them there. The conservative parties couldn't do that, because their real backers were secret.

I had got as far as this when the form from the Manpower Office arrived. I was released from my Diplomatic Cadetship. The *Telegraph* at once offered to put me on its permanent staff, as a 'D' grade reporter, at eight pounds ten shillings a week. There was a catch: they wanted me to go to Canberra for the next parliamentary session, for a month, but after that I could work in Sydney. Splendid! I could come down for at least two of the weekends to see my love. And in Canberra, in the mornings, I would be able to work on my book.

4

When I got to the pragmatic brick of Canberra's Hotel Civic, where the *Telegraph* was paying four pounds a week for my bedroom and meals, I remembered how eleven and a half years earlier I had arrived at the government-owned hostel where I had boarded, Monday to Friday, during my year at Maitland High, as a boy of twelve with a school bag containing a new soap holder, a new toothbrush holder, the new sheets and towels on which my father had printed D.R. HORNE in black ink, thick exercise books with hard covers, a geometry set, newly sharpened pencils and a new foot rule. Beyond thin, sad images of the loneliness of the first day at primary school, it was my first memory of being a new boy. Now, being a new boy had become my style.

As a new boy to Canberra journalism I was shown the ropes by the young woman journalist I was replacing; she was wearing sandshoes, but the sharp vowels of her upper-class voice indicated she was wearing them not from 'bad taste' but from self-confident whim.

She promptly put me on a schedule: when the parliament reassembled next week I would work on Tuesdays from three in the afternoon until mid-night, on Wednesdays and Thursdays from ten thirty a.m. until midnight, and on Fridays from ten thirty a.m. until dinner-time; for the other three days there would be scarcely anything to do. (I would be able to go down to Sydney, or get on with my book.) She organised me into a party of one and took me by bus to Parliament House and showed me the ledge-like balcony (part of 'the press gallery') in the House of Representatives chamber where I was to sit and look for 'stories': that was what I was paid to do – 'cover' the House of Representatives. Then she showed me the adjacent two corridors with small rooms off them where the daily newspapers and the other gallery services had their 'bureaus'. The *Telegraph* 'bureau' seemed smaller than most, with scarcely enough room for its six little tables and a cupboard. Bundles of copy paper and telegram forms were scattered over the tables; on the walls someone had pasted newspaper headings with double meanings. There was no one there.

At lunch at the Civic (soup, entree, main course, sweet, as at Brassey House, but with a fifth course – 'cheese or savoury') she gave me technical information: where the telegram office was, how to type up stories on telegram forms, how to type stories for dictation over the telephone, bus timetables. In the hotel's lounge ('this is the place where they do the hard drinking'), she asked for my report on office gossip. I did the best I could with amusing tales of the enormous room; she gave quick character sketches of Canberra journalists and the newspaper 'bureaus'. The heads of some of the 'bureaus' were said to be untrustworthy, that magic quality that gave journalists a particular glamour. To this was added the extra piquancy that ours was a reformed drunk. She had doubts about him, but the second-in-command was a 'sweetie'. The lounge was empty. The small, chipped wooden tables and the wooden chairs with their stiff, leather seats would not, until the session began, be used by 'the hard drinkers'.

In my bedroom, which I was to share with a *Daily Mirror* reporter, I spent the rest of the afternoon lying on the bed reading *Buddenbrooks* and I went back to it after dinner. The unrealities and insubstantiality of Canberra with the empty *Daily Telegraph* 'bureau', its empty hotel lounge and this room empty of everything except sleeping and storing facilities were replaced by the bourgeois solidity of a Hanseatic town in the nineteenth century.

After breakfast next morning I decided to teach myself more about journalism. I bought two copies each of the *Daily Telegraph* and the *Sydney Morning Herald*, cut out each 'story' in them with a razor blade and put the clippings in piles on the floor according to their categories. I compared in detail the content balance of each newspaper, and took notes on my observations, then when both had 'covered' the same 'story' I compared the way each paper treated it. I had no obvious use for this information, but I had engaged in a ritualistically satisfying intellectual occupation which showed that I was taking journalism seriously. Then I flushed all the clippings down the lavatory in case someone found them and thought I was taking journalism seriously.

After lunch there were several hours in the *Telegraph* 'bureau' in which, listening to the anecdotes of the bureau chief, I felt like David Copperfield. Then I was a new boy again: in the *Daily Telegraph* office in Sydney, not having a typewriter of my own, I had written my copy in longhand but now, when given handouts to 'boil down to a few pars', I had to sit in public in that small office where nothing could be hidden and type incompetently, with two middle fingers, jamming the keys, and xxxx-ing out several words in every line. It reminded me of how, when teaching myself to swim at the shallow end of the pool at the Muswellbrook baths, the important thing had been to look as if I knew what I was doing.

The day before Parliament resumed, the lounge of the Hotel Civic became a movie set for scenes of the arrival of an occupying revolutionary army. Journalists from Sydney and Melbourne – mostly men, some women – came by train or by car and turned the Civic into headquarters for their coming battle. Some unpacked their luggage upstairs in their rooms before they slipped into chairs in the lounge to get on with drinking; others went at once into the lounge, leaving their luggage in the foyer. As a new boy it was my duty to shake hands and drink beers while all these people established how well they knew each other and didn't know me.

At Parliament House the next day, in the corridors and small rooms where the 'bureaus' were, there was now an impression of people as well as of cheap, shabby furniture, while, in the broad spaces below, the politicians were announcing their *camaraderie*. When the House of Representatives met, all the journalists were in the press gallery to hear Ben Chifley proclaim as prime minister that, with victory in the war, the ideals of democracy had triumphed, and the great task had now begun of bringing freedom and lasting peace to a war-weary world: in thanksgiving, he moved an address of loyalty to the Throne. When that was over, and question time had passed, the important journalists left the press gallery. Reporting parliament was left to junior reporters.

For a month, from Tuesday to Friday, I would sit up on the ledge, look down on the politicians and listen to them with one main interest: how much of this talk could be turned into a *Daily Telegraph* 'story'? Or I would sit behind my typewriter in the *Telegraph*'s small, and now overcrowded, office (three extra reporters had come up for the session) and struggle with getting exactly the right arrangement of words to match the *Telegraph*'s style. On the busiest days, when we worked from ten in the morning until midnight, I might write as many as ten to a dozen 'stories', ranging from a few paragraphs to several columns; the next morning, like a schoolboy getting his essays back, I would go through the *Telegraph* to see how many of my stories had 'got in'. Were some of them cut? Had the subs re-written any of the intros? Had they made nonsense of any of them? I could imagine the scene: the sub, seized with fury against the long-windedness of this untrained Canberra reporter, ferociously whittles away until he gets everything wrong.

I did not meet any of the politicians who floated below me like fish in an aquarium: only senior reporters spoke to the politicians. I could not even see clearly the expressions on their faces. I was watching shadows and listening to echoes. My concern was *Daily Telegraph* style. Sometimes in the lobbies or in one of the public areas of Parliament House I would see one of the politicians: unlike the shadows I turned into the precision of a typed telegram, this person was 'real'. But I did not speak to any of them.

Question Time, with which each parliamentary day began, usually provided several 'stories', since the politicians used Question Time to get 'mentions' in the newspapers. The problem was merely which way to write the intro. The Opposition got the credit if I made my intro:

Canberra, Wed. – Australian scientists from the Army Inventions Board should be sent to Japan to examine Japanese war secrets, Sir Earle Page (CP, NSW) said in the House of Representatives today.

The government got the credit if I made my intro:

Canberra, Wed. – Proposals to send Australian scientists from the Army Inventions Board to examine Japanese war secrets will be examined by the Commonwealth Government, the Prime Minister (Mr Chifley) said in the House of Representatives today.

Through the tedium of hours of political point-making after Question Time, the mind partly switched off, but an automatic scanner waited for the sensational – a charge story, perhaps (CHARGES AGAINST HIGH OFFICERS), or an 'incident' (MEMBER SUSPENDED AFTER WILD SCENES), or at least a snatch of dialogue to be used as part of the repertoire of imitations with which to amuse people at a party.

One 'incident' exploded so loudly that it went on echoing. John Dedman, who as Minister for the War Organisation of Industry had already become a threatening figure, said in an excited moment one night: 'The Commonwealth Government is concerned to provide adequate and good housing for the workers. *It is not concerned with making the workers little capitalists.*' We hurried off to our typewriters: for once, a real story had come out of parliament. The next day Dedman tried to explain that he hadn't really meant what he had said, or that what he had said wasn't what he had meant: 'I believe in the right of every head of the family in this country to own his own home,' he assured us. This earned him more noisy headlines: DEDMAN'S SOCIALIST PLAN ATTACKED.

IN DEDMAN'S ONE SENTENCE THE OPPOSITION HAD ACQUIRED material for several elections.

Apart from pure blather, for the most part what was being enacted in parliament was the relaxing of a wartime administration and the beginning of a peace administration, but in four weeks only one new idea emerged which I might use in our book. An Opposition speaker said there were hundreds of thousands of possible immigrants in the refugee camps. For the *Telegraph* this provided a story with the heading LIFETIME OPPORTUNITY FOR MASS MIGRATION, and for me it provided the idea that I could write an angry piece in our book about how the government had failed to consider this kind of policy. In all the noise my only other personal interest was to keep an ear out for examples of illiberalism. An opposition member said radio stations should be prevented from broadcasting 'sensational murder serials' and Calwell, the Information Minister, replied: 'The serials generally emanate from large networks. Perhaps we shall have to smash the networks.' That got in, with the heading: MHR OBJECTS TO RADIO MURDER. In a debate on the new diplomatic service an Opposition member said there should be an emphasis on 'English-speaking countries and particularly the British Empire'. ('Although the United States is an English-speaking country, it is not an English-thinking country.') That got in. In the same debate he said: 'The foulest thing in the world is a cocktail party.' That got in. An Opposition member wanted more censorship of 'cheap cowboy films, serials and musicals' and a Labor minister agreed that films harmed the 'welfare of young people'. That got in. I felt that by this kind of reporting I was still displaying the critical spirit.

When reporting long 'debates' I took some tradesmanlike satisfaction in boiling each speech down to two or three paragraphs so that this was done 'fairly' (each side getting an equal share of space) but with diversity of subject matter.

The very 'objectivity' and 'fairness' of the *Daily Telegraph* style meant that the reporting of parliamentary 'debates' had to be untrue: my reporting would have been more true if the *Telegraph* had let me write prose sketches as I did for *Arna*. I reflected on how correct I was, when making notes for our book, in saying that the most serious distortion in newspaper reporting of parliament was that it made MPs seem better than they were. But, after a month, I had not written any of the book.

TWELVE

A life of mutual independence

I had still imagined that the centre of my world was an apartment in Sydney, where a tall blonde sat on a couch beneath some casement windows, with a typewriter on the coffee table in front of her, and a cup of Turkish coffee beside her as she wrote me amusing letters. But I was now receiving letters of desperation (if still written in an easy conversational style), typed on an office typewriter when some boss wasn't looking, telling me how hateful she found the ways she was earning a living. In one letter: 'It was so bad yesterday that for very pain and sorrow, I wept.' In the next she spoke of 'this sodden state I am in'. In the next she was renewed, because she had been to her dentist: 'I have a great mouth full of teeth. Hundreds of them. All filled.' But, in the next: 'In a sort of way I wish I were dead, you know that.' I didn't know that.

I had kept all of her letters and now I took them out and re-read them. What had mattered about them before was that they were from her – I could imagine her face, in profile, thoughtful, as she wrote them: it was as if I were sitting on the couch beside her – and their general tone was so light and friendly, as if we were chatting over an orange juice, that I hadn't noticed how unhappy she had been with her temporary (and absurd) job. As I read them through again I could see that in a year when I had become a journalist without intending to, she had been passed from office to office, wanting a sensible kind of journalist's job, and failing. After a period of high expectancy, she had seen an executive in one publishing firm but all he had offered was a job in 'social'; there was talk of a position as sub-editor on a magazine with another organisation but the vacancy they had expected did not occur; for two months her hopes were kept up by suggestions of an offer from another firm; when the offer came it was again only a job in 'social'. Now there was talk of sub-editorship on a small magazine in which she wasn't interested.

As I read over these letters, I could hear her speaking her favourite words and phrases and this brought up images of sitting beside the casement window looking at the plane trees outside, or admiring a book of painting reproductions, or watching the pouring of a smooth mayonnaise over the avocado, or putting a Sibelius record on the record-player, or buying smoked eel at the delicatessen, or making fun of economics. Now I was to imagine her as a person with problems. How could I imagine that? I had seen her as someone with 'self assurance': it was she who was supposed to teach me about the ways of the city. And if, as she feared, a large part of the small world of Sydney publishing was closed to her because of some vindictive action of Brian Penton's, what could I do about a matter as complex as that? Had we been part of the society of Paris or St Petersburg in a nineteenth-century novel, on the other hand, I would have been on my home ground.

As I read through the letters again, I heard something else, something I hadn't noticed before, or had chosen not to notice – a silence. There was a constant sprinkling of what I imagined to be cocktail party endearments, but there was scarcely a word about me. To the kind of self-examining letters I had sent Rhodes and Miller from Darwin she had replied in one cool sentence: 'You enumerate your faults with distressing frankness.' Her reply to a long letter on what I self-deprecatingly called 'luv' was again only one sentence: 'People want emotional and economic continuity.' I had written a letter saying that if a chance remark about 'emotional maturity' had been intended as a criticism of me, then here was my reply. No answer. I had read the love verse in her slim volumes: why, in her letters, was there nothing more than the affectionate tone of a good-humoured friend, a manner she used with everyone? In her last letter she had said, in passing, 'I think I will go to England in March. Why don't you come?' What on earth was in her mind that she should say a thing like that, in passing? Why was she speaking of the future at all? The future was unknown. Surely she didn't expect me to speak of the future when I knew all about the paradox of unintended consequences and the vanity of human wishes. The future was an illusion. What frightened me was not that she spoke of a future with or without me, but that she spoke of a future at all.

In my last week at Canberra I had felt like a character in a Chekhov play: I was 'in love', but I was only 'liked' in return. But back in Sydney, after parliament rose, we were together again, apparently with equanimity. There was a new range of anecdotes to tell, about Canberra, with amusing imitations of politicians; I could buy books with some of the money I had saved; she was thinking, after all, that she might go back to writing her verse play. Soon it would be summer and we could lie on the beach. Then I could start writing my book. To be 'Chekhovian' it would be necessary for me to burst out, desperately, with expressions of love, to which I would receive merely cool, if kind, replies. None of that. However, she did say that we must talk seriously. We did. At least she did. She said she was an independent person: I had no rights over her. (*Of course, of course. I knew all about that. I believed in the equality of women. Why bother to say that?*) I mustn't imagine I owned her. (*Me imagine that! I had been secretary of the Freethought Society!*) And I mustn't treat the flat as if I owned it. (*Own it! Ownership was theft!*) Laughter. Light kisses. Chekhov seemed excessively theatrical.

AT THE *DAILY TELEGRAPH*, AS I ARRIVED EACH AFTERNOON IN THE enormous room, there was still the feeling that I was a 'new boy'. What would the Chief of Staff turn me into today? There were still the artificialities of an imposed literary style in which all the words were rationally and mechanically and exactly arranged, with the result that what was written might be accurate, but could never be true. And there were still the embarrassments of dealing with strangers – trying to get the spelling of their names right, getting their ages, turning them into a 'story'. I had gained a reputation for having mastered the office style and was given a number of handouts to translate: this despised task pleased me – it kept me away from strangers.

I was still given light stories (RACE MEETING DELAYED FOR BURIAL ... WAITING BUS PASSENGERS USE UMBRELLA TO KEEP OFF SOOT) but they also gave me intellectual stories (REJECTION OF PORTRAIT ANGERS ARTIST ... POEMS IN 'HERMES' ARE BOGUS) and I had been allowed to meet one politician, an old Minister with trembling hands and a shaking head. I saw him regularly and he provided 'running stories' on Australian angles on the Indonesian struggle against the Dutch and on the future of the Australian coal industry. As I sat opposite him at his desk and tried not to stare at his tremblings, or rang him, looking for a follow-up to a handout, but not being quite sure what he was saying, I had the feeling, for the first time, that there might be some sense in what I was doing.

As soon as I had got back to Sydney, I had been brought down to earth with a 'shopping story': SHORTAGE OF VEGETABLES TO CONTINUE. But I liked the methodical nature of 'round-ups' like this, even if all one was rounding up were the prices of peas and beans, cauliflowers, cabbages and lettuce. When the workers at the main Sydney power house went on strike, I was delighted with the orderliness of doing the 'round-ups' on the effects of this strike. I felt that I had a Zolaesque vision of the complexity of a great modern city. For three days the headlines rolled on. First day: MOST RETAIL STORES MAY SHUT. BUTCHERS SEEK EXEMPTION FROM ELECTRICITY RATIONING. Then: ELECTRICITY RATIONING WILL HOLD UP SHIPPING, ALTER CITY LIFE. The climax: HOW POWER CUTS AFFECTED CITY. DIM OUTS SLOW MOST BUSINESS: LAMPS, CANDLES, TAKE SYDNEY BACK CENTURIES. I was pleased, in particular, with how 'concrete' I had made one intro:

> Sydney bought and sold, made out its accounts, ate its meals, had its hair cut, and generally carried out its business yesterday as best it could by kerosene lamp and candlelight.

On the day I was to write this story, I had said that I would spend the night with my parents (I would 'go home' now and again like this – it showed I didn't think I owned the flat) – but by the time the subs had made their last checks and put all the crossheads into the story I was too tired to spend twenty minutes in a train, after perhaps already waiting twenty minutes at the underground station. Instead, I caught a taxi to her flat, let myself in with the key she had given me, and found her in bed with an officer from the British navy.

It occurred to me later that the way I acted was more Dostoevskyan than Chekhovian. I did not shout love, but yelled out that her poetry was flat in tone and belonged to the wrong school ... that verse plays on radio were a bore ... that she talked too much ... that there was more to life than a good mayonnaise. I turned on the naval officer and bellowed out to him what her age was, then grabbed her passport from the drawer where she kept it and flung it at him so that he could see for himself. The act of throwing was pleasant: I opened a window and tossed out his cap, then jerked the window up as far as it would go and howled into the night, telling the neighbours her exact age. Then I left.

TREMBLING WITH SHOCK, AND MY MOUTH DRY FROM SHOUTING, as I walked the streets I was sobbing, in my mind, but I kept my hands in my pockets and tried to sustain the easy-going pace of someone who, off-hand, had decided to take an after-midnight stroll. After midnight! Where would I sleep? She and I shared a friend – a kind and amusing raconteur who, in some way I didn't understand, made a living out of films, and whom we assumed was a closet homosexual: he would do. I knocked on the door of his flat until he woke up, drank coffee, moved from the angers and sorrows of an implacable pique to the beginnings of tolerance for human folly, then with the first traces of dawn settled down on a couch in his sitting room and slept. I breakfasted with a hangover from grief and went to work in yesterday's shirt.

As I sat in the tram I felt I had been up all night mourning my own death, but I was busy at the *Telegraph*. It was not until eleven o'clock that I left the office with my ears ringing from the headlines: MANPOWER CONTROLS LIFTED and NEW COAL PLAN TARGET: STABILITY, JOBS – and returned to our friend's flat, found not only my suitcase, but her.

We continued our life together, but this time I promised: it was to be a life of mutual independence. When I met the naval officer again at a party, after a conversation about Proust we at once became brothers in literature and for the rest of the evening tested ourselves on novel after novel, taking turns in putting them up and arguing about what each one 'had to say'. It was as enjoyable as writing letters from Darwin. At the end of the party he agreed that my earlier performance had been more Dostoevskyan than Chekhovian.

At work, I wrote stories about Canadian war brides in Sydney, about uniform charges for telephones, the need for more libraries, cures for inflation, the restoration of the post office tower, the turning of munitions factories into peacetime workshops, the first peacetime Melbourne Cup. When I was with her I now saw it was true that I was 'in love' with a woman who merely 'liked' me. But we didn't speak any Chekhovian lines. I didn't know what to say about this. I said nothing. Was even 'like' the right word? Was I now simply a nuisance? Was she slowly getting rid of me in a kindly way? When our friend in the film business invited us, with some others, to a special showing of *Casablanca* and *The Maltese Falcon*, I saw myself as a Peter Lorre figure, an odd bod, an outsider. That would be Dostoevskyan. But I wasn't Dosteovskyan.

This period of reconciliation lasted a fortnight.

Another argument ... another storming out. This time I took my suitcase, and, from the door, threw her the key.

Farewell drinks several days later in the lounge at Ushers. 'We'll stay good friends.' 'See you around.'

PART 4

THE MAKING OF A JOURNALIST
1945–49

THIRTEEN

Someone who lived near the Cross

1

For the next few weeks I was trying to change myself into someone who did not 'live with a woman' and in this turnabout I wasn't sure which novels to consult. I had not been interested in what novels had to 'say' about love, except where love seemed part of some socially interesting obsession, but there were some passages one might look up – in the Stendhal novels, for example (would Balzac also be useful?). However, my books were at my parents' house, in a new bookcase my father had built as part of his occupational therapy, and at a time of crisis such as this I could not be expected to retreat to something as banal as going home. I moved into a second-rate bed-and-breakfast place, down from Kings Cross, and lived out of a suitcase as if I were there only overnight. After a couple of weeks, I left, to go to another rooming house, equally second-rate, moving for no reason except that it made a change. My circumstances now seemed so slovenly (no originals on the walls, no orange juice, no mayonnaise, no record-player) that I again began to see myself as Dostoevskyan, particularly when (although cockroaches were common in these parts of Sydney) I saw cockroaches in my bedroom. Then, as day by day at the *Telegraph* I wrote about dairymen's strikes, or new ration scales for clothing, or the development of helicopters, or delays in meat deliveries, I began to seem more like one of those quiet, set-upon characters in an Evelyn Waugh novel whose passivity provided a basis for the springing into action of others.

Flats were hard to get, and in any case in February I would be back, with my suitcase, in Canberra. I hired rooms in the outskirts of the Cross in two more bed-and-breakfast lodgings and felt demeaned. At parties, I would try to stay overnight, or go home to someone else's place. For several brief episodes I shared a flat. Sometimes I would spend a few days at home with my parents; it was pleasant to be with my books, but I would find the train journey at night after work not only boring but frightening, since I was passing through that long, dark nightmare of the suburbs to which I did not wish to return. At the *Telegraph* I would sit in the enormous room and write, in short, easy-to-read paragraphs, about what had been chosen as the affairs of that day; and the next morning I would see it there in the paper, in black and white, supported by the authority of headlines (UNION SUSPENDS BRANCH LEADERS ... BUS OWNERS WANT TO RAISE FARES ... MARRIED WOMEN FIRST TO BE DISMISSED ... HOLIDAY RESORTS BOOKED OUT) as if it had not been written by a propertyless twenty-three-year-old of failed ambition, carrying his suitcase between bed-and-breakfast joints.

I saw myself as someone who, although a 'reporter', remained detached from what he was creating by his 'reporting', and was even more detached from his readers. When I had been at the university, to distinguish myself from those who spoke of 'the good of the people' in a patronisingly authoritarian manner, I used an expression of patronising tolerance: 'If the people want to make fools of themselves – let them.' This expression was revived, to express tolerance towards the foibles of the readers of the *Daily Telegraph*. In this, the anecdote of how I had spent Christmas dinner became important.

When there was a call for two reporters with no family connections for day shift on Christmas Day I put my name down, although I did not know that the reporter with whom I was to spend the morning alone in the enormous room would prove to be the office's second most persistent monologuist. After we had rung around the surf lifesaving clubs to find out the beach attendance figures and finished the morning's work by telephoning the two main women's hospitals to dig out a human interest story on a baby born on Christmas Day, we went to a faintly lit basement restaurant where there were only four other customers, put paper caps on our heads and, as the monologuist soliloquised on the meaninglessness of existence, ate course after course of the restaurant's fixed-price Christmas dinner. At the appropriate time we snapped open the Christmas crackers and withdrew whistles from them, which we did not blow.

When I met one of my old acquaintances I would use this parable as a way of describing my present condition. As reporters we had done our duty: we had written our story SYDNEY SPENDS FIRST PEACE CHRISTMAS AT HOME; we had put on our party caps and, course by course, eaten our dinner. But we did not have to blow our whistles.

Now that I was again wearing a double-breasted suit I could also see symbols of detachment in my clothes. Double-breasted suits had been banned by the government during the war because they used too much cloth. (In any case, they were somewhat decadent: members of the government all wore single-breasted suits; as diplomatic cadets we had been told that the Minister saw double breasted suits as un-Australian.) When I had been discharged from the army I had bought a single-breasted suit, with a waistcoat, in a respectable navy blue, an outfit so polite that after I resigned as a diplomatic cadet I left it hanging in the wardrobe in my parents' house and assumed I might never wear it again. Now I could wear to the office a light-grey double-breasted suit, and although sometimes I would look down and feel uneasy about the stripe that ran through it, I knew that while I might be writing 'stories' about the effects of the coal strike or the steel strike, I would no more proclaim conformity by wearing a single-breasted navy blue suit with a waistcoat than I would wear a hat.

I SAW MYSELF AS SOMEONE WHO WAS NOW A NATURAL DWELLER within the inner city, with the suburbs a threatening dream. It was only a short tram ride 'into town' or, in the other direction, out to Redleaf, a sharkproof-netted swimming enclosure in the harbour, seen as being somewhat 'continental'. The area between Redleaf and 'town' seemed all that one really need know of Sydney. On working days I would usually read in the morning, perhaps lying around in bed with Flaubert, or sunning myself at Redleaf with Thomas Mann, or taking Turgenev to a coffee shop. I would lunch at 'the Cross', alone or with one of the new friends I had made that month. Then by tram 'into town' to 'report' on whatever it was I was to 'cover' that day.

The two days per week I had off might fall during the week, sometimes inconveniently, so that there was no one to share the daytime with, but if I worked on Saturdays it was on the day shift and I could go to one of the big

Saturday night parties – bottle parties, sometimes in an older apartment with three or four rooms of shabby 1920s furniture, more usually in one of the smaller, newer flats, perhaps in one small, crowded room furnished in 1930s *moderne*. Sometimes I knew the person throwing the party; sometimes I was taken to a stranger's place by some stranger. What remained constant were the bottles (with shortages, they were still hard to get) – at the beginning of the party stacked on a table, full; by the end of the party scattered around, with late stayers holding them up looking for one last drink. On Sunday mornings there were hangovers and always that re-settling of views of human relations which followed the wildness of a Saturday night.

On days off, or at Saturday night parties, as someone who lived at, or near, the Cross I would usually wear a sweatshirt, old trousers and – sometimes – sandals; to this extent, I was ready to be part of the self-assured 'informality' of the Cross, but I also found it necessary to feel detached from the Cross. I saw its illegal nightclub, the Roosevelt, as a place for suckers and racketeers and its theatre, the Minerva, as edging towards the pretentious. Because they were run by European refugees, the delicatessens and continental restaurants were the real thing but the other eating places, with American items on their menus, were leftovers from 'the American invasion' when the Cross had been the favoured area of American soldiers on leave. The surviving 1920s Bohemians of the Cross, if not plain 'ratbags', appeared, at the best, *passé*, and some of its new residents could seem 'phonies' who didn't really belong, or 'spivs' who had done well out of the black market. It was pleasant, however, to be able to walk down the streets lined with trees, awnings and coffee shops, where people could be seen even on a Sunday morning and where there were high, old terrace houses with cast-iron balconies, fashionable apartment houses, narrow jerry-built blocks of flats and an occasional mansion of one of the rich – although not one suburban house, or one suburban garden.

Kings Cross was the principal ritual centre for the festivals of New Year's Eve and on New Year's Eve I had to report the 'revelries' at the Cross (GAYEST REVELS SINCE 1938). Among drunks, voyeurs and show-offs (30,000 of them by my scoring), I walked around for several hours with notebook and pencil, recording the dancing and singing and looking for 'incidents' to phone through from a friendly coffee shop. With the main story gone, at ten thirty I phoned an additional par: in Springfield Avenue a woman's shoe was torn off and raffled. Near edition time I rang through two more pars: a pair of women's scanties had been thrown over the trolley bus line in Macleay Street; there had been a game of two-up in Victoria Street. After midnight I made the story real by recording the whistles, drums, sirens, foghorns, hootings, singings and kissings with which the New Year had been greeted and phoned all that through. As a last paragraph, at one o'clock, so that I could knock off and go to bed, I telephoned that a naked woman had run across Macleay Street.

With its concern with 'facts' and short paragraphs, any act of reporting was an act of destruction: it took me several days to recover from writing this 'story' about the Cross. At other times, however, the declarations of freedom made at the Cross could seem such invitations to conformity that if I went out for a coffee I would protect my individuality by wearing a tie. I preferred the harbourside outskirts of the Cross: Potts Point, Elizabeth Bay, Rushcutters Bay. Walking down Billyard Avenue in sweatshirt and sandals on a sunny day, with the harbour glinting between the trees, or sitting in a Macleay Street coffee shop, reading as people passed by, I could imagine, serenely, that I was home at last: I was someone who lived near the Cross.

ONE WAY IN WHICH I HAD LEARNED TO ACCOMMODATE MYSELF to the collapse of my *affaire* had been to talk about some of its most important scenes so often that they could begin to seem as true as something which had happened in a book. My first choice as partner in this literary ritual was our common friend who made his mysterious living from films and in whose apartment I had taken refuge on the night I found my love in bed with a Royal Navy officer; he willingly coaxed me along with reminiscences about broken hearts and piqued *amours propres* and, for other illustrative examples, drew on his great knowledge of the movies: now and again he would smile, and say, 'You know, I love you both very much, but I don't think you have enough in common,' (which itself sounded like a line from a movie). On one of my nights off he invited both of us to dinner. I could see that perhaps I didn't have much in common with this blonde sitting on the other side of the table making amusing conversation, but this was not the woman I had fallen in love with, and the loss of whose company I still regretted so abundantly: this was the way I had feared she might seem to Jim McAuley.

The other person with whom I was able to talk my way out of a sense of privation was the Royal Navy Officer himself. After our conversation about novels, he became, for the next few months, my closest friend. As a reader of Van der Velde's instruction book on sexual techniques he knew that he knew all about sex. His relationship with his girlfriend was a contract in which they were using their bodies like busy engines for pleasure, and for practice he kept a log book recording numbers of times, methods used and degrees of satisfaction. At a time when he thought he was about to return to England, he had himself photographed with his girlfriend in his favourite sexual 'positions' from Van der Velde. The photographer was so drunk, or so excited, that none of the photographs came out. But he also knew all about novels and as someone who seemed to have read even more novels than I, he also knew that he knew the politics of love. In his zealotry for frankness he unrolled for me, in instalments, the entire chronicle of his experiences of sex and of love – but he was sceptical that anyone else might be as honest as he was. 'There you are ducky,' he would say, if he thought he had caught me out in an inconsistency, 'Repression!' Then (fixing me with the stare of the objectively minded scientist): 'Or are you deliberately lying?'

The use of the word 'ducky' was one of his domineering tricks. In a commanding voice, as if he were reading the BBC news, and with his ruling-class manner – a passing stare, as if there were nothing he didn't know, accompanied by a quick smirk of contempt – he would use 'ducky' to men, women, children and, one suspected, ducks as if differences between the rest of us were of no significance. He had been to one of the 'best' public schools in England, and then to an old university (so that the opening part of the chronicle of his sex life was a paradigm of schoolboy and undergraduate homosexual experience). His father was a member of a family whose males had been part of the governing class in four continents. When, as part of his chronicle, he told the story of his engagement, and its breaking off, to a woman who came from a family similar to his own, his descriptions of the misunderstandings of love and of social commitment sounded like an upper-middle-class English novel, but his descriptions of what was also going on, furtively, in their minds, and down below, between their legs, were so exact that I could not think of any parallel in modern English writing to the surreal juxtapositions he made between the outward certainties of English social forms and the uncertainties of English minds and bodies. I told him he must get it all down as he had told it. He had just finished writing a novel, he said, but it was in the allegorical mode. At parties, in the interest of human liberty, he sometimes unbuttoned his fly and exposed his penis, but he had a firm sense of privacy about his novel and would not show me the manuscript.

Both of us were shouters and laughers and, laughing and shouting, we constantly tried to talk each other down. Our conversation was often pushing and shoving, hugely enjoyable, like a rough game (or what I imagined enjoying a rough game might be); monologues were tolerated only if they had been specifically ordered. There was so much 'effortless superiority', as I had learned to call it, in his voice that at times I felt out-gunned by technological know-how – it was as if his was a superior machine gun, and I would have to keep my head down. I would fight on, shouting out whatever vulgarity might get me a hearing, but he was a master of vulgarity too: the battle would continue.

We were both absorbed in the cults of informality. As soon as he got back to his flat after his day's work in the Navy he would be out of his uniform and into old trousers, sandals and open-necked civilian shirt. If it was my day off I might join him in my sweatshirt and old trousers; we seemed to feel at our best walking along the pavements of the Cross, dressed like stage deadbeats, yelling at each other, sometimes in French, laughing at our own jokes, talking psychoanalysis perhaps, or discussing the coming end of the novel. He enjoyed eating so much that when he thought he was to be sent back to London he decided to organise for himself and his girlfriend a weekend of over-eating, as something to remember when he went back to England's short rations. For this purpose he requisitioned the flat and the services of my lost love because she was so skilled at shopping for food, and such a good cook. I had to be there too: a stranger would put him off his excesses. By several lightning attacks he talked both of us into a reconciliation of convenience, to last the weekend. After a grossly large meal, she and I fell, by accident, into such a quick quarrel in bed that she ran to the kitchen for a carving knife. It was only when all four of us were in the kitchen (all, ludicrously, naked) that we recognised how improbable it was that we were behaving like this. At breakfast we had double helpings of everything and the rest of the weekend was spent as the joke it was intended to be.

Several months later he suggested, one dull night, that we raid her flat. Feeling I was taking part in a rag in a novel about Oxford, I climbed up a tree with him, jumped on to a roof and scrambled over it to her casement windows. We looked in. She was sitting on the couch, with some unknown man, just as she used to sit with me.

SOMETIMES WE WOULD PLAY A GAME: *THINK OF A NOVEL. DESCRIBE the actuality of the sex lives of its characters.* But now that I had found someone else for whom novels provided the main lenses through which to imagine reality, novels could seem too serious for games. This was a subject on which we must get as much as we could out of each other before he went back to London. When we talked about novels, we were deciding existence.

There was, however, one game we played – it went on for most of a night – which seemed to settle things for me for years ahead:

Which are the world's six greatest novels?

He gave me the right to make the first nomination: I began so badly that he almost disqualified me from the game. I had read Turgenev's *A Nest of Gentlefolk* in the army, and taken to its laconicism – I saw myself as a 'superfluous man'; now I had just finished *Fathers and Sons* and the character of Bazarov had seemed so 'real' that in the middle of the last paragraph (which I was reading in a coffee shop) only the quiet optimism of the concluding sentences suppressed my tears. I didn't want any optimism, however quiet. Anyway, there it was: my first nomination – *Fathers and Sons*.

This announcement produced a storm as great as if I had made a speech defending virginity. *If I wasn't going to play the game properly, we wouldn't play it at all! I couldn't be serious, surely?* Fathers and Sons *was not one of the world's greatest novels. It was one of the world's greatest minor novels.* I admitted that I had absentmindedly been taken over by my latest enthusiasm, withdrew my first nomination and then played a card that surely could not be challenged: *War and Peace*! To my surprise, he played, in opposition, *Anna Karenina*.

I had not read *Anna Karenina*. But wasn't that beside the point? Which novel could be better than *War and Peace*? I made my speech, lining up the evidence, beginning with what I saw as the superb presentation of the role of the great man as one who could preside over events with grace, giving them meaning, and then ending with the claim that in any case in all literature *War and Peace* was the most ambitiously successful creation of a whole society, wasn't it? If he didn't agree with that I would make the game unplayable by claiming my favourite Shakespeare work, *Henry IV, Parts I and II*, as one of the world's six greatest novels (as, in fact, I sometimes thought it was).

He accepted *War and Peace* and then made the first of his own nominations: *The Brothers Karamazov*. I found this unexpectedly embarrassing: I hadn't read a Dostoevsky novel since I was an undergraduate, and in my mind the themes of the various novels had run together into one great novel called Dostoevsky in which what really mattered was the kind of reality he created, in which the 'fantastic' was normal. Okay, yes, *The Brothers Karamazov*. As good as any other.

My turn: *Buddenbrooks* – as a huge, complex, ironic construction of bourgeois reality, with extra marks to Mann for producing a lifetime's work at the age of twenty-four. (I was now twenty-four! And proud of *By a Special Reporter*.) From him, another deluge of abuse: *Bullshit! What about* The Magic Mountain, *for Christ's sake?* (For me, what was most remarkable about *The Magic Mountain* was that I hadn't read it, and while one might at least pretend to be humiliatingly honest in talking about sex, being honest about not reading a novel was far more difficult.) I played as hard as I could the themes of *Buddenbrooks*, but he pressed *The Magic Mountain* harder than I could resist. I suggested a compromise: why not both *The Magic Mountain* and *Buddenbrooks? Bullshit again!* Too many others to fit in! We decided to leave the question unsettled. (And I decided to buy *The Magic Mountain* as soon as I could. I had seen it at the English and Foreign Bookshop in a Modern Library edition.)

His turn: *Remembrance of Things Past*. My turn: *Ulysses*. No argument about either, although we did squabble about our reasons for putting *Remembrance of Things Past* on the list. I said I chose it because of its filleting of 'character', its presentation of how social reality constantly shifted and changed like weather, its understanding of the complex geometry of shifting social circles, its great set-piece descriptions of the politics of social intercourse, from a duchess's reception to the putting on of a hat, its treatment of rumour, fashion, deception and the idiocies of conversation. Yes, yes, yes, he knew all about that. He was using his most impatiently sarcastic voice. (He had been listening to me for a long time.) But what about its unsurpassed treatment of the politics of love? I said I found those passages boring. That's obvious, he said, and digressed to present, as ruthlessly as he could, an analysis of my lost love in Proustian terms.

His turn: *Sentimental Education*. This gave me my most disturbed moment. Although I had not read *Anna Karenina* or *The Magic Mountain*, I knew that I would do so; but not only had I not read *Sentimental Education* – I didn't know that it was a book one was supposed to have read. (Where had I seen it? In the Roycroft Bookshop, in an Everyman's Library edition. Another book to buy.) I played *Madame Bovary* in reply, as a study of the banal, illuminated by style. This time he became angry at once. *Sentimental Education* must be on the list. He punched me with reasons, demanding answers. Since the case for *Madame Bovary* was not as obvious as the case for *War and Peace* I gave in, and agreed to put on the list of the world's six greatest novels a third novel which, in fact, I had not read.

With digressions, expositions, and personal abuse, we had already gone on past midnight. We added up the score – six novels. Anyone missing? We ran over names. (We had agreed in advance there were no English or United States novelists worth putting on the list: that had saved time.) Stendhal, for God's sake! We had forgotten Stendhal!

Talking about Stendhal was a simple self-indulgence in which we congratulated ourselves on our mutual agreement; we were two people telling the same anecdotes about the same place even though we had been there separately. Another hour had gone. We had chosen the seven books which were the world's six greatest novels.

It had been one of the most enjoyable conversations of my life.

2

Altogether, I was to spend five months, from October to February, living near the Cross before going 'back' (as I now thought of it) to Canberra. Five months! Passing so quickly! A month wasn't a long time any more. And five months in which, five days a week, the essential underpinning of normality was to arrive in the enormous room, usually at two p.m., and sign the duty book, then wait to be called by the Chief of Staff to discover what particular form reality would take that day, and at the end of a shift to write into the duty book the time at which I had knocked off, how long I had taken for a meal and the total number of hours worked, less mealtime. If I saw old friends at Ushers I told them I was measuring out my life in the duty book.

The whole five months was spent on 'general reporting'. In the duty book each day were recorded the names of those doing specialist reporting. All of these specialists worked in their own cubicles, as did the 'Sporting Department' and, somewhere else in the building, the 'Features Department', the 'Pictorial Department', the 'Finance Department' and the 'Social Department'. The only people with no area of their own were the general reporters and the messengers, who sat on a long form near the Inquiry Desk, waiting for a bell to ring so that they would know what they were to do next.

The slips of paper that told me what to do next did not provide any consistent meaning. 'Light' stories seemed to have gone out of favour in the *Telegraph* that summer. Occasionally I was sent out to 'do a quiz', in which I would ask five or six people the same question. (For example: 'How would you beautify Sydney?') If they couldn't think of their own replies I would suggest answers, then the photographer would take pictures of the people I had 'interviewed', to show that their answers were real. For the several weeks of the 'great strike wave' at the end of 1945 I was put on to 'round-ups' (CANDLES FOR CHRISTMAS ... TRAINS CUT TO ESSENTIAL SERVICES ... 200 HOSPITAL PATIENTS DISCHARGED). If there were any 'university stories' I was given them and I did what I saw as more than my fair share of 'weather stories'. On 14 January 1946, as I walked up to the tram to go into town, I saw outside the newsagent's shop that day's *Daily Telegraph* poster: HUNDREDS FLEE FLOODS! My story! The first time a story of mine had 'made the poster'!

I had come to feel, more or less, that I was part of the general camaraderie of journalists – not only being shoved and shouted at in the bars in the rush hour before the pubs shut at six, or eating quick, furtive meals in cheap cafés, or suffering politely long, boring end-of-the-night soliloquies during a lull in the enormous room, but also being a person some of whose friends were journalists – particularly Rita Dunstan's set which, since it included women, drank not in bars but in hotel lounges, where one could hear what was being said.

I enjoyed ironic conversations with the cartoonist George Molnar about the paradoxes of 'planning', even if he displayed his irony with Hungarian whimsy rather than Australian sardonicism, but he was the principal person who provided what I saw as a chance for intellectual conversation. With the others, it was more likely to be office gossip (which was a safe vehicle for scepticism and wit) or politics (which wasn't – because in politics one had to avoid sounding 'a boss's man'). The *Telegraph*'s editorials thundered against 'planning' and that suited me; but it seemed impossible to make fun of 'planning' without a dash of philosophical anarchism. Yet I couldn't do that in a hotel bar: so how could I make fun of 'planning' without sounding a 'boss's man'?

At times, 'politics' was reduced to one particular question: why had Brian Penton sold out? I had not seen Penton since he had hired me, except from a distance on the few occasions when I was on late stop and he came into the subs' room just before midnight to hold his re-cast conference, but for all of us the *Telegraph* breathed Penton – its attempt to make itself clear to its readers, its policy of educating as well as entertaining, its professed liberalism and dislike of humbug – and now its increasing irascibility with 'planners', 'government muddlers' and the 'self-defeating irrationalities' of striking unionists. We all knew the legends of Penton as a young rebel in the 1930s – wearing sandals and a beret to civic receptions in Sydney and even, it was rumoured, gold, pirate-style earrings, living in Spain on bread, cheese and cheap red wine as he wrote one of his novels, roistering with an Australian bohemian left-wing set in London. Why had he now become a boss's man? This was a question asked even by the right-wingers on the staff. Among the left-wingers – Labor supporters, as well as Stalinists and fellow-travellers (one could not be sure which were which; there were rumours of a Communist Party cell in the *Telegraph* itself) – Penton embodied one of the greatest puzzles of the age: how could an intelligent person not continue to support the ideas of the left? That Penton had been bought out seemed the only rational answer.

As I moved with my suitcase from one second-rate lodging to the next, I was unlikely to be accused of being bought out, but in political conversations with leftwing journalists I would sometimes change shape and colour. Just laugh or nod, instead of disagreeing. Crack a joke, or express cynicism about something or other. Tell an anecdote. Switch to office gossip. Seeing myself as a new boy only pretending to be a journalist, in almost everything I did I was anxious to conceal my own fraudulence. One honest word from me, and they would discover I wasn't a journalist at all.

It was when I saw old friends that I became a journalist. At Ushers bar, and other places where old friends or, increasingly, surrogate friends still met, I was, of course, anxious to pick old fights, but now I couldn't choose my ground. I was likely to be forced away from lecturing on the frauds of representative government and be pushed instead into talking about the *Daily Telegraph*. Instead of listening to what I had to say on Jean-Jacques Rousseau, friends would ask questions about Packer (whom I had never seen) or Penton (whom I saw only rarely and remotely). Those who had remained on the traditional left would attack *Telegraph* editorials and headlines, *Telegraph* criticisms of the government and *Telegraph* reporting of strikes. Andersonians who knew all about the authoritarian nature of modern 'progress' and 'planning' might nevertheless mock the *Telegraph*'s vulgarity or, alternatively, mock its attempts to 'educate the public' or, perversely (and worst of all) praise the *Telegraph* for the wrong reasons. Friends who had married and settled down with careers might compliment me on my unexpected maturity in learning how to take the rough with the smooth: frankly, they didn't know I had it in me. Whatever was said, I was expected to see myself as personally identified by the *Daily Telegraph*, so that while at the *Telegraph* itself I did not feel a real journalist, when I was away from the *Telegraph* and wishing to escape from it, my friends forced me into belonging to it.

AS A 'PHILOSOPHICAL ANARCHIST' I HAD NO CONCERN THAT, IN the reporting of the 'wave of strikes', the unions were coming through unsympathetically. The unionists weren't worker–producers trying to control their own workplaces and liberate the creative spirit. They were just consumers, concerned with making more money so that they could buy more things in a society devoted to commodity fetishism. Anyway, most of the striking unions were controlled by Stalinists. But I had some concern when I was sent north in an office car with a photographer to one of the large camping grounds at Lake Macquarie, a holiday area south of Newcastle, where some of the striking Hunter Valley coal miners were already settling in for Christmas. For one thing, the *Telegraph* was so unpopular that the miners might mistake me for a boss's man and not speak to me, or might even do me some harm. (I got out of the car before we reached the camp and told the photographer to go off by himself and get his pictures, hoping that this might draw their fire.) For another: my grandfather had been a miner and my father had been born in a pit village in the Hunter. Doing 'round-ups' by telephone about the effects of strikes was a matter for detachment; talking to actual miners seemed too real.

I had a splendid day, moving from one tent to the next, passing myself off as someone who was writing a 'holiday story' and mentioning, at appropriate moments, that my grandfather had been a miner. I got it all down – how the miners brought their camp furniture, including beds, tables, ice chests, radios, chairs and even horse-hair couches, how there was plenty of beer in the hotels, plenty of fish in the lake, and good SP betting facilities, how a number of the miners arrived in their own cars. Some sympathetic human interest was added: on Christmas Day whole tents of families would unite for dinner and camp concerts would be arranged. But, so that no one would miss the point, I got a 'good quote' from one of the miners: 'There aren't any gas or electric light or power rationing worries here.'

It seemed my most successful day in journalism. I had gone out to see something for myself and I had been allowed to describe it in something like my own way. Not really my own way. Because it was a 'news story' and not a 'feature' it still had to be expressed in short, simple, single-sentence paragraphs, written that evening, whereas 'feature writers' were allowed slightly longer paragraphs with slightly more complex syntactical structure, and to do one of their pieces they were usually given several days. Nevertheless it was more my own thing than anything else I had done for the *Telegraph*, and the next day, beneath the headings MINERS SETTLE IN XMAS CAMPS. CANVAS TOWNS SPRING UP ON LAKE MACQUARIE there appeared, in italics, four words that marked one of the highest honours the *Telegraph* could pay to a news story: *By a Special Reporter*.

SOME DAYS LATER I WAS SENT SOUTH, IN ANOTHER OFFICE CAR, AND again with a photographer, to Warrawong, a suburb of Wollongong, where there was a strike at the steelworks: I was to write another 'special report', this time on a children's Christmas party at which, despite (it was said) Stalinist union opposition, the children of both strikers and non-strikers would get Christmas presents at a common ceremony. I got there early and was taken to the nearest pub by a striking steelworker who filled me with beer and facts. The toys – dolls, tanks, trains, tommy-guns, prams – had been made in the last six weeks by strikers on the Warrawong Christmas Tree Committee and then painted by a one-armed invalid pensioner. Although the lollies and twenty gallons of soft drinks were 'white', Santa Claus's costume was 'black', because it had been lent by a steelworks manager, and the sledge he would arrive in was 'black' because it had been made on steelworks property; the horse, however, was 'white' – it had been lent by a local farmer. The show would be put on in the Warrawong Hall where, to beat the power restrictions, the lights and the microphone would be run off batteries.

By the time I got back to the steelworker's brick 'cottage' (I had begun to put the Australian usage into quotes, because I now knew that the English gave the word a different meaning) my whole body was fizzing with beer and my mind seemed awash. However, I had kept my notes scrupulously dry and after we had eaten our steak 'tea' (another Australian usage I now put in quotes) I sobered up enough to remember where I had put them. At the Warrawong Hall, as my steelworker host introduced me to some of the 350 'kiddies', he nudged me now and again, indicating which of them were 'black' and which were 'white'. After Santa Claus had arrived in his 'black' sledge driven by his 'white' horse and had begun distributing the toys, they took me to a public telephone and dialled the number for me.

Improvising from my notes as I dictated the simple single sentence paragraphs of a 'story', I became so moved by alcohol in telling this parable of the universality of the Christmas spirit that, between sentences, I several times sobbed into the telephone.

3

I had only just finished reading *The Magic Mountain* before I caught a train down to the country township of Goulburn where a summer school was being held over a holiday weekend; as I sat in the mail train wondering, now that I had read it, whether I believed *The Magic Mountain* was one of the world's six – or seven – greatest novels, I passed through dried Australian landscapes in a heatwave, dusty, and in places smoking from fire like an abandoned battlefield, but my mind was among the fir forests and misty rocks of the Swiss Alps. Above the clattering of the train I could still hear the sheer noise in *The Magic Mountain*, like a series of waterfalls, of all those long, importunate conversations, sometimes lasting for chapters, speaking for a dying Europe, and when I began reporting the summer school ('A White Australia: Australia's Population Problem'), the Australian voices at first seemed thin. But as well as the native-born Australians – mostly professors, lawyers, feminists, 'educationalists', liberal clergymen – there were some 'refugees' who spoke with European voices, if in a subdued tone, as though not wanting to try their luck too hard, and once my mind was adjusted to a more modest pitch, at this three-day conference in an Australian country town where it was so hot that our skin seemed to blister and the hotel bedrooms were like ovens, it could nevertheless seem *The Magic Mountain* all over again: these were still the voices of Europe (even when we lay, for coolness, on the banks of the Wollondilly River).

One of the Australians might have been a character in *The Magic Mountain* itself: W.C. Wentworth, descended from one of colonial Australia's greatest sons, who was on his feet at every discussion, pouring words out in a high 'English' voice, sometimes as sharp critic of sloppy statistics or the misreading of surveys, sometimes as exponent of a brutal *realpolitik*, sometimes as bright ideas man, sometimes as prophet of quinquennial doom. ('In four or five years there must be a world government or there will be no world.') I imagined for a while what it might be like to work for a publication in which I could write an article about this conference as if it were an episode in *The Magic Mountain*.

I kept two sets of notes. One were the snippets that could be turned each day into *Daily Telegraph* stories (Birth control – national need in over-populated countries of Asia ... Australia not defensive outpost of white culture in Oriental world, but cooperative unit in world team ... Need eastern and southern Europeans for immigration ... but many Australians put them in same class as Orientals ... Birth rate will rise only when Australians see sex as merely means to end ... Need for marriage guidance clinics, sex education, community baby-minding services). The other notes were of the key words and phrases used by various speakers. One of them lived in the world of 'on the other hand' and 'it is true that'; another in the world of 'the full cycle of growth' and 'the same rate of increase'; another in the world of 'the rising tide' and 'courting disaster'. It seemed to me that if these words and phrases were put together one could discover, and irrespective of subject, just from style alone, how these people saw the world and what they were 'really saying'. I had no chance of writing such a piece. Perhaps I would simply spend my life keeping two sets of notes, the second of which would never be used?

I spent most of my spare time at the conference talking to Bruce Miller, who was reporting it for the ABC. He didn't have the sense of confused identity I felt among these people in my masquerade as a *Daily Telegraph* reporter. He knew most of the performers, and on the banks of the Wollondilly, at the hotel and at other places where they assembled he would introduce me to them, or at least tell me who they were; in the last session he spoke during the discussion period. Things had changed from the days when I had seemed an intellectual leader: he was speaking of a career that made some sense; my future seemed senseless. Even his clothing seemed sensible: he was in a safari jacket keeping cool, but within convention.

Six weeks later, as I was in the train going back to Canberra for the 1946 parliamentary session, contemplating my life as one who took two different sets of notes, one for the *Daily Telegraph* and one for my own interest, I recognised both that I was sick of being a journalist and that I had no idea of how to earn any other kind of living.

FOURTEEN

'By Donald Horne'

1

During those five months in Canberra I didn't write a paragraph of a novel, but, in its enormous capacity for providing plot and character, drinking was a substitute for novel-writing.

Sometimes the tedium of staying late at Parliament House on a night when parliament wasn't sitting drove us to drink, and there were several drinkers who became legends because they 'got pissed' every night before dinner, but for hard drinkers at the Hotel Civic the time for 'serious drinking' was the weekend. From Friday night to Monday, in bar and lounge, at bottle parties in our rooms or the flats or houses of Canberra friends, a self-contained reality would be constructed in which a new drinking session might begin by telling of the anecdotes of the previous one. When I went to Sydney, as I did, occasionally, for a long weekend or during a parliamentary recess (taking a suitcase of bottled drink with me, each time, because drink was easier to buy at Parliament House than it was in Sydney), I would bring drinking anecdotes from Canberra and exchange them for the latest drinking anecdotes in Sydney.

AS WITH A NOVEL, DRINKING HAD DIFFERENT MOODS WHICH changed according to who the 'characters' were. There were a husband and wife, somewhat older than I, with whom I would quite regularly drink, in the lounge of the Civic; with them I was quiet, steady, rather modest. They would order only small glasses of beer and sip delicately, as if they were professional beer-tasters, so that although, in a night's drinking, we would order and sip and re-order so steadfastly that by the end of the evening we might have drunk ourselves speechless, we had nevertheless done so with great restraint. I felt a significant constraint in their relations with each other, as if they had gone through a catastrophe and re-established, by contract, the conditions under which they would now live together. One rumour was that for a while they had 'split up over his drinking' and that they now drank together to save him from alcoholism. Whatever it was, I found it tranquillising that people could act from an understanding of their own dangers: there was also a perverse reassurance in their being, I suspected, Stalinists or fellow-travellers or at least 'ritualistic progressives'. I had developed a special form of tact for such people if I found them likeable: avoid, absolutely, discussion of the Soviet Union or Stalin, but talk about other matters in a way in which we could indulge, for an hour or two, in the great dream that socialism might not be an illusion.

Drinking with Bill Jenkins was much more a man's affair, carried on with a great deal of shouting and robust joking, but, beneath the noise, with its own subtleties. Bill was big, strong, raw-faced, a journalist from the *Daily Mirror*, a Bondi surfer, a keep-fit man (he several times walked me halfway up Black Mountain), and in Sydney a crime reporter (his brother was a cop) with whom I had shared a bedroom in my first spell at the Hotel Civic where we had at once set up conversational conventions of bluntness and banter, with an unspoken agreement not to 'bullshit each other' and with elements of whimsy that meant we could shout hidden jokes across the Hotel Civic dining room. With Bill, drinking would be done at bottle parties dominated by the forthright manliness of the bottles themselves – so many of them, all standing up so straight – or in the bar, gulping down heavy schooners of gassy beer so quickly I would get the hiccups, and then vomit so that I could continue drinking, as we went on with our zest for a style of conversation that, by limiting itself, might be honest. At one bottle party in a stranger's house, where there was doubt as to whether we had been invited, I was jostled into the backyard by some of the men because I had used 'bad language' in front of women. After they had pushed me down and stood over me, I heard Bill's voice. 'Hey, what are you doing to Don? You know what? I'm going to bash your bloody heads in.' I thought there might be something in the cult of mateship.

Our favoured place for parties was the house of Jack Commins who worked in the press gallery for the ABC, and Joan, his wife, who worked for the *Daily Mirror*; they made a devoted drinking team. Joan Commins was an adept in the art of the send-up (extending it to her presentation of herself), and drinking with her was, for me, an arabesque of satire and fantasy in which we would make up characters and situations and sometimes tease them out, on and off, for a whole evening. Our favourite was to invent a Canberra aristocracy in which we were central members. Some of the characters we invented went into permanent repertoire, so that even when we met in sober work mood in the press gallery corridor we might play a few parts from stock.

If I saw old friends in Canberra, their characters now became defined according to how we drank together. On a night I drank with him in the lobby of the Hotel Canberra Alf Conlon began in his usual drinking style, one of great sincerity as he produced gestures with his glass as reassuring as those he made with his pipe. Discussions were going on about forming a 'national university' in Canberra and, without being definite in any way, Alf seemed to hint that he was central to these discussions even if it were true that he was not, in a formal sense, part of them. After a few drinks he even seemed to be finding a place in this grand design for me: there were half-suggestions – a word with Penton? Editorials? A paragraph? The movements of his glass became less certain: he was talking about General Douglas MacArthur, John Curtin, the winning of the war: now, instead of feeling protected by his benevolence, I felt as if I were alone. With Pritchett, however, drinking had never been more reassuring. On the nights he came to the hotel to have dinner with me we would play chess and sip Madeira: we had reached maturity. I saw us in an oil painting of browns and golds – two men who had reached the autumnal age of twenty-four. A night's drinking with McAuley was full of promise, not because things had changed, but because they had stayed the same. McAuley now had his job at the School of Pacific Administration and a volume of his verse had been published, but he could still drink brandy like a madman, crying out his rage and his fears until blue flames seemed to crackle from his hair. There was also a feeling that things hadn't changed when I had dinner with Jockel (he had married after finishing his diplomatic cadetship and they were living humbly in a shared house): he put drink on the table, but there was a certain reservation in the way in which he served it – even in the way he looked at the bottle that seemed to say to me: *Remember your past excesses and marvel at my moderation.*

OF ANECDOTES TOLD ABOUT THE FAMOUS JOURNALIST-drinkers, the legends of Sid Deamer most held my imagination. He was a liberal who had held significant jobs, so anecdotes about his alcoholic adventures could have moral and even heroic meanings; he was a wit, so anecdotes about him could be enlivened with bitter repartee and smart punchlines; and because he had been an editor the social range of anecdotes was wider – only an editor could have called an editorial conference in the parlour of a fashionable Sydney brothel. When I heard that Sid Deamer had come to Canberra and was at that very moment drinking in the lounge of the Hotel Civic I felt come over me that feeling of *I must meet this man* which I had not felt towards any of the politicians.

He was drinking with one of our groups as merely one among equals. Easy enough to join in. His speech was exactly as it was reproduced in the anecdotes, down to the 'old dears' and 'old darlings' and it came through exactly as I had heard it in the impersonations. Flashing glasses ... sharp eyes ... mobile mouth, welcoming, and then down-turning – dismissive. He was near the end of a long anecdote, told over a small wooden table smothered in beer glasses. He reached the punchline. I thought of an extra wisecrack – a possible twist of the knife. He laughed, leant over, and held my hand in congratulation.

I had attracted the attention of Sid Deamer! Perhaps something might yet come good?

AFTER THE END OF MY *AFFAIRE* IN SYDNEY I HAD AFFECTED A cold approach towards romantic infatuation, passing myself off as one who believed that relations between the sexes were efficiently settled by the regular market adjustments of Saturday night parties (even though these parties often left me entirely unadjusted). At my most imaginative, I saw myself as a male equivalent of a *femme fatale*, a Salammbo of Kings Cross. However, when, at the end of a brief *liaison* with a woman reporter, she said to me, 'Hornie, you have a heart of stone,' I felt injured: how could she make such a shallow observation? At the same time, although our liaison had ended not by design but by a misunderstanding, rather than explain the misunderstanding, I preferred to leave her believing I had a heart of stone.

I was lonely. When I was an undergraduate I would have said, 'I want a woman.' What I needed now was a 'girlfriend'. I found one in the first couple of weeks after being back in Canberra, a woman I met at a party. We were on affectionate terms at the end of our first meeting, and suddenly relations between the sexes seemed pleasantly easy, even normal. I compared everything favourably with my earlier *affaire*: at twenty-three, she was a year younger than I, of no greater social experience and slightly shorter in height; she was writing a novel, but doing it without any fuss. We talked about much the same books and we had the same admiration for Proust (although like the naval officer she was perversely interested in the treatment in *The Remembrance of Things Past* of the politics of love); she discussed my views on social theory with a true intellectual respect (we had a division of intellectual labour: she was intuitive; I was the logician); and she showed, in many ways, that she liked me – at moments of intellectual excitement, hungrily and happily. And our physical relationship was normal in its *milieux*. No enervating life in a comfortable flat. As befitted young people with no place of their own, we snatched our chances where we could.

She was 'foreign'. Her family seemed part of history. As a successful young man, her father had owned a yacht in the Mediterranean: after a revolution in his own country he had escaped and prospered in Canton, where she was born, then sent his wife and daughter to London. She had done her most significant growing up as an impoverished young émigrée of good family in London, meeting her mother's artistic friends, studying drama and ballet, until, just before the war began, the family was reunited and her father brought them out to Australia where he was now living in lessened circumstances. This figure from history, this owner of a yacht in the Mediterranean, was here in a Canberra suburb – a jaunty dresser, with a waxed moustache, his guitar hanging on the wall; at night he would sing old love songs. Her mother would talk a little, laugh, and disappear. They had decided I was very rich.

One morning I arrived at her parents' house and found her in the sitting room, on the floor, surrounded by pages of typescript. With the concentration of a surgeon engaged in a long, complex operation, she was recasting a whole section of her novel. I had arrived earlier than arranged: she was embarrassed and quickly collected the pages together and put them in a drawer. Her novel was not something to talk about lightly: it was something to get on with. But having seen it I began to imagine it, in the drawer where she kept it, growing secretly like a foetus. When she spoke of it at all, she would describe the feel of its growth – its swellings and kickings, as it were – without telling me what she was writing about. But she was happy to tell me who I was and what I should do. She had listened to my anecdotes and imitations – they now made up a considerable body of oral literature – and had decided I should be an Australian Evelyn Waugh: I should write in a 'detached' style, without, however, the traces of distaste that held Waugh's style together. 'Detached' – yes: there were my two *Arna* pieces of two years ago, much praised by friends. But: like Evelyn Waugh? I wanted to be like my 'self'. What would that mean? To put it another way: what did the world 'mean'? My answer was in the language of my grandfather: 'I'm buggered if I know.' Yet using a 'detached' style or any style (and there was no writing without style) would suggest I had an answer.

She was my first novel-writing friend to appear to give thought to what I should write; others were too concerned with their own writing to think about anyone else's and the other friends who urged novel writing on to me were poets and not concerned with the details of an inferior art form. For this reason, what she said about 'my novel' emboldened me, even if it also depressed me when I remembered that I had not, in fact, started writing a novel. What emboldened me without qualification was her analysis of the intellectual differences between us. She saw herself as 'one struggling along a dark path', but I was luminous, quick-witted and clever, with an enlightened 'eighteenth-century mind'. It was a description I liked, especially as it placed me in a century in which I imagined things would have gone well for me – and I wouldn't have been working on the *Daily Telegraph*. She wrote about this to a mutual friend: 'I am going through a terrific anti-romantic Thing inspired by Horne. I have laid aside the flowers and stars of my private world for Horne's ruthless logic – that is, for the time being.'

When we discussed this (I found it a little overdone) I praised the phrase 'for the time being'. That was right: things came and went; nothing was fixed. We then talked about jealousy. She drew on *Remembrance of Things Past* and said she would never be jealous of me, so long as I saved some of my time for her. She had suffered jealousy-sickness in an episode four years ago; she would not suffer it again. About whom had she suffered jealousy? Under what circumstances? I could not allow myself to ask these questions – they might seem to display jealousy. But I felt I had to provide something. I made it up. I said there was a woman with whom I was having an *affaire* in Sydney, called Pat. (There was a woman I knew called Pat in Sydney, but I wasn't having an *affaire* with her.) Did that concern her? Not at all! So far as she was concerned, I could be happy with Pat in Sydney, and happy in Canberra with her. (Many smiles.) I mustn't laugh at her; she was happy.

I was unsure what I wanted our future to be. I thought she might come to Sydney with me for a few weeks of the parliamentary recess (to achieve this, I would have to kill off the '*affaire*' with Pat). I enjoyed our conversations, her company, and the animal convenience of her being there, and the fact that she was more in love with me than I with her seemed an advantage; but there was a difficulty – she didn't 'fit in with anyone I knew'. She became very quiet when I introduced her to hard heads of the Hotel Civic drinking set so I went off and did my drinking without her, and when she was with me at dinner with the Jockels she was an enthusiast at a table of sceptics; I could see Jockel's brown eyes gravely contemplating another of my follies. As it turned out, she went to Sydney for several weeks and I was able to concentrate on hard drinking until a letter arrived which made me see things more clearly.

The letter began with the words, 'Donald the beloved', and ended with an imprint of lipstick, where she had kissed it: alongside she had written 'Please kiss this'.

To my literary taste the letter was overdone; it needed re-writing and toning down, particularly one phrase, 'kissing the air which offers me your lips'. But, beyond that, I now felt she had misunderstood our relations with each other. I didn't 'feel that way about her' – at least not now I had read this letter – I felt persecuted and pursued. The imprint of lipstick on the page seemed not an offer, but a demand. Before I had received the letter her face and her body had moved companionably in my memory; now they were in the way. At once, and impatiently, I saw her differently – every part of her and everything she did and said had become a demand. What I now thought was *She is in love with me and I am not in love with her* and I was offended until, as I went on thinking about it, I began to feel something like acceptance of the situation. I wrote to the friend who had been so kind during my previous *affaire*, 'One thing may amuse you. She is very much in love with me – everything. I flourish on it. I am not in love with her. Not one little bit. It is the previous situation in reverse.' Perhaps, after all, I was becoming mature.

When she returned to Canberra, things between us seemed to go on as they had before, but privately, I could feel aloof. ('Maturity'?) In Sydney for the parliamentary recess, I did not suggest she might join me – there were too many hard heads and sceptics to risk that – but I kept up the fiction of my *affaire* with Pat. A letter from Canberra included a salute to a situation that did not exist: 'I raise my glass to you, my beloved eighteenth-century intellectual. I hope life with Pat is suitably gratifying. Sometimes I imagine her in your company.' In other letters there were reminders of a more significant deceit – that I had concealed my lack of love for her. 'Thinking of you I leapt and ran and voilà I fell. *Le preuve d'amour*,' one of them began. In my earlier *affaire*, I saw myself in love but in the letters I received there had been no talk of love. Now that I professed 'detachment' I was receiving letters which expressed love.

By the middle of June, back in Canberra, I was taken up by parliament, drinking, and the comforts, shames, delights and vexations of my *affaire* when I received another letter in a way that seemed to make everything clear. There was a woman journalist, who sometimes came to Canberra, with whom I would drink coffees at Parliament House while we entertained each other with anecdotes about the peculiarities of colleagues, or of things in general, and on one of these occasions she said a plump little girl with high cheek bones had asked her to give me a letter. As she handed it over she looked waggish.

It was a letter of love in an unsealed envelope written in a style I again found overdone. As I read it, I 'subbed it down' to something cooler and more sparely expressed, but I could not explain this to the sophisticate sitting beside me drinking her coffee. Better to laugh off the unfashionably fulsome literary style. When I saw its author again I explained I had been embarrassed, then told her our *affaire* was over: she was making false claims on me. Everything I had thought about her and suppressed now came out. Not everything: only what was unfavourable. What I had liked in her, and in our being together, was now omitted. As soon as I had said it all, I wanted to kiss and make up; I was faced instead with her fading silence.

It was done on a Saturday afternoon. After it was over, Bill Jenkins and I had a bottle party in his room where 'we all got pissed'. We went to a party where there were 'buckets of booze'. When I got back to the Civic I was 'blind as a bat'.

FOR WEEKS AFTER THAT I CONTINUED TO HAVE ITCHY, IRRITABLE memories of her face, smiling and open, offering an unwanted invitation, but also memories of regret – of a face that looked at me with the thoughtfulness of a victim. In a second phase, I simply 'missed' her – not with the overall sense of a public whipping with which I had lost my earlier love, but in part rationally, and when I put names to what I was missing I found contrasts I hadn't expected: if I thought of the earlier love, I remembered a body that was lazily stretching itself, inside red pyjamas, mauve house gown or two-piece swimsuit, but if I thought of the second, I thought of her body itself, naked. Conversation with the first was style, with the second, content. But why had she written letters to me in such an overdone manner? Perhaps to show her how she should have done it, and perhaps to 'start all over again', I wrote her some letters of my own. The first was a long, cool apology; the second a thorough analysis of our relations; in the third I asked her to come to Sydney and live with me. It was only in my head that I 'wrote' these letters.

2

As I continued to play my lowly function in maintaining the political order, by assisting in keeping up the illusion that parliament mattered, there seemed nothing more to learn. In some of the 'stories' I put together parliament was presented as a great forum of democratic criticism (COMMUNISTS RUN FOREIGN POLICY, SAYS LIBERAL MP ... OR ATTACK ON ATLANTIC CHARTER, 'TWO OLD FOOLS IMPERIL AUSTRALIA,' SAYS LABOR MP): in others it was presented as the centre of government decisions (2500 JEWS TO ENTER AUSTRALIA ... FRUIT PRICES CONTROL TO BE EASED) or it could be a theatre for ritual enactments of freedom (BITTER ATTACK ON SENATE MEMBER: WILD SCENES).

I had no sense of a 'career' (whatever that might mean in journalism). Any ambitions I had were all extraordinary and all involved leaving the *Daily Telegraph*. But when I was tapping at an office typewriter quickly but inaccurately, with only two fingers (an ineptitude which, like not learning shorthand, maintained an amateur status), I continued to be transformed with the desire to get the 'story', no matter how trivial, into *Daily Telegraph* 'style'. One of my exemplary anecdotes was of the time a reporter noted for his shorthand skills and his superb touch-typing came back from a conference to type up his story; he handed it to the bureau chief, who gave it to me, to 'turn it into office style': I 'subbed it down' into *Telegraph* form, giving it a new lead and in general 'pointing it up'. I handed it to the bureau chief. The bureau chief then sent it off in his own name.

THE SECOND-IN-CHARGE OF OUR BUREAU HAD BECOME ONE OF the gallery's quiet heroes, a part for which his modest temperament suited him. He sat at his typewriter 'turning out the stories', a model of good humour, and in the talks we had together, when no one else was in the 'bureau', he was a minor master in gentle irony as we turned life over like garden philosophisers.

We agreed it was absurd that I, a grand master of *Daily Telegraph* style, was still only a 'D' grade, and we discussed how I should get a rise. What could be more humiliating than asking for something for oneself? When, at the beginning of one afternoon, I rang the Chief of Staff from Canberra, I satisfied honour by speaking to him coldly, not so much like one seeking a rise as like one giving him an opportunity to correct an anomaly. I could feel his long, cautious police sergeant's face at the other end of the telephone in Sydney as he coldly acknowledged receipt of my communication. Off to the press gallery for question time, off to coffee where, for once, I was someone wanted on the telephone. The Chief of Staff made his announcement as if it were my fault for not having acted before: he had seen the editor; I was to go up to 'C' grade. Almost six hundred a year! In the week I got my rise I wrote a 'story' about how my group of diplomatic cadets had been appointed third secretaries, on a mere three hundred a year.

But money could not really sweeten the taste of failure of one who at the age of twenty-four had not yet written even an unpublished novel. After months of friendship, in succession, with two people who had mastered the skills of writing unpublished novels and who had given me the chance to say more about novels than I had been able to say before, I had abandoned the idea of writing a book about Australia. That would be mere journalism. But beyond the ritualistically satisfying use of the word 'novel' this ambition had been replaced by nothing. I had a new anxiety: would *Sentimental Education* (I had read it now) prove to be more closely related to my life than *The Red and the Black*? Might I end up simply as one who was moved for a while to do this and that, but lacked the will to succeed? Perhaps, like the two non-heroes of *Sentimental Education*, Pritchett and I would end our days sitting over madeira and chess recalling the time when we thought we might come to something.

I would then remind myself that Dostoevsky didn't write *Crime and Punishment* until he was forty-five. But what would I do in the meantime? I didn't have Dostoevsky's advantages. Exile in Canberra was not as intellectually creative as exile in Siberia. How was I going to extricate myself from the demanding trivialities of journalism? Go back to the university and, under one of the ex-servicemen's schemes, enrol as a law student? Why would I want to be a lawyer? (I knew why: I could see myself as a coolly successful advocate, applying to law the artilleryman's principles of rational concentration of fire: there was many a famous law case won by Horne, KC.) More to the point: a law course took three years. How could I waste three years studying? What would I live on? A student's allowance? There seemed only one way: I must rearrange myself so that I could use my spare time 'to get on with my novel'. At this stage I would drift off into those dreams that so many others shared ... a steady writing routine at my desk ... critical acclaim ... royalties ... lectures on my books at the universities ... the development, through style, of a theory of what existence was like ... plenty of time to read ... a feeling that I was my 'self'.

In any case I must round out my knowledge of French and Russian novels. Perhaps the time had now come to go through Dante, Rabelais, Cervantes, Goethe, Racine, Corneille (at times it was difficult to remember that, in fact, I had not read them). I must get back to reading verse regularly (for a start: a thorough going-over of the French symbolists, English metaphysical poets and Jacobean playwrights, translations of Rilke and Heine). It was a couple of years since I had re-read *Ulysses*. Perhaps I should look into some English novels (there was talk of George Eliot and Henry James)? I must round out my knowledge of modern painting. I hadn't read any William Faulkner. I hadn't read Vico yet! There were gaps I must fill in my history-reading: I must read more Marx, Mosca, Machiavelli. I had read no sociology, nor scarcely any translations from Indian and Chinese classics. Some more Freud? ... Tocqueville? ... Translations from the Arabic? ... Anthropology? I still intended to read most of the books listed in the World's Classics, Everyman's and Modern Library series, and had marked some of them for priority.

Some of my most convincing daydreams came to me sitting in our 'bureau' when it was my turn to do the Sunday evening shift. This was a time when nothing usually happened and I could sit alone at a desk and imagine what it would be like to have an existence over which I could at least believe I had some control. This was also a time when I could wonder what it might be like to be a journalist who met politicians, an experience which came to me only vicariously, through a service the *Telegraph* bought, from the Melbourne *Sun Pictorial*: it included carbon copies of all the *Sun Pictorial*'s exclusive political stories, and although the most important of these did not usually appear on a Sunday evening, there were sometimes 'exclusives' of the second order (NEW MOVE ON HOUSING SHORTAGES or RESHUFFLE SOON ON FEDERAL CABINET) which I would translate into *Daily Telegraph* style, as if I knew politicians who talked about new moves or cabinet reshuffles. Someone introduced me to a politician one night in the lobby of the Hotel Canberra. Other than that, the politicians remained remote creatures in their phantom aquarium.

Occupied with sitting on my ledge in the press gallery watching for movements in the aquarium which might produce *Daily Telegraph* 'stories' or, at an even higher level of abstraction, without any other reference to events, turning other people's work into *Telegraph* 'stories', I had scarcely any sense of actuality. I thought this might come when I was assigned to report the arrival in Canberra of the first two 'international celebrities' I had yet seen – Lord Louis Mountbatten and his wife – but all I could do was to report the reporting: how many journalists and photographers there were, what the celebrities did when asked for autographs, how the celebrities were posed for the taking of photographs. The heading given to the story caught the contrivances of this occasion: FLASH BULBS PRIZED AS MOUNTBATTEN SOUVENIRS.

My only 'exclusives' came from External Affairs Department friends. A 'funny' for the *Sunday Telegraph*: BOARDERS BUTTON UP AT DINNER:

Guests at Brassey House, a Canberra boarding house, are not allowed at meals with more than the top button of their shirts left undone. And three minor 'exclusives' (including FOUR OUT OF 12 DIPLOMATIC CADETS RESIGN IN YEAR) written on lonely Sunday nights.

Moved by boredom and feelings of failure I went back to where I had started and asked the features editor if I might review books again: when the first review was published – of a book on Kipling which allowed me to make fun of imperialism – I became more bold and suggested I write an article for the 'feature page', the most prestigious page in the *Telegraph*. I had an idea: the failure of the diplomatic cadets scheme. And an 'intro': at dinner, Jockel had told me about his financial scrapings. The story could begin: *I know a young Australian diplomat who cannot afford to buy an overcoat.*

AS WITH THE CHIEF OF STAFF, THE FEATURES EDITOR SAID nothing, one way or the other – no idea was a good idea unless the editor said so – but when he telephoned me back, he scattered enthusiasm with the rapid fire of one who had seen the editor, and whose own judgment had now been confirmed. When I started putting my feature article together I found I could write seven more paragraphs about clothing to follow the 'intro'. That 'got people into the story'. Then came a change in images of deprivation:

> I remember other times fingering my sixpences to see if I had enough
> money to buy a round for people I badly wanted to meet. If ever you are
> drinking with an Australian diplomat, don't be hurt if he suddenly pleads
> overwork and disappears. It's simply that he can't afford the next round.

Time for pulling a more serious face: I announced that Australia should have the most democratic foreign service in the world. Then attack the Public Service Board. (Anecdote: One official said, 'In the eyes of the Public Service Board you are very junior clerks.') Then, attack Canberra itself: 'Australian diplomats should be able to put up at least a smokescreen of sophisticated and cultured talk, but in the cultural and social wilderness of a Canberra hostel cadets are not likely to learn very much about the gentle art of conversation. I remember those dreary, desolate days when I had to live in one of those barrack-like institutions.' Follow this with nine more paragraphs getting my own back on Canberra, concluding with: 'The frustrations and inanities of this state of semi-Siberian exile may produce Dostoevskys, but it is not very good training to make you a fascinating conversationalist.' Time to get more serious: there should be an independent diplomatic service, etc. etc. Endpiece: 'Meanwhile there is no more pathetic figure in Canberra than the diplomatic cadet struggling to keep up appearances.'

AFTER I SENT ALL THIS OFF, NOT A WORD. (AND THEY NEEDN'T think I was going to ask them if they liked it.) When the *Telegraph* arrived each day, I would turn to the features page first. Perhaps the Saturday magazine section? On the following Monday, on the features page, there it was, with as full a display as the *Telegraph* had ever given a feature article. First, as a 'strap' at the top of the page: THEY'RE JUNIOR CLERKS TO THE PUBLIC SERVICE BOARD. Then, in 12 point italic, in a box, a recall of my earlier story FOUR OUT OF 12 DIPLOMATIC CADETS RESIGN IN YEAR. After that, in one of those *Daily Telegraph* typefaces I had admired so much when I was editor of *Honi Soit*, the main heading: THE STORY OF THE DIPLOMAT WHO COULDN'T AFFORD AN OVERCOAT. Under that, a blurb: *A bill to make the diplomatic branch independent of the Public Service Board was prepared in 1944. It has been filed away.* After that: *By Donald Horne.* Here was an article by me on the same feature page which had campaigned against book censorship, red tape and Mussolini, the treatment of the Aborigines, addle-pated bungling, Franco, hanging and Hitler.

In the morning, as I breakfasted on praise from the Hotel Civic hardheads, it felt like a scene from one of those Fred Astaire and Ginger Rogers movies in which, after staying up all night, they read the critics and learn that the show will be a Broadway success. In the afternoon there came a token of success beyond any expectations – on my desk, a personal telegram from Brian Penton: *Congratulations on your article on diplomatic cadets. Would you please do me an article on Public Service Board explaining what regulations or prejudices prevent it from giving adequate salaries to specialists. Penton, Editor.* I went on with my usual work, and worked on the article in my spare time. There was not much trouble about it once I had the 'intro':

Some public servants in Canberra have been catching the same bus to work since the first garden was laid in that garden city.

If a new public service face appears in the bus one morning they lean together and discuss how the man belonging to the face has managed to catch this bus and not his usual one. Then they lean back and regard him in hostile silence.

The arrival of a trained specialist in the bureaucracy is greeted with much the same uneasiness as the arrival of a new face in one of these Canberra buses.

The rest was to be a suitable mixture of facts and anecdotes. However I had not finished it when I received a message, on Friday afternoon, that I was to return to Sydney at once. I had been appointed a feature writer.

3

On a wooden wall there was a sign saying FEATURES DEPARTMENT. Behind the wall were two small rectangular spaces separated by an eye-level glass and plywood partition. In one space, set side by side along one wall were the desks of three of the four *Daily Telegraph* writers (the fourth, a foreign affairs writer, had so many files that he was in a room of his own); along the partition were the desks of the features editor and the features sub-editor; in the other space were filing cabinets, piles of old newspapers and empty boxes and a secretary. When I arrived, on the Monday following my return to Sydney, I was put into this back space, with its look of being a neglected spare room, and left to talk to the secretary.

The others did not seem interested in me. Was I too young? Too inexperienced? (Had anyone else become a feature writer after only twelve months as a journalist?) One too many? Or was this simply, again, that I was a new boy? I was left alone in the spare room while, on the other side of the partition, they talked to each other. They went to lunch without me and then prepared themselves for 'the Monday conference', at which, they explained as we walked down a corridor to Penton's office, the feature writers were expected to provide their 'ideas' for the week.

In Penton's room we were arranged around the blue carpet in a form as pre-ordained as that of a nobleman's court or a military parade. The feature writers sat in a row along the far wall at the other end of the room from Penton as if awaiting execution; beside us were the features sub-editor, and the editor of the Thursday magazine (who had her office somewhere else in the building); in front of us, and only a couple of feet from Penton's desk, sat the features editor; beside the desk, and resting an arm on it, sat Sid Deamer. After we had taken up our positions we waited, in silence, as Penton went on writing. When he looked up, it was only at Deamer, to whom he spoke so softly that we could not hear; Deamer said something softly in reply. Then Penton elevated his range to the back of the room and said, 'Well, what are your ideas?' He addressed each of us formally as 'Mister', 'Mrs' or 'Miss' or, in the case of Emery Barcs, the foreign affairs writer, 'Doctor'.

Nothing was to get into the *Telegraph* feature page, or its Thursday or Saturday magazines, unless it had a 'news tie-up'; presenting an 'idea' therefore consisted of summarising a news item of the last day or two and explaining how a feature article might be tied to it. Penton wrote each 'idea' down as we gave it – a feature writer was supposed to provide at least three or four 'ideas' at the Monday conference – but he made no comments. When this was over, he did some more writing. We remained silent. Then he announced the feature assignments for that week, some of them based on the feature writer's own 'ideas' or Penton's amendments of them, other assignments Penton had thought of himself, back in his flat that morning, and about which there had been no discussion. He announced his decisions in a rapid-fire voice – everyone spoke very quickly throughout the conference – and with that there was nothing more to be said. As the feature writer nearest the door was given his assignments he took quick notes and then at once hurried from the room, as if to get on with the job; each of the others in turn hurried out in similar fashion. When I was given my work for the week, like the others, I hurried out to get on with the job – to find that the other feature writers were waiting for me in the corridor, to go for afternoon coffee.

Coffee was taken in a café in Castlereagh Street, with coffee-time expanding or shrinking according to how busy we thought we were. Emery Barcs was always there, partly because his concentration on foreign affairs kept him in his cubicle, with its piles of clippings, some in foreign languages, but also because, as a Hungarian, by taking this afternoon cup of coffee he seemed to maintain self-definition. Sometimes, in his alter ego of 'Esmond Barclay', he was put on to an outside job of the kind the rest of us did (Penton insisted that no Australian newspaper could afford a full-time specialist on foreign affairs and he was determined to prove it), but Barcs would be back by mid-afternoon, giving even a drab Castlereagh Street café something of the feeling of 'the Continent'. When his coffee was finished, with the air of a *boulevardier*, he would take out and light a cheap Australian cigar as if about to consider the latest news from the Balkans (as perhaps he was).

Since his method of working usually kept him in the office, Ronald McKie was also a regular at the afternoon coffee sessions: he would 'get the facts' as quickly as possible, so that he could spend a maximum time sitting at his desk, typing and re-typing until each paragraph came out on its own slip of paper as a perfectly formed *Daily Telegraph* paragraph; he engaged in this process with a casual effortlessness, as if he were occupied in some elegant hobby. At the coffee table, with his bushy moustache, his wide round eyes and his gentle manners, to the *boulevardier* presented by Barcs with wistful melancholy, McKie played the cultivated English cavalry officer (retired, and alternating between his work on an Afghan–English dictionary and a translation of Horace). When Barcs lit his cigar, McKie lit his pipe. The third *habitué*, Zelie McLeod (Penton's 'mistress'), held herself with such confidence and spoke with such authority that to *boulevardier* and cavalry officer she seemed to play *grande dame*. These three, even when the others came, would speak among themselves with a measured *gravitas*, lightened by tolerant traces of worldly humour. There was a sense of bourgeois culture, with talk of concerts and dinner parties, sculpture, the buying of furniture, conversation with *savants*, anecdotes of travel.

A solid sense of an established European culture was to be found around this cheap veneer table in the third-rate Sydney coffee shop. A couple of blocks away, grouped around the two expensive restaurants, Prince's and Romano's, there was the smart, New Yorkerish world of Sydney 'café society'. I entered this world for a couple of hours when I wrote a feature article for the *Telegraph's* Thursday magazine section. Although meant mainly for women, this section presented itself as of general interest so that it would not appear to be patronising women, and it did this with something of a sophisticated style, including ideas lifted from the *New Yorker* (a principal source of sophistication), one of which was the literary form of a 'Reporter-At-Large'. I was to write a 'Reporter-At-Large' on six French mannequins brought to Australia to do some fashion shows, and as part of my 'story' I was to take them to lunch at Romano's. I had, of course, had practice in fashionable dining out – at the Australia Hotel – but Romano's was smarter than the Australia: more expensive and with more waiters and more food cooked at the table. When it was over I was quietly pleased with the apparent skill with which I had ordered lobsters, steak, strawberries and coffees, along with what I now knew to be the appropriate wines, in a smart restaurant in which I was entertaining six young Frenchwomen dressed in the latest from Paris. I had worn a waistcoat, although not, of course, a hat. Another of the ideas the *Telegraph* had taken from the *New Yorker* was that of the 'Profile': on the Saturday following my Reporter-At-Large (FRENCH WITHOUT TEARS IN SYDNEY), there appeared a Profile written by me on John Anderson. The heading JOHN ANDERSON: UNIVERSITY'S STUBBORN NO-MAN spread over two pages; in one corner was a caricature of Anderson; at the other side an 'album' of snapshots from his early life. I had been given a fortnight to write it – an enormous time for a *Daily Telegraph* feature article – interviewing Anderson at the university, checking the story with him at home, even looking over the family photograph album with his wife at Sunday supper; his complicity in writing it was as great as mine. When it was finished, and set up in type, and since the Profile was about a foot too long, I deposited one set of the uncut proofs in the *Daily Telegraph* library for the historical record, sure that at last I had done something worth doing and put the other in the lavatory, for visitors to read. My next story was CAN WE SEE THE FUTURE IN OUR DREAMS?

Feature writing produced its own weariness. Some of it was hack work: there was to be a plebiscite on the monarchy in Greece, so I would look up the library cuttings and put something together for the features page on the king of Greece (GEORGE II, A DAPPER MAN WITH BUILT-UP SHOES); or the Duke of Windsor's house was burgled, so I would go down to the Public Library and write a piece for the Saturday magazine on famous robberies of royal persons (THE MAN WHO TRIED TO LOOT THE CROWN).

Although we shared the same cramped office area and went to the same cheap cafés, any sense of intimacy and trust could go when the subbing began: each sentence was scrutinised by the features editor or the features sub-editor for strayings from office style; words would be moved around or cut out in the process of 'tightening up'; sometimes whole stories would be 're-cast'. It was like being operated on under a local anaesthetic: even if one looked away, or read an afternoon newspaper, one could sense that the subbing was still going on, or even hear the slithering over the page of a pencil. Sometimes the subbing of one feature article might last for several hours of fiddling and, often, argument about what the editor really wanted. One piece of mine for the Saturday magazine was argued about for most of a day: I went home blazing with boredom.

At the same time, I felt more my 'self' than had been possible in the enormous room, or on the Press Gallery ledge in Canberra. One could enjoy oneself sitting in libraries or interviewing experts to find out if tuberculosis and venereal disease would be gone in a few years, or what 'the Old Vic' Company was and what shows it would be bringing to Australia, or what the sociological explanation was of this or that. With some articles, feature writing could seem easy money: one was being paid to indulge in the delights of intelligent curiosity. And although the office style still ran through all things, in feature articles it was forced to run slightly more thinly. Feature writers were permitted two sentences to a paragraph and in their sentence structure were allowed more than one clause. Unlike news stories, which were written to be skimmed, so that the headings and opening paragraphs yielded 'the main facts', feature articles were meant to be read. One could feel a composer's gratification in fabricating the opening paragraphs of a feature article so that they attracted initial attention, quickly tied in the news tie-up, could be understood by a schoolchild, did not offend office style and yet read smoothly enough to 'get people into the story'. Then came the gratification of imagining that the whole story had been constructed so that it flowed on, without giving the reader an excuse to stop reading (a particularly difficult process when hopping around the Telegraph's many limitations on style). There was the particular joy (not always found) of providing a good punchline, so that the reader would have something filling to go away with. Sometimes there could also be the sly satisfaction of writing oneself into an article – I relished in particular the rationality and irony of tough-minded realism – and doing it so indelibly that the subs couldn't wash it out. Stories were ordered by Penton in one of six stock sizes ranging from

800 to 5,000 words – but even 'writing to space' like this could be pleasant and it was a delight to be able to cut one's own copy, thereby reducing the discretion of the subs. I wasn't writing the way I wanted to write (insofar as I knew what that might mean, it still had something to do with my 'detached' army pieces, although by now I had partly forgotten what they were like, or with telling the world how to behave) but the way I was now writing was less unlike how I wanted to write.

There were times when one might preach (YOU FILLED IN 85,000 MILES OF FORMS) or even instruct (MEN DIED FOR THE SECRET BALLOT), as long as it was done entertainingly. And there were the stories, such as my Anderson profile, on which I was happy to receive congratulations. Once, twice or even three times a week, the name was there for all to see, in ten or twelve point type: *By Donald Horne.*

USUALLY THE WORK RHYTHM WAS BOTH PREDICTABLE AND convenient. Monday morning: at home. Monday afternoon: conference and coffee session. Tuesday and Wednesday: do most of the week's work. Thursday: argue with subs. Friday: token appearance in office. With not much night work and no weekend work I had the illusion that I had become an ordinary person; I again began paying predictable visits to my parents for dinner. With such normality, there was a feeling of detachment from the rest of the office with their different working hours. They were the engines which ran the ship. We were the banqueting department.

Detachment went further: because of the peculiar conventions of the news tie-up there was a general detachment from everyone else's sense of reality: we lived in a pseudo-topical world of our own. Scarcely any of the features we wrote 'interpreted the news'. Apart from the short, hard blows Penton dealt out every day in his editorials, the news was simply made up of the 'facts' presented in short sentences in the news pages; the news tie-ups we spent so much trouble getting were usually minor events which almost all readers would have forgotten, if they had any sense, by the time a feature came out or they might never have noticed them. They were there simply to provide excuses for writing magazine articles.

The endless and aimless appetite for news tie-ups could mean that much of Monday morning might be spent dejectedly, perhaps in bed, razor blade in hand, cutting out news snippets that might justify a story, and then trying to contrive what story they might justify. There was always the fear that I would think of nothing: but it was unimaginable that one could arrive at the conference with no ideas. I worked out a joke, to explain my predicament: one day at a conference I would say, 'Look, I haven't got any good ideas for *Telegraph* stories: all I've got are some ideas for good stories.' I got into the habit of lunching well on Mondays, at a small, slightly expensive Kings Cross restaurant, with a world-weary friend who had become a doctor. We would eat minestrone, lamb cutlets, lettuce, salad and cheese, drink claret and a glass of brandy with coffee, and make jokes. These lunches prepared me better than the news clippings for my appearances in Penton's throne room.

Penton could shimmer radiantly with the aureole of success: behind him were the four books he had written and his early brilliant career – Dobell had even painted a portrait of him – and now there was his demonic control of the *Telegraph*, exercised day by day, in a series of conferences which did not end until after midnight, all of them conducted in an atmosphere of impending storm. Throughout the building, if there was any dispute about whether to do this or that, each side would claim it was doing 'what the editor wants'. If the storm broke there could be pens slashing at copy or proofs, demands for the impossible, new policies announced on the spot in repartee, tongue-lashings given in a quick, rough voice, dismissals from the presence. Even if things went smoothly people still waited for the storm. The soft temptations which came at times – jokes, seductive smiles, praise – only made the storms seem all the worse. People talked about his lips: they could leer like a jovial satyr's; they could set primly with the concentration of an assassin.

Penton was driven by an overwhelming ambition to create, perhaps for his own spiritual comfort in an uncertain existence, a tough, empirical world in which there were 'hard facts'. Daily it was the job of reporters to go out and dig for 'facts' and bring them back to the office where they were raw material for a construction process in which they were put together like bricks to build that day's reality. His second obsession was that these edifices of 'facts' should be so floodlit with clarity that the people would then behold them: he was driven on by a desperate faith in the possibility of human communication. If we all worked hard enough purging our short sentences of impurities, then tightening and polishing them, they would shine with the clear light of understanding. He could also seem to be conducting a vast adult education class, in which we should all open our minds and our mouths and start a discussion. He had written a book telling us to *Think! Or Be Damned!* and he violently believed it was only laziness and incompetence that made people so stupid. To help them rise from their errors he wrote daily editorials, and then on Saturdays he used a page of the magazine section, THIS IS WHY WE SAID IT, to repeat what he had already said in his editorials during the week. Penton wanted his readers to see Saturday as revision day.

The *Telegraph* was said to be losing money (the company made its profits from the *Australian Women's Weekly*, and from the goldmines its proprietors owned in Fiji) but its sales were good; Penton's didacticism might have been expected to wreck the sales of a popular newspaper but it was carried out with such verve that he got away with it. Sometimes he would turn against the principles he preached himself and call for more 'light stories'. (He was in one of these moods when my story about the censorship of a film star's thighs struck his fancy.) At one of our Monday conferences he fell into a fury when some serious-minded story was put forward. It was of a kind he would normally encourage. *We're not an educational institution*, he said. *We have to entertain the public.* When we met for coffee we decided we knew what that meant: *the business side were at him again.* But he wanted large sales and commercial success too: to see him being driven in an office car after dinner – cigar in mouth, curly brimmed hat tilted like a buccaneer's, face flushed from wine, Zelie McLeod at his side – he looked like a man who wanted everything.

The Dobell portrait showed him in leering, satyr pose, against a background of red and black which might have set a brothel scene. *Look at those lips*, people would say. How could you trust a man like that? The great public question about Penton may have been whether he had 'sold out', but the favoured personal weakness found in him by office gossip was untrustworthiness: he was said to be 'malicious', 'feline', 'spiteful'; he played favourites, he promoted sycophants. *Is Brian Penton a sadist?* was one of the regular conversations in the office pubs. I discounted this personal gossip. My sympathies were with Penton: I knew what it was like to be a controversialist. Perhaps some of them saw *me* as a Penton sycophant!

When Penton went on holidays and the feature writers were placed in the care of McAlpine, the Editor-in-Chief, the whole office had a vacation from the politics of court life. McAlpine, a tall, lean solitary figure and, when Penton was there, of only very limited executive powers, was an 'old newspaperman' of exotic background, believed to have been an Irish republican in his young days. The rumour that he had known Lenin in Zurich was given credence by the fact that he still wore a wide-brimmed Latin Quarter black hat. His Monday conferences were conducted as if we had all dropped in for a long chat. Decisions about the week's feature assignments emerged only incidentally, among the anecdotes; for a time it could seem that no decisions would emerge. In this new court, I was the favourite; he gave me 'the best stories', praised my pieces at the conferences, had private talks with me about what I was doing, and even took a story away from Zelie McLeod because it was not well done, and gave it to me. Although the others still remained reserved, as if McAlpine were merely a casual visitor in our normal life, I enjoyed being my 'self' at his conferences, talking, joking, telling anecdotes. The whole balance of life on the features staff seemed to be shifting.

Penton came back and at the first of his Monday conferences looked at me and said, 'There seem to be a lot of feature writers.' I was afraid that, after all, the rumours about him might be true. Half an hour later the Features Editor told me I was to be transferred back from the features staff to general reporting. He had nothing else to say. The others went out to afternoon tea. When I went back to the enormous room the Chief of Staff put me on the weather story.

Part of the Royal Standard set

1

The afternoon coffee ceremonies of the feature writers were only one of several social forms in which I had been spinning off into new circles of friendship in the *Telegraph*, some of them so remote from each other that I was the only point of intersection. Most of the people I now mixed with were journalists.

Each of the three pubs next to the office with their fine old English names (the King's Head, the Windsor, the Castlereagh) had its own congregation of *Telegraph* regulars who saw drinking in a particular bar in that pub as a declaration of significant identity, but to me, there had only ever been one bar group to which I belonged – our old group at Ushers Hotel, where sometimes in one afternoon one might find the whole world: Crawford, Conlon, Hope, McAuley, Fraser. In the office pubs I merely moved from bar to bar or from group to group, except when I picked up a scent of the alien: in that case try another bar.

There could be occasions when loyalties seemed expected. I had been turned into an occasional drinking companion – separately – by two of the office 'big names', each of whom used me for monologues, sometimes even for conversations. Both preferred the King's Head saloon bar because it was out of favour that year with most other *Telegraph* drinkers: on one occasion I was in this bar with one when the other came in. It was as if I had been found in bed with a lover. For an hour or so, all three of us drank on, in tension, with subtle, malicious interchanges. For several weeks afterwards I was treated by both as a faithless drinker.

Strolling around the two old buildings that made up 'the office' had become one of the routines by which during a working day I could feel in control of myself. Apart from two forbidden corridors where 'the executives' had rooms, I would visit sections of these buildings to reassure myself that things were still going on in the same way – in the energetic clatter of the composing room, or the orderliness of the *Women's Weekly* offices, or the no-nonsense air of the advertising department, or the locker-room jocularity of the photographic department, or the faded modernity of the *Sunday Telegraph* offices, or the daytime quiet of the deserted machine room, or the sparks and flares of the process engraving department, even the rustle of calculation in the business office (still called 'the counting house' by older hands). I would always walk quickly and intelligently, as if I knew where I was going. Talking to this person or that also became part of the organisation of a day. The Finance Editor was always good for a patch of hard-headed empiricism; I would stand at his door and chat about the world sometimes for half an hour, ready to leave at once if he turned from me to his desk. Pearl's secretary was a clever and amusing informant and she shared many of my tastes in character analysis; we talked about sex but, to my regret, did nothing about it; we drank together and went to some of the same parties but some of our most happily companionable times were spent spinning out our gossiping and wisecracking as I stood beside her desk hoping that a buzz from Pearl would not put an end to our pleasure. The librarian, a devoted monologuist, who wore a new posy in his buttonhole each day, had special lines of reminiscence about the old times, and I had got on to friendly-talking terms with several of the subs, with their reports of the theatricalities of the midnight conference and their absorption in all of the inner technicalities of 'office styles'.

I would meet George Molnar at Redleaf swimming pool, where he would lie in the sun and read, and where there was space for us both to expand; in the office his working area was so small there was scarcely enough room to sit side by side and share our amusement at the endless wonders of the paradox of unintended consequences. He didn't seem 'himself' in the office – Penton was a continuing preoccupation – but there was no avoiding a visit to him in his cubby hole if events had produced the need for immediate examination of some new irony even we had not expected. Molnar was one of the few people who still called me 'young Donald'.

The most intense of these visits was with Peter Hastings who had arrived in the reporters' room with large sad eyes and a lavish moustache, surrounded by mystery and rumour (a career in military intelligence? ... son of an English KC ... *protégé* of the General Manager?). Several months later he was moved into an office of his own as Syndications Editor; it was his job, subject to McAlpine, to buy comic strips, feature articles, serials, photo services, and to sell what he could of *Telegraph* stuff. Hastings and I pranced and squawked like birds in a mating ceremony, exciting each other into trills of ideas, anecdotes, indiscretions, some of it on affairs of the day – politics, novels, Stalin, movies – and some of it on ourselves: as Bruce Miller had once forecast careers for me, Hastings would predict great successes or tragic failures. A lot of our talk was office gossip. Hastings could not believe in the effects of chance. Whatever it was that was happening, somebody *meant* it: make no mistake about it, behind the scenes, something bigger was going on. Gossip went beyond amusing oneself in speculating about human character: for him it was a necessary survival technique in daily life, like checking the temperature – and in the office, it was raw material by which he analysed the state of play in an infinity of office games. Pearl told him something at lunch: what did that *really* mean? McAlpine said something at a syndications conference. What was he really getting at? Gossip was macabre when we considered the remote and terrible Frank Packer. A subsection of our relationships was devoted to close analysis of the character of Brian Penton whom we studied as if he were a character in a Shakespeare play set for the Leaving Certificate.

For most of the time in these office wanderings I would feel like an actor in a low-budget wireless production playing a number of parts. Drinking in pubs was entirely theatrical: formalised manners of mateship between male drinkers allowed no opportunities for sincerity or spontaneity, but different bar groups had different variants of sociability. (I was ready to compare the moving from group to group in the saloon bar of an office pub to the moving from group to group at a Guermantes reception in *Remembrance of Things Past*, but for the moment I lacked friends who had read Proust.) Even in the office I often felt insincere, politely reflecting people back to themselves, like a mirror. I would use one form of down-to-earth language with the Financial Editor ('face the facts' ... 'bloody hard') and five minutes later quite another ('have a fuck' ... 'big tits') in the photographic darkroom. Playing the journalist could be as fanciful as playing the gunner. I was a multi-linguist.

When I was expelled from the Features Department back to the reporters' room, most of those I talked to in my office wanderings provided divinations of what this meant. That I was a pawn in the power play between McAlpine and Penton was obvious to everyone: I had let McAlpine take me up, he had preferred me to Zelie McLeod, therefore Penton had struck me down. What else, for God's sake, had I expected (etc. etc.)? How naive could I get (and so forth)? Hastings had a dozen themes. So much for me: what really interested most of them was to divine the significance of my exile in the wider power play being fought out in the rooms off the forbidden corridors; or to tell exemplary anecdotes about the short, brutish life of the journalist; or to philosophise about how one should conduct oneself in an uncertain world. One of them, however, asked me if I wanted a new job.

Yes. That would show them. *No*, as he at once pointed out, *it could be more subtle than that. They mightn't let you go: you have to test them. Get an offer, then see if they'll match it. They've done this to you, now you have to find out if you can get them to declare that they still want you. If they don't – off you go.* But where would I go? The *Sun* and the *Mirror* were too vulgar. The *Sydney Morning Herald* was too respectable. He provided an unexpected answer – *Smith's Weekly*. Although *Smith's Weekly* was mainly rubbish, it was now being edited by Edgar Holt, who had worked on the *Telegraph* (where he was seen as one of the many brilliant men Penton had offended with his capriciousness) and, in the manner of editors who want to find some sense in what they are doing, Holt was putting some good stuff in, here and there, among the rubbish. Perhaps I might provide some of the pieces of good stuff?

I had already met Edgar Holt. With his black, heavy glasses, gentle manner, pink cheeks, florid bow-ties and kindly wit he seemed someone who might be on a BBC discussion panel, or writing for a London intellectual weekly. Now he received me most jovially. Tea was served, in what I imagined was an English manner. We made jokes about 'Brian', as if, somehow, I really knew something about Penton. He explained to me what he was trying to do with *Smith's*, what part I might play in it, and offered me an extra hundred pounds a year. Well, yes, I said (as I had been instructed to say) I'll have to think it over.

On the way back to the *Telegraph*, still warm from this friendly interview, I imagined that perhaps I might take the job: it offered predictable working hours and a welcome good-bye to the enormous room; I might even like the work; perhaps there might even be a chance to write as I chose. (What would that be?) Back at the *Telegraph*, I reported to the Chief of Staff: *I have received this offer from* Smith's Weekly ... *I don't want to accept it, of course ... But unless you can match it ... Well, I suppose it would be silly to refuse ... Sorry.* Yes, said the Chief of Staff, well, I'll just have to see.

What was I doing? I was acting as impulsively as a Stendhal hero! I might actually have to go to *Smith's Weekly*! Why couldn't I leave things as they were? ... Just as I had had a feeling of love for my regiment (which I despised) when I was offered relief from it, I now had a feeling of nostalgia for the *Telegraph*. Why should I go out among all those strangers?

The Chief of Staff had nothing to say to me that night, nor the next day, but he called me in the following afternoon: yes, they would match the offer, but I had to sign a two-year contract; I couldn't keep on getting rises.

Edgar Holt seemed, to me, ungracious when I told him I would stay with the *Telegraph*. Perhaps it would have been better if I had gone. Perhaps he was serious.

Peter Hastings speculated that the contract might simply mean that McAlpine had won a victory over Penton and if Penton didn't really want me, he'd get his own back on me anyway, contract or no.

Each day I examined the assignments I was given, for signs of what they suggested about my standing on the *Telegraph*. I was taken off weather stories. A good sign. I was put on to a quiz on whether people should be allowed to smoke in cafés. A bad sign. I was sent to the opening of the Archibald Prize: a good sign. They gave my piece a good display and by-lined it *By a Special Reporter*. That was a very good sign. I was given a piece to do on the musician Eugene Goossens. Another good sign. I was put on to a quiz on whether Australian women missed the American soldiers. A bad sign.

2

It was beginning to seem to me that, somehow, I should go 'overseas'. The *Telegraph* had had a number of war correspondents of its own during the war, sharing their cost with English newspapers, and three of these now became people I talked with. All three expressed distress at what the *Telegraph* had now become, with the most esteemed reporters existing as a link between telephones and typewriters, producing 'facts' as factories produced bricks. Having met these three when I was a feature writer, I had not had to observe what happened to them in the enormous room, but when I was expelled from the Features Department I might be sitting at one of the long tables in the reporters' room embarrassed that someone who, on a typewriter which had been with him at Alamein or Singapore or France, was failing to write in office style some small story which in any case might not be used, while I was producing a work of craftsmanship such as TWO DIE, 50 COLLAPSE IN HEAT WAVE or RAIN EXPECTED TO INTERRUPT CRICKET.

Of the three, Sam White spent least time on either drink or talk. He had been a young Melbourne Stalinist intellectual in the 1930s (when he had had a spectacular *affaire*); now he was a European sophisticate, with the tall, glossy-haired, dark good looks, given character by a broken nose, of a hero in a film about the Spanish Civil War or the French Resistance. Tedium would drive him out of the office as soon as the afternoon's work began: a signal between us, as between members of the resistance, and we were in the Windsor's saloon bar. But this was not a place where he could settle down: he needed an *estaminet* rather than a saloon bar and a cognac rather than a glass of beer. He could speak with measured eloquence, but the most communicative parts of our conversation came in signs; sideways looks, raising of the eyebrows, setting of the lips, frowning silences. He was likely to leave his beer unfinished, slap me on the back, grimace, and depart. Life gained meaning after work when he would go to Prince's and drink champagne as part of another *affaire* (with a socialite, on which he was spending his deferred pay). Both conversation and silences were about the life he had left behind in Europe, and the fact that the *Daily Telegraph* offered him nothing but the possibility of annihilation. After one of his most significant silences he had told me he would put all his remaining money into a fare to London, and try his luck in Fleet Street.

The time for drinking with Ronald Monson was within the manly hour from five to six. No subtle signals for this, beyond the simple Australian, 'How about a beer?' With his forthright sunburnt face, with military moustache and good humour lines, and wide brimmed hat always on his head, Monson seemed the archetype of the middle-aged 'digger'. Beginning with the Spanish Civil War he had done more war reporting than anyone else in Australia. His hard bitten, outdoors look gave him the appearance of a construction engineer or a country surveyor, even an explorer; in fact he had been an explorer, in his way – one of his first youthful adventures, his manner of making a place for himself in the world, had been to walk from Cape Town to Cairo, and write a book about it, after which he worked in Fleet Street. Monson was more good-humoured than Sam White about his predicament on the *Telegraph*. He knew that coming back to Australia would be a let-down, but he wanted his children to be Australians; however, he found it necessary to recollect, daily in the pub, between five and six, the time when he had seemed a real journalist. This recalling was a task in which he seemed to find me fitted to assist.

Ian Fitchett was less predictable in the hours when I could assist his recalling of what it might have been like to have been himself: agonies of boredom with his job and disgust for the human condition swept over him so capriciously that several times he knocked me up when I was in bed, arriving with a bottle or two of gin and some large brown paper bags full of oranges and sitting up for hours, even until dawn, pouring gin, squeezing fruit and extending some long tale of ironies and *douleurs*. With his conservatively cut suits, his cropped hair and trimmed moustache, his richly modulated if slightly piping voice and his ability to stride into the reporters' room as if about to close it down, he seemed the least likely of us all to be there. His father had been a lawyer in the Western District of Victoria, the heartland of the Australian gentry, and his grandfather had been a clergyman who had made an international reputation by writing *Deeds That Won The Empire* and other patriotic bestsellers. Fitchett had a sense of honour so lofty and so innocent that no one could satisfy it. Relations with friends should have been those of honour, but friends had always proved themselves bastards; for a time, in the war, soldiering had seemed potentially honourable, but it had been demeaned by the pushy ambitions of those on the make. His paradigm anecdote was of marching into the *Telegraph*'s enormous room in 1940, in full battle order because there had been a city march (he had enlisted as a soldier and only later became a correspondent): he unsheathed his bayonet, lifted it high, then brought it down, stabbing right through the centre of the duty book. The anecdote had a number of uses: it was an image of his high hopes for the morally cleansing action of the war, but therefore also of his later disappointments, and also of his exhilaration in escaping from the enormous room, of his contempt for those who controlled it, and of his return to its imprisonment. As he paced up and down, hitting the palm of his left hand with the clenched fist of his right, many of the sagas he recited of his days as war correspondent in Africa and Asia had something of the same meaning as an Evelyn Waugh novel, but Fitchett's distaste was not as selectively snobbish as Waugh's. He despised the *arrivistes* (and now the 'spivs'), but he also despised those who had arrived before the *arrivistes* and he hated the upper-class English. To Fitchett, at his most disillusioned, all human beings were *arrivistes*, smart-arses without honour. He had built an ironic acceptance of this into his conversational style, with a compulsive use of the word 'villain' as endearment. 'You villain! You villain!' he would say, laughingly, even lovingly, and accept himself as part of general human failure. I bestowed my favourite century on Fitchett and imagined him as an eighteenth-century character – in his concern with honour, in his rashness and, as part of that, in the great dash and selflessness of his gambling. He had won a thousand pounds at the races and, like a true eighteenth-century sportsman, in several successive Saturdays at the racecourse he lost all he had won. Shortly after, he pawned (irredeemably) a star sapphire he had bought in India when he was flush. Any reader of eighteenth-century novels would at once recognise in Fitchett the instinct of an eighteenth-century gentleman.

WITH THEIR ANECDOTES, TOLD IN SYDNEY BARS, ABOUT DELHI, Cairo, Singapore, Rome, New York, Paris, London or Berlin, these three war correspondents who had lost their own wars were reminders that there was a journalists' world wider than that pencilled every day within the blue lines of the duty book. While Penton was on holidays McAlpine had startled me one afternoon by saying that I might be sent to the *Telegraph*'s 'bureau' in London, or perhaps New York. This produced days of private excitement in which I was shocked into imagining that the *Telegraph* might see me as being the person I thought I was. Then, nothing more.

There was no doubt I would go 'overseas', of course, although how I would get there was not a matter to which I had given any connected thought.

'Overseas' had been waiting for me since I had discovered it as a child in my father's war souvenirs and in the *Cassells' Book of Knowledge*. But while there was no doubt that I would travel, there was great doubt as to who would pay the fare.

'Just go to London and get a job.' As we were drinking in the saloon bar at the Castlereagh, Ronald Monson's brave explorer's face would look at me in its kindliest way, as if he were explaining that it was as easy to get a job in Fleet Street as it was to learn the rudiments of Swahili, but I felt a kind of modesty about exposing myself to a foreign newspaper. Why would anyone in London want me? I was, after all, an imposter; I was so unlike a true journalist that there were still times when I was afraid I would drop my mask, 'come back without a story', and resign. Surely, over in London, with their sharp English eyes, they would see through my disguise? And even if I managed to trick them, as I had deceived the *Telegraph*, it would only be because I would have to learn new indignities in the style of some other newspaper and in some other way of not being 'myself'. What was the point of travel if it meant moving from the *Telegraph*'s enormous room to some enormous room 'overseas'? Sam White spoke of the 'opportunities' there were in Fleet Street. What 'opportunities' were there for me, when it was journalism I wanted to get away from?

I could feel a kind of timidity about earning a living: my father had existed within the bureaucracy of the state schools and now received two pensions for his services to the state, as schoolteacher and soldier, and, despite past surface uproar about the 'servility' of the welfare state, there was one quiet, submerged and indestructible part of me where it could still seem that money should forever be growing modestly on small trees as a reward for those who had behaved themselves. In another part, also indestructible, there was even, still, a primary school vision that my career would be assured because, year by year, I would pass from classroom to classroom and come top in all the exams. In other parts of me there were other indestructible memories of daydreams – of how I made my fortune as a liberal lawyer, or of how I had gone down in some celebrated defeat as a bold political leader; I had never imagined myself as a wage plug signing a duty book. I had imagined great liberal causes lost in court, defeats in parliament, suppressions in the street by the Cossacks, books maliciously reviewed, even being mown down in battle, assassinated as a ruler or executed as a rebel: these were all misfortunes that must be sustained – but the idea of being sacked aroused, simply, fear. Yet this was the reality journalists joked about, as in novels of the Great War soldiers in the trenches joked about the shells that had their numbers on them. After the sack? In a rational mood I might consider the despair of taking up an entirely dreary job (the army all over again), but my fears could slip into a chasm of imagination. They were the fears of a child who had read Dickens and to whom scenes of poverty were metaphors for the terror of emotional loss.

To shake myself out of this, I would strike a bargain with my daydreams and imagine that I was successful as an author, but only very modestly: a room in London would do, or a small country cottage without water laid on. To write novels it was, however, essential to be 'overseas'. We all knew that there were no real markets in Australia for serious work, nor any good publishers, but there was more than that to it – there seemed something so dull about Australia that it might not be possible to write well while living in it (except verse, of course: I still imagined that, despite being Australians, Hope, Stewart and McAuley would make their world reputation). It didn't have to be England. Some cheap country in Europe would do: I could be like Penton – live in a European village on rough red wine, cheese and bread while I got on with my novel – or, like Elliot Paul in *A Narrow Street*, hide in a European city and turn one small part of it into a book.

But I didn't have the fare to get to any European country, however cheap. I couldn't save money. It would cost at least eighty pounds to sail to London, and every week my salary leaked out into restaurants, bars, bookshops; sometimes I had to borrow to get into the next week.

Perhaps my best hope was to be sent to London or New York by the *Telegraph*. In my spare time I could then get on with my novel. But how could I write a novel if I was still working as a journalist? (And what would the novel be *about*?)

I was half-offered a job in the British Commonwealth Army of Occupation in Japan, but I was physically unable to imagine myself back in an army uniform. Besides, life was too short to spend two years of it with Australians in Japan. Then a small cluster of my *Daily Telegraph* friends began talking about contracting to join the staff of the *Straits Times* in Singapore, with fares paid. But why would I want to go to a provincial place like Singapore, where there was neither the kind of bar Scott Fitzgerald got drunk at, nor the visions of radiance of Europe.

THE ROYAL STANDARD WAS ALSO AN 'OFFICE PUB', BUT IT WAS several hundred yards down the street from the *Telegraph* and was used mainly for dining and for illegal drinking after the six o'clock closing time by some of the inner circles of the *Telegraph* who did not go to the other pubs. Most of the staff hadn't heard of it. Rita Dunstan's set drank there; Pearl's secretary went to it; Fitchett (who lived there for a while) used it for entertaining; sometimes Penton himself would dine there. It seemed Sid Deamer's favoured pub. The Standard was not only a compound where drinkers could pursue good fellowship to its last, desperate ends; it was also a marketplace for deciding where to 'go on next' and sometimes a command post for organising big Saturday night parties; on Sunday afternoons the upstairs lounge, with scarcely anyone in it, could be a quiet precinct for a respectful sharing of hangovers. In particular, it was a declaration of a certain detachment from the rest of the *Telegraph*. I began to see myself as someone who belonged to the Royal Standard.

In approaching the Standard after hours there was first the ceremony of entry. Someone would unlock the door and conduct an examination. (OK. Come in. He's a regular.) Up quiet, empty stairs, down a corridor and into the buzz and laughter of the lounge, where among the faces of regulars I knew but never met were the 'office tables' and looking at these showed who was having dinner with whom that night. The red carpet, red curtains, round wooden tables and small bar at the end were all routine for a middle-market Sydney hotel lounge but Joe, the barman, an Irishman, provided the hotel with something, apart from our own squabbles, to remember it by. If one shut one's eyes to all this Sydney ordinariness and looked only at Joe, one could imagine it was 'overseas'. With sleepy eyelids lowered over shrewd, narrow eyes and a mouth that scarcely moved, as he dropped his one-liners, Joe cast up reminders of the scepticism of the old world. We would greet him with too much zeal – with their restraint, his hints of welcome were a rebuke (although a gentle recognition that he did, in fact, remember who we were) – and as we ordered each round we would have to joke with Joe, even touch his arm, to draw on his wisdom. We might wonder: 'What does Joe really think of us. What do you think really lies behind that smile?' By the time we were in the dining room sitting around tables with white lace edged linen cloths and eating baked meat as if at a family Sunday dinner, we had become loud laughing people or sharp sarcastic people – in either case, hard-drinking people – and Joe didn't matter any more: he was just the man who brought the drinks. But back in the lounge after dinner when we would all be drunk, Joe would bring serenity to us among our sorrows.

Since everything that happened there was performed on a stage surrounded by critics, the Royal Standard was not a background for the conduct of *affaires*, but I did begin to 'go out' with a 'blonde', a reporter who was one of the Royal Standard *habitués*. She was slender and tall and spoke slowly, with laconic good humour and pure Australian vowels. We had learned to talk easily and honestly with each other, but she aroused my appetites in a most profound way: she lent me a novel. I hadn't heard of either *Appointment in Samarra* or of John O'Hara, but as soon as I read it I agreed that it had caught, in a sharpened and desperate form, the predicaments of some of us at the Royal Standard. I then read *Butterfield 8* and some short stories, partly because the dried-out feel of the dialogue and the general flatness of tone seemed to have something to 'say', and partly for the pleasure of hearing her discuss novels in her casual, hesitant, modest, but honest way. She then made another significant declaration. She invited me to one of the Little Theatres that were the only place where one might see 'serious' plays, to an afternoon and night performance of the eleven acts of *Mourning Becomes Electra*, to which, in an attaché case, she had brought chicken sandwiches on brown bread, slices of fruit cake and some bottles of home-brewed beer. Our *affaire* ended in a fiasco of misunderstanding one Sunday afternoon. There were no last words – I was called to the office – and we stayed 'good friends'. I learned when I got home that Sunday night that, after I left, and before going back to her home, she had given the place I was living in an exemplary cleaning.

ONE NIGHT OUR GROUP WAS SCATTERED IN A RAGGED ARC around several tables in the lounge, and on its outskirts Joe and Rita were trying to soothe a former commando as he cried with rage at the insults life had offered him since the war and then broke off to describe the techniques of killing a Jap in unarmed combat. At another edge of the group one of the most soft-hearted was crying out of sheer boozy sentiment; the tears ran down his cheeks and soaked into his collar. I had seen his face pucker as it turned towards Sid Deamer, who, unaware of its wet edges, was in the soft, happy centre of this ragged arc. 'I love Sid Deamer,' he said. (Not sexually of course: we all understood that.) 'I love that man.' In the upstairs lounge at the Royal Standard belief in Sid was a binding element in our sense of being journalists – belief in his witticisms, the kindness that, we all knew, must lie beneath his sarcasm, his grand record as a newspaperman (he had been a leader of the journalists' union before he became an editor) and, for that matter, as an aviator on the Western Front in the Great War, his liberal mind, his wide reading, his bold campaigns in his editing days against everything that was shabby in the 1930s, from Mussolini to Bondi Beach inspectors. We would never tire of legends of his heroic battles with Packer and sagas of his epic bohemianism: he was the true king, bizarrely returned as courtier to a usurper. When Penton dined at the Royal Standard we knew he was noting who was eating with Sid. One night we watched them meet in the dining room; Sid had been away from the office for a couple of days on a drinking bout: they spoke to each other for only half a minute, both very gravely, their heads down, not looking at each other; Sid came back to our table, with his cheeks sucked in. For a while, he didn't say anything. Penton re-joined Zelie, red in the face and talking angrily.

Deamer was the *Telegraph*'s 'Associate Editor' but so far as we knew this was merely a title of honour. All he seemed to do was write feature articles. Not that Penton treated him as a mere 'feature writer'. He often didn't turn up at feature conferences and if he did he usually sat, lips set, silent, at his place of honour. If he did say anything, Penton would listen with respect, and perhaps even make a note; discussion in front of the rest of us about what 'Mr Deamer' was writing was unimaginable: we assumed they talked about that after we left the room. Deamer had been given an office not much bigger than a broom cupboard; he used it only when he was writing a 'story' – hunching behind a large typewriter and hammering it as if he were in a Vickers Vimy biplane firing his machine gun at Baron von Richtofen. Someone said he had returned to the *Telegraph* with the idea of writing a daily column, but that the column had gone instead to David McNicoll, another returned war correspondent, who had been sent to the United States to meet the columnists Walter Winchell and Drew Pearson so that the column could be based on the latest American models. Someone else said Deamer had suggested a weekly column, but that Penton had appropriated this idea and turned it into THIS IS WHY WE SAID IT. There were other rumours: that Packer consulted Deamer sometimes, privately, without telling Penton what they talked about, that Deamer had influential friends and Packer sometimes used him as a go-between. It was even said that Deamer was an intimate of the unimaginable Ted Theodore – Packer's partner, chairman of the firm, once a union leader, then Labor Premier of Queensland, then a Treasurer in a Labor government, a character from history who, unaccountably, was now wasting his time in business, making money.

I had been intrigued when Sid Deamer told me he remembered our first meeting in Canberra, and startled when he recited the wisecrack I had made that night to cap his anecdote. From this episode he had constructed some picture of me or, more particularly, of my 'mind', that I could not altogether understand, but whatever it was he found noteworthy, he relished as if it were an acquired taste: my 'mind' wasn't for everyone. Sometimes he would break off one of his speeches and grasp my arm, then shake it and look into my eyes, as if we were separating ourselves from the others. 'You would understand that, with such a mind,' he would say with a significant look which I would return, although I did not understand the significance. His admiration for my 'mind' seemed to suggest to him that he had 'discovered' me: when he had returned to Sydney from Canberra, he explained, he had told Penton 'all about me'. Whatever this meant, there was no one among them from whom I could be more delighted to receive praise than Sid Deamer: I would even listen to his monologues with pleasure – great complex arias, filled with movement and presented with the greatest animation; sometimes they were so complex that one lost track of what they were all about, but they were conducted with such enthusiasm that there was pleasure just in the sound of his voice, or even in watching his face and the movements of his hands.

I was, of course, aware of how 'Proustian' it was that I had now entered a *salon* in which my mind could be admired, close-up, by someone whose face I had first seen, in 1936, in an advertisement for 'the new *Daily Telegraph*'.

There was another element of the 'Proustian', almost the beginning of a Deamer novel: at the time when as a student I was hearing the first anecdotes of Sid as legend, his eldest son was at the university in the unlikely form of a 'public schoolboy' who moved in 'society'; already emblazoned with public schooldom in ox-blood sports jacket, grey flannel trousers, white shirt and maroon tie, Tom Deamer became almost a caricature of 'playboy' when, one winter, hobbling on a stout walking stick, he displayed in the Quadrangle the most fashionable bone fracture available in Sydney – an ankle broken while skiing. There seemed no entering his remote and enclosed world of expensive pleasure and when I first met his brother, in the *Daily Telegraph* reporters' room, on his first day as a journalist, his aloofness also seemed to be warning me that trespassers would be prosecuted. Now Adrian and I both belonged to the Royal Standard set. In fact, people put us together as a pair, even as brothers. We were of much the same height, of similar colouring, much the same age; both of us had incomplete university careers and insignificant war records; we were equally sceptical about what we had seen about journalism; and, after we had met, we had quickly gained the belief that we could talk to each other honestly, although it seemed to me as an ex-Andersonian that he had more 'illusions' than I, and was somewhat weak on the paradox of unintended consequences. There were times when, with Adrian beside me, I would feel I was in the uneasy presence of some other 'self'.

To the Royal Standard set, what mattered about Adrian was that he was Sid's son. Would Adrian have Sid's genius? Did he have the same character as Sid? Adrian could be as scathing as Sid, but did he have Sid's charm? Above all: did Adrian realise how lucky he was to be the son of Sid Deamer? While, for Adrian, drinking at the Royal Standard was like drinking at a permanent celebration to honour his father, Sid had an itch to disparage Adrian in public. (There was gossip that Tom had been Sid's favourite son, and that Sid had never been altogether satisfied with Adrian.) At one of the Royal Standard dinners sarcasm from Sid reached such sharpness that it produced an incident we all talked about for weeks. I was not there, but the witnesses gave much the same description: Sid was goading Adrian and, after one smarting crack, Adrian picked up a small glass jug of Worcestershire sauce and threw the sauce at his father. It ran down Sid's face, over his clothes and onto the white linen tablecloth. As we talked about this – using this event to analyse Sid, Adrian, our 'selves', life – it was as if the incident had been re-played in slow motion, like a cricket shot in a newsreel, so that it developed new meanings it could not have had at the time.

SIXTEEN

Living in a mixed neighbourhood

1

There was still a shortage of flats in Sydney. Questions of 'key money', 'knowing the right person', and general arguing and bargaining seemed technical matters beyond my patience or knowledge. (I hadn't read a book on how to get a flat.) They also seemed beyond my pocket: how could I find 'key money' when I saw my salary each week meticulously accounted for on hotel cash registers, taxi meters and restaurant bills? Years ago, as one of the recognitions of 'growing up', my father had given me a wallet but (perhaps for that reason) I went on keeping my money in my trouser pocket. Carrying money in a wallet would give too much dignity to it. When two disagreeable friends continued to send me letters about money I owed them – £10 in one case, £4 in the other – I asked Fitchett's advice. With the spirit of one who was about to present me at court, Fitchett marched me through the streets to a satisfactorily ancient city building ('Balzacian') and introduced me, as if doing them a great honour, to two old brothers who were in the business of money lending. I borrowed £20 from them, at some high rate of interest; as I signed the papers Fitchett joked, as if saving them from embarrassment in dealing with the gentry. Now I too was part of an eighteenth-century novel.

Insofar as I had developed any idea at all of normal living arrangements, it was that I might again fall in love with a woman 'with a flat of her own'. This time, of course, we would share the costs, share the work, 'respect each other's independence', etc. The question was settled differently when, early in my brief 'career' as a feature writer, Sam White lumbered across to me (his walking style had such dignity it could give the impression he was leading himself in procession) and made signs that a conversation was about to begin: he was paying what seemed the large sum of £4 a week for a studio flat ... he spent very little time in it ... I might care to share it with him, paying half the rent. If he decided to go back to London, I could take it over without key money.

At first I scarcely noticed either the flat or its neighbourhood. The flat was merely the place where Sam and I camped. We did all of our eating (separately) at restaurants. On the day I arrived, apart from a delicacy Sam's mother had made for him, there was nothing in the refrigerator. I was working day shift, he night. After work I would stay out late; after his work, he would go to Prince's and stay out even later. Usually I was asleep when he came back but I was likely to wake as he came down the corridor and into the flat. We would usually then express some new degree of disgust at what life in Sydney was offering Sam White. This emotional depth-finding reached bottom the day Packer called him in and told him to stop going to Prince's. If Sam were awake, we would talk again in the morning; then I would go up to the Cross, to Cahill's, to have breakfast. At weekends we might both be in the flat for several hours together. We would speak to each other cordially, but with restraint. It was only after Sam flew back to London on his expensive air journey that I felt able to notice (since it was now 'mine') what the flat was like. I was to live in it for three years.

It was in a narrow, four-storey block, with a façade of brightly coloured bricks, some of which, in a smart late-1930s manner, were given a slightly Aztec arrangement reminiscent of the new kind of 'intimate cinema' then being built; it contrasted with the straight-up and-down 1920s liver-coloured brick on the opposite side of the street. The street was St Neot's Avenue at Potts Point, down from Kings Cross. (I looked up St Neot in the Public Library, discovered that 'Neot' rhymed with 'feet' and composed a limerick about him.) It may have been one of the first streets in Sydney devoted entirely to flats built in the modern style.

This impression of modernity continued behind the plate glass doors of the foyer, in the floral pattern of the wall-to-wall carpet and in the vase of fresh gladioli on the table of mahogany veneer. It extended down the long, carpeted corridor whose stucco, also in the manner of a cinema, was marked out to look like honest stone. Some of the modernity had rubbed off in 'my' flat but several small parts of the green wall-to-wall carpet were threadbare, one corner of the mirror on the dressing table was slightly tarnished, an edge of the mahogany veneer on the dining table showed a thin crack, the seat of the lavatory bowl was unhinged, and one of the cream tiles near the electric cooker was loose. The flat was so small – about four yards wide and six yards long – that any further deterioration would transform it from 'modern' to 'run-down'.

Compact as a ship's cabin, it was assembled on 1930s 'space-saving' principles. The 'daybed' was a 1930s space-saving idea, so in this flat two daybeds were set flush beside the walls, with large drawers beneath them to save further space, and small shelf recesses in the walls beside them; on sound space-saving principles, the dining table was set out from the wall between the two beds and some shelves ran up the side of the larger of the beds. 'Built-in furniture' was another space-saving idea, so there was a large built-in combination wardrobe and dressing table, covered, like all the other woodwork, in mahogany veneer. In the bathroom, the lavatory bowl, wash basin and shower recess almost touched each other, but the triumph of space-saving was the 'kitchenette'; shelves, cupboards, sink, bench, small electric cooker and small refrigerator were all contained in one large cupboard with doors that could be shut, so that one could imagine the kitchen was not there. As with a window in the background of a Dutch painting, an illusion of spaciousness was provided by two plate glass doors leading onto a small balcony that overlooked the garden of the flat next door (and provided, as I found out, an occasional temptation to peeping Toms and cat burglars).

I had been brought up to believe that it was the duty of every young Australian male to accumulate enough money for a deposit on a house and furniture of his own: as I approached my twenty-fifth birthday I had five shillings in the savings bank, and I could not imagine any circumstances, beyond writing a bestseller, in which I would save enough money to buy a house. But I had taken one step on the road to normalcy: I was renting a furnished flat I could not afford.

ON THE DAY SAM WHITE LEFT FOR LONDON, ADRIAN DEAMER arrived to share the flat and the rent but since he went to his parents' house each Friday night and did not come back until Monday evening I had a long weekend to myself; this gave me enough time, among other things, to develop a sense of neighbourhood greater than any I had known since I had lived with my parents. My earlier diffuse, general sense of belonging to 'the Cross' became more particular now that a small part of the Cross, if only by weekly rental, belonged to me: I had become someone who lived at Potts Point.

On the face of it, this was an address of ambivalent meaning, with both the connotation of a funny stage name suggesting extreme ordinariness (*Enter Mr and Mrs Potts, carrying hotwater bottles*) and the connotation (as in 'he's a big pot') of a residential quarter for the rich. It had, in fact, been a quarter for the rich – some old mansions were still there (including the house Frank Packer lived in when he first married; we regarded it with astonishment because, unlike anything else we knew about Packer, it could be seen) – but these old houses had been taken over by the military or turned into restaurants, or subdivided into apartments. Several of the largest blocks of flats, Macleay Regis in particular, were regarded as classy, but more in a New York than a London way. There was nothing ordinary, in a Sydney sense, about Potts Point.

Like the rest of the general area of 'the Cross' it was mainly flats, or at the least 'rooms' or 'bed-sits', and its two main thoroughfares, Macleay Street and Victoria Street, encompassed the whole Kings Cross experience. With their plane trees, both could seem 'continental' but Macleay Street was seen as elegant, sophisticated, modernising, 'European' in its restaurants, delicatessens and other speciality shops, although also partly, and stylishly, 'American' (more exactly, 'New Yorkerish') in some of its building styles, while Victoria Street was seen as part of the old Cross – down-at-heel, with connections with criminals and prostitutes, something seedy left over from the 1920s. Its terrace houses provided a dilemma in taste. I had been brought up to see terraces as something that should be pulled down, and when the cast iron was stripped off their balconies and fibro walls were put up to turn the balconies into rooms, terraces could seem halfway to demolition; but I was now partly aware that a terrace house could be respected as 'old' or 'European'. Sali Herman, a European painter who lived in Sydney, had painted pictures of them as if they were part of the old world. He had also made a painting of the long steep stairs which had been built down the cliff face from Potts Point to Woolloomooloo, so that when I walked down these steps and looked over the shabby rooftops of Woolloomooloo to St Mary's

Cathedral, set on the edge of the park that rose at the other side of the valley, I knew that I could imagine I was in Naples.

It was also seen as characteristic that Potts Point was 'mixed'. In one corner were the buildings that led down to the Australian Navy's dockyard; in another was a fashionable convent school for girls. (This seemed like France.) There were mixed nationalities, of course – a Czech grocer, a German delicatessen keeper, a Hungarian coffee shop proprietor, an Italian greengrocer, a Serbian restaurateur, and so forth. In social class: at one extreme – a penthouse in Macleay Regis, at the other – a room-to-let in Victoria Street.

In Park View in St Neot's Avenue we were also 'mixed'. In the flatette to one side of me was a musician, a noted piano-player and harpist whose harp, kept near the door, defied space-saving principles; the man who lived with her sang at clubs and receptions; her son and daughter were on their way to careers in the theatre. In the flat on the other side, in the near squalor of males unconcerned with housekeeping, lived a quiet gentleman from England, an accountant, and his two richly spoken sons, one studying for the bar, the other a full-time thinker. In others there were a woman doctor, a skilled tradesman and his dressmaker wife, a woman journalist and the male schoolteacher she lived with. And, as it turned out, although it was several weeks before I learned this, in another flat was Douglas McCallum, returned from the army, now finishing his university degree and living with a woman of seraphic beauty (whose affection for him had developed from a Sydney University Dramatic Society production of *Candida* when they were called upon to kiss). Douglas had fallen in love with a woman who had a flat.

I had 'done the shopping' before, for my mother, and for my former love, but now I did it for myself, or for Adrian and me, partly buying the kind of things I would have bought in Muswellbrook when I was sent out after school – a pound of short loin chops, two pounds of potatoes – but also buying some of the things my earlier love had taught me to buy: smoked eel ... avocados ... T-bone steak ... gorgonzola. There were some things I would not risk: I would not dare to cook aubergines, but on one occasion I cooked calves' liver exactly as she used to do it. I would always make the coffee her way, and spice the tomato juice in the way she had taught me.

There was the rent to pay each week and the newspaper bill, money to leave out for the milkman, decisions about what kind of bread to buy, checking the shelves in the kitchenette to see what was 'running out': washing-up to do – and the house-cleaning. I began to feel that in some ways I was becoming 'practical', just like most other people in the world, although in this I would feel housewifely resentments towards Adrian; since he was there only during the week he did less than I. One morning we quarrelled over a dirty sock he had left on the wall-to-wall carpet.

It was also possible to 'entertain' – most ambitiously, over the weekends, when on several occasions I even cooked a special dinner, although with a great amount of uncertainty and cursing and, on one occasion, a hand burnt when some fat caught on fire – but during the week there were a few people who might 'drop in', and the flat had become one of the places one might 'go on to' after drinking at the Royal Standard. If too many 'went on' to it, most had to sit on the floor.

I had never thrown a large party of my own, but after several months at Park View, I began, with a woman friend, to plan one. It was to be held on the roof, which offered views of the city and the harbour. We worked all day preparing what my mother, when she had thrown bridge parties at Muswellbrook, would have called the 'savouries', which we arranged on the new plates I had bought. Before the party started the roof laundry was set up as a bar, with sheets over its laundry equipment and a display of all my new glasses. Extra ice was kept downstairs in the refrigerator. 'Everyone' was there – the entire Royal Standard set, other people from the *Telegraph*, Douglas McCallum and some Andersonians, some of the other Park View tenants, a few survivors from my days in the Ushers bar, and my former love and the man she had now married. On the roof, people broke a plate and a few glasses and crushed some of the food underfoot, but other than this they seemed happy simply talking (some of it with actions – Sid Deamer almost fell over the railings); for a large part of the night a group around Douglas McCallum sang blues. As they argued about the world, those who stayed downstairs in the flat made a more sullen kind of party, which reached a point of definition when my former love, intending to throw her whisky and water over her husband to bring him to his senses, threw the glass as well. His cheek split open: as the blood spread over his shirt and spilt on to the wall-to-wall carpet we shouted advice, both medical and marital, did some first aid, called for a doctor and argued about the meaning of existence. At the moment of greatest noise, Rita

Dunstan came in, a vision of reason from the roof, and said in her calmest and most mature contralto, 'Donald, we've run out of ice.' This surrealist juxtaposition passed us from the tragic to the humorous.

When the doctor arrived, Fitchett, who had now also come down for more ice, took the doctor aside and told him he had been having trouble with his shin. The wounded were evacuated. The party calmly settled into two parts – the innocents on the roof, and those of us who had seen blood. Fitchett came out at his most eloquent. When the party was over and we were hosing down the mess on the roof he was in his best lyrical-narrative form; downstairs, when we did the washing-up, he moved to the mock epic. With the dawn, he mixed one last drink before he went home.

I had not yet put a deposit on a house. But I had now thrown a large party.

2

In sharing a flat Adrian and I found we could make many of the compromises of companionship without adopting the manners of male mateship, unlike my experience when sharing huts in the army or rooms at the Hotel Civic. When we talked together I usually sounded almost like my 'self'.

We spent a lot of conversation on the accountancy of existence, showing a special concentration on making up the accounts on life at the *Telegraph* and the Royal Standard, but also striking trial balances on family life, school life, the absurdities of our life in the armed services, and, to some extent, sex life. Overall, in attempts at honesty (which we both rated above almost everything), a lot of this went further, and was much more particular, than had been customary with my university friends: it seemed based on actual experience – almost like the pieces I had written for *Arna* when I was in the army, but not like anything I wrote now. However, there was one feeling of difference I wouldn't admit to (and here manners came into it) although we both knew it was there: I saw myself as someone who had read more books.

Reading novels had again become a private pleasure, as it had been in the army, but there was no one any longer with whom I could argue about the world's six best novels as if we were settling the nature of existence. My imagination was still 'bookish', but how could I now use books in conversation? Since I did not read to engage in traditional bookish conversation but to put together some view of things, I was likely to be frustrated even more by bookish styles of conversation than by the conversation of those who didn't do much reading; there was even less to say to those who had learned the bookish style without having read many books.

The other intellectual difference between Adrian and me brought us together, because we enjoyed arguing about it: we disagreed on 'politics'. At what I saw as the trivial level, this meant that, in some way, he believed in the Labor Party, and I didn't. Nor did I believe in its opponents, and I had not registered as a voter: the Australian political system had failed me but it was the Labor Party that was in power and I would still make libertarian lunges at trades union prejudices on women and race, and 'Catholic Action' prejudices on censorship, to which could now be added (and this was where we would begin our disputes), the extra delight of attacking its policies on 'welfare' and 'planning'. These could produce a splendid range of terms of abuse: *'étatiste'* ... 'meliorist' ... 'voluntarist'. When these words began to be used, we rose above political parties and really got going. *Was there any point in individual human endeavour when matters were determined by social forces? How could one believe in action when all the evidence was that most of the consequences of our actions were not what we had intended?* In such shouting matches, it was not, at heart, Adrian I was angry with, but myself: upbringing and temperament had made me an optimist, but now, by intellectual training, I was a pessimist. If I didn't keep on shouting, I might forget.

As someone who thought of himself as having drunk deeply of Old Word scepticism, I saw Adrian's simple belief in innate human goodness as Rousseau-esque. (I had forgotten that Rousseau was also a part of the Old World.) So when he told me of the sense of freedom he and Tom had sometimes enjoyed as boys playing tennis without any clothes on, I knew I had him. *That's you,* I said. *Beautiful young, naked people living in amity in a garden of innocence! Life that is one long afternoon of tennis!* But in our 'hardheaded' belief in 'saying what we thought' and 'cutting out the bullshit' we were both innocents, imagining words without consequences. We were joined in this by Gwen Tanner, a secretary on the *Telegraph* of such great style and beauty that she was the talk of the office, and whose wit was as sharp as wisecracking in a good Hollywood movie. As well as going to the movies she listened to the wireless (which for some years I had put behind me as 'low-brow') and even knew popular songs; out of this and the stimulus of her family, she had constructed a tough Sydney version of wisdom, with a laconic throwaway style. I was as entranced as Adrian by her white skin, her red lipstick, her elegantly cut jet black hair, her earrings and her sharpness, but it was Adrian who dared her wit, and began to 'take her out'. Sometimes the three of us would sit in the flat together, almost unable to speak because of the consequences of our frankness. From Adrian I would learn about the other side of Sid, the reverse of his bohemianism – his substantial house on the North Shore, with its tennis court and grounds; his games of contract bridge with respectable neighbours, his wife's knowledgeable and indefatigable interest in home and garden – and his oscillations between these two lives, sometimes disappearing for days, and then coming home, tight-lipped, ready to speak only when the guests arrived for bridge, whereupon the show would go on again, as usual. There was one anecdote Adrian told that, to me, as self-appointed student of his innocence, seemed significant: when Adrian was a child and his father was still a light in the world, Sid returned home at breakfast-time, his arms filled with flowers; Adrian could not understand why his mother did not admire their freshness and colour.

In our conversations, Sid was often with us, now that Adrian could watch him in all of his waywardness, as well as see him, tightlipped, at home. It was over this period that one of his escapades provided another anecdote of the caprices of power. Sid had not been seen in his broom cupboard office since the Monday afternoon; day after day there were more and more unanswered messages on his desk – at first concerning the correction of proofs, the inspection of artwork and other feature writer business, then concerning a deputation which had come to see him and had come back the next day. The messages from Penton became shorter and sharper. On the Friday there was a message that Packer urgently wanted to see him. This, of course, was the end. On the Monday night and Tuesday afternoon he had been seen at the Royal Standard, but then had left, taking off with him one of the Royal Standard set, who returned to the office briefly, late on Friday afternoon, to resign. He would not tell us what had happened to Sid. Adrian learned that Packer had phoned Sid at home. The family spent Saturday without Sid, but speculating what he would do now that he was about to be sacked from the *Telegraph*. He was back the next morning, and sat through a traditional Sunday lunch, saying nothing. Packer was on the phone. They could hear Sid take the call: 'Yes, Frank ... Yes, Frank ... Thank you, Frank ... Yes, Frank ...' When it was over he came back to the table, even more tightlipped, and said with the greatest exasperation, 'Frank has made me a director.'

By the Sunday, several months later, when I was invited for afternoon tea at the Deamer house in Turramurra because Adrian's mother had decided it was time she met his friends, Sid had slipped away from the *Telegraph* to start a column on the *Sydney Morning Herald*. One Royal Standard speculation was that Sid's resignation from the *Telegraph* provided the real meaning of his week's disappearance, because the *Herald* position was already lined up and, for Sid, going on an old-style bender was a polite way of leaving a job. This explanation suited those who wanted to see Sid as a person of elfin wiles. Of those who preferred him as gallant victim, the Penton-haters explained that Penton was so angry at Sid's appointment as a director he had forced him out, while the Packer-haters said that making Sid a director was Theodore's idea, not Packer's; it was part of some boardroom power play in which later, by forcing Sid out, Packer had fought back. Those who hated both Penton and Packer could put both these explanations together.

There he was, on our Sunday afternoon, drinking tea among all these young people (for once, I felt a 'young person') in a large, light sitting room with a handsome outlook over lawns and flowers, while from the tennis court came happy cries and the click of racquet on ball. With chintzes, antiques, copper objects and valuable china surrounded by young people holding cups and saucers, and 'balancing plates', the sitting room seemed a setting for a country house comedy at the Theatre Royal. I remembered now that Sid was English (those 'old dears' and 'old darlings'): there was no doubt about the Englishness of his wife, Dolly, as she sat there, a duchess in an antique chair, and regulated the passage of food, people and conversation. I had not before been in such a large house, and certainly never a sitting room that might have been on the stage. When Dolly directed me to sit on a *pouffe* I did not know what she meant. Was this a homosexual joke? When I found that I was to sit on top of a large leather thing looking like a cushion while I drank tea and ate cake, I felt the need to clown my way out of it; instead, I sat there, and felt a fool. (But 'feeling a fool' also seemed English. There was a BBC show I had heard in which one of the characters, a silly ass, kept saying, 'I say, I am a fool!')

Most of what I knew about drama came from books rather than the stage, but I knew enough about life to recognise that if this were a play it would not be a country house comedy: it was merely the first scene in which we would all seem at peace; soon we would be shouting, crying, screaming, as we tried to say who we were.

SEVENTEEN

The *Sunday Telegraph*
Beach Girl Quest of 1947

I was now being given occasional reprieves from my state of exile in the reporters' room. I might still find myself writing pieces such as TERRIFIED KITTEN CAUSES PEAK-HOUR TRAFFIC HOLD-UP, but I was also doing an occasional feature article or a background piece explaining something or other in simple sentences (WHAT YOU NEED TO KNOW ABOUT TARIFFS). Towards the end of February I was lifted up two floors and placed on the staff of the *Sunday Telegraph*.

Except for Cyril Pearl, alone in his editor's room, we were divided among a few glass and three-ply cubicles whose partitions were so designed that standing up one could see the whole *Sunday Telegraph* staff; but this appearance of communality had no relation to the sense of civil war that came from the rivalries between two of the *Sunday Telegraph*'s three sub-executives. A hidden hand had descended to demote the News Editor to Magazine Editor and promote the Magazine Editor to News Editor. As with a disturbance to natural order in a Shakespeare history, after these two men changed cubicles everything else became unsettled. Pearl alone remained above these calamities; in the mornings we would see him walk down the corridor between the cubicles carrying an old leather briefcase, smiling serenely, but looking straight in front of him. If the door of his office was opened we might hear the sound of his typewriter, but there were no Penton-like conferences, nor any other contacts. It was rumoured that he was fed up with the *Sunday Telegraph*. Adrian Deamer was also working on the *Sunday Telegraph*, and over lunch or beers we would talk about how things would have gone on quite differently had we been editors. Even the distribution of by-lines seemed to do more harm than good. Sometimes they were given; sometimes not; sometimes a mere *By a Special Correspondent* was bestowed instead of a proper by-line. As proofs came through on a Saturday afternoon, we would look for the by-lines and feel elation, pique, or scorn.

My principal business was to report the *Sunday Telegraph* Beach Girl Quest. It was on this subject on my first morning that I had my only interview with Pearl, who told (in words) what I was supposed to do, but also told me (in sad eyes and sad smile) that one must accept these things and make the best of them. I was to provide, in photograph and story, 'The *Sunday Telegraph* Beach Girl of the Week'. There was a pretence that, with a photographer, I was 'touring the beaches in quest of Beach Girls' but in fact all the girls had written in asking to be chosen. They had then filled in forms giving their height, their age, their jobs and ambitions, what beaches they swam at, where they lived, the colours of their hair and eyes, and their waist, hips and bust measurements. This information had been used in sorting them out so that there was variety between them, in terms of social class, height and colour of hair. There was to be no variety in their bust sizes.

I would interview them so that to the information provided I could add, under two headings, the 'human interest' expected to distinguish one Beach Girl from the other. Under 'Man's Angle' I would report on their attitudes towards marriage and what their hobbies and sporting interests were. Under 'Woman's Angle' I would report on their tastes in cooking, clothes, perfumes and cosmetics. After the interview I would call a photographer and we would go by an office car to whatever beach this week's *Sunday Telegraph* Beach Girl was supposed to have been spotted at. She would then be photographed in a swimsuit standing, sitting, lying and arching her back, first on some sand, then on a rock. I had instructions, several times renewed, not to leave any young woman alone with a photographer in case he asked her to pose with her clothes off.

By April the 'quest' was finished and for a week my job changed to writing plugs, mostly in the *Daily Telegraph*, for the various public spectacles throughout the state in which the twenty-two young women would be displayed; at the last of these, the judges – a sculptor, a painter, a French mannequin and Frank Packer's wife – would announce the winner of the *Sunday Telegraph* Beach Girl Quest. In writing anticipatory stories about the six parades and the Beach

Girl Ball I projected clichés of 'mounting excitement' in daily headlines: JUDGES OF BEACH GIRL CONTEST ANNOUNCED ... BEACH GIRL REHEARSAL (with a photo of the radio personality Jack Davey) ... JUDGE SEES PROBLEMS (the French mannequin had said judging 'would be as difficult as in many Paris beauty contests') ... Then came the climax of the first period of excitement: BEACH GIRLS PARADE TOMORROW. JACK DAVEY COMPERE FOR BONDI SHOW

THE SECOND PERIOD OF EXCITEMENT BECAME NUMERATE: 6,000 WATCH BEACH GIRLS PARADE ... 1,400 EXPECTED TO SEE BEACH GIRLS ... 1,500 FAIL TO SEE BEACH GIRL PARADE ... I became part of a travelling show of twenty-two Beach Girls, various performers from radio, screen and stage, several *Telegraph* executives and three senior police officers.

The police were there because the takings from the various parades were to be donated to the Police Boys' Clubs; to them the whole 'quest' was simply a small but significant incident in power stratagems within the NSW Police Force which seemed to spread out into the whole community. When they discussed their moves I felt I was in a 1930s film on the secret manipulation of power in a big city; nothing was what it seemed; somewhere behind it all was Edward G. Robinson or James Cagney. A young woman would come out in a 'Sunshine Colony playsuit', we would smoke our cigars and see her as part of the struggle for police power in Wollongong.

Our search for the ideal Beach Girl had also become an aspect of a power struggle within the *Telegraph* organisation. When the parades began, our travelling show was joined by a confidant of Frank Packer and by a salesman from the Advertising Department, both of whom could find hidden significance in almost everything and whose presence set off reverberations in the civil war within the *Sunday Telegraph*. In these moves Packer's confidant seemed highly amiable (he called me 'Donnie' and would sometimes give me a friendly hug), but back in the *Sunday Telegraph* the News Editor told me: 'Watch out for him ... you can't trust him.' The News Editor was so concerned that the Advertising Department was too prominent in the conduct of the parades that instead of my travelling by the bus, which in any case, was crowded, he ordered an office car to take me to the parade in the country town of Cessnock, thus making a counter-assertion of the prestige of the *Sunday Telegraph* over the Advertising Department.

Remote from these manoeuvres, Pearl first appeared at the gala parade held in the last week, at the Stadium, where he shone with detachment and intelligence, with a special set of the face that seemed to warn us all that he knew what he was doing and that nothing would surprise him now. He came with Frank Packer, and together they cast up such emanations of power and knowledge that they looked as if they knew everything and could do anything. For most of the show I could see only the backs of their heads, but they were clearly the backs of the heads of powerful men.

I saw Pearl again at the Beach Girl Ball at the Trocadero and, since my prime concern was to avoid admitting I couldn't dance, I spent as long as I could in sanctuary at the police table, where no time was going to be wasted on dancing when there were so many significances to look for. Now Pearl's aureole of power had gone; he was sitting several tables away from the official party where Packer presided (this placing was taken by office people to be a snub to the *Sunday Telegraph*), and although from a distance there was interest in watching for signs of Pearl's intelligence at play among what seemed dreary people, it was now clear that it was his being next to Packer at the Stadium which had added the glow of power to the brightness of his intelligence. Power was Frank Packer's business.

Packer had the build for it; he was both tall and thickset, with a fist that could fell an ox and a boot that could kick a mule; standing, he had the bulk of a gorilla, but he walked with a certain swaggering daintiness. In the same way, although, with its heavy jaws, sharp teeth and sloping forehead his head had some of the features of a Neanderthal Man, other parts had elements of the 'handsome' so that, as I watched him in the flickering lights of the Beach Girl Ball, I could see a Jekyll and Hyde alternation; while he could scowl, as if deciding on immediate decapitation, or stand in the confident posture of a conqueror about to set a city to the sword, as he moved among his guests and talked, he was also able to bestow gracious smiles, or make gestures of 'charm'. There was never any doubt that he was prince.

Packer displayed power; his wife displayed glamour. With her mink and diamonds, and a splendid smile on a handsome face, she was a film star in a New York nightclub. At the end of the week, on the night of the final parade in the Sydney Town Hall when the winner was to be announced (I had already written my story: BONDI GIRL WINS 1947 BEACH GIRL CONTEST), she seemed to be looking at me. Overawed, my imagination jumped: if I were in the position of Pearl, or Penton (I would not be, of course, since I would, instead, be a novelist) but if I were, and had to deal with these people, I could imagine myself dealing with Packer in great, reverberating arguments – everyone knew this was the only way to deal with a man like that – but how could I feel at ease with a film star, with a perfect smile, wearing mink and diamonds?

After it was all over, and I got back to the office to add a couple of paragraphs to what had already been written, I heard that Packer wanted to congratulate me. There could be no other reason why he had called for me. I went along the forbidden corridor and through an empty anteroom into what, with the books lining its walls, seemed to be a gentleman's study. There Packer sat, behind a desk the size of a dictator's in a movie, with a desk lamp as bright as if we were about to play the third-degree scene.

He began shouting as soon as I reached the door. As I stood in front of his desk the room seemed to shake as if it were a hurricane and I was in the ship's cabin with a mad admiral. *Why had I taken a car to Cessnock?* ... The car was authorised, and I ... *Where's the authority?* ... Well, I had spoken to ... *I'm telling you there wasn't an authority* ... What I was trying to say ... *I don't care what you're trying to say! Why would you want a car? What was wrong with the bus?* ... There wasn't a spare seat on the bus ... *Are you too grand to travel by bus?* ... I said there wasn't a spare seat on the bus ... *You didn't need a seat! You could have stood up!* ... Well, I thought there were laws against that ... *Don't try to be smart with me, Mr Horne! You're sacked!*

There were a few more exchanges, and some repetitions, but when I got back to the flat and began talking about it, this was all I could remember, along with the feeling of fright which came from being in the presence of a man who could kill me with one hand. I stayed awake for a couple of hours – not, as yet, from anxiety about what would happen next; it was a sense of physical shock that kept me awake. It was as if I was back in the army and I had again been hit over the head.

*AS IT HAPPENED WHEN I GOT TO THE OFFICE THE NEXT DAY, THINGS
seemed to have been sorted out. I wasn't quite sure how it had gone, but it was said
that Mrs Packer had intervened ... In any case I had my job back. In fact they had
put me on to the features staff ... When I went to the Features room Mrs Packer
was already there; she was explaining it all to me, and smiling ... She made me a
cup of tea ...*

When I woke from this dream it was Saturday morning; I didn't have a
job, and on the chair where I had thrown my trousers was what was left of a
week's salary.

In the office pubs that afternoon I told the anecdote of my dismissal again
and again – by now I had perfected an impersonation of Frank Packer – and
in return received explanations, in varying orders of probability, about which
office manipulations had made me their innocent victim. The usual view
was that the News Editor, to protect himself, had 'put me in' by not himself
taking responsibility for ordering the car. The general opinion was that I
would probably get my job back; the thing was to return on Monday and see
if Packer had cooled down. This advice was accompanied by outpourings of
anecdotes of famous Packer sackings, all more interesting than mine. That
night, I was at Peter Hastings's most ambitious party: the Royal Standard
set were there, along with other elements from the office; even the Chief of
Staff. More anecdotes ... more advice ... but also a conversation with the Chief
of Staff. With the preoccupation of someone who was giving the matter full
and immediate consideration, he listened, nodded, turned his eyes away from
me in a gesture of judicial impartiality, sucked his pipe and told me to come
and see him on Monday afternoon. Well, that settled it. Everything would
be all right. I was able to indulge my Sunday morning hangover without any
special anxieties; when I saw the Chief of Staff on Monday the main question
would be to help this awkward man through his embarrassment at admitting
a mistake.

In fact, on Monday, as soon as I entered his cubicle he frowned me into a
chair and lectured me for 'taking advantage of a social occasion' at the Hastings
party. Then he announced that Mr Packer had made a concession: if I paid the
sum of £14, the estimated cost, including overhead charges, of taking the car
to Cessnock, I would be permitted to keep my job. In my reply I used the
word 'outrageous'. *There was no need to get emotional,* he said. *The question was*

simply whether I would accept Mr Packer's offer of a compromise. No! *Then his instructions were to dismiss me on the spot.* Could I see Mr Packer myself? *Of course not. Mr Packer was a busy man.* Could I see Cyril Pearl? *Mr Pearl was not available. But Mr Pearl had put through a payment of £20 overtime. I could pick this up at the pay office with any other monies that were owing to me. His instructions were that I should go to the pay office and then leave the building.* At the pay office they asked me to sign a statement that I was receiving the money 'in full and final settlement of all claims'. I said I wouldn't sign that. They told me to leave the building.

Talking about what I should now do took another day's discussion in the office pubs and a long telephone call from Hastings. Someone arranged an interview with the secretary of the journalists' union, but when I saw him he seemed scarcely interested; the fact that I had a contract with the *Telegraph* wasn't a concern of the union's, he said, I would have to see a lawyer about that. All that mattered to the union was that I should have been given a conventional period of notice. They would take that up for me. Of course, if I really had committed a misdemeanour there was nothing they could do. He hoped I understood that.

Then he thought of a tactic that seemed to give him fighting spirit. He would dictate a letter. Nothing to do with the union. I would sign it as a personal letter. As he dictated this abusive letter, it seemed just what was needed ... 'most tyrannical and oppressive' ... 'morally and legally unjust' ... 'ludicrous' ... 'full rights under my contract'. That was the only language Packer would understand.

Sustained by greed (I might even be able to bluff Packer into paying me salary for the nineteen months which were the unexpired part of my contract), and with angry words of self-righteousness, I took a copy of this letter back to the office pubs. Bad luck, one of my chief advisers said: I had fallen into a trap. The very phrases I had most liked – 'tyrannical and oppressive' ... 'morally and legally unjust' – were taken verbatim from a notorious letter Penton had written at a time when he was in dispute with the union. Packer would recognise these words. Penton would never forgive me. The union secretary was using me as part of his vendetta with Penton and Packer.

The next morning, a telegram came from the Chief of Staff: *Please telephone me personally.*

'Oh yes, Mr Horne. Thank you for ringing. Mr Packer would like to see you at three o'clock.'

Three o'clock. Packer stands up when I come into his office, face all smiles ('creaking', as I put it in the subsequent anecdote, 'with old world charm'). He motions to a chair. We sit down, two men talking together reasonably. He had the wrong picture in his mind the other night, he says, but he's banged a few heads together and he's found out the truth. (Smile.) He wants me to come back. (Smile.) A great future awaits me at the *Daily Telegraph*. (Stand up.)

We shake hands. The next day I am back working in the enormous room. It is three months before, cautiously, they put me on to an interesting story.

EIGHTEEN

Settling down?

1

One night a friend dropped in with an Englishwoman who had, I learned, just divorced her Australian husband. It was a hot night and we sat on the roof drinking until early morning. Ethel lived a couple of blocks away, in a converted room in one of the terrace houses I still half-felt should be pulled down, but that to her represented one of the 'English' aspects of Sydney. The next day we went on the first of a number of walks around the Cross and its environs (she had not been living there for long) and, over the weekends, through Woollomooloo 'into town'; on these walks I had intended to show off the Sydney I now thought of as my own, but she showed me instead aspects of the 'old', so that what had seemed most decrepit in Sydney or most imitative, could now seem most genuine. She was slightly taller than I, a few months older, and spoke exotically in the kind of 'high', 'clipped' English voice I had been brought up to hear as a voice of command. As we walked, I could feel I was being introduced by an expert guide to an engaging view of the world, in which terrace houses or St Mary's Cathedral were merely an insubstantial fringe for images of the antique. When she talked about the village where she had been born (memories of which seemed the main love in her life) we entered the heartland of her sense of the authentic: as we walked down some street at the Cross where new façades had been put up over old houses to give them a veneer of modernity, she might instruct me about patterns on porcelain, or hallmarks on silver candlesticks, or she might recall how, until just before the war, the road running through her village (where three hundred people lived) had still been a simple, unpaved lane of sand; or describe the woods belonging to the

Duke of Buckingham which half-enclosed the village and provided stories of favourite walks, haunted trees, pheasants and gamekeepers (gamekeepers!). In particular, there was the feeling of honesty and authenticity given to life by building materials: at a crossroads near the village an old farmhouse still had a thatched roof; at a village a couple of miles away, she told me, there were six thatched roofs and a dozen cottages that were half-timbered – I developed a special warmth of sentiment towards the timber beam. Her father was a moderniser: he had stripped his farm buildings of their thatched roofs and replaced them with asbestos roofing, covered the plain, old red bricks of the house itself with stucco and, in the hall, boxed in some old beams. When she inherited the house she intended to strip off the stucco and expose the beams: that would make things real again.

At about the time Adrian moved out of our studio flat and she moved in, we began to exchange lives. As if making a customs declaration, I insisted on telling her about such *affaires* and encounters as I had been able to experience. (One had to be frank about these things, didn't one?) In return, she told me about the failures of a marriage that had been made in the village church early in the war, and un-made, several years later, in the divorce court in Sydney. I took her through my collection of didactic anecdotes, a recital that, on and off, took several weeks. In return, she told me the tales of a social worker – she was now training as a hospital almoner – and tales of her youth.

I had a picture of two girlhoods. One was a picture book story of a young child living happily in a comfortable nursery with pets to love, woods to walk through, a nanny and maids, and, remotely, but with some reassurance, a mother and father to meet at certain hours of the day. The other was like a school novel of the bleak kind: a girl sent to a fashionable boarding school her parents couldn't afford which had a strict regime and where a characteristic sound was the slap of gym shoes on the floor.

In our exchanges of experience, telling each other about ourselves, sometimes over dinner tables, sometimes until late in the night, sometimes just walking down the street, we could seem to be building new 'selves', in a kind of joint experience that accommodated each of us to the other. I was beginning to talk about the kinds of ordinary things in my life that had previously not seemed worth talking about.

WITH DOUGLAS MCCALLUM AND HIS WOMAN FRIEND, ETHEL AND I formed a 'foursome', visiting each other's flats whenever we felt like a talk, as if they were extensions of our own. McAuley lectured Ethel on English nature verse; Fitchett took us for a roast pork Sunday dinner at Petty's Hotel where he decided to nick-name her 'Atlantic' after a brand of petrol called 'Atlantic Ethyl'; Adrian had her invited to Turramurra where she fitted perfectly into the English tea ceremony; when former diplomatic cadets came through Sydney we would take them to dinner at the restaurant around the corner. I tried to begin to explain to her the mysteries of Andersonianism; Rhodes lectured us on the derivation of the name of her village. The flat now seemed full of things – not only her clothes, her electric iron and so forth, but with objects she had taken away from her marriage, and with new things we bought. I saw this as my main contribution towards making things more comfortable for living together. For my part I hired a carrier to bring to the flat from Denbigh my books, and the bookcase made for me by my father.

ON CHRISTMAS DAY I TOOK ETHEL TO VISIT MY PARENTS AT Denbigh, explaining how it had first been given its style by Nanna and Pa. The twenty-minute train journey through the suburbs which had seemed a symbol of defeat in a period I now saw as 'like something out of Gissing' had become nothing more than an occasion for amusing anecdotes about the illusions of a boy and the lost illusions of a young man. My mother, who had been waiting for us on the front verandah, said 'Welcome to Denbigh!' as if she had ordered the blowing of a fanfare, and she opened the fly-screen door as if it were the raising of the portcullis of a famous castle. The dog barked welcome ... Janet was in a party dress ... Nanna was all smiles as she brought out the traditional Christmas morning port to drink beside the Christmas tree ... My father cracked the traditional jokes. We walked around the rooms inspecting the 250 or so framed photographs on the walls as if they were ancestral portraits painted by Old Masters, and walked around the back garden as if it were a great park designed by an illustrious landscape gardener; then, in a ceremony of sincerity, we settled into the kitchen and while the last preparations were made for the Christmas meal, Nanna told stories about the famous things that had been done and said in her kitchen. After that, we often went to Denbigh on Sundays.

While Ethel kept her end up with the grown-ups I would talk to Janet, then walk in the garden and stand in front of some part of it – the chook run, perhaps, or the fernery, or the guava tree, a reminder of 'bilious attacks' brought on by gluttony, or the fig tree where I would sit among the branches and think about how I would like to live forever at Denbigh; or the old stable, which had once been a reminder of the miraculous time when Denbigh had its own horse, but now, against all expectation, had become the place where my father wove baskets as part of his occupational therapy; or the hedges, behind which 'Mick' and I used to play our most private games; or the rustic arch over the entrance to the cement path which led, between the two perennial gardens, to the outdoor lavatory, a reminder of those journeys 'down the back' that now seemed a memory of some earlier social order, as did the space beneath the aviary where the empty bottles used to be kept, a reminder of the bottle-oh – and of the milkman, the baker, the iceman and the clothes prop man in their horses and carts ... or the workshop, the centre of life for Pa ... or the lattices that kept the world away from our life at Denbigh. When Ethel said the garden reminded her more of an English than an Australian garden it occurred to me that Pa was so proud of his family's early Australian connections that in reconstructing his boyhood memories of colonial gardens at Camden and ignoring current suburban fashions, which lined up a garden like a small parade ground, he had put together something that was now un-Australian. Perhaps I might write a 'decline' novel about an 'old' Australian family, living on in an age of impostors, of rich people like Frank Packer.

Usually, we would arrive in time for a midday 'roast dinner'; occasionally, not until an afternoon tea of sandwiches and cakes; on visits of greater than usual sincerity we would arrive early and sit in the kitchen for morning tea and hot scones. So that my mother's love could gain full expression in food, we always stayed for 'tea' (always, now, in quotation marks); then, if no one else was around, we had to play bridge so that we could eat chocolate gingers and sugared almonds, and then, when the rubber was over, leave, and go back to what was now our own world.

2

All around me people were 'settling down': into marriages, careers, householderships, parenthoods and opinions, and because I had now been working at the *Daily Telegraph* for more than two years friends would say, 'Well, Donald, you seem to have settled down.' To demonstrate my integrity as a fundamentally unsettled person, I would jab with some offensive word or lay down a quick barrage of offensive opinions; yet, in a kind of a way, in our shabby, space-saving flatette at Potts Point, I was afraid, at times, that even I might be 'settling down' (although not, of course 'selling out').

We had arranged things in the flat so that the worn-out sections of the carpet did not show; we put a vase in front of the tarnished parts of the mirror and when we had a telephone installed we placed it over the cracks in the mahogany veneer. My father built me a second bookcase and I was again regularly buying books. However, I could not believe that I had yet fallen into respectability. It was true that the flatette's mean pretensions to modernity might seem to say otherwise; contrasted with the rundown generosity of the colonial sandstone house in the city where some Andersonians were now camping, our flatette could seem scandalously petit bourgeois. So it was – but flats were hard to get ... and after all it was at the Cross, not in the suburbs. In any case, I owned next to nothing; I had nothing in the bank; I was living with a woman. How could one call that 'settling down'?

I was becoming, in a minimal sense, 'domesticated', but surely that was not bourgeois but task-sharing? Unless I was rostered for weekend work at the *Telegraph* Ethel and I did the week's shopping together; in fact, until I had passed on all the shopping knowledge I had acquired, I saw myself as more experienced in buying exotic foodstuffs than Ethel, although when we were cleaning the flat, I acknowledged her superiority (which could mean that she did more of the cleaning). An American cookbook, *The Joy of Cooking*, became one of the bases of our living together. I learned from it how to carve a pheasant and how to mix a gin fizz; reading *The Joy of Cooking* was a civilising experience. It would be consulted each weekend for new dishes and we would eat them as if they were magic food giving our relationship new meanings; while preparing the dinner parties we gave it would lie open on the table as if it were the holy book from which we could obtain all guidance.

Were dinner parties a sign of 'settling down'? To some of the more puritan Andersonians they could seem irredeemably bourgeois – who could imagine John Anderson giving a dinner party? – but I saw them as resuming, at last, those festivals of the good time that had illumined my boyhood. Ethel and I would spend most of the day preparing for a dinner party: shopping, cooking, arranging the flat so that it would look like something else – and then sit there with the bottles out and the glasses on a dressing table that had for the night become a sideboard, listening for footsteps to come down the corridor.

McAuley and Norma had 'settled down' at Bellevue Hill in a larger flat, and they had bought furniture and furnishings of a kind that, in their design, showed a McAuley view of the world. They went bird-watching. Now they were having a baby. On the first night Ethel and I went there for dinner, McAuley carved the lamb in vertical rather than horizontal slices. This was something so unknown to me that I thought he had made a mistake but after Ethel told me that this method of carving was appropriate to this particular type of joint it seemed another example of how McAuley, having decided to 'settle down', was eager to make an expert job of it. If we met, he and I would still drink as much as before, even if it were now table wines and a somewhat higher quality of brandy, but other than this there was a feeling that we had both put childish things behind us; in my case it was not obvious that I had put anything in their place, but, late in the night, when the brandy was burning our brains, if McAuley became mystical, as he usually did, he became mystical about the virtues of domesticity. Then as tobacco smoke and brandy fumes poured out of our mouths we would fall into more familiar themes, and lament the crises of our times – the failures of progress, the treachery of intellectuals, the sterility of modern life, the coming catastrophes. After a night like this it would be all the more difficult to wake up the next day and again persuade myself that I was still a reporter on the *Daily Telegraph*. That was proof that I hadn't 'settled down'.

As well as my own sense of domesticity there was a wider sense of shared domesticity – in the joint life in our block of studio flats; but all this standing around for hours chatting at open doors was surely bohemian and communal rather than bourgeois and suburban? Borrowing a clove of garlic from a neighbour and then being invited to have a drink and a talk about the theatre while she made a Russian salad was, surely, not 'settling down'?

And the way in which Ethel and I, Douglas and Jean could seem a 'foursome' might have come from an operetta on bohemian life: either pair would 'drop in' on the other and we might lounge around for a whole afternoon, or a whole evening (sometimes both), smoking and drinking coffee, spinning out long threads of conversation. In this conversation there was another proof that I had not 'settled down': I saw Douglas as one of the few who, like me, was firmly set against the way the intellectual tide was flowing; we were odd men out in a world of 'ritualistic progressives' and 'left-wing authoritarians'. Most of those who had 'settled down' were not only in danger of disappearing behind the privet hedges of their suburban front gardens; fed on Beveridge and Keynes, they were also settling into what I saw as prevailing drifts towards an acceptance of government 'planning' as the principal basis for human betterment. They had not read Sorel on the producer ethic. Not even John Anderson on the servile state. They were likely to be rationalists ... miserable idiots who had never heard of the paradox of unintended consequences. Even worse ... *étatistes*, fools who trusted the state.

Trust the state! It was enough to blacken the blood of two retired philosophical anarchists drinking coffee in a Kings Cross flatette. The state! The censor of books! Suppressor of sexual freedom! Enforcer of monogamy! Suppressor of abortion! Enforcer of conscription! Hangman! Shutter of pubs at six o'clock! How could these idiots see the state as a centre of benevolence and rationality simply because it 'planned' the economy and bribed people with pensions? Even Douglas did not fully understand the dangers of 'planning' and of the welfare state: as part of a course she was doing as a trainee almoner Ethel had to write an essay on some proposed anti-tuberculosis legislation that included a provision to make chest x-rays compulsory; I suggested she devote her essay to exposing this as another trend towards state authoritarianism and servility, but Douglas warned her that this might not altogether satisfy the examiner.

It was not just a question of the state. Some episodes in our conversations as a foursome were duologues between Douglas and me on the decay of the proletarian movement: as he smoked his pipe and drank his beers and I smoked my cigarettes and drank my gins, we both knew that if one were to avoid the bourgeois style, then it was the workers one must, in particular, avoid, since it was in the proletariat that bourgeois values now flourished most rankly.

Above all, there were the frauds of Stalinism. This was a theme on which we could enrage ourselves systematically. On our side there had been some rays of enlightenment – *Darkness at Noon* and *Animal Farm* had popularised for some people what we already knew – but so many intellectuals knew nothing of all that solid stuff, fully documented, in all those sensible books on Douglas's bookshelves: the Stalinists were still making gains in Europe, large parts of Asia seemed about to fall, but all around was intellectual illusion. To be an anti-Stalinist intellectual as late in history as 1947 seemed a gallant and lonely stand.

I had learned from Douglas that there were new breeds of Andersonians at the university who had become more Andersonian than Anderson, wanting to revive an earlier and truer Andersonianism and hold it up against John Anderson himself, whom they saw as having now become, in some ways, 'reactionary'. I met some of them at a weekend conference 'camp' organised by one of the student societies, at which I was to give a paper on criticisms of the capitalist press. I was sharing a hut with the classical Andersonians and was not much aware of the modernising Andersonians who were also at the conference – until I gave my paper, when I found they were criticising me almost as much as the Stalinists. I had intended to infuriate the 'ritualistic progressives' and 'authoritarian leftists' by defending the capitalist press against 'illiberal attacks'. But here were Andersonians attacking me. Andersonians were not supposed to attack each other. They were expected to unite against the illusions of the rest of the world. I sent a copy of my paper to Penton. Several days later the *Telegraph* published it, in full, in two parts, under the heading A REPORTER ON THE PRESS. The next week I was assigned to write some feature articles and was given other 'good jobs', with flourishes of by-lines. At the beginning of 1948 I was reinstated on the features staff – restored to my rightful condition.

3

For the next two years I was a feature writer, with scarcely any upset to a predictable Monday-to-Friday routine other than an occasional significant frown from Penton at the Monday conference that would set me silently wondering whether I had fallen out of favour. Work would not begin until after lunch on Monday and, beyond a brief, polite appearance on Friday mornings, was usually over by Thursday night. For the three busy days in the middle of the week a pleasant sense of deadline anxiety gave some entrepreneurial sense to what we were doing. It showed we weren't just clerks: we were getting a show on the road. Then, with the long weekend I was able to get back to reading at least one novel a week and we could throw a dinner party any Saturday night we wished. There were times when I really did fear I was settling down.

But even being a feature writer kept me somewhat 'unsettled'. Long, brittle battles of attrition could be fought stolidly, sentence by sentence, and sometimes word by word, over 'copy' for the *Telegraph*'s Saturday magazine. Its sub-editor saw himself as the custodian of office style and defended it with a battery of sharp pencils in five different colours. The artificiality of the specific 'news tie-up' still prevailed, so that it continued to be difficult to write about anything that mattered, and there were times when I had to pound out so many stories that I would use one or two pseudonyms. Some of the stories were shamefully silly; for others, particularly a 'Reporter-At-Large' or a 'Personality', I was tempted to be my 'self', writing as I had written my fugitive articles from the army, but I couldn't do this: it would not be in office style. In scarcely any of the stories could I see my 'self' and then only as part of the mimicry. There were some evenings when, paralysed by headache, I would wonder how I could go on the next day. But all the time there was the bright reward of not having to perform in the reporters' room.

At the least, whatever it was I had to do, I felt that I knew how to do it, whether it was MALES' LAST MARKS OF SUPERIORITY, or WORLD RESOURCES ON EBB, or ARGENTINA'S LOST PARADISE – THE FALKLAND ISLANDS, or ZOO SOON TO HAVE ITS OWN GORILLA. In the army, I had learned all the drills and successfully pretended to be a gunner; now I was successfully pretending to be a *Daily Telegraph* feature writer. Even the other feature writers now seemed to have accepted my disguise. I enjoyed our afternoon coffee ceremonies and developed rituals of conversation with all of them, and we exchanged dinner parties with some of them.

There were the pleasures of being paid to go off to libraries to find something out. There were people to meet, and although I still felt shy with strangers and uneasy in the artificialities of 'the interview', there were anecdotes to pick up from these ritualised meetings, on which I might 'dine out' (as I would now put it).

At times I could put up an 'idea' for a 'story' that touched on some part of my other world with its afternoons with Douglas McCallum, smoking and drinking coffee, or its evenings over brandy with McAuley: when *Meanjin* magazine was refused a subsidy because it was not seen as 'literary' I had a 'news tie-up' for a piece on the difficulties of running little magazines; when the American, Hartley Grattan, produced a book on Australia I was able to thump the typewriter about Australia's 'prolonged cultural adolescence', as I would have done if I had written my own book on Australia (a project that now seemed difficult to imagine).

I enjoyed instructing ignorant readers in the background to what was happening in the world. Britain devalued the pound, so I was able to write DEVALUATION AND WHAT IT MEANS. The House of Lords was to be reformed, so I could give the readers a lecture on upper houses; when there was talk of electoral changes in Australia the readers received a lecture on voting reform. The partitioning of Palestine produced three background lectures; when Ireland declared its independence I wrote GREAT DAY FOR THE IRISH – AFTER 779 BLOODY YEARS; when the Old Vic Company put on *Richard III*, the readers were lectured on the politics of Tudor England; there was a United States presidential election, so I was able to instruct readers in the United States political system; as background to one of the insurrections of Southeast Asia I wrote MALAYA – LAND FLOWING WITH TIN AND RUBBER.

For a Christmas present, Ethel had given me a subscription to *The Economist*. As I read it each week I would underline all the important passages in ink, put them by and, later, do revision by looking over the marked passages. In this I was particularly taken with hard-headed concerns about the allocation of scarce resources. There were two tough sentences in particular that *The Economist* often used: *You can't have your cake and eat it* and *You can't get a quart out of a pint pot*. When I saw one of these, I might underline it in red ink, a colour used for especially significant sentences. I had taken to inserting into conversations the phrase 'the marginal principle' (I had even re-read parts of my despised economics textbooks) and there could be a special delight in lecturing readers on all the tough decisions they now had to make on economic policy: INFLATION: BEWARE OF 'ARTIFICIAL PROSPERITY' … A WELFARE STATE DOES NOT RUN ON AIR … THE DANGERS OF AUSTRALIA'S MILK BAR ECONOMY.

The Economist was offering me, weekly, more lavish helpings of unpalatable truths than sometimes, despite my keen appetite for the unpalatable, even I could properly digest. I knew that there was usually 'little ground for optimism' and indeed most occurrences were 'disastrous at home and ruinous abroad'; that almost always 'there was very little room for manoeuvre'; that ambition should always 'shrink to sensible proportions'; that one was usually 'down to the last weapon in the armoury'; that in any situation 'the frailty of the whole structure' was about to be revealed; and that there was an obverse side to every medal. Most important of all, whether one was discussing the development of backward areas, the industrialisation of Albania, or the surveying of the Amazon, there was one certain immutable principle: above all, we must *increase productivity*.

As part of the enjoyment of hard-headedness there were, as well as the gratifications of fact-facing, the satisfactions of plain talk and straight thinking. While Penton continued his terror campaign in which he faithfully protected *Telegraph* readers from the evils of abstract nouns, the passive voice, long sentences, complex syntax and general gobbledegook, I now began writing articles against the specific absurdities of bureaucratic officialese and academic jargon; then, as a logic-chopper, I was entranced when Penton asked me to give the cadet journalists lectures on straight thinking. Straight thinking! This could be as good as an argument in the old days at the Ushers bar. I began with a savage assault on loose usage, followed this up with an awesome revelation of the six great fallacies and a thorough debunking of the misuse of expert opinion, then came to a climax with a tirade against the abuse of statistics. The cadets were to sit for an examination in straight thinking, but when one of them put it to me that straight thinking shouldn't get in the way of their careers I made sure they all passed, even if some of them passed more than others. Someone on the ABC heard about these lectures, and I gave a three-part radio series called 'Do You Know Your Own Mind?' I hoped that John Anderson hadn't heard of this indulgence in popularisation.

Penton dominated all – in his presence, when we paid court to him at the conferences and, in his absence, in our conversations, in which he was a standing item on the agenda. He would read our 'stories' in typescript, after they had been 'subbed', but before they had been 'set'. Occasionally a story might be rejected, usually because it was 'too dreary'; sometimes he might cross out a paragraph or two because they weren't in office style; occasionally, at a Monday conference, he would congratulate one of us on a 'story'. Like a message from heaven, word would sometimes descend that the editor had just read one of our 'stories' and found it good.

I was drawn closer into his presence when he sent for me one afternoon to discuss an idea for a story. This time I was not at the other end of his room, but in the very chair where Sid Deamer used to sit, right beside Penton's desk; he talked to me with as much joviality as if we were having a coffee together. Not long afterwards he instructed that he was to see a particular story of mine *before it was subbed*. It came back unmarked. As such, it was as inviolate as an authentic manuscript in a glass case. Then, on another occasion, he called for me as well as the 'story'. I sat in front of Penton as he read my 'story', pen in hand turning over the slips of copy paper, altering nothing; he laughed, then threw it back to me across the desk and said 'Good!' A few weeks afterwards I was given a rise, to the top of the journalist's scale.

There were pleasures in this but given all the anecdotes of Penton's rages and his inconstancies, there were more fears than hopes. What disasters might come if Penton 'took me up'? When one night he invited me, offhand, to have dinner at the club where he dined regularly with his mistress, I saw myself as becoming one of those favourites of a medieval king I had read about as a boy in *The Story of the British Nation* – I would be taken up for a while; then I would be beheaded. As it turned out, the dinner was to discuss a 'story' with a man who would provide some information. With jokes, business talk and anecdotes, it seemed a perfectly ordinary dinner; as a student of *The Joy of Cooking* my main impression was that the French dressing was too vinegary, but I assumed that Penton liked vinegar. The next week, however, my anxiety returned. Penton invited me to spend Saturday with him on his yacht, the *Josephine*.

The yacht was rumoured to be a company yacht, but like anything else connected with Penton, through its very connection with him it became his. He was said to sail it every weekend and in his office were coarse-grained, tough-looking, action-packed photographs of the *Josephine*. When he had first captained it in the Sydney–Hobart yacht race, one of my jobs on a dull night as a general reporter had been to interview him about the fast time the *Josephine* had made on its run back to Sydney; there was an inference in the 'story' that Penton had, as it were, won the race backwards. This had been the only time I had heard him talk about the *Josephine*. Scarcely anyone on the *Telegraph* had been on the *Josephine*. It belonged to one of the sides of Penton's life in which, I assumed, he had 'sold out'; his crew were said to be mainly 'business people'. But we all knew that skippering the *Josephine* must bring out the worst in Penton. We would imagine him, piratically tyrannical, astride the sloping deck of the *Josephine* bullying his scurvy crew. And now I was to be bullied. I had never set foot on a yacht. How would I know what to do? Penton would throw me overboard.

Ethel had also been invited. She had been on a yacht, so was able to give me a background briefing and advice on what to wear. When we arrived at the *Josephine* on a sunny Saturday morning, Penton was giving directions about making the salad. The opening conversation left me with nothing to say – it was about a big boxing match of the night before – but when we set off sailing, I found I was not expected to do anything and there was no need even to talk; I could simply sit and enjoy an unusual experience. At lunch things became more usual, with a lot of drinking of red wine and a lot of shouting, so that I was able to be my 'self', if in a modified version. After lunch I fell asleep, and when it was all over we went to the bar of a local pub where the noise was so great I couldn't hear anything. It hadn't been so bad after all.

In her voice of command Ethel insisted we must make Penton understand that outside the office we were all social equals. To demonstrate this, she proposed a plan of greater daring than any I could have imagined: if Penton could invite us out on the *Josephine*, then we could invite him and Zelie to our flat for dinner. When they accepted, we spent several days narrowing a list of French recipes from *The Joy of Cooking*; on the Saturday morning of the dinner we shopped more carefully than usual and cleaned the flat more fastidiously; in the afternoon as we got on with cooking there was double-checking of all the recipes and an even greater attempt to make the flatette look like somewhere else. When the sherry, whisky and gin bottles were standing on the dressing table and the uncorked table wines were breathing on the balcony and the port and brandy bottles were waiting on the kitchen shelves, the question became: what should I wear? There were rumours that, off-duty, Penton still kept up old habits of informal dressing – this was something on which he hadn't 'sold out'; but of the other two we had invited, married friends of Ethel, we had no idea what the husband, a former Stalinist, would wear. I made a compromise: I would wear a tie, but not a jacket. When Penton arrived he was in some nautical gear, with his hairy chest bared to the waist, but the former Stalinist was done up in a three-piece suit as if about to review the May Day march from the top of Lenin's tomb. I sided with Penton and took off my tie: the former Stalinist seemed to tighten his defensively as, at once, he attacked the capitalist press. Penton shouted a counter-offensive; as they bellowed at each other they shovelled down course after course without appearing to notice what they were eating and gulped down our carefully shopped for wines as if they were water; they made so much angry noise that two neighbours came to the door offering help.

The former Stalinist and his wife left early, immediately after the first round of coffees. The dinner seemed an unparalleled fiasco. But here was Penton, now that they had gone, reclining on one of our daybeds as if it were a couch at a Roman banquet. He had enjoyed the cooking enormously – he loved experimental cooking, he said; he had enjoyed the argument enormously – he loved arguing. He stayed on for several hours, drinking brandy, joking, arguing, tale spinning, shouting, and assuring me of a bright future on the *Telegraph*.

A BRIGHT FUTURE ON THE *TELEGRAPH*! SEVERAL MONTHS LATER, when I met him in a corridor, Packer made the same threat. Whenever we passed each other we had developed the habit of joking about my being sacked – on his side: 'Stolen any more of my cars lately, Mr Horne?' ... on mine: 'I think I might take a drive up to Cessnock, Mr Packer!' – but on this particular corridor-passing he had stopped and said he would send for me soon; it was time we had a good talk about my career. (My career!) Obviously, I wouldn't want to stay a mere feature writer ... it was time I was groomed for an executive position. He'd put me on the subs' desk – give me all-round experience ... (wave of the hand) ... teach me the ropes. I must come and see him: he had plans.

There were rumours that I was a poor relation of Packer. This was seen as the only rational explanation for my 'selling out' by writing articles making fun of the Chifley government. Yet when I wrote pieces such as POLITICIANS HAVE BEEN FOOLING US ON HOUSING, or PUBLIC SERVICE – GROWTH OF A LEVIATHAN, I had no images of Packer as an audience. I couldn't, in fact, imagine him reading a *Daily Telegraph* feature article. Nor was Penton in my mind, except for the need to keep within the vocabulary and the syntax of office style. If I were to imagine anyone who might approve of CANBERRA MAKES ANOTHER GRAB, or YOU MAY GET A JOB IN THE DEPRESSION BUT NO CHOICE, it was likely to be John Anderson or the editor of *The Economist*. But images of Anderson could produce pulsations of anxiety. I was meeting him again in quite new circumstances, at Andersonian drinking parties where he was called 'John', and although he seemed so taken up with cracking jokes or tippling or singing blasphemous songs that it was unlikely he would attack what I wrote in the *Telegraph*, I would sometimes feel ashamed, as I wrote an article, of what might from his viewpoint seem its weaknesses. I could imagine being derided for some fault in THE PIPE DREAMS OF OUR PIECRUST POLITICIANS, or CHIFLEY TAXES US SO WE CAN'T SPEND, THEN SPENDS FOR US and I would then, in my mind, argue out this point with Anderson, and then rebut myself with arguments he might use. What particularly concerned me (but what could I do about it?) was that I was engaging in the sin of popularisation.

I knew, of course, that events were historically determined and that nothing I wrote was going to make the slightest difference to anything: what I was doing was exposing folly (and enjoying doing so), not changing people's opinions. In fact, insofar as I imagined a model reader for what I was writing, it was most likely to be someone whom it would enrage. My favoured imaginary reader was a person whose illusions I was exposing. In AUSTRALIA'S DIPLOMATIC GROWING PAINS: WE ARE NOISY BUT ARE WE GETTING A BETTER NAME? I imagined myself enraging most of the External Affairs Department. When I wrote CANBERRA – CITY OF DREADFUL NIGHTS, I hoped to enrage most of the inhabitants of Canberra. There could, however, be subtleties in irritating these imaginary readers: when I wrote HOW THE ALL-POWERFUL STATE DESTROYS UNIONS I imagined myself, of course, angering those who most believed in trade unions, because they also believed in all-powerful states, but I also imagined that I would irritate those who mistrusted unions – by writing into the article the argument that it was a free trades union movement that made a society democratic: so that was one for them, too. In what seemed my lonely warfare against the fantasies of those who believed in the state, the idea of 'Star Chamber methods' was one of many necessary devices, but when I wrote BEHIND CLOSED DOORS THEY DECIDE IF YOU NEED A PENSION, I not only wanted once again to goose the *étatistes* – this time by describing how people could be refused pensions because they were 'undesirable', 'not of good character' or 'not deserving' – I also wanted to have a go at the moralists by suggesting that conventionally immoral people were nevertheless entitled to pensions.

In this readiness (in the interests of exposing folly) to be surrounded on every side by enemies, it was not I, but my intellectual critics, who had 'sold out' to statism, etc. I enjoyed writing two articles about the Commonwealth Office of Education and its Current Affairs Bulletins ('oversimplified and lopsided') and Discussion Posters ('presumably for people too stupid to understand the Current Affairs Bulletins'). I felt old, and deserted, when, in protest against my articles, there came in the mail, from Bruce Miller, a note formally abandoning our friendship and returning to me all the letters I had written to him while I was in the army.

PENTON HAD SO ENJOYED MY PIECES MAKING FUN OF OFFICIALESE that at one Monday conference I suggested an entirely un-*Telegraph* idea: a short satire for the Saturday magazine. *A satire? Readers wouldn't understand satire! Well, what was the idea anyway?* Well, the news tie-up was an industrial dispute at a radio station about which union's members should push the button that switched on the electric fans. I wanted to write a satire, set in the future, about a 'Politicians' Equity' and an industrial dispute about which politicians should push the button to open new schemes. Chifley had said a golden age was coming to Australia: I would call my satire 'The Great Crisis of the Golden Age'. *Well, try it out. Have something else ready in case it falls through.*

When it was done, Penton kept on repeating 'Marvellous!' as he read out the best bits. Later he took it into Packer. He called me in again: Packer thought it was marvellous, too, and he suggested that a set of mock government regulations I had composed should be printed in small capitals.

'Packer understands,' said Penton. 'He's seen regulations printed like that. The small caps were entirely Mr Packer's idea.'

For the next twelve months I 'did a Golden Age' about the follies of the Chifley government, and other contemporary follies more or less every second week. (*Not too regularly*, Penton said. *People might get bored*.) Drafting them could be done at home, where I could scribble, like a writer, rather than sit in a cubicle, like a hack. There were no 'facts' to get, no 'interviews'. I just had to use my imagination. In the second of the 'Golden Age' series, I solved industrial disputes at the main Sydney power house by closing it down. In the third fable in the series, I eradicated bad conditions on the coalfields by forbidding miners to go down the mines, so that the coalfields could be turned over to the pursuit of happiness; then the problems of soil erosion and introduced pests were solved by abolishing farming; at the end I had Australians living on an income earned by exporting bits of the Great Barrier Reef, cricket stars and other national treasures, so that they could devote themselves to courses in raffia work, folk-dancing, pottery classes, communal rug-weaving, popular psychology. When the time came for Penton to announce that he thought the series should have a rest, a new rumour had joined the rumour that I was a poor relation of Packer's – it was that I was his illegitimate son.

4

ALMOST EVERYONE NOW SEEMED TO THINK I WAS 'SETTLING down', although that was not how it seemed to me sitting at my typewriter, surrounded by enemies, pursuing the lonely task of exposing the follies of *étatistes*, the crimes of Stalinists and the illusions of meliorists who thought you could get a quart out of a pint pot or have your cake and eat it. It was true that I didn't drink so much – or at least not so often: pub-drinking meant less now (all that noise in which I couldn't hear myself). There was an occasional unexpected pub binge, but only with friends, to show that we hadn't changed. There was 'civilised' drinking with meals and, if someone dropped in, some 'quiet drinking' in the evening – even, at times, some wild drinking – but usually it was only Sunday mornings that were devoted to the pains and complex pleasures of hangovers. Surely drinking a little less regularly wasn't 'settling down'? In fact, I still had the same solid evidence that I had not 'settled down'. Our flat was the same. It was small, wasn't it? It was rented, wasn't it? I didn't own any furniture, did I? And even if my bank account had grown a little, it was only so that I could later spend what I was saving, wasn't it? It was true that I liked to imagine I had become more good-humoured, more worldly perhaps, more tolerant of the deceits that kept things going, and with a greater reliance on illustrative anecdotes, including imitations, as a way of giving an idea of what life was really like. If I felt an anecdote coming on, I would stand up and do it with simple actions as if playing a character part in a corroboree. But to hell with bourgeois standards of good manners: anger could still seem the most sincere of the emotions. Fighting my good fight in pub arguments and at Saturday night parties, I still saw myself as able to put on a brawl about any of the principal illusions of the age.

I met Andersonians now only through Douglas McCallum, who would interpret them to me and tell me how they were changing, and although I could go on feeling that Anderson's sad, brown eyes were staring over my shoulder while I was writing a *Daily Telegraph* piece, I still thought of myself as an 'ex-Andersonian', although I had no clear idea of what it was that I was now 'ex'. Of course, I would say, Anderson wasn't altogether wrong: his aesthetic and his ethic were, of course, bullshit, but he was right about conflict. (Wasn't he?) One must continue to ask of a mind or a society: 'Of what conflicts is it the arena?' (Mustn't one?) And, of course, he was right about uncertainty. (Wasn't he?) And, of course, Anderson was absolutely correct in his attitudes to servility. (Wasn't he?) Yet how could I be an Andersonian when I wrote *Daily Telegraph* articles, or read pieces in *The Economist* that expressed interest in the revitalisation of British farming?

Sometimes I would imagine that all that I had abandoned were the central secrets of Anderson's philosophical 'system'. But I had never properly understood this system. In any case I went on using phrases I had picked up in the main quadrangle in my first year at university. 'But, don't you see, you idiot,' I would still shout, 'that when I say "The book is on the table" *I am taking something to be the case!*' I still knew that facts were occurrences in space and time (although I couldn't imagine what that meant), and that all A are B. After I had written a piece on Sartre for the *Telegraph* Saturday magazine, I wondered if I might become an existentialist. I plunged into the deepest end of existentialism, so deep that I couldn't understand what I was reading. Guiltily, I then tried several popularisations, but I was shocked to find that existentialists thought individuals were 'free'. Were existentialists mere 'voluntarists', 'individualists' and 'social atomists'? Existentialists did not seem to believe that all A are B.

Although I could defend my beliefs like a crusader, there were other times when I could become ashamed and alarmed by a feeling of secret weakness as I realised that I had been upholding as eternal truth some opinion I had just made up. It was as if I were merely trying it out for size (*What would it be like to believe that?*) and could throw it away if it didn't fit. There was no premeditation about this playing at belief – my mind would suddenly and innocently fill with some unexpected way of seeing something. On the occasions when I would *deliberately* pretend to opinions I didn't believe, out of politeness, because they were similar to those of the person I was talking to (and this was never done dogmatically or angrily, but always thoughtfully), there was guilt, but also excitement, in pretending that I was learning what it might be like to be someone else. As a student I had written a poem about the treacheries of Alcibiades and as a diplomatic cadet I had written a tutorial paper on them: sometimes I could see myself, with loathing or delight, as an Alcibiades of opinion, as a traitor who, despite all the noise he was now making, might later change his mind. Such deceits applied only to beliefs, of course, never to anecdotes. One could make up a belief, but never an anecdote. Inventing an anecdote would be lying.

I knew, nevertheless, that a time of enlightenment would come to me. I remembered how, as a schoolboy, I would go for long walks, trying to think a new thought and not being able to raise one. I knew the time would come when I would think some thoughts. Then I would really know what I believed existence was like. I would then be able to start writing a great novel.

FRIENDS OLD AND NEW PARADED THROUGH OUR FLAT LIKE photographs in a family album. Usually I was not D.R. Horne, angry shouter – that was for strangers: among friends anger was only for those who if I didn't shout at them would accuse me of 'settling down'. So, pending the time when I made the final accounting of what the world was like and what I was to be, I took the second pathway of deceit and tended to be close to what they wanted me to be. ('Gaining experience'. People were characters in a novel. I was 'gathering material'.) To Frank Rhodes, I would continue to play young promise, or (I suspected at times) failed promise; while for us, he played something of the role of intellectually enlightened uncle. When he came for a meal he would give us great trouble by insisting on something simple (for owners of *The Joy of Cooking*, how could cooking be simple?) but he would bring a book as a gift and after the meal we would laugh for hours at the follies of Australians. When we dined formally with McAuley and Norma we played grown-ups; when McAuley dropped in to our flat by himself, we drank wildly, and played the old days. In either case we could share the delights of re-telling the disasters of the age and the ironies of progress. If the brandy was running freely his mysticism became even more puzzling than before, since so much of it was now connected with revelations gained from village life in New Guinea. On one strange evening he said he admired the Quakers. (The Quakers!)

Friends from diplomatic cadet days would pass through Sydney from New York or Jakarta, Paris or Bangkok, and offer anecdotes as gifts – anecdotes of the United Nations Organisation that made it sound like meetings of the 1941 Students' Council, or of Evatt and his entourage that made them sound like a medieval court, or anecdotes about the signing of the Australian peace treaty with Thailand that sounded like scenes from early Evelyn Waugh. I could not offer, in return, the personal anecdotes of a well-travelled man, but I could at least spray around the worldly wisdoms of *The Economist*: Could Britain really pay its way? Would the Belgian coalition hold together? Were the Chilean trades unions viable? Could Tito have his cake and eat it? When John Rowland came back from Moscow we had a special dinner. (A friend who had been to *Moscow*!) Fitchett would still sometimes drop in, and when he did, I would become a character in the later Evelyn Waugh regretting the passing of the gentleman. Massey Stanley, back from Japan, would sometimes descend on the flat and carry us away on a fanciful adventure. On one occasion he had assembled his Sydney journalist friends so that, dressed in a Japanese gown, he could cook Japanese food, using authentic Japanese utensils; on this occasion, I played, quietly and insignificantly (but noting, I hoped, their illusions) the young journalist, but I now understood that the part that Massey wanted me to play was that of a sharp-minded, intellectual son. When old Canberra friends came down for a weekend we would, sometimes, join in a weekend's ceremonial drunkenness, returning to the complex parodies of court life with which we had amused ourselves in Canberra.

In a bizarre night with Conlon, former Gunner Horne sat around as Conlon again explained, this time with assistance from a school atlas borrowed from the bookshelves, how the Pacific War had really been won: in his comments, Gunner Horne drew on his knowledge of Clausewitz, Frederick the Great, Liddell Hart and ancient Chinese military philosophers. One of our woman friends would tell us about the two men, one a homosexual and the other a virgin, who were declaring their affections; therapist Horne lay on his couch and played the psychoanalyst for her. With Adrian Deamer, either comrade Horne tried to speak a language of friendship or Dr Horne denounced soft-minded progressivist folly. With George Molnar, jester Horne was whimsical. With feature writers, by-line Horne was soft-spoken and blasé. With old friends, met again by chance, Young Donald acted out anecdotes or D.R. Horne shouted abuse, according to how they wanted him. With new friends, sophisticated Horne would drink coffee as they talked about their work or their sex lives. When questioned about his novel by any of these people, novelist Horne would explain that perhaps he hadn't yet written a novel, but at least he was living one.

Douglas was now married to a social worker friend of Ethel. Even more than before, I felt part of a 'foursome'. Ethel and Ann shared the mysteries of social work just as Douglas and I shared the mysteries of our education. Ethel had brought Douglas and Ann together at a dinner at our flat, and they had gone off reciting Louis MacNeice to each other; a few months later we were at the registry office, in the first booking for the morning, to watch them being joined together in the name of the State of New South Wales. Off they went in a plane to Brisbane where Ann's parents lived, and when they came back with long anecdotes of family celebrations it reminded me of those times of sharp character interest and warm affection when my mother would return to Muswellbrook from a family wedding in Sydney, and I would sit and listen, until I had heard it all. As a 'foursome' we had no quarrels; we walked into each other's flats as if we were part of the one family. We had no secrets ... we shared friends ... we talked over anything at all that concerned us, from private affairs to public opinions, without dissimulation. When the four of us were sitting around drinking coffees, bonded by the calm blue haze of tobacco smoke, with

Ann and Ethel jolly, me doing imitations and Douglas thoughtful, there could seem a constancy in existence, a recollection of the certainties of childhood.

I SEEMED TO HAVE SETTLED DOWN WHEN I WENT TO SEE MY UNCLE Loy in the warehouse where he was in charge of hats. (*Hats*, my mother would say, *are Loy's real love*.) I had finally agreed to buy a hat, and Ethel had already detected in him an eye for quality in men's clothes and had suggested I see him; he had himself said to me, several times: *Don, it's time you wore a hat*. A hat seemed all that was left to buy. I had a supply of the white shirts that had come into fashion; I had bought a modern-style dinner jacket secondhand (deceased estate, scarcely worn) and stocked up on imported Irish linen handkerchiefs and Italian silk ties, bought through Uncle Loy; I had a good pair of black shoes and a good pair of brown shoes, in a brand recommended by Fitchett (the brown shoes were not to be worn, Ethel told me, with dark clothes), and although at times I was afraid that the drape on my new navy-blue double-breasted suit was 'exaggerated' and the shoulders too padded, the new light-grey double-breasted suit seemed the most elegant thing I had ever worn. But a suit like that still represented an assertion of difference; wearing a hat was an assertion of similarity. Apart from the army, I had not worn a hat since I had been at Maitland High when, with a school crest on my hatband and pocket, a school tie around my neck and a school badge in my lapel, I had festooned myself with declarations of what had proved to be my last loyalty.

When I went to the warehouse, I couldn't make up my mind between two hats, so I bought both. One had a narrow brim and was of a brown felt so soft that it might, when touched, be expected to purr; its crown was arranged in something of the style of a 'pork pie hat', but was more expansive, so that it gave a different impression altogether; it was a foreign hat, but not too foreign. Sometimes I would take it to the office with me. I would hold it as if I scarcely noticed it, in my hand, tentatively … I would never go so far as to put it on.

The other was a snap-brim grey felt with the width of rim universal when I was a boy, but it was more individualistic than those hats of my father's generation (I certainly wouldn't wear one of those!). Where it turned up, the rim was curlier, almost buccaneerish, like the hat Penton wore, and where it turned down it was snappier, with just a touch of the 1930s movie gangster about it; the fold down the centre was deeper, and more assured than those tentative dints in the hats of my father's friends. When I tried it on I turned the hat onto the right-hand side of my head, and pulled the snap brim down hard over my right eye. As soon as I looked at it when I got back to the flatette, I realised that I would never wear this hat: it had too much of the past about it, even in its differences. It remained stored in the wardrobe.

I MAY NOT HAVE BEEN WRITING A NOVEL BUT I WAS TURNING Ethel's life into a series of books. Her life as a social worker – she was now almoner to the Queen Victoria Homes for tuberculosis patients – made up one of the small library of novels I kept up-to-date in my head. That particular 'novel' had two *milieux*: there were the magic mountains of the two TB sanitoria, both out of Sydney, where she entered on her index cards what the patients declared to be their problems (some of these sub-plots could show twists as unexpected as a radio serial); and there were the conflicts, backstage quarrels with the secretary, talks with the chairman, differences within the board, the ambitions of doctors, nurses and matrons. And there was Ethel herself, when I met her at Central Station every Wednesday evening, back from one of her magic mountains, walking down the platform towards me, already smiling as she thought of what she was going to tell me after dinner. Another of my Ethel 'novels' turned into the story of her first marriage, a tale of the innocence of a young middle-class Englishwoman, gullible from boarding school; with the transition from well-bred innocence to hard-gained experience, this had something of eighteenth-century novel about it, but it was presented mainly in contemporary cinematic scenes – air raids in London, a wedding in an English country house, life on a wartime convoy from England to Australia, quarrels about the washing-up. And there was Ethel herself, telling the story, with the good humour of one who had survived misfortune. Another 'novel' was really a collection of droll stories (or was it a picaresque tale?): this came from her recountings of the lives and loves of a friend, an older woman, whose confessions (*Rabelaisian? Balzacian?*) of her adventures with various lovers seemed literary enough to be un-Australian. This was the Ethel who was part of my world of the anecdote.

My favourite Ethel 'novel', however, was a multiple-volume family chronicle of English village life as seen by the small gentry. Her own village was as real as a book: there was nothing she told me about the village, whether it was about the woods, or the village postmistress, or the spinney near the orchard, or the rector, or the first primroses in the front garden – that I had not read before. Her picture of the village's social hierarchy was as familiar as poems about the falling of autumn leaves or the coming of April showers. My sense of complete familiarity extended to stories about other villages, and about her uncle's house and her maiden aunts and her North Country cousins, one of whom was a squire. From books, I already knew more about the gentry view of English village life than I knew about many aspects of Sydney.

One whole volume of this Ethel series was devoted to her father who had, we assumed, married her mother for her money. Her father came from a lower reach of the English middle-classes than his wife, who was heiress to two respectably sourced private incomes and daughter of a gentleman who could spend the day in his study, reading. Ethel's father came from a long line of market town doctors; he had worked on farms in Canada before the Great War, where he gained what was to prove an expensive appetite for agricultural improvement, and during the war he became a captain in the army; after the war, with no money of his own, he had no prospects until, with his wife's money, he could become what he assumed life had intended him for – a gentleman farmer. 'The captain', as he was known in the village, had farmed on modern principles: each year, as the farm lost money, he would introduce further costly improvements. There was no year in which the farm made a profit; by the beginning of the Second World War he had disposed of his wife's entire fortune other than what had been put in trust for Ethel.

As she talked about him in our flat, his presence could seem as real as that of an oversimplified character in a novel. He would wake early – his shaving mirror was placed near the bathroom window so that his face could be seen by the farm hands in the farmyard at milking time – and when he came down, at the same time each morning, to exactly the same breakfast, he would pause in the hall to check the thermometer and tap the barometer; then he would go into the dining room and ring the bell to summon breakfast. Every weekday, wearing leggings and hacking jacket, he would superintend the farm work and the gardening as if making an inspection of a position on the Western Front, or sit at his desk as if sending off a military despatch. He dined at noon, usually on soup, roast meat and pudding; he rested, and then resumed his tour of the battle zone. Occasionally he would change into flannels and play a set of tennis; he usually joined his wife in the drawing room, or the garden, for tea; he would change for supper (which consisted, every night, of soup, sliced ham and salad, cheddar cheese, and rice pudding). After supper he would drink coffee in the drawing room and listen to the BBC; before going upstairs he would pause in the hall, check the thermometer, tap the barometer, and wind the grandfather clock. On Sundays he went to the morning service where his friend, a retired colonel, read the lesson. His grandest outing was to attend the Bedford assizes as a juryman; on these occasions he would hire a car and chauffeur for the day.

Now details were coming in letters from Ethel's mother of the collapse of the old order. The multi-volume family chronicle seemed to be reaching its *dénouement*. The farm had lost even more money in war than it had in peace. Some of the fields had been sold. The garden had fallen into ruin. The house could not be kept warm. Letters came asking Ethel to agree that her father should borrow a certain amount of what had been put into trust for Ethel, but no sooner had Ethel signed the papers than her father died and the money she had given him was lost among the debris of the farm. The farm was sold, to a dealer, at a low price, at what was then said to have been a rigged auction. Ethel's mother kept only the house and one small field, but the story of decline continued, in letters that told of how the tennis court had been turned into a hen run, the vegetable garden had been taken over by brambles, the rose walk had been smothered by briars and the herbaceous borders given over to bindweed. The cellar had flooded; there had been a fire in the orchard; the drains had broken down. These familiar fictional metaphors of social decline matched *The Economist*'s statistical metaphors of how England was living beyond its means, but if we could get to England (perhaps it was now time to marry?), Ethel would be able to put her mother's and her own affairs in order. As with *The Economist*'s Britain, Ethel's mother would have to realise she couldn't have her cake and eat it.

5

When it came to our marriage, to keep the different worlds separate, I invented new rules for celebrating marriages. It was a compromise in three parts. My mother would have the traditional Denbigh wedding breakfast – but on the weekend before we were married. A week later we would be married in the early afternoon in the flat of a friend of Ethel's and the only people there would be my parents, my grandmother and Janet (who would wear a new dress). This would be followed by afternoon tea. Later in the day we would go to a buffet dinner party, arranged by Zelie McLeod. Here we would be with 'our own friends'.

The function my mother arranged was less a wedding celebration than a commemoration of her memories of the great days of Denbigh. As was traditional, the furniture was cleared from the large room that had been built onto the house by Pa's rich aunt, the family great hall where bodies had once been laid out and mourners kept an overnight vigil, the ballroom where, during the Great War, the send-offs and welcome-homes had been held for 'the boys', and the banqueting chamber for twenty-first birthdays and family wedding feasts. Once again the furniture was piled up in another room, china and cutlery and trestle tables were hired from the School of Arts and the tables were arranged in a big 'U', with bottles of beer and chicken-and-ham salads on them, and then trifles and wedding cake. Aunts and uncles, great-aunts and great-uncles, cousins and second cousins reminisced that this was just like the old days – even the younger ones who knew of the old days only from family legends. My mother had arranged for the main toast to be proposed by Uncle Alf, who as a former Mayor of Manly and as someone who had once contested pre-selection for the Senate, was our family's tribute to success. When it was over, just as they did in the old days, we gathered in the drawing room, held hands and sang 'Auld Lang Syne'. For the bonding itself, we would have preferred a civil ceremony but these were performed only in a registry office; as a compromise, I hired a retired congregationalist minister who was said to 'do' a private wedding ritual scarcely touched by religion. We were married standing in front of a card table on which were laid a sherry decanter and six sherry glasses, a plate of small daintily cut sandwiches, of the kind

The Joy of Cooking told me were *canapés*, some chipolata sausages, some 'savouries' skewered on toothpicks and, for Janet, a bottle of lemonade.

We had already received some presents from 'our own' friends – wine glasses, wooden salad bowls, a coffee grinder, earthenware casseroles, a cocktail shaker, brandy balloons – and some of these were used for the buffet that Zelie had arranged in her flat. Here the food was what we were used to up at the Cross: there were a couple of French stews, some boiled rice, a lettuce salad, some red wine from the Hunter Valley. Not too much fuss. Informal. Some guests sat on cushions on the floor. The champagne for the wedding toast had been donated by Penton (the only man without a tie and, for that matter, the only man with his shirt unbuttoned almost to the waist). When he made his speech Penton seemed at his best – jovial, witty, with a touch of send-up. 'Everyone' was there – including a drunken gatecrasher, whom (to my surprise) I threw out when I discovered he was lurching around saying our marriage would not last for a year.

I felt content with this division of myself into different worlds. It was a simple matter of preferences. Some people liked chicken-and-ham salad for weddings. Some liked chipolata sausages and savouries on a toothpick. I happened to prefer a French stew and some red wine from the Hunter Valley.

NINETEEN

Selling out?

At the Denbigh wedding celebration, relations who read the *Telegraph* said to me, 'My word, Don, you've done well.' But I did not see myself as having 'gone up in the world' from my family. Unlike Julian Sorel, I had not been taken up by a rich family. I was simply someone who lived by typewriter and pen and happened to be more aware than most of the danger to freedom in compulsory chest x-rays and other excesses of *étatisme*. I had not been inside the house of a rich family, nor did I want to be. Rich people in Sydney were not out of a novel by Stendhal or Mann or Turgenev; if they were 'out of a novel' at all it would be an Arnold Bennett novel, or something by Upton Sinclair or Theodore Dreiser; so there would be the same difficulties in talking with them as in talking with my family at Denbigh. The nearest I got to the rich was an evening arranged by Ethel as a farewell to one of my diplomat friends leaving on a 'posting', at the nightclub Prince's, one of the two assembly rooms for Sydney's 'café society'. I wore a dinner jacket and 'black tie' when practically no one else was wearing one; everything was more expensive than we had intended: we had a 'bad table' near the door, among other outsiders, well away from the dance floor where there were the table-hopping and shared fellowship of the people who really belonged. Since I did not dance, a large part of the evening was spent in politely standing up as others left for the dance floor or came back from it. Towards the end of the evening, Frank Packer came in: was it me he was glaring at so vacantly?

I was still (and self-contentedly) property-less, with no intention of acquiring anything (apart from books, a few wine glasses, wooden salad bowls and earthenware casseroles) and although my name might appear in the *Daily Telegraph* two or three times a week, it was on the jackets of books, not in a newspaper, that I wanted to see 'By Donald Horne'. Reminders that I was now aged twenty seven and had not yet written even one novel could strike me momentarily senseless with disbelief. Sometimes when I woke up from sleep to contemplate some alarming failure – a recurrent theme was that I had not had enough *affaires* – I would then slide into a more general sense of disaster, with the recognition that since I had stopped being a student I had simply been wasting my life: I had not 'written anything'. To punish myself, I would work out what age the first-year students now at Sydney University had been the year I had enrolled. The first time I did this the answer was that they had just started at high school; next year it would be that they had just begun primary school; soon that they had not been born.

'SETTLING DOWN' WAS NOT THE ONLY CHARGE I WAS READY TO clear myself of. There was also the question of 'selling out'. The Chifley government seemed likely to fall, ending a decade in which some of my lost friends had seen government planning as the rational way ahead for humankind, and here I was making fun of it as a dream of a 'Golden Age'. Former friends would say: *Horne has sold out to Frank Packer*, or even *Horne is a fascist*. Horne would grow very angry. These people hadn't troubled to read the right books, he would think. But even Horne was concerned with one particular question: he had for several years become used to seeing 'progress' as an illusion and some of his best imitations were of Labor politicians – but for years Horne had been singing left-wing songs from university revues making fun of 'the reactionaries': these songs were still one of his acts at parties. Would he now vote for the reactionaries? Horne wasn't on the voting roll. Horne wouldn't vote at all. So he went on writing satires on progressives and singing satires on reactionaries. The Chifley government should be defeated, Horne thought. But the Menzies opposition didn't deserve to win.

One particular problem pressed most heavily on Horne: the opposition parties wanted to ban the communists. What was Horne's reaction to that? Well, no one yielded to Horne, of course, as an opponent of the Stalinists but, frankly, Horne would see the ban as an attack on freedom. But, what would Horne do if Penton told him to write an article saying the communists should be banned? Well, of course, Horne wouldn't write the article. (Horne worried about this: where would he get another job?) At one ideas conference in Penton's room he thought the test was about to come, but all that Penton wanted was an article listing the laws already on the statute books that could be used against the communists. Well (thought Horne), that was all right. (Wasn't it?) He didn't like the heading they put on his article, THESE LAWS COULD CURB THE COMRADES, but, after all, the article was just explaining the position. (Wasn't it?) Horne went on worrying. He decided the opposition parties didn't mean what they said. They wouldn't really try to ban the communists, would they? So that would be all right. (Wouldn't it?) In any case (thought Horne), by that time I might be out of this damned country.

WHEN MASSEY STANLEY, WHO HAD PREVIOUSLY BEEN A MODEL of informal dressing, came into my cubicle wearing a three-piece grey suit and a grey homburg I understood at once he was proclaiming that in some significant way the world had changed. A few movements of the eyebrows indicated that I was to come down and have a drink with him: in the bar he told me he 'was going into PR'. 'PR' was something new, and I soon began to understand that some of this activity had something to do with the elections that would be held at the end of 1949. The opposition parties were 'using PR'. Penton had begun to speak of 'PR' too. Of the kinds of people with whom he had private sessions in his office (was it with some of them that he negotiated the continuing details of his selling-out?) some were in 'PR'. I met some 'PR' men: they spoke quickly and cleverly, but with enormous gravity, of 'mass opinion' and, obliquely, of private manoeuvres and public campaigns.

Penton told me I was to 'liaise' with an old hand, a 'PR' man, once a Labor supporter but now 'on the other side', who, among other things, was running a 'research service'. ('Research' was also something new.) When the old hand's firm released a 'research report' I was to summarise it in a *Daily Telegraph* feature article. After some months the old hand invited me to have lunch with John Carrick, the new secretary of the Liberal Party, a 'keen young ex-serviceman', he said. We met at the Millions Club, a second-rate club with a grand name. I chatted away during the lunch about how a great leader must learn to preside over events and always expect the unexpected. Then a more ambitious luncheon was arranged, at the Hotel Australia – W.C. Wentworth would be among those there (he was standing for parliament that year) and, most significantly, R.G. Casey, an imperial Australian whom Churchill had made Governor of Bengal. (He had therefore become known in Massey Stanley's Canberra column in the *Sunday Telegraph* both as 'the Proconsul' and as the 'Tiger of Bengal'.) Now that the proconsul was making a political comeback and again standing for parliament, there were those, the old hand told me, who thought it would be Casey who would take over as soon as Menzies had again demonstrated his incompetence as a prime minister.

I didn't have much to say at this lunch: the talk of these men whose party had been out of power for almost a decade was mainly political dirty stories about the deceits of politics, discussed with the excitement of soldiers talking about sex after they had been deprived of it. The proconsul, whose fiercely sincere moustache and general elegance outwardly suggested an aristocratic detachment, was as excitedly talkative as the others, but it was W.C. Wentworth who made the straightest running: 'the people' were going to vote the government out anyway, he said, because they were sick of it, but his own party must add honour to this process of revenge by having 'positive policies'. To support this argument, he produced a metaphor he liked so much that he repeated it several times: 'The party's ambitions are a naked woman,' he said. 'We must clothe her with reason.' Each time he repeated the metaphor he moved his hands through the air, outlining the naked body of his party's desires, and by his metaphor, gave the lunch its only literary flavour.

When the lunch was over, I went back to the old hand's office: the point of all this, he explained, was that Casey was to come through as a statesman concerned for the well-being of the nation, who would produce positive policies for the future that rose above mere considerations of party gain. It would be Casey who spoke up for Australia. That was where I came in. (*Don't worry, he said, it's all been cleared with Penton – but don't discuss it with him: that's important.*)

They would like me to write some statesman-like newspaper articles for Casey, then they would place these articles over Casey's name in the newspapers all over Australia. I could write about 'increasing productivity', for example, or, most of all, about the need for 'national development': that kind of thing.

They had noticed I had a talent for popularising economics. Five or six articles. Perhaps more. At £20 a time.

TWENTY

Like life in a minor novel

On the evening before Ethel and I were married, Penton, who had arrived without warning at our flat with a wedding present, said to Ethel: 'How will you like living in New York?' When we returned from our honeymoon, he said, the *Telegraph* would send me to New York: I was the obvious choice. What must I do but pass this piece of gossip on to Peter Hastings (speaking to him confidentially at Zelie's party, and instructing him to tell no one)? And what must he do, I learned later, but at once go to McAlpine and put himself forward for the job? And what must Packer do, I also learned later, but adjudicate between McAlpine (for Hastings) and Penton (for Horne)? And what must Hastings do (I learned years later) but say he would do it for less than they were going to pay me? When we returned from our honeymoon I was told Hastings had been given the job.

But now we were off to London anyway. I had saved some money, somehow, and added to it the money from the articles I had written for Casey, and Ethel had a nest egg, to which she had added some money borrowed on the reversion of her mother's estate. 'Reversion of her mother's estate'! That sounded like something from an English novel. At times it seemed that all of us would soon be in England. The McCallums would go to Oxford, of course, so that Douglas could take a second degree and Adrian would, of course, get a job in Fleet Street. Others were also on their way to Oxford, or to Fleet Street, or to establish themselves in the theatre, or in painting, or even in advertising, or just to 'go over there for a while', on a working holiday. When the Old Vic company came to Sydney with its three plays, for the three Saturday afternoons on which we saw them we seemed that much closer to London. At the end of this season we had a party in our flat – almost a cocktail party except that, of course, in the English manner we were just 'having some people in for drinks' – and almost everyone at the party spoke of how it would be when we got to England. I scarcely used the radio, but when I did it was usually to listen to *Much Binding on the Marsh*, taken from the BBC. When I turned from *The Economist*, it was to the book reviews in the *New Statesman*.

It was not, I told myself, that I had any 'illusions' about England (or, of course, about anything): how could I, when to *The Economist*, of all those who wanted to get a quart out of a pint pot, the English seemed the blindest and greediest and when, every week, *The Economist* warned me that nobody owed the English a living? It was more that life in Australia seemed so thin and insubstantial. Even the soil was blowing away: in two successive hot, dry summers, westerly winds lifted up the thin topsoil of the eroded outback into long storms of dust that stretched out across the breadth of the state, making the air in Sydney as thick as a brown fog, and then spread over the Tasman Sea, colouring pink the snowfields of New Zealand. Was that the kind of country in which to write a novel?

AT TIMES I WAS IN BED, SLEEPLESS WITH AN IRRATIONAL excitement matched only by boyhood anticipations of visits to the department store dream worlds at Christmas. My imagination would wander between Eliot:

> Unreal City,
> Under the brown fog of a winter dawn,
> A crowd flowed over London Bridge, so many
> I had not thought death had undone so many

and Ward Lock's *Guide to London*: London Bridge, the most famous of all the bridges across the Thames, connects the City with Southwark.

Where England shone brightest was as a splendid living museum. Apart from Waugh, English fiction seemed in almost as bad a way as English drama. (Terence Rattigan! Christopher Fry!) I would be able to feel part of a continuing 'tradition', with an assured sense of familiarity with the first primrose, the class system, the bookshops in Charing Cross Road, Westminster

Abbey, the National Gallery, thatched roofs, the Flying Scotsman, the Houses of Parliament, the Old Vic, and with Ethel's village – the woods, the spinney, the Council Houses.

I again began reading English novels: they might not be 'great', but could one go through life simply re-reading the same couple of dozen novels? I began trying 'minor novels' with Hardy, unread since high school: clumsy, perhaps, but satisfyingly sceptical. Conrad (also not read since schooldays): not only sceptical, but 'French'. Even Wells, in *The New Machiavelli*, was sceptical. There was more to the English, perhaps, than I had imagined (although they were still, of course, 'minor'). Then I read Samuel Butler. Splendidly sceptical! Best of all – George Gissing, discovered, appropriately, in a secondhand bookshop. *The New Grub Street* was not only 'French', it was despairing about journalism. And the feeling in it of desiccation in London life, confined and third-rate, seemed the closest I had read to a description of life as I saw it in Sydney. However, I felt some guilt that furtively picking up copies of minor English novels in secondhand bookshops or in cheap editions provided evidence that I really was 'settling down'.

When Penguin reprinted the 'Tietjens' tetralogy of Ford Madox Ford (whose existence was news to me) I found the strangeness and disjointedness of these four novels 'life-like' – I would read passages out to myself as if I were a classroom sharing this discovery – and argued, for a season, that as a picture of 'decline' they were ahead of Waugh. *Brideshead Revisited* had been a nasty shock to us all and for a while, until *The Loved One* came out, we were afraid that Waugh, like Eliot, might collapse into trivial pieties. I re-read my Penguin copies of all the Waugh novels from *Vile Bodies* to *Put Out More Flags* and reassured myself that I could still tell anecdotes from Waugh which matched my own anecdotes of absurd randomness and unintended consequences. Waugh's general distaste for the inadequacies of all human activities reminded me of McAuley in a non-mystic mood, on a rough night, speaking more and more coldly.

As a way of imagining what to make of existence, 'gaining experience' had produced for me nothing more than character parts for anecdotes. This was not enough. One must 'write'. And to 'write' meant writing a novel. My *Arna* pieces on aspects of the army, drawn from life, seemed 'mere journalism' now. Nothing more than *reportage*. Any fool could write like that (though even a fool could not write like that for the *Daily Telegraph*, since it didn't match the office style). Of course I could write about myself and tell some anecdotes. But that wouldn't be 'writing'. That would be mere autobiography.

It was now becoming clear that, until I had a thought, I would have to content myself with writing a 'minor novel', perhaps something in the style of Evelyn Waugh. Now I had an idea. It had come from forty or so letters received from the Education Department in my five-year resistance campaign against the demand that I should repay the allowance of £120 paid to me, at £40 a year, when I was bonded to the department as a university student. The story of this campaign had become a prime anecdote and if put on as a turn in the flat it would be illustrated by quotations from the letters themselves, taken from their folder and held up for all to see.

The hero of my novel (not really a hero, of course – imagine that! a hero! – but, as in the Waugh novels, a passive victim) would be engaged in a correspondence similar to mine (about something or other, to be decided when I started writing the novel on a ship taking me to London) with some government department (name to be thought up when I got on the ship). There would be a big bust-up scene (I could imagine that already) ... he would go to the newspaper (I might call it the *Daily Trumpet*) ... they'd take him up ... it would become a political 'affair' ... the politicians and press would use him for their own purposes. There would be great, hot clouds of political rhetoric as in the imitations I did in the flat; and great, cold slabs of officialese, as in the 'Golden Age' series. At last! Twenty-seven was not too old to write a novel! And to start it in a ship on the way to London!

BOOK THREE

PORTRAIT OF
AN OPTIMIST

PART 1
TRAVELLER
1949–54

ONE

Getting away

1

Which way should I begin the novel?

'Edging his way between the milling, perspiring suburban housewives who crowded the city's pavements, Adam Richmond lit a cigarette.'?

'Edging a way along the narrow pavements, Adam Richmond lit a cigarette.'?

It was my first full day at sea in the SS *Moreton Bay*, and I was sitting in a canvas chair on the poop deck rewriting the first sentence. Even the clichés of the weather – 'fresh breeze', 'blue water', 'bright sun', 'blue sky' – were part of the sense of deliverance from Australia.

On departure day, our cabin had seemed abasingly small, with twenty people in the passage outside passing around the cheese straws, cakes and sandwiches brought by my mother, as if we were back in the days when she threw tennis parties. I was wearing the same double-breasted light grey suit and Italian tie I had worn on our wedding day and Ethel was in the same blue and white silk dress, but after lunch we were too weary to change into more informal clothes, although, from her voyage to Australia with her first husband, Ethel knew this should have been done. We sat on a wooden bench, Ethel upright, holding her back straight and her head high, in the manner I admired, while I sprawled in one of my more nonchalant poses, as if to put the uncomfortable bench at its ease. (Ethel told me that deck chairs were not put out until the first full day at sea.) We looked at the ocean and assured ourselves that somehow we would be able to afford what we were now about to do. 'Most of the others are like us,' said Ethel. 'What they own is on their backs.' We walked around and then through the ship, among all these baffled Australians, some of whom were lost. Ethel gave names to the public rooms: smoke room, forward saloon, aft saloon, writing room – while I tried to convince myself the ship was unlikely to sink. There were two other uncertainties: we had not yet decided whether to give the stewards preliminary tips; and I had been too late at the purser's office to enrol for the more prestigious, and more convenient, 'second sitting' in the dining room. (We were obviously second-sitting types.) Only someone we had nick-named 'Colonel Pepper' seemed to know absolutely what should be done. After lunch, this Englishman returning Home had changed into tropical kit and then walked around the main deck three times, taking possession of it in the name of the empire.

The cabin seemed larger the next morning when the steward came in with early morning tea. A cabin steward, as in a Somerset Maugham novel? Not on this shipping line. On voyages out, its ships brought immigrant 'New Australians', and on voyages home it was the cheapest going. At least the steward was wearing a white jacket, if unbuttoned at the top and slightly soiled, and, with his white face and North Country accent, he was authentically exotic. The flowers that had been brought for our farewell were still fresh. A greaseproof wrapping was still around the sandwiches packed by my mother in case the ship didn't give us lunch.

At breakfast we contemplated the complexities of the voyage – providentially, with companions, since Gwen Tanner was going to England to try her luck, along with a friend who, like Gwen, had been a secretary at the *Daily Telegraph*. Gwen's shrewdness at once illuminated the dining room. We would be able to have wisecracks at breakfast! With her laconic Sydney wit sharpened from all those movies and radio shows and with my anecdotes, imitations and one-liners, enormous opportunities for laughter and gossip opened behind us: there was all the old *Daily Telegraph* life to reshape as a Marx brothers movie.

And, on this voyage of hope, we had before us the spectacle of our fellow passengers – but not to be taken up too soon. Ethel warned that one must be cautious about making premature friendships, otherwise for the rest of the voyage one might be landed with unwanted people. So by the time we were sailing on the northern edge of the Roaring Forties we had cautiously befriended only two others. When the ship began rolling, its decks wet with spray and its steel plates rasping, Gwen had sunk into her cabin with the despair of seasickness and doubtful whether London was worth such pain and melancholy. Sitting almost alone in the desolate smoke room, proud of our strong will to survive, and wanting someone to talk to, Ethel and I risked speaking to a 'couple' somewhat older than us – an Australian professional man who looked like a golfer and his wife, an Englishwoman – and found ourselves playing bridge. I was unprepared for feeling so grown-up.

The heavy seas calmed. Gwen was back. The smoke room was again crowded before meals, so that we could continue to display the important distinctions between those who sat in the smoke room and those who didn't and, of the smoke room *habitués*, between those who sat 'on Tony's side', favouring one waiter, and those who sat on 'Eaves's side', favouring the other, known by his surname – appropriately so, in the view of those of us on Tony's side who preferred Tony's directness to Eaves's greater formality. But while Ethel and I were, by nature, on Tony's side, the couple we had played bridge with had already established themselves on Eaves's side. There would be problems of definition.

It was only when we left Australian waters, after our last meal in Australia at Perth, that our true voyage commenced. It was then that we changed our Australian pounds into English sterling. Goods were duty-free. Ship's movies were on twice a week. Deck games were available. Shipboard life had begun. (*By God I was glad to get out of this country.*) As we sailed the Indian Ocean, approaching the Equator, we would check each morning at breakfast that the 'fresh breeze' was 'still with us'. We would plan part of our deck life in the sun, to 'get a good tan'; the rest would be spent on what we had learned to call 'the weather side of the ship'. We 'spent our days lazily', in the companionship of mild games of deck tennis, or sitting in deck chairs admiring 'the calm blue of the sea', or writing on the poop deck, or gossiping on Tony's side. The nights could seem 'romantic', with flying fish and phosphorescent waves and suggestions of concupiscence in 'the heat of the tropics'.

In the dining room and the smoke room Gwen and I made fun of the English food – we had never before seen people put on the one plate boiled, baked and mashed potato – and mimicked English accents of servility or of command. We told speculative stories about our fellow passengers and made allusive jokes. And now there were additions at Fremantle to the 'young group' (of which we were a part), who were moving to England as naturally as flocks of migratory birds, seeking (according to taste) enlightenment, careers, fame, opportunity, relief from Australia ... As the ship's satirists, Gwen and I developed languages of our own, with secret jokes.

At the same time Ethel and I kept up games of bridge with 'the couple' and they were declaredly not part of the young group. There seemed to be something in Ethel that found reassurance in the stolidity of bridge-playing and knitting and the conversation of this 'professional man' – who, on one occasion, went down to his cabin to get a clipping from *Tight Lines*, a fisherman's journal, and show us an article he had written about preparing flies for trout-fishing. I settled into bridge, again grown-up. In a further act of treachery, when he offered to use his influence to move us to the second sitting and sit at his table, we deserted Gwen and accepted.

THE DAY BEFORE WE REACHED THE EQUATOR WAS OUR FIRST wedding anniversary, and at breakfast I decided to begin a book of our marriage, made up of descriptions of all our wedding anniversaries. I wrote notes on how Ethel and I sat on the deck after breakfast gossiping with Gwen, how we played a game of deck tennis until it was time for the smoke room, and how, when I tried to buy a celebratory round, Tony insisted on shouting. This section would give an idea of our casualness. After an afternoon spent in our cabin I took notes on how, as a celebratory gesture, Ethel put on the blue and white silk dress, along with the same clip and earrings and the same white shoes she had worn when we were married. When I wrote this up it would be the romantic bit. Then would come social comment. It was the birthday of the professional man and he was celebrating with pre-dinner warm beers in one of the largest, hottest and stuffiest cabins: some of the ship's officers were there and this gave an opportunity to describe their combination of pretension and scruffiness. As well as describing the Chicken à la King at dinner and the bottle of Moët bought to go with it, there would be a greater attempt to give a feeling of the presence of Ethel. This would be the banquet scene. For the rest – the purchase of two long Elegante cigars, the round of liqueurs, the descent to beers in the smoke room – I would use the light satirical mode.

As the years passed, I decided, I would write up social observations in this way for each of the celebrations of our marriage.

AS WE SAILED ALONG THE COAST OF CEYLON, KNEELING ON Ethel's bunk and looking through the open porthole at the dark shapes of land, I was transfixed with excitement. Here I was, about to set foot on a foreign country; and when the dawn came up, revealing white beaches fringed with palm trees, I swore I could smell in the breezes the tang of Eastern spices.

By nine o'clock we were walking the streets of Colombo, two whites led by a 'self-appointed native guide' in bare feet and green sarong who was gently shooing us towards a shop where Ethel 'placated him by buying a few oddments'. But 'there was no shaking him off'. I offered him an English sixpence, but even that didn't get rid of him. Now we were surrounded by 'swarms of natives' trying to sell food, peanuts, postage stamps, geegaws. A small boy insisted on being photographed with a cobra around his neck and then demanded money. 'The crowds gathered around us to see the fun.' I offered him Ceylon cents. 'Only English money, master.' When I gave him the English sixpence a rickshaw driver also demanded to be photographed. We only got rid of him when the taxi dropped us at the hotel. I gave him one rupee 'to reward him for his trouble'.

Rhodes had given us a letter of introduction to a former student, now Burmese *chargé d'affaires* in Ceylon. He affably showed us into a legation car so that, before lunch, we could see the sights. On the way to Mount Lavinia we passed 'a native bazaar', and marvelled at a road crowded with bullock carts, rickshaws, bicycles and spanking new cars blowing new horns. *Character interest*: 'Here, a half-naked native carrying a basket on his head, there a wealthy Sinhalese woman, dressed in sari and jewels, taking her ease in a rickshaw, and around the shops groups of natives, standing or squatting, exchanging gossip.' Bustle everywhere, and (extreme symbol of nativeness) 'some of them already stretched on the pavement, asleep'. *Tourist inspection*: 'A little, fat priest showed us around a Buddhist temple. A family was leaving flowers on the altar in the Buddhist fashion.' *Generalisation*: 'There is always the sweet smell of tropical flowers in a Buddhist temple.' *Sophisticated tourist scepticism*: 'The temple was brightly painted, rather gimcrack, modern – probably designed for tourists.'

At the Mount Lavinia hotel, at the end of a large, cool spacious lounge we 'sipped our beers' beneath the 'whirling fans', looking out to the sea while 'attentive waiters bustled'. At lunch with the diplomat and his wife the clichés of tropical splendour overwhelmed us, with 'vast, cool spaces', 'teeming waiters', 'whirling fans', 'sea breezes' and, outside the hotel, on one side the 'clear blue' of the Indian Ocean and on the other two miles of 'green lawn and waving palms'.

After lunch, as the legation limousine honked its way through 'the Pettah, the native quarter', constantly held up by bullock carts with little tinkling bells or natives slowly crossing the road, we penetrated the very heart of the native experience. There seemed 'millions of tiny little open air shops and several thousand different smells'. At one stage a whole street was blocked 'by a great crowd chuckling at the antics of a man with a snake around his neck who was selling some form of native medicine'. The driver had been trained by the British and we noted how he bumped natives away with his car, but in his own way he was 'just as stubborn as the other natives' in his insistence that we go to the museum. 'Master would like to go to the museum?' 'No,' we would reply, 'we want to see the people.' Suddenly, we were in front of a large, dilapidated building: 'Master, here is the museum.' (A wily native.)

At the museum ('shabby with tropical decay') where the throne and other treasures of a defeated order were displayed as trophies, along with piles of gold objects and thousands of gems, we passed from the native experience to the jewel experience – a transition maintained over tea in the diplomat's hotel apartment. His wife ('small, pleasant, pretty') seemed festooned with gold and rubies. Even her eyes (set in a 'perfect pale olive skin') seemed like jewels and much of the talk was about the jewel purchases we must make in one of the hotel's shops. (Rubies? Gold? Where would we get the money? When Ethel said she would buy some moonstones, I felt easier: moonstones sounded reassuringly cheap.) Despite the insignificance of the purchase, the diplomat went with us to do our bargaining, 'beating them down in the best Oriental fashion'. The rest of the evening was set in scenes of modified Oriental splendour – the apartment itself, with its 'superb view', the pressing of bell buttons to produce servants, a five-course dinner of English food, with dance band and dance floor – and the bowing and scraping of waiters, to whom the diplomat's wife gave orders with 'imperious waves of the hand'.

We all had to be back on the ship by eleven o'clock and as we sailed out of Colombo Harbour, displaying to each other our jewels, we offered anecdotes about successes and failures of bargaining. When Ethel told of how our own haggling had been done by a Burmese diplomat and one of the wiseacres said 'Obviously that native was getting a cut', this became an anecdote of the voyage.

I SEEMED TO HAVE PUT A WEEK'S ENERGY INTO OUR FOURTEEN hours in Colombo and pleaded the effects of 'something I ate in Colombo' as excuse for withdrawing from what was left of shipboard ceremonies. We were now crossing the Arabian Sea, in such heat and with such surrender to laziness that even the occasional games of deck tennis were abandoned. When we got to it, Aden did not seem familiarly 'exotic', like Colombo, but uncomfortably foreign: perhaps because it was night and, with only a short stay, all we saw was from a taxi ride through huge stone walls into a 'native town' inside a crater, with men in fezzes and turbans sitting in open-fronted shops in dirty, flat-roofed buildings, drinking coffee under the light of oil lamps. Our driver, an Ethiopian, added to the foreignness with tales of polygamy and of King Solomon, to whom he seemed to credit the building of all large stone structures throughout the world. In the climax, a visit to some old reservoirs (part of Solomon's international public works program), we stood in the dark listening to the cries of small Arab boys. ('The English are very nice people. Throw us a penny, sahib.')

Deck tennis was resumed in the Red Sea ('sparkling blue ... fresh breezes'). December was beginning and we now had eight of the ten hours we must gain before earning the privilege of being on Greenwich Mean Time. Five weeks behind us. Another two to go. Our next duty was to pass through the Suez Canal but while several of the Australians stayed on deck all night, awaiting revelation, Ethel and I did not take up the story until dawn, when we looked through our porthole at a bank of reclaimed mud beside a huge swamp. The travel experience resumed when we docked at Port Said 'surrounded by scores of little boats' from which Egyptians 'shouted their wares' and passed objects to us on poles. There was new evidence of the exotic: as they checked our passports the Egyptian police were armed with rifles (it was rumoured they were looking for Jews) and we found our letters had been opened by the censor. (One of them, from my mother, was largely about Nanna's chooks.)

When we set foot on shore we walked into the now familiar experience of travel as an encounter with pedlars and entertainers to whom one would at first 'fall victim' and then 'give the brush-off', but we were rewarded with an example of the refinement of the old world. The language of social improvement in Sydney had long promised that one day there might be pavement cafés, but they were still illegal. Now in Port Said, for the first time in my life, I was sitting in one, outside the Eastern Exchange Hotel, sipping Turkish coffees, watching passersby, enjoying 'the leisurely, civilised atmosphere' and having my shoes polished. On a walk I took notes on a Greek Orthodox funeral, an Egyptian auction sale, with a group of black-veiled women in one corner, one of whom lifted her veil to spit, and food markets where meat hung on hooks, as expected covered with flies. We went back to the Eastern Exchange for lunch (French cuisine!) and then again sat outside sipping Turkish coffees, and relaxing in the 'leisurely, civilised atmosphere' for which we were intended. In this way, with so much of the day spent in or outside the Eastern Exchange Hotel, Port Said introduced me to anticipations of European maturity.

And now we were sailing across the Mediterranean into a European winter of, as it was turning out, blue skies and sunshine. We read the ship's news, participated in the daily guessing about how many miles we had travelled in the last twenty-four hours, drank our early morning tea and took our saltwater baths, gossiped, listened to the weather forecasts as if we could do something about them, played deck tennis, and twice a day progressed from deck to smoke room to dining room to saloon to cabin. To demonstrate that we were Australians and that Australia was a funny country, we of the young group would call out to each other in exaggerated Australian accents, use outlandish Australian expressions and do imitations. I produced a small magazine that made fun of our homeland (it was run off on the duplicator in the purser's office) and one night we put on a short satirical concert in the aft saloon in which my contribution was to give a mock schoolroom 'recitation' of a satirised version of Dorothea Mackellar's *My Country* that began:

I love a sunburnt country;
A land of dawdling trains

We continued, however, to mock 'the Poms'. It was not in the English themselves but in the institutions of England, whether it was thatched cottages, scientific research or the West End theatre, that we sought hope.

The 'beautiful Mediterranean weather' followed us to Malta, where we engaged in another and different foreign experience of walking through the streets of a Catholic city (Catholic churches everywhere, Catholic bells ringing) followed by the again different foreign experience of having lunch (through a connection of Ethel's) in a Royal Navy mess in the presence of what seemed confident British power – to which we said farewell with a midday view of Gibraltar with those 'blue skies and blue seas' I had made much of in letters to my mother. We were already listening to the English weather forecasts and engaging in banalities about the possibility of snow for Christmas.

2

Between the two acts of throwing pennies to Arab boys at Aden and then of staring at the banks of the Suez Canal, the essential demand on us as tourists crossing the Red Sea had been to witness and, preferably, to take part in the fancy dress ball. Ethel and I had talked ourselves into entering the Best Dressed Pair section, as 'Hornes and Haloes'; so Ethel had become an angel by putting together a costume of sheets from her bunk, wire from the ship's carpenter and silver paper from the smoke room stewards, and I had changed into a devil by attaching to myself two horns and a tail, made from Ethel's shoe trees, and a cotton-wool beard dyed with red ink from the purser's office.

When I awoke the next morning, with our cabin a mess of red ink, cardboard, cotton wool and silver paper I recognised that we had engaged in an enterprise it might have been more prudent to avoid. Couldn't I (at the best) merely observe such acts? (In fact, if I was to be an observer, *why couldn't I observe something less banal?*) The cabin steward had not yet arrived. Ethel was still asleep. The only sound suggesting movement was the hiss of air as it came through the porthole. My brain seemed to have been stunned by the clichés of the voyage, with only occasional moments, such as now, when I went on a private journey I did not discuss with anyone: I began to dream of being a writer interested in everything – internationalist, versatile, generalist, above all, *critical* – critical of both the specialism of the academies *and* the inanities of commercialised 'popular culture' and, in particular, of the vapidities of middle-brow culture, the greatest of all enemies. (One must be equally severe, of course, on mere reactionary nostalgia.) If there was ever another *avante garde* I would join it.

There was a pile of unread *Economists* in our Sydney flat and I had taken them on board and read them carefully, underlining wisdoms such as 'The simple test of all policy must now be whether or not it serves the purpose of reducing costs of production' and pieces of knowledge on Bulgaria's tobacco crop or the uprising in Burma. It was only when I had finished this underlining that I had realised I had not brought enough books to read – an omission that for most of my life would have been as unimaginable as not bringing my head. However in a packing case in the ship's hold was a selection from my library. When we got to England I would begin the reconstruction of my 'self' by re-reading the novels, then I must read more history, more political theory (to begin with I must revise Sorel's theory of the producer ethic and I must re-read Mosca) and I must put them together – novels, political theory, both with serious concerns. Most importantly I must get back into the habit of reading verse. I could see the bindings of the secondhand books I would buy in Charing Cross Road as the ample feast of London spread before us.

On one of the nights we were sailing up the Red Sea there had been a discussion over on Tony's side about what we were all going to 'do'. In the middle of such practical discussion I felt as useless as when people had asked me 'What are you going to do when you leave school?' Then, I had simply lied. This time I had said I would 'look around'. Before I had left Sydney, Frank Packer had given me three letters, one to his own London editor and one each to the features editors of the *Daily Mail* and the *Daily Express*. The three letters were in my cabin luggage. In that sense I had nothing to worry about. But why would I want that kind of job? How to un-become a journalist was the problem.

And my novel. Usually I could believe that the writing was going well, and I had thought of a title: *The Richmond Affair*. But after the few hours we had spent in Port Said it had occurred to me that from 'sharp observation' I might have written a prose sketch. Why not that rather than a novel? If *Ulysses* was the last of the great novels, why was I writing a novel? In any case, would people see my novel as 'too thin'? Perhaps they wouldn't understand that 'thinness' was what I meant?

Of course, living in Ethel's mother's house for a few weeks would provide time to sort things out. But until I 'decided what I was going to do', how could I tolerate the flatness of living with Ethel's mother and her two old friends, already dismissed by Ethel as 'the dowagers', leading their middle-class lives in an English village? Ethel found some of her principal meanings in the house, the garden, the 'village characters', the woods, the country walks. Perhaps I might accommodate myself to such familiar literary values. But what would we talk about over dinner?

AS WE APPROACHED THE BAY OF BISCAY, ON A DAY OF FIERCE lashings from the ocean, with the ship again groaning and the decks impassable, we heard that the Chifley Labor government had been defeated in Australia. Good. That should put an end to the excesses of 'planning'. Labor's defeat in New Zealand the week before had been taken by Gwen as an omen and now she feared that her two communist brothers would be sent to jail. *Nonsense: banning the Communist Party was just election talk. Nothing more would be heard of it.* But the great shadow of my new cynicism about the Left could fall between us. How to explain the tragedy of politics, that it was only revolutions that could produce great change, yet all revolutions must necessarily be betrayed? And that what mattered in politics was not what people said they wanted to happen, but what actually happened.

And in the Britain we were now approaching (I would then brood) 'socialism' was another name for control by the state, and for servility. I still had in mind a photograph of Attlee, taken after the war, in black top hat and morning dress, glittering with medals, standing beside King George. What was 'socialist' about that? In the meantime, if I could not avoid journalism for a while there was this question: how could my light (so bright in *Daily Telegraph* feature articles in Sydney) illuminate the errors of 'post-war' Britain? I had enjoyed preaching to Australians, especially in satirical articles. Would there be a place for my kind of preaching in Clement Attlee's England?

AS WE WENT THROUGH THE SLOW BUSINESS OF BERTHING AT
Southampton I read in a letter from my mother that Frank Rhodes had been
found dead, floating upside down in some baths in Sydney Harbour (that were
known as a pick-up place for homosexuals).

TWO

Homecoming

Westminster was just as every writer I had read on the subject had imagined it. The light was already beginning to fade. (Unreal City, under the brown fog of a winter noon!) We walked around the Houses of Parliament, the Abbey, and on to Westminster Bridge, where I stood admiring the familiarity of mists, remnants of river traffic, London taxis – and the sign of an ABC tea house. (Over buttered scones and crumpets weeping, weeping multitudes droop in a hundred ABCs.) As in a movie, Big Ben struck four. The street lights were on, recalling all the exotic capitals of northern Europe, 'wrapped in darkness'. In our taxi ride from Westminster to Piccadilly past thoroughly familiar façades and monuments (so that it was like looking at postcards), it already seemed night. Overwhelmed by clichés, we added one more: we had an English 'tea', then retreated to our hotel, ordered hot baths, and after a few sandwiches delivered to our room on a silver tray, fell asleep.

ON OUR MORNING TRAIN INTO THE COUNTRY THE PALE SUN WAS out as it had been when we came up from Southampton, again startling in its sickliness. Inside the carriage there were only dispirited 'post-war' people in shabby clothes, and when we arrived at the railway junction town where Ethel's mother was waiting with a taxi, in the drabness of brick and bitumen she seemed one of them, a small old woman swathed in an old grey coat, with a grey hat pulled down over her ears as if there were nothing more she wanted to hear.

In the taxi she became 'birdlike', speaking quickly with an upperclass enunciation, but jerking her words almost into a modest unintelligibility as if she had no particular right to be heard. We drove along a narrow road, with hedges defining the fields, then in a quick diversion, down what Ethel remembered as a sandy lane but what was now a bitumen-paved road, past hawthorn hedges and elms, we approached the village, first manifest in several morose blocks of semi-detached brick buildings with bare gardens and low, neatly clipped privet hedges ('council houses' – another English word, like 'hawthorn' and 'elm'). After a row or two of what in Sydney eyes were slums, a couple of farm walls and a few specimens of suburban Gothic, we reached the high hedges of the house, now denuded of its farm, that was for Ethel her most prevailing symbol of order and content.

We went up two flights of stairs into what had been, when Ethel was a child, the maids' attic and earlier, before her father had moved in as gentleman farmer, a farm loft. These two rooms, crowded with cheap secondhand stuff, were presented by Ethel's mother as the 'flat' she had prepared for us. We thanked her for her trouble.

On our tour of the house we could not look into the two main bedrooms – these were the rooms of 'the dowagers' – not only old friends of Ethel's mother, but now also paying guests. Ethel's mother had made her own bedroom in a cell-like space near the stairs, as if she were doing penance for the decline in her fortune. It was in the kitchen that we found the first signs of sociability. With a fuel range heating the room, and cooking giving it savour, three village women were bustling around the table – one part-time cook, one part-time cleaner, and the third with great authority but no immediately defined business. She was the only one of the three who in the excitement of reunion did not revert to an earlier style and call Ethel 'Miss Ethel' as if there had never been a war, or a Labour government. In a conversation of complex reminiscence but undoubted love of the subject, the five women seemed to dispose of ten years' village gossip in ten minutes.

From all that Ethel had said, I had a neat plan in my head of the garden and the field next to it (called 'the dinge', Ethel had said) but when we walked into the garden we found the rose pergola overtaken by brambles and the nut walk almost a 'jungle trail'. Instead of naming shrubs Ethel gave names to weeds. The lawns had been dug and turned into vegetable plots (that had now been abandoned and taken over by what Ethel identified as bindweed). The tennis court had been invaded by long, tufted grass; a section was wired in, with some pullets scratching in the dirt. The cucumber frame in the kitchen garden had collapsed; and most of the glass in the hot-house was broken. The orchard was a wilderness; the field was in the possession of one sad cow, a few hens and five roosters, two of whom, as we stood at the gate, jumped up and tried to bite me. The elms were said to be infected with some disease; parts of them were already dead.

For lunch, we sat in the dining room, amongst relics of mahogany and silver, to a formally served meal of watery soup, stale fish, cheddar cheese and an indeterminate pudding. We took our coffee in the drawing room, the largest room in the house, furnished in no particular style and with no sense of a family presence. Outside, I could see, in the pale sun, through the bare branches, the village green – a small patch of unkempt grass, with a modest war memorial on it, against which a dog cocked its leg. After one cup of weak coffee, served from a silver pot, Ethel's mother said it was time for her afternoon nap.

Ethel's vision of the village was given more life on our walk up the hill – the 'cottages' and several gentry houses had a genuine nineteenth-century appearance and the church, set on the top of the hill, although locked, yielded what Ethel claimed to be evidence of Norman origins. The air was still light enough for an encouraging view over miles of fields with their clumps of trees, with half a dozen or so small villages set between them, although on one edge the suburban brick of the rail junction town spread into this calendar-art scenery. We strolled for a while through the edge of a forest (now neglected) belonging to a great nobleman, one border of whose estate joined the village. Ethel retold the stories she had already told me at bedtime in our Sydney flat of gamekeepers, pheasants and 'shoots' and we identified the tree that as a girl, following village custom, she had known as 'the wishing tree'. We made (or affected to make) wishes.

It was almost dark as we walked down the hill and into the drawing room, where a peat fire had been lit. (Coal, in short supply, was saved for the kitchen range, which also worked the hot water system; in the other rooms there were small, fragile electric heaters, with tarnished fittings of some antiquity.) A silver tea tray was brought in, with silver pot, silver milk jug and silver sugar bowl. The bread was stale. (I was told later that stale bread was preferred because it sliced more thinly.) The cakes were both stale and shop-bought. Passing them around appeared to be essential to the tea ceremony.

The amount of passing increased when the 'dowagers' arrived and (first things first) attended to their appetites. At once they seemed dames in a pantomime. Both of them were old and fat, but while Lily was fat and dumpy, as if stuffed with pillow cases, Rose, although fat, held herself very straight, so that her bust swelled out, like Queen Mary's, into a declaration of basic principle. When the eating was finished, Lily sank into what appeared to be her usual state of self-contemplation, but Rose, knowing that Ethel had been away for almost ten years, found it necessary to command the conversation.

She wanted to tell us what she and Lily had been doing that day (all of this with a rhythmic emphasis on key words: Oh, I *do* think they're *such* nice people ... It is so *very* important, isn't it? ... Really I do have *such* a lot to do tomorrow). At the end, duty called: she must solve the *Daily Telegraph* crossword puzzle. She took out a small sheet of composition board, fastened the crossword to it with a bulldog clip and called on our help in this national task. Between calls such as 'Missouri's southern peat-bog in four letters' (Oh, I *do* wish they wouldn't use these American references) and 'Renunciation of underworld – a sort of miracle in ten letters' we went on with scattered conversation. Except for one break of concentration when, leaning towards me and smiling, she said 'There are a lot of names of flowers, aren't there?', Lily remained slumped in contemplation of her own wisdoms. She was not concerned about my answer.

FOR THE NEXT FORTNIGHT WE FITTED OURSELVES INTO A SYSTEM which began when, after breakfast, Rose and Lily 'attended to their affairs' in the room that used to be Ethel's day nursery, then posted their mail and 'walked the dog'. Lunch (announced by the sounding of a gong) was of continued dullness, although Rose used it to issue a number of significant public announcements on what she had read in the *Daily Telegraph* at breakfast; it was followed by coffee in the drawing room, when we were expected to help with that day's crossword puzzle. All three old ladies retired to their rooms for a nap, then re-emerged for tea, when there was more stale food to eat. What happened before the evening meal (also announced by a gong) was indeterminate (there were sounds of movement in their rooms); the evening meal was more of a supper than a dinner and of a blandness established fifteen years before to suit the stomach condition of Ethel's father; it was followed by a rubber or two of bridge, played in the drawing room. Lily, who had been a widow for almost thirty years, recalled how on one occasion she had asked her husband to make up a four. 'No thank you, my dear,' he had said. He had then lit a cigar, and died. By playing bridge, we were postponing death.

Ethel and I would spend the morning on long walks in the nobleman's woods. Ethel would teach me the names of the trees, and both of us would speculate about how it was that the dowagers so dominated her mother. The weather was fine, and mild, although wet enough underfoot to warrant the moral fortitude of gumboots: we walked for miles, planning how we would make things better.

Of the few welcome-home lunches and teas Ethel was invited to (at which we inspected various kinds of old people, old houses and old furniture) the most significant was a visit to the large Victorian house, with damp moving up its walls and only a few rooms still habitable, where Ethel's two maiden aunts were presiding over the dissolution of her senile Uncle Charles. The dowagers – from the perspective of old family friends – had several times speculated about how 'the aunts' would manage the fortune they were soon to inherit; Rose would give Ethel sidelong looks. Would the embarrassments of this fortune pass to Ethel? Overall, there was much talk of the calamities that could befall 'estates' under a Labour government and of the general diminutions of British power that came with such a disastrous turning away from the natural order. The affairs of Rose and Lily were in confusion but they talked about this with great openness, and considerable repetition, since it was a matter of public interest, as yet another example of what was happening to Britain under 'Mr Attlee'. Their own 'estates' appeared to have been invested in such concerns as Argentine railway shares that, having been symbols of British power, now became symbols of British decline.

THIS WAS TO BE MY FIRST 'REAL' CHRISTMAS. IT WAS NOT PLASTIC holly that festooned the hall, and it was real mistletoe (looking like a weed) that was fastened to a beam. The carol singers were singing in a cold English winter night; there was no snow, but there was at least a statistical possibility that there might have been; the Christmas tree had grown its roots in Europe, and the fourteen-pound turkey had been fattened in Old England.

The younger brother of Rose and Lily, a sixty-year-old civil servant in a minor government department, came down with his wife for Christmas. He was seen by his sisters as having 'never quite grown up', but he organised us into an extensive season of charades and pencil-and-paper games, so that we seemed to be setting the scene for a murder in a detective novel set in an English country house.

Out of curiosity I went with them to church on Christmas morning. The church was cold, the performance perfunctory. Christmas Day was to be hallowed more by the King's Speech than by the church service. Straight-backed, Rose listened to most of it standing to attention.

THREE

What could be more interesting than the village?

1

The mild weather had gone. Although there was no snow to write home about, there were frosts and frozen pipes. If Ethel and I went for our morning walk early enough there was a crunching under our gumboots and when we found a small pond frozen over I felt like an explorer discovering some new sea. Ethel added a new habit to the household: a daily peat fire in the hall would cheer us up. The small, antiquated electric heaters in the other rooms teased us with the prospect of warmth without satisfying it, but in the bathroom there was not even this. The bathroom, and village bathing habits generally, confirmed my Australian prejudices about the uncleanliness of the English. A maturing scepticism might be turning me into something of a 'conservative', but I still saw a bathroom as a natural human right; yet in all the unconverted cottages in the village the weekly bath night began by people heating water in pots and pans over the kitchen range and then pouring it into a tub in the kitchen. None of them had bathrooms. Half were not even connected to the main water supply, since this cost ten shillings a year in water rates and many villagers preferred to get their water free from one of the four village taps (which sometimes froze in winter and sometimes dried up in summer). To them, free water was a natural right. Our own bathroom was icily cold and almost as primitive as the country bathrooms of my Australian childhood; I noticed with alarm that Ethel's mother and the dowagers did not bathe daily. The first feature article I wrote for the *Daily Telegraph* was headed: IF YOU'RE GOING TO ENGLAND TAKE YOUR OWN BATHROOM.

If I was going to see myself as a conservative (with some suitable qualifying adjective placed in front of it – radical? anarchist?), contrasting my enlightened conservatism with crass village reaction could be useful. The opportunity came when, as a compromise measure, it was decided, after fifteen years of controversy, to install one street light in the village as a purely experimental measure. Although not a naive reformer, I believed in street lights. The village conservatives did not. Among our old ladies the reaction was 'Really, one might as well live in the council houses and have done with it', but the postmistress expressed the widest range of opposition: the rates would go up; the village children would smash the globe; the light would attract bevies of giggling teenagers. In any case, if there were to be lights, surely the village gentry could put them up outside their houses. As Australia's expert on English village life, I wrote another article for the *Daily Telegraph* (HOW THE LIGHTS CAME TO OUR VILLAGE), presenting the village as an example of amusingly stupid conservatism. I warned my mother not to write about this article in her letters.

Although seeing myself as a true, if pragmatic, conservative fallen amongst people who didn't understand true conservatism, I had otherwise become transfixed by Ethel's view of the village and of the past and become part of it, like a ghost. One of the important forms of my enchantment came from the naming of things. In the woods (nature was the part of our life that was most faithful to the past) Ethel would point to one tree and name it 'beech' and to another and call it 'oak', and they would come to life, as if in an animated cartoon. One part of the garden would be designated as the area where primroses would appear, another as the place where we would see daffodils. We would stand in the churchyard and identify village family names and then look out over the plain and recite the names of other villages. I learned off the names given to all the fields; I knew the difference between 'woods', 'forest' and 'spinney'; I taught myself the difference between 'rector' and 'vicar'; I learned the names of the styles of domestic and farm architecture in the village. How lucky, as an Australian, to be married to an Englishwoman, I would say. I was being taken behind the scenes.

Another part of this process of enchantment was that I was absorbed in the sense of order of the household – the sounding of gongs, the set meal times, the ordained movings from one room to the next, the times for walking, the times for privacy – so that it could seem part of some autonomic social system. In obeying these movements, I recognised that all we were imitating had in fact gone when the gardener went into the army and the two maids went into munition factories and Perón had taken over the Argentine railways, but nevertheless we could even find ourselves following our old ladies to the village hall into the worlds of the Mothers' Union and the Women's Institute, for their annual parties. We played General Post, Musical Chairs and Pass the Parcel and watched two concerts, with patient boredom.

The result of this enchantment was that in two months we made only three moves outside the magic circle of village and woods. The first was the most touristically satisfying – to the county town, by bus, where, rapturous in the inconvenience of sloping floors, low ceilings and bulging walls, I was able to lunch in an inn that was 'partly eighteenth-century' and, after visiting a church that was 'partly thirteenth-century' with a font that was 'partly Norman', a pub whose windows were 'partly fifteenth-century' and a museum of Roman and Saxon relics whose building was 'partly seventeenth-century', we had tea and crumpets in a café that went back 'partly to the fourteenth century'. The second journey was a reminder of the inadequacies of the present – a day in London for the January sales, with spare time only for a newsreel. The third was a long walk to the nearby small town, where we had a tea of buttered toast and cake in front of a large fire, visited an antique shop, then walked through a nobleman's park. My energies were turned almost completely inward, towards the ways of our household, the mysteries of the village and, more obscurely and only occasionally, into myself, for living like this.

My principal act of rebellion came when a friend of Rose's arrived in the village to give a lecture with slides on missionary work in the Yukon. I volunteered to run the projector. The absurdity of this imposture, along with growing irritation at the lecturer's use of a clicking device to order me to put on a new slide decided me to sharpen the parody. I put in the second last slide upside down, and then, in correction, the wrong way round. The evening was to conclude with a hymn, the words of which were on the last slide. After I had shown the words back to front several times and then upside down 'the meeting dissolved into laughter'.

2

On a day when Ethel's mother and the dowagers were away on a Women's Institute outing, we locked the dining room door, went through the cupboard where she had thrown her papers, and put them in piles on the dining room table. It took us a couple of hours to sort them and read them and afterwards we knew nothing more than we had already known. Piecing together lawyers' letters, bank statements, final notices and letters from mortgagors showed that in maintaining his patriotic position as gentleman farmer, Ethel's father had gone through her mother's maternal fortune and he would also have gone through her paternal fortune if her father had not thought his daughter an idiot and tied up his money in a trust so that she couldn't throw it away. Facts had to be faced. There was nothing we could do.

It was the same story we had already told ourselves in Sydney. There was no sense of joy evident in the profligacy with which Ethel's father had spent her mother's money. In his private habits, as distinguished from his public extravagance as someone who threw away money on his farm, he was a puritan. As if he had set up platoon headquarters in his own house, 'the captain' had established a rigid timetable for wife, daughter, dog, two cats, two maids, cook and gardener. He had also established timetables for his farm labourers (of whom he had too many) but it was not altogether clear that they took this into account. (There were rumours that he was fleeced right and left.) When he ordered new clothes they were of exactly the style of those they had replaced. The were ordered from the same shops. He ate the same types of meal, at the same times, year after year, as if the house were an unambitious private hotel.

If he had lived on his wife's money instead of wasting it on developmental projects for his farm he would have given better service to wife, daughter, king and country. His excesses lay in the very rectitude and normality of his behaviour, and in its fanciful sense of order. To him, rational economic calculation, if he had heard of it, would have seemed un-British. I imagined how it would be to write an article on 'the captain' in the hard-headed, pragmatic mode, for *The Economist*, explaining how Britain could no longer afford such expensive concepts of virtue.

As to Ethel's mother, it was for her neurotic self-abnegation that I gave her bad marks. I did not find her grotesque, as Lily and Rose were, nor a symbol of national disaster like 'the captain': in fact, when the dowagers were out of the way, it was established that we could talk to each other but only so long as we contained ourselves within the humorous, anecdotal style. She carried one great advantage over the dowagers. She was soundly connected with eighteenth-century gentry – on her father's side, through a celebrated admiral; on her mother's, through a minor figure in the English Enlightenment. (Such concern with maternal and paternal lineage, with failing estates, with inheritances and with questions of whether wealth was old or new – previously matters merely of literary concern – were now part of my life.)

In contrast, the dowagers' father had 'come from nowhere'. As a young man, he had set up a small factory which made him a fortune, which he trebled during the Great War. So here were the dowagers – Rose, at least – professing all the beliefs of an upper class in which, according to the rules taught by my reading of bourgeois novels, they were in fact, intruders.

Literary caricature still seemed the only mode in which to assess them. They were real because they were like people in books. The rhythms of Rose's sentences would throb through my head like oversimplified dialogue in a novel. (It is so *very* important for the village that nice people should behave like nice people: *don't you agree?* ... There are *such* a lot of things that need to be done in the village: *aren't there?*) Ethel and I collected anecdotes in which we cut the dowagers out into absurd stereotypes of hypocrisy: in this historical set they were the greatest of all betrayers of the past. Thus on one occasion after Rose had again declared herself on 'the sacred working class' (after all, where would the sacred working class be *if it weren't for us?*) even Lily broke her usual silence at lunch to complain about the greed and self-interest of the workers; then in mid-afternoon we found her climbing the stairs almost on all fours (she was short as well as fat), with a small wastepaper basket clutched to her large breasts. When we went to her help, we noticed two eggs at the bottom of the basket. Ethel checked – Lily had stolen two of the eggs set aside for selling to the village and, judging by the warmth of the saucepan, she had boiled them as something to go on with between lunch and afternoon tea.

For the dowagers, the working class provided their principal explanation of the sorrows of poor little England, and when I began my counter-offensive against Rose's dining room sermons, it was usually within the discourse of class conflict. For one luncheon address her homily was on the present disrespect of the lower orders for their betters. (It's been just like the French Revolution, without the bloodshed, although I wouldn't put that past some of the people we have as lords and masters these days: *would you?*) Under my cross-examination, she put up the aristocratic argument that some (such as herself) had inherited the quality of leadership, and they exercised it for the good of all. I subjected this position to close analysis then, cut her down with one question: If it was one's duty to respect one's betters, whom did she respect? There was a long pause. (Which of her betters was she contemplating? Leaders of industry? Archbishops? Colonial governors? Dukes?) 'Well,' she said, 'I give my respect to His Majesty the King.'

It was at bridge that I most clearly saw our old ladies as usurping members of a deceived class. Whenever I 'made up a four', I won. These victories came from my utter confidence in their weaknesses. Ethel's mother was easily frightened out of bidding; Rose was easily provoked into over-bidding; and Lily, since she relied on cheating, could be bamboozled by holding up the cards so that she couldn't see them. I was never again to have such success at cards.

3

Despite his betrayal, I was writing to Peter Hastings, who was now pursuing what might have been my career in the *Telegraph*'s New York office; and here was I writing to him about the 'characters' who were essential to the village as stage set. I sent off pages to Hastings, as if they were extracts from the journal of an explorer.

Of the people we met, only five households were seen as being, in varying degrees, 'like us'. In one lived Elsa Macpherson, an object of suspicion to the dowagers because she had been deserted by her husband and was living alone in her converted cottage with her small son. But she had been educated at a private school. She had taken a degree. She lived on a small private income. And, having abandoned a Scottish accent, she spoke 'like one of us'. so the furthest Rose would go in public denigration was to say that she was *such* a pretty little thing. The Grimsteads, the family in the other converted cottage, also spoke like one of us. Grimstead was merely a County Pest Officer, but Rose excused him ('Quite nice people are forced into *such* funny occupations these days') because he and his wife treated her with such politeness. Ethel and I at once befriended Elsa and the Grimsteads; we talked amongst ourselves as if we were mid-twentieth century people, even if it was essential to our theatrical constructions that most of what we talked should be village gossip. The nearest household with which our old ladies had any real communion (an occasional afternoon tea, perhaps twice a year, since it was a village away) was that of a retired colonel, a butterfly collector, who saw himself as one of the few genuine aristocrats to have survived an unpleasantly democratised world. 'I am pure Dane,' he told me, referring to the invasions of England in the Dark Ages. He was undoubedly 'like us'. (His wife, a genuine Colonel's lady, clearly did not regard the dowagers as 'like us'.) The Rector was, of course, an essential part of the social order and 'no doubt a perfectly nice man in his way', but the Rector was 'not really one of us'. This was a matter of accent, education and general demeanour (there was never any specific reference to 'birth'). No one in the household or in the other households we visited could give any information about how life was lived among the village Wesleyans.

Our neighbours, the Whites, who were now renting what was left of the farm, gave the old ladies a problem in social categorisation: accent and background were against Jim White (it was true that he had been an officer, but it was only in the air force), so Lily and Rose decided against him. But they could not class him with the other village farmers since Ethel's mother liked the Whites. The Whites were alone among the farmers in being allowed into the drawing room. For Ethel and me the Whites were also fellow beings with whom we could speak more or less as we chose; but some barrier had fallen between them and our other set of fellow beings in the converted cottages up the hill. Ethel and I found ourselves with two classes of fellow beings neither of whom felt fellows to each other.

There was a woman schoolteacher in the village, with whom I had an intelligent conversation on one of our expeditions to the village hall. But, despite her *grande dame* manners she was the daughter of a villager and had married a villager, and even our friends in the converted cottage found her pretentious (which meant she was acting as if she were one of them). I put in a word for her at lunch. 'No doubt they are very nice people,' said my mother-in-law, 'but they are people with whom we don't happen to have anything in common.'

More generally, in this part of the country, the wild cards were the parsons, who provided one of our most satisfying areas of gossip. In one parish there was a rector, a former army chaplain, who so bullied his churchwardens and other stalwarts that most of them had defected to an adjoining parish. But in this parish services were 'high' rather than 'low', so that while the 'low' rector now conducted services in an almost empty church, the 'high' vicar of the adjoining parish doubled up on Sundays, providing a menu of both 'high' and 'low', changing on the hour. In our own parish Ethel remembered an earlier rector who had taken his loss of faith so seriously that he got out his razor and cut his throat.

And through an informant we learned spicy bits about the sex lives of two other parsons. One had for several years been infatuated with a female member of the choir – a teenage school girl when it started, and now a shop assistant. Their most companionable moments were believed to occur in a nearby woods. In another parsonage, on most mornings the vicar's wife would get up early and cycle down to the milking shed, where she and a local farmer engaged in various kinds of sexual pleasures, the details of which were regularly given to our informant. After she had concluded, she would cycle home, prepare her husband's breakfast and take it into his bedroom. On one of these mornings she had found him masturbating.

AS SOON AS DOUGLAS AND ANN MCCALLUM ARRIVED FROM Sydney (they travelled on a sister ship to ours) and found a flat in Oxford, where Douglas was to take a B.Phil. (seen as a less flashy degree than a D.Phil., which was really for American and colonial consumption), we invited them over to the village. When they walked onto our stage set, Douglas's Oxford connection, his pipe-smoking and his diffidence seemed to go down well with the old ladies; as did Ann's affability and, for that matter, her precise diction. They seemed to pass muster as a colonial version of 'one of us'. There was a pleasant element of sheer imposture in what we chose not to reveal of ourselves.

We took Douglas and Ann off to Elsa's and the Grimsteads' converted cottages and went for walks in the woods, but my principal concern was that in the short time of their stay they should be thoroughly schooled in the social structure of an English village.

Almost all of the conversation was village gossip; now and again I would recognise that Douglas and Ann might have been silent for a quarter of an hour or so, and could not possibly have known what we were talking about. It was up to them to learn. This was the way to discover England. What could be more interesting than the village?

FOUR

Getting on with it

1

It was like the sensation of immobility one gets in a dream ... I was in the village, and I could not move ... This was reality. It was when I thought of getting a job that life seemed unreal. Yet there were Douglas and Ann settling in, like normal people, at Oxford, with Douglas reading for his B.Phil. and Ann working as a social worker with an Oxford hospital; in London, Gwen Tanner (who had arrived in London with £5) had become secretary to the managing director of a men's clothing retail chain and then, after he had propositioned her, had left and become a secretary at the London office of the Sydney *Daily Telegraph*; Adrian Deamer was on his way over to England and no doubt would get a job in Fleet Street.

But what was there, really, for me to 'do'? As soon as I had arrived at the village I had ordered *The Times*, the *Manchester Guardian* and the *Daily Express* and I would read all three of them after breakfast. If this was Fleet Street, how could I work in it? A job on *The Times* or the *Guardian* seemed beyond Frank Packer's field of influence, and in any case they seemed to come from some club that was not likely to have me; and the *Express*, although obviously a daily masterpiece of brilliant contrivance, was, fundamentally, turning all the 'news' into diligently crafted fairy tales. I put Packer's letters away and asked the bank to send over most of what was left of my money.

Towards the end of February; we broke from our seclusion and after a couple of days with the McCallums at Oxford, spent (on a last bank draft from Australia) a week or so in London. It was time to cash in Packer's letters and settle my affairs. I put this off from day to day, in favour of undertaking the common tourist experience. In one part of this, there was the taste of 'civilised' living – of going to the movies on Sundays (to see Brighton Rock, banned in Sydney, along with Sunday movies); of 'dropping into a local pub with a friend' (with women standing at the bar as well as men – impossible in Sydney); of trying out a different style of national cuisine in each meal we ate in restaurants in Soho; of going to plays in the West End of a kind seen in Sydney only on an occasional tour, with the extra experience of satirical revue, at the Lyric in Hammersmith, of a kind we couldn't imagine in Sydney. As another part of the tourist experience, there were all those buildings to see that were familiar since I had read *Cassell's Book of Knowledge*. For most days we walked through the sections of Ward Lock's *Guide to London* that had been selected as priorities on our voyage from Sydney. The third part of the tourist experience – the prospects of the National Gallery, the British Museum and other art museums – was so enormous that I did not enter any of these buildings. (What could I learn in a couple of hours?) But they were there. With the exception of the flatness and warmth of the beer, London clearly illuminated the provincialism of Sydney. Even doing the sights of the ruins left by the Nazi bombings supported this experience: the Nazis had never bombed Sydney.

As one day followed another, and money drained off, I would put away until the next day the dreary task of looking for a job. On the third-last day I rang the *Daily Express* and the *Daily Mail*. An interview? Yes, well they'd see me, but there definitely weren't any prospects for feature writing. Well, fuck them. Who would want to write that kind of drivel? *No thanks*. On the second-last day I saw Clarrie McNulty, the *Telegraph*'s London editor. He smiled as at a secret joke when he read Packer's letter, before dropping it into the waste paper basket and arranging for one of his staff to take me to lunch at the Press Club. Well yes, he said, they would go on sending to Sydney any feature articles I wrote. If published – five guineas. I decided to save money by cutting down on cigarettes. I would be a freelance.

And here was an idea: in the constituency of which the village was a part, the national election provided exactly the view of British politics I wanted, now that I was a sophisticated liberal-minded and pragmatic conservative. The sitting member, a Labour man, had been to Eton and Oxford, and had played cricket for his county; the Conservative contender had left school at fourteen and 'started life' as a messenger boy. I wanted to do a five-part series, putting the general election into a broad social and indeed world perspective. I had to settle for one short piece: OUR VILLAGE TAKES THE ELECTIONS QUIETLY.

THE WEATHER WAS GIVING PRELIMINARY INDICATIONS OF WHAT I imagined would be the delights of spring, as unknown to the Sydney experience as bars opening on Sundays. It was warmer, with much more sun and more bird song, and I found I could now sit in the front garden, in the mornings, to read the papers (clipping out interesting pieces – if I was going to be a freelance I would need my references) and also to 'get on with my writing'. Tiny leaves were beginning to appear on the hedges and on the trees; walks in the woods, amongst trees whose names I now knew, became my spring rite.

'Getting on with my writing' had been the greatest pleasure of the four months or so since we had left Sydney. It was a physical pleasure, amongst others, with the feeling that I was carrying on some ancient handcraft, with a ceremonial feeling that this was going on in a magic circle of concentration. On the ship, a deck chair; in the village, an easy chair in front of the peat fire in the drawing room when no one else was there; and now a kitchen chair, taken into the front garden for the morning sun. Typing out the first draft was more like 'work', and so was the disappointment that could come from reading the typescript, as if someone else had written it and not got down what I meant, but this could be followed by the comfort of getting paper on my knee again, and crossing out and rewriting and transposing, enlivened by the faint smell of ink. A rough outline was written on pieces of paper and when as work was done I crossed out a section of this outline there was an even greater satisfaction than that obtained in counting a day's words. But the outline was constantly scribbled over and then rewritten because of another delight: following the sheer logic of their conversational styles, the characters were moving off in directions other than those I had imagined.

Elsa also became part of the process of writing, especially in sustaining faith. We would drop in to see her at any time, morning, noon, night. There was always coffee and talk we couldn't share with anyone else: knowing things others couldn't know, we would smile at our shrewdness and giggle at our irrelevance. And, other than village gossip, which was as customary an opening to a social occasion as offering cigarettes, much of the talk was about my novel. Neither Elsa nor Ethel had any doubts that the best thing was the dialogue, but, overall, there was such a shared feeling of belief in its prospects that Ethel and I began to discuss whether she should borrow a couple of hundred pounds on the strength of the trust fund her mother's father had set up. This seemed a sensible idea. (Entirely unlike the way his wife's money was wasted by Ethel's father.)

I would finish my last revisions in July. Elsa had volunteered to type out the final draft. The manuscript would be off by August. Ethel had borrowed enough to see us through the summer, along with whatever guineas I earned in freelancing. Usually I didn't doubt that after this I would be a writer.

2

As the feeling that our existence in the village was fiction grew firmer, I had begun to think that perhaps I was also living out, in a kind of trial run, what could be my second novel. When I realised how my debates with Rose had become stylised into simple repetitive caricatures, some of the dialogue for this second novel seemed to be already reaching the rehearsal stage.

But now, as 'characters', Rose and I were beginning to develop. My uncharacteristically polite silence dissolved as Rose continued to provide instruction on the events of the day and the meaning of life. The period of great debates began when I found myself forced to instruct the old ladies in the Whig interpretation of British history. Rose had seen the past as a pageant of English kings and queens assisted by a variety of English geniuses – Shakespeare, Charles I, Charles Lamb, Florence Nightingale and other 'people like us' who showed the way to the lower orders; and beyond England was the glory of Empire (now diminished by Mr Attlee) in which English genius enlightened the lesser breeds, whether in Delhi or Melbourne. I had begun my course of instruction in the past by pointing out that the Welsh, Scottish and Northern Irish were also 'British': she found this analysis unconvincing, disposing of it with her usual form of dismissal (Oh, if you say so). Our real battle was then fought. When I gave the view of British history I had been taught in an Australian country schoolroom, where the principal dates had been printed on a chart on the wall, from 1265 – SIMON DE MONTFORT

SUMMONS PARLIAMENT – to 1928 – COMPLETE WOMEN'S SUFFRAGE – this was news to Rose, to whom the last great constitutional reform appeared to have been Magna Carta. I produced evidence. The most contemporary work of reference in the house was an edition of the *Encyclopedia Britannica* which still included articles by Macaulay (whom I referred to as '*Lord* Macaulay', to increase his authority with Rose) and I read out extracts from these. She merely amended her usual form of dismissal by saying 'Oh, if you and Lord Macaulay say so', as if this would-be 'lord' was as discredited a witness as I was.

When I tried to instruct her in the tenets of British liberalism she ended our debate by saying 'Oh, you might as well vote for Mr Attlee and have done with it' – a statement so grossly offensive that there was an intervention from Ethel's mother. She usually sat through our exchanges in a state of anxious silence, as if she were reliving her humiliating childhood, but this time she said: 'Rose, you are going too far.'

It was in this context of political, historical and constitutional discussion that the Australian question came onto our agenda. At first, discussion was of a general kind. Oh, I don't suppose you have villages like ours in Australia. Really, I can't imagine a countryside without our dear little villages. Do they have woods and lanes in Australia? ... Of course Australia is a very democratic country, isn't it? I *do* think it is *such* a pity when everyone is reduced to the same level – don't you? ... Australia must be a wonderful country. I have heard *so* much about it. A friend of mine was going there once but her mother persuaded her not to. When the word 'colonial' declared itself, I tendered the Statute of Westminster and what I hoped would be other decisive evidence. Rose remained unconvinced, but she did not dismiss my submissions with her usual, Oh, if *you* say so!, perhaps because there was at least a *prima facie* case that this might be a subject in which I would have some superficial information unknown to her (although my overall interpretation would, of course, be false).

The discussion as to whether Australia was still a colony remained open, but rather than argue it directly we began to fight it out on the streets of Sydney and in the paddocks of the Australian countryside. Rose had now become obsessed with putting Australia in its place in conversational asides such as 'I suppose Sydney is quite a large town really: would the population be a hundred thousand?' or 'It must feel *so* strange to be surrounded by all those spaces!' As I issued population statistics, export figures, details of national income and other evidence of national maturity, I became a patriot despite myself, but I could still be left with nothing to say when confronted with *pensées* (delivered while staring thoughtfully at the window) such as 'The Australians I have met have been very *loyal*' or 'There must be some *very* fine people in Australia'. I began to imagine that in my second novel there would be a character called Mrs Blair-Jones, and she would be based on Rose. I would marry her to a non-communicative colonel. The character of Colonel Blair-Jones would be based on Lily and he would show a taciturnity equal to Lily's with a normal conversational range running from 'I dare say!' to 'Quite!'

The arrival of the McCallums was the beginning of a colonial invasion. Rose had found them 'very nice people indeed', but they were followed by a Canadian cousin of Ethel's mother whose talkativeness outdid even Rose's: apart from meals, the dowagers retreated to their rooms, abandoning even the after-dinner rubber of bridge. The main offensive began with the next visitor – Douglas's former 'mistress', Jean (who had been living in Borneo for a couple of years). Jean's affable outspokenness brought into the open subjects the old ladies had never considered. She spoke softly and pleasantly, nonchalantly smiling their indignation away; so that although what she said may have outraged the dowagers, there was nothing in her manner of saying it they could seize on as bad form. Ethel's mother yielded to this geniality, chatting to Jean with an openness and pleasure she could not find when talking with me: although Jean was probably the most outspoken person she would ever meet, she took Jean's side in most of the discussions and was several times heard to say that old people should be careful not to get into a rut. I had imagined I might call my second novel *One Can Always Tell a Gentleman*: it would be essential to this theme that, despite attempts at a born-to-rule manner, Colonel and Mrs Blair-Jones should not really be gentlemen. In this context Jean was one of nature's gentlemen. Perhaps I should put in a character like Jean?

The essential non-gentlemanliness of Rose and Colonel Lily again came out when we invited down for a weekend 'Gaga' Beaton and his wife, Coral. I had met Gaga when he was a sub-editor on the *Daily Telegraph*, a position he loathed and had been reduced to by economic circumstance, but now he was taking what he hoped would be one of their regular spells in Europe, thus restoring some of the meaning he expected from life. Gaga had a 'small, private income' (which, as befitted a gentleman, had shrunk in value due to careless investment); he had been born with gentlemanly expectations and was brought up partly on the French Riviera by a mother who had retreated there from Australia and, as a young man (he was older than me) he had lived, so far as he could manage it, a life of amusement. All of this gave him the worldly ease of manner of one who could see the enjoyment of leisure as part of the natural order, and he could seem at home not only in England, but on 'the Continent' (to which, although they could not afford it, the old ladies would go on a regular two-week pilgrimage each year, with a hired limousine and chauffeur, on an expedition planned by Rose).

On the first night, comfortable in his plum-coloured smoking jacket, Gaga went down well with the dowagers, not least because he shared their view that things were getting worse and worse: they could not see that people like them might be part of Gaga's concern. On the next day we went to a point-to-point put on by a hunt club run mainly by city barristers and other 'weekend gentlemen' from London who kept houses in the country. One of those who had entered a race was a London lawyer who kept a house in a nearby parish. Long ago marked down by Ethel's father as not a real gentleman, he hired a couple of horses each year, paid for their stabling, trained for three months, and then failed to finish the race. On this occasion he fell off at the first jump. Another *arriviste* had bitten the dust. Throughout the day, amongst all these *parvenus*, Gaga and I both played gentlemen (in my case, by nature, in his, by birth): we had assembled several appropriate delicacies, some from the food parcels my mother had sent us and some brought by Gaga, whose favourite shopping was for delicacies, and we had our lunch from the boot, surveying these flashy newcomers and assembling a stock of anecdotes for the colonial spring offensive over dinner. We discovered that for both of the dowagers the hunt club was one of the signs of the county's firmament, and that one of their favourite examples of what it might mean to be a gentleman was the lawyer who had fallen off his horse. I might also put that into my second novel.

MY NEW CONCERN WITH GENTLEMANLINESS BEGAN TO DIMINISH when we were at Oxford with the McCallums. Douglas and Ann had tolerated an obsession with village gossip but they would not go as far as talk about gentlemanliness: in any case, they had Oxford gossip, even if it was somewhat muted and as out of key with the England of our earlier expectations as almost everything else we were to see in this 'post-war period', a phrase that seemed to suggest that things were now defined by their past, not their future.

There was abundant serenity in sitting with Doug and Ann in front of the fire in their flat, drinking mugs of coffee and talking about the changing shape of the world, or standing with them in some faded pub swapping anecdotes and drinking warm, watery beer. It was comforting to think of Douglas at his books, and of Ann working as a social worker at her hospital, Monday to Friday, nine to five. Unexpectedly, compared with this worthy ordinariness, our own life in the village suddenly seemed bizarre. Why was I living like that? There was nothing bizarre about writing a novel; but why couldn't I be writing it in some mean basement flat in London, doing a bit of freelance on the side, while Ethel was working as a social worker at a hospital, Monday to Friday, nine to five?

When we passed from Oxford to London, where we had been lent a Hampstead flat for a fortnight, I found pleasure in pale faces and grey streets; there was more to see in staring at one's fellow passengers in the Underground than in looking for primroses in the woods. In any case, the weeds would soon be in flower in the bomb sites in the ruined City: that seemed more my kind of flower. I also felt thoroughly at home with the two main problems that had given interest to this fortnight in London. The first was that, seen close-up, the West End theatre was rather shabby and limited. We enjoyed going to revivals – *Hamlet, The Heiress* – but what else was there, apart from satirical revue? Here was a thoroughly familiar circumstance: the present was letting me down. As we had dinner with Gaga Beaton, in a restaurant he had chosen because of its associations with the end of the nineteenth-century, while he and Coral would tell us about the 'shows' they had seen (travelling by bus and sitting in the grand circle; in a busy week they would go to three or four shows) I would rail against the West End theatre as revealing the many intellectual inadequacies of the age. The second problem was one which could be solved only by living in London: we had gone to the latest Epstein exhibition, and that was comprehensible, but when we went to the National Gallery, I could scarcely get beyond the first court. Here was an encyclopedia of paintings: how could I 'do' this in an afternoon?

Then, on our first night back in the village, over coffees in Elsa's cottage, we picked up the gossip about who had done what and to whom. Elsa had stop-press news: the new rector had arrived – an Oxford man, with a young lively wife who seemed just like Elsa and Ethel and me. They had moved into a few rooms in the twelve-room rectory – the rest of it remained abandoned – and there were rumours that the young wife had said she would do something about the acre of brambles and thickets that was all that was left of the garden. I decided I should have a clergyman in *One Can Always Tell a Gentleman*.

3

Ethel could now imagine a future based on reconstruction of the past. When we first arrived she had detailed, room by room and flower bed by flower bed, what used to be. Now she was projecting what might now become – the repair of fences, the revival of vegetable-growing, the reform of the hen run, the repainting of walls, the exposing of beams. The drains in the dinge must certainly be attended to. Could mushrooms be grown in the old dairy? Should the orchard be replanted?

In these dreams we found two allies in the part-time cook and the part-time odd jobs man. With her round, red face and steady gaze, Mrs Dulwich was honesty embodied. When she and Ethel were alone in the kitchen she would, in her own manner, open a new topic for the reform programme. She devoted most of her time to an exposition of the petty thefts and general rule-breaking of the dowagers, their attempts to exceed authority (specifically, their attempts to bully Mrs Dulwich), their laziness, and scandalous anecdotes about the avarice of their father. Our other ally was Brown (as Ethel's mother called him, although, in the democratic style, I called him 'David' and he agreed not to call me 'sir', but 'Mr Horne'). With wise wrinklings around eyes and mouth and a gaze as steady as Mrs Dulwich's, Brown would lower his head and adopt a helpfully thoughtful expression as we raised plans for restoring the glass house, or putting the dinge under potatoes. Our working relationship with Brown and Mrs Dulwich sustained my belief in the true wisdom of the people.

They were both put down as characters for *One Can Always Tell a Gentleman*.

After a morning's writing, in the afternoons I would try to help Ethel in her great task of getting things back to where they had been. The hens were her first objective. They were scarcely laying, and when they did it was often in a hedge. We read Ministry of Agriculture pamphlets and began contemplating the relative virtues of different styles of keeping hens. In the meantime, there were the existing hen houses to patch, a task that had very great difficulties, since I was unable to hit a nail straight on the head.

My part of our programme of regeneration was the garden reclamation plan, at least in its primitive first stage, of weed destruction. Apart from mowing the lawn when told to as a boy, I knew nothing about gardening; when in my first year in high school I had been sentenced to path weeding for an hour a day I had doubted whether I could survive such tedium. But what I was doing now was not weeding. It was pioneering.

The twitch was the easiest to remove. I spread weed killer according to the instructions on the packet, and, as other people might watch their flowers grow, after breakfast each morning I would walk along all the paths watching my weeds die, then return to the house and describe to Ethel their death pallor, and their screams.

The kitchen gardens were the largest expanse to be reclaimed. The remains of last year's nettles were carted off and exultantly burned, then, with fork and spade, with my corduroy trousers tucked into the captain's gumboots, I started a detailed and ruthless eradication. Beneath the dead brown matter on top, inside the earth, the nettles had developed a complex and interlocking system of juicy, vigorous roots. All of these had to be pulled out of the earth, taken off in the wheelbarrow, dried out and burned. Only then would the kitchen gardens be freed. The networks of nettles extended into my dreams – usually with a low, fatalistic sense of anxiety as if I would remain forever in an earthy sub-world of slowly and inevitably extending roots.

It was against the brambles that the main force of the attack now moved. It was not just a question of digging out roots: the brambles had intertwined with the roses and hundreds of snips with the secateurs were needed to extricate the wood of brambles from the wood of roses. The main effect was fairly quickly gained: one could again walk through the rose walk, although for the rest of the summer I would still spend occasional half-hours extracting

– as if they were shrapnel or shattered bone – small pieces of dead bramble from among the roses.

The superficial weeds in the flower beds were easily forked out, but the bindweed defeated me. Its roots were like long, white, thin worms stretching into infinity. I would dig along the length of a root, delicately, with a fork, so that it didn't break, playing it out as I went, but this period of pleasant elasticity would end with a snap and the rest of the root would spring back into the soil and, often, not be found. A stone wall ran at the back of the herbaceous border: perhaps down amongst its foundations, safe from my probing, were the central forces of bindweed, ready for a summer expansion. These extraordinary events gave me another idea for my second novel: I would have some Australians come to the village (it was, of course, going to be set in a village); they would modernise hen runs, reclaim gardens, and introduce the village to the spirit of pioneering.

I DEVELOPED EVEN MORE FAITH IN THIS IDEA WHEN ADRIAN Deamer came to stay with us in the middle of May, only a few days after he arrived from Australia. Ethel and I knew he had come intending to resume his *affaire* with Gwen. Of course he denied this: he had simply come to get a job in Fleet Street, and so forth. It made a better story to imagine he had sailed to England in pursuit of love.

Adrian had a wider vision than mere wilderness clearing: when we discovered an old croquet kit among the rubbish in the summer house he contemplated the recovery of the tennis court as a lawn on which we could play a rough game of croquet. Adrian showed the way with a brilliant achievement: he knew how to scythe. Amongst the extensive range of garden tools rusting in store rooms and potting shed we found both scythe and sickle and we recaptured the simplicities of the peasant experience as, under a warmish sun, Adrian scythed his way across the tennis court. We had found, abandoned amongst the nettles, a garden roller, entwined with the dead remains of many seasons' weeds and we used this to roll the scythed grass; then we cut it more finely with a mower, rolled it again a number of times, and were able to offer a sporting croquet lawn. Croquet rules were found in the old edition of the

Encyclopedia Britannica: making fun of ourselves as we did it, we played ironic games of croquet every day after tea, and sometimes after supper.

When the old ladies went off on their annual pilgrimage to the Continent we had the house to ourselves, rearranging meals so that we had dinner at night, breakfast in the front garden, tea in the main garden, snacks in the kitchen. We invited in our friends from the village, cooked our own kinds of food, got up late, went to bed late, and acted as if we owned the place. Sending ourselves up as 'Horne, Horne and Deamer, Interior Decorators', we painted the woodwork in the dining room a new colour, papered the walls, took the doors off the cupboard, and displayed the glass.

The three of us went for outings and we would comment on what we saw with appropriately worldly equivocations. In the woods the bluebells were out, and the beeches were in leaf; Adrian now had to be instructed in all those names Ethel had bestowed on things. On one splendid morning when there was a cuckoo in the dinge we ran around giving mock cuckoo cries; on a walk one afternoon we stood in our tracks as a skylark rose above us, singing; after dinner one night we sat in the front garden and listened to the extravagances of a nightingale. Elsa had become an honorary Australian and we continued to use her converted cottage as a coffee shop, especially at night when we would talk, tell jokes, do imitations, sing, and give Adrian detailed instruction in village gossip. For a day or two Adrian and I helped Jim White on his farm, enjoying the authenticity of drinking tea in the kitchen while we cooled down. For one stretch there were almost two weeks of successively sunny days. It was as if we were shooting stock footage to provide cliché scenes of memorable contentment for half a dozen films, symbolising the carefree life, and, later, its transience.

FIVE

One can always tell a gentleman

1

When the second draft of *The Richmond Affair* was fully typed there was comfort in going over it, typescript on knee, pen in hand, changing things: thinning out words was more familiar than unearthing the roots of bindweed and nettle. The next stage of revision needed a flat top rather than a knee and scissors and paste, so that whole parts could be moved from one place to the other. Between meals I took over the dining room table, shutting the door as if the dining room were an operating theatre which must be kept surgically clean. By July, when Elsa began her first job as a typist of literary manuscripts (her 'small private income' seemed to be becoming smaller), it was to type out the final draft of *The Richmond Affair*.

As a result of Elsa's belief in the manuscript, what would happen next was also planned. She knew a minor contributor to a minor London weekly and she invited him and his companion to the village for lunch, with the hope that he would take an interest in *The Richmond Affair*. Although London was only an hour or so away by train, he acted as if he had been despatched to Afghanistan. It was a fine day, with some sunshine, and we spent most of it in a picnic party at the edge of the woods, looking out over our large and picturesque plain, which, in this light, seemed at its best. A village was alien to him – he was even concerned about the effect on health of so many trees – and that one village inhabitant was, unaccountably, Australian made stronger the sense of surrounding threat. Towards the end, he and his companion sat on the outskirts of our party, looking out over the plain, while the rest of us got on with the village gossip. When some clouds came up he inquired about catching an earlier train. *The Richmond Affair* had been mentioned but he had restricted himself to giving the name of A.P. Watts, a literary agent. Could we say he had recommended us? Well, no, perhaps not.

WITH THE MANUSCRIPT ON ELSA'S DESK, ETHEL AND I WENT OFF with Gaga Beaton and his wife, on what was to be the first sightseeing tour of my life: in Australia, when I was a child, car travelling had been confined to a 'spin' in one of my uncle's cars – and on these all we would stop to look at were a few famous 'views'. In Sydney our real past was geological: our human past was merely something to be pulled down. If one wanted to look at old artefacts there were the museums. Now Gaga had bought a 1933 Wolseley and, with touring maps and a guide to cheap private hotels, he had planned a week's tour of the West Country.

We photographed ourselves lighting cigarettes in front of Stonehenge, and looking through telescopes at Land's End, but these photographs were taken mainly to send home to my family. Apart from the disagreeable food we congratulated ourselves on the civilised nature of our progress: with only two cathedrals, one ruined monastery and one stately home on Gaga's list, there was appropriate time to 'see' what we did look at. While I was inspecting the outside of the Deanery in Wells, it occurred to me that I had looked at scarcely anything in London with my own eyes: we had simply 'done' some sights.

Except for Bath, our overnight stands in private hotels were in undistinguished provincial towns, and this gave us a chance to go to the local theatre (if a touring company was in town) or to drop into local pubs and feel we were tasting some of the undistinguished life of provincial England. From this we gained confidence that we were not merely being conned by the past. But it was the past we were after, so that it could illuminate us with its authenticity.

We seemed to find authenticity most convincingly in Bath and, in Cornwall, Polperro. Polperro displeased us, as we had expected, because of the swarm of tourists that had settled on it, their cars parked in long lines at the approaches and their bodies jostling in the 'narrow, twisting streets'. But this was itself a spectacle: I had never seen a place so taken over. The slender houses with their juttings-out and slopings seemed *papier maché* (for a film set), not stone (for history). But as we were driving away we imagined Polperro in winter, when it went back to its authentically sullen stoniness. I had not before seen such a model of the idea of 'Fishing Village'; in Bath I saw for the first time a model of how the ideas of 'Reason, Elegance and Order' might be represented in a town. In Polperro I had imagined myself as a pipe-smoking author in a polo-necked sweater living in a small stone house beside the harbour, lifting his eyes to watch the boats come back with their catch; in Bath I imagined myself as a person of reason.

In our inexpensive private hotel in Bath, with its faded furnishings and dispirited food, Gaga and I were at the top of our aristocratic form, manifest, in his case, in his ability to open his lips and show his teeth in a way that might seem a smile but was really a sign of languid contempt. I began to wonder if in *One Can Always Tell a Gentleman* I might establish a scene in Bath – some *arrivistes*, perhaps, not knowing how to behave in their expensive but elegant hotel?

PREPARATION FOR WRITING THE GENTLEMANLY PARTS OF *ONE Can Always Tell a Gentleman* was helped when Ethel and I spent a fortnight with her cousin, who was a squire in the Peak District. Now I would be able to see a North Country squire, direct in manner and self-assured, a person without southern corruption; the kind of eighteenth-century type I wanted.

During the train journey to Sheffield through the Black Country we passed landscapes as desolate in their own style as the desert landscapes I had seen on my way to Darwin as a soldier (but, through literary creation, more familiar than the Australian desolation) and with its haze of light blue smoke and grey and dead honeycomb of mean terraces, Sheffield seemed historically accurate. That was almost all we were to see of the Industrial Revolution. The large upland village where we were staying had once depended on lead mining for a living, but the only contact it now seemed to have with industry came from the fact that some Manchester and Sheffield businessmen used it as a retreat (where they were mildly mocked for their attempts at gentlemanliness). Industry, commerce, trade and finance were activities pursued in despised cities on the fringe of the heather moors of the Peak District. Our only expeditions beyond the village were to the Palladian showing-off of Chatsworth and the medieval domesticity of Haddon Hall, and to spectacular views of undulating green turf and loose stone walls. The only other reminder of the Industrial Revolution came on a visit to another cousin of Ethel's, sister to the squire, a woman of strong character living alone in a stone cottage on the moors, and to reach this we passed an old factory of grey stone placed in a small village beside a river. The sight of this early survivor of the beginnings of the factory system provided the greatest shock of historical authenticity I had known since we had arrived in England.

THE HALL WHERE THE SQUIRE LIVED WAS PART OF THE VILLAGE, and made of the same stone. Built in the seventeenth century, it had eighteen rooms, although only one bathroom (a space partitioned off from a corridor), and as the day proceeded there was progression among the range of public rooms, beginning with the breakfast room and ending in the drawing room. Upstairs I was given a desk in the corner of the library. For good measure, we slept in a four-poster bed. Even the garden had maintained a gentlemanly assurance, unlike the wilderness in which I had absurdly played the part of pioneer. Words like 'conservatory' or 'kitchen garden' or 'orchard' meant what they said and the garden was still part of the sense of ordained progress. While we were there it was the turn of the raspberries, blackcurrants and red currants to control what happened in the house – there were daily pickings of the fruit and daily makings of excellent 'summer puddings'. All the fruits and vegetables had their seasons to be picked, cooked, eaten, sold, given away, preserved or stored. Even the lawns and flower beds had their seasons as the places for taking tea on a fine afternoon.

This sense of gentlemanly assurance was given a realistic and modern feeling by the fact that Ethel's cousin no longer had enough money to keep the place up. They could run to a daily help and 'a man', but those parts of their daily lives that were not spent in moving, in the traditional order, from one room to the next, were largely spent in getting on with dusting, cleaning, scrubbing, polishing, gardening, patching, weeding – so that when we sat down with them in the morning room or on the terrace, or wherever it was one was expected to sit at a particular time of day, it was as if the stage hands, having set up this traditional scenery, then became the actors. I appropriated The Hall as the principal setting for *One Can Always Tell a Gentleman*. I would bring it into play several years after its founding family had ended.

One more thought for this yet-to-be-written novel: the North Country. Ethel's cousin was adequate as eighteenth-century squire; although he was not a boozer or a fox hunter, he was intelligent and even amusing, and he was as straight as a die. And throughout the day we spent with his sister she stared at me with such determined frankness that I felt she had seen into my innermost fraudulence. In my novel the squire and his sister would be but a memory of how much better things used to be before Lily and Rose moved in as Colonel and Mrs Blair-Jones.

There was something else I had wanted – some sense of what, apart from eighteenth-century gentlemen, had made Britain 'Great', and that was to be found in a romantic view of nineteenth-century North Country business enterprise. We had Sunday morning sherries with a rich Manchester businessman but he seemed concerned entirely with making a good impression on the squire. In our two weeks in the North Country I did not see any business enterprise.

BACK IN THE VILLAGE, THERE WAS THE LATE SUMMER TO contemplate. I had bought the *Penguin Vegetable Grower's Guide* and was writing myself general position papers on plans for the kitchen gardens now they had been reclaimed; Ethel was contemplating uncovering all the beams that had been concealed when the house had been 'converted'; we were both reading Ministry of Agriculture pamphlets on efficient egg production. It was time we brought to the egg industry some of the spirit of nineteenth-century North Country enterprise. One enterprising plan had already failed – but in a fiasco sufficiently ironic to make a good anecdote: after reading in a magazine called the *Smallholder* about the nutrient value for hens of sunflower seed, we had planted several rows of sunflower seed alongside the fence dividing garden from field; but, not aware of the principle of deferred gratification, the hens had broken into the garden and eaten the seeds. Now we had a plan: the hens would be housed in 'folds', that were moved every day. Moving to the fold system seemed one of those tough, pragmatic decisions *The Economist* would approve as the kind of change that could again make Britain 'Great'.

After some freelancing work covering the tennis season at Wimbledon, Adrian now had a regular job, on fourteen guineas a week, as a reporter on the *Daily Express*: he would still spend occasional weekends with us, and so now would Gwen. (*Those two seem to be coming together again.*) They were both able to keep straight faces when we talked about hens or kitchen gardens and when we dropped into Elsa's for coffee or over to the Whites' for afternoon tea; village gossip had become a part of Gwen's repertoire of wisecracking. If the four of us played croquet it became not so much a game of croquet, as a game about playing croquet – usually in a comedy of manners, but sometimes in a Marx Brothers presentation.

And now, in the middle of these pastoral scenes there was glorious news about *The Richmond Affair*. In August, when Elsa had finished the typing, I had bought a manila folder, trimmed it to the page size of the typescript, anchored it with paper fasteners fore and aft (was that what one did with a manuscript?) and posted it to A.P. Watts, who had already said they would look at it. Less than a month later a letter came back saying YES. There were two sentences and for several days I couldn't keep my eyes off them: 'We have now placed your book on offer in a likely quarter. I shall report to you again, as soon as I have good news for you about it.' 'Isn't it wonderful news about your novel?' my mother wrote in her next letter. 'Our blessings go with it in hoping it will be a best-seller.'

I was in London several days later. Because the filth in the air got into my scalp I had just bought a hat, a light grey trilby, although I was not sure what to do with the brim. Should I snap it down in the front, as they did in Sydney? Or let the brim softly curl upwards, in a manner reminiscent of the homburg, but not so pompous? I was sitting in a bus, looking out at an unexpectedly sunny, if somewhat dusty, London and for the first time I felt that in my own way I might belong to this city. The brim was snapped down, in the Sydney style. On an impulse of confidence and companionship with my new environment, I touched the brim in a gently, upward caress. It sprang up. I was wearing a hat in a London manner.

We were approaching Trafalgar Square. Again on an impulse of happiness, just as a young man in a nineteenth-century French novel might, at some moment of joy, make his first visit to a brothel, I got out of the bus and made what I saw as the first of many visits to the National Gallery. I was about to become a Londoner. I would have time to master the Gallery.

ETHEL MADE THE DECISION. SHE WOULD BORROW A COUPLE OF hundred more and for six months we would rent a cottage in Cornwall. I started planning *One Can Always Tell a Gentleman* and had a few goes at the opening chapter. Through an advertisement Ethel decided on a cottage – in Polperro, at £54/12/- for the six months. We could live on cheap fish. We were spending practically nothing on alcohol. I had almost given up smoking. Now I would start my second novel.

2

The cottage (part of a terrace built for coastguards) had two rooms up and two rooms down, with narrow, creaking stairs and no bathroom, although a porcelain hip bath had been installed in the kitchen beside the box for the coals. The terrace was a solitary building on the hill above the village and facing away from it. Looking across a steep valley to the Cornish Sea, we felt quite alone. A fine set of windows across the front room caught a wide view and, for most of the day, the sun.

I had notes on the structure of *One Can Always Tell a Gentleman*, a draft of its opening and a sketch map of the village I would set it in. This village would be called 'Rottenham'. That seemed to catch what I wanted. I must rush at it, with a daily ration of words large enough to finish a first draft by Christmas. On our first day, however, I would take things easy until after lunch. We hobbled down to the village, on a road so steep I was afraid I would fall over, into the web of narrow streets that provided just what we had expected – a village drained of tourists and restored to the authentic. We spent time admiring the neatness of the little harbour, walled into a small inlet in a gap in the cliffs, and then leant over the stone walls of the little river that plunged through the village as we chose individually shaped whitewashed stone houses to approve. Polperro seemed a museum of the authentic past. Behind a rough black wooden door, in a small stone shed with lobster pots piled in the rear, we looked over a box of diverse types of smallish fish from the day's catch and for a few pence bought some pilchards – a fish we had not imagined outside a can. In an epiphany of the authentic, we saw a fisherman making a new crab pot out of willows, and Ethel, who was better than I was at talking to strangers, discovered he was making 'crappots' out of 'willies'. Perhaps we should establish a notebook of local dialect? We already knew from our summer holiday that 'pol' meant 'pool', 'pen' meant 'headland', the town Fowey was pronounced *foy* and the town Mousehole was pronounced *mowsel*. When our four trunks arrived, unpacking became a ceremony in improvised song, mime and dance, celebrating liberation from the dowagers and restrictions on our lives, even freedom from having to talk about the village. This house was ours (for six months). These were our things, brought from Australia. We would put them where we liked and do with them as we chose.

For me, the most meaningful unpacking was of the selection I had made from books brought from Australia. After a fine lunch of pilchards and bread and butter, when I lit the coal fire in the front room and settled down to rewrite the opening paragraphs of *One Can Always Tell a Gentleman*, beside me, near the wide windows where the sun was shining through, they were there: Dostoevsky, Tolstoy, Mann, Flaubert, Stendhal, Proust, Joyce – as relevant to what I was doing as the view of the valley and the English Channel.

I had to rewrite what I had already done because on the train I had decided to make the two central characters Americans, not Australians. Obviously, this would sell the book in the United States. The character of the husband would still be inspired by some view of myself as a passive person (something I had never considered until we came to England), but now it had to be rewritten so that I spoke like a passive person educated at Harvard. Although she showed the same energy, the character of the wife drew no inspiration from Ethel – that would make the book too 'real' and distract from the comedy. (It would also place a greater strain on my powers of self-examination than I wanted to bear.) I had no one person in mind, but the character seemed to be coming out like some version of Gwen. I had no idea how Gwen and I would talk if we were Americans.

For three weeks I spent most of the day sitting in the front room writing my novel with a fountain pen into a large exercise book held on my knees, or sitting at the table, typing up what I had written. In the mornings we would have breakfast in front of the window, looking out to the Cornish Sea and, on most days, absorbing the sun: then, with the care of an alpine climber, I would descend on the village for *The Times*, the *Daily Express*, and the *Manchester Guardian*, and on Sundays, the *Sunday Times* and the *Observer*. Later in the morning, Ethel would walk down to the village to buy the day's fish and other provisions, but also to make discoveries about the people. Beyond passing the time of day or discussing the weather or the price of fish, I spoke scarcely to anyone. I didn't need people. Since I was writing a novel I was inventing my own people.

Before lunch, as if I were looking from an observation balloon, I read the newspapers; then I would bring myself down to earth and, as a potential freelance, clip out useful items about what was said to be happening in the world and put them into manila folders. I did not even read some of the clippings: all that was required was that I should put them in the appropriate folder. 'The news' was mainly a land of shadows. Stalinism, certainly, was real: ... The Korean War was real, and so was 'the next war', which we would sometimes write about in letters, as if we were already looking back on it ... And 'the Cold War' was real not least because the Americans were giving it a bad name, with Senator Joe McCarthy as such an instructive specimen of American nastiness ... The failures of 'planning' were real, of course, and increasingly self-parodic ... What was most believable in the newspapers were reports of the continuing failures of progress. But the reality of even these was suspended slightly outside the magic circle of writing my second novel.

Over lunch, again eaten in front of the window, and usually with the sun still warming us, Ethel would report on the morning's findings. After lunch, we would have the day's principal walk: we had bought an ordinance map and we intended to walk over the territory thoroughly. Then I would light the fire and we would have tea, again in front of the Cornish Sea, now seen under a fading light. Later, with the comfort of drawn curtains and a glowing fire I would get on with more writing. Before supper (eaten on our laps in front of the fire) was the time for revision. After supper we would read and talk and attend to the fire. If I had written a particularly amusing passage I might read that out.

Ethel was untwisting from the disillusion of finding such disorder in the very house which for her had seemed a symbol of eternal order: compared with the frustrated busyness of reforming household and hen-yard she now 'didn't have much to do', and had resumed reading. Each night she gave special thanks that she did not have to play bridge and we both were grateful for the quietness, after spending so long with two old ladies who had been brought up to believe that it was imperative that for every moment someone must be 'making conversation'. We were awe-struck with the luxury of being able to sit side by side in front of the fire, reading, and speaking only when we had something to say.

BECAUSE THERE WAS SO MUCH WRITING TO DO, OUR WALKS WERE of only an hour or so. But at the end of the three weeks I needed a Bible. I had my leftist parson character alternating in his conversation between quotes from the Bible and quotes from Marxist texts (thereby getting rid of two faiths in one) but while I seemed to have remembered more than enough sentences from Marxist texts I had no textual memory of the Bible. We decided to walk the three miles to Looe (a 'typical' Cornish fishing port), buy a Bible, then get to know something about Looe, to amplify my knowledge of Cornish ports. I had discovered, for instance, that Looe sent twenty ships to aid Edward III at Calais when London sent only twenty-five. (*Did you know the rafters in the chancel in St Nicholas Church were made from the timbers of a Spanish warship? Did you know that Looe was, until the 1832 Reform Bill, a famous rotten borough?*) I was passing from a romantic view of the North Country as the centre of nineteenth-century enterprise to a romantic view of the West Country as the centre of enterprise in the Elizabethan age. As an enthusiasm it had replaced an obsession with village gossip.

When we got to Looe itself I was not ready for a megalopolis of four thousand people, amorphous, incomprehensible, indifferent, anomic. As we shopped for a Bible my arms and legs drooped; my stomach turned sour and stale. My eyes began to hurt. The headache started when we visited the Church of St Nicholas, where the sunken vestry was 'of special interest'. I couldn't think. (Perhaps I might faint?) We stole a Bible from the church, and caught a taxi home, back to our magic circle.

IT HAD BECOME AN IMPORTANT PART OF OUR DAY TO OPEN THE curtains each morning and discover which scene the window was now framing. Several days after our retreat from Looe, following a scene of black clouds and drizzles of sleet, we woke and drew the curtains to find, framed in the window, a snow scene. (Once, when I was a child, when there were rumours of snow in the Blue Mountains we had loaded ourselves into an uncle's car but by the time we got there the snow had melted.) After several days of 'Sunny Scene, Cornish Coast' our window then framed 'Gale in Cornwall', with a sky black enough and waves wild enough to take us to the cliffs for greater realism. But the sound effects were not as good as from our cottage where the whistling in the telegraph wires gave a more authentic representation of high wind in Cornwall. The scene framed by the window was supplemented by other daily observations, of which the most important was the movement of the fishing boats. Whether or not the boats went out and, if they did, what was caught, were important demarcations of the day, reported on by Ethel from her contacts in the fishing world and demonstrated in what she bought for a few pence from the stone shed with the black door – pilchards or mackerel usually, both delicious when cooked fresh, sometimes whiting (after we had learned to follow the local way and soak it in salt overnight to give it flavour) and, as a special treat, lobster. Sometimes there were rumours of crab. But Ethel discovered that the fishing itself didn't amount to much any longer: what mattered was the tourist industry (in which the fishing boats were essential evidence); in fact a number of people in the village took their wages from the tourist trade in the summer and in the winter went on the dole. Then came information about the resentments roving through the village about the 'foreigners'. Not us – as a fellow subject people, Australians were acceptable, provided they didn't stay for too long. The unacceptable foreigners were the English, who had invaded Cornwall from across the Tamar River and were the main entrepreneurs of the tourist industry. One of them, from the North Country, refused to eat local fish, preferring stale cod railed down from Grimsby.

I myself learned nothing about the natives of Polperro apart from the images and anecdotes brought up the hill with the day's fish by Ethel. In any case most of them did not live in the postcard-like part of the village ('the narrow, twisting streets clustered around the harbour') but in some straight streets of more ordinary houses hunched into the narrow valley, and these few streets seemed to be grouped not around the harbour, but around the ugly Wesleyan chapel. Of the farmers whose fields we passed on our walks into the interior we learned nothing: we did not develop with the farmers that keen sense of communion that united us with the fishermen from eating, daily, what they sold us. Ethel got to know some foreigners who were living in the village for a season to escape the world and gave them character names – 'Mrs Bits and Pieces' for a woman who seemed all over the place, 'Mrs Double Front' for a woman of *petit bourgeois* pretension – but these scarcely seemed the real Cornwall.

The 'real Cornwall' was something I read about and developed for myself during walks. Walks along the cliffs, one of our favourites, recalled the kinds of tempests and wrecks popularised in nineteenth-century lithographs, along with schoolboy tales of derring-do among smugglers and revenue men. If I was by myself, my favourite walk was down a steep hillside to Talland Sands – a small, shallow, rocky, seaweed-infested and unswimmable bay which had a steep little valley behind it and, beside the beach, a ruined house built of stone. On the other side was a path to Talland church, which I had marked down as one of the places we must take our visitors to when they came, because it would provide the substance for one of my lectures to them. If the church was not shut there were mouldering stone and intricate wood-carving to look at, but when I gave my lecture the point would be that Talland church represented the plight of the Church of England in Cornwall and, beyond that, nothing less than the need for adaptability in all human institutions. Talland church was alone in the field, no longer surrounded by a village, but it still had a parson; he conducted his services but (apart from a few Catholics who celebrated mass, furtively, in a garage, with an itinerant priest) almost everyone went to the ugly Wesleyan chapel, which was where people lived. In the eighteenth-century, when the Church was indifferent to change, Wesley had preached his message of faith in the open fields of Cornwall: Methodism conquered all. Here was an instructive tale; a lesson to Mr Attlee's England.

During our inland walks, when we were stared down by cows who stood above us as we moved along a sunken lane, the mud and bare branches were reminders that in the upper world it was winter and not just a series of 'Scenes from the Cornish Coast' framed by a large glass window. In the spring we intended to go for longer walks and even take bus trips. We could cross Bodmin Moor into the territories of Arthurean myth – Dozmary Pool, Slaughter Bridge, Camelford (Did you know that 'Camelot' became a rotten borough?) and the stones of the castle above Tintagel Bay, and find contrasts between legend and tourist experience. What I most wanted for my lectures, however, were physical metaphors, like Talland church, of 'real' legend. Near Lostwithiel there was a famous battlefield from the Civil War: that would do as a reminder of how the Cornish usually supported failures. The engine house of an abandoned tin mine would be a good symbol of the ruthlessness of industrial change, while the white slagheaps, open pits and smoking chimneys of the St Austell china clay mines would be a reminder of the necessary price of progress. (Did you know that, apart from China, Cornwall has a monopoly of high quality kaolin?) There were other intimations of a lively past: Gibbon had once been the member of parliament for Liskeard; it was in Cornish mines that Richard Trevithick had experimented with the first high-pressure steam engines (Did you know that?); and Humphry Davy, inventor of the miner's safety lamp was Penzance-born. With Plymouth to the east and Fowey to the west, there were reminders of West Country seadogs and the lost spirit of English enterprise. We would go to Fowey in the spring, perhaps even Plymouth (although a place so large might give me a headache) and seek exemplary reminders of the seadogs.

ETHEL'S MOTHER WAS OUR FIRST VISITOR. SHE STAYED FOR A fortnight and, again, there was the realisation of how comparatively normal she could seem when extracted from her companions and, again, the realisation that she 'was doing her best to like me' (or perhaps did like me). There was no need to lecture her on examples of the decline of England. She was herself a prime example of this process. Instead, I told her stories about Cornwall without drawing didactic lessons. Successful. Much laughter. The more serious lectures would begin when Gaga Beaton and Coral come down to spend Christmas, and, in the new year, Ann and Douglas and Adrian and Gwen (who, having married in October, had become 'the Deamers').

I had not finished the first draft of the novel. There seemed no good reason for ever stopping the flow of its amusing conversation. But at our wedding anniversary dinner it had been agreed that over Christmas I would take some days off. I took a few notes on this dinner: 'House said to be three hundred years old. Perched on a rock by the harbour. Walls two feet thick.' I didn't get around to writing them up.

We considered our Christmas dinner to have been celebrated in gracious style. With the Beatons we were seated in front of the fire around a table brought in from the back room and decorated by Ethel with moss. Some sprigs of holly stolen on a walk from a nearby wood were placed in the room, but they were used evocatively, so that it was clear that we thought it amusing to bother to put up holly. All four of us helped prepare the dinner, with considerable wit (wit was my main contribution), then we sat round the candle-lit table enjoying our feast and making fun of a meretricious world. But there was no place in this festival for lectures on the true meaning of Cornwall. Even when Douglas and Ann arrived to replace the Beatons (with only two days' writing time in between) there again were no occasions for delivering the Horne lectures on Cornwall. Ann was ready to listen, if with a certain quizzical tolerance, but Douglas seemed preoccupied, even morose, as if doubting whether there was any point in being at Polperro, not expressing any enthusiasm for even the cliff views. (He was writing a thesis on Max Weber, some of whose works were now being translated into English. I knew nothing about Weber: was there something in this unknown German that had made Douglas sad?) He did take me aside, however, to read me a most serious letter from Sydney: the 'Andersonians' were about to split. Some of them found Anderson's concern with Stalinism excessive; they were about to form a group of their own with an anarchist bias. They might call themselves 'the libertarians'. What frictions in old friendships might we not see now? The McCallums' visit, however, was mainly a re-enactment of happy days spent by the four of us in Sydney, and it reached its climaxes after tea, when the curtains were closed and there was no reason to remember that we were in a coastguard's cottage above the Cornish Sea.

I had imagined myself at least gaining some hearing time from Adrian and Gwen, but their visit overlapped with the McCallums'. However, I had my chance, on a visit to the Polperro pub (where Ethel and I did not go when we were by ourselves: we felt we could not normally afford to drink alcohol). After we had got through several mugs of watery beer, when I let myself go on

Cornwall, they seemed to be listening. There were some laughs. But I felt so strongly a presentiment of a kind I had never known before that, after a while, I stopped talking.

What might I be in twenty years or so? A pub bore? Fat? Bald? Losing my teeth? Telling the same anecdotes over and over again?

OTHER PRESENTIMENTS HAD COME FROM THESE VISITS. ALL SIX OF our visitors now had jobs, while Ethel and I were living, however cheaply, on Ethel's borrowed pounds. Ann was still working at her hospital. Douglas knew that when his degree was concluded he would be given a three-year job at Oxford. Gwen was pulling in £6 a week as a secretary. Adrian was a fourteen-guineas-a-week man on the *Express*, with anecdotes to tell of the kind I might once have told. Coral was doing some part-time work. Now even Gaga had a job – in the *Telegraph*'s London office (the job I should have got!). 'It seems,' he had written to me, 'an agreeable and leisurely office.' (*Agreeable! Leisurely! My God, if I had that job I'd make it something more than 'agreeable' and 'leisurely'*.) Even worse, after a long period of no news, a letter came from A.P. Watts telling me *The Richmond Affair* had been declined by Gollancz. Not that this mattered. One would expect Gollancz to decline it. Why did A.P. Watts send it to Gollancz anyway? (*Did A.P. Watts really know what they where doing?*) They had sent the manuscript to Eyre and Spottiswood. I thought I detected a certain confidence in their letter. Meanwhile, there was my mother writing to Ethel 'I do hope everything will be all right ... I wonder what plans you have for the future ... I am just wondering what Donald will be doing.' What Donald was doing was finishing the first draft, and then worrying about taking it all apart and putting it together again. Ethel read the manuscript very thoughtfully while I sat there wondering what she was going to say: when she gave me her report, I took notes, then read through the manuscript myself and made my own 'report', which we then both discussed. Out of this came pages of queries and instructions: 'Do John and Elsa Thrumm really seem like Americans? ... Cut down on descriptions of hens ... Must have a new Ch VIII and a new Ch X ... Cut out reference to "taut lips" ... What is the secret of the most successfully funny bits? ...' I drew up a diagram of the plot and theme structure, indicating how many pages were given to this and how many to that, then cut up the carbon copy into corresponding batches. Another two months work.

It now seemed the most natural thing in the world that one of the day's principal divisions should be between the periods when I sat writing by the light that came through the large window and those when I sat writing in front of the fire, or that one of the day's principal decisions was whether our after-lunch walk would be along the cliffs, or along the Talland path, or along one of the farmland lanes, or that the two principal relations we had with 'reality' were either the changing views of the Cornish Sea framed by a large window or items clipped out of *The Times* and the *Guardian* and put into folders.

I wrote off to Australian friends, trying to evoke the reassurance of living in this fixed world. As one might expect from a poet, Jim McAuley gave me the most satisfactory answer:

> It is strange how the mere repetition of the homely details you
> supplied evokes a composite atmosphere of Hardy; George Eliot;
> H.J. Massingham and Angela Thirkell. I shall expect at least one of
> your novels to be saturated with Cornish sailors, lobsters, vicars,
> bouncing lasses and other essences.

But nothing about the kind of verse he was now writing (surely he must soon have enough for a second volume) and something profoundly troubling in the next paragraph (this from a one-time jazz pianist – glass of neat gin on the piano, playing the blues at dawn, at the end of the party): 'My sole material concern is somehow to buy a house. Our chances with the Ryde Council housing scheme are still good, but they do move slowly.' McAuley *settling down*?

Disturbing news of other friends 'becoming normal': Bill Pritchett back from the Australian diplomatic mission in Jakarta 'with a charming Dutch wife'; Pritchett, Jockel and others now moving along their careers in the diplomatic service; Alec Hope now Professor A.D. Hope, although he had not yet published even one volume of verse (was Hope running out of steam?); other friends settled in as teachers (teachers!). Another friend wrote that he was thinking of buying a car (buying a car, when in my thirtieth year, the only capital equipment I owned was a portable radio set that needed attention!).

Our life in Polperro, or at least my perceptions of it, seemed to reach a quiet and satisfying climax when Elsa stayed for several weeks, with her son. I relished improvising long stories for him, with actions, and made-on-the-spot jingles, and I was gratified again to be talking with Elsa in our soft, wry mode, but her visit brought the extra pleasure that I could engage in a kind of final revision of Polperro – going on all the walks and showing all the things we most liked to my only sympathetic audience.

TOWARDS THE END, AS WE WERE PACKING TO GO BACK TO THE village, Ethel began to imagine we could run a guest house in Polperro: I would help in the summer, when things were busy, at least until I was getting my royalties. (The latest letter from A.P. Watts about *The Richmond Affair* began: 'I am sorry we are not yet in a position to send to you any good news'.) Just as, in our summer dreams, we had discussed setting up as smallholders, with ducks or mushrooms or angora rabbits or whatever caught our fancy in the latest Ministry of Agriculture pamphlet or in that week's issue of the *Smallholder*, we now again got out pencil and paper and attempted calculation. There was an old house for sale, three floors of it, plus cellar, right beside the harbour. Ethel had looked it over and already got the price down a bit. That would do. She had worked out how much to borrow, on expectations from her trust, for down payment and working capital and how much we would pay on the mortgage. This all seemed rational, but as someone whose only asset was a portable radio it frightened me even to contemplate such risks. My ideas of investment came mainly from eighteenth- and nineteenth-century novels in which decent people, falling into the hands of rogues or becoming victims of circumstance, lost all they had and were thrown out into the streets. Our summer dreams had involved nothing more than setting up a little working capital to buy modest items such as piglets or seed potatoes but this latest plan meant buying a house! I was not emotionally ready to buy a house.

There was another concern: while raising sunflower seeds or angora rabbits was a natural activity, bringing one closer to the earth, running a guest house was 'small business'. What would I be expected to do in such a *petit bourgeois* enterprise? – wait on them at table? Make their beds?

Of course, all this was 'simply a game'. But playing games was how I had fallen into the disaster of becoming a journalist. When re-reading *The Charterhouse of Parma* and *The Red and the Black*, I marked passages in them, remembered from when I read them as a gunner with the excitement and horror of realising that Stendhal *understood* me. Like Julien Sorel, I didn't really have my head screwed on right. Like Fabrice I could talk myself into anything. (Perhaps Ethel really wanted to run a small business!)

ON OUR LAST DAY IN POLPERRO WE TOOK, IN FAREWELL, OUR TWO most favoured walks – in the morning, along the Talland path to the beach; in the afternoon, along the western cliff. Then, in a last farewell, we stood and looked at the harbour. I felt I was saying goodbye to my life.

SIX

As it happened that summer

1

There had been some reminders of the existence of Europe when we went to Polperro: Brittany and Normandy lay across the water and on some nights we would listen, for a while, to French radio. But – unless the third world war came – there was no hurry. The Beatons, naturally, were Francophiles – Gaga was inclined to drop into conversation key words such as *bordello*, *bistro* and *bidet* – so the Beatons had already 'had a trip'; of the others, only the McCallums had so far been to Europe, and then only for a very cheap week in Paris.

It was Frank Packer who sent me to Europe. Menzies, as prime minister, had told Packer (in confidence, of course – not the kind of thing that should get around) that there would be war in the late spring: the Soviet Union would invade West Germany. Or that, according to the London editor, was what Packer thought Menzies had said. It was now early spring: time to investigate. Packer told them to send Horne. (At least Frank Packer had some understanding of the talents of Horne.) There was an economy drive ... Still, they would pay a contribution towards expenses and a higher rate than usual for an article: altogether they wanted eight or so feature articles. That would leave a profit after paying expenses, and, anyway, the articles would probably be syndicated and earn more. It was only at lunch with Ethel (we had both come up to London for this consultation) that I recognised how poorly I had bargained. Still I'd see something of Germany. (Was I actually becoming like the male American in *One Can Always Tell a Gentleman* – a passive participant?) *What had gone wrong with me?*

As the train went through the lowlands of Flanders in failing light, I was obsessed with my own excitement; absorbed in the convincing monotony of flat farmland and rows of poplars seen through light rain; re-fighting the Great War. By Brussels, it was dark and thundery, but there was the extraordinary excitement of knowing that the yellow lights through the window, and the bustle, were from the railway station of one of the cities of Europe. The gale had made the train late, and as the night got darker, it added entrancement to a border crossing in which the German border police were dressed as if in a spy movie. My hotel in Köln (as I now knew it), was one of a group of three tall, slender buildings with a carefully composed late imperial bourgeois assurance, but now set alone, beside a tram track, in a field of flattened rubble.

After breakfast I walked, until my cuffs and collar were red with brick dust, through the rubbish heap, some of it smoothed out, most of it still in lumps, that now made up most of Köln. Entering a lane between some sheds, I found myself amongst a crowd moving past the plate glass of jewellers' shops, cigar stores and food shops with piles of smoked ham, French wines, imported sausages, Scandinavian lobsters, sides of pork, pyramids of eggs, mounds of grapefruit. If one kept one's eyes on all this expensive stuff lit up behind glittering glass it was possible to forget the wasteland. After my first day in Köln, I walked only along these magic tunnels. Everyone knew that to clean up the rubble would take fifty years.

That evening I was again out among the ruins (not rubble this time, but broken buildings), lost, with light snow falling, having got off at the wrong tram stop on the way to the house of an Australian official: the one sound thing in a street of ruins seemed a large, prosperous suburban house, ablaze with light as if it were defying a blackout. In it I found a caricature of an eccentric but good-humoured English gentleman. He told me he was an intelligence officer and he insisted on a couple of stiff whiskies and sodas and some brisk conversation before promising me lunch the next day and lending me a car and driver to take me to the large house of the Australian official, again among the ruins. It was being used that night for a chamber music recital, so after our dinner we assembled in a big reception chamber full of Germans to listen to a quartet play pieces by Bach, Haydn and Brahms, and then enjoy a supper of sympathetically provided delicacies. Until I was back among the ruins, it was as if there hadn't been a war.

At lunch the next day, over red steaks and red Bordeaux, the intelligence officer told me of interviews he had arranged for me with people in Bonn who were engaged in some of the more clandestine activities. By now my assignment seemed easy enough: from the newspaper clippings I had collected in England I already had enough for ten articles: what I needed in Köln were anecdotes and impressions, to make the newspaper clippings real. It was one thing to be told by *The Economist* of the count-us-out slogan REMILITARISIERUNG OHNE UNS but it had more impact when I saw it lettered on a broken wall in a desert of crumpled brick.

In Bonn I did more of what might be expected – background interviews with Australian and British officials, front-line interviews with Germans from ministries, clandestine interviews with clandestine Germans, typical interviews with typical Germans. Some of my most memorable scenes were of eating: at one restaurant, the most expensive in Bonn, I saw Ludwig Erhard, the Economics Minister, Europe's greatest symbol of the belief that 'miracles' could result from liberating the spirit of economic rationality, puffing a long, fat cigar after a complex meal, his chubby, red cheeks swollen with food, a caricature of the bloated capitalist. Suppers were with German families – frugal meals with a thin tomato soup or bread and cheese (but with excellent beer), or potatoes and vegetables, taken in apartments where the floorboards rattled and the scratches on the furniture were honourable scars. I talked to the wives and took notes: meat only on Sundays, fish once a week. I could see the story line – DON'T BE FOOLED BY THOSE BULGING SHOP WINDOWS: FEW WEST GERMANS CAN AFFORD CREAM CAKES. Meanwhile I had coffee in cafés where the cakes were piled up with inches of whipped cream.

At the Finance Ministry I was given enough statistics to pad the bottom of my suitcase with papers inches thick; from the Foreign Ministry I attempted (but failed) to learn how, in one set of movements, to transfer umbrella from right to left arm, raise hat, and unglove right hand so that it could be shaken; in the more clandestine reaches of the Ministry of All-German Affairs I was let into what were supposed to be secrets of the propaganda war. (Why were they telling *me*?) When, after a course of instruction in Soviet propaganda, I learned that one of these was to spread rumours of coming war, I mentioned Menzies's belief that there would be war in the late spring. They looked at me significantly. (*What were they thinking? Was Menzies a Communist plant?*)

After one day of such conspiracy talk, and a large dinner eaten alone, I slept uneasily. The hotel was near the railway station and sometimes rattled with the trains. I started awake at the first, slight hissings of what in several seconds would obviously be the final explosion. The atom bomb! I was out of bed, screaming ... It was a train at the station, letting off steam.

Now that I was in Europe I used some of the time for tourism. In Köln, the only monument to other days that seemed to have survived, apart from the basic elements of the railway station, was the cathedral, but even that had been weakened by the bombing. Only a fifth of Bonn had been destroyed and I took time off to experience creaking timbers in Beethoven's birth house, to walk along the banks of the Rhine, to stroll in the forest on Venusberg above the town, to discover 'the baroque' in cathedral and castle, and, with astonishment, the rococo – I had never imagined that the central affirmation of a city – its town hall – might be presented with such light-heartedness, in pink and grey and gold. However, the feeling that the Germans didn't really know how to be European disappeared as I travelled by train to Frankfurt, along the banks of the Rhine and then the Main. This was what German tourism was expected to be: romantic gorges, rushing whirlpools, outcrops of harsh rock and, perched on escarpments, Rhine castles.

At Frankfurt the railway station gleamed with brightly lit and confidently decorated eating places, cigar stands, jewellery shops, newsreel theatres and expensive food stores: at one end of the concourse they had put up a huge advertisement in coloured glass – but the shattered glass of the roof had not been replaced. This would make an appropriate feature article anecdote. Outside, in a street of spanking new shops and hotels, cinemas, cabarets and restaurants, with sparkling plate glass and glittering neon signs, legless veterans sat on the pavements, singing 'Auld Lang Syne': another feature article anecdote.

I had got all I was to get from Frankfurt. I might as well have caught the next train home. As had happened to Sydney during the war, Frankfurt was suffering its 'American invasion': the Germans spoke English with American accents and, unable to understand what I was talking about, several asked what dialect I was speaking. On my first day, when I went to the United States headquarters in the I.G. Farben building (it seemed a universal belief that the bombers had spared this building so that it could become United

States headquarters), I was fobbed off by some public relations sergeant who also found it hard to understand my dialect: that night I went to a political cabaret, where I wondered which of the songs and skits were making fun of rearmament. I did not want to go back to England early, lest I should seem too superficial, but there was not really anything more needed before writing my articles.

In the interests of international amity, the British had established a library in Frankfurt, and the French a restaurant: feeling like a reporter in Evelyn Waugh's *Scoop*, I spent most of my time reading in the one, and eating in the other. I needed solitude: I had lost some of my confidence in the operation of the free market.

The closing feature article anecdote of my journey came when I got back to London. I was to spend the night with Adrian and Gwen in their flat at Maida Vale, but when I arrived earlier than expected, a tenant from across the hall invited me to wait with him and his wife. Apartment, wife and husband were all dully suffused with the sense of shabby defeat that still seemed the prevailing English mood and he met my anecdotes about Germany with petit bourgeois self-righteousness. The mood changed when I said that all the Germans I had spoken to professed ignorance of the killing of the Jews: assuming the mantle of the British race, he declared that Hitler's only error with the Jews had been that instead of killing them he should have castrated them, and then made them do some work.

*

The nearest thing to a popular war film in West Germany this year has been *Laurel and Hardy in the Foreign Legion*, which draws capacity houses wherever it shows.

This box office showing is a pretty fair indication of where the Germans themselves at present stand on one of the crucial issues of the day: Should the West Germans rearm?

They don't want to become the foreign legion of the Western democracies.

With intros like that, the eight feature articles were easy to construct but they left me with the combined feeling of both satisfaction and emptiness that had been a part of my condition as a feature writer in Sydney. It was satisfying that they were perfect specimens of *Daily Telegraph* style, but this process of turning them into someone else's language had meant that I had not been able to say anything I really wanted to say. (Perhaps I would never be able to say anything, except in anecdotes and imitations? Would I be merely part of 'oral tradition'? And, in that, would I end up a pub bore?)

A message came that they liked my articles. Yes, they would put them together as a big series. Then, still editor, but now dying, Brian Penton came back from his latest stay in hospital and, just after my series had begun, dropped it so that he could find enough room to spread himself on the state of the free world. Parts of the rest of the series were used, in separate bits, scattered over several weeks. Attempts to syndicate them failed: the other Australian newspapers did not share Packer's interest in West Germany. When it was all over, Ethel worked out that I had not made any profit. Still, I had 'been to Europe'.

2

When I had said goodbye to Polperro harbour I had felt that I was also saying goodbye to *The Richmond Affair*, at least for a while. The confirmation came when A.P. Watt sent back the manuscript 'very reluctantly'. They had offered it to eight publishers, they said. Well, to hell with eight publishers – they were only British publishers. I would finish revising *One Can Always Tell a Gentleman*, and send it off to the United States: in New York they would know what to do with it. Then I would revise *The Richmond Affair*. One expected setbacks, I said to Ethel and Elsa.

In the meantime, however temporarily loathsome it might seem, perhaps I should get a job? Peter Hastings and I wrote several letters in which, as part of our general discourse on the dangers of work as a way of life, we discussed his attempts to place me in the Melbourne *Herald*'s London office, but it turned out that the *Herald* preferred their own. Gaga Beaton arranged an interview with the London office of Qantas, which wanted someone 'on the PR side'. When, to my dismay, they seemed to show some interest, I set up satisfactorily impossible conditions. There was an advertisement for a script-writer for Pathé Gazette, a newsreel company with a jocular style that turned my stomach. In my application I promised to help them reform their present style. Sometimes I imagined making a round of newspaper offices, but surely it wouldn't come to that? By the time Rose had begun making small speeches on the state of the labour market ('There are so many opportunities nowadays – of course, one cannot always get exactly what one wants') it was early autumn.

Such efforts as I made at freelancing also failed. I seemed to have such contempt for journalism, or for myself as a journalist, that, with one exception, I offered articles only to magazines I despised. The exception was *Punch*, to which I sent a piece reflecting some of the calmly assured inanities of Rose's dinner-table conversation. It was at once accepted and later published under a pseudonym. I sent two more pieces. They came back, rejected, but with expressions of interest. *Good! I wouldn't have to write any more of that!* To Ethel's suggestion that I might go and see someone at *Punch* I said they could go and get stuffed. What I wanted to work at were potboiling pieces for popular magazines such as *Everybody's* and *John Bull* that had had their day: surely it would be easy enough to churn out this passé stuff to a failing market, without thinking about it? After I had finished my West German series, I tried several historical storytellings, of which the first was:

OXFORD – ITS GREATEST BRAWL
For three days the converted medieval town was a battlefield as ancient scores were settled in the long-drawn-out dispute between 'town' and 'gown'.

None of them wanted my historical storytellings. I tried biographies tied to anniversaries ... WELLINGTON – HE BATTLED ALONE and THEODORE DREISER – HE GREW UP WITH AMERICA ('Seventy-five years ago a skinny, buck-toothed little boy might be seen hanging around the slushy railway tracks and shunting yards of the fast-growing manufacturing centre of Terre Haute in Indiana, USA'). No one wanted any of them. By autumn I had given up imagining I might make a living by writing rubbish for magazines I despised. On the back of the last returned manuscript I scribbled a poem on aspects of English civilisation:

A sprouting crop of TV masts
sucks friendship from the air
and blows it through the sitting rooms
where lonely women stare

in double-fronted solitude
at silly things on screens.
In the garden men stake out
their artichokes, or beans.

Within these damp-proofed monuments
an austere web they weave
of manly anonymity
and female make-believe.

There wasn't the slightest possibility that anyone would want to publish that.

ALL THAT WAS PUBLISHED THAT SUMMER WERE A FEW PIECES accepted by the *Telegraph* at their ordinary rates. I declared myself on subjects such as the vicious practices of 'price-propping', the pampering of British farmers, and proposals to decimalise the British currency, and I provided a village piece on the caprice of paper-and-pencil games. Wondering what they thought about this back in Sydney (Penton was now dead), I wrote to the *Daily Telegraph*'s features editor. Sure, yes, of course, they 'liked my stuff': the London office left 'plenty of ground to cover'. A pity about the airmail delays: a couple of my pieces may have missed out because of that. Of course, sometimes there simply wasn't room: a couple of other pieces missed out that way. What the features editor really wanted to say was how lucky I was to be away from it all: 'How I envy you your pigs and fowls and distance from a newspaper office.'

He also wrote how he and all the feature-writers were buying motor cars – Morris Minors, all of them. 'For all of us, the idea of owning a car is economically mad and financially unsound but we propose to sell our cars at a fabulous profit when the next war breaks out.' Now everyone seemed to be buying motor cars! The Deamers had bought an old taxi for £125 ... The McCallums had bought a 1934 Vauxhall for £60 and whimsically christened it 'Sir Henry'. (*Why were they all buying cars?*)

Seeing myself as of a practical turn of mind, I realised that what really mattered was *One Can Always Tell a Gentleman*. I tried it on Peter Hastings, so that he could apply a good New York eye to it. Yes, on the whole he liked it – but 'dialogue needs controlling. The whole thing too long. Needs a different ending.' He would try it with a New York agent. ('That's a wonderful idea trying to sell the novel in New York', my mother wrote; 'Surely it must happen. Here's hoping it comes off!') The New York agent was gentle when he rejected it. ('We often make mistakes and may be wrong in our judgement. You should try this on someone else.') After my revision (along lines suggested by Hastings, so that he could try it directly with a publisher), the next rejection was encouraging: they found it interesting; all that worried them was that the two American protagonists 'were not portrayed authentically enough'. It was now high summer.

I had myself been uncertain of the credibility of the American characters. I had another go at them. The next rejection was even more encouraging: 'good touches ... excellent characterisation in some of the minor local personages ... amusing sidelights'; all that was wrong with it, really, was that 'we feel that the work is too British on the whole for us'. I would revise it again. Hastings was as pleased as I was. I felt very confident now (although my mother was getting restless; 'Any word yet about your novel?') It was autumn.

As Hastings and I exchanged the names of New York publishers, I turned to what now seemed another good idea. The *Observer* was running a short-story contest for which the theme was Christmas. I would enter this contest and win it. My story would be set in a converted cottage in a village like ours, with three of the people I knew there, all in various ways betraying each other. (A normal Christmas situation.) The tone was struck in the first few words: *It was dull sort of weather. Washing the dirty dishes was not long finished.* That caught the spirit of Christmas. Then I would catch the boredom and falsity of Christmas afternoon chatter: *'Is it twenty to or twenty past,'* Dorothy asked. *'It always is when someone stops talking.'* The anti-romantic climax would be reached in a scene of betrayal in the woods: *Her prim mouth quivered as she pressed herself and her layers of clothes and corsets against him giving one last pat to her hair.*

I felt confident when the final draft was typed and sent off.

BECAUSE I HAD TO CONFRONT AND CONQUER SO MANY DOUBTS, I felt the self-assurance of one who knew he would soon be established as a novelist and who in the meantime could make a living writing articles in an outmoded style for outmoded magazines: alternatively one whose irresistible talents the *Telegraph* would soon recognise or who could, if he stooped to it, work on the PR side for Qantas or take up some other such absurdly irrelevant and temporarily demeaning position.

Running beside this self-assurance was another strain of confidence that came from Ethel's belief that we could support ourselves from some kind of small business, although I felt endangered when she went through a period of investigating a laundrette as the material base for my novel-writing. So far as we could work it out, compared with what we had known in Sydney the development of laundrettes was in a pre-modern condition in London. I had made jokes about how from our humble origins in running one laundrette in a back street in Hampstead we would soon become the laundrette barons of the United Kingdom, but I was seized with fear when Ethel went to see the Bendix company and then the bank. She 'laid all the facts before me'. In typed figures and pamphlets, she 'put forward a serious business proposition'. Terrified by prospects of mortgages and uneasy about personal humiliations (*What was I supposed to do? Stand around in a white coat and give out the change?*), I stopped making jokes. Our next investigation was into raising goats.

In the meantime we settled that we would go seriously into the egg business. We bought secondhand breeding arks and watched our chickens proceed from chick mash to growers' mash and growers' pellets. We had read further pamphlets on egg production and decided to abandon the fold system in favour of the deep litter system: we would take over the large shed in the field and the hens would be housed there giving a certain amount of freedom without the disadvantages of free range; and as the straw matured it would generate its own warmth. The shed was cleaned out, the inside walls were white-washed, the straw was laid, the nesting boxes were dusted with insecticide and the hens installed – a ceremony that was followed by a celebratory tea.

Now we could get on with our next project – the raising of pigs, a matter in which, to my surprise, I took some of the principal theoretical initiatives. A pig, I would say (in the hard-headed manner of *The Economist*), was simply walking bacon, and I constructed a graph on the maximisation of profit in pig-raising showing exactly the stage when the revenue and expenditure curves were furthest apart; this seemed so instructive that I tried to interest some of the farmers in it. But pigs were a sideline for their wives. The farmers provided the food, the wives sold the pigs. The more fat on the pig, the greater the wife's takings (and the greater the farmer's loss). I contemplated developing this as an allegorical tale of the economic irrationalities of modern England and sending it to *The Economist*. I did develop it as a feature article for the *Daily Telegraph* but they didn't use it. In the meantime we had the old pigsties in the field re-bricked in places and white-washed, a load of potatoes arrived and we covered it in straw; when the six Large Whites arrived, twice a day Ethel or I would put together, on Ministry of Agriculture principles, some combination of pig mash, potatoes and household scraps, and as we approached the pigsties we would call out 'Pigs, pigs, pigs'. I would tell anecdotes about the intelligence of pigs and their cleanliness.

This had been the summer of the garden revolution, in particular in the recreated vegetable gardens. Ethel had called the flower beds into some kind of order but the real creative impulses were going into rows of French beans and scarlet runners, of green peas and broad beans, of lettuces, radishes, carrots and beetroot. None of the onions had bolted; the tomatoes were safe in the restored greenhouse; the sweetcorn had matured. The cucumber plant and the marrows had flourished. There were even rows of parsnips, and turnips and a swathe of potatoes. If a vegetable came into glut we used it in healthy peasant dishes; and where possible, we preserved surpluses, for the lean winter months; while Ethel was preserving fruit in the kitchen I might be in the cellar salting the beans in a large earthenware crock. And by the autumn I had turned my reading of the *Penguin Vegetable Growers' Guide* into a full year's vegetable-growing programme (including vegetables I had never heard of) expressed in diagrammatic form over several pieces of paper stuck together: we would grow some of almost everything. Perhaps I could not arrange my life as I wanted it, but by this arrangement of plants I could at least in one sense appear to be making things as they should be.

In future the planning would be based on a rotation of the three kinds of crops – a suggestion that seemed to cause as much comment in the village as my chart on the principle of marginality in pig production. There was talk of 'Mr Horne's rotation'.

3

There I was, lost among the vegetables, in my cravat, my corduroy trousers and my tweed jacket patched at the elbow, looking like a stereotype in an Ealing Studio comedy ... why was that? I knew I wanted to 'be a writer' there was no question of 'why?' there – but why was I writing a novel about stereotypes in an English village? Why hadn't I worked out some form of writing of my own (not necessarily a novel at all) – prose sketches, perhaps: if I wanted to write about a village, why not do it like that? Perhaps I had handed myself over – out of politeness – to a loyalty to Ethel. (That would mean that I had become part of a vision of a secure past that had never existed, with an affectionate commitment to the impossible.)

Even my reading of novels had been deliberately changed to what I saw as the second-rate: I spent most of the summer reading Trollope – thousands of pages, all the Barsetshire and Palliser novels and some of the others, page after page, novel after novel, no sooner putting one down than I started the next, just as Trollope himself would begin writing the next as soon as he had finished the last. In the *Observer* I read each weekend the columns 'In the Garden' and 'Open Air', passing from contemplating the possibility of gardening in tubs to the breeding habits of the Manx Shearwater. If I wanted to think of a 'society' or of the political life I was no longer likely to think of Tolstoy or Sorel. I was more likely to quote from feature articles in *The Economist* or leading articles in *The Times*, or even splash stories on the front page of the *Daily Express*. Sometimes I would make a note on the aphorisms of the village postmistress.

I would still sometimes say to people that I was optimistic by temperament and pessimistic by education but in public affairs I was left with no respectable way of expressing optimism. Life is tragic or comic, I would say: it is not progressive. In my Andersonian scepticism towards government planning I now not only saw myself as conservative, I had also become a supporter of the Conservative Party. Not on libertarian matters – censorship, abortion law reform, and so forth (*never!*) – but I had moved from being an anarchist small 'c' conservative to being a *liberal* capital 'C' Conservative. For the first time, I not only opposed a political party: I supported the other one. I was more sceptical than ever before of what I saw as Labor's fantasies of rationality – in the very season in which part of my imagination was taken over with ideals of planning a vegetable garden with thorough rationality.

For Jim McAuley and Norma, buying a house was now the main preoccupation. Ann McCallum and then Gwen Deamer had announced that they were going to have babies (*babies!*). Everyone was buying motor cars. They were all becoming 'ordinary', and they were doing it in conventional ways. I had more adventurous schemes for achieving ordinariness. I didn't want to become ordinary in the same ways as other people.

Yet there were days when I felt so bored or so sorry for myself (displaying symptoms of neurasthenia, shock, stomach disorder, severe headache) that I might have been a child, face to face for the first time with the prospect of meaninglessness. Even looking at the spines of books could set it off. (*Why should I ever again do any reading?*) Alternatively, while doing some simple task – in the middle of picking the runner beans, perhaps – I would be caught by a terrible fear: so much unread, unheard and unseen! There could return the Polperro image of the pub bore of twenty years into the future, windbagging away. Behind his back people would talk about him as someone of failed promise. Sometimes I would put myself on the sick list and retire to the bedroom, feeling cankered, mangy, rotten to the core.

Yet although I did not see myself as calmly set amongst familiar ways as I had in the paradise of Polperro, I had not returned to the need to negotiate a new normality every day. Even meals with Rose and Lily were less like a continuing conversation with strangers in a railway compartment; in any case, since we had a lot of friends stay with us that summer, we frequently overwhelmed them. Like a game of croquet, or a walk in the woods, the dowagers were one of the attractions we could promise visitors.

Ethel's mother continued to approach me with some loyalty of her own, offering this gift in chance conversations when the others weren't looking, usually in corridors or in the kitchen, or in asides when others were talking, as if there really were something between us; but now there were other comforts of familiarity. We had been given a sleek grey tabby cat, whom we called 'Kitten', even when she had kittens of her own: Ethel bought a dog whom we called 'Rufus' because this was the nearest I could get in Latin (lacking a dictionary) to the apricot colour of his coat. I gave Rufus the same trust I had given Zac and he made a lively and amiable companion.

Rufus and Kitten were two of the three 'real friends' I had made in the village. The third was a human. Elsa's nerves were on edge, from loneliness, from worries about money and from the fragilities of her relations with others, but between us she and I seemed to have created a friendship, defining its terms and conditions so that we could feel easy with each other and, when we were alone, we could move beyond the fictions of the village. At times the question would come into my head: would I be more my 'self', living in some small converted cottage with Elsa?

I COULD IMAGINE I MIGHT SOMETIMES MAKE AN INDIVIDUAL new friend, as I had with Elsa; but would I ever again have a feeling of belonging to a circle of friendship? Was this an illusion peculiar to childhood and youth? Now and again a survivor from my days as a diplomatic cadet would visit Britain, usually as a member of some Australian diplomatic delegation, or on leave from an Australian mission in Europe, and we would invite him out for a weekend; but it would take so much time to make sense of the bizarre environment of the village that not much energy would be left for reviving friendship. It was only with Douglas and Ann and with Adrian and Gwen that we could regularly and easily re-weave tapestries of old friendship. At the end of that summer Adrian and Gwen spent the better part of their holidays with us. The four of us relived the splendours of the previous summer, but with more assurance. We knew the village better. We knew how to handle the dowagers better. We knew the rules of croquet better. For several days Adrian and I worked on Jim White's farm, helping with the hay, and with baling the straw. Memories of Adrian and me, stripped to the waist, on top of the hay cart, or of all four of us playing croquet, were later to provide nostalgic images of companionship almost as strong as memories of sitting in a nondescript Sydney café talking about Picasso.

AS SOON AS HE GOT BACK TO WORK AFTER THIS SUMMER HOLIDAY, Adrian was sacked in a last-on first-off *Daily Express* economy drive. Several weeks later Gaga Beaton was sacked in a *Daily Telegraph* economy drive.

In the autumn, Ethel and I went to Paris, where we spent the rest of the money she had borrowed.

SEVEN

What do you hope to do, Donald?

1

Gaga Beaton had recommended a cheap Left Bank hotel (one pound a day, bed and breakfast) because of its faded elegance and because part of it had been built, or so he thought, in the seventeenth century, but such fragments of possible authenticity could not save me from a recurrent sense of fraudulence while we were in Paris. I had read all those great novels but, so far as anyone could tell, as we walked along the Quai d'Orsay on our first morning we might just as well have been tourists.

To begin with, I felt fully at home as we crossed the Pont de la Concorde. I had crossed my first bridge over the Seine in the New South Wales Art Gallery when I saw Marquet's *Le Pont Neuf*, and I had written a poem to it in 1940 when Paris fell to the Germans. But after crossing the bridge I was just like any other visitor, gawking at the grand vistas of the Place de la Concorde as if I knew nothing about it. In fact, I could not recall reading any descriptions of this area after the guillotine had been taken from it in 1795.

In a walk of a mile or so to the Place de l'Etoile there was too much unnecessary detail and too little of the panorama obtained from fictional accounts of the Avenue des Champs Elysées and when we reached the Place de l'Etoile, the Arc de Triomphe exploded in a storm of fury as Ethel and I argued about the possibility of crossing through the traffic. She went over to the Arc de Triomphe alone while I stood on the pavement. There was some of the familiarity of a French movie as, after this scene, we sat over a drink and a snack in a café, recovering belief in the possibility of human communication; but familiarity dissolved when we took what seemed a cross-country walk to

the Eiffel Tower. To get more of the feel of Paris, we had decided to go by
back streets but in a number of squabbles over the map we were overcome
by the difficulties of navigation. Our sense of the familiar was regained over
cream cakes and tea in an expensive café in the Rue Royale, where we saw a
woman seat her poodle on a chair beside her, feed him titbits and then, in a
moment of passion, hold his head between her hands and kiss his mouth –
that was very French – but what seemed most French was the long walk up
the drab hotel stairway with its faded wallpaper and the resumption of our
quarrel in a shabby room, behind gauze curtains and brown shutters, sitting
on a bed with a well-worn white coverlet, debating the possible general failure
of our relationship and perhaps of human relationships in general, and then
subsiding into reconciliation, followed by a splendid dinner.

It was what I didn't know, and therefore had no expectations about,
that went down best, so that we could use words of discovery, even if the
same discoveries had already been made millions of times. Thus while I had
expectations of *boulevards* and *quartiers* and therefore when visiting them
could not behave to the measure of my literary experience, I had no expectations
about the squares of Paris, and was therefore able to attach to them, as if by
my own discovery, the clichés of tourism – so one of the discoveries of the
voyage was what the Europeans meant by *square, place, platz, piazza*. And
while touring the vaulted rooms, iron grilles and spiralling staircase of the
Conciergerie was entirely familiar to anyone who as a schoolboy had 'done'
the French Revolution – yes, obviously, that was the Galerie des prisonniers
and that was the cell where their hair was shorn before they mounted the
tumbrils – I had not known that elsewhere in the same palace was the glowing
miracle in stained glass of the upper chapel of Sainte Chapelle. I didn't know
that lightness of touch was allowed in Gothic. I had also not known, until
we visited the Musée Carnavalet (recommended by Gaga Beaton) that there
could be a museum of social history – made up of bits and pieces of ordinary
things; nor, until we visited the Jeu de Paume, that there could be a whole
art museum devoted to just one period; nor, until we saw Marie Antoinette's
Hameau where she played peasants that aristocratic taste could be quite so
foolish. But our four-hour visit to the Louvre was a shambles. I repeated my
old vows – back in London, painting by painting, I would master the National
Gallery – and from future visits to Paris over a lifetime I would master at least

parts of the Louvre. Our one-day pilgrimages to Chartres, to Fontainebleau and to Versailles satisfied us – there was plenty of that kind of thing in literature – and (when we learned to take them more easily) so did our 'strolls along the Seine', or even some of our 'aimless strolling'. It was the authenticity of the eating experience however, that most precisely matched expectation, even to hearing a waitress pronounce '*hors d'oeuvres variés*' or smelling freshly baked bread on a Sunday (very *The Narrow Street*). But although I knew what *flâneur* meant, the night of our promenade along the Grands Boulevards was a washout. We lost our way several times. We weren't sure where we should drop in for coffees and cognacs. Our expedition to Montmartre was ludicrous; the Moulin Rouge was merely a tourist stage prop. In Montparnasse we visited the Dôme but there hadn't been any Hemingways there for some time. We enjoyed walking around the Sorbonne and 'the Latin Quarter', but as *voyeurs*. The Bois de Boulogne no longer rattled with the equipages of the rich and their courtesans and when, in remembrance of literary things past, we tried a reminiscent stroll through the Faubourg St Germain we were not sure of the way.

WHEN ATTLEE ANNOUNCED AN ELECTION, MY CONSERVATISM stepped one pace forward and I at once saluted and accepted the call to arms. If Churchill was to win, he had to win our village. In all the land, our constituency was one of the most narrowly held by Labour. It was here that the truth of the paradox of unintended consequences must be upheld, or it would not be upheld at all.

Without anyone asking him to, the designer of Horne's pig profit-maximisation graph and re-inventor of crop rotation was ready to show the villagers how to 'get in the vote'. (I had read about 'getting in the vote' in D.W. Brogan's *The American Political System*: there would be a few local variations.)

Since there was no Conservative branch in the village it was up to me to sound the bugle: I summoned to a special meeting in Ethel's mother's drawing room the most reliable elements in the village – most of whom had not been invited into the drawing room before. Having sounded off against the tyrannies of socialism, the farmers and the worthies of the parish council appointed me chairman of a committee, whose members I would now choose;

the dining room became village campaign headquarters. It took days of confidential discussion to prepare a dossier of all registered voters and mark them 'C', 'LAB', 'LIB' or '?' and to put a '?' against all 'LAB's' and 'LIB's' who might be worth canvassing. Day after day, on information provided, notations were expanded. '+' and '−' were introduced to indicate degrees of certainty, 'x' to indicate people who might need cars to bring them to the polling booth and 'xx' to indicate people who might be so negligent of their democratic rights that they might not be in the village on polling day. As information about conversions came in, there could be triumphs in the committee room. A 'LAB' might move to a 'LAB?' then to a 'C??exLAB'. A few moved finally to a 'CexLAB', or even a 'C+'.

On polling day our job was to arrange that those we had marked down as certainties got to the polling booth, while the '?'s were left at home. Two of our observers sat in a car outside the village school working shifts and marking names. Lists were handed in each hour: towards the end of the day we brought in the stragglers. By the end of the day we had collected all of our vote. There were rumours that some of those who were still 'LAB?' on our dossiers were now 'C's.

With the Conservative victory, it was obvious that our village branch had been among Churchill's foremost shock troops of intellectual sceptics. Our new Member was knighted and my reward was to join the Conservative Party and call a meeting to reconstitute a village branch – at which I declared myself president and, then, in what I saw as an episode of Napoleonic audacity, turned into vice-presidents (and charged them a donation) most of the people such as Lily and Rose who would normally have constituted the committee and done nothing on it, and put on to the committee people who had just swung from Labour. Power and honour in the village lay with the organisers of Christmas parties, bring-and-buy stalls and duck raffles, and now we would have some of this at our disposal. It could become a brilliant Conservative season, culminating at the end of summer, 1952, in a grand fête in our reclaimed garden, the first garden party in the village since before the war. The more 'villagers' who had a hand in organising these activities, the stronger their allegiance to the party of the people.

As well as the day-to-day agitational struggle of whist drives and raffle tickets, I had to push on with the important propaganda work of the party:

as in television, we would have panels of speakers in the village hall and with the help of a young woman in the village I founded the *Village Newsletter*. When the Conservative agent visited us, with a guide on how to set up a Conservative branch, I offered to rewrite the guide for him. At about this time, there was a thunderclap from Australia: Jim McAuley had engaged in a most unconservative act. He had become a Catholic.

ALTHOUGH A RUNNING DOG OF THE PARTY OF CAPITAL, I HAD NO capital, and one of the smallest incomes in the village. Most of my freelance ventures had failed; and New York reactions to *One Can Always Tell a Gentleman* continued, at the best, to be polite rejections. When the time came for selling the pigs we watched them with dejection as they were loaded into the death wagon, but the bacon factory cheque showed a fifty per cent profit on capital invested. With Horne's principle of profit maximisation thoroughly vindicated we now had a chance to 'plough back our profits' and buy a greater number of pigs. Here we were on the edge of thoroughly scientific pig farming: but, apart from the egg money, we now had nothing left to keep us for the next few months. Expansion in the pig business would have to be delayed until I got an advance on my novel.

After he was sacked from the *Daily Express* Adrian had gone onto unemployment relief at 22/6 a week while Gwen took up temporary secretarial work at seven guineas a week. He had made some money out of freelancing and now he was serving time as a wire editor on Associated Press, a loathsome job in which success was measured in the number of short filler pieces registered each day in the London evening papers. Gaga Beaton was living on an overdraft. We were living on our pig capital. It was a time for desperate measures, if only to stop my mother from writing Ethel such desperate letters, ('I do hope Donald can get something concrete in the way of work and in the meantime I still hope for the novel – what wonderful news about the McCallum baby') or even addressing her appeals to me directly ('What I wonder about most of all is what will you do? Do write and tell me what you hope to do, Donald'). I swallowed one lot of hopes and began sending *One Can Always Tell a Gentleman* to publishers in London: perhaps something would be fixed up there, until the real settlement of hope was reached in New York.

As the polite and sympathetic rejection notes began to come back I decided I must make another revision of *The Richmond Affair*. In the meantime, I might win the *Observer*'s Christmas short-story contest; first prize £250.

Christmas was splendid. We had two lots of friends staying over the Christmas season, so that the dowagers, laughed about in walks in the woods or in private sessions in unoccupied parts of the house, merely became part of the general quaintness of a village Christmas. When it was all over, I wrote a piece for the *Daily Telegraph* headed IT'S STILL MERRY ENGLAND. But of the 7,000 entrants in the *Observer* short-story contest the winner was someone I had never heard of called Muriel Spark whose piece, praised by the judges for its 'gaiety, originality and crisply poetic treatment' to me seemed fanciful rubbish. My worst suspicions were confirmed: the *Observer*'s judges admitted in the following week's issue that they had decided they could not publish in their Christmas number 'a story likely to arouse feelings of disgust or unrelieved gloom'. Unrelieved gloom was what I had intended.

WE WERE ABLE TO LEAVE OUR PIG CAPITAL IN THE BANK OVER January, when a week in London for the *Daily Telegraph* covering a Commonwealth Finance Ministers' conference earned me more than enough to live on, with the egg income, for the rest of the month. It was easier money than pigs and hens: an official I had known in Canberra would spend a few minutes with me each day, providing enough for more-or-less exclusive stories such as BREACH SEEN IN LONDON TALKS or EMPRIRE PLAN FOR NEW U.S. AID. To spice the story there could be threat-talk of 'complete bankruptcy of the sterling area' and hope-talk of 'new kinds of dollar loans'. I ended with a round-up feature article: WE'LL GET THROUGH, YOU KNOW: WE ALWAYS DO.

I stayed with the Deamers for my week's freelancing, sleeping on the couch in their London flat – in what had once been two large reception rooms on the ground floor of a house in Maida Vale, now sparsely and shabbily furnished and only partly warmed by two small electric heaters, with a kitchen under the stairs that had a bathtub in it, concealed under a wooden lid. London seemed dark and filthy as I passed through it by buses that moved slowly in sticky traffic, between the faded 1920s elegance of the Savoy Hotel where the

Australian politicians were staying, and the tarnished 1930s *moderne* of the *Daily Telegraph* office, and it seemed crowded and smelly as I made my daily journeys in the Underground back to Maida Vale, where we could still have a good laugh over old times as we ate our meal in the kitchen or sat in front of one of the small heaters in the partly abandoned reception rooms. Not long after I got back to the village, Gwen gave birth to a daughter.

FOR FOUR MONTHS I LIVED OUR VILLAGE LIFE WITHOUT RELIEF; I now felt we could not afford even one day in London. Nevertheless for most of the time there seemed to be sustaining activity, as if, after all, this was what I had really meant to happen. There was the regularity of meals, walks, hen-feedings, newspaper readings, visits to Elsa, playing with Rufus and Kitten. It was necessary, on walks in the woods, to observe whether flowers were blooming in the correct sequence and whether the various kinds of tree were coming into leaf in the appropriate order. The vegetable garden expanded and flourished like a well written novel; except for a few minor revisions, almost all the plans I had made for it were being achieved. The village Conservative Party branch met regularly in the dining room, with regular self-congratulation on our planning for the summer garden party and I brought out two issues of the *Village Newsletter*; I was now a member of the central constituency committee, where I could see a possible coming struggle for power by the simple Tory democrats such as me against the strong stockbroker and London lawyer 'weekend gentleman' element. For reading, I had now taken up a regular study of biographies of British politicians from the 1890s to the 1920s. There was regularity in writing an occasional freelance piece, and the predictability with which they were knocked back. Fiddling around with revisions for one or the other of my manuscripts was something I could regularly settle down to, even if it might mean that for a morning I now did little more than turn over the pages and brood about the inadequacies of the publishing industries of New York and London. When we had friends for lunch or staying with us over a weekend I could act as if all this was something that might puzzle them, perhaps, but was exactly what I had intended.

IT SEEMED PARTICULARLY SIGNIFICANT TO MAINTAIN THIS FALSE front of dedicated eccentricity when Clarrie McNulty, the *Telegraph*'s London editor, was added to our invitation list and came down several times, with his wife, for a Sunday lunch at a time when we knew the dowagers would be out. He paid a top price for our eggs but what might be wanted out of McNulty, some time or other, was (if I still really wanted it) a job: when he was with us it was very important to keep up the appearance of being someone who might even 'return to journalism', with the right offer. He would bring a bottle of port and the four of us would sit over it, after lunch, wisecracking and swapping anecdotes until the light began to fade and he drove back to London. It had to be very clear to the McNultys that they were dealing with equals.

It also seemed important to maintain a sense of equality with the Johnstons, because George Johnston, who had been a journalist in Sydney, was now London editor for the firm that owned the *Sydney Sun* and for all I knew there might be a time when he would offer me a job. But maintaining an illusion of equality with George and Charmian, his wife, was not possible to control. This was not because of the glow of purpose and prosperity that came out of George's commercial success as a journalist, nor the flashiness of their pricey American car, nor the expensiveness of their clothes, nor their general air of a wholesome Norman Rockwell liveliness; we could match all that with our own well-bred shabbiness and our eccentricity in living in a village. Where they gained unmatchable social eloquence was in both being published novelists.

I SCARCELY EVER ENJOYED THE OLD KIND OF CONVERSATION AND when I did meet someone from 'the old days' I might skilfully make 'real conversation' impossible by reducing the world to village gossip. I had almost given up reading: sometimes I would sit in the drawing room, looking at the pale sunlight reflected in the glass shelves of the bookcases, unable to imagine any interest in any book. I studied all the contract bridge columns and chess problems as carefully as I had once read *The Economist*. Ethel had given me two packs of patience cards and a book of rules for patience games: I would sometimes spend hours playing out some of the more intelligent of them, allowing myself only a minimum of cheating. I took up cryptic crosswords; there were days when I would tackle crosswords in both *The Times* and *The Guardian*. Even sightseeing seemed beyond interest. Ethel would suggest bus trips to some nearby county – they wouldn't cost much – but what was there worth seeing? I would walk through the woods up into the village churchyard at the top of the hill and look over the plain: nothing worth seeing.

At last, in May, Ethel tempted me – with a trip back to Cornwall. She had read an advertisement: some rich man, living at Looe, was advertising for a literary assistant. We booked in at a hotel we couldn't afford, arriving a day before the interview so that we could go on old walks (which simply recalled failed hopes). The interview was a fiasco: a young man, already with a small court of enthusiasts, was concerned with the 'acceleration of world economic expansion' and 'the mobilisation of the world's social and economic resources'. He would set up a research institute to 'create a comprehensive and objective long-term social and economic blueprint'. To this purpose he wanted a literary assistant to put his ideas into a book. Good pay. Separate accommodation. Good living expenses.

Despite the embarrassment of having to be polite to this lunatic, the incident cheered me. And we stayed overnight in London on the way back to have dinner with the Johnstons in their apartment and hear their reactions to *One Can Always Tell a Gentleman*. On the whole, good – worth revision. Parts of it made them laugh out loud. They read out their most favoured bits. Then: the conversations were too long ... the characters were too cardboard cut-out ... But that was what I wanted: long conversations between cardboard cut-out characters! Nevertheless it seemed worth having another go. And now I had won a literary competition. In March someone had told me that *Bandwagon*, a magazine I had never heard of, was running a competition in which humour was the test. There had been 300 entries and my piece, 'Appointment in Barnhampton', a satirical skit both on England and on John O'Hara's *Appointment in Samarra* was placed first. It would be published in August.

Winning the competition helped me restore some earlier version of my 'self', but in my mother it brought out cries of hope and hatred. To Ethel she wrote:

Surely in the name of all that's good it must lead on to other things. Everything is most unfair. My dear, I have been wondering and worrying about your financial affairs. Surely Donald has reached the turning point and things will brighten up for you both. I do hope the novel will be accepted. Most people read absolute muck these days. I do hope Donald has some luck about a job.

And to me:

There must be lots of editors who if they knew of your ability would roll down the red carpet for you. We drank a little toast to you last night and wished you all good luck for the future. I have worried and worried about the financial side and how you are making out. If it's a matter of money could I send you some? It doesn't seem quite right to see dumb clucks of men earning good money and your ability is overlooked. Donald, you must win in the end and, my God, it will be through sheer tenacity.

And now the light that came from winning a minor literary competition in a magazine I had never heard of shone even more vividly after the success of the Conservative fête: curiosity attracted even Labour voters. Most of the work had been done by Ethel and her helpers or by the mounting of traditional stalls, some of which seemed to go back to village fairs in the Middle Ages: my specialty had been conceptualisation and publicity, but towards the end I had decided to improvise a topical Punch and Judy show, using the now-restored summer-house, suitably draped with old curtains. I made up a skit which relied for its laughs on local allusions, with a certain amount of improvising on events in the fête itself, but nevertheless with a certain (if subtle) concentration on the anti-socialist message. Elsa helped me and when we emerged from behind the curtains we felt that in this expression of the continuity of folk culture we had to some extent overcome the alienations of the age. As they began pulling the stalls down I felt at one with the people: we Tory democrats more properly understood the wisdom of ordinary persons than Labour intellectuals. When the money was counted in the dining room, confidence in the people further increased. Secure in my communion with the *volk*, and confident that my literary style would now receive its proper recognition, I began again to imagine studying the paintings in the National Gallery.

2

McNulty rang. Was I busy? Well, not really … Perhaps I might care to come up to London and discuss a small proposition?

I arrived in London with time enough to visit the National Gallery and look at 'the primitives', a term then used to describe those fourteenth- and fifteenth-century painters in Italy and the low countries who were seen as tooling up for the Renaissance.

In the afternoon, McNulty explained that the *Daily Telegraph* was paying the Australian golf professional Norman von Nida to lend his name and his comments to coverage of the British golf tournament season. Did I know anything about golf? (The accurate answer to McNulty's question was no. I had even forgotten the difference between 'shooting a birdie' and 'shooting an eagle': Adrian would have to remind me.) 'Yes, Mac, I grew up in a golfing family.' Well, the problem was that von Nida was playing in all the main tournaments. He couldn't be everywhere at once. If I was interested in taking it on, I would sometimes have the by-line *By Norman von Nida* and sometimes *By a special correspondent.*

Fine, Mac. Before catching the return train I was able to spend some more time at the National Gallery for further study of 'the primitives'.

For five weeks my significant walks were not through the woods but around British golf courses, sometimes with von Nida himself, sometimes looking for highlights from other players, and sometimes – at what seemed great personal risk – in hurrying back to the telegraph office in the face of hostile golf balls. Von Nida was seen as having a fearsome temper, but he and I were able to respect our almost complete lack of interest in each other by adopting a laconic amiability.

For the *By a special correspondent* pieces I had studied the technicalities of golf reporting and was able to write paragraphs such as these:

At the 450-yards third he sank a 30-footer for an eagle.

He smacked his tee shot almost dead at the 224-yards sixth and
holed the putt on a tricky green for a two.

Apart from mastering this language, the trick in being a golf writer was to
stay near the clubhouse as much as I could with the real golf writers, and
pick up the gossip. Since I wasn't writing for any newspaper they had heard
of, the real golf writers gave me a kind of honorary status as I joined the
free chicken-and-champagne lunches in the refreshment marquee and the
pink gins in the afternoon. I still maintained coverage of 'the Von's' lonely
campaign, however, so I arranged for a despatch rider on a motor bicycle to
be waiting near the ninth hole, where, like a war correspondent on the field
of battle, I would type out the *By Norman von Nida* part of my despatch on
a portable typewriter and the despatch rider would go off to the telegraph
office. I could then stroll around the course like a real golf writer, admiring
style and making up sentences: 'Bobby Locke, in yellow cap and blue plus
fours, looking as if he had stepped out of one of the testimonial ads that had
made his fortune ...' 'Our own Peter Thompson, an honest tradesman, in
maroon sweater, grey slacks and wearing on his head not a golfer's cap but
an eyeshade.' I rang the London office and asked if, when it was all over, they
would like an atmosphere feature article for the sporting pages. No, there
wasn't room for atmosphere feature articles in the sporting pages.

BACK IN THE VILLAGE, ALTHOUGH IT WAS UNCERTAIN WHERE
my next cheque or my next free chicken-and-champagne lunch would come
from, I felt as if I were rolling in money and confident about my future as a
satirist. I even shared my imitations of famous professional golfers with the
dowagers and enjoyed unprecedentedly affable relations with Ethel's mother
when I found she had been reading the golf reports in the London papers
because she thought that anything I did should be followed with interest.
Nothing more seemed to be coming from *Bandwagon* – satire wasn't their line
anyway – but Adrian rang to say he had just had a significant bus conversation
with a common acquaintance of ours, once the keenest of *Daily Telegraph*
sub-editors and the one most enthusiastically addicted to its belief in a sharp,
'factual' style. The sub-editor had said he was working on a new paper in Fleet

Street that was, partly, to be satirical: would Adrian like to contribute some satirical pieces? Try Donald Horne, said Adrian: he won a competition for satire.

The small suite of offices of this paper was, strangely, in the *Daily Mail* building (a funny place for satire) – in a distant corner of an insignificant floor. A notice proclaimed the *Weekly Overseas Mail*. 'Don't pay any attention to that,' said our sub-editor acquaintance when he interviewed me in room A3. He explained that the *Weekly Overseas Mail* was a scissors-and-paste job put together by two old hands: it had been coming out for years, telling British people in the colonies what was happening back home. Now it was being used as a way to overcome the rules for newsprint rationing. A new paper could not be started, but existing papers were now allowed to expand. The *Weekly Overseas Mail* sold only a few thousand copies but (here was a clever idea) a domestic issue was now being brought out that, apart from the masthead, was entirely different. Without any promotion it was already selling 70,000 copies. Promotion would begin in a few weeks. There seemed no limit: One million? Two million? Three million?

He showed me a copy of the *Weekly Overseas Mall* in the form that still went out to English exiles in Singapore or the Gold Coast, and then told me that the 'domestic edition' might, at first glance, seem like *Reveille* (a tabloid, done on newsprint, but apparently with no news at all – its front page featured a 'cover girl' each week, with either uplift or cleavage or both, and scattered around her, crazy headings. It seemed the most depressingly stupid thing I had ever seen on a newsstand). It wouldn't really be like *Reveille*, he told me. It wouldn't be exploiting sex, for instance: the 'girls' would just be there to give a feeling of jollity. There were office rules that navels must not be shown in pin-ups and that navels were to be erased if they appeared in joke illustrations. And it wouldn't be a 'news' paper, really. It would be a lighthearted entertainment. What was wrong with that? In fact, there would be opportunities for really intelligent lighthearted reporting satirical stuff. That was where I came in. Interested?

He gave me a couple of assignments; I stayed with the Deamers for several days, sleeping on their couch, and there my stories were, next week, in the *Weekly Overseas Mail*: THE RITZ'S GEORGE GOES ON HOLIDAY AND BATHS GET UNDER HIS SKIN.

When I was given some further assignments (again sleeping for several nights on the Deamers' couch), we seemed to have lost an interest in satire – perhaps the editor (whom I hadn't met) had changed his mind – but we were still determinedly lighthearted. In that issue they published four perky little stories of mine. One had some connection with reality (it was based on the plumbing difficulties of our railway junction town): BLOOPS BLEEP BECAUSE OF BATH NIGHT. The other three were beat-ups: YOUR SMILE GIVES YOU AWAY (Watch that smile! They're taking smiles more seriously now), WOMEN ARE SUPERIOR TO MEN (Men ... compared with women you're about as streamlined as an old steam tram) and WHAT ARE YOU AFRAID OF? (You're not afraid of anything? Nonsense! You must be afraid of something.) As I sat in the train going back to the village I could feel the five- and ten-pound notes in my trouser pocket.

The sub-editor had taken me through the domestic edition, to give me some idea of its formula: wholesome pin-ups and illustrated jokes to convey light-heartedness; MAIL BOX (short pithy letters) and AUNT SALLY (pert replies to readers' questions); STAR DESTINY; an advice column; STRANGE BUT TRUE; JACK JOHNSON'S RECORD ROUNDABOUT; SHOW BUZZ; a centre spread pot-pourri of pictures and a back-page 'feature' picture spread; two pages of sport; a women's page (in which the words 'cosy' and 'warm' were much used in headings). Put like that, it could sound just like any other low-grade magazine, but the presentation of each of these regular features was so bizarre, with crazily lettered headings, irregular type settings and strangely chopped-about presentation of the pictures that the pages looked like some newspaper version of children's graffiti. And set between these regular features, were 'news' stories that were devoid of any conventional meaning. Some were lighthearted snippets; a few were pseudo crime busters; some were simply bits and pieces of disconnected chatter, with headings that jumped around and funny drawings.

I was absorbed in the cynicism of the hard-headed theorising that lay behind the production of all this claptrap, and in the meticulous craftsmanship that went into making it. With the five- and ten-pound notes in my pocket I had a sense of piratical adventure – after all, this didn't really do anyone any harm. I could feel the pulsations of the future. (*One* million ... *Two* million ... *Three* million.) But what most kept me in an acquiescent daze as in the third week I was taken into Room A1, the editor's office, for my first interview with him, was that these people had asked me to do something for them. I did not have to demean myself by asking them. I had not made myself part of that bustle of self-declared ambition that seemed to make up Fleet Street or, for that matter, the world.

The editor was dressed as if for the City, in a dark pin-striped suit. His bowler hat was on the stand in his secretary's office. He spoke with a tender smile, looking at me with large, sad eyes. They were very pleased with my work, he said. Now they would increase the payment rates and they would like me, although I wasn't on the staff (there were difficulties with management about setting up staff), to have a desk and a typewriter in Room A6 and to act as if I were on the staff (except that at freelance rates I would, ha ha, earn more money). They appreciated the bright pieces I was doing, and there would be more where those came from, but now they wanted me to produce stories that would match some headings he had already written. He gave me two of these headings, each written on a separate sheet of paper. The first was I CHANGED MY SEX AND MARRIED. That was a good heading wasn't it? Could I get a story to justify that heading? They needed it quickly to use at the end of their present run-up period ('We're putting on sales every week without any promotion and we need newsy headings that are eyecatchers on the stands'). The second, WOMEN WHO MURDERED FOR LOVE, would be part of their promotion drive when they went for the first million. It would be a series, just a write-up of old murder trials but it made a good heading. They would need that quickly, too. 'We're relying on you.' He spoke with the soft voice of command, but as between equals. We might have been discussing buying futures in lead-zinc.

I at once wrote the story for I CHANGED MY SEX AND MARRIED but, to give it greater verisimilitude, I did not hand it in for several days:

> Ten years ago, I, too, changed from a woman to a man. It was in 1942 that my sex was changed. I was 20, and as far as everyone knew, I was a young woman. My interests were not those of a normal young girl. I was ashamed of my hairiness and worried almost to desperation that my interests lay more in the direction of women than men. As a woman I had always been mannish, but as a man I felt – somehow – womanly.

There were twenty more paragraphs of this. When I went to the small hole in the wall where contributors were paid I found I got not the expected £20 but £50. (Was that how one felt at the races?) I met my deadline for WOMEN WHO MURDERED FOR LOVE, with a piece that began:

SHE WAS DECOY FOR HER HUSBAND'S KILLER

A woman stood by the dock of the Old Bailey, two nurses holding her up. Her face was dead white, even to the lips.

and ended:

A love affair, created in dreams, created in a world of fantasy, crashed to its final tragedy with the hangman's knot. NEXT WEEK: SHE STROKED HIS HEAD, AND GAVE HIM ARSENIC

I was now earning so much as a freelance that the editor had me put on the staff – at twenty guineas a week, plus some English-style 'fiddle' about tax-free expenses that, they assured me, would get past the Inland Revenue and add some pounds more to my effective income. Before joining the staff, I sold them, as a job lot for £100, all the freelance pieces (suitably revised) rejected by other English magazines. We put some of this plunder into improvements in house and garden but Ethel insisted I should buy some new clothes – a dark, slightly waisted overcoat with a touch of the eighteenth-century about it from Aquascutum in Regent Street, and a stylishly cut (but only quietly so) suit, in a colour soon to be known as 'charcoal grey', from the equally esteemed Jaeger shop nearby. I might be engaged on a piratical course, but at least I would appear as a gentleman pirate. As I walked through London with hat on head and pigskin gloves and umbrella in hand, in my Aquascutum overcoat and my Jaeger suit, who was to know that I was on assignments such as VICE TOUTS SHOCK TOURISTS IN WEST END or lighthearted pieces such as CORSETS FOR MEN? OH DEAR, NO!

The main exception to the generally respectable look of us members of the staff of the *Weekly Overseas Mail* were the two survivors from the original and genuinely overseas edition: they stayed on in Room A5 for a few more months in their cosy old clothes, cutting out and pasting up, for fewer and fewer pages as more and more of our features moved into their space. In Accra or Kuala Lumpur instead of WHAT THEY ARE TALKING ABOUT AT HOME, expatriate English would now have to get used to headings such as HIS HEART'S NOT IN HIS STOMACH: THE RECIPE FOR A HAPPY MARRIAGE IS STILL LOVE.

Apart from a general need for 'sales' I had not seriously thought about journalism as a business, but that was how the brightest and best of us saw it at the *Weekly Overseas Mail*. When they came in, the reader surveys were handed out and discussed. We knew the main promotion plans. We were instructed on the importance of the on-sale situation. We understood the need for writing cover headings first so that stories could then be written to match promotion strategy. Such calculations gave an atmosphere of intelligence and rationality to our proceedings that could distract us from the triviality of what we were doing: in fact, as we made hypotheses about social behaviour, discussion could rise to levels of intellectuality of a kind that seemed largely to have gone from my ordinary conversation and if rationality failed to relieve the tedium of INNOCENT YOUNG CHILDREN LOCKED UP WITH CROOKS or SHE JILTED 53 MEN, there was always bonhomie. I shared Room A6 with at first one, and then two other reporters; we cultivated amiable relations and told jokes, but revealed none of the cynicism with which we were deliberately fabricating our bits of rubbish. We would speak gently, even protectively, of our readers and the harmless amusement we were giving them. I developed a comforting parallel: it was as if we were knocking off B grade movies for the first half of a cinema programme – not art, of course, but harmless. Meanwhile the great dynamo that justified everything drove on and on: the sales had reached half a million.

For a while I kept the weekly surpluses from my freelance money in my pocket, to remind myself of what it was like to have money again: at about the time we reopened our bank account I began travelling into London every day, rather than once a week and then living with the Deamers. But now Ethel had come to town and we both stayed with the Deamers while she looked for a flat. The *Daily Express*'s economy drive was over and Adrian was back with the *Express*, but Australia seemed a better country to bring up children; soon the Deamers would go home. Douglas now had his job at Oxford but even the McCallums might later go home. Gaga Beaton was back for a limited period at the *Telegraph* and the Beatons were living in a maisonette, tastefully if transiently, furnished, since it belonged to an antique dealer who saw its furniture and *bric-à-brac* as interchangeable with the rest of his stock; but the Beatons would go back to Australia later. The Hornes were staying.

Now the Hornes had signed a lease for a furnished flat near Red Lion Square, WC1 – just down from Bloomsbury, and within walking distance of 'the office' – and they would use it, Monday to Friday, and then spend the weekends in the village. Six guineas a week, but Brian Beddie was now in London, to take a Ph.D. from the London School of Economics with a thesis on the elusive Max Weber (would the mysteries of Weber's writings make Beddie as sad as they seemed, for a season, to make Douglas McCallum?), and Beddie would be our lodger at £4/10/- a week, with full use of the flat over the weekends although he could come down to the village any time he felt like it. Before he went off to his room 'to get on with his work' Beddie made splendid company as we sat around the coal fire in the flat after dinner, reminiscing about our days as diplomatic cadets in Canberra, and, for that matter as gunners in Darwin or students at Sydney University; but, more importantly we had endless anecdotes to laugh over about the ironies of unintended consequences, the fatuities of Stalinists, the absurdities of planners and, in general, the concluding whimperings of the modern world. Then, every dark morning, like a character in a London novel, I would walk down Chancery Lane to Fleet Street, then across Fleet Street towards the Embankment in my Aquascutum overcoat and Jaeger suit.

Until I got there, I would usually forget that I might be about to write I BECAME A DOPE ADDICT AT SIXTEEN or interview a psychic animal healer. The further my *Weekly Overseas Mail* stories kept me from interviewing people, the better I liked them. An occasional piece really did seem like 'light reporting' but even then, by the time it had been presented with silly headlines, staggered type and absurd illustrations it lost its 'reality'.

When, to give it greater verisimilitude, I suggested the by-line By *J.W.S. Freund* for the series on parapsychology that bore the headline DO DREAMS FORETELL THE FUTURE? (Johan Wilhelm Sebastian Fraud, I thought to myself), the editor called me in to praise my subtlety. We planned another series by J.W.S. Freund, TRAGIC SECRETS OF THE LONELY. I wrote the blurb first (that was the way they did things in Fleet Street): *The cold grip of loneliness is everywhere, even among those who do not live alone. Must some people stay friendless? This dramatic new series shows that they certainly need not.* Appeal to hope through despair. The editor agreed and when I worked out a formula for J.W.S. Freund pieces he acknowledged a fellow craftsman. According to my formula there would be anecdotes in ordinary type, with a use of italics to point up key sentences: after one or more anecdotes there would be a philosophical bit in black type, with a few 'hard words' readers had never heard of put into black capitals, to gain their respect. Occasionally a whole paragraph would be run in black capitals. This would be a paragraph that gave readers advice about how to handle their own problems. As I wrote the series, I also put in the appropriate type directions.

When the work was too boring, or when its humiliations could not be endured, I would go to newsreel theatres, sitting in the dark, watching Donald Duck, ALBERT SCHWEITZER WINS NOBEL PEACE PRIZE, Pete Smith's Sporting Specialties, BRIGHTON MAN BUILDS HOUSE WITH MATCHSTICKS, Looney Tunes, COMMUNIST PARTY CONGRESS IN MOSCOW. Or I would go to the National Gallery, where by now I was passing from 'mannerist' to 'baroque'.

At the end of each day's inventions we journalists would make a last joke and go off to the mysteries of our dwelling places, knowing nothing more about each other than when we had first met. A couple of us did make several visits to a local pub, where, instead of the jostling and guzzling and yelling of the Sydney journalists' bars, with their ostensible openness and sincerity, there was a cultivation of gentility, with modulated accents, beer-sippings and quiet pipe puffings. All that came out of these visits was that a drinker who professed an exact knowledge of the sexual problems of the Duke of Windsor produced a set of obscene handkerchiefs. Nevertheless beneath their affability I could sometimes see the ambitions of those around me, and their envies. They were stirred by rising sales not, as I was, for the novelty of it, but for the sake of their careers. (Careers! To me, the *Weekly Mail* – as it had now become – was just a passing adventure, altogether improbable except as a parody of the Fleet Street experience.) Were they saying anything about me behind my back? Me – the invisible man, merely observing their desperate situation. Surely they didn't think that I ...?

WE ALL RECEIVED AN EXTRA WEEK'S PAY TO CELEBRATE THE *Weekly Mail*'s first million. As I went back to the village that Friday in our 'businessman's special' (the train that transformed us into weekend gentry) I reflected that perhaps the only gulf that divided me from the other businessmen was that they were making more money – there they were in the City, all the week, buying cheap and selling dear, or in the futures market, cornering bananas, or at the Law Courts, making the worse argument appear the better; and there was I, also in the City, dealing in harmless drivel with the same elements of calculation as theirs – but at a higher level, perhaps, since the best of us at the *Weekly Mail* were, really, rather clever. There was one way in which I had a clear advantage. My dealing in drivel was only a passing adventure, but their dealing in bananas or legal sophistry was a life sentence. When I resumed my career as a writer it would be all finished. In the meantime, unlike them, I didn't have to believe in what I was doing.

EIGHT

Surely I must be learning something from this?

1

With Ethel's mother and the dowagers away, and with the *Weekly Mail* money in our bank account, we were able to celebrate Christmas in a way that provided material for cheering letters to my family. We 'tarted up' the drawing room with coloured paper and tinsel and a five-foot Christmas tree that cost almost as much as a week's lunches of herring and mackerel a year before at Polperro, and held a cocktail party for our village friends and those few members of the village Conservative committee who would not be affronted by a choice between dry sherry, gin-and-tonic and scotch-and-soda. The hall was smothered with holly and balloons to make it a suitable milieu for the distribution of mince pies to carol singers and over the festive season itself a log fire blazed in the hall. In the dining room there were just hints of Christmas decoration – a few sprigs of holly, an absurd lone balloon.

Firelight and candlelight were the essential decorative devices for the two feasts, of which the centrepieces were a twenty-pound turkey for Christmas night, stuffed in a way I had read about in *The Joy of Cooking*, and for the next night a brace of pheasants, presented in a style recommended by Mrs Beeton. The Johnstons were with us for Christmas, and the Beatons, each 'couple' coming out of their cars with armfuls of things to eat and drink for our several days of gracious gluttony – and, in the Johnstons' case, also with their two children. With our large supply of eggs, we were able to offer 'traditional breakfasts', presented on silver serving dishes; we walked in the woods each morning, then went motoring, with an alfresco lunch. Tea yielded to drinks before dinner. Day and night we talked and laughed – long anecdotes, wise fables, one-liners. It was no surprise when, several months later, George Johnston offered me a job in his office, as correspondent for the Sydney *Sunday Sun*, at the same basic salary as on the *Weekly Mail*, but with three expense account fiddles instead of one. I felt I had served my time and should now enter a period of rehabilitation. At the *Weekly Mail* the duller members of the staff were astounded that 'having got my foot into Fleet Street' I should go back to a mere colonial newspaper; they were looking for a cosy lifetime existence. The two brightest writers thought I was imprudent not to wait until the paper sold two million, so that I could leave, at a time when it had curiosity value, for a job on one of the London dailies. (When that time came, they both did this: one of them was later knighted.) To the editor, my departure threatened the end of J.W.S. Freund, until we reached an arrangement that I would write an occasional series at £100 a go, to be advertised on posters in the underground railway. As I went up and down on the escalators I was to read headings written by me to appeal to the lonely, the unhappy and the credulous.

There were six of us on the staff of the *Sun*, sitting at desks three-a-side, facing each other like cattle in their pens at a show, with at one end, in a small office, George looking out on us. We all saw ourselves as stars, and none of us had enough work to do. Four concealed this by sitting at desks most of the day; two by scarcely appearing and then, when they did turn up, by pounding their typewriters with intense conviction. Our amiable relationships suffered their greatest test in the flood of George's conversation at lunchtime sessions at the press club, where he showed off not only as anecdotalist but also as adult education lecturer: a long reminiscence about a truck ride when he was a war correspondent in China might be followed by a seminar paper on the principles of Confucianism. At a time when he was thinking about writing a novel set in the Stone Age – it was to begin with an Aurignacian boy and girl making love in a swamp – after he had sent Charmian out to do some research, we had several weeks of discourse on topics such as single- and double-edged harpoons and barbed pointed flints.

An essential tool in my work at the *Sun* was the razor blade. Each morning I would go through my set of London dailies and slice out any items that might be treated in some way that would interest the editor of the *Sunday Sun*;

the base of my week's work was the grading of piles of newspaper clippings. Occasionally, I would send myself out on a 'follow-up' (I did not initiate any 'stories') but in most cases I would simply 'do a rewrite', sometimes a 'think-piece', being careful to keep most items fairly small, since the *Sunday Sun* was a broadsheet with make-up problems and little bits from overseas were useful as fillers. It was important not to send too many: there had been complaints about cable costs. In the opening weeks my masterpieces were a front-page story on Malenkov, culled out of the London weeklies, and another front-page story, CHANCE TO SPLIT FROM REDS IN CHINA, based on a magazine article. The *Sunday Sun* assignment had been despised before it was given to me. Now it was attracting more by-lines than went to anyone else. Having successfully made the first careful approaches to each other by which we might agree to an intimacy in which we could gossip about the others, I had taken to having lunch with Hazel Tully, who sat at the desk next to mine, at a restaurant which served three-course French meals at a fixed price (half a bottle of wine included). Hazel was a Queenslander, outwardly a 'true Aussie', slow-spoken, with a skilful grasp of the laconic punchline; as a warmth of friendship developed in giggling about the follies of colleagues I found these lunches, held once or twice a week, as successful a distraction from the tediums of 'work' as sitting in newsreel theatres or visiting the National Gallery. (At the Gallery in my time at the *Sun* I 'did' the nineteenth-century and after.) It was at one of them that Hazel told me how the feeling was growing that everyone should take turns at the *Sunday Sun* assignment, so that there could be a fairer distribution of by-lines. My great moments with the *Sunday Sun* had come with the Christie murders, which prompted me to get on a bus and go out and see for myself, standing outside 10 Rillington Place while we heard the police rip out floorboards as they looked for more bodies. My first story made the front-page lead:

FOUR VICIOUS MURDERS
Maniac Kills Women
All Die At Full Moon
By Donald Horne

A hunt is on throughout Britain for the man – believed to be a maniac who strangled four women. 'The Clockwork Man', they called him – a thin, precise sort of chap who has strangled four women. Always the gentleman. Always well dressed. Always raising his hat.

I followed the story right through – in spring, with Christie's arrest and his appearance in the Clerkenwell police court; in early summer, with his trial and his hanging; in late summer, with a psychological study by me in the *Sun* company's one intelligent magazine. The principal instructive anecdote of that summer became the contrast between the meticulous and ordered suburbanite ('his only indulgence a cup of tea') and the 'sex monster', all of whose articles of attire, including his boots, were, according to police evidence, stained with semen – but whose craziness was still so meticulous that he put together trophies from the pubic hair of the women he had killed.

When I talked about Christie with friends, all of this was intended to be a parable of the irrationality of rationality and therefore as something more to hit 'progressives' with. But as 'the Christie story' developed, Sunday by Sunday in the *Sunday Sun*, it was also the story of Timothy Evans, an illiterate hanged a few years before, mainly on Christie's evidence, for a 'sex murder' which was the same as Christie's; I got as much space in the *Sunday Sun* for the Evans story as for the Christie story, and in the course of writing it I found myself being transformed, at least on this 'issue', from conservative to progressive. As a liberal conservative I had turned a tolerant eye on hanging. Hanging was not a question, like censorship or abortion, on which one must oppose the intervention of the state. After all, it was only murderers who were hanged. (In any case, mightn't execution be more humane than life imprisonment?) But when I decided Evans was innocent, there was a difficulty in continuing to believe that the issue of capital punishment concerned only murderers. As, with razor blade and typewriter, I fought this great summer battle for minds in the suburbs of Sydney against what seemed a cover-up by the rulers of England, I was taking one small, dangerous step back on the path of progressiveness.

My general conservative line still held firm: within the *Sun* office, since this was the summer of Elizabeth II's coronation, there was progressivist illusion to confront on the subject of the monarchy. The *Sun* itself was an afternoon daily and for coronation week most of us would work for its 'exclusive coronation coverage': George had arranged for me to write a daily personalised column; he would provide the front-page purple prose; Hazel would do the women's angle (where necessary wearing a tiara); others were to concentrate on this and that. On the day itself we would be deployed at strategic points throughout the celebratory areas of the city. I shared in the general derision – how could one survive without derision if one was a journalist turning existence into 'stories'? – but I felt bound to confront the shallow rationality from which the others, with George as the most derisory, argued their general principles. I was, however, more Whig than Tory. (In fact the only use I had for the word 'Tory' was to associate it with 'democrat'. The real Tories might be too stupid to be trusted with something as important as a sceptical conservatism.) I couldn't really *believe* in the monarchy – that kind of belief was for Rose and Lily – but one had to recognise that societies were not rational, etc. (*Didn't one?*) Symbolism was unavoidable in human existence, etc. (*Wasn't it?*) These Hanoverians, brought over to England for this job, provided a harmless enough symbolism. (*Didn't they?*) That was why we had brought them over.

For my last column on the night before the day itself I strolled the streets with Ethel and Beddie; we were at one with the people as they settled on the pavements for their long, patriotic task.

I had to be in place by six a.m. the next day in the assigned viewing stand and by luck I found there a woman with whom I had had a small *affaire* eight years before. She had brought more than enough alcohol for us to be drunk by midday and we staged a revival of the mood of eight years before, in which what most mattered was to be amusing. In any case it was a grey day, with stretches of rain, and as we looked out (from beneath our canopy) on the people, who were alternately bawling out 'Land of Hope and Glory' and being patient in the wet, I was beginning to tire of folk festivals. When the procession returned from the Abbey, however, its colour and rhythm and sheer bulk mesmerised us into silence. Our silence was not unappreciative (although elements of it may have been due to sobering up) but it so enraged one of the patient people on the footpath that at one climactic moment he turned on us and shouted 'Why don't you cheer?' As befitted members of a free press, we tried to look objective.

On the way back to the office I found myself walking beside a Guards officer, who was clanking with metal and creaking with leather and, when I bumped into him, he seemed as large as a monument. My umbrella handle caught in the hilt of his sword. For a few feet he dragged me along with him, a helpless and rather absurd civilian.

I WAS TO WORK IN THE *SUN* OFFICE FOR ONLY EIGHT MONTHS, FROM late spring to early autumn, but it was a period that caught in my imagination as my typical working experience in England. The week would begin by riding in the village handyman's van to catch the businessman's express to London, sitting in a carriage disguised in a suit as dark (if more fashionably so) as all the others, then taking a taxi at the other end to Fleet Street, where the razor blades lay in a box. Not much to cut on a Monday morning – it was more a time for gossiping about how we claimed to have spent our weekends and, if George wasn't there, for gossiping about George. As we went about our disparate tasks, our common moments of truth came with the airmailed parcels of newspapers and magazines published by the *Sun* company: we would inspect these (without comment) to see how many of our stories were run and which of us had got by-lines. There were times when most of us would eat together at the Press Club, but that was usually when George had in mind one of his seminars – on Cretan ruins perhaps, or the Gothic style. 'George and Charm' also had their night-time relationships with some of us, but never all of us together. (That way we could gossip more freely about the others.) It was only when Ethel and I were having dinner with 'George and Charm' that one of them might ask about my unpublished novels. 'Oh,' I would say, 'I'm giving them a bit of a rest.'

Apart from lunches with Hazel, my most successful escapes from the enfeeblement of office life were still to be found in newsreel theatres and in the National Gallery (where I had now gone back to the 'primitives' to do revision). There were times, however, when I could not escape regret at the inanities of 'work'. To begin with, I could ease myself out of acknowledging its shams by recalling how much worse it was when I was on the staff of the *Weekly Mail*. Then I began having headaches: some days I would go home early, or come in late, with some weak excuse (but then most of us in the *Sun* office, including George, were full of weak excuses). One Monday morning I awoke with such a bad attack of the horrors that Ethel rang the office to say

I had a gastric upset: I spent a couple of days lying upstairs, aching with the dejection of exile. By Wednesday morning I was back with my razor blade, trading jokes.

Luncheon life began to expand. Gordon Jockel was now with the Australian diplomatic mission in London and although I went only once to the large, ugly house he and Gwen had rented in Surrey, we would sometimes have lunch at his club. In a typical Jockel declaration of the down-to-earth, this was the Royal Automobile Club where, he said, there was the best-value lunch in town. Despite myself, Jockel and I were back to where we had always been: he the hard-head, me the slightly suspect intellectual, although there was something less puritanical about him now, with hints of indulgence beyond exercise and sport, and even a confessed new taste for classical music. I was carrying out my autodidact's art course at the National Gallery. He was buying gramophone records. Bill Pritchett had been in the Australian diplomatic mission in Berlin and had now moved to Bonn. When he came to London we met in a bookshop before going to lunch. That was like the old days.

As well as former diplomatic cadets, there were those past student acquaintances who were gaining 'academic' careers by acquiring Ph.D.s – among them Bruce Miller, who put aside for a day the quarrel on the future of education that had divided us some years before to allow me to survey the dining room in the London School of Economics: as his research specialty, he was considering taking up the Commonwealth of Nations. Even more strangely there continued to be 'Andersonians' who, like Douglas, had come over to pick up second degrees. Formerly a closed sect, Andersonians now seemed to be all over the place. If a new one turned up, it was likely to be with alarmingly new ideas about what it might now mean to be an Andersonian.

Other than Hazel, my most regular luncheon companion continued to be Gaga Beaton, whom I would meet at a place of his choosing. We would eat frugally; Gaga had again lost his job at the *Telegraph*. He had some commitment that occupied him once or twice a week; otherwise he was a man of leisure. This new commitment seemed to give his life a purpose it had lacked and he had now stopped complaining about the kinds of people who had jobs. I assumed he had some small, satisfying business connection – until I found out he was drawing unemployment relief and that his commitment was a call at the local labour exchange.

2

London was all around us – theatres, cinemas, concerts, galleries, lecture halls – but what seemed to matter most about London was 'coming home', four nights a week, Monday to Thursday. Along Fleet Street; up Chancery Lane; across High Holborn; into Red Lion Street. What's for dinner? Since neither of my novels had been published I did not yet see myself as having the full intellectual rights of a Londoner; in any case, beyond reading the weeklies and the quality Sundays, I could still feel an exile from intellectual life – partly from a kind of shyness, lacking a certainty in style, from new political distrusts.

I looked at a street map, once, in the office. I hadn't realised I was within walking distance of almost everything worth seeing in central London. The British Museum was closer to where we lived than the office; yet I had never walked even there. Even Red Lion Square, at the end of our street, I looked at only once. We walked nowhere. Apart from my long programme of self-guided tours of the National Gallery, we saw nothing. We lived in some kind of other world, with the 'real' world – the world of the village – again opening out to me when I caught the train on Friday afternoon and closing behind me when I left on Monday morning. Ethel enjoyed more of the real world of the village than I did: she would catch an early train out of London on Fridays and a later train back to London on Mondays, giving her the better part of four days.

To conceal myself like this seemed a privilege: I did not see myself as a polite prisoner of Ethel's obsession. If I wanted intellectual life, it consisted in having long talks in our flat in Red Lion Street, amid much laughter, with Brian Beddie. For a while I took to sketching. That was safe, since it was obvious I had no talent for it. Even my reading remained dull: the contemporary novel having deserted me, it still seemed more satisfying to read history or biography and make up novels in my mind. And there was still my own existence. I could contemplate parts of that, even if doing so could give me a headache. Surely, I would say to myself, emerging from pains in the stomach brought on by contemplating one of the many unsatisfactory aspects of my condition, surely this is at least an *experience? I must be learning something from this.* (But what could it be? Was I ever likely to describe myself, walking home, across High Holborn, into Red Lion Street, and asking what was for dinner?)

The world of the village even came into London – with eggs to sell to the favoured, or tickets in the latest Conservative raffle: it was an amusing challenge to wishy-washy progressivist bullshit to sell tickets in the duck raffle of a village Conservative branch to someone in a bar in Fleet Street. Selected people from the *Sun* office were invited to the village to stay with us for weekends – on one occasion we put on a panel of Australian speakers in the village hall for a Conservative branch quiz on Australia – thereby carrying the addictions of village gossip right into the workplace, among the typewriters and razor blades.

With autumn I again began to survey the garden with the eye of a conqueror. Here was a world where I could still exercise will. In the house, Ethel sought for stability by restoring the past: at least in the garden I could play progress and move into a future. I would put down more new lawns; I would thin out the nut walk and build three new paths through new areas now being opened up to civilisation. I had bought a good book on how to reproduce a shady woodland garden and I was planning artificial banks and rock outcrops to separate gardens from field. Inside, Ethel was extending the area of colonisation. The large barn next to the dining room, empty except as a place to store apples, would be converted into our own sitting room. Some of its barn-like character would be preserved in the high wooden ceiling, but we would cover its walls in hardboard which could then be wall-papered; we would put in French windows, build floor-to-ceiling bookshelves and lay down wall-to-wall carpet. I had now sent for the rest of my books, most of which were still in Australia; there could be no greater mark of our determination to stay where we were.

I would sometimes stand in the barn with its aroma of rotten apples and catshit and imagine how satisfactory it would be when the French windows were installed and the carpet was down and I would be able to sit at my desk, Rufus at my feet, Kitten in my lap, writing another novel. I still saw myself as an itinerant. Certainly, I now had a few possessions, but even gypsies had possessions. It was this sense of transience that made it easier to accommodate myself to the improbability of being a Conservative. As one success followed another – the duck raffles, the *Village Newsletter*, the meetings in the parish hall, and a second and even more successful garden party – I could maintain an anecdotal detachment: there was nothing in all this for me. But I was growing in local prominence. We now had as secretary a Captain somebody, retired from something, and now that the day-to-day affairs of our branch of thirty members were in his good hands, I could concentrate on the broader issues. The constituency agent held up our branch as a model to others. The local member came to see me a couple of times; he seemed to be a Tory democrat too. There was talk of my attending regional conferences and since I was, notoriously, from a Dominion, I was appointed to something called the Conservative Commonwealth Council that met occasionally in a hall in Westminster. A few people in the party began to ask had I ever thought of going into parliament?

3

It was October when the news came through that our moderately amiable existence in the *Sun*'s London office was to be no more. The first rumours were that by some *coup* Frank Packer was about to seize the firm that published the *Sun*. Packer's father had controlled the *Sun* when Packer himself was a young man and Packer had built up his own publishing business by two spectacular *coups* in which he had terrified the *Sun* into buying him off to prevent him starting an opposition afternoon newspaper. Both family connection and reason (his printing presses had nothing to do in the afternoons) suggested the *Sun* was Packer's by right. The rumours included stories of Packer celebrating his just and historic victory in advance at Prince's, his favourite nightclub, the exultant baron, drinking French champagne, surrounded by women in diamonds and boasting of whom he would sack, whom he would hire, how he would alter the machine-room rosters, how he would change the colour supplements.

The rest of the *Sun* staff saw Packer as the worst of evils; for me his arrival would mean that I might now come into my own. The others called for a champagne celebration at a Fleet Street bar when we heard that, in a counter-*coup* carried out at a midnight meeting on the very eve of battle, the directors of the *Sun* had sold the firm to Packer's morning-paper rival, the *Sydney Morning Herald*. Then came the 'days of uncertainty' as rumours began of the *Herald*'s unexpected toughness. Already there was talk of 'heads rolling'. (Had the *Sun*'s directors themselves been double-crossed?) In the London office morale sagged. There was a period of panic. Looting set in (we raided the stationery cupboard and carried home in triumph stocks of writing paper, glue, razor blades, paper clips). For much of the time the staff was 'in emergency session' as we analysed each new rumour – much of it at the Press Club, in a circle at the bar, listening to George explain that he would do the best he could for us.

Now it was my turn to be at the centre of some unexpected move. I suggested to McNulty that Packer could hire me and Jack Pollard, the *Sun's* sporting writer, for his London office. That would show them. The teleprinters exchanged signals. Packer said yes. Everyone could now understand that Horne wasn't someone who would stand about waiting until others decided what they were going to do to him.

MY HOLIDAYS HAD ALREADY BEEN PLANNED TO BEGIN IN THE next week, so the Horne *coup* was followed by the Hornes' fortnight in Dublin. As it turned out, Dublin was even more familiar than I had expected – partly because of the Irishness of Australians (so that a pub crawl with an Irishman who took a liking to us over whiskies in a professedly literary bar became 'typically Australian') and partly because it was reminiscent of *Ulysses*. (The pubs we went to were all 'something out of Joyce'.) We worked at our tourism as hard as our guide books and our muscles allowed, taking in everything, from relics of the Celtic golden age to the first typewriter with Gaelic characters. Including background reading, I thought that for the first time I had 'done tourism' in an intelligent way. At this rate, in less than two hundred years I might gain at least a superficial coverage of some of Europe.

Unlike the English, the Irish hadn't 'burdened themselves with economic controls'. However my belief in the necessary rationality of the free market was surprised by the sight of beggars in the streets – not only beggars, but cartoon beggars wearing rich people's cast-offs, as in the English comics I had read as a child. Like Charlie Chaplin's little man, one of them shuffled from one rubbish bin to the next wearing a bowler hat. These unusual sights prompted us to an act of welfare. The breakfast brought to our room every morning contained two sausages, two cutlets, two fried eggs, two rashers of bacon and two grilled tomatoes. This was much more than we could eat and, since much of our lunches and dinners also seemed to be the kind of thing we might have for breakfast, there seemed no surprises left for the rest of the day. Yet if we didn't eat all of it the maid would reprove us. After a couple of days we decided to put what we couldn't eat into the *Irish Times*, wrap it in two parcels, and place them in the rubbish bins in the streets, so that the humorously clothed beggars could make a nutritious find. However it occurred to me that, by doing so, we were interfering with the free market.

SINCE ETHEL AND I SEEMED TO LEAD SO MUCH OF OUR CON-versational lives in the presence of others, we again admitted, as we had at Polperro, that we had wondered what we would have to say to each other. The true answer, at least in my case, remained private: all we seemed able to say was what we talked about in the presence of others, and most of it about the village, which perhaps now had become our only shared reality. My tourism was a private journey, even if accompanied publicly by a companion.

So were my jitters about whether I had been too rash in prompting Packer to hire me. Why did I sometimes have to do things just because I had thought of them? When the next economy drive came, how would Packer feel about having a London office with thirteen people in it, two of whom had been taken on simply to spite the *Sun*?

When I came back from Dublin and began work in the *Telegraph* offices the staff treated me as a new boy in the playground. The office was moving soon: in the meantime there was no desk and chair. Perhaps I could just borrow whatever space available? In this treacherous environment I became a kind of staff freelance, operating mainly out of the office, coming in with his pieces – but, more importantly, his ideas for features. As long as my idea went off on the teleprinter to friends in Sydney I knew I would be all right. 'My God,' they would be saying, 'there's been a change for the better in London since Donald came back.' By Christmas I was writing something like one and a half feature articles a week for the *Daily Telegraph* and a monthly piece for one of their magazines. Here I was, again doing what I had learned to do eight years ago, although now in an office in which there was no praise.

When, after a *Telegraph* lunch thrown by Packer at the Savoy, I found myself as drunk as I had ever been, it seemed natural towards the end of the afternoon to drop in on George Johnston and the others and call them out for a few sorrowful drinks, so that we could join in regretting the past. I may have been as drunk as this before, but never so expensively. When some of us moved on to a bar, it was the whole experience of journalism I was cursing; but by the time I called on George and the others to share my rage, my curses seemed to have narrowed to details of the humiliations of my present position in the *Telegraph* office in London. And now I was not so much angry as belly-aching. What I most hated in other drunks was self-pity – of the drunk's tetralogy *jocose, bellicose, lachrymose, comatose* I preferred cracking jokes, although anger and passing-out were also honourable – but here I was with the tears pouring down my cheeks, in a bar, in front of George and the others, who were saying, 'Look what Packer's done to Donald.' Someone took me home – up Chancery Lane, across High Holborn, into Red Lion Street, bawling all the way.

AFTER CHRISTMAS WE MOVED TO A NEW SUITE OF OFFICES WITH enough space and enough chairs and desks for double the staff. (The room I was in was shared by four other writers and between us we had nine desks, arranged in varying patterns of territoriality.) I was getting a more comfortable feel for the office now. The news room was still somewhat faded in spirit, but down the corridor there was an air of bustle and expansion in the offices of a London book publishing firm Packer had bought, and next to us were three women writers for Packer's extravagantly successful *Australian Women's Weekly*. They could give us a sense of really being in the middle of things, with the latest gossip from the Palace, or on a new Chelsea interior decorator, or on the new Paris fashions. One of them, Patricia Rolfe, became my confidant, as Hazel Tully had been at the *Sun*, although with an extra literary finish since Pat was also writing fiction: we would relish long, bitching lunches, in which we could delightfully mock the inadequacies of McNulty and almost everyone else in the office and wonder that they could not do things as we would, if we were in charge.

Pat had become one of those who would stay with us for weekends in the village, where her practice of actually looking down her nose at those of us she was about to put in their places made her an even greater deterrent than Gaga Beaton for use against the dowagers, whose bourgeois fussiness was exposed by her nonchalance and controlled urban wit. In any case our new room was finished. My books had come from Sydney and were laid out in the floor-to-ceiling bookshelves. Now we had our own part of the house. The desk was there, and an enormous amount of writing paper I had taken from the *Sun* at the time of looting: any weekend now I would start on my third novel.

Perhaps my period of exile was over. I seemed to be getting back into things.

PART 2

ADVENTURER
1954–58

NINE

The temptation of excitement

1

For the next few months I was able to rush from one diversion to the next. The first began when a letter arrived from the executive council of our Conservative branch telling us it had reluctantly accepted our MP's decision not to run in the next election. A couple of weeks later, the MP himself arrived, carrying a different message. Could he see me? Yes, of course. Scotch? Soda? Ice?

He wanted to explain that he wasn't as young as he used to be, and it was true that all-night sittings and the Conservatives' narrow majority had taken it out of him. (Nod from me.) And then, of course, there was that time, during an all-night sitting, when he had fallen down the stairs. I'd heard about that, of course? (Wave of the glass.) It was all over the constituency in no time, spread by his enemies. (Since I hadn't heard a word about this, I gave a nod that might mean anything.) It's true, he did go to the constituency council, but he hadn't actually spoken of resigning. Something less than that. The agent would confirm this. But the hunting and stockbroking set who ran the council didn't want him, of course, and (he was sorry to say) they had outsmarted him. But since then he had been on a holiday. He could assure me that now he was extremely fit. (Nod.) It wasn't just himself he was thinking about. (Nod. Nod.) This was a swinging constituency. It needed a man of the people, to hold it for the party. (Nod. Nod. Nod.) The next election wouldn't be as easy as they thought. He had come to me because our village branch was a model for all England.

Horne the ward-heeler jumps in. *Grass roots support. We will fill the hall with the people.* The Member will give his annual address, I will ask him a question. He will admit he now realises he must not desert the constituency. He will lay himself at our disposal. (*Thunderous applause*, followed by retreat of hunting and stockbrokers' faction.) We arranged to hire a bus to take our village branch to the annual general meeting. Liaison work in neighbouring villages produced the promise of another busload of faithful, and an extension of fraternal relations to a large party branch in the constituency's one manufacturing town produced promises of two more busloads. Then the opposition struck back: the executive council – the junta – asked me to second the vote of thanks for their year's work.

(*Did they think they could buy me off with that?*)

Here was a chance to show what a wily foe they were trying to silence. I passed on to Jim White the task of putting the key question to the Member – we rehearsed it together in his cowshed – and, on the night of the annual general meeting, as seconder of the vote of thanks, I gave a five-minute speech praising the executive council for doing all the things it should have done but everyone knew it had left undone. Loud laughter from the hall. Even smiles from some of the more reasonable members of the junta.

After our victory, the junta resigned. Perhaps we might in a year or so let in one or two of those who had smiled, if by that stage they had fully demonstrated their continuing loyalty to the party. Now the whole constituency must be thoroughly reorganised. A newsletter in every village. A fête in every garden. I was thrust upwards into the structure of the party, onto a regional council. You must become better known regionally, said the agent. That will help you get selection, said the Member.

People have begun to talk like this but I scarcely think about it. Obviously, if it happens, I will be an enlightened Conservative MP making intelligent speeches. And it will leave me time for writing.

NO TIME FOR WRITING AT PRESENT. FOR THAT MATTER, NO TIME to thrust upwards through Conservative Party branches. Packer has ordered me to Kenya, to report the Mau Mau uprising: and here I am, rushed off with scarcely enough time to look at a map, flying overnight on a plane that has its final break-down in Uganda and while I would be charmed if we could spend a few hours, or even the night, on the shores of Lake Victoria, my new friend the foreign correspondent tells them again and again: we must fly to Nairobi at once, we are *the Press*. We arrive at Nairobi before sundown and spread ourselves over a splendid dinner in the New Stanley Hotel. Each night we will soak in our baths, change into our suits, put on our ties, assemble in the grill at seven, order martinis, and again exchange our views on the ironies of the world; the ironies increase over Grand Marnier and coffee. For years afterwards, I will begin dinners with martinis and end with Grand Marnier.

The foreign correspondent, who works for one of the less successful Fleet Street dailies, a 'popular paper' with falling sales, interprets his being sent to Nairobi as part of some power play in his office that does not seem to his advantage: they have sent him out here while they wonder what to do with him (he suspects) now that he is back from New York. It's true this Kenya story has become rather hot – 'warm' might be a better word – but none of the star names of Fleet Street have been seen; in fact most of the Street is still relying on stringers. Why on earth is an Australian paper sending someone here? he wonders. (I do too.) In Nairobi he must maintain a personal presence. No daily news coverage. Not even scoops. It is literary presence that is needed: he must give a sense of special occasion to this Mau Mau story because it is now he who is writing about it. We will, of course, work together, he and I: with our different deadlines and countries of origin, we are not competitors. (Do I detect a sense of amusement at the thought of my being a competitor?) We toast our forthcoming collaboration and congratulate ourselves on our mutually enlightened scepticism. (Along with my lack of competitiveness, it is for my general style – unexpected, he feels, in an Australian – that he has decided to honour me as his dinner companion.)

For the next three days I feel like a gold digger shovelling up the easy stuff – with daily news pieces (NAIROBI BECOMES CITY OF FEAR ... PLANES HUNT FLEEING MAU MAU ... MAU MAU TERRORISTS STRIKE AGAIN) and the first of what will prove to be eleven feature articles. The foreign correspondent is spending most of his time with 'settlers', especially the European members of the Legislative Council. He has his angle. He will denounce the governor's softness. By agreement, I concentrate on army PR people, who lay it all out for me, with daily handouts about what they say happened yesterday and background briefings of horror stories. I assemble many details of the killings by the Mau Mau of a couple of dozen whites and a few anecdotes about the killing of a couple of thousand blacks. Spice is added with details of secret and terrible Mau Mau oath-taking ceremonies. (When I write these up it seems essential to make generous use of the words 'blood' and 'semen' but I doubt whether the *Telegraph* will print the word 'semen'.) With a furtive leer that reminds me of when I was about to see my first filthy postcard, in the playground of Canterbury High, one of the PR men slips me some photographs of Mau Mau hanged in the courtyard of Nairobi gaol – killed in job lots, half a dozen at a time. Their heads are gravely inclined, as if there were still some intellectual puzzles they wanted to ponder before their necks were broken.

We do not speak to any government officials, and certainly not to any Indians or 'Africans' (as we have learned to call the black people). The New Stanley Hotel does not let in even the Aga Khan, a number of whose followers make up part of the commercial element in Kenya, and who visits the colony often enough to keep a private box at the racecourse. Africans enter my world as servants and drivers, apart from pavement encounters on my early-morning walks to the telegraph office (where a large poster says: SHUSH ... *someone may be listening ... guard your tongue* ... SHUSH).

At dinner each night, from martinis to Grand Marniers, as the band plays, again and again, the theme song from the movie *La Ronde*, a sexual allegory of the decadence of late imperial Vienna, we have better things to talk about than Africans.

One of the army PR men is an Irishman, who is not really PR but someone seconded from his regiment (a move that, he suspects, may record the end of his army career). Having taken a fancy to me as a conversational companion, on the fourth day he 'lays on' a Land Rover, with African driver, so that he can show me the Rift Valley. We pass miles of Africans, waving and smiling from among the leaves of banana trees, then we move over the escarpment that divides the 'white highlands' from this great landslip with its old volcano craters and its pastel colours. Our first stop in the valley is the Navaisha Sports Club (described as 'cool, stone-walled') where a hallful of 1920s-looking settlers, festooned with revolvers, sporting rifles, shot guns, hunting knives and belts of ammunition, speak some of the languages of revolt against a governor who is too soft on the blacks. Outside, under one of the pepper trees, a woman with a pearl-handled revolver at her waist says she is too angry to sit inside with all these traitors whose words don't match their deeds. She invokes the spirit of 1922, when the settlers made credible their talk of armed rebellion.

After the meeting disintegrates from an angry mass into groups of departing families, the Irishman and I drive through ancient landscapes as if it were the moon, or the Australian outback. Talk rushes by like the wind. Then I understand that what he is now saying is that the settlers have reached the end of the road. This Irishman is a romantic. He 'loves Africa'. I am not sure which Africa it is that he loves. Some of it seems the loyal Africa of the King's African Rifles, when district officers were gentlemen, faithful tribesmen were rewarded, and the natives knew that if they were faithless their villages would be burned down in reprisal. Some of it is a reconciled Africa of the future, when the settlers have all been sent home and there can be some new kind of relations between gentlemen and natives.

For the moment, the 'Africa' I love is the Africa of the movie travelogue and the *National Geographic* magazine. I photograph strangely shaped hills, waving natives and a small lake entirely fringed with hundreds of pink flamingoes. By the time we have tea with one of the settlers (served by 'polite, barefooted natives') it has become 'Africa, continent of contrasts'. As we look out over the hippopotamuses wallowing in Lake Navaisha the settler says he has installed electric fencing to keep them off his lucerne crops.

There must be three feature articles in this day so far. Then, to cap all other anecdotes, at dusk, just before we reach the road leading back up the escarpment, the motor engine stops. The driver understands almost as little about motors as I do. (What if we have to spend the night here? Are there lions? Are there Mau Mau? Yes, says the Irishman. There are a few gangs. A carload of settlers was fired on last week.) (*Later*: Do we have any weapons? No, says the Irishman: carrying guns is provocative. All you must do is drive fast and you're safe.)

A passing army sergeant does whatever it is that fixes the engine and we drive on to a settler's lonely farm, for dinner. Another anecdote:

Over dinner, settlers and their wives retell horror stories of meals in lonely farm houses with guns on the table and the door into the kitchen locked, to keep out the servants (as our door is locked tonight). During one such recital my foot steps on an electric light flex and pulls a plug.

We are in darkness. Silence. (Is that click the 'quiet loosening of a safety catch'?) When the light comes back, the settlers all have their guns out, pointing them, as it happens, at each other.

I send off cables – news stories, feature articles, special reports, always before breakfast, so that during the rest of the day I can see more of Africa. My knees are so sunburned that they begin to bleed and I have swallowed so much red dust that for a day I lose my voice. A small dog bites me. In the wildlife park I see giraffes courting and then mating; I see a jaguar killing a deer and baboons scratching their arses like old men. On a day's expedition with the commander of the African 'Home Guard' we tour cedar and bamboo forests on the slopes of the Aberdare Mountains ('the principal Mau Mau hideout'), driving 'through red dust lanes, with sporting rifles held between our knees'. We visit half a dozen fortified villages, walled off like castles, with poisoned bamboo spears sticking up in their moats and the Indian store, because it is made of concrete, turned into the castle's keep. We inspect guards of honour armed with spears and shotguns and clothed in cast-off army greatcoats and old blankets. We watch displays of shooting skills with bows and arrows.

Just before I leave Kenya, the Irishman and I spend a day in a Land Rover in the Fort Hull district where, the day before, a district officer was killed and mutilated. (This time the army insists that we are armed, with forty-fives.) We photograph the district officer's Land Rover, which was also mutilated, and I get hitherto unpublished details about what was done with his head; then we drive on to Filo's Bar, run by an Indian, the last place of its kind before the Ethiopian frontier. I buy cigars and a bottle of champagne. As we ride back, smoking cigars, singing dirty songs, with forty-fives at our waists and champagne inside us, we are fired on, several times, from long grass on either side of the road. 'Don't stop!' says the Irishman, 'Never stop!' I struggle with the lanyard on my forty-five, then turn around and fire one commemorative shot at the long grass. After several more bends in the road, a young leopard leaps at our Land Rover. At the hotel that night my friend the correspondent is missing; I have a tray sent up to my suite, and enjoy 'a rare moment of solitude' and think about myself and Ethel.

AS WELL AS MASTERING AFRICA I HAVE BEEN GAINING CLOSER realisations of the 'settlers'. It seems extraordinary that a people so highly armed and so argumentative have not, in a mutual shoot-out, performed an act of self-genocide. In one of my special reports I point to the symbolic significance of the reiterative playing of 'La Ronde' in the New Stanley Grill: it is the end of another empire. The foreign correspondent and I drink with settlers in one of their clubs, where they repeat brutal anecdotes of famous drunks shooting out light bulbs in the days when men were men and you could kick a black up the arse. An English lord calls a press conference and announces a new plan. We spend more time talking about the conspiracies of the settlers than we do about the Mau Mau. We go to a meeting of the Nairobi Jockey Club in one of the private boxes and it is astonishing to see how much they can eat and drink when they are at play. When they start talking about an army officer who has been sentenced to five years in jail for cutting off the ears and the balls of a 'suspected terrorist', he is seen as one of the victims of the liberal prejudices of the age. I make notes on one of the great issues that divide the settlers: the moderates would send RAF bombers to the Aberdares to blast the Mau Mau into submission; the extremists would use poison gas.

A group of us at the New Stanley throw a large, drunken lunch that includes a settler who, given the emergency, has returned to the colours and is done up in what seems a uniform of his own design, that makes him look like Hermann Goering. In the late afternoon, over the scotches and pink gins, he begins crying. Upstairs, his young wife, who looks like a 1920s beauty, is in bed with the second journalist of her day. La Ronde.

When the foreign correspondent and I pursue our amiable dinners in the New Stanley Grill, as night after night we order the same food and drink, we treat each other as equals; but during the day, when it comes to journalism, he sometimes reveals, in a warning flash or two, what he sees as his upper hand. He imagines that I am dependent on him for my daily news pieces (I have written so much that I am ashamed to confess to him that I have also been writing special reports) – yet he can have seen scarcely anything of Africa beyond what he cannot avoid between the telegraph office and the New Stanley Hotel. (Then I learn that he has been paying one of the porters to deliver his cables.) He has not sat in a lonely police outpost surrounded by barbed wire entanglements or seen a truckful of 'suspected terrorists', all freshly captured in the Aberdares.

When the first of his set-pieces is published and his paper splashes it as the front page lead, he rings me in my room to come and see the congratulatory cable. I am writing, daily, better stuff than that – but not a word from the *Telegraph*. Are they using anything? Is it the kind of thing they want? Or do they not give a fuck what I write? My uncertainties develop into the anecdote of my world scoop, which is to become one of the most often told anecdotes of my repertoire as a journalist.

One afternoon I was drinking with some settlers and one of them told me a secret he had sworn not to reveal, but I was only writing for an Australian paper, so what did it matter? One of the Mau Mau leaders, who had taken the pseudonym 'General China' and had been captured by the army some time ago, was now being used to negotiate a secret truce through the Mau Mau underground. This secret dealing, one of the greatest acts of treachery in the long history of betrayal by the British government in Kenya, had already been going on for twelve days. If word got out, all hell would break loose: at long last the settlers would storm Government House. But word might not get out. There was no overt censorship on news from Kenya, but if the army were suspicious, they would certainly clamp down. The telegraph office had spies from all four warring sides – settlers, Mau Mau, government, army. If someone tried to cable out the shameful truth the army would at once step in.

It was late at night. If I filed a story now it would attract attention. But what would I file at breakfast time tomorrow? My brilliant solution seemed worthy of a character in Evelyn Waugh's *Scoop*: I sent off to the London office (who relayed all my copy to Sydney) a rather vague piece that in itself did not make sense. Then I sent to McNulty at the telegraphic address of the book publishing company he also ran (that would put them off the scent) the following cable: THE TWO SONGS ARE QUOTE REMEMBER CHINA UNQUOTE AND QUOTE TOKYO BAY IS NOT FAR AWAY UNQUOTE ... Mac would get that: 'General China' was featured in the news and the Japanese surrender at Tokyo Bay was still in living memory.

Instead of going out to discover Africa that morning I stayed by the phone. Mac's reply came quickly: MESSAGE UNDERSTOOD STOP PLEASE ARRANGE TO BE PRESENT AT FLAG DAY CEREMONY CONGRATULATIONS. (Clever McNulty.)

The army commander called a press conference that afternoon. He was about to pass on to us some confidential background information, he said, on the understanding that we did not use it. If we did use it, there was no likelihood that it would be published: the appropriate arrangements to suppress the story had been made in Fleet Street. When I went up to him after the meeting and told him I had already sent the story he said yes, he knew that.

His bluff worked for only a few days, then the story was in any case released.

It was not until I got back to London that I learned that the *Telegraph* had run my world scoop, but only down the page, as a mere rumour. Since it was exclusive they could not really believe it was true. Several days later when the story became official and everyone else had it, they gave me a front-page lead.

As it turns out, I discover that the *Telegraph* has given me three other front-page leads as well. *Daily* and *Sunday*, they have used everything I sent them and used it with great vigour. Mac tells me they took radio campaigns to advertise two of my specials. Why didn't you stay on? he asks. Why didn't you suggest it? I think.

BACK IN LONDON, MY MIND REMAINS HOT WITH 'THE RAT-TAT-TAT of Patchett guns' as British troops 'scour the cedar forests of the Aberdares' or 'the tinkle of ice in pink gins' as settlers confront their end, or 'the slow drip of blood' in bestial oath-taking ceremonies in Mau Mau hideouts' or, for that matter, 'the slither of grass as a jaguar pounces on its prey'. As I go through the papers with a razor blade in the London office waiting to pounce on my own prey, if there is the slightest movement in East Africa I write yet one more feature article, explaining this latest twist in events to the readers of the *Daily Telegraph*. I begin to read books on Kenya, on East Africa generally and then on anywhere in Africa: week by week I watch for news on Africa in *The Economist*. I find that I have lost most of my interest in the garden, and even in village gossip.

Horne of Africa then becomes involved in some combination of spy novel and Ealing comedy. It begins when I summon a meeting in the village hall to tell Conservatives or anyone else who cares to listen about the situation in Kenya. My talk is of a somewhat ironic vein. At the end, I tell how I had heard of plans for psychological warfare against the Mau Mau by letting off green smoke from the craters of extinct volcanoes, spreading rumours based on ancient tribal prophecies, sending live messages through amplifying systems in the Aberdare forests: that kind of thing.

When one of the gentlemen from up the hill comes down to see me some days later he is even testier than the character I turned him into in *One Can Always Tell a Gentleman*. (I must remember this when it comes to the next revision.) He has heard about my talk in the village hall and he wants me to understand he doesn't give a damn about my views but do I realise that everything I said about the psychological warfare plans was top secret? As he proceeds, he gives me many more top secrets – not only about the plans but about the top secret committee in London (of which he is a member) which is preparing the plans. It is evident to him that I am part of a conspiracy (whether consciously or not he doesn't know) and this conspiracy is being mounted by some counter-faction in the intelligence world which clearly wants to discredit what his committee is doing. I will hear more about this, he assures me. I am summoned to two separate confidential meetings in London with officials who have not, I suspect, disclosed their full identity.

Now I am privy to at least one of the secret idiocies of the state, I am beginning to feel that I really belong to this country.

NO TIME TO WRITE A NEW NOVEL WHILE I AM LIVING OUT ONE of Evelyn Waugh's, although I must find time at once to get on with my upthrust through the branches of the Conservative Party. No time for that either, as it happens. I am sent to Helsinki, on another adventure.

This time it is my idea. A Soviet agent in Canberra has defected and one of the results has been a retaliatory expulsion of the Australian diplomatic mission from Moscow, and who should be *chargé d'affaires* of the Australian embassy but Brian Hill, a diplomatic cadet with me ten years ago? Obviously, the *Telegraph* must send me to Helsinki to pick up an exclusive interview when Hill and party arrive from Moscow. Frank Packer says yes.

My own arrival in Helsinki is rich in anecdotes, of which my favourite becomes the story of how I spent my first night in Helsinki in the Palace Hotel's luxurious sauna bath with two drunken Lapps, and the second in the YMCA, which, because of its strange initials (NNYK) and my own paranoia I imagine to be a Soviet institution. I stay awake most of the night waiting for the first move from the notorious NNYK. With the President of Iceland and entourage on a state visit, a conference of Scandinavian cooperative societies and a touring group of sixty midwestern US editors, Helsinki is booked out, but when the cooperatives' conference ends I am installed, as befits me, in the Palace Hotel, where I order champagne and salmon steaks and book two telephone calls a day to Brian Hill in Moscow.

There are delays: I must 'keep the story going'. In this the calls to Brian are a mainstay but I also discover (and to that extent invent) a minuscule 'Australian community' in Finland, in whom I try to arouse enough interest in the arrival of the Australians to provide me a story or two. I even ring the Soviet Embassy to ask for a visa so that I can fly to Moscow and interview the Australians: their refusal makes another story. Not that I want to waste time beating up stories for the *Telegraph*. I have all Finland to learn about. Even on the first day I visit the Finnish parliament, collect statistics and arrange interviews. The *Telegraph* may not be interested in Finland but I am: the prospect of learning about all Scandinavia opens up. And, for a diversion within these diversions, there is the small British diplomatic community, into which I have entered because 'the Brits' handle Australian affairs in Finland and they are now relying on me for advice about what to do about the mysterious Australians. I have just discovered Anthony Powell's novels, and the British community in Helsinki reminds me of the British community in his novel, *Venusberg*. I imagine having an *affaire*, as in a Powell novel, with the wife of a minor 'Brit'.

Even the presence of sixty midwestern editors at the Palace Hotel provides 'experience'. Apart from a brief encounter with two tourists in London that provided an anecdote of American innocence abroad, I have had nothing to do with travelling Americans. It now occurs to me that I have had nothing to do with Americans at all, except for writing a book in which the two principal characters were Americans. (Perhaps, after all, George Johnston was right, and that was a mistake? Should I rewrite the book and turn them into Australians?) Even during the 'American invasion' of Australia I do not recall even speaking to an American: my closest personal contact with Americans has come from reading about them in Peter Hastings's letters. I know, of course, that they have not been as sophisticated in handling the Russians as 'we' would have been. (Although I know that 'we' are also as mad as hatters: planning to set off green smoke in extinct volcano craters.) In these soft-looking, self-regarding people I meet in the Palace Hotel I find nothing to change that impression. I am delighted when, on several occasions, Americans ask me for various kinds of directions ('Where is the toilet? Where is Denmark?'). They have taken me for a Finn.

My coming to Finland has precipitated a minor 'Fleet Street invasion' of Helsinki. When the *Sydney Morning Herald* executives hear of my going to Helsinki they make arrangements with the *Daily Express* on a share-expenses basis that the *Express* will send a reporter and this in turn prompts two other Fleet Street papers to send reporters to match the *Express*, and other papers to at least activate their stringers. A special reporter from one of the wire services arrives. Of all of these, I favour the man from the least successful, and also the silliest, of all the papers in Fleet Street – about the same age as the foreign correspondent in Kenya (again older than me), even more urbane and enlightened and a shade more liberal (but with no progressivist illusions, of course). We dine each night under chandeliers, in a room decorated in red and gold in a restaurant that, we have heard, goes back to Tsarist times. He cannot imagine why his paper has sent him to Helsinki. But then why did they send him to France last month? Or the month before to Italy? Or the month before to Lichtenstein? It is a habit Fleet Street newspapers have, of sending reporters to other countries, and even his comic book follows this tradition. He shares my interest in Anthony Powell and we chat in a fine, amusing style. Since his deadline is later than mine I promise him a few pars from my exclusive interview. (His paper would probably not give the announcement of World War Three more than twenty paragraphs.) The other journalists manoeuvre around me unsuccessfully, but I have nothing for people who don't know how to sit under chandeliers and talk about Anthony Powell. When the day comes, two of them try to outsmart me by going overnight to the frontier to meet the special train the Australians are on. Brian Hill won't speak to them. I have breakfast with the Hills and get more than enough. AUSSIES FROM MOSCOW GREETED WITH SONG says my front-page lead. IT WAS A FINE MOMENT TO BE AN AUSTRALIAN (ENVOY'S STORY) says my exclusive interview on page four.

I have given my friend from Fleet Street both stories to pick over for his few paragraphs. It is all somewhat too serious for his paper, but I also mention that the Hills' younger child broke a glass while we were having breakfast. He writes an exclusive story of eight paragraphs for his paper about the breakfast misadventure of 'Baby Hill'.

BACK IN ENGLAND, I REALLY FEEL ON TOP OF THINGS. LIFE IN THE room with the nine desks seems disconcertingly confined to the usual – lunches with Pat Rolfe become longer and our conversation more pungent about mismanagement in the London office – and the latest reordering of the garden and the planning of the next Conservative fête seem disconcertingly predictable, but I am restructuring the programme for my next novel. I have been to my first regional Conservative Party conference. My head is filling with new knowledge, gained from books and journals about Africa and now Scandinavia. I am bursting with new experiences from two continents.

In this state of high *élan* I now embark on my most disastrous adventure.

2

PACKER SEEMS TO HAVE BEEN MOOCHING AROUND LONDON, ON and off, for weeks. He spends some days in Paris and makes a brief trip to Rome (leaving after the first few hours, it is said, because Rome seems too old) but London is his centre of business and pleasure. When he sits in the 'visiting executive's office' we feel he is there even if we don't see him, although occasionally his big body passes the open door of our room like a huge shadow. On one occasion I met him in the lift. He is in full morning dress, and he congratulates me (with a bluff shyness) on my Kenya and Helsinki expeditions (and also lets me know that 'there were those who didn't want me to send you'). He spends more of his time, however in his suite in the Savoy, when he isn't hobnobbing with Fleet Street big shots making deals or engaging in strenuous forms of pleasure. His wife (McNulty tells us) is trying to encourage 'Frank' to relax but one of his greatest pleasures is still his daily phone call to Sydney where (says McNulty) his executives line up, waiting their turn to be told what to do.

A friend from Paris is visiting London for a few days: I hear from him that the people who publish *Reveille* are planning an Australian edition and this has brought out Packer's sense of adventure: he wants to beat them at their own game. He will make a blitzkrieg launch of an Australian version of the *Weekly Mail*. This is told as just one more illustration of Packer's compulsive gambler's spirit – there are hundreds more where this anecdote comes from – but to me it reopens memories of my three and a half years' neglect by the *Telegraph*. Packer himself has admitted that there were those who didn't want him to send me to Kenya, or even Helsinki, but is Packer himself now turning against me? *For Christ's sake, who knows more than I do about this kind of publication?* I storm off to McNulty: *Why aren't they getting the benefit of my experience?* McNulty's main response is dismay that I have heard about what is for the moment the *Telegraph*'s top secret. Then I am even more insulted when McNulty tells me Packer has already chosen an editor. It is to be one of the people here in the *Telegraph*'s London office.

This scene is set on a Friday afternoon. The weekend is given over to obsessive fear and hatred. Each night I wake up several times with shock and loathing. Through the day I contemplate human folly. Whatever, on the outside, I may appear to be doing, on the inside I am brooding over this outrage. But (at the same time): Why should I care? (*Because for Christ's sake it's so fucking stupid not to draw on my experience.*) But didn't I hate the *Weekly Mail*? (*That is not the point.*)

As well as anger, envy and pride there now comes another, and deeper, temptation: the temptation of excitement. What an experience it would be to edit this thing myself! I wouldn't want to make a career of it, of course. I see it as a brief, piratical adventure. Go out there. Kick it off. After six months come back. (I imagine the last page of the first issue as it goes to press ... in my mind I design layout sheets and production schedules, call for market surveys. Shining down on us all, like a great sign in the sky, is the sales curve. The circulation figures rise and rise.)

But why degrade myself with such drivel?

To this the answer is that it doesn't do anyone any harm. It's better than progressivist claptrap.

I might as well edit something before I leave journalism.

It would get me a free trip to Australia.

Nobody who matters here need ever know about it.

My interior debate always comes back to: *It would only be for six months.*

On the Monday morning I leave a memo with McNulty for Packer, telling him that my medium-term plan is to enter the House of Commons but as a short-term interest I might be able to interest myself in this new venture.

I am called in at once. After a slow start, with uneasy jokes about the House of Commons, the rest of the interview goes like a gale. When it is finished I have to spend some time putting things back into order, so that I can remember what Packer said.

– Yes. The job is yours.

– Stay there for six months, yes.

– Salary? Double your present salary.

– Something like a professor's salary? (How much do professors get?) Very well. It's only for six months.

– You must leave for Sydney in three days.

– Well, a week.

– Well, not later than ten days! Remember this:

ABSOLUTELY CON-FIDENTIAL. If *Reveille* gets wind of this it's all off.

– You're not to say you're going to Australia. We'll say you're going on holidays.

– When you get to Sydney we'll spread new rumours. We'll say you're starting an intellectual weekly. The *New Statesman*, we'll call it. That's a good idea.

Packer flies to New York that afternoon and he won't be back until after I leave. But from New York he rings me twice in one day. When I am in New York, he says (until then I didn't know I was going to New York), as well as buying pin-ups I must buy some astrology notes: there is a woman there I should see – he has arranged it: she lives in Park Avenue, her husband is a newsprint tycoon and Packer does business with him ... I must make up my own mind about whether to buy, or course. The second time he rings it is to say can't I leave sooner?

The *Weekly Mail* is going halves with Packer in our privateering expedition. I am given an empty back room upstairs in a building in which they organise their competitions and promotions, and from which the *Daily Mail* Ideal Home Exhibition is run, the most successful thing the *Mail* still has going for it. For cover in our conspiracy, the Ideal Homes people are told I am planning a special secret promotion drive for one of the *Mail*'s publications. I am in a maelstrom of improvisation. It is essential for our blitzkrieg that I assemble reserves large enough to draw on for the first six months. I fill a large cardboard box with drawn headings taken from the *Weekly Mail*, tearsheets of stories for which they own the copyright, five hundred drawn jokes and as many picture spreads (already retouched – that will save time). I list special series they can quickly buy copyright for, and other features and picture spreads, categorise them and give them code names. They can buy batches of this stuff when I cable for what I need.

At a safe place I have conferences with the editor of the *Weekly Mail*. We compare the distinguishing characteristics of our two 'managements' and discuss staff requirements, reader surveys, promotional devices, layout techniques, production schedules and the central mysteries of profit and loss. I go to sleep pondering the marginal utility of allocating extra resources to sales promotion, I wake up weighing the balance between gaining sales and satisfying advertisers' prejudices.

What I am embarking on can at times seem a question of rational decision; at other times, of daring adventure and desperate gamble. I go back to my ponderings on Napoleon and Kutuzov that had followed my reading of *War and Peace* in an army hospital in 1942. Whatever happens, if it is successful, one must look as if that is what was meant to happen.

Naturally in my conversations with the editor I keep quiet about all of this intellectualising. At first he lectures down to me, but although I haven't edited anything bar the *Village Newsletter* since *Honi Soit* thirteen years ago, I know how to act like an editor. At our third meeting he says he didn't know I had it in me.

It is at this meeting that we have our first disagreement. He assumes I will call it the *Weekly Mail*. No, I say, I'm going to call it *Weekend*. He doesn't like this: he wants my one to be as close as possible to his. He even talks for a while of taking this up with his management, then yields. I give him some advice: when the time comes, he should rename his one *Weekend*. It's a title that says it all – relaxation, escape, even the time of the week to buy it.

On the one hand, I know that my comic must make a profit, so the more of his stuff we can use, the better, because it's cheap. On the other hand, I know that we can't simply turn his into mine: mine must be Australianised. I get some dummy layout sheets and begin scribbling on them. I am trying to work out my own, Australian, formula. Then a thunderbolt from New York.

Packer rings to instruct me that almost all the pages in *Weekend* must be exactly the same as the *Weekly Mail*: each week they will fly out to Sydney the mattes which mould the metal and all I need do is to have holes cut in a few of them and in those spaces put some Australian stories. We'll save money that way. Later in the day I will ring him back and resign. This simply can't work: he just doesn't understand, etc., etc. My God, if it's going to be like this, the sooner, etc., etc. Well, so far as I'm concerned, if that's what Packer thinks, then etc., etc. In an emergency meeting with the editor we both agree that, even allowing for our own differences of opinion, *Weekend* must be more Australian than Packer is allowing for. Then it occurs to the editor: maybe what Packer suggests is not physically possible. The *Weekly Mail* is slightly longer than the normal tabloid size: do the *Daily Telegraph* presses produce a normal tabloid length paper? I ring McNulty. We get the measurements and compare them. We have Packer there: what he wants can't be done. You'd better ring him up and explain, says the editor. No, I say, quick as a flash, he'll think I'm just making excuses. He might call the whole thing off. Let him find out later. Fuck him. (I don't say 'fuck him' out loud: the editor of the *Weekly Mail* doesn't like swearing.)

ON THE FLIGHT TO NEW YORK I AM, TO BEGIN WITH, FURIOUS. McNulty has booked me economy class! (What other betrayals am I about to experience?) I calm down: even if I am seated beside some detestable American who wants to talk about all the duty-free shopping he has done, these are the first moments of doing nothing I have enjoyed for ten days.

I seem filled with farewells: Rufus, Kitten, an unexpectedly affectionate farewell from Elsa, a clandestine dinner with McNulty; a hail and farewell from the managing director of the *Daily Mail* company who swooped around the side of his desk, clutched my hands and held them while he spared me a few minutes' rapid talk, intently; eye to eye, man to man; and Ethel, standing at the gate that separates those who stay from those who depart.

When we had come to England four and a half years before, we had brought with us, borrowed at the last minute for things we couldn't fit in, a leather suitcase of my father's. It was the one in which he would pack his and my clothes (there weren't many of them) when, three times a year, we went from our country town to the city for the school holidays. Now in this receptacle of childhood innocence are five hundred jokes, several dozen pin-up pictures, sheets of tearsheets, and fifty drawn headings with words on them such as I MARRIED THE WORLD'S STRONGEST WOMAN and HOW TO RECOGNISE THE FACE OF YOUR IDEAL MATE.

PACKETS OF OTHER FEATUES AND PICTURE SPREADS WILL NOW fly out ahead of me from London to Sydney. Not being able to sleep on the plane and having my first chance to think for ten days, I have written out a list of possible selling stories for the first two months. If things go wrong in making *Weekend* Australian, this list will provide a fallback position. I have also thought of a telegraphic address for *Weekend* – it will be BRIGHTPRESS SYDNEY – and I have decided that I must have a plastic ruler of a kind I have seen in London, with inches on one side and ems, the printer's measure, on the other. This em ruler will be my sceptre, emphasising that I will be a working editor, butting into everything.

By the end of my first day in New York another parcel is on its way to Sydney, flying ahead of me: it contains fifty pin-up photographs. I have been worried by the insipidity of the *Weekly Mail* pin-ups and decided to get some of my own. But how does one buy pin-ups? Does it matter that the women in them don't really look like human beings? I know we mustn't flagrantly exploit sex, and that the 'girls' are just there to make the readers feel lighthearted, but even if, for commercial reasons, they must still be idealised, isn't there some way of making these women more real? Will having real-looking women throw the readers into a state of heavy-heartedness?

Have I overdone it? I have been given an address in lower something street and I spend my first morning in New York in a small office with batteries of filing cabinets containing thousands of photographs of female flesh. This is the first decision: if the pin-up girls in *Weekend* are going to seem more real, then I must go for legs or breasts. Since breasts seem more human than legs, I go for breasts. The man in charge then asks me if I am going for uplift or cleavage. I decide that cleavage seems less contrived than uplift and in any case I have read somewhere that uplift was going out of fashion. Having declared myself for cleavage, I must answer one of the great questions of our times: how much cleavage? Perhaps all fifty of the photographs I have bought 'show too much'. What will Packer say if he finds out that I have bought a hundred large breasts at up to $5 a pair and we might have to throw them all out?

I spend the rest of my first day in New York sleeping, and wake at dawn realising that there is no need to be in New York at all. I am there because it seems necessary to Packer that, as an act of propitiation before beginning some new enterprise, one should pay one's respect to the power of the two great English-speaking metropolises (one of which I have lived in, so he doesn't have to send me to that). His own movements are based on a calendar of annual pilgrimages and these can seem essential to the continuing renewal of his affairs. In sending me to New York he is allowing me to acquire grace.

Unfortunately he hasn't sent me to New York for long enough to see all the museums, walk the streets, go to the theatres, sit in the bars and drink bourbon. But I can do a little of this, since all that remains to be done is an hour's work – in seeing the Park Avenue astrologist. How many museums, streets, theatres and bars can I visit in two days? After breakfast I ring the *Telegraph*'s New York office, where I am expected (unnecessarily) for a full day's 'briefings', to say that I must spend time on urgent pin-up purchases. OK, but they'll still expect me to lunch. I spend the whole morning at the Museum of Modern Art where I stay on longer than I expected, astounded by an art museum that is as accessible as a department store.

The New York office cannot be avoided. Its editor and his offsider must be 'briefed' on this new enterprise of Frank's: Frank has told them they must help me all they can. They take me to a very courteous lunch, in which I discover that I cannot sit with these intelligent people and confess the details of my fatuous enterprise. Knowing what *Weekend* will be like is a matter of experience, not of talk. If I use words to describe the 'product' itself this will not convey all the rationality that goes into its construction. If I describe the intelligent calculation needed for its construction this will make the product sound much less trivial than it is.

The question doesn't come up. What I am really going through is not a briefing but a 'getting to know each other'. I am an executive. You are an executive. He is an executive. Our 'conference' fills out the afternoon – over lunch, then back at the office, where I seem to become familiar with every desk and filing cabinet and paper clip. There are also hints, slight openings out of executive-level gossip; not about Frank himself, for whom they express absolute loyalty, but about his entourage. I don't know some of the names but I can see that it is by this kind of gossip that we are establishing ourselves as fellow 'executives'.

My hour with the Park Avenue astrologist is spent in an apartment in which precious objects are displayed as if it were a museum-palace – the kind of movie set in which you might meet Bette Davis in one of her classier roles, perhaps with Claude Rains or Adolph Menjou. The astrologist pours Scotch into glasses as large as small buckets and adds a hailstorm of ice and then pours another round before we 'do business'. When we start 'doing business', she inclines towards me a cleavage more generous than any shown in the fifty pin-ups I have purchased.

Next morning, I walk from the Algonquin, where I am staying because of its literary associations (none are now evident) back to the Museum of Modern Art where I intend to spend the day, although the New York office thinks I have a hard day ahead of me bargaining over pin-up supplies. (They offer to take over this responsibility but I explain that buying pin-ups is a specialist business.) The route from the Algonquin to the museum is to be my New York street-walk. It is now officially a heatwave and what I am passing through are stock movie images of urban heat, lacking only the shots of children dancing in water spraying from fire hydrants. I spend all day in the Museum of Modern Art (where else could I learn as much as this?). When at the cafeteria at lunch and in some of the galleries I find myself 'throwing glances at' or perhaps even 'exchanging glances with' solitary women it is as if we are playing that moment when Cary Grant captures the gaze of Katherine Hepburn. I am now too old for a simple boy-meets-girl scene; in the late afternoon in a bar when I meet a friend from student days I haven't seen since 1948 she and I compare notes on the ageing experience: here we are, both of us now in our early thirties and (especially since we drink so much) we are like something out of a John O'Hara novel. She lives in the top apartment of a brownstone house (which is, of course, very New York) and when she stands me at a window from which we look out at New York's dreaming spires and says that normally we would 'make love', but she will be getting married next week this also seems like a movie. A French movie.

On the plane I discover that McNulty has again short-changed me. This is not even an economy flight. It is a special holiday excursion flight, so low down the scale of esteem that when we change planes at Chicago I have to queue to buy a lunchbox since the plane does not serve food. I get my own back at the St Francis Hotel, itself one of the most expensive in San Francisco, by ordering a particularly pricey dinner (beginning, of course, with martinis and ending with Grand Marnier, with three half-bottles of different kinds of French wine in between) although noting, of course, how tasteless all this American food can be.

I have only a morning in which to 'do' San Francisco, but it does not have a lifetime's movie-going and fiction-reading to give it meaning, as New York does, and so far as I know it does not have any great museums, so a morning's tour does not seem as absurdly short as three days in New York. All I have to direct me are disconnected memories of Jack London, Dr Fu Manchu, goldfields ballads, railroad barons and the great earthquake of 1906. Of these, the earthquake is the most real. Not only did I see the Clark Gable/Jeanette MacDonald vehicle *San Francisco* when I was at high school; my mother's Aunty Florrie went to San Francisco after the earthquake, with Uncle Arthur, who hoped to make some money there as a builder; Aunty Florrie told us many stories about San Francisco, sitting in the breakfast room at Denbigh. I settle for the earthquake and get up early to walk through the reconstructions of Nob Hill and Telegraph Hill, then have as expensive an early lunch as I can extract from the menu of the St Francis Hotel, before embarking on the Pan Am clipper flight to Australia.

What seems the most self-willed level of existence, whether in airport or in air, by night or by day, is working out the formula for *Weekend*. I work over it until I run out of layout sheets, but there does not seem any way in which all these little bits of rubbish ('light, amusing material') can be spread over thirty-two pages without revealing their own trashiness. *Weekend* may be a series of sideshows but there must be some limit to the length of a sideshow alley, otherwise the sameness of what is offered will mean that the public won't walk to the end of the alley. When he spoke about thirty-two pages Packer did not seem to have given the figure any particular attention, and he doesn't seem yet to have any particular selling price in mind. (Is this the way gamblers go on?) I make an entrepreneurial decision, based on reason: *Weekend* must not be more than twenty-four pages. As soon as we get to Sydney, I'll ring up Packer and tell him. Twenty-four pages makes a saleable package, I'll say. It gives some sense of variety and therefore value.

By the time my first entrepreneurial decision is made it is mid-morning on our second day and we are well on our way to Nadi, Fiji. But during the night I have made an even more important entrepreneurial decision (or is this simply mere gambling?): we must sell half a million copies. That will be the measure of success. There is no rational reason for choosing this figure – its value comes from the emotional appeal of the phrase 'half a million', a larger-sounding sum than 'five hundred thousand' but also because of the casualness of 'half', something within reach. 'Half a million' will remain with me as a prompting to action and a reminder of failure for nearly nine years.

With the big decisions made – twenty-four pages, half a million – the journey takes on a morally discomforting level of existence. There is on the flight a fellow I knew as a student, now in a university job as an 'educationalist'. He has been in the States 'doing research'. While I was making the big decisions about *Weekend* I had to put off talking with him. But now we can talk. One part of the conversation is comforting: I can reassure myself of my own probity by inwardly scorning 'educationalism' as one of the more virulent forms of progressivism, and, for that matter, dismiss academic careerism as one of the most pernicious ways of selling out. But how silly I feel when he asks me what I am now 'doing'. I can't answer him honestly, of course. Security is far too tight for that. *But, my God, what am I up to?*

3

There is a passage in the 'Overture' to *Swann's Way* in which Proust recalls how, when they heard from the far end of the garden the timid peal of the visitors' bell, they would say: 'A visitor? Who in the world can it be?' For me, the equivalent memory was the click of the gate in the lattice that divided the front garden at Denbigh from the back. At Combray, they led such a restricted life that they always knew it would be Charles Swann. At Denbigh we lived such a public life that it could have been a selection from thirty or so aunts, uncles, cousins, great-aunts, great-uncles, or second cousins once removed, who had just opened the lattice gate.

In England, in my dreams, I still went back to Denbigh. Now I am back. My father seems as cheerful as I remember him to have been, idealised as in a snapshot, before his 'nervous breakdown' but also, even tonight, constrained as if he knows this won't last. My mother is happy without any equivocation (Donald, you look *so well*), trilling comments on everything I say. Janet is excited (a brother back from 'overseas'!) but, more significantly, now a woman of eighteen. In Nanna I still find comforts of earthiness and common sense. She now seems someone who no longer needs to know anything new. But it is the house itself I must also welcome. They understand this. We all share the Denbigh cult. As I walk from room to room I am walking through our past, and paying respect to it. All of the dozens of family photographs are still in the same places on the walls, as if to confirm that any kind of life considered to be worth living ended somewhere between fifteen and twenty years ago. The table is still in the kitchen where, on Sunday morning, we would have tea and hot scones to get ourselves ready for the task of eating the Sunday roast. My grandmother's bedroom is still a museum of how things were in those days – framed photos of boys in uniform, paintings of birds, lace hangings, a fan, a bottle of smelling salts. I walk out into the garden and stop at the lattice gate. I open and shut the gate to hear the click that used to tell us that some of our family had decided to 'drop into Denbigh' and have a cup of tea and a chat.

Back in the drawing room, we are seated around the coke fire. On the mantelshelf is the clock whose chimes I would hear when I was lying in bed (although not as clearly as the chimes from the clock in the church steeple at Muswellbrook: they told the whole town the time). I do the inventory: vases and bowls are where they always have been; the radio is in its corner; the chairs and sofa have been re-upholstered; the gramophone has gone; the cut-glass vase is on top of the pianola.

My father is the first to go to bed. He has reported on his form in the lawn bowls he plays twice a week, and on the basketwork he practises on the other days in a converted stable in the back garden. Nanna is the next to go: she has reported at some length on her successes at the housie-housie games she and Aunty Florrie go to three or four times a week and she has given me the run-down on what has happened to some of the more distant family relations (always one of her specialities). She has even provoked me to speak openly and naturally, with anecdotal material, of something from my own experience – my life with hens, gardens, pigs, and (if in a restricted version) dowagers. Nanna has the knack of keeping what we talk about to subjects and styles familiar to her. Janet goes, after providing anecdotes about life at the Teachers' College. (This is something nearer to what I want to talk about. Perhaps, later, I might be able to talk to Janet about Picasso?)

I am alone with my mother. We are allowing the coke fire to die down We are unable to use directly any language of love and openness, but we do so indirectly, through reminiscence, so that in the repetition of anecdotes we provide symbols of what might have been open speech. Then she talks about her life as a clerk in a government department – she took up working for money while I was away and it has now become the normal part of her existence: Nanna's old-age pension and Dad's pensions as ex-soldier and ex-teacher are not enough to keep the household going. But, my word, it's hard going, Donald, to have to come home from work and then cook the tea, although Nanna does the vegetables. There's one thing, though: Dad and Nanna get on so well! They always have their early-morning cup of tea in the kitchen and have a talk before the hens are fed.

She is down to whispers: Dad is very tense. He is no better at all, really. Still, there's no point worrying. And he does seem to enjoy the bowls. So that's a good thing. There's this, though. (She didn't want to write to me about it in letters in case it worried me.) He has a 'heart condition', *angina pectoris*. Still, the doctor says he might live for years. By now the fire is almost out.

I sleep in the room that was Uncle Loy's bedroom after the Great War, and then became a dining room that was not used. I slept on a couch here the night before my grandfather's funeral, when his sons and my father kept vigil over his body, drinking cups of tea and sometimes talking. When my parents and Janet came to Denbigh during the Japanese war the room was rigged up for me, as a place to come to when I was on leave, and it has stayed like that. The desk reminds me of high school days; it is as if I could sit down again at the desk, finish my French prose and then solve a problem in trigonometry.

4

As I drive in a taxi to the city through some of the older suburbs and then pass what seem half-derelict small factories, Sydney seems shabbily unambitious. (Six months and I'll be out of it.) I have explained to my mother that she won't see much of me for the next few weeks: I will be working night and day. I'll have to stay in town. (How can I get ready for something as outlandish as the launching of *Weekend* in a household where people sit in the kitchen drinking early-morning tea before they feed the hens?)

Someone from the office was supposed to have met me at the airport to tell me what arrangements have been made: the sight of my suitcases should stir things up. But as I load them into a lift in the *Telegraph* building all that the sight of them seems to stir up is a polite 'Have you been away, Mr Horne?' from the lift driver; and when I line them along a corridor of one of the suites of executive offices, I am at first asked to take them away. No arrangements have been made. Well then, ring Packer for instructions. If they won't, I will. No need, the Boss's call from London will come through later. Well then, I'll talk to the Boss. There is some disquiet: it is obvious that no one considers me initiated into the mysteries of a call from the Boss.

With nothing to do, I wander up to the feature writer's section, now made up of two partitioned cubbyholes and an overcrowded open space on the fifth floor. After we engage in attempts at old familiarities I drop false hints about starting a weekly intellectual magazine. These fabrications are pleasant to tell (how wonderful if they were true) but I can see that they are already arousing ambitions among some of these former colleagues.

WHEN AS A DIPLOMATIC CADET I HAD READ DENIS BROGAN'S *The American Political System*, I recognised as a revelation the section where he developed his statement that a president ruled through his 'court'. Packer is a baron: I will now understand lordly leadership. As soon as I use the phrase 'the Boss' I feel part of Packer's court. To adopt such an expression of shared abjectness is to have sworn an oath of fealty. To working journalists Packer is 'Packer'. To us executives he is 'the Boss'.

David McNicoll, the Boss's Editor-in-Chief, has invited me to lunch with Tony Inglis, who has been made an executive, it is said, because of a connection with a friend of the Boss's wife. Both McNicoll and Inglis are silver-haired and gentlemanly. McNicoll has the smooth amiability of a 'sophisticated American' – Dean Acheson, perhaps – while Inglis professes some of the gruffness of an Australian gentleman. It is a courtiers' meal – amusing, anecdotal and allusive, with perhaps (I am not sure) gentle digs at some of the less gentlemanly of the Boss's courtiers – but much of the talk is about racing, stock exchange gambling and what is left of Sydney's night-club set. Perhaps I will find no friends in Packer's court? Nothing I can talk about?

It is not till much later that I am told the Boss's call from London has come through. The telephone through which his judgments are announced rests on the huge desk in his office (which is to say his throne room), with the result that even when he is in New York or London his presence still seems to dominate this room. He tells me he has been kicking a few backsides; I'm to stay at the Australia Hotel; he'll be in Sydney in a few days and then he will kick a few more bums. I tell him I think we should make it twenty-four pages not thirty-two. Do that, he says. Twenty-four pages. And we'll charge threepence.

STAYING AT THE AUSTRALIA HOTEL IS A TURN-UP. IT IS JUST DOWN the street from the *Telegraph* building and, despite its degradation during 'the American invasion', it is still seen by most (or it was when I left four and a half years ago) as Sydney's top hotel. The Boss keeps a suite at the Australia (one of several maintained in different parts of the city, I learn later – primarily for visitors, but for those who keep in with Tony Inglis, one of whose functions is supervision of *Telegraph* flats and suites; it is also useful for liaisons). I am put into a single room: the suite will go to the editor of the *Weekly Mail* when he comes out to help with production. 'I want you to be close to the office so that you can get on with the job,' Packer had said on the phone. (Although I have begun calling him 'the Boss', out loud, as a gesture of freedom I will go on thinking of him as 'Packer'.)

There is not much job to get on with. Someone has hired office space for *Weekend* in another building and McNicoll expects to hire a reporter in a day or two: other than this, no one has done anything. The early indications are (we are to have a big conference tomorrow) that the facilities are 'simply not there to do the job'. The 'office space' is a single room with a long table and a few chairs, four blocks away, and with only one phone. I unpack the treasures from my suitcase and lay them out in categories on the long table, then go back to the Australia, ring room service, order a dozen oysters and a half-bottle of champagne and get on the phone to invite an old friend to dinner.

In presiding over our conference the next day, McNicoll seems the only person prepared to begin with the working hypothesis that bringing out *Weekend* might be possible. I am told the composing room can't provide the irregular typesettings necessary for the messiness of *Weekend*'s layouts, a style of layout which, in any case, they say, went out years ago. No one can comprehend that this kind of messiness is essential in maintaining *Weekend*'s fairground appeal but it wouldn't matter if they did understand: these are the men who know about the machines and they say that what I want is not possible. The same goes for the kinds of headings I want to use: neither the art department nor the process engravers will be able to handle so many headings and anyway headings like that are old fashioned. The way out is simple. I will have to make *Weekend* more like other papers. So far as office space is concerned, another no. There is definitely no space in the *Telegraph* building. I will have to make do with the room with the long table. And so far as anything else is concerned: also no.

Is the conqueror of nettles, maximiser of profits in pigs and purger of corrupt Conservative Party branches going to be thwarted? For the moment – yes: wait till Packer comes back. There is, however, one debating point I can score: when a schedule is produced that shows the absolute necessity for a four-week production period I say that if this is so, then we should have started production a week ago. Not that this smart-aleckry gets me anywhere. All the more reason (I can imagine them saying) for dropping the whole thing. There are suggestions that when the Boss gets back to Sydney he will see at once that none of this can be done and drop the whole thing. The Boss is like that.

Each morning I go down to the long, lonely room and sort out the pictures, jokes, tearsheets and drawn headings brought in my suitcase or airmailed out. I want to have basic material for the first four issues arranged in page folders. Here you are (I'll be able to say to the chief sub-editor when I have one), here's page seventeen, the beauty page and page nineteen, the short-story page. These are the folders. I even get some of the copy ready for the printer. Here you are (I'll say to the chief sub), pages ten and eleven, SHOW BUZZ. I've already marked some of it up. When McNicoll hires a reporter – the rest of the staff will not assemble until the day we start production – I assign him to write a series of articles on bushrangers. That will give us Australian content.

In the afternoons I go on reconnaissance expeditions. First to the agencies who syndicate pictures and features, to see what they have, and then into enemy territory, the composing room itself. It is clear there is no mechanical reason why we shouldn't maintain messy layouts with irregular settings: it will cost a bit more, but that's my business. They don't want to do this because that's not what they're used to. Armed with this intelligence, with the confidence of one who has already brought enlightenment to an English village, I take on the composing room. Its overseer looks as if he'll have a stroke, but I win the argument. This is done partly through sheer vigour but more particularly through generous mentions of what is wanted by 'the Boss' (who, of course, has no views at all on irregular settings). But what good has winning an argument done me? They still won't give way on the schedule. Well, wait till the Boss is back in Sydney (I say). You won't last five minutes.

Nor do they. As soon as Packer gets back, this big man sits behind his big desk, puts me in a brown leather chair and says 'Watch this!' He speaks to each of them himself, in turn, on the special office intercom that wires him into his executives ('Ah, Les just come up here for a minute'), tilting his head appraisingly towards the microphone, and swivelling his eyes towards me to make sure I am enjoying it. He calls them in one by one and puts on his show. In this splendid performance, as Packer tells each of them to do what I have asked for, he is thoroughly confident and competent. Some are charmed into it by a few jokes. Others are outwitted by Packer's knowledge. When they suggest a mechanical difficulty he seems to have an empathy with all the machinery he has stored in this building and speaks of it as if it is part of him; he knows what it can be forced to do. If need be, he frightens them by suggesting a solution so outlandish that, to put off disaster, they think of something better. When it all seems to be over I wonder how I can survive such a victory. They'll all have it in for me now.

Well then, who do I want as assistant editor, someone who can take over when I leave? He pulls a face at the name I suggest. 'You can have him, but he's no good. Anyone else?' I name a 'top reporter'. 'He's yours.' What else? Well, the accommodation. I begin by suggesting there might be some difficulties in producing *Weekend* four blocks away from the office, in one room, with all of us sitting around one table, and with only one telephone. I see him frowning. He is ready to spring. (I have mucked this up: it is now my turn to be gulled into doing the impossible.) But he hasn't listened to the last part of what I said. What has inflamed his imagination is that I seem to be trying to produce *Weekend* four blocks away, outside his control. 'You've got to do it under this roof, where I can keep an eye on you,' he says. And then, into his intercom: 'Ah, just come down and see me for a minute.' And then: 'What's all this about no office space?' As in one of those scenes in a film when someone, in one move, finishes off a game of draughts, it is all settled. He closes down a profitless activity and moves two small departments around. My old friends, the features staff are turned out of their cubbyholes. When our production week begins, *Weekend* will take that space over.

THE *WEEKLY MAIL* EDITOR ARRIVES SEVERAL DAYS BEFORE production week, and amongst other things we 'do a few pages ourselves', with layouts and marked copy all put into folders so that they can go straight down to the composing room at eight thirty on the morning of the first production day. As troubleshooter, he will solve the emotional problems of sub-editors suffering from shock at our bizarre layout styles, irregular settings, hyped-up paragraphs and ridiculously worded headings; above all, if, down in the composing room they say something can't be done, he will show them how to do it. He is to give me full protection from the enemy within.

Starting day is as disordered as I have hoped for. The staff McNicoll has hired have been told to arrive at seven thirty, for what until then, is their mystery assignment. Apart from the reporter who has been doing undercover work on bushrangers, I meet them for the first time. There are eight – twice the number Packer had wanted, four less than I had asked for. (He has warned me that when things settle down he may sack some of them.) They have arrived before the furniture, so that towards the end of my inspiring speech to this hastily shanghaied crew, exhortations about our great adventure are interrupted by men carrying in the desks and cupboards and chairs. Despite this anti-climax, we are now at sea. The time has come to open the sealed orders. Now these people thrown together on this mysterious voyage can learn the meaning of their strange mission. (Other metaphors are assembled but this one seems the most satisfying.)

The whole week is like a rough surf in which I must keep my head. I am explaining to a reporter the mysteries of *Weekend* style when someone from the business office arrives and provides a lecture on the functions of Editorial Purchase Orders, Contributors' Claims, Office Stationery Requisition Orders, Staff Appointment Forms, Staff Recommendation for Promotion Forms, Staff Termination Forms, Car Vouchers, Petty Cash Vouchers, Staff Expenses Claims, Process Engraving Orders. He warns me that all of these have to be counter-signed and that there can be weeks when Packer may call for them and draw a line through them all, with NO scribbled at the bottom followed by a big *FP*.

Then I hear that a sales promotion conference has been called for *Weekend*. Perhaps I will leave it to the sales promotion manager? Not likely! Who does he think he is? I'm not going to leave anything to anybody. We argue over whether it will be in his office or mine, an argument he wins because my office is so small. (In fact my secretary has already given notice.) Packer has ordered £5,000 on sales promotion for each of the first two weeks, then £3,000 for each of the next two weeks: after that he will decide whether *Weekend* is worth promoting. The stakes are on the table.

I find it easier to explain the meaning of *Weekend* to perceptive people from an advertising agency than it has been to explain its mysteries to puzzled (and perhaps already somewhat rebellious?) writers and sub-editors. For the first two weeks (we decide) the main sales pitch will be WEEKEND – AUSTRALIA'S BRIGHTEST NEWSPAPER, with the selling features subsidiary to this message but giving it credibility. In the next two weeks the order will be reversed: selling features first, general image subsidiary, but adding a necessary background of emotional warmth. We will take newspaper ads and radio commercials – all over Australia. The map of Australia appears in my head no longer as the schoolroom chart, emphasising my insignificance, but like a map spread out at a campaign headquarters as we plan an invasion.

Well, I enjoyed that. Now back to the reporter to whom I am explaining the mysteries of *Weekend* style.

Each day at lunchtime the visiting editor and I get away from the roar of confusion by strolling down to the Australia Hotel and then enjoying a large, and to some extent leisurely, lunch in the dining room, with all the other businessmen. This is one way of reminding ourselves that we are executives and that executives must take time off so that they can stay on top. Each evening we remain in the office after the others have left so that we can finish any talking that still has to be done about the day's fiascos. Then we go back to being gentlemen. We return to our hotel rooms to do whatever it is one does in hotel rooms: in my case, I enjoy the luxury of ordering a half-bottle of champagne and drink some of it while I am in the bath. We meet for pre-dinner drinks, then treat ourselves to a long, relaxed dinner. No talk about the production of *Weekend*, although in our general philosophising about the human condition we can gossip about courtiers we have met in Packer's entourage and speculate about the 'character' of the newly arrived *Weekend* staff.

His particular interest is in philosophising about the executive condition. He describes executive life in his own organisation: already two younger men have been promoted to higher positions, bringing up the question, has he peaked already? If so, well then he must bear it. To him one of the least satisfying features of the executive condition is that it allows this (sweep of the hand at businessmen like ourselves enjoying expense-account meals), but what he would prefer would be free refrigerators and free washing machines. It is in the pleasures of home life (and the consolations of his religion – he is a Catholic) that he finds the principal satisfactions in existence. We get to the office at eight o'clock each morning to show that as well as being executives we are working editors.

On Wednesday I overrule one of his decisions.

He recognises that I am the boss.

It is all right for him to be concerned with what is happening hour by hour, but I have to look ahead week by week. By the middle of the week I am briefing writers on the second issue. By the end of the week the subs will have to get down some early pages for the second issue. No trouble about that. The folders with copy in them are already here in my desk. On Friday we will be having the cover conference for the third issue. By the time that issue is on the streets he will be back in London. I am here to stay – for six months. After that the 'top reporter' will take over. Packer was right: the man I chose as assistant editor is no good. Too old. Next week he can go back to where he came from (which seems to be what he wants) and I'll promote the 'top reporter' to assistant editor, with the glittering prize that in six months he can be an executive.

Despite all my planning, the production people are letting us down. I have drawn up a production schedule. Along the top are the page numbers, linked in twos, corresponding to the formes in which pages go to press – pages one and twenty-four; pages two and twenty-three, and so on. Along the side are:

Copy to subs
Copy to artists
Copy to comps
Art copy to engravers
Layouts to comps
First proof
Final proof

By Friday afternoon there are only two sets of pages with ticks against 'Final proof' – and we go to press on Monday with no work over the weekend! Packer agrees to bring in a special composing-room crew for Sunday afternoon.

IF KUTUZOV, IN *WAR AND PEACE*, COULD SET AN EXAMPLE BY dropping off to sleep during the Battle of Borodino, the London editor and I must take Saturday off. (There is nothing we can do anyway: all the machinery is engaged in producing the *Sunday Telegraph*.) I arrange for a hired limousine with liveried chauffeur to take us to some of the famed beauty spots of Sydney and environs, an expedition I enjoy like a child, since it is a reminder of the days when one of our car-owning relations would take us to some of Sydney's 'beautiful views', but although I lecture him on our Australian talent for improvisation, the London editor is obsessed with all the missing pages.

On Sunday morning we get into our sports jackets and play hunt the blocks: there are something like fifty individual blocks from the process engraver still missing. Packer comes in for a while, and enjoys the anxiety. On Monday morning I know it is my task to stay upstairs, sitting in my editor's cubbyhole getting on with the muddle of next week's issue and maintaining calm but towards the end I go down to the composing room. Some of the formes are already lined up to go. Then off they move, one by one, like ships from a harbour. I stand by a printer's stone and help with one of the last pages. When they have all gone we organise a faint cheer.

Over a celebratory drink Packer says yes, when things are going well, you can have your intellectual weekly.

TEN

Our one great enterprise

1

On the day after the first *Weekend* was published, Packer arranged for stacks of it to be placed in the lifts of the Australia Hotel. In a liftful of people there confronted me a cover girl stretching diagonally across the page, with three headings disposed around her body:

I MARRIED THE
WORLD'S
STRONGEST WOMAN

and

THE FACE
OF YOUR
IDEAL
MATE

and (to show we were really Australian)

BUSHRANGER CUT OFF THEIR HEADS

No one in the lift knew I was responsible for this rubbish. Nor would I want them to know. I preferred to see editing *Weekend* as a private exercise, an 'experience', gaining me wisdom. If I weren't producing it, wouldn't someone else be doing so? (Not, of course, so successfully!)

If someone had turned on me in the lift and said, 'How can you produce this rubbish?' I would have had a number of answers ready. The short answers were: 'It's just like a B grade movie' and 'Don't you think I wouldn't be happier in Polperro writing novels?' or 'Look at the afternoon papers: aren't they simply comics pretending to be news?' Then there was a more abusive answer: 'Wasn't a large part of our society intent on producing worthless absurdities? Where would you find serious intellectual journalism in Australia anyway?' I was already developing the line that at least *Weekend*'s vulgarity spoke with the vigour of the ordinary people. But my particular concern remained that, as an 'experience', editing *Weekend* would teach me all I need know about action.

But how could I both edit *Weekend* and remain my 'self'? I had an answer: I would be here for only six months. And on that very day when I had imagined what was in the minds of those strangers in the lift, hadn't I twice heard the pounding of the press that printed *Weekend* and hadn't the circulation manager confirmed that *Weekend* was selling out in Sydney and Melbourne and they were reprinting?

This euphoria lasted for slightly more than two months. I had a strong wind behind me – every Friday I would receive a memo on the sales figures and they stayed comfortably steady, at the rate of 420,000 to 430,000 a week, enough to blow me confidently through to the next week: these flimsy carbon copies of the circulation reports that went to Packer at the end of each week could excuse almost everything.

2

After the first two weeks of disorder it was obvious that producing *Weekend* from my cubbyhole had the privacy of a dugout in a trench during the Great War. When I complained to Packer, he came up to the fifth floor, walking into every room 'Who are you? What do you do? Why do you need all this space?' and then, on the spot, like a commander in the front line redisposing his troops, he rearranged the office space so that the *Weekend* staff had more room and I was given an office appropriate to an executive, with a red carpet and a view of Hyde Park. I at once told the sales promotion manager that, in future, conferences with the advertising agency would be held in my office not his. Before the first conference I could not resist rearranging things on my desk so that it could seem appropriate to an occasion so advanced in style as a sales promotion conference.

Now there were available all the rewards that came from sitting behind an executive desk. One of these was that the office intercom extended into my new executive-style office and for a while, in this time of rumour and excitement, Packer would ring me with ideas (most of which, to me, showed childlike misunderstanding of the uniqueness of *Weekend*) or he would ask me to come and see him, perhaps to look at some feature he had just bought for me (that I didn't necessarily want). Whenever I heard his voice on the intercom (usually a little hoarse) I was likely to fear he had caught me out in something, and when I was summoned down there was a spectacle of the vast desk, and his own bulk: if I looked at his fist, which he would sometimes shut, I could see it as a club that could knock my brains out: even his teeth, which were rather small, seemed sharp enough for a nasty bite. But all this imagined violence was merely potential. He was treating me as if we were in this great adventure together – although perhaps with the understanding that there was nothing else we had in common.

The most gratifying moments behind my desk came from the enormous satisfaction of taking papers from the IN basket, 'dealing with them' and then throwing them into the OUT basket. All the paper that went from one tray to the other! – layouts to knock back; copy to rewrite; artwork to deride; page proofs to slash at; forms to initial; memos to check – but also there was the weekly reward of ticking away at columns in a production schedule until there were no more spaces to tick. There were also the grand theatrical spectacles of ideas conferences, cover conferences, layout conferences and general staff conferences when it seemed essential that I should put on a turn – funny, threatening, subtle, coarse: whatever seemed necessary to keep our show on the road. On one occasion I tore up some copy and threw it out the window: that would give them something to remember.

This was done with calculation. But there could also be the embarrassments of rage. Doing unpleasant things sometimes necessitated working up an emotional charge, just to get something done. I began to accustom myself to fits of anger, as an efficiency device. But I also learned how to simulate it so that although I remained the savage guardian of the *Weekend* style I could do this without wearing myself out. There was, of course, also praise, usually proclaimed publicly at conferences, but seeming even more effective if I hurried out of my office and bestowed it on the spot 'That's exactly the kind of thing we want. More like that, and we'll hit the half-million.'

These devices were intended to work on the common assumption that we were all bonded together in this one great enterprise. We could be cynical about it and make jokes about the silly headings and our other enormities – that could give moral release. The only belief that was required was that by combining our energies and our intelligence we could produce the right sales figures. (But what about those who didn't share this great objective? I was aware of one or two of them grumbling and spreading dissatisfaction. As soon as I could manage it, I would have to let them go.)

NOW I WAS LOSING THAT SENSE OF A NATIONAL EMERGENCY THAT had marked the opening production of *Weekend*. Copy was being set in advance and galley proofs of advance copy would hang in the subs' room on spikes, where they seemed as comforting a symbol of good husbandry as smoked hams in a peasant's kitchen. New and even more rational production schedules were devised. A new system of IN and OUT trays was organised near the subs' desks. I was even finding a bit of time to wander around. The *Telegraph* building seemed as thick with character interest as my own extended family had become when, as a schoolboy, I had first discovered the idea of 'the Dickensian'. A stroll around the building produced much more gossip than a week in an English village, because these were people I was engaged with, producing character in action – the chief of the art department, as sharp-witted as a 1930s barber; the composing room overseer, seeming on the edge of nervous breakdown but with enough cunning never to cross it; the head of the machine room, cheerily ready to give whatever it might be a go; the production manager, keeping an engineer's eye out for 'the practical difficulties'; the business manager, with glasses that glinted like coins; the circulation editor in his bow tie, done up like all old-style picture show man. I had plenty of company.

THE KIND OF EXCITEMENT THAT SUSTAINED ME DURING THE DAY burst out in other, and more conventional forms, at night. With bottles of champagne in their ice buckets and even caviar and *paté de foie gras* being trundled to my door, life continued full tilt in my room at the Australia Hotel, but now my main way of spending money (and in this case mine, not Packer's) was in dining out as part of an *affaire* that was as demanding by night as *Weekend* was demanding by day. (My marriage with Ethel had fallen apart in an unexpected exchange of letters that seemed to blow everything up: I was now in a state of revulsion against every meaning conveyed by the phrase 'the village'.) It was like Nairobi all over again, in that there were martinis at the bar and Grand Marniers with the Turkish coffee. Instead of 'La Ronde', the hit tune now seemed to be something that had as its refrain 'Let me go, let me go, let me go, lover'. (Love was much in my mind.) Sometimes I would not be back at the Australia until dawn.

I could now talk about all this – love, dawn, circulation figures, the Boss – in long dissertations with Peter Hastings, who seemed to find an excitment of his own in the detail. Hastings had joined our 'team' after Packer started the *Junior Telegraph*, having enjoyed his gamble on *Weekend* so much that he tried to repeat this pleasure a month later by taking another idea from Fleet Street, this time based on material bought from the *Junior Mirror* in London. He rang me from Melbourne. Did I want the *Junior Telegraph*? Yes, why not. As well as posters saying I MARRIED THE WORLD'S STRONGEST WOMAN we now had up on the wall posters saying WHAT'S HAPPENED TO OUR POCKET MONEY?

Hastings was back from New York with nothing in particular organised for him: why not make him editor of the *Junior Telegraph*, with me presiding over its fortunes in some Tolstoyan sense, seeming to be responsible for what was, in any case, going to happen? Now I could have a real companion for lunch: we would go off together and make enormous jokes that helped us accommodate ourselves to what we were doing and make some sense out of it. There was no point in having 'an experience' if there was no chance of talking about it. But how could long lunches and nightly celebrations survive if *Weekend* was merely coasting along on 420,000 sales? If we were to make the half-million, we needed another big effort before Christmas. Packer had cut weekly promotion down to £400; I needed some demonstration that it would be worth putting extra chips on the table. For this purpose the November 6 issue would do the trick. I had assembled three splendid cover headings – HOW MURDER CHANGED MY LIFE; MY BEAUTY SECRETS: BY ELIZABETH TAYLOR; LET'S PEP UP THE TESTS: BY SID BARNES – and Packer had responded by agreeing on £1,000 for promoting that issue. If I got results I could ask for a whole new promotion campaign.

While the November issue was printing, a national dock strike began and, with only enough newsprint for his whole firm to last him a week, Packer cut the *Weekend* print run and cancelled the sales promotion. The next week *Weekend* was off the streets. The following week there was an emergency issue of only sixteen pages. We approached Christmas with sales running at only 360,000.

I gave the memo I wrote to Packer a catchy heading:

WEEKEND – MORE QUALITY, FEWER PAGES, MORE PROFIT
Not much was lost from *Weekend* when during the strike we cut it down to 16 pages.

Why don't we improve it by running it at 20 pages not 24, when we are back to normal?

This could produce a greater *appearance* of value – which is all that counts – without producing any sense of loss. And it will save £800 to £900 a week. If you could possibly let me have a decision this morning I could go ahead.

The memo came back from Packer with a pencil scrawl:
Yes go ahead – *FP*

No sales were lost, but there was no answer when I sent Packer a memo reporting this success, and nothing more than another scrawled GO AHEAD on a memo in which I suggested that the *Junior Telegraph* would also be improved by reducing its number of pages. Was I, for some reason, out of favour? Hastings had several years more experience than I of gossiping about the moods of Frank Packer and over our lunches he built up a theory that I had been stabbed in the back by one of the Boss's court. Why didn't the intercom ring any more? Who was the knife man? When would I again be called downstairs? The answer came when Packer called me down to say 'the party is over' and that *Weekend* was to be just a normal part of the firm's operations: the staff was too large and my salary was disproportionate. On the question of the staff, I won the battle. On the question of my salary I said if my salary were to be cut I would go back to London.

He said he would think about it.

(*Go back to London!* What would I do in London with a failed marriage and no job? Work on the *Weekly Mail?*)

The bluff came off, but in a state of delayed shock I now became so enraged that I sent a memo of complaint. Later in the morning I saw Packer in the lift. 'I've accepted that,' he said. 'What is "that"?' I asked. 'Your resignation,' he said.

Hastings and I were obviously going to need a very large lunch. 'Go down and apologise,' he said. Packer agreed to see me as soon as I asked, whereas on other occasions one might wait for an audience for days. 'I can see now that the memo might have seemed discourteous,' I said. 'I can assure you it wasn't meant to be. You are someone for whom I have the greatest respect.'

He was affable. I had been man enough to admit my mistake. In any case, he had intended to let me move into an office flat for a while – they had one vacant in Marton Hall. He supposed that since I wasn't resigning I might as well go there.

When the six months were up, things just went on as usual. It was not agreed either that I should go, or that I should stay.

WHAT WAS AGREED WAS THAT THE PRICE OF *WEEKEND* SHOULD go up to fourpence. There was something that promised fun, since Packer had said there was to be no extra promotion money, nor any extra editorial spending. I devised a stratagem that delighted my small court of cynics. We were charging more and offering less, so we must make a Napoleonic move. The price increase should be announced with the heading: HERE'S WONDERFUL NEWS FOR YOU! and I had an artist draw an emotionally appealing penny. (The drawing had to be sent back several times before it had all the warm humanity that was needed.) Beside this imaginatively satisfying coin we then grouped another heading, which said: GET THAT EXTRA PENNY READY! and this was presented with such friendship and open-heartedness that the whole thing could seem like some new and exciting game in which readers could earn a right to *Weekend* if they could find a nice enough penny.

Another success! When the figures came in we found that *Weekend* sold as well at fourpence as it had at threepence. Life was mostly illusion. Boldness was everything. As much in an extension of our lunch-time sense of ironic humour as anything else, Hastings and I decided we would increase the sales of *Junior Telegraph* by increasing its price from fourpence to sixpence. How could I lose? Either this manoeuvre came off – then, good! – or it failed, and I would have more time for *Weekend*. In fact, sales held. But the office faction supporting *Chucklers' Weekly* (another of the Boss's enterprises) moved against us. We proved defenceless against the forces of *Chucklers' Weekly*. The Boss sent a memo ordering the burial of the *Junior Telegraph*. Packer had now engaged in the thrill of a different and enormously more profitable chase: he was applying for a television licence. Hastings and I buried the *Junior Telegraph* quietly one midday and, as colleagues in children's journalism, had our last ironic lunch.

I HAD TO 'PRESS ON, NEVERTHELESS'. (THE CLICHÉS OF SCHOOLBOY adventure stories were never far from my mind.) I fired off other memos, intended to display the toughness of Horne on Resolution Island: *Weekend* must have its own circulation manager, 'even if he is a second-rater'. No answer. Our advertising manager was following a philosophy of defeatism. No answer. Then a memo headed WEEKEND – INCREASE WEEKLY PROFITS BY £500. That would show how ruthless I could be. Expenditure on *Weekend* must be cut down to size, I wrote. (Surely that would attract him.) No answer. I went ahead and cut costs, without any praise from downstairs. At the staff conference at which I presented these decisions, after ten years reading of *The Economist* I was able to point out (as if *Weekend* were Britain) that, 'after all, nobody owes us a living'.

The intercom did not buzz any more. There were no more memos. No more calls downstairs.

Hastings could provide explanations of astonishing subtlety even for events that to simpler minds might seem to require no explanation, but even Hastings could not match my mood of betrayal. We still had occasional lunches now that he had been made Chief of Staff of the *Sunday Telegraph* and at these, when we discussed my 'case', he was inclined to the simple explanation that Packer was preoccupied with television.

But when a memo finally arrived from Packer, it could be given greater significance than that. He told me that *Weekend* should now be given a definite place in the organisation: he had put it under the administration of Tony Inglis, who would maintain particular responsibility for publicity, advertising and circulation. As to me: 'Mr Inglis will supply your needs and fight whatever battles are necessary'. Packer had deserted me. What would be the point of fighting battles if they were to be fought not by me but by Tony Inglis?

3

I was now learning to break from the habit of dropping French phrases into conversation – it had been part of an earlier literary allusiveness which had helped assert what one was meant to be but I would still use these phrases in conversations with myself or even in the letters that I began but did not finish, so that when I was moved into an office flat at Marton Hall, I thought of it as a block of serviced 'apartments' (a word with French connotations) which were favoured as *pieds à terre* by business firms and rich 'country people'. *Pieds à terre* could seem so much more apt than ... what? Was there any equivalent in English? How could there be? This apartment was in the central part of the city, if down a relatively quiet street, so I gave everything about it a 'continental' aura, when I was not favouring it with New York associations. Living in a flat in the centre of a city was not Australian.

Not that I noticed what surrounded me. I would make my own breakfast and then walk to the office, eat out expansively for lunch and dinner (I was getting the flat rent-free, so there was still plenty of money to waste) and spend the nights in what were proving to be the disasters of an *affaire* that was now developing both the tragic intensity of grand opera love, remorse, jealousy and rage and the disarray of bedroom farce when Packer, for reasons of his own, flew Ethel out to Australia where, failing reunion, she set up for a while on her own. Hastings gave long, thoughtful *recitatifs* explaining everything, in turn, if in different ways, to the three principals. It was only some weeks after I had arrived at Marton Hall that I walked around the area at night and, even more grimly, on a Sunday morning and looked at it. What *longueurs* there were to be found in realising the shabbiness of the streets once the people were out of them. All of Sydney seemed second-rate and run-down: I saw myself as an exile from the old world – itself shabby, but with a shabbiness rich in meaning. Australia was mindless, I would say to myself. Where were the art museums and theatres, the intellectual debate? It was true that, apart from my long private relationship with the National Gallery (I talked about this with no one), I had known scarcely anything of intellectual and artistic life in London, and despised most of what I did know. But it was there. In such moods I would still imagine that in due course I would return, even if I now imagined it not as a return to England, but 'to Europe'.

My apartment was made up of a single, long room, with a bathroom and a kitchen that could be disguised as a cupboard. There was a parquet floor in several shades of blonde wood that had once been in good taste; the fittings and surroundings of the two daybeds were also in blonde wood, as were bookshelves, wardrobe and cupboard. The room came together as a shabby monument to the aesthetic aspirations of the late 1930s. Even if I was not already engaged in the disasters of my *affaire*, the loneliness and meanness of this – what shall I say? habitat? – no, *milieu* is the better word! might have driven me into one.

When I spent an evening by myself I could find a mean satisfaction in lying around in this outmoded furniture exhibit and sharing with it a sense of exhaustion. Since I hadn't read anything by him other than *Brighton Rock*, although I had seen some of his movies, I bought all the novels of Graham Greene and when I read them, one after the other, like someone chain-smoking, I knew I was reading them in a situation as 'seedy' as that of a Graham Greene novel.

But what was most disheartening about these novels was a trick I discovered in their composition. At first I admired their simple style, which seemed to grow even more laconic as he wrote more – perhaps he had gained confidence to cut more out. Then I found a distraction in these careful silences. Every few pages he would put in gratuitous reminders of the actual, in asides such as *His son sat at a table out of earshot with a glass of orangeade and a bun* – when the existence of the son or what he did was quite irrelevant to everything else Greene was saying at the time. I knew all about this trick. We would instruct *Weekend* reporters to make copy seem 'real' by putting into an interview, for example, such meaningless asides as 'He coughed' or 'She smoothed out a wrinkle in her dress'. George and Charmian Johnston had wanted to make my second novel seem more real by putting in this type of corroborative evidence. For several weeks after finishing the Greene novels I returned to the ambition that I would write an eccentric Thomas Love Peacock piece, all stereotypically intellectual conversation, no description. (Who would publish that?)

My predicament would reach its most characteristic form when I dined by myself, in the restaurant in the basement of Marton Hall. It was a failed restaurant, most obviously and painfully at night when there was scarcely anyone else, perhaps no one else, in it. As I ate my fried oysters and fried parsley served in a 'basket' of fried potato, followed by *filet mignon*, rare, and then apple strudel and drank a half-bottle of white and a half-bottle of red, the owner was likely to keep on pestering me with much the same inquiries every night about whether I was satisfied with the food and drink. Sometimes he would stand behind my chair, without speaking. I could hear him breathing. By the time I called for a Grand Marnier and a moderately-priced cigar he would again open out on what was for him the only true topic of conversation: how could he save his business from ruin? With cigar waving from one hand and a fountain pen making notes with the other, I would enter into a 'conference'. We planned brochures, to be distributed in all the Marton Hall apartments; then we spoke of organising 'good PR' in the Sunday newspapers; we contemplated various changes in food style; I improvised a redesign of the layout of the menu card; we imagined how we would redecorate the restaurant. None of these proposals actually was put into practice. I had become a character in a Graham Greene novel.

THE PREFERRED THEME FOR MY THIRD NOVEL (*IT WAS 1955! I WAS thirty-three and I had not yet published a novel!*) was not of Peacockian characters making conversations that no one would want to read, but of the sad fate, borne stoically, of some person of gentlemanly disposition who was being done in steadily, chapter after chapter, in a continuing decay, by the kinds of spiv who now seemed to run the place. Usually they were merely crass money-making upstarts, but, as well as being one of nature's gentlemen in an ungentlemanly age, my hero was also a 'true intellectual' among the false intellectuals of our time. I had no belief that there ever had been a gentlemanly age, but I did feel that once there might have been true intellectuals, although I was not sure when – in the eighteenth century, perhaps, or perhaps briefly in our own circle in the early 1940s, at Sydney University. Now and again, if I met a survivor from that time (which I did rarely) we might spend most of our conversation regretting the intellectual sell-outs that surrounded us – sell-outs to literary gushing, to progressivist illusions, to academic careerism.

In this mood of despair about the inadequacies of the age, I turned Tony Inglis into a sympathetic character (although of course, only partly so) in some of the drafts I worked out in my head for my third novel. He was not an intellectual at all, and that was to his credit – better not to be an intellectual than to be an intellectual in quotation marks – and not being an intellectual made him indifferent to what others might see as the meretriciousness of *Weekend*. He agreed with me that if this was what the people wanted, let them have it. Throughout our relationship (our offices were side by side and when he lost his temper I could hear him shouting) he kept up the admirable practice of never showing any interest in the contents of *Weekend*. To him reality was contained in 'the black book'. This was a book, almost as long and as wide as a small desk, into which each week were written estimates of *Weekend*'s weekly costs and estimates of what money came in, set against each other in some detail and then balanced off so that a declaration could be made, as if a judge were handing down a sentence about whether *Weekend* was guilty or innocent. I had no regular right to know the secrets of the black book, but I soon persuaded Tony that I should see it weekly. Without this common rational language of profit and loss, how could we talk to each other?

I was now beginning to give even some members of the staff a certain provisional trust, however sceptically. In particular, I now had relatively stable dealings with my new assistant editor and my new chief sub-editor. At that time, these seemed my only two stable emotional relationships, except perhaps for the excitements of declamatory lunches with Hastings. Tony Inglis, of course, could not really be trusted, and my 'love life' was still as melodramatic as a nineteenth-century Italian opera.

This provisional trust began partly from exhaustion. The replacement of one assistant editor by another in the first production week had been merely recognition of one mistake amongst many – it even took us a couple of issues before we had time to rearrange the desks more efficiently – but when I put in the 'top reporter' as assistant editor it was only a week or so before I knew I had made another mistake – in appointing a 'hard news' reporter of great energy and skill who was trying earnestly to look as if he belonged to our travelling fun fair. It took me some weeks to get around to saying this to him, but once I did get it out, he was up and out of my room like a gentleman. When Hastings and I talked about it later, the main part of our analysis was concerned with whether I would ever accept as an assistant someone who really might be able to succeed me.

There was no doubt that, whatever his talents might be with *Weekend*, Larry Boys, the next assistant editor, would never really be a 'boss'. From the very first issue Larry had seemed to know what to do by producing 'news stories' that could sustain headings such as GIRLS BAR AUSSIES FROM BEAUTY SHOW or SHE'S A BUBBLY GIRL WITH AN ITCHY BACK that must have been true, because there were names and photographs; he even seemed to know how to evoke enough of this kind of mystery to pass some of its secrets on to others. In fact there seemed to be one part of his brain that actually thought in *Weekend* heading styles. I could see him, along with others, as a character in a novel I would never write.

When I offered him the great prize of becoming assistant editor he 'needed a little talking into it'. He was some kind of intellectual but he kept it quiet. He even had some kind of left-wing opinions – I was never to know and certainly didn't care what these or any other of his opinions were – and there were also other compartments of his life that were, apparently, not compatible with being an 'executive'. I was not to learn anything about these, either, apart from the particular significance he seemed to give to getting drunk on Friday nights, but then there were weeks when I seemed to be drunk every night, although not, it was true, with the staff. I only trusted him within limits but I was sure he would always do what was agreed upon. I knew he was a bullshit artist and a talented flatterer, but surely I had earned at least a little flattery; if I was to be flattered, it was better to be flattered by someone who could do it with sensitivity. On the first occasion when he came in to see me, bearing the full responsibility and title of assistant editor, I knew I had made the right choice. For weeks the normal tone of conversation in my room had been that of the shout or the threat. When Larry Boys came in, it was of soft humour.

The new chief sub-editor, Jim Murrant, had been thrown up by a great crisis that had manifested itself in the subs' room at the very time when sales had fallen, and also at a time when as I drifted into sleep (often at dawn) I had begun to see myself being sent back to London by Packer either to starve or to sink into a miserable success in the worst of all of Fleet Street's sideshows. The subs had 'taken me on'. They thought I couldn't do without them. Well, they had a second thing coming. No compromises. They had made the mistake of challenging D.R. Horne, the man who could do anything. If they didn't like the way I was running things then they could all piss off. Who did they fucking well think they were? Jim Murrant and I could produce *Weekend* by ourselves. Jim had just turned twenty-one and even at the age of thirty-three I still had a certain amount of vigour left. After this trial of strength and the quick victory that followed, a new order was established. There were new faces in the subs' room, new ways of doing things. Jim Murrant became what may have been the youngest chief sub-editor in the history of journalism in Australia.

I decided to 'take him up'. He was someone to whom it was worth giving advice. He would be my first Marshal. We did a certain amount of drinking, had some lunches, even a dinner or two, and after he had married I went out, on a couple of drunken nights, to the garage where he and his wife were established in a distant suburb, on a block of land he had bought and on which he was now about to build his own house. With Tony Inglis, after discussing the black book in clipped, ironic phrases, like two experienced staff officers standing over a map in a château during the Great War, there were occasions when we might go to the private bar at Adam's and continue our sceptical conversation over martinis and Scotches; but Tony and I always treated each other with the reserve of characters in a Ford Madox Ford novel. Reserve was maintained equally strongly between Larry Boys and me. There were times when Boys, in his 'handling' of me would descend to such humility that in anyone else it would have seemed a gross insult, but he was able to do this with such diffidence that it left open the possibility that he was, after all, joking. Yet there were no dinners with Boys, only lunches, and as a protection against intimacy we talked *Weekend* all the time. There was the danger, in dealing with Larry, of moving from the control of a character in Ford Madox Ford to the gush of a Dylan Thomas poem. Although I treated both Inglis and Boys with reserve (even if drawing on different literary analogies to do so), I cultivated a kind of reckless openness with Jim Murrant. I didn't conceal myself nor did I conceal what I thought about the staff, although not a word did he ever get out of me about Packer or the 'executives'. This was the magic part of me that must remain a mystery. We played buccaneers, laughing at our own outrages, anecdotalising them into legends and philosophising about life. With audacity anything might be possible.

What was possible in this life comfortingly stripped of false intellectuals was that there were times when I sat by myself so miserably in my new exile in the blonde wood furniture exhibit in Marton Hall and was so convincingly overcome by headaches, sweating, stomach constrictions and other nervous disorders that I decided these were not 'psychosomatic' and that there really was 'something wrong with me organically'. Usually I would brood my way through such an episode until I was rewarded with the solace of mere unhappiness. Until the next time, the incident could be dismissed as a *malaise*: things could seem better by putting it in French, and making it seem a necessary part of the human condition. Twice I was so seized by so many symptoms that I rushed myself off in a taxi to Alf Conlon, now simply a doctor, keeping myself under observation as if I were an accident case in an ambulance. He went through the tests. I was quite fit. 'Anything worrying you?' 'Who, me? Nothing!' On both occasions I was the last patient that night. I stayed and swapped stories about the old days before going back to dine by myself, later than usual, in the basement restaurant, where we might discuss the possibility of putting up a neon sign outside, or introducing table napkins of different colours.

AS THE MONTHS WENT BY, INGLIS, BOYS AND MURRANT WERE part of the new normality that began each morning when I cooked my breakfast at Marton Hall and then walked through shabby streets to the office. My desk routines were standardised by the calendar of regular conferences: almost every hour there seemed to be some kind of conference; and to these predictable movements in and out of my room was added the inexorable movement of papers from IN tray to OUT tray.

The true measurements of existence seemed to come in the weekly arrival of the circulation reports and my weekly inspection of the black book. While I was inspecting the black book no one was allowed to see me. Its principal headings of analysis were to become as important to me as a chart of the nervous system to a neurologist. If anything had gone wrong, it was here. For years afterwards, at any time of diagnosis, I would first write down on my clean sheet of paper the headings NEWSGATHERING, PRODUCTION, PUBLISHING, SALES PROMOTION that added up to the larger heading COSTS and then headings SALES and ADVERTISING that, more modestly, added up to the headings of REVENUE. This was practicality. I wished I could fit my life under similar headings.

But this was only one of the many glosses I could provide on my 'learning from experience'. The *Weekend* staff provided what I saw as a creative confusion in which the only true stability was the predictability of the unpredictable: there was some lecturing to be done on this. I found undergraduate memories of Heraclitus useful: if there was some new shift in the policy or even a new format for production schedules, I was likely to remind a staff conference that all was change and that, as Heraclitus had said, one could not step into the same river twice.

Apart from the weekly inspections of the black book and the arrival at the end of each Friday afternoon of the circulation reports, among my most significant weekly confrontations with reality were 'cover conferences'. As week after week, sales showed no increase, Boys, Murrant and I would go through the same old ponderings. Should we have more girl and smaller headings, or larger headings and less girl? What mattered most: heading? girl? general impression? Was our use of colour over-done? Did splashing colour on the cover attract more attention than large black headlines? What exactly was it that was likely to make more people buy *Weekend* when they went into a newspaper shop? Back at Marton Hall I would sometimes still think of the map of Australia: all those Australians out there – how could we induce more of them to buy *Weekend*? Sometimes, just for a try-out, we would abandon some of the wisdoms I had brought out on my lonely flight across the world. (I had already made a legend out of my founding of *Weekend* in which this act of cultural diffusion was given some of the historical significance of the bringing of the potato to Europe.) Instead, we would revert to contests and other stunts used by more conventional magazines. One of the 'world stars' who came to Australia that year was the singer Johnny Ray, who had a habit of throwing his jackets to fans. By arrangement with his entourage we put a heading on our cover: TEAR A PIECE OFF JOHNNY RAY, and offered readers, at a shilling a slice, sections of what was alleged to be one of his jackets. Seven thousand readers sent in their shillings. Then we launched an Ideal Girl competition, which culminated in a big show at the State Theatre at which I made a speech that included phrases so coy that I continued to be ashamed of them for many years. Our contest season reached its height with an idea of the Boss's (passed on through Tony Inglis) that one of our contest prizes should be a racehorse. We launched this under the headline WIN A £1,000 RACEHORSE and several months later, on the day the winner of the contest first raced her horse I found myself at a midweek race meeting at a suburban racecourse with Tony Inglis and David McNicoll, feeling as if I might look like a passable imitation of an ordinary Australian, if without a hat. None of these stunts put on sales but there could be wisdom even in these failures – for (as I would philosophise as we chose the next cover girl or wrote the next cover heading) what would have happened if we hadn't had them?

I could feel a victim of my own decisions, but never behind my desk. There, there was always something new. Having picked up the phrase 'tonal quality', for several weeks I studied photographic printing and process engraving and then launched a crusade to benefit humanity by improving the tonal quality in *Weekend*. When someone said there were on sale in England sets of lettered headings the use of which would cut down on artists' time, cables went off to London and emergency supplies were flown to Australia: *Weekend* became the centre of a technological revolution. To attract extra advertising, I decided we would have four special pages dropped into the New South Wales print run. (Well, it was worth trying.) With such excitements I did not have to spend all my time with ludicrous headings, ridiculous stories, bizarre photographs and grotesque layouts.

Not that we were ashamed, of course: there could still be pride in considering how clever we were to contrive such stuff and, if this failed, there was honest delight in mischief and sardonic front-line wit. For me there was still also the reward that at least this was not middlebrow intellectualism: it expressed some of the vigour of 'the people'. I was delighted to receive a message from London that over in the *Weekly Mail* they found in *Weekend* 'tremendous Australian vitality'.

BY THE MIDDLE OF THE YEAR I HAD RESUMED SOME KIND OF working contact with 'the Boss'. Despite Inglis's uneasiness (which only ended when he was shifted from *Weekend* altogether) this contact with Packer was to remain, but it was sporadic and it was beyond my control so that, if there was a call from the Boss on the intercom, or a memo, or a summons downstairs, like most of the other 'executives' I got into the habit of assuming that I must take post to protect myself from a new threat. Perhaps he had vetoed all the contributors' claims? Or wanted to kill *Weekend*? Or treble the size? Or sack the staff? Or make me editor of *Chuckler's Weekly*? During the year I read A.J.P. Taylor's *Bismarck* and took a special fancy to the descriptions of how Bismarck so delighted in crises that if affairs were quiet he would create a crisis of his own by not attending to his papers. Packer found crises such an essential part of his metabolism that he could not even trust us to create them for him: in his role as 'the Boss' he developed his great visions at home, or over dinner tables, or in New York or London and then rang us so that we could share them; but to sustain his pleasure he also kept large reserves of potentially excitable material in the stacks of papers that covered most of his grand desk. If life seemed too secure, he could at once, and at random, seize a document from one of these piles, scribble on it and (as he would put it) 'set a cat amongst the pigeons'.

Over the eight more years in which I was to stay with him, the only occasions on which I could again feel at least a temporary *rapprochement* with Packer would come now and again when he saw a part for me, as proven buccaneer, both reckless and careful, in some great new adventure that might amuse him. After he had again set me off into the emergency mode I would prepare dummies in double quick time, construct tables of figures showing estimated costs and revenue at different levels of sales and advertising, and then construct a memo that was buoyant with the hope that we were all young again and anything could happen. The Boss would lick his lips and call for more. Then 'the others' would get at him, with wiser counsel. By the end of the eight years I would feel like an organiser of royal revels for a monarch who adored mock battles as well as real wars.

In the first of these excitements, in the middle of 1955, I was called down to see the Boss – no sign of Inglis – and taken in for a drink, in the kind of extended cupboard used by the Boss as an executives' watering hole. He spoke with the kind of bounce he had used when I had been first inducted as an editor in London, speaking directly, with shared enthusiasm. He had been thinking about *Weekend*. Sales of 375,000 were good for a magazine. But sales *weren't going up*: if we didn't do something, *Weekend* might just wither on the vine. (The fear that the whole show might just wither on the vine seemed to be one of Packer's great promptings to action.) There was a sales base, wasn't there? Well, couldn't we build on it and widen the appeal? Put in an extra eight pages. Put up the price to sixpence. Put in a short story. That would help hold readers. That would make it solid.

Make it more solid! What did he think *Weekend* was? *Weekend* wasn't solid: it was ephemeral! But when I was in his drinking cupboard with his whisky in my hand I simply couldn't say 'You don't understand anything at all about *Weekend*.' I said I would give it thought and write him a memo. Then, for a few minutes (something I had not done with him before) we made conversation. After that, something just as unexpected: 'Donald, you're doing a good job'. I went back to my office tempted by the excitements of something new – and tempted by that praise. I spent several hours perfecting a thoughtful memo, both optimistic and cautious, elaborating on his idea as a practical proposition but also putting up a plan so that it would be postponed until next year. 'Thank you,' he said in his memo reply. 'Yes, I am willing to stand this over until next year. Go ahead and prepare the detailed plan.'

Several months later I was called down to the boardroom, where he was surrounded by his production executives and financial advisers. There were samples of paper on the table, each marked as to quality and cost. No discussion. I had been brought down to get my orders. The Boss said he had some spare printing capacity in his rotogravure plant. *Weekend* was to be printed in rotogravure. I was to prepare some dummies.

I had a whole new style of *Weekend* made up, appropriately modified for rotogravure, and run off as a test on various kinds of cheap paper. They all looked shoddy and deranged even beyond my own planning. These were all sent down to him, with profit and loss estimates, and with a memo from me telling him that *Weekend* would go down the drain with all of them because the paper was no good. Another amiable reply: 'OK, hold it till next year'. I could work something out by then.

BUT IN THE MEANTIME I WENT OFF ON AN INVIGORATING RUN OF my own choosing, not discussed with anyone. I went through the spiritual preparation for this new trial in a state of retreat during a strike in July, that had left *Weekend* bare except for the two secretaries and the junior typist. I came in each day and sat at my desk performing the offices of 'catching up' (not much fun with nobody there) meditating upon our long failure to regain 400,000, let alone half a million, and contemplating one of life's most significant mysteries: here we were keeping *Weekend* so 'clean' that we were removing navels from drawings, yet *Weekend* had the reputation of being sexy. On the third day of this retreat the method of salvation revealed itself. If *Weekend*, although 'clean', already had the reputation of being sexy, then we might as well make it sexy. They had had their chance. In the very first issue of *Weekend*, in welcoming readers as well as promising them AMAZING PICTURES, SPARKLING GOSSIP, SHREWD ADVICE TO THOSE WITH LOVE TROUBLES, WITTY EXPOSURES OF RACKETS IN AUSTRALIAN LIFE, and all the rest of it, I had said:

> There is nothing dreary – or dirty – in *Weekend*. You can read it from cover to cover – and *enjoy* every word.

If they didn't want it 'clean' they would have to have it 'dirty' – but not very sexy, otherwise *Weekend* might be prosecuted or banned. I took out the pin-up photographs I had bought in New York and had kept in a sealed package in a filing cabinet. For the first time, I made what was to become one of the most meticulous weekly decisions of my professional career: how far down, with safety, could one reveal a cover girl's 'cleavage'? There was no question of revealing nipples, or even a suggestion of the aureole of a nipple, or even the impression of a nipple through clothing. Nipples still did not exist. There was 'uplift', and that was still necessary, but 'uplift' was a matter of bulges. The safest 'cleavage' photos were those of breasts artificially pressed together so that they looked like buttocks. I was myself, if anything, put off by big breasts, but it became one of my Friday afternoon exercises, while waiting for circulation figures, to examine the pin-ups that had been left by the syndication agencies that week and make fine judgments about the cracks and bulges, with special concern about which could be used on the inside pages (where one 'could get away with more') and which met the stylised convention of a cover. We would never speak of 'tits' or use any other word that would suggest any kind of levity or even humanity about this part of the body that now seemed to have become so essential to our commercial enterprise.

After three months sales had risen by more than forty thousand.

ELEVEN

Two years in the life of Captain Horne

1

With Larry Boys and Jim Murrant providing week-by-week emotional continuity, I could now see the staff as being permanent enough to arrange a formal farewell when one of them left. Before this, they had arranged their own send-offs – drinking sessions in one of the office pubs had become one of the essential rituals of the now developing anti-Horne cult – but on this occasion I wanted to indicate that there could be people I was not necessarily pleased to see leave. That it was the office boy we said goodbye to showed the others how far they had yet to go.

I could still maintain suspicions and dissatisfactions towards this and then that member of the staff, but when Tony Inglis suggested they deserved a party, things seemed quiet enough to say yes. He and I would pay for it and we would use my flat at Marton Hall. Since it would be a simple six-to-eight Friday night drinks session, there would be no need to worry about the noise: in fact he would arrange for a hire car to call for him at eight – that would make sure the party ended on time. As it turned out, the party did not end until after midnight, when the fire brigade arrived, a useful ending to what became an anecdote illuminating the noise and senselessness of my new condition.

I had decided that martinis should be the only drinks and bought enough bottles of Gordon's gin and Noilly Prat for two or three parties, although as it happened we got through all of that, and the rest of the drink in the flat as well. I kept a scorecard of my own consumption, until I stopped counting, but it was untrue, as the anti-Horne cult alleged the next week, that there was a specific order as to how many martinis each member of the staff should drink. Phones rang with complaints, there were knocks on the door, and after the hire car driver had been waiting for three hours someone went down and punched him. By then only 'the stayers' remained, including the staff member who at that time seemed to be 'next for the jump': when this malcontent took off his shoes, I saw this as such an impertinence that to remind him who was boss, I threw his shoes out of the window. Jim Murrant went down to the lane behind Marton Hall to get them back, and, while he used the lid of a garbage can as a shield, we pelted him with empty gin and vermouth bottles. I fell asleep in a flat whose floor was heaving like the deck of a ship, awash with spilt martinis. The flames seemed to be shooting right up the wall from the lane when the fire engines came, their sirens screaming, but I went back to sleep: it would need more than a threat of incineration to get me out of bed. It was only on Saturday morning, as one of the many shocks of a return to reality – including threats of eviction and, if I understood what he was saying, from Packer, threats of the sack – that I learned that the departing staff had set light to the large rubbish containers in the lane in an attempt to smoke me out of Marton Hall.

Packer had summoned me to his office, where it took a few minutes to understand that while he was handing down a weighty reprimand he was also enjoying details of this escapade. When he had finished, in a way I had noticed before, there was a hint of a sunny smile. 'Well,' he said 'it seems to have been a good party.' This was Packer the 'playboy'.

Larry Boys was not exactly the playboy, more the wild roisterer, a Friday night bohemian – and part of his party performance came from songs and guitar. He wrote a lament, to commemorate what was now becoming our legendary party, which had as its refrain:

When sirens call
At Marton Hall

The Marton Hall party seemed (at least to me) to have brought us all more together. We were Captain Horne, the gentleman desperado, and his merry crew, working hard, playing hard, as we sought relief from life's desperate dilemmas. I began to drink with the staff – but 'having a drink with the staff' was a favour conferred only intermittently and arbitrarily. Jim Murrant remained my only true drinking companion – just the two of us, jointly admiring our own audacity – although I had also got into the habit of 'sneaking off for a quiet one' with a writer who was becoming the chief purveyor of our outrageous 'news' stories. As masters of the humorously allusive, he and I could say everything about what we were up to without ever being specific. I also began the technique of having a 'quiet drink' with others during the day, not at the end of it (thereby marking a special significance). This would be 'just to talk something over': it was more likely to apply to the women than to the men. Not many of the men had mastered the art of the quiet drink but I trusted the women.

There were no more Marton Halls, although we had all learned the song, but occasionally I might go to a staff party, usually as part of Larry Boys's Friday night experience (for which he would always prepare himself by going home to get his guitar and put on an Hawaiian shirt). In one part of him, Boys would make something instructive out of my being there, drawing attention to the essentially democratic and human qualities of 'the editor'. But another part of him obviously felt invaded, although I was nothing more than, or little more than, one of 'the others' at these functions. I could feel most isolated, and even *old*, at parties at which the new rock 'n' roll music was played. At one of Boys's parties they seemed to play 'Rock Around the Clock', over and over, for most of the party. I knew about rock 'n' roll from reading about it in *Weekend* and later we exploited the sales possibilities of Elvis Presley (improbable as it might seem that someone so unwholesome in conventional terms should be a 'popular idol'). But I did not expect to find that kind of thing in my private life. At parties one should keep in touch with the people by singing the blues or working-class ballads, or by playing jazz.

I seemed to be again a kind of waif – a waif on a good salary, and wearing dark grey suits made in London, living in a serviced apartment in the centre of the city (for which I did not pay rent) and every night dining out expensively, but owning nothing, apart from the books now accumulating on the shelves of blonde wood above the daybeds in Marton Hall. ('My real books are over in England,' I would say, if a guest began looking at the titles.) I was drifting from day to day, held together (if by anything) by a belief that *Weekend*, a publication that, when I thought about it honestly – which was not often – gave me psychosomatic pains, should sell half a million copies.

After my *affaire* had shuddered through the last of its several endings, I had taken up the party habit again, drifting, amongst other things, around the fringes (or was it some future centre?) of people in, or near, 'the theatre' … People I met at one party could lead to another and thus I put myself back to where I had been when I was living at Kings Cross ten years ago, before I had met Ethel, passing from one acquaintance to the next and sometimes not even remembering names. But now I was approaching thirty-five, when all around me were old friends with young children; my Ealing Studio anecdotes about English village life seemed so bizarre that it was better not to tell them, and my belief in nineteenth-century novels could find no expression among people who had never heard of *Sentimental Education*. I couldn't even dress properly: I was likely to turn up anywhere in one of my dark grey suits. When I went down to Melbourne to spend a Christmas with the Deamers – they had two children now – on Boxing Day they took me off to a party where some bohemian left-wing bore, who had trapped me in the kitchen and into an argument in which I revealed my reactionary views, then said that, judging from what I was wearing, I was either an accountant or a dentist.

It was when I bought a Sunbeam electric frypan that I began to relocate myself. The cooker in the kitchen in the Marton Hall flat was not an object around which one could develop a new sense of identity but the electric frypan shone with those images of progress that had illuminated my unhappy adolescence when I went to an Electrical and Radio Exhibition in Sydney Town Hall and contemplated the more optimistic potentialities of the age. That had been twenty years before: since then the potentialities of the age had been expressed in the deaths of tens of millions and my own education had developed in me a scepticism about all progress, but as I contemplated purchasing a Sunbeam electric frypan I returned to some of the very roots of my experience. Perhaps salvation might still come from buying some new object for a kitchen.

In at least this way now in communion with modernity, I developed a small repertoire of electric frypan dishes – most of them French recipes for cooking chicken, converted into the vocabulary of electric frypans – and from this there came a small and fitful aura of domesticity. I was in the habit of going out to Denbigh where, after dinner, my parents and Janet and I would play bridge (when my mother would always serve chocolate gingers and sugared almonds): now I was able to invite them to Marton Hall and cook them a chicken dish in some French style. When the McCallums came back to Sydney with their two young sons they also got their chicken dish cooked in a Sunbeam electric frypan.

The Boss finally expelled me from Marton Hall but although I would now have to pay rent, I felt a sense of deliverance. Now, in at least one way, I would become somewhat more normal. I chose a furnished flat in Kirribilli, just across the Harbour from the central city. Jim Murrant helped me with the move and, once I was unpacked, instead of going straight to the office, we 'cracked a few beers' and sat in a large, sunny sitting room, looking out at the Harbour as we talked. I caught ferries to work; became a recognised customer in some of the food shops; went for walks; 'entertained'.

In Kirribilli there were blocks of flats, large houses turned into separate apartments, and even some terrace houses, so that there was no suggestion that it was merely suburban, and it was given extra texture from being built on a peninsula surrounded on three sides by the Harbour. The McCallums had bought a house a few neighbourhoods away and there was no denying that their house was itself 'suburban', but they still held parties as if it was ten years ago and we were all living at the Cross. And they would introduce me to novelties – playing Tom Lehrer records after lunch, or passages in German from *The Threepenny Opera*. In any case the very suburban qualities of the house gave an extra, if furtive, satisfaction when I began to go there for an old-fashioned roast meat lunch on Sundays, and after lunch, with whomever was the youngest child at the time on my knees, we would resume an old conversation.

As things were going, I might have spent the rest of my life living like this. All that stood against that probability was my naive belief – founded in belief alone – that at some time I would effect my own rescue.

2

Reading books was now returning as an essential part of my bodily activity – in some ways more fully than for years, but no longer with the sure sense of anticipation that life might be reconstructed by reading the next book. With no great novels left unread, I continued to tolerate 'minor novelists', preferably bought, as I had acquired Graham Greene, in batches, although I was ready to read Anthony Powell's *The Music of Time* in single volumes as they came out, with his 'characters' becoming part of my range of acquaintance: in fact, I was 'keeping up' with Anthony Powell characters more fully than with most of my old friends, who had, in effect, dropped out of the series. Joyce Cary's writing was the 'discovery' of one of these organised reading seasons – the two trilogies and then, out of sequence, *Mr Johnson* (whose central character reminded me of one of the views I had of myself – as someone attached to a world belonging to other people and regarded by them, at the best, with bemusement). The trilogies were just what I wanted: in each of them, one man, two women, each presenting entirely convincing views of much the same events, and all three views contradictory. (I found Cary's books were also what I wanted in another way, when I read that he was forty-five when his first novel was published. Time yet.) The next year, on a visit to New Zealand, where Packer had sent me to arrange distribution of *Weekend*, I discovered the first two volumes of a translation of Robert Musil's *The Man Without Qualities* in a bookshop in Wellington and, since I had the flu I spent most of a week in my room in the Hotel Waterloo, alternately sleeping and then drowsily reading about the Vienna of *The Man Without Qualities*. When I got back to Australia, my memories of New Zealand were that it was unknowingly on the brink of the Great War, in the grip of an influenza epidemic, and obsessed with puzzles about the meaning of life and of the Austro-Hungarian Empire.

There was, however, something about the texture of these two volumes and their principal concern – the difficulty of finding if there was anything to believe in – that posed a highly practical question: 'was this the last of the great novels?' I couldn't answer the question. Volume three of *The Man Without Qualities* had not yet been published. But perhaps it was a 'great novel': the first two volumes when I was reading them, fevered, aching and rheumy in a lonely hotel room, had forced on me a melancholy that brought back that characteristic nineteenth-century 'great question' I had first put together at the end of high school: if existence is meaningless, how can it matter what one believes, or what one does? Now a smart-arse, I was likely to put aside such a 'great question' as essentially superficial. If I was inclined to melancholy I was more likely to fall into wonder at the strange form of my failures. But phlegm and headache and sweatiness made me reconsider how easily we construct 'meanings' for existence and can then escape such a 'great question'. As I saw it for a day or two in the Hotel Waterloo, what had happened to me was that I had constructed a 'self' that I now denied every day of my life. Why had I done that? Why not, now, at any cost, walk out of the buffooneries of my well-paid role as hired jester and, in some way, act more like my 'self'?

When I recovered from the flu back in Sydney I abandoned such questionings as adolescent, even 'undergraduate', and returned to practical matters such as sales figures and profit-and-loss estimates, in my reading time turning to histories and biographies of London political life before and after the Great War. Lloyd George, Churchill, Birkenhead, Beaverbrook and other daredevils of an age of great adventurers now became part of my range of acquaintance. In the paradoxes and ironies of power – matters on which I was always ready for a new theory – these London desperadoes of forty or fifty years before were as real as Frank Packer. One night I might be reading about how Edward Carson had dealt with Bonar Law. That would provide one theory about how things were run. The next morning some question might come up about relations between Tony Inglis and the Boss. That cast up a contradictory theory.

Even in my continued reading of whatever books were being published about the Nazis, it was the ordinary I was looking for. Some of the Nazis seemed very ordinary. I sometimes daydreamed a game in which I went through my own past and present acquaintances and picked similar types to some of the Nazis so that I could wonder who would be the Nazis if we were all let loose? And I would be grateful for anecdotes of the muddles and blunders of the Nazis: how very ordinary it was that what concerned them most was keeping their own private power, which they did in conflict and confusion. Most of them were simply crawler bullies (so like so-and-so or what's-his-name in the *Daily Telegraph* building) who try to get to the top in any period where there seems a main chance. Ambitious power men like this were everywhere, messing up everything. When I found Alvin Gouldner's *Patterns of Industrial Bureaucracy* in a bookshop, there revived old visions, begun as a diplomatic cadet at the time I had discovered Mosca and Michels, that reading sociology might be as good as reading a novel. This 'case history of the bureaucratisation of a gypsum factory' made a good story well told and intelligently analysed. Perhaps that was what had happened to the great novels? Had they become sociology? To anyone who did not interrupt I would lay down the law about Gouldner's theory of 'The Problem of the Successor' or of 'Punishment-Centered Bureaucracy'. That was the kind of thing you could apply direct to the *Daily Telegraph* organisation. I tried some other books of sociology: *Juvenile Delinquency in an English Middletown*; *The Analysis of Political Behaviour*; *Negroes in Britain*; *A Study of Rural Economy in Yunnan*.

APART FROM DOUGLAS MCCALLUM, OF MY EARLY UNIVERSITY acquaintance only Jim McAuley survived as someone I might see from time to time, usually at dinners, with him and Norma (who had become a great cook). He was a poet still, but with only one slim volume published and that in Sydney not London, his 'genius' had not yet been recognised; and he was not even a literature professor. Instead, he had some job lecturing trainees for the Australian colonial service. (How 'typical of Australia' to waste McAuley like that!) Instead of anarchist, loner and jazz player, he was now suburban landholder, Catholic family man and, it was sometimes rumoured, writer of hymns, yet, on our first meeting, we drank ourselves silly in a city pub, then stayed up all night drinking brandy in his house out on his suburban plot, breaking off only when the chirping of birds was joined by the early-morning crowing of waking children. And I had been able to pass over what had seemed the intellectual calamity that McAuley now believed in God: he had not spoken of religion directly, only of art and ceremony, and while religion was there in the verses he had shown me during the night it didn't seem to be doing any more harm than the other kinds of mysticism that had always given mystery to his verse (and angered John Anderson).

We had been able to distract ourselves from our differences by litanising our common scepticism about 'progress', putting the word into ironic quotation marks simply by raising the eyebrows when using some phrase such as 'Whig interpretation of history' or 'Oslo lunch'. By this mutual tact I was able to continue to disregard McAuley's belief in God. There was some embarrassment, however, when his second slim volume came out, since some of the pieces in it showed the unanticipated bad taste of speaking directly of religion. I could not believe my own eyes when I read in his 'Letter to John Dryden' such reassurances as that *Christ was the Word, the source of unity, the Reason of man's reason, and its Light.* But there was enough of the old charm to divert me from this Salvation Army preaching. In any case, verse no longer had that central place in human guidance I had given it when I was an undergraduate: apart from the verses of old friends when they were published, I had given up reading poetry. There was another matter in which we might embarrass each other: my continued, if modified, belief in novels. Although McAuley seemed to be reading more prose than before, almost all of it still ran second to verse in seriousness, and some of the novels I was now reading were seen by him as specimens of depraved modernity. We scarcely spoke of novels, except those few that were part of his own canon.

Both at the McCallums' and at the McAuleys' (although in this period of exile scarcely anywhere else), I could still discuss the great affairs of the world and, after Khrushchev's secret speech, we could do so with the complacency of at last being able to demonstrate that, all the time, it was we who had been right and the Stalinists who had been wrong. Ever since the Andersonians had first instructed me in these matters, in 1939, we had confronted this superior Stalinist insolence that it was we who had been the dupes – of Trotskyist lies, fascist lies, capitalist lies – and there was no evidence any of them would accept that would suggest that anything at all had ever gone wrong in the Soviet Union. Now we had them! From Khrushchev himself! But now that there was proof even Stalinists would have to accept, I no longer met any Stalinists.

The events of 1956 in Hungary were no surprise to us but there were people in Australia (I heard from somebody) who were leaving the Party over it. Well, more fool them for joining it. As to Australia – there were certainly no grand generalisations, and not even very much detail. What was going on in Australia? Ten years ago, I had planned a book about it. What was going on? Not in politics, of course. But what was happening in Australian *society*? ('society' was a new word). As to politics – politics in Australia seemed a provincial revival, put on by old, decrepit actors who had not learned their parts, but McAuley seemed to take an interest in it: he had some special concern with denigrating the Labor Party. There had been troubles in the party, to which I had not paid much attention. The existence within it of a Catholic conspiracy had been revealed. The party had split. This scarcely seemed news:

even when I was a student 'Catholic Action' had been one of the words used by the oracles who revealed to us what was really going on in Australia. In this connection McAuley seemed very troubled about the communists, but how could he imagine Australia was important enough to have a communist problem? There was some talk from McAuley of time running out, of its being 'five minutes to midnight' ... and when I was at the McAuleys' I would pull a serious face as we contemplated our imminent annihilation. At the McCallums', however, we took a more generous view.

When McAuley told me he was to edit a quarterly intellectual journal published by a strangely named organisation, 'the Australian Committee for Cultural Freedom', this seemed, for a short season, to be one of the most interesting developments in what there was of intellectual life in Australia. The magazine, to be called *Quadrant*, would be something like *Encounter*, he said, and for me *Encounter* had now replaced *The Economist* as the most trustworthy source of periodic enlightenment. Although I could still be attracted by detail in *The Economist* I now preferred the broader horizons, presented in a more intellectual context, in *Encounter*, in which I could consider questions such as whether the European world order which was now breaking up was from the first inherently contradictory, or questions such as whether it was true that as in all else, William Blake's relation to tradition was one of extreme paradox? When I read *Encounter* I felt part of a communion of those who could use the modes of a common intellectual discourse to discuss anything. As we *Encounter* readers passed from art to history to general questionings of the human condition, no specialist languages divided us.

The *Encounter* style seemed to reach its most urbane in the travel pieces, of which they ran one or two in every issue. I admired, and even studied, the techniques by which wise generalisations were projected out of a myriad of particular observations, yet I was also aware that this was a style that was beyond me. When I opened an issue of *Encounter* and read some such introductory paragraph as:

> This spring, Leningrad's sky, filled with grey clouds, had a vast
> melancholy, and in the misty distances the city looked flat and indistinct,
> almost levelled out on its horizon to a smoky relief of long, uniform
> buildings over which here and there the spire of a tower rose or the gold

of a minaret gleamed forth. It was raining; or rather the atmosphere was so humid that it covered everything, the marble walls of the great public buildings and the trees in the parks, with a thin film of gelid moisture.

I might study such a passage for a while, but I would grow uneasy with the realisations of my own incompetence. I would never have thought of a juxtaposition such as 'It was raining; or rather the atmosphere was so humid that it covered everything'; I would not be likely to set a scene with phrases such as 'misty distances' and 'vast melancholy'; and I would certainly never have invented 'a thin film of gelid moisture'. On such an occasion I might get out one or both of my rejected novels, and turn over their pages, feeling some unease as I meditated on their simple prose constructions.

I became aware of what was 'contemporary' from reading *Encounter* (it was an easy way to keep up with what was happening in London or New York) and even 'radical' (in that it seemed to find a special savour in revealing the follies of much that was conventional) but, to McAuley, *Encounter* (though somewhat untrustworthy for these very reasons) was soundest in its anti-communism. Both of us respected its scepticism towards many of the illusions of progress although I also envied its coolness (why couldn't I write like that?), which McAuley seemed to see as intellectual softness. It was *Encounter* that *Quadrant* was to resemble, if perhaps with somewhat more intellectual toughness, and it seemed to me essential that I should have some part of it.

I suggested to McAuley that he bring to my office the publisher, Richard Krygier, a Pole who had escaped, eventually to Australia, from the Stalinists. When they came I had removed from view all evidence of the dastardly deeds usually performed in this room, although, just as I had never raised with McAuley anything connected with how he actually practised his religion, he had never referred in any way to the nefarious manner in which I earned (if that was what I was doing) my living. I sat the two of them opposite me and gave a lecture on print runs, production schedules, distribution patterns and other information – but as soon as I had begun this it occurred to me that everything I was saying was unrelated to the actual problems of the magazine they were to produce, even if bringing it out seemed too important for me to have nothing to do with it. *Quadrant* would represent 'our' breakthrough. (Even if the 'we' I had in mind had some years ago ceased to exist, was there nevertheless a certain characteristic state of mind that might be reanimated in others?) For the first issue, under the name of D.R. Horne (my serious name) I wrote a favourable review of *The Decisive Battles of the Western World*, Vol III by Major-General J.F.C. Fuller, in which I was able to reveal the paradoxes of the unintended consequences of the actions of both Woodrow Wilson and Franklin D. Roosevelt. I was not invited to write for *Quadrant* for awhile.

There was a Christmas party for *Quadrant*, in the converted wool store near Circular Quay where the Australian Committee for Cultural Freedom had its offices. Given its name, some of the Committee seemed a curious lot – they included lawyers and union officials who spoke of the Labor Party split as my father and his friends used to speak of the failed offensives of the Great War, going over it all again in the same anecdotes, and again counting their dead. Some of them were not intellectuals at all. When one of these, an orthopaedic surgeon, and (I learned later) a Catholic, said to me: 'How long do you give us?', asking this with the anxiety of someone who was afraid the drink was going to run out, I said I thought the party would last another hour or so. 'I don't mean that,' he said. 'I mean how long do you think it will be before the Red Chinese take over Australia?'

WHILE ANTI-STALINISM HAD IMPELLED SOME OF THE ANDERSON-ians into membership of the Australian Committee for Cultural Freedom, Douglas (who called them 'the Australian Committee of Cultural Arseholes') was in some undefined stage of negotiation with the breakaway Andersonians who had declared themselves 'the libertarians' and who, although also, of course, anti-Stalinist, had gone off in some way of their own, exploring the anarchist potential of being an Andersonian. (In this they were more Andersonian than Anderson, who had now assumed a position so inherently contradictory that it was no longer available for imitation.) In their secular aspects, as drinkers, gamblers and fornicators, the 'libertarians' saw themselves as 'the Push', with their favourite hotel bar, their own parties and the habit of forming into gangs which would gatecrash and then tyrannise other people's parties. It was only in this last, and threatening, manifestation that I was likely to meet them collectively.

I could not find any form of reconciliation with the Push. This was partly through a sceptic's scorn for their romantic playing with anarchism. (Of course, we would all be anarchists if it were possible but haven't these people yet realised that anarchism simply doesn't work?) In any case, also because they seemed so male (the very fact they were 'great womanisers' emphasised their maleness) and, as part of this (through some despair of their own) so anti-intellectual. Not that in other ways I wasn't myself 'highly critical' of intellectuals, of course, but (I would say to myself) mine was a distaste for intellectuals in quotation marks, not for intellectuality. Didn't I entirely support their opposition to censorship and other suppressions of freedom? Of course I did and here I was forced to part ways with McAuley. In fact, to be perfectly honest, there were times when I could understand how the libertarians might see me (if they saw me at all), in my dark suit, as someone who had sold out but then (I would say to myself) it was they who had sold out – on any commitment to the practicality of the possible.

WHEN I WAS AN UNDERGRADUATE I HAD SHOWN AN INSTABILITY in knowing who I was. I seemed to be showing this again. When I was with McAuley, I was aware of the ironies of 'progress'. When I was with the McCallums I was gently aware of the virtues of what remained of true liberalism. When I was reading *The Economist* I was spellbound by the charms of fact and detail, and when I was reading *Encounter*, by the charms of style and generalisation. I knew what I wanted. I wanted a style that was tough (like McAuley's), liberal (like McCallum's), informed (like *The Economist's*) and urbane (like *Encounter's*). Yet when I heard myself in some argument (or thought, yet again, of my review of *The Major Battles of the Western World*, Vol. III) I could hear myself as D.R. Horne, angry, ill-informed shouter. Some of what I read was so removed from my characteristic modes that at times in reading a book I would slip from pleasure to a sense of parody. Even at the best, I could not usually find any match to what I wanted, although in one of the continuing series of my seminars on the problems of D.R. Horne, I thought for a while that I knew what to do. Some of it was prompted by the McCallums' gramophone record of Brecht songs (translated impromptu by a friend, Henry Mayer, who gave them an extra roughness) and from an osmotic process in which discussion about the plays themselves seeped into me with my scarcely knowing it. This came when Packer sent me, for a few weeks, to Britain at a time when the Berliner Ensemble had come to London and Brecht's work was providing that year's revelation. I conjured up visions of what it would be like to write a novel that escaped all the hindrances of the London literary mind. There would not be one paragraph of sensitive psychological study. The plot would be all over the place, pushed recklessly by events. The writing would be the kind of thing one might find scrawled on a fence. There would be no 'vast melancholies' or 'thin films of gelid moisture'. It would be a crude story of the conflicts and frivolities of men who enjoyed the thrill of the chase. I made a few notes: 'Anyone who has ever started anything can recapture in it all the brilliant improvisations, sleepless nights, cheerful doggedness, black despair, unexpected triumphs, sudden disasters and endless, restless tossings and turnings of the difficult business of trying to pull something off. This is something that someone who has never started anything will never understand.' Then I discovered later that, in *The Threepenny Novel*, Brecht had already written this novel.

3

Ethel had stayed in Sydney, working, and when we had agreed to try to establish some kind of reconciliation I hired a huge apartment at Kirribilli, looking out across the Harbour to Circular Quay. Perhaps something smaller might have worked ... Ethel flew back to England. Now here I was in England myself, for six weeks. Despite our failure at Kirribilli, I spent most of my time in Ethel's company (if company is the word) – some of it in the village and the rest in a serviced apartment in London – in what we presented to each other as a last attempt to discover if, through our being together, even now, some new form of marriage might emerge. At the end, after a drunken farewell at the airport bar, as I got even more drunk on the airline's wines (this time I was travelling first class), it seemed that we had merely wasted six weeks.

I had known this would be so on my first morning in London. It was still dark when I had woken up in my separate bed in our rather expensive hotel and then, with the beginning of dawn, when I heard the clip-clop of horses' hooves outside I went to the window: in a street still lit by lamps, a troop of Life Guards was riding by. Obviously, with cavalry outside, it was Vienna, 1913, and, like a character in *The Man Without Qualities*, I was expected to ponder life's meaning. Ethel remained sleeping as I examined the futility of my journey (both to London and through life). After that morning, however, I was concerned (as she was) with the details of ensuring that our outward relations remained 'civilised'. The last thing we could do was to speak to each other seriously. The result was that the principal concern in these six weeks was not reconciliation, but 'remaining civilised'. This alone was enough to make reconciliation impossible.

There was one night when civilisation failed. This followed a dinner in London and then a champagne party in our train compartment on the journey back to the village: both dinner and champagne drinking were carried out in company that made our mutual politeness particularly timely, but at the same time particularly testing. When we got back to the house and Ethel discovered she had no key, as a joke I kicked in one of the glass panels in the door to 'my study' (with my books still on its walls and the desk still there waiting for me to write my third novel). This got us inside the house, but it also produced the hot argument we had, presumably, been awaiting as people wait for a thunderstorm to clear the air – and then an event that seemed one of the least characteristic of my whole existence. Consumed by alcohol, rage and self-pity, when we broke off, instead of retreating to the separate bedroom in which I was then sleeping, I went down to 'my study', wall-to-wall with failed aspirations, and as if I were an incompetent actor overdoing a part, I fell into a fit of manic laughter and sobbing. All that seemed left of anything I recognised as myself was the realisation, my God I've got *hysterics*. Continuing this tenth-rate melodrama, Ethel came downstairs and also over-played her part: as a therapeutic measure, she slapped my face.

These unexpected scenes of violence produced what nothing else had achieved: we spoke to each other seriously. The experience was not repeated.

In the village some things still seemed to be moving along with the rhythms we had started. The garden and the hens now proceeded on automatic control; the Conservative fête was being planned along the lines we had established, and although the *Village Newsletter* had not come out recently there were plans to revive it. Ethel now had a car, but the decisive change was that she had bought a large house near Earls Court, which had been converted into bedsits of various sizes, and it was about her tenants that she now engaged in 'village gossip'. I looked over this establishment: by careful contrivances there were enough hints at 'elegance' in it, mainly in the wallpapers and the shape of the chairs, for the rents to be kept high. Ethel was what she wanted to be: someone running a business. If I had stayed with her perhaps I would have sat in one of these rooms, on an elegant chair, in front of a typewriter, writing another novel no one would publish.

Apart from the Brechtian revelations of that year, the tedium of the London theatre had in any case moved beyond Christopher Fry and Terence Rattigan. The kind of revue put on at the Lyric had gone commercial and died of its own successes but the Royal Court was providing an alternative. Since it was the year of *Look Back In Anger* we liberal conservatives had to make up our minds about what we thought of the idea of the angry young men. I was inclined to rate *Lucky Jim* as good and *Look Back In Anger* as medium, but I failed *The Outsider*. On the whole, to me, 'The Angries' were a Fleet Street stunt. We went to almost as much theatre in a few weeks as we had been to in all of my previous time in England and I gave the National Gallery a thorough revision, right through, from Giotto to Gaugin. Nevertheless there came over me some of the same wasting disease that had made me so dispirited when I had lived in England. This time I was at least able to get on with my reading – book after book after book, from Isaac Deutscher's biography of Trotsky to *Lolita*. I hadn't enjoyed such a period of reading for years.

4

When I was a child I had once found a verse anthology somewhere and put it amongst my own books. There were several passages from Shakespeare's plays in it. I was very young: this was before my mother had bought me my own Shakespeare on time payment. What I most remembered from these extracts was the stage direction: *Alarums and Excursions*. It was beginning to seem to me now that if what I was supposed to be gaining was 'an experience' it was an experience in alarums and excursions – but in themselves, with no plot ...

WEEKEND'S COMMERCIAL EXPLOITATION OF SEX HAD BEEN salacious rather than erotic. Visually, it was a matter of choosing two or three photos each week of female breasts arranged so that they projected the concept of breast. Verbally, it was a matter of ensuring that the words 'nude' and 'sex' occurred in two or three headings each week, and thereby projected the concept of sex. It was in the cover heading and the poster that these two words had their greatest illusory power. I would plan the poster first, so that it would stand out well in the street: if you had too many words in a poster they would be too small. There should certainly never be a heading any longer than: LOVE LIFE OF A PRUDE NUDE although even something as brief as this had too many letters running horizontally. Something like: ALL SEX NO BRAINS would go into a larger type and was therefore likely to get greater attention from the gutter. One of the creations on which I most congratulated myself was: SEX MUST STOP. Not only did this provide a heading that even those who were three-quarters blind could see: given our habit of writing the poster heading first, and then the story, it also provided one of the more interesting challenges.

But there seemed a limit to the sales we could attract by this kind of thing. Let's try something else – we would tone *Weekend* down a bit and as a compensation for a less energetic projection of salacity we would bring the number of pages up to forty and the price from fourpence to sixpence. The manoeuvre succeeded: for a time sales were running at 450,000 a week and then for reasons I could not understand they rose to 460,000 – a disconcerting success since it had not come out of any memoranda, or new strategies or any individual action of mine. I couldn't leave things like that. I must do something new. The plan was so cynical that parts of it shocked them in London.

It was that we would further increase the appearance of 'quality'. What concerned them was that I had written that I was going to put in an OPINION section and a few other features that, with a slightly more orthodox use of headings and layouts, would produce a 'more permanent type of paper'. 'Our kind of journalism does not have opinions,' said the letter-in-reply from London. 'We are offering entertainment of the cinema, circus and the music hall kind – not opinions.'

I wrote most of the OPINION pieces myself, under the pseudonym of 'The Gunner', and when that seemed established I ruthlessly piled in more and more orthodox features of the kind they wouldn't run in London: LIVING HISTORY by F.L.T. Prowsett (an invented name that had more than a hint of sober scholarship about it); VOICE OF THE PEOPLE; SECRETS OF THE SURGERY; SPOTLIGHT ON THE NEWS; OUR WORLD BY C.S.T. ESDALE (another scholar). There seemed no end to this new sales pitch. We even put in a penfriends column. I could not think of anything more cynical than that.

Sales went up. We were now running at 480,000. Well then, another bold move. Something that might be as ordinary as one might find on the poster of a sensational afternoon newspaper. I tried: IS PRINCESS MARGARET ON THE SHELF?

WE MIGHT LOSE IMMEDIATE SALES, BUT IN FACT THE ISSUE reached our highest sale – 485,000: only a few thousand behind the half-million. I followed this the next week with something even bolder: instead of a girl, I put a dog on the cover. We lost 20,000 sales. What did that matter? Most of them came back in the following week. The point was (I would say) that all over Australia people would have been talking about how daring *Weekend* was to have run on its cover not a girl, but a dog.

Again something new: a reduction in the number of pages, from forty pages to thirty-two. I knew already that reducing the number of pages could increase the illusion of quality. Hadn't that been the basis of my first clever memo to the Boss more than two years ago? I sent my plan to Packer. No reply. No reply was a good reply. Do it anyway.

Again we got away with it. *Weekend* became that rarity in cheap magazines – a publication making a small profit on sales alone, before allowing for revenue from advertising. I wrote another memo to the Boss, reporting that *Weekend* had now become a 'much more permanent type of magazine' and more likely to attract advertising. No direct reply to this, but a reply came indirectly a week later in the form of a barrage of thunderbolts. When I was called to Packer's suite a couple of his people from the business office were standing beside him with, in their arms, all the black books from the company's publications and looking like fully briefed officers of the Inquisition. Along with an assortment of petty cash vouchers, contributors' claims, advance purchase orders and other pieces of paper signed by me that week, the *Weekend* black book was spread out in front of him. He looked up as if it contained all the previously unknown details of my criminal record. You're running a bloody expensive magazine, etc., etc. All this extravagance (pointing to petty cash vouchers and other forms) must stop, etc. Sack three of your staff. All expenditure must be authorised in advance. Why do you have to buy photographs when we have photographers, etc., etc.

It was only when he moved to the language of rational persuasion and asked for cooperation that I began to listen sympathetically. Profits were down. Costs were up. All the publications had to organise economy drives. (Well, that was quite reasonable. The whole firm would collapse without profits. Here was the Boss, battling his way against the storm.) I expressed sympathy and said I would like to put my proposals to him later. He tossed all the forms I had signed over to me: each of them was slashed across with a pencil and signed 'NO'. I saw him twice more and by the second interview the intrepid Boss seemed weary: he had been up on the bridge for two days fighting the storm. My main argument was that I had already cut out eight pages a couple of weeks before. Wasn't that enough? I had made my savings already. Not good enough. Save some more. In the last interview I was able to protect most of what mattered but I agreed that we could safely cut sales promotion. Over the next few months sales fell by 40,000.

BY THEN IT WAS 1957 AND THE MUCH-DELAYED PLAN TO PRINT *Weekend* in rotogravure could be delayed no more: it must be implemented by February. I sat in my Kirribilli flat, alone, or with Jim Murrant, planning the production schedules or the column widths of the new, better *Weekend*, I would sometimes look through the window at the ships moving in the harbour and have the feeling that I was also planning those.

We were supposed to be giving our magazine an illusion of quality that would attract advertisers, increase sales and justify charging an extra penny. But the newsprint the magazine was to be printed on was low-grade and the more 'quality' we introduced in artwork and production techniques, the shoddier it looked. Perhaps low-grade presentation would combine with low-grade paper to produce an illusion of quality? It looked worse. In some form of self delusion we finally kept our eyes away from the realities of what we were doing. But the first issue looked as uncomfortable and dispirited as we had expected.

I had my eyes on something more important than realities. I was waiting for the sales figures. Five-hundred-and-eight thousand! We had cracked the half-million! I had to shut the door and suppress some tears. When I 'regained control of myself' I called in Jim Murrant and asked him where were the thanksgivings for my own great contribution to this success. After the excitements and disasters of the last two and a half years, I felt surrounded by people with neither gratitude nor imagination.

When at the end of the day the staff came into my room and gave me a pewter tankard on which was inscribed:

D.R.H.

From the Staff of Weekend

to Commemorate the Record

500,000

I made only a short speech in reply – a quarter of an hour or so – reminding them of my lonely flight across half the world to bring the secrets of *Weekend* to Australia, and of the continuing need for the virtues of loyalty and audacity. We all went off to an office pub at which I drank out of my pewter tankard. Perhaps this was what my life was to be? A series of improvised stage skirmishes, so insignificant that they needed no dialogue, merely stage directions? *Weekend* was never to sell half a million copies again.

In the period of build-up for our offensive I had seemed again to enjoy Packer's special favour. Here was something diverting. He left for London not long before the launch, but he sent me a cordial letter. What went to my heart was that it began 'Dear Donald' instead of 'Memo: Mr Horne' and it was signed with a simple 'Frank' (Frank!). Then he gave me a present. Just as the headlines of launching *Weekend* had been given extra disorder by the *Junior Telegraph*, the launching of the rotogravure *Weekend* was followed five days later by the launching of another magazine for which I had some responsibility – *Pictorial*.

Although *Pictorial* was necessarily second-rate because of the small staff and the small resources, it provided intermittent deliverances from *Weekend*'s fairground noises, and, unlike *Weekend*, it was second-rate by accident rather than by design. In any case, Packer had given me a second present. He had appointed his son, Clyde. Although we never finally established who did what, it was enough for me that whenever the Boss sent us a memo my name came before Clyde's.

Clyde was twenty-two and, given his coming inheritance, he was obviously ready for 'executive responsibility': if it was left a bit longer it might be too late. We established an eating relationship – lunches, and occasionally a long dinner at a failing basement restaurant across the road. At these meals we had established a common interest in *Pictorial* and in office gossip, but both were likely to be talked about in an elevated style that, as with Hastings, might lead into more general discussion: the nature of power, perhaps; the mysteries of existence. At work, if one of us had something to talk over, he would visit the office of the other, always (as if bearing a gift) coming in with a joke.

There were times when Clyde would speak as if he would have been happier just to have gone off somewhere and been some other version of himself – becoming a suburban solicitor was one example – but most of the time we both accepted that he was crown prince. A few of the older hands in the firm referred to him with deference as 'Mr Clyde', as if they were servants at the Packers' house, but Clyde would usually handle his position with modesty – to the extent of referring to his father as 'the Boss', as if it were true that Clyde was working his way up from the ground floor (as an editor). We engaged in such tact that no one listening to us would have seen him as a twenty-two-year-old heir to millions and me as a thirty-five-year-old windbag and failure.

BY THE SECOND HALF OF 1957 – THREE YEARS AFTER MY HISTORIC voyage – I was engaged in yet another new normality: on the one hand running a *Weekend* that had disappointed expectations but that at least seemed to be travelling fairly steadily, and on the other hand presiding over a failing magazine that did not know its own name (*Pictorial* had now become *Pictorial Show*). I had begun to write learned tracts on subjects such as the difference between fixed costs and run-on costs, presented in a detached, 'realistic' style, in which *Weekend* was merely 'a marginal product of the firm', and annexed to these would be substantial statistical tables, nicely ruled up. Packer would settle into his studious mode when I gave him one of these reports and he would read it with the attention of someone settling down to a good book on a train journey, making no comment, however, except to ask for more. By now I was keeping in my desk a dozen or so manila folders containing statistical tables that tabulated sales 'breakdowns', costs 'breakdowns', advertising 'breakdowns' and other kinds of 'breakdowns' (although not my own).

By such acts I was still able to give myself the amusement of imagining myself, despite the alarums and excursions, as rational. Not that one couldn't be rational about alarums and excursions: my reading had instructed me in the need to preside over unexpected events as if I knew what was happening. Perhaps few of our individual plans succeeded in exactly the way they had been planned, but other plans succeeded in spite of the planning. Despite individual senses of failure, an elation of success would often sustain us. It was as if an overall success might be built out of a series of particular errors.

Even rage could be made to look as if I meant it. The incident in which I had torn up a reporter's 'story' and thrown the pieces out of the window had now become an exemplary legend, warning those who worked for me of the penalties of not taking our craft seriously. And I had become notorious for my sackings. Confronted by the mysteries of sales (market research now showed that the typical reader of *Weekend* was a young housewife with two children), I would thrash around, hiring, firing, hoping I might finally get it right. (I was delighted when I read that Harold Ross was once heard to say, with desperation, when he was editing the *New Yorker*: 'Christ, I'll hire anybody'.) But while in hiring someone I could be sceptical, or sometimes even quixotic, dismissals were final acts that had to be performed with absolute conviction; for this purpose, without even thinking about it (but how otherwise might I have done it?) I would always become very angry. It was their fault, not mine. And there were plenty of other jobs they could go to.

Gradually, despite all my doubts, there seemed to be a greater proportion of 'permanents' on the staff. Some of them had respectable journalist 'careers' behind them, later to be resumed; others picked up respectable 'careers' when they left. A spell on *Weekend* seemed to offer a relief from the ambiguities of being a more ordinary journalist. On *Weekend* we knew we had carried journalism to the point of fatuity: in acts of parody we had brought out some of its fundamental principles. Perhaps this was why so many who might not have been expected to do so served their time in this madhouse in which expense accounts were likely to carry items like 'Cost of plastic bloomers' or 'Cost of false nose and beard'. From the windows of our asylum we could meditate on the insanities of those outside.

Things toughened up even more when Pat Burgess arrived. When Larry Boys left to go back to Britain he told us Burgess was the person to appoint, so Clyde and I took him to lunch in our failing basement restaurant. After lunch, he walked out on his job on the *Daily Mirror* and signed up with us. I knew as little about Larry when he left as when he had started, but with Pat there was the frank, open style of Australian mateship, in which we did not necessarily say everything that was in our minds but could appear to do so. One of our favourite forms of converse was the tough anecdote reminding us of the quirks of existence. Like two animals engaging in some playful sparring, on a Monday morning we would warm ourselves up for the week by an exchange of exemplary tales and loud laughter; no conference was too important not to be illuminated by the wisdom of some relevant anecdote. The more important the conference, the more it had to be informed by such wisdoms. Pat was tall and tough. He kept 'fit', and 'could more than look after himself'. On one Monday morning, after a weekend in which he had got into some kind of brawl, I looked at his large, strong fist as it lay on my desk: there were small cuts and some discolouration around the knuckles.

We reached our most characteristic anecdote in an episode that began when we were drinking in one of the office bars and were joined by a journalist whose brother I had just fired. I didn't quite understand that what this journalist was doing was slowly pouring a glass of beer over me.

How should I react? With *sang froid*? Make a joke? This was really a matter for rage and revenge, and a certain amount of self-justification from D.R. Horne, angry shouter. To some extent, D.R. Horne might even enjoy self-pity. Burgess and I had a long, revengeful, expensive red-wine dinner at Adams and then the next day, at one of the Greek clubs, an even longer white-wine lunch, lasting until well into the afternoon, with bottle after bottle coming to our table. We drank our two other companions insensible – and then moved on to the private bar at Adams to get on to the hard stuff. By then it was clear what a man must do: I had rung up my assailant from the

Greek's and challenged him to a beer-throwing duel, to be held when the bars had cleared, after dinner. Why not bring Frank Packer into it? The fellow I had challenged was some kind of minor executive somewhere in the *Telegraph* organisation. Didn't Packer have any loyalty to senior executives? Eaten up with pique at Packer's faithlessness, I left Burgess in the Adams bar, broke through the normal defences that surrounded Packer and explained that I was about to challenge one of his minor executives to a duel. He said I was too short to take on someone as tall as that, but if it came to a fight, the first thing to do would be to kick this fellow in the shins, to bring him down to my size. If it came to a fight! What did I know about fighting? There was a lane outside the Adams private bar. Burgess took me out there and gave me a few emergency lessons in self-defence.

When we arrived at the hotel, two schooners of beer had already been placed on the bar, like duelling pistols, and the journalists who had come to see us play out our high noon had formed a semi-circle of space for the contenders. A long, challenging speech from me. Something from him. Blah blah. Nothing much happened. I had a technical victory.

IT SEEMED OBVIOUS I HAD TO MAKE EVERYTHING CLEAR TO everybody. We all must take an absolutely intelligent and rational interest in everything. For most of the time this would come in exhortations at the weekly tribal ceremony of the general staff conference, but the need to cast light on sloth or ignorance could sometimes be so immediate that I had to shoot a memo up into the air like a signal rocket, so that at once the charge could begin. There were memos on when black paragraphs were admissible, where by-lines should be placed, or on the use of cellulose tape. When one issue of *Weekend* appeared 'too grey, sludgy, dreary and indigestible', a memo was sent off to proclaim 'Twelve New Rules'. For a season of three months I produced a weekly 'Bulletin', sometimes of a dozen or more pages. In some bulletins I composed helpful hints on themes such as What to Do Before Starting a Layout or How to Maintain Good Taste. Twelve Hints for Writing Good Blurbs was followed by Twenty Two Rules for Writing Good Blocklines. There were moments when things seemed to be going well ('this story was an object lesson in the brisk, businesslike style of reporting that gets the story over with, breathlessly, quickly and strikingly – light in tone, anecdotal, provocative'); but more often there were moments of despair ('There is always a tendency for regular weekly features to become routine, slapdash, humdrum; they suffer from a nervous debility or inferiority complex. Life hardly seems worth living').

In July I had what seemed the most clear-headed of all my ideas. What we needed was a grading system of symbols for every story, every illustration, every heading and for the impression every page made as a whole. Henceforth all reporters were to label each of their stories with these symbols, and as the stories passed through the hands of news editor, assistant editor, production editor and chief sub-editor, they would do the same. And each week, after an issue was printed I would label everything. We would be thoroughly rational.

AS WHEN I WAS A STUDENT, I WAS STILL READY TO CHAIR discussion groups on the subject of who or what I really was, but mostly this subject now had to be discussed by Horne himself, sitting on his own case. The only person who might join me was Lillian Roxon, a former member of 'the Push'. (Or was she still a member? We kept most of our lives from each other.) In the testing business of 'earning a living' she had been writing advertising copy for a department store of declining profitability, and when she asked for a job, and I gave her one, it was the acknowledged sense of parody in what we were doing that made working on *Weekend* a kind of liberation for her. It was this sense of parody, of not being at any time altogether serious about ourselves, not to mention anyone or anything else, that framed the entire way we treated each other. Our cast of characters went well beyond *Weekend* – one of the most important roles was played in our conversations by Lillian's 'invention' of her Jewish-Russian mother – but it was talking about *Weekend* that would often set us off. It was like putting on a carnival hat. It got us in the mood. If *Weekend* was possible, then what wasn't? Lillian told me later (years later, when she was living in New York where she was later to die) that on nights when she couldn't sleep she might sometimes read over her favourite *Weekend* bulletins, to reassure herself that life could seem orderly.

TWELVE

Laughing all the way

1

By August 1957, Clyde and I had decided it was time to throw a large party. We hired a second-rate basement restaurant, and two bands: to show our strength, we would invite all the executives, from the Boss down, and as many of the *Weekend* cover girls as we could find. Speeches would run for half an hour and supper-time would start with a fanfare, after which the chorus line from the Tivoli, Sydney's main vaudeville house, would dance down the stairs doing the can-can. No sooner would the can-can finish than two footmen would carry in a large *papier maché* pie, out of which a girl would spring, fully unclothed apart from a G-string.

The party was an excellent *mêlée*, with enough fiascos to please the sardonic – the bands clashed, something went wrong with the arrangements for the *Weekend* cover girls, and there were a few parodies of bar-room brawls – but all this merely added to the creative confusion. I was delighted with the speeches with their mixture of ironic praise for *Weekend* and tales of my own legendary toughness (Captain Horne and his scurvy crew), and the can-can was perfect. As a fiasco, so was the girl in the pie. In the kitchen just as they were getting the act ready it was discovered that the bottom of the pie had come unstuck. The naked girl had to walk in on her own two naked legs, with the two footmen holding the pie so that it concealed the rest of her. There was some disorder when the pie was put down: because the naked girl found it difficult to curl up inside it, there were minutes of unrehearsed fumbling. Then, when all was settled, there was a roll of drums; followed by nothing. The girl could not burst through the *papier maché* crust. She knocked on its inside, and whispered. The footmen lifted off the crust. Another roll of drums: when the naked girl found herself in all the glare and glitter of the El Morocco restaurant, surrounded by the Tivoli chorus, with drums rolling from a Latin American combo and a jazz band, and some dozens of drinkers viewing her, she realised she did not want them to see her nipples. A hand went over each nipple. Even then she could not leap out of the pie. As she lifted a leg to step out of what was left of the pie she understood that the bit of material fastened around her crutch might lift up and the Tivoli chorus, Frank Packer and some dozens of staring drinkers might see what lay beneath. Her two hands played between the three parts she wished to conceal, as if she were dancing a fan dance, standing, leg bent, inside what remained of a *papier maché* pie. When someone put a jacket over her, she ran out of the room. As we boozed on until three o'clock in the morning, it was often agreed that the episode of the naked girl was 'very *Weekend*'. By putting on these revels we had proved to be significant fools in Frank Packer's court. The Boss himself had enjoyed it.

Clyde and I continued to have occasional dinners at which we drank champagne and brandy and philosophised about what existence really was – although, being 'realistic', never about what it might become. Several times he took me to an expensive 'night haunt' where I shared for an evening, with some self-consciousness, the night life of a young heir to a fortune. He would tell me stories of life back at 'the Taj', as he called the Packer mansion, set up behind trees and walls on one of Sydney's hills of prime real estate, sometimes speaking as if it were a five-star hotel noted for its excellent room service and fine cuisine; at other times as if it were an observation ward in which the rest of the inmates contemplated his father's moods of anger and fear. Frank Packer was going through a bad stretch, dissatisfied with everything, moved by doubts they could only speculate about. None of their remedies worked – golf, amusing dinners, even chess lessons.

Some of Packer's executives would discuss as one of the great problems of the age: How can we get Frank to relax? I did not make friends with any of Packer's intimates, although I did develop working relationships with some of the more junior men now coming up. I saw the others as mere court favourites. How 'good it would be for the firm' if I could let the Boss know what was really in my own mind! From gossip passed on by Hastings and sometimes by

Clyde I heard suggestions of what seemed many types of conspiracies against me. I would say it was like being an old hand in the Great War – you wouldn't hear the shell 'with your name on it'. No compromises!

My relations were with Packer alone: the marks he made on paper, the crackling voice over the inefficient intercom, the court rituals across his vast desk set the limits of my possible. He was also of enormous interest – better than any of my books – as a model of the playfulness of power, providing a pass key to political history and providing me with enough anecdotes about power – in particular, running things by means of a court – to shout down any idiot at a party. And there was another interest. This big, strong man with his redoubtable scowl was like some stormy mountain in which I imagined that, somewhere, there must be at least one place that was peaceful. Each time I entered his office I would hope that this would be the occasion when I could find some openness in what we said to each other – not the front-line wit of which we were both masters (although he found only his own wisecracks funny), and not friendship (what would we talk about?), but some small portion of mutual understanding.

Clyde was also likely to see Packer as surrounded by a court of flatterers: he had been brought up with it, at home, where the most successful courtiers would be in attendance on roster. He took me out to the Taj one afternoon when there were no other Packers in it and showed me the poker table where the Boss played for big money, the billiards table, the small office where the Boss read through the files he brought home, the tennis court, the swimming pool. In the servants' wing there were some pensioners and retainers. At fixed hours, as part of the Boss's bounty, several courtiers were allowed to use the swimming pool and there was a duty round for the Sunday tennis parties, with a mixture of regulars and others for the Sunday dinners.

Clyde shared with me the belief that 'the Boss should get to know me better'. It was Clyde who arranged for me to be at one of the dinners, but at this dinner Packer seemed to be in a fearsomely uncertain mood. He arrived late for the drinks tray ceremony, acting for a few minutes as if he were some shy stranger obsessed by the blackness of his own uncertainties; he then put on the geniality of a host (at which he could be convincing) but as we were eating the main course he asked his plate 'What does a man do when he can't get on with his own family?' He again became meditative when we were gentlemen over port, but as soon as we joined the ladies he called for his car, said he had some work to do and gave me a lift into town, sitting in the back, silent except for heavy breathing.

Now he was trying to kill *Pictorial Show*. Not that I hadn't lost interest in it myself, but if Packer wanted to kill it, I wanted to save it. At a meal at his favourite society nightclub, as he hurried through his grilled lamb chops and treacle tart, I made an emotional appeal to brute pragmatism based on a ruthless analysis of overhead charges. He seemed to be thinking about something else. The best I could now do was to fly to Adelaide and try to sell a half share in *Pictorial Show* to Rupert Murdoch, a young provincial 'tycoon' who enchanted me with his reasonableness as he displayed charts of future growth and tables of statistical projections – even if this was not my idea of behaviour for a 'newspaper proprietor'. (There seemed nothing Napoleonic about this intelligent young man.) Murdoch was acute enough to recognise what a bad deal I was offering him in *Pictorial Show*. I fell back on the last measure of desperation – a long memo to the Boss. It came off. But we were to swear a great oath that if *Pictorial Show* lost more than £200 a week, we would kill it with our own hands.

Clyde was created Managing Editor, Subsidiary Publications just before *Pictorial Show* folded. He was now in overall charge of me.

PACKER HAD HIS COURT; I HAD MINE, WITH A GREATER SENSE OF cohesion because a change in office space had given us our own floor, in a separate building, where we could imagine we were a bit on our own. Packer owned a small building, Adam's Chambers, next to the *Daily Telegraph* building (it overlooked Hyde Park) and one quiet weekend our desks and cupboards and filing cabinets were moved in. A former editor and a former editor-in-chief had earlier been shunted off to the rooms I was to have as my office, to which even their nesting material had been transferred – the dark glass-topped desks and the blue carpet that had been the executive colour in their day. To make room for us, they were retired from the firm. (A farewell dinner was not needed. They had already had their dinner.)

There were scores of buildings like Adam's Chambers in Sydney – leftovers from late nineteenth- and early twentieth-century endeavour – offering single rooms or suites of rooms for the city's smaller commercial and professional enterprises. Unlike the main building, it was not a beehive of partitions. There were solid rooms, with doors. And with a wide corridor, an ancient lift, faded paint and all these separate rooms, we could imagine we were conducting our own separate business. And here I reached new visions of the ritual significance of 'the conference'. Conferences were rostered in increasing number and complexity. There were specialised conferences (sometimes on the hour) on every aspect of the magazine I could imagine, and then the weekly general conferences which the whole court was expected to attend. On special occasions there were extraordinary conferences, summoned without notice. ('What's he up to now?') At all these conferences, although I was happy for others to play bit parts or to provide feed lines (Lillian Roxon was becoming even better at this than Larry Boys had been), it was obviously necessary for morale that I should keep the main character parts for myself. As bard, I would recall, when necessary, the great legends of *Weekend*. As community crier, I would proclaim the latest edicts. As public orator and poet laureate I would mark, with appropriate solemnity, all special occasions. I must also be my own court jester and my own lord high executioner. After all, I knew all about leadership from reading nineteenth-century novels, political biographies, sociological studies and schoolboy adventure yarns. I knew that it was my heavy task to personify events. A non-stop show must be put on that would entrap the imagination. There were some disloyal elements, of course, who thought all they had to do was to work five days a week, from nine to six, without looking as if they were participating in our great drama. They were the ones who ended up getting fired. (There were others who knew their part in history but they didn't do a full day's work from nine to six. They were also likely to get fired.)

IT WAS AMONG THE BLOCKLINES TO THE 3,000 ILLUSTRATIONS IN *The History of the British Nation* that I had first learned my lessons about the perils of rulers. I knew all about false favourites, conspiracies, treacheries, madmen, obsessions. At times when I sat there on a Friday afternoon, alone, waiting for the circulation figures to come in their sealed envelopes as if they were reports of the latest disasters of battle, I felt like a king in one of the 'illustrations specially painted for this work' – alone in his throne room, chin in hand, waiting for the next betrayal.

Nevertheless after Larry Boys departed as my most trusty flatterer I still maintained three relatively steady favourites in this small court. Lillian Roxon, who had the advantage of holding no power at all and of knowing all the rhetoric of our great drama, was a clandestine favourite: it would be 'bad for the rest of the staff' to know that a mere reporter and Show Buzz editor was favoured in joking meetings in which we amused ourselves by sustaining most of our mutual inscrutability. Pat Burgess and Jim Murrant were favourites, *ex officio*. With Pat I could continue to have sardonic but 'matey' conversations at an intelligent level (there was a lot to be learned about life each Monday morning), although all we saw of each other outside the office was in occasional lunches or in bouts of shared boozing. As a *protégé*, Jim Murrant was in a less certain position – things were no longer as simple as they had seemed when the two of us, one Christmas, had got *Weekend* out between us – but I had invited him and his wife several times to my flat for dinner, feeding them Frenchified food.

Jim and I were at our merriest when we were given the great sport of planning something new – even, on one occasion, a new afternoon newspaper in a week in which Packer's imagination was reaching its furthest boundaries. Whatever it was going to be we now had our routines: sheets of dummy paper, plastic em rules, scissors, paste and bottles of beer would be assembled on the largest table in whatever flat I was living in, and off we went, laughing all the way.

It was this routine that moved into action when Packer told me to work out a new kind of *Weekend*, to come out in February of the next year – BIGGER ('*Weekend* will be nearly TWICE as BIG'), BETTER ('16 MAGAZINES in one'), BRIGHTER ('*SIZZLING WITH VARIETY*') – and higher priced ('*But you'll pay only twopence more*'). By October it was time to give substance to this: we would have some trial copies printed in a 'dummy run', but first we would spend a day at my flat, away from the office, and plan a paste-up.

Jim and I were sitting at the dining table considering whether ten pages of fiction would be too much, or whether a hundred jokes would be too little, or some such other question, when we remembered that this was the night when Sputnik would be most easily seen in Sydney. We went out on to the verandah.

The Harbour Bridge was on our right, Circular Quay was ahead of us. We searched the stars to see if any of them were Sputnik.

2

As I moved from one furnished flat to the other, the manuscripts of my two novels were carried around with a few other possessions. Sometimes I would think about revising one of them, but when a fire broke out in one of the flats and I came home to the mess and saw the two manuscripts, undamaged in a cupboard, I wished they had been burned.

Not long after, at one of the McCallum's parties I was taken to task by a drunk whose first novel was about to be published by Gollancz (the publisher who was first to reject the *The Richmond Affair*): in the frank style I professed to admire, he told me everyone saw me as a curious example of an early promise that had failed.

IN GAZING BACK, FROM MY PRESENT PLACE OF EXILE, OVER WHERE I had been, I felt like someone standing on a hill watching his own shadow lose itself across the plain as one false trail led, confidently, to the next. I looked up a quotation from *Remembrance of Things Past* (I had marked it years before, without thinking about it much) of how one's actions were generally 'dictated by previous actions the prime motive of which had already ceased to exist'. That hit it off. Now one thing had led to another and here I was. (Banal terms like these seemed 'not inappropriate' to my condition.)

But if I was a victim of my own chance enthusiasms, hadn't I also been – in an obsession with 'the village', the vegetables, and so forth – a victim of my own passivity? Why had I gone on for so long – *immobilised*? I was talking all the time about boldness and risk, but, somewhere, did I lack boldness, or at least a coherent boldness? (Or was I lost among the runner beans and the beetroot simply because I had been overcome by a bold passion for the mundane?) But why ask '*why*?' as if I were analysing a character for Intermediate Certificate English?

I HAD BEEN FRIGHTENED OFF EXISTENTIALISM BY THE ANDERSON-ians: now I gave it another go. Was I simply a prisoner of my own dithering? Why not, with one mighty leap, declare that the bars were not there? I couldn't be everything I wanted to be, but surely there was *something* I could declare myself to be – something rooted in some sense of conviction? I was free to choose. Why hadn't I chosen?

Chosen *what*? I had written down that existence might in itself be meaningless, but we provided a working basis for our thinking and acting by: *Ritual* (secular or divine). *Art. Faith* (secular or divine). *Rhetoric. Knowledge. Et Cetera*. What did I have? I had the ritual of *Weekend* editorial conferences.

ANOTHER APPROACH: MY FATHER HAD SAID, 'BE YOURSELF, Donald'. After I had been instructed by the Andersonians that the mind was 'a battleground of passions' I had accepted that there wasn't a 'self' for me or anyone else to be. But now I had a thought. Surely, at least, I *knew what I was not*. For one thing, I was *not*, in myself, the editor of *Weekend*. For another, I was *not*, in myself, a courtier of Frank Packer. In fact almost the whole way in which I was spending my life provided a series of examples of what I was *not*. My actions were rooted in rubbish.

THERE WAS A KIND OF LITERARY 'SELF' I IMAGINED I HAD constructed out of my experiences, and the books, movies, paintings, conversations I had come across. This was more a 'self' of observation than of exposition – a kind of concealed vantage point from which to put together shreds out of which one might imagine a fabric of existence. I used to say that I wasn't able to write a nineteenth-century novel but in my mind, although not on paper, I had a way of living, through characters and anecdotes, a kind of live novel. But from what I had learned of the German idea of *Bildungsroman* – of finally constructing a 'character' for oneself after many a false trail – I myself needed a new 'character'.

At least: what was some distinctive way in which I could put things down on paper? Here I was, aged thirty-five and I didn't have a literary style – a 'voice', a way of organising words that constructed at least an external self. I could imagine no greater failure.

WAS BEING HARD-BOILED THE PROBLEM? (AS A SEVENTEEN-YEAR-old student, I had written in my diary: *Why do I sometimes still give a horrid sneer?*) Was I cynical rather than sceptical? Not ironic, merely sarcastic? Would it help my style if I could recover some of the optimism I grew up with, before I was educated into pessimism? Recover optimism, but qualify it with touches of pessimism, and put that together? Perhaps even become a bit more sorry that things were as they are? Or at least better humoured about it? (Or more 'detached'?) Wouldn't it be smarter to be more concerned with others? This took me back to my High School musings when I went for a day's walk with my father, wondering about what it meant to be good. Perhaps it was important in gaining a style to become a 'better person'.

3

As it happened, there was now a chance for what I saw sometimes as 'liberation', other times, more modestly, as 'a reconstruction', or at least as a relief from exile. It had opened out earlier in the year, when I pushed myself downstairs to see Packer to play my one wild card – his promise, or half-promise, made two and a half years before over a celebratory Scotch on the day the first issue of *Weekend* came out, that if *Weekend* made it he might (at least that was my memory of it) give me 'an intellectual weekly like the *New Statesman*'.

So there I was in my charcoal grey suit, with a silk handkerchief in its breast pocket and shirt cuffs with gold links dropping below its sleeves, while on the other side of the desk on which we had had all those dealings about petty cash vouchers, staff sackings and epic visions of expansion, Packer sat in his white shirt, jacket off, showing he was one of us. I had a memo describing in a couple of paragraphs a proposal for a weekly magazine that would concern itself with Australian society at large, with foreign affairs, with social, economic, political and cultural questions; it would have a lot of book and arts reviews; it would fill a gap in Australian life. (To show that it was going to be coolly detached, I would call it *The Observer* – although I didn't want to bother him with details about 'cool detachment'.)

I knew how wary I had to be. He might not remember the *New Statesman* promise (if it was a promise). But there was almost a nod. I was half there; part of the legend was that in person-to-person deals Packer was as good as his word. But would he be as good as his word here and now, over this prodigious desk piled up with files and memos some of which he would never answer? Or would he give me his word that he would be as good as his word, but only at some more appropriate time? When sales hit 600,000? When advertising quadrupled? When he had won the Melbourne Cup?

There must be no suggestion of *give me a magazine or I'll go*: if he was offered an opening in repartee I would be out of the door as quickly as it took him to say 'I'll accept that offer'. A few weeks before, an ancient executive who was kept on as a reward for fidelity had said that a lot of holidays were owing to him. 'Well,' said Packer, seeing the chance for a wisecrack, 'I think it's time you took one long holiday, Jack'. We all went to the farewell dinner.

Why did Packer give me the go ahead (with that movement of the lips that suggested he was learning how to smile)? Perhaps because, like me, he also suffered from the sheer silliness of *Weekend*. His wife hated it. Menzies used his position as prime minister to nag him about it. The editor of *The Australian Women's Weekly* had spoken privately to him about it (and about me). Perhaps he said OK because he liked new things as a remedy for boredom, and as a gamble. Perhaps he was being generous ... Perhaps, somewhere, there was a Frank Packer in the alternative, who thought this kind of thing worth doing ...

But it was not to be a weekly, he said. A monthly. And not before the end of the year. And only if things were going well.

I had it! An intellectual magazine! With a bit of luck, I was saved!

4

There had never been anything in Australia as comprehensive as this magazine I was planning. At that time almost everything that now makes up intellectual life seemed to be missing, even to the extent that the number of foreign books banned each year was greater than the number of books published in Australia. Like messages from the gods, signs of hope flashed occasionally from 'overseas' – Patrick White's *The Tree of Man* had been praised in New York, and in London several exhibitions of Australian paintings and *The Summer of the Seventeenth Doll* had good reviews – but when that was over we would go back to moving around in our customary greyness. At home a theatre trust had been formed (named after Queen Elizabeth) and it had organised a ballet company and an opera company and it was now engaging in occasional entrepreneurship in 'serious drama', but the usual place to see 'serious drama' was still in the 'little theatres' and hardly any of it was Australian; the film industry had evaporated. In Sydney, a satirical revue company, on the London model, had gone professional, and that was something to talk about. Other than that, we had long conversations about the latest foreign movies. The 'university poets' (all of whom I knew) had changed some of the scene, and the quarterly 'little magazines' ran articles of general intellectual interest but there were hardly any academic journals and scarcely a book about Australia seemed worth reading – the architect Robin Boyd's *Australia's Home*, and the historian Manning Clark's three selections of Australian historical documents were the exceptions. In journalism the one advance was that John Pringle had come from *The Times* to edit *The Sydney Morning Herald* and he had put into the *Herald* feature articles and book reviews worth reading (some of them even written by people I knew).

In the discussion of public affairs a rather grandly named Institute of Political Science put on a big annual summer school (especially popular with 'refugees', who made a good weekend out of it, getting in a bit of golf as well, and reminding themselves of what used to go on in Europe) and out of this, each year, there came one book. But these summer schools, and the Institute's journal, *Australian Quarterly*, along with a sister Institute of International Affairs (which also had a journal) were just about all there was. The universities produced nothing. Yet amongst some of the people I knew there seemed to be enough talk to fill a dozen summer schools.

Some of them were 'political scientists' – a term that, despite the Institute's name, we really hadn't used before. I had started meeting 'political scientists' at the McCallums' parties – Douglas had now become one himself (and I had put him down to write on the Soviet Union; Ann, of course, was down for reviewing books). Brian Beddie had also become a 'political scientist', with a lecturing job in Canberra, and he had introduced me to two other young 'political scientists' who might write for us – Arthur Burns, who, at a picnic on the banks of the Molonglo, had delivered a breathtakingly brilliant impromptu on strategic policy; and Sol Encel, Polish-born but brought up in Melbourne, who had instructed me on the careful research he was doing on the background of business executives and government officials. (Social research! We must have some of that!) And I discovered that Political Science parties in Sydney were just my style, with plenty of angry shouting, although there was also more quietly spoken talent – Dick Spann, a professor from England, had exactly the remote, detached style with which I wanted to replace my own angry shouting (when I remembered that this was what I wanted to do); Hugo Wolfsohn, a German-Jewish refugee showed a quiet, quick and stinging wit (another way of replacing angry shouting). But the greatest potential talent of *The Observer* was Henry Mayer, himself an angry shouter, another German Jew (educated in Germany, Switzerland, Italy, England and, after being transported to Australia in the *Dunera* through some wartime stupidity, Melbourne, where he picked up some transplanted Anderson): he would write in every issue of *The Observer*. Peter Hastings would write for us, of course – it would offset the tedium of his job as Chief of Staff of *The Sunday Telegraph*. And there was Des O'Grady, a wan and remote young Catholic who had come in one day with a note of recommendation from McAuley: I gave him a job on *Weekend*, so he was part of the strategic reserve. Perhaps Lillian Roxon might write some pieces? I had also imagined (without thinking about it) that all of 'my old friends' would also write for *The Observer*, but, when I began to think about it, I recognised that, apart from McAuley and the McCallums; they were doing something else.

BY MAY, THINGS WERE LOOKING PRETTY GOOD FOR *THE OBSERVER*. For once, something was proceeding without haste, and with no fiasco. I had received the printing quotes and the newsprint samples and sent Packer all the figuring, assisted by Alan Ratcliffe who had been given to me as 'manager' for *Weekend* and anything else (such as *The Observer*) that came up, because his father, a rich accountant, was Packer's tax and general financial adviser. Alan had one of those long, bespectacled faces that denote detachment, intelligence and coolness under fire and a rather languid delivery that he used in 'exploring a topic', sometimes for weeks, over the oysters and before the chess at the lunches we often had in my office. In June I appointed as associate editor George Baker, hiring him on the spot because he seemed to know a little about a lot and was as conservative as one might expect from the son of a family of rich New England squatters, with enough family obsessions to make a Victorian novel, but also as amusing as one might expect from someone who had taken a minimum kind of degree at Oxford, where, the McCallums told me, he had lived up to standards of expensive eccentricity that might have amused Evelyn Waugh. Now and again Baker would come into my office with a dignified sideways movement and report on the new contributors he was lining up but our main work was done over long lunches at Adam's Hotel, beginning among the polished wood and gleaming brass of the private bar, where I would drink a couple of martinis while Baker sipped his dry sherries and then in the dining room, ingesting alcohol, fat and nicotine. By August we had decided on the allocation of space within our forty-eight pages; by September we had a long policy document; by October we experimented with design and printed several trial dummies, and I hired as our second staff member Peter Coleman, when he came into our office, one day, looking for someone else: we had a talk, he told me he had lost belief in the Ph.D. he was doing in political philosophy at the Australian National University – he had been an Andersonian and, in London, a student of Michael Oakeshott, the conservative sceptic. I enjoyed the talk; he had no experience in journalism. He seemed just right for the job.

Baker was tulip-shaped and waistcoated, speaking a quiet, controlled Anglo-Australian, with much use of raised eyebrows and downturned lips. When Hastings and I were having *our* lunches, at an upstairs fish restaurant, we were pretty clear that he was a frustrated homosexual: we would sometimes imagine Heath-Robertsonish devices for masturbation packed away for use in his lonely room at the fashionable Sydney golf club where he stayed. But he was getting down, onto unusually long sheets of paper, descriptions of what we had decided (over our lunches) about what we were going to do with *The Observer*. Its tone should be 'moderate to the point of coldness', with 'feeling' being expressed by irony. (That's why it was called *The Observer*: it was standing by, watching.) Even when we spoke of communism, we would speak with a deliberative restraint. We knew, after all, that *The Observer* was being directed mainly to 'an educated, but classless group found in universities, in the public service, and in all kinds of niches in private firms'. These new people did not really know what they thought, or where they were going, but since for the moment they 'had nothing to guide them but the kind of cynicism which is all that remains from the leftist enthusiasm of the 1930s and the authoritarian provincial spirit of the 1940s', it was up to us to tell them who they were. (All of this suited my mood as someone who wished to abandon angry shouting, but there were times when I felt uneasy: Would it miss the point? Alternatively, would we actually be able to get people to write like this?)

But what a feast we were preparing (all of it to be served in the cold, detached style that was to be the specialty of our house). THIS MONTH 'varying from solemn to lighthearted and from national to international', would put the world into place; then we would broaden out into THE NATIONAL SCENE, intricately diverse, treating politics 'in the English manner' so that it was presented as theatrical performance, and BEYOND THE SEAS, for which we planned the special novelty of developing 'a foreign policy based in Australian self-interest'. Some of the main courses would include PROFILE, ('individuals examined from the perspective of the institutions of which they were a part'), a PROSE SKETCH ('vignettes of Australian life concerned with some form of social embarrassment'), REPORTER AT LARGE (on a major topical event, giving 'examples of the general social frictions and outward social formalisms marking Australian social life') and then we would have a monthly EVERYMAN'S GUIDE TO THE SOCIOLOGY OF AUSTRALIA – an article best knocked together, we thought, in a brainstorming session over a long dinner. We had not yet agreed on where to have the dinner.

There would, of course, be a big piece each issue on 'some Australian problem' and we would go for notes on the professions and on farming (taking farming seriously would surprise our kind of reader). We would have columns of food, and wine, and fashion, and sport – all from an intellectual angle: that would also surprise everyone. In THE ECONOMIC WORLD I would get my own back on those who had tried to teach me economics. We would display 'a constant hesitation to accept any of the present received economic wisdoms' and, as realists, we would not concern ourselves overmuch with what the people 'controlling the economy' thought they were doing. What would matter would be the actual effects of the actions of those who thought they were 'controlling the economy'. And here was another good idea: our BUSINESS section would be concerned not with fantasies of profit maximisation but with treating business as material for social observation. One of the most important sections would be the lavish attention we would give to ARTS and BOOKS: a real move away from the tattiness of the newspapers. I gave George Baker a filing cabinet and it was understood that this would become a storehouse of future articles. Baker and I began to have regular conferences in the office itself. (I was now able to do in a newspaper office something I wanted to do.) He had long lists of the contributors he was dealing with. (My God, *The Observer* was going to be good!) The first issue would come out on 14 November 1957. I would sometimes go to sleep thinking about how even if I had not yet found a literary style, nevertheless, through the collectivity of this magazine, I would at least establish a personal style.

THE OBSERVER WAS NOT TO COME OUT ON NOVEMBER 14. I WAS again in a state of battle. This battle began with an article attacking *Weekend* in *Truth*, a Sunday scandal sheet run by one of Packer's rivals (who on one occasion had arranged for Packer to be beaten up). There was nothing to concern oneself with in an attack by *Truth*, but it was followed by attacks by the Melbourne Catholic weekly, the *Advocate*, with stories headed SEXY PUBLICATION CORRUPTS AUSTRALIAN YOUTH and OBJECTIONABLE PAPER A DIGRACE TO AUSTRALIA. When the first reports on sales in Melbourne showed a drop I made appointments, first with a 'prominent Catholic layman', second with a monseigneur, then for an audience with the archbishop, Daniel Mannix, whom I regretted disturbing on such business when I would sooner have interviewed him as a 'figure from history' (as I might be able to do once I had *The Observer*).

Embarrassment in concerning myself with such matters seemed to give a kind of acceptable detachment when I spoke to the prominent layman (with whom I had dinner) and then, across his desk to the influential monseigneur. They did not act as if I were the kind of person who would be producing an 'impure publication', but they were entirely unable to listen to my analyses of content, expressed in column inches, the details of our inhibitions, and other careful assessments of what was actually in *Weekend*. Since they had images of what it was they wanted, arguments on detail were of no use to them. What seemed to attract their attention was that I spoke quietly and reasonably and did not appear to be engaged personally in the corruption of youth. There was no real sign that they were interested in *Weekend*. They would be quite happy to attack some other publication: almost any publication. It was general images of the world that disturbed them.

This insouciance became a dinner-table anecdote when I learned how it was that Mannix had come to speak about *Weekend*. The monseigneur had not heard of *Weekend* until he attended a communion breakfast of Victorian railwaymen at which the prominent layman made his speech attacking *Weekend*'s depravity as part of a national tragedy in which we were 'breeding effeminate boys and masculine girls'. In his own speech, however, the monseigneur at once joined the attack, which was expressed in rhetoric understandable at a communion breakfast of Victorian railwaymen. After lunch, when he was driving with Mannix to the opening of the annual fête of the St Joseph's Babies' Home and Mannix had asked for ideas for a speech, the monseigneur had mentioned these sexy publications that were corrupting the Australian youth. Mannix had never heard of *Weekend*, but he thundered against it at the annual fête of the St Joseph's Babies' Home. He 'assured his audience' that 'if his voice carried any weight' it would be in favour of 'suppressing this form of most objectionable literature'.

'Literature?' Perhaps Mannix had thought it was a book by some infamous literary personage of secular humanist persuasion? By the time I went to see him in his palace, a very old but princely figure sitting up stiffly as he gave me audience, he could not remember the name *Weekend* and at once indicated he had not seen a copy of it. I gave him my 'facts' as quickly as I could, and then spent half an hour speaking with him as a figure from history.

By moving from cathedral to palace and back again I made myself seem someone seriously engaged in negotiation, even though all I was doing was being polite, and in my last conversations with the monseigneur and the prominent layman it appeared that at any further communion breakfasts or annual fêtes at which they would defend youth from corruption they would be happy to use some other examples than *Weekend*. But when I got back to Sydney I discovered that the *Catholic Weekly*, the New South Wales equivalent of the *Advocate*, had spent most of a page attacking *Weekend*'s 'undue emphasis on violence, sadism, cruelty and horror', its 'provocative headings' and its overall formula of *True Confessions*, sexy cartoons, crime, film star scandals and strip-tease pictures' (Untrue! Untrue! Well, perhaps 'provocative headings' was true).

As a professional I was being publicly humiliated: the idea of even suggesting we were exploiting an interest in violence, sadism or cruelty had never been part of our formula. Sexy cartoons! – when we were still painting out women's navels! *True Confessions*! Didn't these idiots know that the *True Confessions* idea was an altogether different formula? It was true that *Weekend* was largely rubbish. But they hadn't complained about that.

Clyde and I invited the editor of the *Catholic Weekly* into my office and for two hours threw logic and facts at him until he broke down, called for some aspirin and a glass of water and made a full confession about his lack of editorial freedom. A long lunch at Adams should fix him, we decided, but, first, I must see the cardinal.

Although a prince of the Church, Cardinal Gilroy did not have Mannix's stiff bearing. Instead of an impression of a gracious head, held aloofly high, there was an impression of badly made false teeth, displayed obsequiously, and when Gilroy spoke of 'our Lord' I felt an affront to my understanding of European history: Gilroy was not using the language of a cardinal, speaking in a worldly way; he was using the language of a Salvation Army chaplain. However, whereas with Mannix I was more concerned with presenting myself as one who was politely paying court, with Gilroy I did attempt to present matters of fact and of logic. I even went so far as to ask for some specific guidance as to how much exposure of a woman's flesh was acceptable to the Catholic Church, in Sydney, in 1957. I laid before him some of the latest issues of *Weekend* as if they were sinners awaiting an announcement of penance. He preferred not to examine them but to arrange for a monseigneur who knew about such matters to come and see me.

This second monseigneur and I met on a Saturday morning, in a man-to-man chat about the sexual habits of adolescents that had something of the YMCA about it. When this was over I began to feel that in Sydney, also, in seeking their images of a corrupt modern society, the Catholics would be ready to find something other than *Weekend* to attack.

When I had been invited to Sydney University by the libertarians to defend *Weekend* I found myself addressing an overflow lecture theatre in the same room in which I had made my first public appearance as a student, seventeen years ago, defending (as a poet) good verse against bad. What was I to say? I certainly wasn't going to deny that *Weekend* was merely a commercial venture, that it was of no literary or intellectual merit and you wouldn't catch me suggesting that there was something wrong with 'exploiting' sex or crime stories: it just happened that in this case that is not what we were doing. Look, here's the evidence. Listen to this: In the last twenty-six issues of *Weekend* only four of the cover girls showed any cleavage. No, what the Catholics are really objecting to is that *Weekend* is not presenting the Christian icons of woman as mother. Yes, in its own way *Weekend* presents a view of life and these people want to suppress it. (A good chance to bring out some populist arguments here.) *Weekend* represents one of the suppressed elements that 'does not find expression in the public culture'.

I was pleased with this line of argument and with its use of words like 'public culture'. Now I would be able to get on with beginning my own regeneration, by producing *The Observer*. An informant rang from Brisbane to say that at the end of the week there would be gazetted a ban on *Weekend* in Queensland.

Clyde and I flew to Brisbane where our lawyers told us nothing could be done and then – because we stood there and said something had to be done (and perhaps also because Clyde was a Packer) – they developed a plan to prevent the ban from being gazetted. Triumph: an interim injunction. And a victory for an established figure of speech, the censor was censored.

When it came to trial I was to develop an anecdotal repertoire that served me for years. Our next astute move had been to hire Sir Garfield Barwick (Frank Packer's idea), an advocate with an irradiant reputation for clever courtroom strategies, who was to win our case partly through the very act of lending his presence to the Queensland Supreme Court. For storytelling there were tales of both his boldness and his economy of effort – and also of the way he relaxed by entirely dominating conversations, one anecdote leading at once into the other so smoothly that there was no physical possibility of interruption.

My prize performances came from learning off pages of the transcript and acting them out. Of these the most telling was the anecdote of the extra nipple. It began with their man identifying a nipple in a pin-up picture, after which 'the following interchange ensued':

BARWICK: Can you show me where this is? I am sorry to interrupt you, but I would like to see it.

THEIR MAN: My friend would like me to point the nipple out to him.

BARWICK: I would. My glasses are not strong enough.

THEIR MAN: See?

BARWICK: (*addressing the judge*): Does Your Honour see what my friend means?

HIS HONOUR: I can see what he means. I would say it was probably a nipple, but I do not know whether it is the right place for it.

THEIR MAN: There is a faint suggestion – all these things are suggestion – in the top right-hand one, the biggest one, of just the beginning of a nipple. There is a slight discolouration.

HIS HONOUR: There is a mark there, but I would suggest that she is probably deformed if that is where the nipple is. (*Barwick produces gold-plated Parker pen and induces Their Man to ring two marks on the one breast.*)

BARWICK: I suggest, Your Honour, my friend has found a nipple in the alternative. (*Laughter in court.*)

5

It is almost Christmas. Packer has said *The Observer* should come down to thirty-two pages, be put on cheap newsprint and come out fortnightly, not monthly. When I decide I must get away for a few weeks, George Baker arranges a berth for me on the *Polynésie*, a Messageries-Maritime combination of 'cargo vessel' and 'cruise ship' that makes a regular round trip to New Caledonia and the New Hebrides. On the day I leave, the temperature has hit the century for the second day running. The sky is dark with dust. Bush is burning. As the ship sails through the Heads (Ethel and I set out like this for England eight years ago) I seem one of a group of refugees leaving the doomed city.

I spend most of each day in a deck chair, so far as possible thinking of nothing – although there are occasional intimations of the spiritual presence of Frank Packer: he has written me a long letter about what should happen to *Weekend* – 'the period of trivia may be passing ... we may be pursuing a course which is in dying demand', and so forth – in the longest and most thoughtful communication I have received from him. Perhaps, after all, Packer and I might be able to talk to each other. We could sit there, side by side, thinking out loud. His letter ended: 'Anyway, this is something for you to chew over'. (What could be more reasonable?)

When Baker suggested a 'cruise' on the *Polynésie* I imagined myself entering a Somerset Maugham novel about polite people on a 'luxury liner'. Perhaps I would have an 'intrigue'? When I learned that the *Polynésie* carried only a couple of dozen people and relied for its business mainly on cargo, the word 'freighter' set me off to imagining myself joining a ship on a foggy night at Rotterdam or Ostend. I was now in a Simenon novel. After a couple of days on the *Polynésie* I discover that in fact I am in a Kingsley Amis novel. My fellow passengers are holiday-making Australians who would never read either *Weekend* or *The Observer*. I throw myself into desperate alliances with one group after the other, but I am now playing Lucky Jim, and thereby making a mess of everything.

The third part of my private voyage begins on the day when we go in the ship's launch to picnic on a 'tropical island', where I feel the contentment of one who is caressed by clichés. The beach is a semicircle of white clichés. The water is turquoise cliché. The fish flash with brilliant clichés. The water laps gently on the clichés. Apart from our feeding periods I spend the day by myself floating on the turquoise water; sitting on a rock listening to it gently lapping; snorkelling (improbably) and observing the brilliantly coloured fish.

All that is worth thinking about now is *The Observer*, and, through it, my regeneration.

IT IS COMPANIONABLE TO SEE CLYDE PACKER AND GEORGE BAKER on the wharf when the *Polynésie* returns to Sydney but odd, since it is a Saturday, that they should want to take me at once to an office empty of staff. Also odd that it is to Clyde's room that they take me and that he then sits behind his desk, as if in judgment. He is about to perform some stern but unavoidable executive function.

He does this in the kindest way. I will be enormously busy launching the new *Weekend*. It has therefore been arranged that George Baker will edit *The Observer*. I will always be, of course, the most honoured of its contributors.

I SPEND THE SUNDAY AT KIRRIBILLI, LISTENING TO THE ANIMALS roar from the zoo, and in an animal rage of my own. I am looking to the future, seeking revenge, and – right back to that deceitful night in 1941 when my friends saw to it that I was not reappointed editor of the student newspaper. I catalogue the past, listing its treacheries.

PACKER IS IN LONDON. FIRST THING MONDAY MORNING I INSIST on seeing his stand-in, with Clyde, now silent. By all means make whomever you wish editor of *The Observer*, I say. And make whomever you wish editor of *Weekend*, too. Just give me my air ticket so that I can fly back to London. Of course, if you would like to ring up the Boss we could all discuss it together?

It is over in ten minutes. Victory to D.R. Horne, angry shouter.

6

On the night we put *The Observer* to bed in the composing room of the private printery that had been given the job, it was like doing business with the Marx Brothers. The men in the composing room, and their machines, seemed intermittently frozen by some external force, George Baker was seized by an inner intellectual experience that would leave him in silence for minutes on end, and Francis James, the printer, put on a series of funny hats: near dawn, when he came out of his shower room naked, he was wearing a Mexican sombrero, standing there, in his little boy mood, waiting for a laugh. As I left at dawn, to get a few hours sleep, I noticed that there seemed to be some problems with the printing press itself. It was new and this would be the first publication it printed. They were experimenting. A couple of hours later I was awoken by Alan Ratcliffe, on the phone. 'Donald,' he said, at his coolest, 'the first issue of *The Observer* is now being printed.

Significant moment.

'Something went wrong with the press,' he said. 'The first copies came out backwards.'

www.ingramcontent.com/pod-product-compliance
Lightning Source LLC
Chambersburg PA
CBHW021926110726
47901CB00003B/731